P9-DEZ-811

Visual Basic® 6:

ENVIRONMENT,
PROGRAMMING, & APPLICATIONS

Alan Eliason and Ryan Malarkey

An Imprint of Macmillan Computer Publishing

VISUAL BASIC® 6: ENVIRONMENT, PROGRAMMING, & APPLICATIONS

Copyright© 1999 by Que™ Education and Training

All rights reserved. Printed in the United States of America. No part of this book may be used or reproduced in any form or by any means, or stored in a database or retrieval system, without prior written permission of the publisher, except in the case of brief quotations embodied in critical articles and reviews. Making copies of any part of this book for any purpose other than your own personal use is a violation of United States copyright laws. For information, address Que Education & Training, Macmillan Computer Publishing, 201 W. 103rd Street, Indianapolis, IN 46290.

Library of Congress Catalog Number: 98-89114

ISBN: 1-58076-272-7

This book is sold as is, without warranty of any kind, either express or implied, respecting the contents of this book, including but not limited to implied warranties for the book's quality, performance, merchantability, or fitness for any particular purpose. Neither Que Corporation nor its dealers or distributors shall be liable to the purchaser or any other person or entity with respect to any liability, loss, or damage caused or alleged to be caused directly or indirectly by this book.

02 01 00 99   4 3 2 1

Interpretation of the printing code: the rightmost double-digit number is the year of the book's printing; the rightmost single-digit number, the number of the book's printing. For example, a printing code of 99-1 shows that the first printing of the book occurred in 1999.

Trademark Acknowledgments

All terms mentioned in this book that are known to be trademarks or service marks have been appropriately capitalized. Que Education & Training cannot attest to the accuracy of this information. Use of a term in this book should not be regarded as affecting the validity of any trademark or service mark.

Microsoft and Windows are registered trademarks of Microsoft Corporation.

Screens reproduced in this book were created using Collage Plus from Inner Media, Inc., Hollis, NH.

Composed in *AGaramond* and *MCPdigital* by Que® Education and Training

Photo Credits

Part I: p. 1, MDA

Chapter 1: p. 3, Sheena Luu and Christopher Porter

Chapter 2: p. 19, From H. Holgate, Royal Commission: Quebec Bridge Inquiry; p. 26, Courtesy of Professional Engineers Ontario

Chapter 3: p. 37, Gordon C. Andrews; p. 49, Courtesy of Professional Engineers Ontario

Chapter 4: p. 55, Formula SAE team, University of Waterloo

Chapter 5: p. 67, Dwight Aplevich

Chapter 6: p. 81, Dover book of public-domain illustrations

Chapter 7: p. 99, Dwight Aplevich

Part III: p. 147, © National Maritime Museum, Greenwich, London

Chapter 9: p. 131, Adapted from Charles Minard, Figurative Map of the Successive Losses in Men of the French Army in the Russian Campaign 1812-1813. Paris, November 20, 1869

Chapter 10: p. 149, Dwight Aplevich

Chapter 11: p. 163, Gordon C. Andrews; p. 164, Courtesy: National Research Council of Canada

Part IV: p. 221, Dwight Aplevich

Chapter 15: p. 223, Midnight Sun Solar Rayce Car Team

Chapter 19: p. 289, © De Klerk / Alamy

Chapter 20: p. 317, DILBERT © 1999 Scott Adams. Used By permission of UNIVERSAL UCLICK. All rights reserved.; p. 321, DILBERT © 1999 Scott Adams. Used By permission of UNIVERSAL UCLICK. All rights reserved.

Chapter 21: p. 329, Chipworks; p. 336, M. GOETZE. DEVICE FOR PRODUCING DIMPLES. No. 560,351. Patented May 19, 1896 PWWves es gj ib UNITED STATES PATENT OFFICE: http://www.google.ca/patents/US560351.

PUBLISHER:
Robert Linsky

EXECUTIVE EDITOR:
Randy Haubner

DIRECTOR OF PRODUCT MARKETING:
Susan L. Kindel

OPERATIONS MANAGER:
Christine Moos

DEVELOPMENT EDITOR:
Songlin Qiu

PROJECT EDITOR:
Laura N. Williams

COPY EDITOR:
Jill Bond

TECHNICAL EDITOR:
Alfonso Hermida

SOFTWARE COORDINATOR:
Angela Denny

TEAM COORDINATOR:
Melody Layne

BOOK DESIGNER:
Louisa Klucznik

COVER DESIGNER:
Nathan Clement

INDEXER:
Cheryl Landis

PROOFREADER:
Sheri Replin

LAYOUT TECHNICIANS:
Steve Balle-Gifford

Jeanette McKay

ABOUT THE AUTHORS

Alan Eliason is a Professor of Management Information Technology at the Atkinson Graduate School of Management, located at Willamette University. Dr. Eliason specializes in information systems and management, Visual Basic, database design, and data communications. He has published more than 20 books on topics related to information technology.

Ryan Malarkey is president of Malarkey and Associates, a software development and corporate training firm located in Portland Oregon. Mr. Malarkey specializes in database and client/server application design. He conducts workshops on Visual Basic, Java, database design, and client/server development.

ABOUT THE TECHNICAL EDITOR

Alfonso Hermida has a Bachelor of Science degree in Mechanical Engineering and two Master of Science degrees in the areas of Dynamics and Space Systems. He has worked as a software consultant, taught at various engineering colleges, has authored various books on computer graphics, and has worked as a technical editor and consultant for various publishing companies. He currently works at NASA/Goddard Space Flight Center, where he has worked both as a Mechanical and Electrical Engineer in the Electromechanical Branch. Alfonso wrote his first computer program on Apple II and hasn't stopped since. He has developed computer programs in the areas of computer graphics, numerical methods, artificial intelligence, robotics, structural analysis, and currently develops digital signal processing (DSP) and mechanism control applications. Alfonso has programmed in C/C++, Fortran, Pascal, Lisp, Prolog, Java, assembly, and all flavors of Basic.

ACKNOWLEDGMENTS

Many people were essential in helping us write and polish this book. Foremost, we would like to thank the students who attended our workshops and gave us comments and suggestions on improving the chapter materials. There is no substitute for teaching from materials which are to be included in a textbook. Students identified topics considered essential to learning the language, and pointed out the inevitable errors that come into a book with over 500 exercises. Our students made this a much better book. To all our students, thank you.

Book projects are hard, always harder than you expect when first undertaking them. We especially would like to thank our families for their indulgence for the time spent away from them during the busy months while we brought this volume to completion.

We must also mention the marvelous development team at Que Education and Training. Special thanks is given to Randy Haubner, Executive Editor of Que E&T; our wonderful Development Editor, Songlin Qiu; our amazing Technical Editor, Alfonso Hermida; our watchful Copy Editor, Jill Bond; Project Editor, Laura Williams, as well as all others who helped to coordinate this difficult project.

INTRODUCTION

Visual Basic is the most popular programming language for the world's most popular operating system. By encapsulating the complexities of the Windows application program interface (API) into easily manipulated objects, Visual Basic is the first language people consider when they want rapid application development for the Windows environment. The capability of custom controls to easily extend the language has made Visual Basic a popular choice for an amazingly wide variety of programming tasks.

However, the easy accessibility of the language and its enormous breadth pose challenges to both the students and the instructors. Students approach the language from a wide variety of backgrounds and abilities: Some are new to programming; some have extensive programming experience in other languages (often character-based procedural languages); some want to learn the language to accomplish a very specific task.

Frequently, instructors are challenged by the variety of students who come together in a course. A senior engineer from an aerospace company sits right next to a programming neophyte. Some students are comfortable working with a visual programming environment, while others find the design paradigm quite difficult. Consequently, teaching materials must be flexible enough to accommodate a broad range of backgrounds.

Key Features of This Book

Because knowledge is cumulative, each chapter of this book builds on the previous one, as the concepts and exercises become progressively more challenging. The material begins with easy-to-learn design environments and computer programs that require no previous knowledge of programming. This book, therefore, works well for the beginning programmer.

All of the chapters contain essentially the same elements which are designed to explain the concepts involved in developing Visual Basic programs and guiding the students through putting these concepts into practice. The chapter elements are as follows:

- Each chapter begins with a brief overview of what to expect in the chapter and a list of tasks that students will be able to perform after reading the chapter.

- Each chapter is organized around **Chapter Objectives** that distill the tasks into meaningful units of explanatory text and exercises.

- Visual Basic concepts are introduced and put into a practical context. We have discovered that the best way to learn the language is to work through a large number of exercises. To this end, each chapter contains several hands-on **Exercises** for students to study and complete.

- Each chapter contains a **Chapter Summary** of the key concepts.

■ Each chapter ends with a set of **Skill-Building Exercises** that call upon knowledge acquired in the chapter. These final exercises provide opportunities for students to wrestle with programming problems on their own so that the concepts and techniques presented in the chapter become solid skills.

New Features

We provide a more comprehensive examination of object types, variables, and collections in this book than in previous editions. We have reorganized the sequence of chapters so that "Object Types, Variables, and Collections" (Chapter 19) and "Class Modules" (Chapter 20)are introduced after a full introduction of Visual Basic's design environment, control structures, and sequential file processing. This should better accommodate the needs of beginning programming courses.

The Applications section of the book emphasizes "Modular Design" (Chapter 21). It adds a new chapter on "ActiveX Data Objects" (Chapter 25) and provides a greatly revised introduction to Visual Basic's use as an Internet application development environment, discussed in "Visual Basic Internet Application"(Chapter 27).

Chapter 18, "Sequential File Processing and Error Trapping," has been greatly expanded. It provides more complete coverage of sequential file functions and statements, features of the Common Dialog control, and error trapping. Chapter 17, "String Functions," also gives comprehensive coverage to the new string functions included in Visual Basic 6.0.

Each chapter contains seven or more skill-building exercises, which, when added to the exercises contained in the text, makes the book rich with examples. We have discovered that by working through several sets of exercises, students are able to learn and retain Visual Basic's concepts and details—of which there are many. We keep telling our students that Visual Basic is not all that difficult to learn; however, there is so much to learn.

Prerequisites

A working knowledge of Microsoft Windows 95, Windows 98, or Windows NT Workstation (4.0) is assumed, as is familiarity with the use of a mouse, basic file-handling skills, and basic editing skills. For example, students should know how to create directories and subdirectories, open a file and save it to a disk, and know how to cut, copy, and paste text. Students should also be conversant with basic computer terminology, such as *icon, window,* and *menu bar.*

Organization of This Book

To simplify the learning process required in mastering Visual Basic, this book follows a three-part sequence of general topics: environment, programming, and applications.

Part I: Environment

The first section of this book addresses the Visual Basic design environment, teaches programming, but very little. We stress the importance of design in visual programming and the event-driven nature of the language. In this way, we can introduce the standard Visual Basic controls and reveal the nature of an event-oriented language to those students who come to Visual Basic from other programming backgrounds.

Part II: Programming

Part II is more challenging and contains some complex, yet important, subjects. We introduce core programming concepts, some of which will be new to most students—including those with previous programming experience. These include standard Visual Basic data types, conditional tests, variable and procedure scopes, loops, user events, single and multidimensional arrays, numeric and string functions, file processing, object types, and class modules.

Contrary to our own expectations, this portion of the text would prove the least adaptable to the needs of a wide variety of students, the opposite has proven to be the case. The topics in this part of the book often lead to our most successful classroom experiences.

Part III: Applications

Material from Part I and Part II is combined in Part III for the building of actual Visual Basic applications. We introduce application development with a heavy emphasis on application design, Visual Basic's extensive record-handling routines, and Visual Basic's built-in Jet database engine. Some books slight the record-handling to focus more attention on databases; this one gives appropriate attention to both.

This part of the book becomes challenging when Data Access Objects are introduced and used in the exercises (important in database applications). This final part also examines using ActiveX Data Objects (ADO) for data access, working with objects from Microsoft Office, and building Internet applications.

Appendices

The appendices in this book provide a handy reference for two important topics: the entire ANSI code as supported by Microsoft Windows, which is frequently referred to in this text, and the collections, properties, and methods of various Data Access Objects, which are vital to the chapters in Part III.

PART II: PROGRAMMING   123

ENVIRONMENT

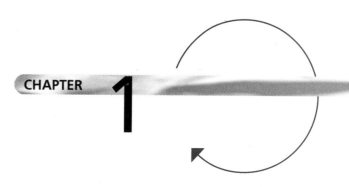

RUNNING A VISUAL BASIC PROGRAM

Welcome to the world of Visual Basic. Released by Microsoft in 1991, Visual Basic was designed to be a visually oriented programming language in contrast to the popular languages of that time (Pascal, C, COBOL, and FORTRAN). Although Visual Basic is similar to QBasic—the procedural language supplied with every version of MS-DOS beginning with version 5—it contains important extensions that make it more of an object-oriented language.

The newest version of Visual Basic is more object-oriented than ever. It is capable of handling software development projects of enormous scope and depth. Visual Basic now is one of the most flexible and powerful visual object-oriented computer languages available, and it remains the most popular language for the world's most popular operating system.

One way of describing Visual Basic's nature is to say that when the computer programmer develops programs in Visual Basic, data is more often than not approached as an object rather than just numeric or text information. Data objects, like real-world objects, such as desks and chairs, have properties. Desks and chairs could be said to have a "LegCount" property, which describes the number of legs for that object, whether it is a three-legged stool or a four-legged desk. Similarly, a data object that held information about a store's customers might have a CustomerCount property. Unlike the "LegCount" physical property of a real-world chair, you can easily change the CustomerCount property of a data object.

Objects in Visual Basic have many features that are introduced in this chapter and explored throughout this book. When you complete this chapter, you will be able to perform the following tasks:

- Comprehend the basic concepts of object-oriented programming
- Understand the Visual Basic design environment
- Understand the essential programming components of Visual Basic
- Understand the three key object features: properties, methods, and events

- Be able to launch Visual Basic
- Be able to use Object Browser to examine Visual Basic objects
- Be able to run Visual Basic programs

Chapter Objectives

Every chapter of this book contains a set of objectives. Read through them prior to reading each chapter and review them at the end of the chapter to determine whether you have realized the objectives. In this chapter, you will not write a Visual Basic program. Instead, you will explore the Visual Basic program design environment and run several sample Visual Basic programs.

Before you turn on your computer and start working, you should consider briefly the Visual Basic programming language to understand how it differs from other types of programming languages. Consider the Visual Basic architecture and learn a number of terms, including forms, controls, properties, methods, events, statements, and system objects. The objectives of this chapter are as follows:

1. Learning how Visual Basic differs from other programming languages
2. Understanding the relationship of Visual Basic to Windows
3. Understanding objects as instances of classes
4. Running sample Visual Basic programs

Objective 1.1   Learning How Visual Basic Differs from Other Programming Languages

Of the 1,000 or so computer languages that have been developed, each language can be categorized based upon the following criteria:

- Low-level or high-level
- Procedure-oriented or event-oriented
- High-visual or low-visual
- Interpreted or compiled

Imagine: 1,000 or so languages! Where does Visual Basic fit? This section helps to explain not only where Visual Basic fits, but why it is different from many other programming languages.

1.1.1   Low-Level and High-Level Languages

A computer language can be described as a low-level or high-level language, based on how close the language is to machine language (which depicts a low-level language) or to English (which depicts a high-level language). Look at what is meant by this difference in language.

Low-Level Languages

Low-level languages are machine-oriented. These languages work close to machine language, which is limited to 0s and 1s. Why only 0s and 1s? This is the language the computer understands. By making a language closer to 0s and 1s, the speed at which the computer processes data improves.

An example of a low-level language is assembly language code. With this language, such instructions as the following tell the computer to save, move, add, and store the results of processing:

```
PUSH BX
PUSH AX
MOV  AX, @A
MOV  BX, @B
ADD  BX, AX
MOV  @B, BX
POP  BX
POP  AX
```

Assembly language code uses mnemonics (memory aids), for which such words as ADD and POP make it easier to remember what an assembly instruction does. While not quite 0s and 1s, you deal with the exact steps the computer must take in processing data when programming in assembly language.

Low-level languages are said to have a *one-to-one relationship* with the computer: A programmer must write an explicit instruction for every operation of the machine. A low-level language is precise. Programmers use low-level language code for tasks such as writing operating systems (the software that enables your computer to operate).

High-Level Languages

High-level languages are more people-oriented. These languages have a one-to-many relationship, in which one instruction leads to a series of machine-level instructions. These languages feature more English and English-like words. In Visual Basic, examples of these English-like words are If, Else, Dim (for dimension), and OpenDatabase.

Because of this one-to-many relationship, high-level languages are easier to learn, use, and understand; however, they do require more machine time to translate a single instruction into a set of machine-level instructions.

Programmers (those who write computer programs) use high-level languages in writing application programs. A high-level language such as Visual Basic, for example, would be used to write the instructions for processing a company payroll. Application programs define the ways by which users are able to use the computer.

1.1.2 Procedure-Oriented and Event-Oriented Languages

Besides low-level and high-level languages, computer languages can be classified as procedure-oriented or event-oriented. *Procedure-oriented* languages tend to run without human interference or the taking of some action by the user: a computer program is executed by a simple run instruction, and usually runs from top to bottom, with all the code executed until the program ends. Event-oriented languages are different in that they depend on the user: They wait for the user to take some action before they execute. As you will soon discover, the program waits for an event (or happening) to occur before beginning a program execution.

Procedure-Oriented Languages

Prior to 1990, most commercial high-level languages were *procedure-oriented languages*. The emphasis in writing a computer program was to identify a set of processing tasks and to describe the steps important to each task. Collectively, the set of tasks represented a procedure: a listing of a set of tasks required to perform an activity. As an example, consider the procedure required in processing an employee paycheck, in which the steps of the procedure are expressed as tasks:

1. Get employee name.
2. Get hours worked.
3. Get hourly wage.
4. Multiply hours worked by the hourly wage to compute gross pay.
5. Compute taxes based on gross pay.
6. Subtract taxes and other deductions (such as union dues) from gross pay to compute net pay.
7. Print the employee's check.

This procedure could be used in writing a QBasic program. The following code listing shows a partial QBasic program written to print an employee's check. Although you may not know the QBasic language, you should be able to understand, step-by-step, how the computer processes an employee paycheck.

```
'Compute and print a payroll check
'Initialize variables
emp.name$ = "Roger Rabbit"
pay.date$ = "06/15/99"
hours.worked = 40          'Total hours worked
rate = 7.50                'Pay per hour
tax.rate = 0.25            'Tax percentage

'Compute gross and net pay
gross.pay = hours.worked * rate
taxes = gross.pay * tax.rate
net.pay = gross.pay - taxes

'Display the results
LPRINT TAB(40); "Date: "; pay.date$
LPRINT
LPRINT "Pay to the order of: "; emp.name$
LPRINT
LPRINT "Pay the full amount of: "; gross.pay
LPRINT TAB(25); "---"
LPRINT
LPRINT TAB(40); "--------------------"
LPRINT TAB(40); "W. Pinchpenney, Treasurer"
```

Event-Oriented Languages

Event-oriented languages became possible with the advent of the Macintosh operating system for Apple Macintosh computers and Microsoft Windows for MS-DOS computer systems. Both environments were designed to bring hardware and software together into a standard user interface by employing a *graphical user interface*, or *GUI* (pronounced goo-ey). A GUI simplifies learning—once you learn how to work with one application using the interface, it is easy to learn another application because the interface remains the same.

An event-oriented language implies that an application (the computer program) waits for an event to occur before taking any action. What is an event? It might be the press of a key on the keyboard or the click of a mouse button. With these events (there are many types), the computer waits for a key press or a mouse click (pushing a button on a hand-held mouse).

1.1.3 Low-Visual and High-Visual Languages

Computer languages can be described as having a *low-visual* or a *high-visual orientation*. Prior to 1990, most languages were low-visual languages, so programmers had considerable difficulty designing the computer forms and reports, data entry screens, and navigation tools by which to move from one area of a computer program to another. High-visual languages greatly simplify the tasks of designing forms, screens, and navigation tools. For this and other reasons, Visual Basic is known as a *rapid prototyping language*. Its design tools let you quickly design a version or prototype of a computer application.

Low-Visual Languages

Consider how a low-visual language differs from a high-visual language. Low-visual languages are not supported by a GUI. Instead, the programmer usually works with a blank terminal screen, adding line after line of instruction to that screen. After the instructions are entered, the programmer issues a Run or Execute command to execute the instructions. Only at this time do visual images appear on the screen. Those of you who use common DOS-level commands, such as Copy, Del, or CD, use a low-visual language.

High-Visual Languages

High-visual languages are supported by a GUI design environment. Figure 1.1 shows the Visual Basic design environment after startup. The appearance of the design environment is conceived to improve speed in program design and can even be customized to suit your needs. At the top of the screen is a menu bar, which contains the File, Edit, View, Project, Format, Debug, Run, Tools, Add-Ins, Window, and Help menus. Below the menu bar is a toolbar (see Figure 1.2).

Menu bar   Project Explorer window   Properties window   Toolbar

Toolbox   Form window

Figure 1.1   *The integrated Visual Basic design environment contains a menu bar, a toolbar, a toolbox, and three types of windows: Form, Project, and Properties.*

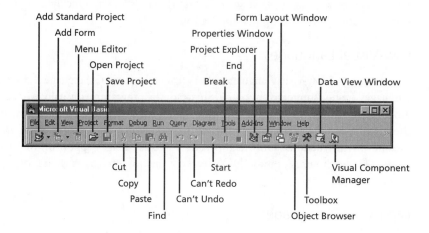

Figure 1.2   *The Visual Basic toolbar contains commonly used icons designed to speed your design.*

The buttons appearing on the toolbar allow quick access to the most commonly used commands. Figure 1.3 shows the toolbox, which you can drag around the screen and place where you want. As you work your way through the exercises contained in this book, you will become familiar with the use of each tool in this toolbox. Finally, the Visual Basic startup screen often contains a Form window, a Project (Explorer) window, and a Properties window. Figure 1.1 shows all three of these windows. Chapter 2, "Writing and Running Your First Visual Basic Program," asks you to use each in constructing a Visual Basic program.

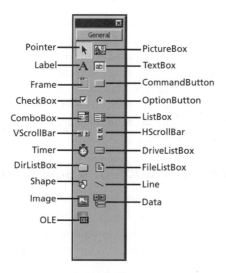

The controls shown in the toolbox are labeled:

Left column: Pointer, Label, Frame, CheckBox, ComboBox, VScrollBar, Timer, DirListBox, Shape, Image, OLE

Right column: PictureBox, TextBox, CommandButton, OptionButton, ListBox, HScrollBar, DriveListBox, FileListBox, Line, Data

Figure 1.3   *The Visual Basic Standard toolbox contains the standard controls to use in constructing a visual application.*

Pause and Breathe for a Moment!

Looking at the toolbar and toolbox the first time might fill your heart with fear. You might exclaim, "I can't remember what all those icons mean!" With Visual Basic, help is readily on hand. To quickly identify a control, just let your mouse pointer linger over an item in the toolbox. A ToolTip appears by your pointer and identifies the control. The same applies for buttons on the toolbar. You also can click the button you want to inspect and press the Help key: the F1 function key on the keyboard. The Visual Basic Help screen appears with a description of that button.

1.1.4   Interpreted or Compiled Languages

Computer languages can be *interpreted* or *compiled*. An interpreter executes a program, while a compiled language uses a compiler to translate the high-level language into machine language. Visual Basic now is both an interpreted language and a compiled language. The developer has a choice when creating a Visual Basic executable whether to make a compiled program or an interpreted program. You will create both types of programs in an exercise in Chapter 2.

The main advantage of an interpreted language is immediate response. Program development often goes faster because the code instructions can be easily modified and immediately tested without being compiled (or translated) first. This saves you considerable time in writing and testing a program. The main disadvantage of an interpreted program is speed of execution—especially in processor-intensive instructions. An interpreted program must translate instructions each time a program is run. This is not required of a compiled program.

The advent of compilation in Visual Basic versions 5 and 6 has dramatically sped up numeric calculations and most other computations. The speed by which forms now load into memory in Visual Basic is one of the language's more dramatic speed improvements. Compilation alone, however, does not guarantee speed. Design of a program is one of the more important determinants of performance. Visual Basic programs, whether they are interpreted or compiled, rely upon other runtime libraries of functions in order to execute. These libraries are probably the largest factor in Visual Basic performance.

1.1.5 The Recent Evolution of Visual Basic

In the last several years, Visual Basic has evolved rapidly. Until recently, Visual Basic was a proprietary language used only by Microsoft products. Microsoft now licenses Visual Basic for Applications to those software developers who want to add programmability to their applications. This will increase Visual Basic's prevalence.

Visual Basic now is the universal macro language for the Microsoft Office suite of applications. The newest version of Word, for example, has migrated to Visual Basic for Applications. Other large programmable applications, such as Microsoft Project, also use Visual Basic for Applications.

Another important development of the Visual Basic language is the advent of the *Visual Basic Scripting Edition* (also known as *VBScript*) for developing Internet-enabled applications. The capability of Visual Basic to create downloadable ActiveX components and the capability of VBScript to manipulate Internet browsers and Internet documents (HTML documents) suggests Visual Basic will play a major role in the explosion of Internet and intranet applications.

This text assumes that you have the Learning, Professional, or Enterprise Editions of Visual Basic. All chapters other than the database chapters can be completed using the Learning Edition of Visual Basic, but you will need the Professional Edition to work with databases in Chapters 23, 24, and 25, and the Internet applications in Chapter 27. Microsoft Office also will need to be installed on your computer to take advantage of Chapter 26, "Working with Objects from Microsoft Office," which introduces working with Microsoft Office applications from Visual Basic.

Objective 1.2   Understanding the Relationship of Visual Basic to Windows

All application programs (the kind of programs developed with such languages as Visual Basic) must be developed to work with a specific operating system. Application programs interact with operating systems by using operating system functions that applications developers can exploit. These functions usually are referred to as application program interface (API) functions. API functions allow programmers to add such functionality to their programs as opening and saving files, checking system hardware, using the computer's internal clock, and, in the Microsoft Windows family of operating systems, creating, modifying, and communicating with Windows.

The Windows API is enormously complex. It has over 800 functions, some of which can perform a wide variety of tasks. The value of Visual Basic is that it greatly simplifies Windows programming. Visual Basic encapsulates the Windows API into objects that Visual Basic programmers can manipulate. For example, when you use the C programming language, creating a program that greets the user with the message "Welcome to Visual Basic" can take several lines of instructions. In Visual Basic, however, the same program requires only a single line.

1.2.1 Forms and Controls

What, exactly, does the phrase "encapsulates the Windows API" mean? *Encapsulation* is a key concept for any object-oriented programming language. It refers to the capability of an object to hide its internal workings from other objects. In turn, the object allows itself to be manipulated by the programmer and other objects through the use of three key object features: properties, methods, and events.

Consider two kinds of objects that you have seen in the Visual Basic startup screen: forms and controls. Figure 1.1 shows a Window that contains a *form* named Form1. This form acts as a container for controls. You could think of Form1 as a blank piece of paper that you must fill in. You use this blank form to design the user interface for a Visual Basic application. When you begin the design of a Visual Basic program, you start with a blank form and, with a set of tools, begin to design the user interface.

The tools you use to construct the interface are called *controls*, which are attached to forms. Examples of controls are shown on the toolbox and include a text box (a box the user types text into), a command button (an onscreen button that the user can click), and a label (an area on the form to place a text heading) (refer to Figure 1.3). If the toolbox is not visible, select View, Toolbox on the menu bar, or click the Toolbox button on the toolbar to display it.

Because forms and controls are objects, they can be manipulated by properties, methods, and events. Consider each of these object features in turn.

Object Properties

A property is a named attribute of an object. Properties are used to change the appearance and behavior of objects, such as forms and controls. These properties include attributes affecting the color, size, and name of the object.

Take an everyday object, such as a shirt. Suppose that you write the following:

```
Shirt.color = "Blue"
```

In Visual Basic, this would tell you that you have an object named Shirt. One of the properties of the shirt is color. You can change the color by assigning a new one, such as "Blue". You might want to set another of the Shirt's properties as the following:

```
Shirt.launder = "Clean"
```

as opposed to

```
Shirt.launder = "Dirty"
```

In the example, the condition of the shirt—clean or dirty—can be set directly. Wouldn't it be great if your shirts were always clean?

For a Visual Basic object, such as a form, you can write instructions to alter it. The following instruction changes the color of a form named Form1 to blue:

```
Form1.BackColor = vbBlue
```

Object Methods

The concept of an object method is more difficult than the concept of a property. Methods are computer instructions (code) held by an object that operate on the object's data. Methods are written in a different way than properties. The syntax (required way) for describing the application of a method to an object is written as follows:

```
Object.Method
```

Perhaps an analogy will make methods more understandable. Suppose that you had a very compliant dog named Sparky. By invoking the following methods of Sparky, you would get the behavior from Sparky that you desire:

```
Sparky.eat
Sparky.bark
Sparky.scat
```

Object methods in Visual Basic are similar. One method for a List Box control (a control that displays a list of different text items) is the Clear method. To clear the contents of the list box, you would write the following instruction:

```
List1.Clear
```

When working with object properties in Visual Basic, you are either assigning them a new value (for example, Form1.BackColor = vbBlue), or you are reading their values (for example, mycolor = Form1.BackColor). Object methods, by contrast, are invoked with the Object.Method syntax (for example, List1.Clear). The distinctions between object methods and object properties will become familiar to you as you work more with Visual Basic objects.

Object Events

While the value of a property can be set and a method can be invoked, an object event is an action taken by the object when notified by a message. An object event might be a mouse click. The handling of object events is an operating system responsibility. The Windows operating system sends messages to windows (objects) for different events.

Remember the words message and action. If the user clicks a mouse button on a Visual Basic form, the operating system sends a message to the form. The Visual Basic designer can choose to execute code (the action) in response to the message or ignore it. An image on a form, for example, might be programmed to take some action when it is clicked. It might take some other action when it is dragged across the form. The Visual Basic programmer writes coded instructions for the events that should be assigned to the form or control. Visual Basic code, for example, executes instructions by invoking a form's Print method when the user clicks the form:

```
Private Sub Form_Click
    Form1.Print "You clicked the form!"
End Sub
```

1.2.2 A Closer Look at Encapsulation

Object properties, methods, and events make up what is known as the objects *interface*. This interface may be considered the public view of the object, and it describes how that object can be manipulated. Objects also have a private view: the data and code that the object does not expose to public view, but retains in order to execute its functions. When you invoke the Clear method of a List Box control, for example, you do not know how the list box clears its contents. It just does it, and you know that it works. To illustrate encapsulation, conduct a brief and simple exercise.

Exercise 1.1 Illustrating Encapsulation

In this exercise, you don't have to write any code. You simply run an executable that is included on the companion disk.

You must have Visual Basic installed on your computer; otherwise, the executable will not run. Using the Windows Explorer, you can run the Demo1.exe program from the companion disk (in the Chapt01 folder) or copy it to your computer's hard disk and run it from there.

1. To run the program, click it. You should see the interface shown in Figure 1.4. The program consists of only two TextBox controls placed on a form. No Visual Basic code was written at all.

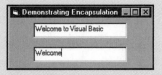

Figure 1.4 *This application places two text boxes on a form and contains text that you must type in or copy and paste.*

2. Set the insertion point in the upper text box, and type the text **Welcome to Visual Basic**.

3. Select the text you have written using your mouse (or hold the Shift key down and use the directional keys—-the keys with arrows point up, down, left, and right).

continues

Exercise 1.1   continued

4. Copy the selected text onto the Windows Clipboard (Ctrl+C).

5. Using the Tab key, shift to the lower text box and paste the text (Ctrl+V) from the Clipboard into the lower text box.

6. Using the Backspace key, delete the word Welcome, the text that you pasted.

7. Exit the application by clicking the Close button in the upper-right corner of the form or using the System menu (the choices presented when you click the small button in the upper-left corner of the form). Do not save this application before exiting.

Consider all the functionality contained within this application without a single line of Visual Basic code being written. Three windows—a form, and two text boxes—were created. One of these windows, the form, uses the default colors specified in the Windows Control Panel. This form can be resized, minimized into an icon, or maximized to fill the entire screen. It can be moved around the screen with the mouse.

The two text boxes allow the user to erase existing text and type text. Text could be copied and pasted. The text controls even indicate the user's location by displaying a cursor.

How does the `TextBox` control manage the insertion point? How does it "know" to erase text when the Backspace key is pressed? You don't know. That's the private view of the Text Box object. You don't really have to know the inner workings of the Text Box object. It works, and you can use it to build your own applications. That's the power of encapsulation!

1.2.3   Visual Basic Statements and Instructions

The discussion of objects and encapsulation in section 1.2.1, "Forms and Controls," uses several lines of Visual Basic code, including examples of object properties being assigned values and methods being invoked. The terms code and instructions can be used interchangeably, but the term statement means something specific in Visual Basic.

Visual Basic Statements

A statement differs from the assignment of a property or invocation of a method. Consider the following definition: A statement is a reserved word that causes a computer program or the operating system to do something. Statements are instructions (code) that are built in to the Visual Basic language. Methods are code held by an object.

If you look at the Visual Basic Help, you discover that some keywords are state-ments. For example, the keyword End is a statement that ends (stops) the execution of a Visual Basic program. The keyword Kill (sorry, this is in the language) is a statement that deletes a file from a disk.

As another example, the statement to force explicit declaration of all variables is written as follows:

```
Option Explicit
```

In this example, no reference to an object is required because the statement is built in to the language.

Visual Basic Program Instructions

Methods, statements, and Visual Basic instructions are different. An *instruction* is simply a line of code in a Visual Basic application. Instructions contain the names of constants, variables, functions, properties, methods, and built-in Visual Basic statements. The rule to remember regarding instructions is that all instructions begin with a statement or the invocation of an object method. For example, an instruction beginning with a statement is as follows:

```
End
```

The following is an instruction beginning with a method:

```
List1.AddItem Entry
```

The method is AddItem and the object is List1.

Finally, some instructions beginning with methods or statements also contain what are known as *statement* or *method arguments*. Consider the following:

```
Form1.Move Left + (Width \ 10), Top + (Height \ 10)
```

In this instruction, Move is a method and Left, Width, Top, and Height are proper-ties of the object, Form1, that are used as method arguments. An example of a built-in Visual Basic statement that takes an argument is the AppActivate statement:

```
AppActivate "Calculator"
```

In this case, the statement shifts focus to a running instance of the Calculator util-ity bundled with Windows.

This all may seem a bit confusing right now, but you will get used to working with objects, methods, and statements once you begin writing Visual Basic programs.

Objective 1.3   Understanding Objects as Instances of Classes

In Exercise 1.1, the two text boxes and the form are referred to as windows as well as objects. In a Windows program, just about everything that you see onscreen is a window, and many items that you don't see are windows.

In a standard Windows word processing program, such as Word or WordPerfect, every button on the toolbars is a separate window. Every open document is a separate window, as are the dialog boxes that permit you to select different font properties, and the rulers that allow you to set tabs and adjust page width. These windows are objects, which have their own properties, methods, and events. The Windows operating system sends messages to the windows to respond to user events.

1.3.1   Object Classes

How many different kinds of windows can there be? As many as a programmer can imagine and create! The design of the Windows operating system provides several standard window types called classes. There can be many classes of objects in addition to the standard types. Whether you know it or not, you probably are already familiar with several standard Windows classes and their behaviors, including the following:

- `Button`
- `ComboBox`
- `Edit`
- `ListBox`
- `Scrollbar`

As you might suspect by now, some of the controls in the Visual Basic toolbox are related to these standard Windows classes. A `TextBox` control, for example, is closely related to the base Windows Edit class.

A class is like a cookie cutter: It defines how an object should look and behave when it is first created. To work with Visual Basic objects, you first use this cookie cutter to cut out the uniform shape of your object. After you have this basic shape (called an instance of the class), you can manipulate the object by altering its properties or by calling one of the object's methods to make the object behave in a certain way.

Visual Basic often creates an instance of a class for you. When you add a `TextBox` control to a form, Visual Basic creates an instance of the Visual Basic Text Box control class. After it is created, you can manipulate it. To alter text displayed in a text box object named `txtDisplay`, for example, you would execute the following instruction:

```
txtDisplay.Text = "Welcome to Visual Basic"
```

In other circumstances, you will be required to create an instance of the class (an object) yourself. In this book, you will even define your own classes and then create multiple instances (objects) from the class you have defined.

1.3.2   Invisible Objects in Visual Basic

Not all objects in Visual Basic are visible and displayed to the user. Neither are all objects windows. Visual Basic contains system objects that are available to use, although they are not displayed in the toolbox, including the following:

- **App**—Stores information about the application, including its name, path (where it is stored), and the files it requires. This object can also activate an application.

- **Clipboard**—Temporary storage location. It allows text, graphics, and computer code to be transferred from one part of an application to another part or from one application to another.

- **Screen**—References the entire video display screen. It manipulates the size and placement of forms onscreen.

- **Debug**—Permits the display of information about a program while it is being developed.

- **Printer**—Determines how text and graphics are printed on a page and how output is sent to the printer.

These are system objects because the Windows operating system keeps information about each one. For example, when you set up Windows, you must designate the computer printer to be used to send output to the printer. When a specific printer is selected, Windows stores information about its makeup, such as the paper width and length. In Visual Basic, you never have to use your printer's name in a program. Instead, you can instruct your printer to print directly by using the Printer object.

System objects will become important later. For now, you should simply be aware that they exist and of what they do.

1.3.3   Software Components

After all this discussion of classes and objects, you might be asking yourself, "Why all the fuss about objects? What are the advantages of using objects?"

The real benefit of objects is that, developed properly, they provide software that is reusable and robust. The continuing dilemma of software development has been to create reliable code much faster and at lower cost. Some claim that it is an impossible task. More than a few software developers have a large sign posted above their doors: "Software Developed: Fast, Cheap, Good. Choose Two."

Although object-oriented design has certainly not proved to be a magic bullet to shoot the beast of software development costs, it has helped create reliable, reusable software components. Visual Basic components include the following:

- Visible controls (the tools represented in the Visual Basic toolbox)

- Software libraries that can be reliably used by many applications (ActiveX DLLs)

- Executable programs that can be used by other programs (ActiveX EXEs)

These components make single or multiple objects available to the developer.

Different types of software components are introduced and used in this book. You will build applications using software components, and in the case of ActiveX DLLs, build a software component yourself. Software components make possible rapid development of applications by acting as the building blocks of an application. Each software component provides a particular service to the application. One way to think about software components is to see them as servers to client applications.

How do you know which software components are available to you? Visual Basic provides the Object Browser utility to enable you to examine your choices.

Exercise 1.2   Launching Visual Basic and the Object Browser

In this exercise, you will start Visual Basic and then use Object Browser to examine Visual Basic objects. You are provided step-by-step instructions. Don't be alarmed if you see unfamiliar windows. The Visual Basic environment is explained in greater detail in Chapter 2, "Writing and Running Your First Visual Basic Program," and Chapter 3, "Adding Controls and Event Procedures to Form Modules." This exercise assumes Visual Basic has been installed on your computer.

1. Start Visual Basic from the Windows Start menu.

2. When Visual Basic launches, a dialog box similar to that shown in Figure 1.5 appears. If this dialog box does not appear, select Project, New from the Visual basic menu.

Figure 1.5   *The Visual Basic startup dialog box contains several types of new projects, including the Standard EXE project.*

3. Click the Open button for a new Standard EXE project (or click OK if you opened the dialog box from the Visual Basic menu).

The Visual Basic design environment will appear. It should look somewhat similar to the design environment you saw illustrated in Figure 1.1. It will appear similar, but not identical. As you will discover in the next section of this chapter, the Visual Basic design environment is almost infinitely configurable by you. There really is no standard Visual Basic design environment.

4. Press the F2 key or select View, Object Browser from the Visual Basic menu. Object Browser will appear as shown in Figure 1.6.

5. Select the VB library from the combo box in the upper-left corner of Object Browser, as shown in Figure 1.6. (You have used this kind of Windows object before, but you may not have known that was called a combo box.)

Figure 1.6   *The VB Object Browser lists the software classes available to you from the Visual Basic class library.*

6. The classes through which you can scroll are listed on the left-hand side of Object Browser. Select the TextBox class of the VB library and then examine the properties, methods, and events of the TextBox class in the right-hand list box.

Notice that the Object Browser icons indicate whether the class element (called a class member) is a property (the icon depicting a small hand holding a piece of paper), a method (the icon depicting a small green rectangle), or an event (the icon depicting a small thunderbolt). Figure 1.7 shows these three icons.

continues

Exercise 1.2   continued

Figure 1.7   *Object Browser displays information about classes, in this case the TextBox classes, and shows properties of the class, class events, and class methods.*

As you examine the TextBox class and select different properties, methods, and events, observe the bottom of Object Browser where the class member is described.

Objective 1.4   Running Sample Visual Basic Programs

Given this brief introduction to Visual Basic, it is time for you to become more familiar with the Visual Basic programming environment. Still, you are not expected to write a Visual Basic program at this time; right now, you'll start Visual Basic and become a bit more familiar with the way in which the environment can be configured. Then, you will run three sample programs stored on disk.

1.4.1   A Quick Tour of the Visual Basic Design Environment

The Visual Basic design environment is almost infinitely configurable. This makes it difficult to describe a standard Visual Basic user interface. It depends upon the way the design environment was last configured.

There are two overall design environment choices: MDI or SDI. The abbreviation *MDI* stands for *multiple-document interface*, and it is the default Visual Basic setting. It features an overall container window and movable and dockable windows inside the container. It is the environment displayed in Figure 1.1. The abbreviation *SDI* stands for *single-document interface.* It features free-floating windows on the Windows desktop, which is the environment that would be most familiar to you if you have worked with previous versions of Visual Basic.

Whether the environment is MDI or SDI, the Visual Basic startup environment frequently displays the windows and utilities listed in Table 1.1. These windows and utilities are described in detail in Chapter 2 and Chapter 3.

TABLE 1.1   Visual Basic Startup Windows

Window	Description
Project Explorer	This window is frequently positioned on the right of the the modules that make up a Visual Basic project.
Form module	This window displays a form, if a form is selected for viewing in the Project Explorer. This form is the "canvas" upon which controls are placed.
Properties	This window displays the properties for whatever object has the focus—whether a module or control.
Toolbox	This window displays available controls for placing on forms.

The MDI Design Environment: Using Dockable Windows

The multiple-document interface for Visual Basic was introduced in version 5.0. It enables you to configure the Visual Basic design environment in many ways, but it can be confusing. In order to use it effectively, you must have a large screen set to a fairly high resolution; otherwise, you will quickly suffer from screen clutter. It also requires that you know how to work with dockable windows, an interface feature designed for those who prefer to use a mouse, rather than the keyboard, as a principal input device.

If you have not used dockable windows inside a container before, you might find them frustrating at first. Dockable windows allow you to take any window inside a container and dock it on the perimeter of the container. As you move a window inside a container by keeping your mouse button depressed on the window title bar while moving it, an outline of the window is displayed. The width of this band gives you a visual cue as to what you can do with the window. A thick band outline indicates it will become free-floating if released by the mouse button. Figure 1.8 shows the toolbox docked to the right-hand side of a form.

Figure 1.8 *The toolbox will be docked at the side of the Visual Basic form when the Dockable command (right-mouse button) is selected.*

Given the capability to dock any window at any position in the Visual Basic MDI container, it is possible to customize the environment to your liking. Many developers prefer to dock the toolbox at the bottom of the container in order to make room for form design.

To view a window or toolbar that is not displayed, choose <u>V</u>iew from the Visual Basic menu to see a list of windows and design-time utilities.

The capability to dock windows within the MDI environment can be controlled through the Docking tab of the Options dialog box (choose <u>T</u>ools, Options). If the docking option for a window is not selected (see Figure 1.9), it will remain free-floating.

Figure 1.9 *The Docking tab of the Options dialog box presents many possibilities for docking the Visual Basic windows and design tools, such as the Color palette.*

The SDI Design Environment: Using Free-Floating Windows

The single-document interface, the one preferred by the authors, essentially makes all windows free-floating outside of any container. This increases the amount of screen "real estate" available, which is important in the rich (and often times cluttered) design environment of Visual Basic. The SDI design environment is probably also more familiar to you from working with other Windows applications, including earlier versions of Visual Basic.

To move to an SDI environment, select the Advanced tab in the Options dialog box (by choosing Tools, Options), as shown in Figure 1.10. After you select the SDI environment, a dialog box will appear, informing you that your selection will take effect the next time Visual Basic is launched. To view the SDI environment, exit Visual Basic (by choosing File, Exit), and launch Visual Basic again. You will now be in an SDI environment similar to the one you see in Figure 1.11. To view individual windows and toolbars, you can make selections under the Visual Basic View menu.

Figure 1.10   *The SDI selection in the Options dialog box creates a design environment in which windows remain separate and are no longer docked.*

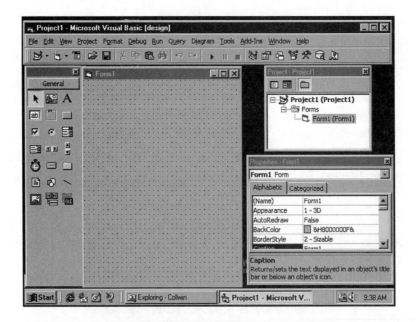

Figure 1.11   *The Visual Basic SDI features free-floating windows, and is good to use when you have a small screen.*

1.4.2   Running Visual Basic Applications

Now that you are a bit more familiar with the Visual Basic design environment, let's run several Visual Basic applications.

Exercise 1.3   Running the Screen Blanker Demo

Run the Screen Blanker Demo, which is named blanker.vbp and is located in the Blanker folder placed in the Chapt01 folder on the companion disk.

1. Start Visual Basic from Windows.

2. Use the mouse to select File, Open Project. If a dialog box appears asking you to save a file, click No.

3. Find the Blanker folder contained inside the Chapt01 folder on the CD supplied with the text.

4. Double-click blanker.vbp to open the application, or select the file and click the Open button.

---

5. Choose <u>R</u>un, <u>S</u>tart from the Visual Basic menu, or press F5. This runs the Visual Basic application.

6. When the Screen Blanker Demo appears, click the Start Demo button. (This button is a control that begins an event. Can you tell what the event is?)

7. Click the Stop Demo button and experiment with the other choices found under the <u>O</u>ptions menu. Open Options and make a selection. Click Start Demo to begin another demonstration.

8. Choose <u>O</u>ptions, E<u>x</u>it to exit the application and return to the Visual Basic design environment.

What does this demo tell you about Visual Basic? With Visual Basic, you can write any number of graphics procedures. The demo should reinforce the fact that Visual Basic is a visual language.

Exercise 1.4   Running the Controls Demo

This application demonstrates some of Visual Basic's controls.

1. Use the mouse to choose File, Open Project. If a dialog box appears asking you to save a file, click No.

2. Find the Controls folder contained inside the Chapt01 folder on the CD supplied with the text.

3. Select the controls.vbp file, and click the Open button.

4. Select Run, Start from the Visual Basic menu or press F5.

5. When the Controls application appears, click the various buttons of the Main application form to see key properties of different Visual Basic controls demonstrated.

6. Select File, Exit to exit the application and return to the Visual Basic design environment.

This demonstration illustrates some key features of Visual Basic's standard controls, including the use of a Command Button, Label, Text Box, Check Box, Option Button, and Image Box controls.

Exercise 1.5   Running the Calculator Demo

This final demonstration application illustrates how you can use Visual Basic to create a simplified calculator. It is the type of application that you should be able to develop with this language within a relatively short period.

1. Open and run the calc.vbp file. This program is found in the calc folder inside Chapt01 folder placed on the CD supplied with the text.

2. Observe the design of this application. Numeric input keys and operator keys are placed on a form with a space for displaying output.

3. Run the application and experiment by making calculations. Notice that input is limited to mouse clicks rather than the pressing of numeric keys. Also notice that input is not permitted in the area that displays the results of calculation. You soon will learn the different kinds of controls that allow user input and those that are used primarily for display.

After experimenting with the calculator, you can close it by double-clicking the application's System menu icon (the box at the upper-left corner of the window) or by clicking the standard Close button in the upper-right corner.

Chapter Summary

Visual Basic is a high-level, event-oriented, high-visual, and compiled or interpreted language. As you will come to appreciate, Visual Basic uses a large number of English words, waits for an event to occur before taking any action, and features a GUI in support of its high-visual orientation.

Visual Basic has a close relationship with Windows. Visual Basic's main characteristic is the encapsulation of the complexity of Windows into objects that are easily manipulated with simple coded instructions.

Objects are manipulated by exposing properties, methods, and events. A property is an attribute of an object, while an event is an action recognized by an object. A method is code executed by an object that acts on data held by that object. The invocation of the `Form1.Hide` method, for example, triggers code held by the form that hides it from view.

Properties, methods, and events serve as the object's public interface. The structure and means by which an object holds data or executes its methods is hidden from view (encapsulated), while its public interface makes it usable to other objects and to program instructions.

Visual Basic has both visible and invisible objects. Forms and most controls are examples of visible objects. Five system objects are examples of invisible objects: the `App` object, the `Clipboard` object, the `Screen` object, the `Debug` object, and the `Printer` object.

Objects are instances of classes. Classes define the default properties, methods, and events of an object. Objects in Visual Basic are created during design time when controls are added to forms and created dynamically by coded instructions. The Object Browser utility in Visual Basic enables you to examine the classes available for use by your application and the object properties, methods, and events defined by the class.

A statement is a reserved word that causes a computer program or the computer to do something. The Beep statement, for example, tells the computer to make a sound.

An instruction represents a line of code used in a Visual Basic application. Every instruction begins with a statement or a method.

Visual Basic's design environment can be designated as an MDI (multiple-document interface), featuring dockable windows inside a parent container, or an SDI (single-document interface), featuring free-floating windows.

Skill-Building Exercises

The programs for these skill-building exercises are found in the skill-building folder (SB01) inside the folder for Chapt01 on the CD that comes with the book. This first set of exercises asks you to examine sample programs to work more with the Object Browser.

1. Open and run the MDI (MDI\Mdinote.vbp) and the SDI (SDI\ Sdinote.vbp) samples. Based on these samples and the material contained in this chapter, describe the difference between MDI and SDI. You may get an error stating that the DBGrid32.OCX cannot be found. If this occurs, select Project, Components from the menu bar to open the Components dialog box. Scroll through the list of components and check Microsoft Data Bound Grid Control and Microsoft Bound List control. Click on OK. Now your program should run.

2. Start Visual Basic in MDI or SDI mode, depending on the settings on your machine. Choose Tools, Options, and click the Advanced tab. Perform one of the following steps:

   ■ Click SDI Development Environment if it is not checked, and exit Visual Basic. Start Visual Basic to note the difference in the development environment.

   ■ Click SDI Development Environment if it is checked (to uncheck it), and exit Visual Basic. Start Visual Basic to note the difference in the development environment.

3. Open and run the Alarm Clock sample. This sample is placed in the folder alarm, placed inside the SB01 folder. Select Run, End to close the program. Examine the design of the alarm clock form. What type of control has been placed on the form? What happens to this control when the program is run?

4. Open and run the Alarm Clock sample again. When the display appears, click the right mouse button to set the alarm time. What happens when this time is reached?

5. Open the Alarm Clock sample once again. Click the Object Browser button on the toolbar and select the Project1 library (not the VB library). What are the members of the class `AlarmForm` (shown in Bold), and what types of members are they: property, event, or method?

6. If your computer has audio speakers, turn them on. Open and run the ATM sample. This sample is placed in the folder named ATM, placed inside the folder SB01 (Go to the path or use the student disk.) When the display appears, enter 123456 as the PIN number. Withdraw $100.00 from the checking account. What message is stated to end the transaction?

7. Open the ATM sample once again. In the Project Window, click on `frmOpen`. Click the Object Browser button on the toolbar, and select the ATM library (not the VB library). Click on `frmOpen` to examine the members of this form. Find the member `command1_click` and double-click on this member. This will open the Visual Basic code for this button. What is the purpose of the `command1_click` member?

WRITING AND RUNNING YOUR FIRST VISUAL BASIC PROGRAM

In Chapter 1, "Running a Visual Basic Program," you learned how to run a program that had been made for you. You probably noticed that when working with Visual Basic, several types of windows could be inspected—even though you were not asked to examine any one window in detail. In this chapter, you learn about three types of windows:

- Project window
- Properties window
- Code window

You will learn how to move from one window to the next in writing a Visual Basic program. You also are asked to write and run several simple Visual Basic programs.

In working through the exercises in this chapter, you will master a number of new tasks, including how to do the following:

- Open a new project
- Save a project
- Name a form and a project
- Remove a form from a project
- Add a form to a project
- Print a form, form text, and code
- Write a `click()` procedure
- Write a `KeyPress()` procedure
- Change font size, style, and type
- Change the window state

Chapter Objectives

The tasks for this chapter are distilled into five objectives that teach you the fundamentals of writing and running a Visual Basic program, as follows:

1. Understanding the concept of a Visual Basic project

2. Learning how to manage Visual Basic projects

3. Opening the Properties window and changing form properties

4. Opening the Code window and writing Visual Basic instructions

5. Producing a compiled application from a Standard EXE project

Objective 2.1   Understanding the Concept of a Visual Basic Project

Every Visual Basic application is defined and saved as a project. Each project, in turn, consists of a collection of files. These files can include modules, insertable objects, and a single resource file. Projects themselves are tracked by a project file, which has a .VBP extension.

Form modules, as discussed in Chapter 1, are first seen as windows with a caption, but little else. Form modules contain coded instructions called procedures for the form itself and for the controls and insertable objects placed on the form. Other modules include standard modules and class modules. You will learn the differences among these types of modules as you progress through this book.

The tools of the toolbox represent controls and insertable objects. The toolbox can be made visible or invisible by choosing View, Toolbox. When visible, the toolbox contains a set of icons, each representing a standard or a custom control. A Visual Basic project always includes a set of standard controls and can also include custom controls. Each custom control has an .OCX extension. In this chapter, you are asked to write some beginning Visual Basic procedures for forms. In Chapter 3, "Adding Controls and Event Procedures to Form Modules," you will add procedures for standard controls.

Projects also can include a resource file, which can contain either binary data, such as images and sounds, or string data. Resource files need to be created by a Windows resource compiler (typically a C or C++ language compiler), or, for string data, you can use the string editor table bundled with Visual Basic.

2.1.1   The Files that Make Up a Standard EXE Project

In working with Visual Basic, you are asked to work with different types of files. Each file type is given a unique file extension, which enables you to identify it. Visual Basic contains over two dozen types of files, each of which has a different extension. Table 2.1 shows eight common file types contained within a project, their extensions, and their meanings.

TABLE 2.1   Common File Types

Type of File	Extension	Description
Basic module	.BAS	Each coded module is saved as a file.
Class module	.CLS	Each class module is saved as a file.
Form module	.FRM	Each form is saved as a file.
Binary	.FRX	Each Icon or Picture property value is saved by Visual Basic in .FRX form.
Log	.LOG	A file for logging loading errors.
Resource	.RES	A project can have a single resource file for storing binary and string data.
Project	.VBP	Each project is saved as a file.
Workspace	.VBW	Each workspace for a project is saved as a file.

This file notation is used throughout this book. When you save a form, it is saved with a .FRM extension, and all event procedures written for that form are also saved in the .FRM file. Because procedures are not saved as separate files with their own unique extension, they become bound to forms. When you write and save a coded basic module (also called a standard module), it is saved with a .BAS extension. Coded modules are thus different from event procedures written for forms. Coded modules are not bound to forms.

In Figure 1.5, you saw that Visual Basic can be used to create different types of projects. For now, you will be creating only Standard EXE projects.

2.1.2   The Project Window (Project Explorer) in the Visual Basic Design Environment

Whenever you begin a Visual Basic program, you begin a new project. Each project usually contains several forms, several standard and class coded modules, and often custom controls. The Project window displays a list of all modules assigned to a project. Whenever you begin a new project, a default Project window is created (see Figure 2.1). If the window fails to appear or is hidden, choose View, Project Explorer; press Ctrl+R or click the Project Explorer icon. In addition, you can set your environment to remove the docking of the Project Explorer. This setting is controlled by choosing Tools, Options, clicking the Docking tab, and turning off the Project Explorer and Object browser selections.

Figure 2.1   *This Project window reveals that Project1 contains a forms folder that is limited to a single form.*

Figure 2.1 illustrates a Project window that contains three small icons on the left-hand side of the Title Bar. The leftmost icon permits you to view code, while the middle one enables you to view the underlying object (which in this case is the form). The third icon, the folder, is important when projects become large and contain multiple modules or when projects are combined. With large projects, all forms are placed in one folder, and all code modules are placed in another folder. Toggling the folder icon enables you to organize similar modules together, so that form modules are contained within one folder, code modules in another, and class modules in a third. The icons within the Project Explorer window act as a collapsible tree to show or hide the modules contained within these folders.

Objective 2.2   Learning How to Manage Visual Basic Projects

In this section, you learn how to open and save a project, add and delete files from the Project window, give an object focus (further explained in section 2.2.5, "The Concept of Focus"), and use the other File commands provided with Visual Basic. You also will work through several exercises to test your knowledge of the concepts presented.

2.2.1   Opening, Saving, Adding, and Removing Projects

Whenever you open Visual Basic, you always start a new project; however, there are File commands that enable you to work with both old and new projects, and File and Project commands for working with old and new files. The File menu on the menu bar contains six commands designed for managing projects, as follows:

- **New Project**—Starts a new project. If you are working on a project, this command prompts you to save the current project. It then closes the current project to enable you to start a new one.

- **Open Project**—Opens a saved project. Before opening a project, this command asks if you want to save a current project, if one exists.

- **Add Project**—Opens a saved project and adds it to another, provided one exists. A Visual Basic application can contain any number of projects.

- **Remove Project**—Removes the selected project from a project group.

- **Save Project As**—Saves the current project to a disk. This option always prompts you for a project name. Use this command to save a project for the first time or save a copy of an existing project. When first saving a project, you are asked whether or not you want to save each form and module associated with a project.

- For each form or module, you can assign a name. You should name each form with a name other than the default name (such as `form1.frm` and `form2.frm`); otherwise, you will only save the most recent form1.frm and find it impossible to retrieve the form you thought you had saved. You should also name each project with a unique name, or else Visual Basic will assign every project the same default name.

- **Save Project**—Saves the current project to a disk. This option saves all forms and modules as separate files. It creates a file with a .VBP (Visual Basic Project) extension. If the project is being saved for the first time, this command prompts you for the project name. If saved earlier, it updates the .VBP file.

The .VBP file is saved as text or in ANSI (American National Standards Institute) format. This enables you to inspect its contents with any text editor. Each project contains one—and only one—.VBP file, which provides a description of the project, showing the names of the stored files and other descriptive information.

2.2.2   Naming a Project

Each time you begin a new project, the default name, Project1, appears at top of the form. Unless you change this name, every project you work on will be named Project1. To change the name, choose Project, Project1 Properties, and then type a new project name (see Figure 2.2). For example, you might enter **Project2_1** for this initial project.

Figure 2.2   *The Project Properties dialog box is used to change the name of the project from the default, Project1, to a name of your choice.*

33

Exercise 2.1   Using the Save Project As Command

This exercise asks you to do very little, but it does introduce you to the file naming conventions. Start Visual Basic, and perform the following steps:

1. Open a Standard EXE new project.

2. Choose Project, Project1 Properties and change the name of the project to **Project2_1**. Click OK. This new name should appear on the topmost title bar of Visual Basic.

3. Choose File, Save Project As. A dialog box appears and asks whether you want to save the file as Form1.frm. If you click Cancel, the form is not saved and you have to rebuild it if you need it. Imagine that you spent hours perfecting a form. Unless you save it, your work will be lost.

4. Before you click Save, navigate to the location where you want to save the file, and assign a name to the form. Assign a unique name—something other than the default, Form1.frm. You can use the notation F2-1.frm to indicate that this form goes with Exercise 2.1 (not very clever, but it works). A more descriptive name would be better.

   If you want to store the form on a diskette placed in the A: drive of the computer, navigate to the drive and type **F2-1.frm**.

5. After you save the form, a second dialog box appears that prompts you to assign a name to the project. Again, assign a unique name (not the default, Project1.VBP). You can call it P2-1.VBP to indicate that this project goes with Exercise 2.1. Here, too, a descriptive project name would be better.

   If you want to save the project on a diskette placed in the A: drive of the computer, navigate to the drive and type **P2-1.VBP**.

2.2.3   The Add File and Remove File Commands

Files can be added to, or removed from, the .VBP project file using the file commands contained on the Project menu. When adding or removing files, keep in mind that you are adding or removing files from a project. The following are two Project menu commands that you will use often in this book:

- **Add File**—Opens a dialog box that enables you to navigate the Windows file directory to identify a previously saved file and to add the file to a project, for example, an .FRM (form), .BAS (coded module), .CLS (class module), or .RES (resource file) . This command is especially important when you use a file built for a different project. Simply identify the file name, and click OK.

- **Remove <Name of File>**—Removes the file from the current project that is active (has the focus, a term that is described next).

Other Project menu file commands include Add Form, Add MDI Form, Add Module, and Add Class Module. These enable you to add new types of forms and modules to a project.

2.2.4 The Save File and Save File As Commands

The following are two File menu commands that are used to save a particular file rather than an entire project:

- **Save File**—Saves the form or module that is active (has the focus). If the file has previously been saved, this command updates the file. If the file is new, this command prompts you for the name of the file and, once entered, adds the file to a project when the project file (.VBP file) is next saved.

- **Save File As**—Saves the current file to a disk. This option always prompts you for the file name. Like the File, Save Project As command, File, Save File As is used to save a file for the first time or to save a copy of an existing file.

You will find file commands most useful when you want to use the same forms and modules in different projects. There is nothing to prohibit you from using the same form in dozens of projects because each form is saved as a separate file.

2.2.5 The Concept of Focus

The concept of focus is important in Visual Basic. The object that is selected (such as a form, control, or menu bar selection) is said to have *focus*. In order for Visual Basic to know which file to save, it is necessary to click the object to give it focus, making it the active object. Likewise, to remove a file, the object must be given focus. To remove a file, open the Project window, click the file to remove, and choose File, Remove and the name of the file to remove will also appear. An alternative is to display the Project Explorer, click the file that you want to delete, and right-click to produce the shortcut menu shown in Figure 2.3. The concept of focus is discussed at length in this book. There are even unique events, such as GotFocus and LostFocus, that deal with this issue.

Figure 2.3 *Display the Project Explorer and right-click to reveal several file options, including a command for adding a form to a project.*

Exercise 2.2   Using the Remove and Add Commands

This exercise assumes that you completed Exercise 2.1 and saved the form as F2-1.frm.

1. Open a new Standard EXE project, and change the name of the project to **P2_2** (click Project, Project1 Properties).

2. Choose Project, Remove Form1. Form1 must have the focus because it is the only object assigned to the project.

3. Choose Project, Add File. Navigate through Windows to the location where you saved F2-1.frm, and add this form to your project (see Figure 2.4).

Figure 2.4   *The Add File dialog box lists saved forms that are available to add to a project.*

4. Open the Project Explorer Window, and give form F2-1.frm the focus.

5. Choose File, Save File As (or click the right mouse button). When the dialog box opens, navigate to the location where you want to save the file, and name it **F2-2.frm**.

6. Open the Project Window again and observe what happens. The name of the form has been changed and assigned to the new project.

7. Choose File, Save Project As. In this instance, you can name the file a different name or select P2-2.vbp.

2.2.6   Other File Menu Commands

Besides the four Project menu commands and the two file commands found on the File menu, the latter also contains the Print and Print Setup commands and the Make Project1.Exe commands, as follows:

- **Print**—Displays several options for printing information about a project (see Figure 2.5). You can print the form image, code, or the form as text, and you can choose to print information for a module or for the entire project.

- **Print Set<u>u</u>p**—Launches the standard Windows Print Setup dialog box.

- **Ma<u>k</u>e Project1.Exe**—Creates an executable application. Project modules are compiled into a single .EXE file. This file is either a P-Code interpreted executable or a native code executable file. (The two code formats are explained in section 2.5.1, "Interpreted P-Code," and section 2.5.2, "Compiled Native Code," later in this chapter.)

- Both types of executables require runtime files. The Visual Basic Setup wizard can help you determine which runtime file your application requires. (See Chapter 22, "Creating an ActiveX DLL," for more information about the Visual Basic Setup wizard.)

Figure 2.5   *The Print-Project dialog box enables you to choose the parts of an application that you want to print.*

Exercise 2.3   Using the <u>P</u>rint Command

This exercise is designed to show you the type of information printed for a project.

1. Open a new Standard EXE project.

2. Choose <u>F</u>ile, <u>P</u>rint.

3. When the dialog box appears, click Current <u>P</u>roject, <u>F</u>orm Image, <u>C</u>ode, and Form as <u>T</u>ext.

4. Click OK.

What is the difference between the <u>F</u>orm Image and the Form as <u>T</u>ext choices? Why is there no computer code?

Objective 2.3   Opening the Properties Window and Changing Form Properties

Besides a Project Explorer window, each form (or control) contains a Properties window. As stated in Chapter 1, "Running a Visual Basic Program," a property is a named attribute of an object. Properties are used to change the appearance or behavior of objects.

Figure 2.6 illustrates the default Properties dialog box for a form. If this box is not visible, you can bring it into view by pressing the F4 function key, or choosing View, Properties Window. With the form having the focus, you also can press the right mouse button and select the Properties list item.

Figure 2.6   *The Properties dialog box of a form contains the built-in form attributes that you can change.*

You can set over 50 properties for a form. Although this number seems over-whelming at first, some properties are used so frequently that they represent an initial set to remember:

Caption	FontName
Name	FontSize
BorderStyle	FontBold
MinButton	FontItalic
MaxButton	FontStrikethru
ControlBox	FontUnderline
WindowSize	ForeColor
BackColor	StartUpPosition

To simplify this list somewhat, the items can be grouped by their uses:

- Seven properties deal with the way in which the form or text appears on the display screen (Caption, BorderStyle, MinButton, MaxButton, ControlBox, WindowSize, and StartUpPosition).

- The identification of an object is specified by the Name property.

- Font settings are controlled using the Fonts dialog box (FontName, FontSize, FontBold, FontItalic, and FontStrikethru).

- Color settings (ForeColor and BackColor) use a special palette.

You can change most property settings in the following three ways:

- Click the property to highlight it, and enter (type in text) the new property setting in the text box.

- Double-click the setting to view the alternative settings.

- Click the down arrow to open the drop-down menu for property settings.

Properties for fonts and colors launch a separate dialog box for you to enter settings.

2.3.1   Changing a Caption

The Caption property enables you to change the title that appears on the top of a form. Instead of Form1, use the Caption property to add a title. To change the caption, select Caption in the Properties dialog box and type the new title in the text box next to the property name.

2.3.2   Changing a Form Name

The Name property specifies the name of the form to be used in writing Visual Basic code. Remember the following rule: the name, not the caption, is the identifier. When writing coded instructions, the Name property appears as the object name. To change the name, select Name in the Properties dialog box and type the new name.

2.3.3   Changing the Border Style

The BorderStyle property enables you to change the appearance of the form's border. To change the border setting, double-click the current setting to reveal other choices, or click the down arrow to open the drop-down list of the six options.

If you are uncertain about the six border choices and their precise effects, click BorderStyle to give it the focus in the Properties dialog box, and press F1 (the Help function key). Visual Basic Help displays the six style choices and explains their effects, as shown in Table 2.2.

TABLE 2.2   Settings for the *BorderStyle* Property

Setting	Style	Description
0	vbBSNone	No border or border-related elements.
1	vbFixedSingle	Can include Control menu icon, title bar, Maximize button, and Minimize button. Resizable only using Maximize and Minimize buttons.
2	vbSizable	The default. The size can be changed using any of the optional border elements listed for setting 1.
3	vbFixedDouble	Can include Control menu icon and title bar; can't include Maximize or Minimize buttons. Not resizable.
4	vbFixedToolWindow	Under 16-bit versions of Windows and Windows NT 3.51 and earlier, behaves like Fixed Single. Does not display Maximize or Minimize buttons. Not resizable. Under Windows 95, displays the Close button and displays the title bar text in a reduced font size. The form does not appear in the Windows 95 taskbar.
5	vbSizableToolWindow	Under 16-bit versions of Windows and Windows NT 3.51 and earlier, behaves like Sizable. Does not display Maximize or Minimize buttons. Resizable. Under Windows 95, displays the Close button and displays the title bar text in a reduced font size. The form does not appear in the Windows 95 taskbar.

The online Help is one of Visual Basic's strongest features. Remember, the F1 key is your friend! Use it often. The language is just too vast to remember all of it.

2.3.4   Disabling the Minimize Button

With the first two border styles, the Minimize button appears unless it is disabled by the Minbutton command. To disable the button (and remove it from the form), double-click the MinButton property to change the setting to False. (With this property, there are only two choices: True and False.)

2.3.5   Disabling the Maximize Button

With the first two border styles, the Maximize button appears, unless it is disabled. To disable the button, double-click the MaxButton property to change the setting to False. (Like MinButton, only two choices are available with MaxButton: True and False.)

2.3.6   Disabling the Control Box

With the first three border styles, the control box appears unless it is disabled. To disable the box, double-click the `ControlBox` property to change the setting to `False`. (The two settings for `ControlBox` are `True` and `False`.)

2.3.7   Changing the Window State

The `WindowState` property determines the appearance of the form at runtime. Table 2.3 shows its three settings.

TABLE 2.3   Settings for the *WindowState* Property

Value	Setting	Description
0	vbNormal	The form appears in normal size (the default).
1	vbMinimized	The form is minimized and appears as an icon (either on the taskbar or above it) when the application is run.
2	vbMaximized	The form is maximized and expands to fit the entire screen when the application is run.

2.3.8   Changing the Background Color

Part of the enjoyment of working with Visual Basic is the ease with which colors can be added to a form. Color settings are expressed in hexadecimal notation (base 16). The designers of Visual Basic did not expect you to work with hexadecimal numbers and instead provided a color palette. To open the palette, double-click the `BackColor` setting and click Palette. When the Color palette appears, click a color to change the background color of the form. Following the click, the hexadecimal number assigned to the color appears in the text box.

2.3.9   Changing Font Properties

When working with text, Visual Basic enables you to change the font (or text style) with which you are working. To determine which fonts are available on your system, open the Properties window, highlight Font, and click the ellipsis button to the right. A dialog box appears for setting numerous font properties, including Name, Bold, Italic, Size, StrikeThrough, and Underline.

2.3.10   Changing the Foreground Color

The `ForeColor` property determines the color of the text and graphics to be displayed. This differs from `BackColor`, which determines the background color of the object. To set this property, double-click `ForeColor` and click Palette. Make the color selection using the palette.

2.3.11 Changing the Startup Position

The StartUpPosition property specifies the position of the form when it first appears. Table 2.4 shows its four settings.

TABLE 2.4 Settings of the *StartUpPosition* Property

Constant	Value	Description
vbStartUpManual	0	No initial setting specified.
vbStartUpOwner	1	Center on the item to which the UserForm belongs.
vbStartUpScreen	2	Center on the entire screen.
VbStartUpWindows	3	(Default) Position in upper-left corner of screen.

Objective 2.4   Opening the Code Window and Writing Visual Basic Instructions

The final type of window discussed in this chapter is the Code window. To open the Code window for a form, click the Project Explorer and click View Code, or choose <u>V</u>iew, <u>C</u>ode. This opens the window shown in Figure 2.7. The object shown is the Form; the procedure is shown as Load(). The title bar reads Form1 because you have not changed the name of the form.

Figure 2.7   *This Code window shows the start of a* Form_Load() *procedure.*

The Code window contains the first two coded instructions, which are entered for you. The first combines the name of the object with the name of the event procedure. This coded instruction is shown in the following example, in which Load() is a special type of event:

```
Private Sub Form_Load()
```

It occurs when a form is first loaded. However, suppose that you want to change the event from Load() to Click(). By selecting Click (click the procedure list box and scroll to Click, as shown in Figure 2.8), the first coded instruction changes to the following, in which Click() is another type of event:

```
Private Sub Form_Click()
```

Figure 2.8 *The code window now shows the start of a* Form_Click() *procedure.*

It is triggered by a mouse click.

The event now has been changed from occurring at the time the form is loaded to the time when the form is clicked, with the user controlling the time of the event with the click of the mouse.

The ending instruction stays the same. It reads as follows, which means the end of the procedure (Sub):

```
End Sub
```

Exercise 2.4 Adding a *Click()* Procedure

In this exercise, you begin a new project.

1. Choose File, New Project and open a Standard EXE project. If the last project is still onscreen and has not been saved, you will be asked whether you want to save changes to P2-3.vbp? Click No, unless you have already saved it. Either way will not lead to problems.

2. When Form1 appears, press F4 to open the Properties Window. Change the name of the form to **frmEvents**.

3. Double-click to open the Code Window for frmEvents.

4. Change the project name to **Project2_4**.

5. Change the procedure name from Form() to **Click()** in the procedure list box. Your code should read as follows:

```
Private Sub Form_Click()
End Sub
```

6. Type the following to create the procedure:

```
Private Sub Form_Click()
    ' This procedure will display a message on the form
   frmEvents.Print
   frmEvents.Print
   frmEvents.Print   " When you click, look at what happens!"
End Sub
```

continues

43

Exercise 2.4   continued

7. Close the Code window by double-clicking the Control box icon.

8. Choose <u>R</u>un, <u>S</u>tart, click the Start icon on the toolbar, or press F5 to run your procedure. When frmEvents appears, place the mouse pointer on the form and click. What happens?

9. Click the form again. What happens? It makes you want to click forever, doesn't it?

10. Choose <u>R</u>un, <u>E</u>nd from the menu bar or press the End button on the toolbar to return to the design of frmEvents.

11. Save this form and project. You can call the form **F2-4.frm** and the project **P2-4.vbp** if you want to use them in later exercises in this book; however, this is not necessary. Continue with the next exercise using the same form.

Exercise 2.5   Adding a *KeyPress()* Procedure

In this exercise, you add a second procedure to a form. Figure 2.9 shows the revised form. This exercise assumes that you have completed Exercise 2.4 and are using that form.

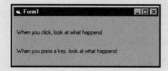

Figure 2.9   *Adding a* KeyPress() *procedure to the form places more than one procedure on the same form.*

1. Choose <u>V</u>iew, <u>C</u>ode from the menu bar. The code you wrote for Exercise 2.4 should appear.

2. Choose KeyPress from the Procedure list box, and observe what happens to your code.

3. Type the following to complete this procedure:

```
Private Sub Form_KeyPress (KeyAscii As Integer)
'This procedure will display a different message on the screen
  frmEvents.Print
  frmEvents.Print
  frmEvents.Print "   When you press a key, look at what
➥happens!"
End Sub
```

4. Close this procedure (using the Control menu icon) and run the revised program. Following are the four ways to run your program:

- Choose <u>R</u>un, <u>S</u>tart.

- Choose <u>R</u>un, Start with <u>F</u>ull Compile.

- Press F5.

- Press the Start button on the toolbar.

This time, press F5 to start your program; then, as a test, do the following:

   a. Click the form.

   b. Press a key.

   c. Press a second key.

5. Click the End button on the toolbar to stop your program a different way, or choose <u>R</u>un, <u>E</u>nd to stop the program.

6. When you are returned to Form1, double-click the form to open the Code window. What code appears?

7. Scroll through the list of procedures in the Procedure menu. Coded procedures appear in bold.

8. Save this form and project at this time. You will be asked to work with the form and project in the next several exercises, but it is wise to save your work periodically. You can save your form as **F2-5.frm** and your project as **P2-5.vbp** to keep your examples in sequence. Name the project **Project2_5** before saving.

Exercise 2.6   Changing the Font Size Property

In this and the next two exercises, you change the properties of the form used in Exercise 2.5.

1. Choose <u>F</u>ile, <u>O</u>pen Project, if necessary, and select <u>V</u>iew, <u>P</u>roject Explorer. Or you can also click the Project Explorer icon to open the Project window. Click the View Form icon.

2. Click the form to give it the focus, and press F4 to open the Properties dialog box.

3. Click font and change the font size to **18** points (or to another size if this size is not available on your system).

4. Run the program. Click to display the first sentence. Press a key to display the second sentence.

5. Exit to continue with the next exercise.

Exercise 2.7   Changing Font Style Properties

In this exercise, use the form from Exercise 2.5 once again.

1. Open the Properties dialog box and open the Font dialog box by double-clicking the Font property. Change the Font to Bookman Old Style (or another font if your system does not have this font installed).

2. Change the style to bold and italic.

3. Run the revised program. Click to display the first sentence (it should be in bold and italic). Press a key to display the second sentence.

4. Exit and save your project at this time. The next exercise asks you to begin a new project.

Exercise 2.8   Adding a Message to a Form and Changing Property Settings

In this exercise, you write a new procedure and change properties.

1. Open a new project.

2. Add the following `Form_Click()` Visual Basic procedure to the form:

```
Private Sub Form_Click()
    'This procedure will display a Happy Birthday message
    frmEvents.Print "                HAPPY"
    frmEvents.Print "                BIRTHDAY"
End Sub
```

3. Change the following form properties:

Property	Setting
Backcolor Palette	= &H00FF00FF& (light purple)
BorderStyle	= 1 'Fixed Single
Caption	= Today is the day
Font Style	= Italic
Font	= Arial
Font Size	= 24
ForeColor Palette	= &H00FF0000& (blue)
WindowState	= 2 'Maximized

4. Run your program.

5. Exit and save your program. Give the form a unique name, such as **BDAY.FRM**. Give the project a similar name, such as **BDAY.VBP**.

Objective 2.5   Producing a Compiled Application from a Standard EXE Project

This final objective asks you create an executable file from a completed Visual Basic application. Two options are available: under the Compile tab of the Project Properties dialog box, you can select Compile to P-Code or Compile to Native Code (see Figure 2.10). Compiling to native code is the default.

Figure 2.10   *The Compile tab of the Project Properties dialog box enables you to control the way in which you compile your completed application.*

2.5.1   Interpreted P-Code

By selecting P-Code, the modules of your Visual Basic application are compiled into what is called *pseudocode* or false code. An interpreter program that then produces machine-language instructions reads the coded instructions. All versions of Visual Basic prior to Visual Basic 6 were interpreted from P-Code.

Interpreted programs offer some advantage. Applications can be designed rapidly because new code can be tested immediately, without time-consuming compilation. They also offer some security advantages in networked applications. You can rely on the interpreter to serve as a buffer between an application and computer hardware. This is the security model built into the Java programming language, for example. To their disadvantage, interpreted programs tend to run slower than compiled programs.

2.5.2   Compiled Native Code

With Visual Basic 6.0, you can create native code compiled applications: The compiler takes the modules of your project and creates a machine language compiled application. Although the native code executable does not require interpretation, it still depends on other files to run. These files mainly consist of the object linking and embedding (OLE) libraries that make up the ActiveX architecture upon which Visual Basic is based.

One way to think about the difference between interpreted and compiled programs is to compare it to translating a letter from English to German (or another language). A compiled program translates the entire letter once, producing machine language instructions. An interpreted program translates each letter every time the letter is read, producing P-Code, which translates into machine language.

2.5.3   The Make Tab of the Project Properties Dialog Box

When you decide to create an executable, the Make tab of the Project Properties dialog box comes into play. The Make tab presents general attribute options for your executable, including the title of the application, the icon used to represent the application when it is minimized, and different version options (see Figure 2.11). The Make tab also enables you to set command-line arguments for your application, should you decide to use them.

Figure 2.11   *The Make tab enables you to set version numbers, version information, application, attributes, command-line arguments, and conditional compilation arguments.*

Exercise 2.9   Creating an Executable Application

This exercise asks you to create a make file from the Happy Birthday application created in Exercise 2.8.

1. Open Exercise 2.8 if it is not onscreen.

2. Choose File, Make Project2-8, if this reflects the name you gave your project.

3. When the Make Project dialog box opens, select a file name, such as **BDAY1.EXE**, and click OK. That's it. You have created a native code executable file. Remember that native code is the default.

4. Choose File, Make Project2-8 again, and when the dialog box opens, click Options.

5. Click the Compile tab.

6. Click Compile to P-Code, and click OK to return to the Make Project box.

7. Select a different file name, such as **BDAY2.EXE**.

8. Close Visual Basic, and start Windows Explorer. Locate both BDAY1.EXE and BDAY2.EXE. Click BDAY1.EXE to run the program. Close BDAY1.

9. Click BDAY2.EXE to run the program. Close BDAY2.

Chapter Summary

This chapter explained the Project Explorer window, the Properties window, and the Code window. In addition, it taught you how to design, program, and run several Visual Basic programs and, in this way, how to manage projects.

By now, you should know that every Visual Basic application is defined and saved as a project. Each project, in turn, consists of a collection of forms, controls added to forms, and procedures. In this chapter, your attention has been limited to the use of a single form and writing procedures for that form.

The Properties window shows the attributes of an object (such as a form) that can be modified. In this chapter, you studied several form properties. You learned to change the caption, name, border style, Minimize button, Maximize button, control box, window state, background color, foreground color, start up position, and font properties of a form.

The Code window contains the instructions for event procedures attached to an object. In this chapter, you learned three types of event procedures: Form_Load(), Form_Click(), and Form_KeyPress(). These are only 3 of the 16 standard events that can be attached to a form.

Managing Visual Basic projects requires considerable care. Each project should be given a unique name, using the Project Properties dialog box. When saving a form, each and every form should be assigned a unique name. The same is true of a project. Forms are always stored as separate .FRM files, with controls bound to the form. When you decide to delete a form, all controls placed on that form are also deleted. Projects are stored as .VBP files. These are text files that can be edited with a text editor.

Although it was discussed only briefly in this chapter, the concept of focus must be remembered. The object that is active (such as a form, control, or menu bar selection) is said to have focus.

With Visual Basic, it is easy to create an executable file. After an application is designed, choose File, Make Project1.EXE to create a file that can be executed outside the development environment.

Skill-Building Exercises

This set of skill-building exercises asks you to work with properties of a form and to experiment with several types of events: KeyDown(), KeyUp(), MouseDown(), and MouseUp(), Activate(), Click(), and Resize(). You are also asked to work more with the Object Browser.

1. Change WindowState of Exercise 2.8 from Maximized to Minimized, and run the Happy Birthday application. What change occurs?

2. Design a form that contains Form_KeyDown and Form_KeyUp events. Display "Hello" with keydown and "there!" with keyup.

3. Design an application that contains two events: Form_MouseDown() and Form_MouseUp(). When the MouseDown() event occurs, display the following message on the form:

   When you press the mouse button, this message appears.

   When the MouseUp() event occurs, display this second message on the form:

   When you release the mouse button, this message appears.

4. Design an application that contains the events Form_Activate() and Form_Click(). For the Form_Activate() event, display the following message on the form:

   Please click the mouse.

   For the Click() event, display the following message:

   Thanks... That feels better!!!

5. Redesign the Happy Birthday application to display the following:

Happy
Birthday

   In this design, lines are placed across the form. In addition, use a Fixed Dialog border (setting 3), and experiment with new colors.

6. Design an application that uses the Form_Resize() event. When the form is resized, display the following message:

   You resized me
   by making me bigger or smaller.

ADDING CONTROLS AND EVENT
PROCEDURES TO FORM MODULES

So far, you have learned how to add controls to a form, but you have not yet done it. In this chapter, you add controls to form modules and attach event procedures (Visual Basic code) to a control. How can you do this before you understand the Visual Basic language? Whether you knew it or not, you wrote some Visual Basic code in Chapter 2, "Writing and Running Your First Visual Basic Program." The Print method, for example, is part of the Visual Basic language.

In this chapter, you will write several additional Visual Basic instructions. The instructions take you through the steps slowly to help you gain confidence in working with the language.

You will master several tasks in working through this chapter, including how to perform the following tasks:

- Add a control to a form
- Change the properties of a control
- Add a procedure to a control
- Write an assignment statement
- Use the Dim and remark statements
- Use the Print and Cls methods
- Assign text to a text box
- Assign a caption to a label

Chapter Objectives

The four objectives of this chapter introduce you to adding controls to a form and writing event procedures to display information:

1. Understanding standard toolbox control objects

2. Adding a control to a form and setting its properties

3. Coding an event procedure for a control

4. Changing object properties with coded statements

Objective 3.1   Understanding Standard Toolbox Control Objects

Remember from Chapter 1, "Running a Visual Basic Program," that a control is an object attached to a form module. The designers of Visual Basic decided to provide a number of standard controls (located on the toolbox) to represent the standard types of objects to be added to a form. You can also purchase custom controls, which have an .OCX extension when installed. To help you remember the differences among controls, tools are grouped into the following four initial categories:

- Text controls

- Containers for groups of controls

- Button controls

- Scroll bar controls

There are still other controls on the toolbox, but the preceding four categories represent a significant number. Remember that by letting your mouse cursor linger a moment over one of the controls in the toolbox, a ToolTip will appear to identify it.

3.1.1   Text Controls

The following four controls deal primarily with text. The left-hand side of Figure 3.1 shows how these controls appear on a form.

- **Text Box control**—Places text entered by the user on a form. Information that the user types appears in the text box. A text box also can contain default text to enable the user to bypass the control if the text does not need to be changed.

- **Label control**—Displays text entered by the program designer. The user cannot type or directly change a label.

- **List Box control**—Displays a list of items. The user can make one or more selections from the list. With a list box, the Visual Basic designer can add or remove items from a list.

- **Combo Box control**—Combines the features of a list box and a text box. This control gives the user the choice of selecting an item from a list or entering a value from the keyboard.

Figure 3.1 *These standard controls are used in designing the majority of Visual Basic applications.*

Two of the text control objects—the text box and the combo box—permit the user to enter data into a program. On the other hand, a user can make a selection from a list box, but can't enter data. Similarly, a label cannot be changed; however, because labels are read-only, they are often used to display the results of processing.

3.1.2 Containers

Containers house or contain (like a bucket) a set of controls. When a container is repositioned on a form, the controls contained within it move with it. There are two types of container controls, as follows:

- **Picture Box control**—Used to store or contain a graphic image, such as a bitmap, and to display the results of graphic methods. It also can serve as a container for other controls, such as a group of images or a toolbar.

- **Frame control**—Used to provide a rectangular area on the form where other controls can be placed as a group. It often serves as a container for a group of buttons, such as a set of option buttons.

The middle portion of Figure 3.1 shows how these controls appear on a form.

3.1.3 Buttons

Buttons are controls that users click to turn on or off. The button manipulation action (for example, a single mouse click) invokes an action called an *event*. The middle portion of Figure 3.1 shows option buttons, check boxes, and a command button. The following describes the button controls:

- **Option Button control**—Allows the user to make one selection from a group of choices, similar to a multiple-choice question. Several option buttons are usually grouped inside a frame or picture box. When one option within a group is selected, all other options are canceled. This is called exclusive choice. You should use option buttons when you want the user to make only one selection.

- **Check Box control**—Enables the user to turn an option on or off, or set a value to true or false. Check boxes can also be grouped. Unlike option buttons, however, any number of check boxes can be selected. This is called *non-exclusive choice*: selecting one does not cancel the others.

- **Command Button control**—Places a button on a form that the user clicks to invoke an event.

3.1.4   Scroll Bars

Scroll bars enable the user to examine a list when the entire list does not fit on a screen. You can add both horizontal and vertical scroll bars to a form (see the right-hand side of Figure 3.1), as follows:

- **Horizontal Scroll Bar control**—Provides for easy navigation through a long list of information, or enables the user to set speed, quantity, or quality. Placement is across the screen.

- **Vertical Scroll Bar control**—Same as the horizontal scroll bar except that placement runs down the screen.

The 11 controls described in this section do not take into account all of the standard controls found in the toolbox. In this chapter, you will use only the command button, text box, and label controls. In Chapter 4, "Learning to Think Visually," you will use check boxes, option buttons, a frame, a combo box, a list box, and scroll bars.

Objective 3.2   Adding a Control to a Form and Setting Its Properties

With the preceding brief overview of several different types of controls fresh in your mind, consider the procedures for placing a control on a form, and once positioned, changing the properties of a control. As a rule, the properties of a control should be set before event procedures (that is, coded procedures) are written. This practice enables you to prototype your design before you begin the code-writing process. A prototype in this instance is a partial, but not full, representation of your finished design.

3.2.1   Adding a Control to a Form

There is a long and a short procedure for adding a control to a form, and each method has merit. The following is the long procedure:

1. Select the control you want from the toolbox.

2. Make the form active by clicking it to indicate where you want to place the control. This step changes the pointer to a crosshair.

3. Drag the handles on the control to size it the way you want.

The short procedure is simply the following two steps:

1. In the toolbox, double-click the control you want. This places the control on the active form.

2. Move and change the size of the control as needed.

Figure 3.2 shows how you move a control. Click the center of the control and drag the control to a new position. To change the size of the control, click one of the handles (the small black boxes), and drag the control in a horizontal, vertical, or diagonal direction.

Drag the corner handles to size the control in two directions.

Drag the center handles to size the control in a single direction.

Click in the middle of the box to move the control.

Figure 3.2   *To size a control, use the square handles on the sides. To move a control, click the center of it and drag it with the mouse.*

When placing controls such as option buttons within a frame or picture box on a form, the longer procedure binds the control to the container. (You are asked to use a frame in Chapter 4.)

3.2.2   Setting Properties for a Control

After adding a control to a form, you can modify the properties of the control. Control properties work in the same way as form properties: they can be used to change the appearance or the behavior of the control. Figure 3.3 shows the Properties dialog box for a command button. Like a form, you can set a wide variety of options for a command.

Besides Caption and Name, command button properties include ways of changing the appearance of the text on the button, the size of the button, and even how you want the cursor to appear when it is placed over the button (the MousePointer property).

Figure 3.3 *The Properties box for a command button contains a Caption and a Name property and a host of other properties.*

Exercise 3.1 Examining the Control Property Box

In this short exercise, you add a command button to a form and change its properties.

1. Open a new project.

2. Double-click the Command Button control. If you place the wrong one on the form, select <u>E</u>dit, <u>D</u>elete to remove the control from the form.

3. With the Command1 button onscreen, move it to the left-hand side of the form (see Figure 3.3).

4. Change the Name property to **cmdTest**.

5. Change the Caption property to display the string **Test Properties**.

6. Change the Style property to **1-Graphical**.

7. Change the BackColor property to red or some other color on the palette menu that appears in the BackColor property dialog box.

8. Change the Style property to 0-Standard. Notice the effect on the button.

9. Run the project. Click the form and the cmdText button. Can you determine why nothing happens? Because you have not indicated what action (that is, what event) is to take place when the button is clicked, the piece missing is a procedure.

10. Exit to return to the form.

Objective 3.3   Coding an Event Procedure for a Control

Adding a control to a form and setting the control properties set the scene for adding a procedure. Remember that a control will do nothing in an event-oriented environment unless an event procedure is attached to it. To add to this concept, more than one event can be associated with a single control, as with a form. In Exercise 3.2, you will examine the various event alternatives for a single control.

3.3.1   Controlling Naming Conventions

When adding a control to a form, a default name is always assigned to the form or control unless you decide to change it. For example, the first command button added to a form is named Command1, and the second is Command2. In this text, you are to follow a command syntax by adding a name prefix to a control (and many times to forms). If you decide to add a command button to a form and change the command caption to Start, for example, you would name the control cmdStart. The cmd is the command prefix. The prefix always tells you what specific control you are working with.

The exception to the preceding rule is when you are working with labels that have no effect on the input or output to a program. Because changing the name of each control takes considerable time, you should often leave label conventions (Label1, Label2, and so on) alone, unless the content of a label is determined by a procedure. This separates labels whose content is determined by a procedure from those whose content is not determined by a procedure.

Table 3.1 shows the controls, the default names, and the name prefixes that are used in this book for the 11 controls defined in Objective 3.1, "Understanding Standard Toolbox Control Objects."

TABLE 3.1   11 Controls

Control	Default Name	Name Prefix
Text Box	Text1	txt
Label	Label1	lbl
List Box	List1	lst
Combo Box	Combo1	cbo
Picture Box	Picture1	pic
Frame	Frame1	fra
Option Button	Option1	opt
Command Button	Command1	cmd
Check Box	Check1	chk
Horizontal Scroll Bar	HScroll1	hsb
Vertical Scroll Bar	VScroll1	vsb

Exercise 3.2   Adding a Procedure to a Command Button

For this exercise, write a procedure and attach it to a command button. Figure 3.4 shows how the form will look when you run the program.

Figure 3.4   *In this display, the user is expected to click the Start button to display the message on the form.*

1. Begin a new project or continue the last.

2. Add a command button to the form.

3. With the form active (not the command button), press F4 to reveal the properties box. Make the following changes:

   ```
   Name = frmMsg
   Caption =  A Printed Message
   ```

4. With the command button active, press F4 to reveal the properties box. Make the following changes:

   ```
   Caption = Start
   Name = cmdStart
   ```

5. With the command button still active, double-click to open the Code window. Enter the following code, between the `Private Sub cmdStart_Click()` and the `End Sub` instructions:

   ```
   Private Sub cmdStart_Click()
    ` The Start command button is used to display a message
    Dim message As String
    frmMsg.Print
    message$ = "Welcome to Visual Basic"
    frmMsg.Print  Spc(20); message$  ` prints 20 spaces followed
   ➥by the message
   End Sub
   ```

6. Save this project.

7. Close the Code window and run the program. Click the Start button to test the program.

8. Exit and open the Code window to examine the other types of events that can be assigned to the `cmdStart` control. For example, rather than writing a `cmdClick()` procedure, you might write a `MouseDown()` procedure, such that when the user presses the mouse button, the message appears onscreen. As another alternative, write a `MouseUp()` procedure.

3.3.2   Coded Statements and Methods

In the preceding procedure, you wrote several coded instructions, which introduced two different programming statements and a method: the `Dim` statement, an assignment statement, and the `Print` method. You also added a remark or comment to your code and used the `Private` keyword.

The *Dim* Statement

The `Dim` statement is used to declare variables and to allocate storage space. The statement begins with the keyword `Dim`, as in the following:

```
Dim message As String
```

It declares the variable message as a string of characters. As a string, it can contain characters, including blank spaces and punctuation, as well as numbers.

When typing statements, observe that the Visual Basic editor changes keywords to blue. If your statement is correct, the word `Dim` and the words `As String` appear in blue. This tells you that the syntax used in writing the statement is correct. If you make a mistake, as in the following code in which the word `String` is misspelled, the blue markings will not appear:

```
Dim message As Sting
```

The Assignment Statement

With an assignment statement, you use an equation. The value expression on the right side is assigned to the variable on the left. The syntax for the assignment statement is as follows:

```
[Let] varname = expression
```

The syntax states that the keyword `Let` is optional. In this book, you are asked to follow a syntax that does not use the keyword `Let` in your coded instructions. The dollar sign ($) is also optional. You could have written the following:

```
message$ = "Welcome to Visual Basic"
```

Because the dollar sign ($) is optional, you could have written the following, for message has been declared as a variable of type `String`:

```
message = "Welcome to Visual Basic"
```

A string expression must begin and end with quotation marks. If you write the following, omitting the quotation marks, you will be in error:

```
message = Welcome to Visual Basic
```

The Remark Statement

In Visual Basic, any statement that begins with a single quotation mark (`'`) or the keyword `Rem` is a remark, as follows:

```
` The Start command is used to display a message
```

You use *remarks* or *comments* to describe the purpose of a procedure, as well as key features of a procedure. Use remark statements to document how your code works and to provide other types of important coding information. Also, be careful when writing the statement: Use the apostrophe (') which is the same as the single quotation mark and shares the quotation mark (") key, and not the grave accent (`), which can be found on the tilde (~) key. In writing the procedures in this book, the apostrophe, rather than Rem, is used. This enables you to place remarks to the right of an instruction, as in the following example:

```
Print      ` This instruction displays a blank line
```

When writing remarks, use the color code returned by the editor to determine whether your statements are correct or incorrect. A correct remark statement will, by default, be shown in green.

The *Private* Keyword

All control procedures are preceded by the Private keyword by default. This keyword makes the procedure accessible only in the form module in which it is declared. The meaning and uses of the Private keyword, as well as other keywords that can be used in procedure declarations, are discussed in detail in Chapter 10, "Defining the Scope of Variables and Procedures." For the time being, all procedures you write will use the Private keyword.

The *Print* Method

The single method used in Exercise 3.2 was the Print method. A method differs from a statement, such as an assignment statement, by specifying the behavior of an object. The following statement features a period (.) to separate the object from the action to be taken:

```
Form1.Print "Message to be printed"
```

That, in turn, is followed by a space, so that the following instruction would be in error:

```
Form1.Print="Message to be printed"
```

The syntax used for the Print method itself is quite complex and deserves special attention. You consider that notation next. After you understand this syntax, you will be able to understand the syntax designed for all methods.

Understanding Syntax Notation

The Print method enables you to display information directly on a form or in the Debug window. The method contains a complex syntax, which uses brackets, braces, pipes, and parentheses. Consider what this all means. The complete syntax is as follows:

```
[object.]Print [{Spc() ¦ Tab() }] [expression list][{; ¦ ,}]
```

Table 3.2 explains the components of the syntax of the Print method.

TABLE 3.2   Syntax of the *Print* Method

Component	Description
object	Indicates the object (for example, the name of the form, not the caption) on which the expression list will be printed.
object.Print	Signifies a method rather than a statement, even though the object name is optional.
[ ]	Indicates an optional component. It does not have to be included in a Print statement. In the preceding syntax, everything is optional except the word Print.
{ }	Indicates choices. You can select one from the list. As an example, you can select a semicolon (;) or a comma (,), but not both.
expression	The string to be printed. If no expression is indicated, a blank line will be printed.
¦	Means or. For example, you can select Spc() or Tab().
Spc()	Invokes the space function. For example, Spc(20) provides a blank space of 20 characters.
Tab()	Invokes the tab function. Tab (2) means to tab two columns to the right. When you use the tab function with Print, the print surface is divided into a set of fixed-width columns.
;	A semicolon places the cursor immediately after the last character displayed.
,	A comma places the cursor in the next print zone. Print zones begin every 14 columns on the screen.

In the next example, the following instruction produces a blank line:

```
frmMsg.Print
```

Therefore, the following instruction would print the message Welcome to Visual Basic 20 spaces to the right:

```
message = "Welcome to Visual Basic"
frmMst.Print Spc(20); message$
```

Remember that object is optional. In Visual Basic, if an object is not specified, the default object is the form. Although the instruction Print can appear to be a statement, it is a method without the object specified (form in this instance).

The *Cls* Method

A second method that often is used when displaying text with the Print method is the clear or Cls method. This method clears printed text or other graphic output from the form. The method can also be used to clear graphical output in a picture box. The complete syntax for this method is as follows:

```
[object.]Cls
```

The name of the object is optional. Thus, to clear text from a form, you could have written the following instruction:

```
frmMsg.Cls
```

Observe that if you specify the object, the name of the object is required, not the caption.

Exercise 3.3   Adding a Second Command Button and Procedure to a Form

For this exercise, you add a second command button and a control procedure to a form. Figure 3.5 shows the completed form.

Figure 3.5   *Adding a Clear button will enable the user to clear the text displayed on a form.*

1. Begin a new project or continue with the last one.

2. Add the Start button and code required in Exercise 3.2, if necessary.

3. Activate the form, not the button, and press the F4 key if the form properties box is not visible. Change the caption to **A Printed Message**, if necessary.

4. Add a second command button and move it to the right of Start.

5. Activate the second command button, and press the F4 key to reveal the control properties box. Make the following change:
   ```
   Caption   =  Clear
   Name      =  cmdClear
   ```

6. With the command button still active, double-click to open the Code window. Enter the following code:

```
Sub cmdClear_Click()
    ` This single instruction clears the screen
   frmMsg.Cls
End Sub
```

7. Close the Code window and run the program. Click Start and click Clear. Click Start and click Clear again.

8. Save this project. You will start a new project in the next exercise.

Objective 3.4   Changing Object Properties with Coded Statements

Besides changing the value of properties using the properties box, the assignment of a property can be done using code. In this section, you examine the assigning of text to a text box and the assigning of a caption to a label using code.

3.4.1   The Text Box

You can set properties of objects using the properties box or set within coded procedures using assignment statements. Visual Basic follows a specific syntax for each property setting. The following is the complete syntax for assigning the Text property to a combo box, list box, or text box:

```
[form.] {combobox ¦ listbox ¦ textbox}.Text [= stringexpression]
```

The syntax indicates that text can only be used with a combo box, list box, or text box, and that one of these choices is required.

With a text box named txtDisplayIt, you can use this syntax to write the following:

```
Form1.txtDisplayIt.Text = "Welcome to Visual Basic"
```

With this instruction, the string expression Welcome to Visual Basic is assigned to the Text property of the object txtDisplayIt (which is the name given to the text box).

The corresponding instruction can be used to assign an empty (or zero length) string expression to the Text property:

```
txtDisplayIt.text = ""
```

Exercise 3.4   Adding a Text Box to Display Output

In this exercise, you add a text box to a form to display output. (You will use labels in Exercise 3.5 to display output.) Figure 3.6 illustrates the completed form. Because this exercise is similar to the previous one, you can copy and rename the last exercise to save time.

Figure 3.6   *This display prints a message inside a text box rather than on the form.*

1. Start a new project.

2. Change the caption of the new form to **More Beginning Displays**.

3. Add a text box to the screen, and move it and change its size to take the shape illustrated in Figure 3.6. The Text Box control has the letters ab on it.

4. Change the following properties of the text box, removing Text1 from the Text property, leaving it blank:

   ```
   Text   =
   Name   =   txtDisplayIt
   ```

   (The second statement changes the name of the object.)

5. Add a command button, and change the following properties:

   ```
   Caption  =  Start
   Name     =  cmdStart
   ```

   Position it as shown in Figure 3.6.

6. Add a second command button, and change the following properties:

   ```
   Caption  =  Clear
   Name     =  cmdClear
   ```

7. Activate the cmdStart button, and open the Code window. Examine the objects from which you now can select. Click cmdStart to open the pull-down menu. The objects cmdStart, cmdClear, and txtDisplayIt now should appear on the list.

8. Enter the following statements:

   ```
   Private Sub cmdStart_Click()
       `The .Text property displays a message in the Text box
       txtDisplayIt.Text = "Welcome to Visual Basic"
   End Sub
   ```

9. Close the Code window, activate the Clear button, and open the Code window.

10. Enter the following statements:

```
Private Sub cmdClear_Click()
   `This single instruction clears the Text box
   txtDisplayIt.Text  = ""
End Sub
```

11. Run and test your program. Click Start and click Clear. Perform this sequence several times.

The Text *MultiLine* Property

Open the text box and examine the 40 properties. Of these, the MultiLine property is important. Setting this property to True enables a text box to accept and display multiple lines of text at runtime (that is, when your program is running). Setting the MultiLine property to False restricts text to one line and ignores carriage returns. The syntax for the MultiLine property is as follows:

```
[form]textbox.MultiLine = {True ¦ False}
```

The Text *Alignment* Property

The MultiLine property is important, in part, because of its effect on the Alignment property. Unless the MultiLine property is True, the Alignment property is ignored. Following is the syntax for the Alignment property:

```
[form.]control.Alignment [= numericexpression]
```

As an example, Table 3.3 shows the settings for a text box.

TABLE 3.3   Text Box Settings

Setting	Description
0	Text is aligned to the left (the default).
1	Text is aligned to the right.
2	Text is centered.

3.4.2   The Label

The label differs from the text box in that information can be displayed, but not changed by the user. Like the Text box, the Label features close to 40 different properties. Of these, the Label caption, autosize, wordwrap, and borderstyle are especially important.

Assigning a Value to the Caption Property of a Label

A label has a caption, rather than a text property. The complex syntax for this assignment is as follows:

```
[form.][control.]Caption [= stringexpression]
```

Although the syntax appears somewhat less complex than the syntax for the Text property of a text box, the caption property is held by a much greater number of objects. The Visual Basic Help contains an "Applies To" section for the caption property, which indicates that a caption applies to a dozen standard objects, such as a form, command button, and label.

In Exercise 3.5, use labels with borders rather than text boxes for displaying output. This practice is desired when output is not to be changed by the user. Usually, you never have to be concerned about whether a caption will store a sufficient number of characters. When used with labels, the length of a caption is unlimited. When used with a form and all other controls, the length is limited to 255 characters.

The Label *AutoSize* Property

The properties associated with a label are also numerous, many of which fall outside the scope of this chapter. Like a text box, the text in a caption of a label can be aligned using the Alignment property. The three settings are the same as with a text box: Left, Right, and Centered.

A property unique to labels and picture boxes is AutoSize. Set this property to True when you want the size of the label to change automatically to fit the label caption. Set it to False to keep the size of the control constant. (The contents are truncated if the text exceeds the area of the control.) False is the default.

The Label *WordWrap* Property

Closely associated with the AutoSize property is the WordWrap property. When set to True, the text wraps and the label control expands or contracts vertically to fit the text and the size of the font. The horizontal size doesn't change. When set to False (the default), text doesn't wrap, and the label expands or contracts horizontally to fit the length of the text and vertically to fit the size of the font and the number of lines.

The Label BorderStyle Property

Another useful label property is BorderStyle. You use this property to add a border to a label to make it appear as a text box. The syntax is as follows:

```
[form.][control.]BorderStyle = {0 ¦ 1}
```

Set this property to 0 when you don't want a border (the default for the Image control and Label control), and set it to 1 for a fixed, single border (the default for the Text Box control and Picture Box control).

Exercise 3.5   Using Labels Rather Than Text Boxes to Display Output

The purpose of this exercise is to introduce you to the use of labels. You use three labels to display a user's first name, middle name, and last name. In addition, you add three labels not affected by coded procedures, and the command buttons Start and Clear. Figure 3.7 shows the completed design.

Figure 3.7   *This display uses read-only labels rather than text boxes to display a person's name.*

1. Begin a new project.

2. Change the following form properties:

   ```
   Caption  =  Displaying your name
   Name     =  frmName
   ```

   Observe that you should use the prefix frm with a form.

3. Add the three labels, and change the captions to **First Name**, **Middle Name**, and **Last Name**.

4. Add a First Name display label, and change the following properties:

   ```
   Caption      =
   Name         =    lblFirst
   BorderStyle  =    1 - FixedSingle
   ```

5. Add the Middle Name display label, and change the following properties:

   ```
   Caption      =
   Name         =    lblMiddle
   BorderStyle  =    1 - FixedSingle
   ```

6. Add the Last Name display label, and change the following properties:

   ```
   Caption      =
   Name         =    lblLast
   BorderStyle  =    1 - FixedSingle
   ```

7. Add the first command button, and change the following properties:

   ```
   Caption  =  Start
   Name     =  cmdStart
   ```

8. Add the second command button, and change the following properties:

   ```
   Caption  =  Clear
   Name     =  cmdClear
   ```

continues

67

9. Open the Code window for the Start command, and enter the following code:

```
Sub cmdStart_Click()
    `Program to display first, middle, and last name
    lblFirst.Caption = "Alexander"
    lblMiddle.Caption = "Graham"
    lblLast.Caption = "Bell"
End Sub
```

10. Open the Code window for the Clear command, and enter the following code:

```
Sub cmdClear_Click()
    `Program to clear all display labels
    lblFirst.Caption = ""
    lblMiddle.Caption = ""
    lblLast.Caption = ""
End Sub
```

11. Run your program. Test it by clicking the Start and Clear buttons several times.

12. Save your form and project.

3.4.3   The *With* Statement

At times, it might be desirable to change several properties of a control, such as a label, all at once. An abbreviated way to do this is by using the With statement. Consider the following code, which changes three properties of the label named lblMine:

```
Sub cmdChange_Click()
    `Program to clear all display labels
    With lblMine
        .Height = 200
        .Width = 300
        .Caption = "This is a new Caption"
    End With
End Sub
```

The syntax of this statement is quite straightforward. It reads as follows:

```
With object
    [.property = expression]
End With
```

Table 3.4 explains the components of the With statement.

TABLE 3.4   *With* Statement Syntax

Component	Description
Object	The name of an object or a user-defined type (required)
Property	The property of the object to be executed (optional)

Exercise 3.6   Using the With Statement to Modify Several Properties of a Label

This exercise asks you to modify Exercise 3.5. (Steps 1-8 in this exercise are the same as those in Exercise 3.5.)

1. Begin a new project.

2. Change the following form properties:

   ```
   Caption = Displaying your name
   Name    = frmName
   ```

   Observe that you should use the prefix frm with a form.

3. Add the three labels, and change the captions to **First Name**, **Middle Name**, and **Last Name**.

4. Add a First Name display label, and change the following properties:

   ```
   Caption     =
   Name        =  lblFirst
   BorderStyle =  1 - FixedSingle
   ```

5. Add the Middle Name display label, and change the following properties:

   ```
   Caption     =
   Name        =  lblMiddle
   BorderStyle =  1 - FixedSingle
   ```

6. Add the Last Name display label, and change the following properties:

   ```
   Caption     =
   Name        =  lblLast
   BorderStyle =  1 - FixedSingle
   ```

7. Add the first command button, and change the following properties:

   ```
   Caption = Start
   Name    = cmdStart
   ```

8. Add the second command button, and change the following properties:

   ```
   Caption =  Clear
   Name    =  cmdClear
   ```

9. Modify the cmdStart_Click() procedure as follows:

   ```
   Private Sub cmdStart_Click()
     `Program to display first, middle, and last names
     With lblFirst
       .Caption = "Alexander"
       .BackColor = vbGreen
       .Alignment = 2
       .Height = 400
     End With
   ```

continues

```
        With lblMiddle
          .Caption = "Graham"
          .BackColor = vbGreen
          .Alignment = 2
          .Height = 400
        End With
        With lblLast
          .Caption = "Bell"
          .BackColor = vbGreen
          .Alignment = 2
          .Height = 400
        End With
      End Sub
```

10. Test your code. What are the advantages of the With...End With structure?

Chapter Summary

The objectives of this chapter introduced you to 11 controls found on the toolbox and instructed you in the use of three of them: a command button, a text box, and a label. The various types of controls are easier to remember if you group them, as follows:

■ Four controls are used with text:

1. Text Box control

2. Label control

3. List Box control

4. Combo Box control

■ Two controls are containers, as follows:

1. Picture Box control

2. Frame control

■ Three controls are buttons, as follows:

1. Option Button control

2. Check Box control

3. Command Button control

■ Two controls are scroll bars, as follows:

1. Horizontal Scroll Bar control

2. Vertical Scroll Bar control

You can add a control to a form by double-clicking the control, or by clicking the control and dragging it to change its size on a form. You can set control properties after the control is placed on the form. Double-click the control to open the Code window and add an event procedure to a form.

Add name prefixes to forms and controls to help in the management of objects in a design. Adding the name cmdStart tells you that the object is a command button with a likely caption of Start.

The Dim statement, adding remarks to code, the Print and Cls methods, and assignment statements were used in writing the exercises for this chapter. You use the Dim statement to declare variables. Use a single quotation mark (') to add comments (remarks) to code. The Print method displays characters on an object, such as a form. The Cls method clears text or graphics from a form or picture box.

Assignment statements are used to assign property values to an object within a coded procedure. When writing an assignment statement, the syntax associated with the object becomes important. The complex syntax for the Text property of a text box is as follows:

```
[form.] {combobox ¦ listbox ¦ textbox}.Text [= stringexpression]
```

Following is the complete syntax for the Caption property:

```
[form.][control.]Caption [= stringexpression]
```

Text boxes and labels are used for different purposes. You use a text box when you require the user to enter values to be used by a procedure. You use a label to display output when the user is not allowed to change the display.

Skill-Building Exercises

This set of exercises asks you to work with properties and events, including the MouseDown() and MouseUp() events. The last two exercises ask you to use the With statement to modify several properties of a control.

1. Modify Exercise 3.2 using the MouseDown() and MouseUp() events. Leave the Start button on the form. When you click the Start button, change the Click() event to a MouseDown() event to display the following:

   ```
   Welcome to
   ```

   Write a MouseUp() event to display the following:

   ```
   Visual Basic
   ```

   Before you print either message, add 20 blank spaces to the Print statement.

   When you run this program, the MouseDown() action displays the first part of the message. Releasing the mouse button completes the message. Display this as the caption of the form: **A Printed Message**.

2. Place two labels on the screen, changing the caption of the first to **Click here**. For both labels, make the following property changes:

```
Alignment = Center
BorderStyle = 1 - Fixed Single
```

Write a `Click()` event for the first label. When you click the `Click here` label, display the message `Welcome to Visual Basic` in the space set aside for the second label. Change the caption of the form to **Working with Labels**.

3. Modify Exercise 3.5 using Figure 3.7 as a guide. Rather than using a Start button to display the name, modify the design so the user must click the label `First Name` to display the first name of the person, the label `Middle Name` to display the middle name, and the label `Last Name` to display the last name. Remove the Start button from the design, but keep the Clear button.

4. Design a form with two multiple-line text boxes and two command buttons, one named **Start** and one named **Clear**. In the first text box, display a person's name, such as Alexander Graham Bell. Place part of the name on one line of the text box and part on a second line. In the second text box, display the person's address, such as 7677-5678 Telephone Drive. Once again, display part of the address on one line and the remainder on the second line. Use a larger font size, such as 12. Change the caption of the form to **Name and Address**.

5. Design another form with two multiple-line boxes, but no command buttons. Above the first text box, add the label **My name is**. Above the second text box, add the label **My address is**. Write a `Click()` event such that when you click the name text box, the person's name appears. Then, write a double-click event to clear the text box. Write a second `Click()` event to add the address in the second text box; write a double-click event to clear the address in the second text box. Use a larger font size, such as size 12. Add the form caption Name and Address II.

6. Revise Exercise 3.4 to include `With`, `EndWith` statements. When the user clicks on the Start button, change the text to **Alexander Graham Bell**, the background color of the text box to blue, center the text, and change the foreground color of the text to white.

7. Add three labels to a form, and then write a `Form_Click` procedure that contains `With`, `EndWith` procedures. For the first label, change the caption to **This is the first label**, left-justify the caption, and set the background color to red and the foreground color to yellow. For the second label, change the caption to **This is the second label**, right-justify the caption, and set the background color to white and the foreground color to blue. For the third label, change the caption to **This is the third label**, center the caption, and set the background color to blue and the foreground color to white.

LEARNING TO THINK VISUALLY

Visual Basic requires you to give special attention to the design of forms before beginning to write computer code. This might be a somewhat different task for those who have programmed before. The Visual Basic designer must be much more concerned with the user interface, compared to earlier programming languages. Some might say that the designer must be *artful* as well as *logical* in the design of a computer application.

In this chapter, you continue to learn about controls in the design of Visual Basic applications and to practice working with the controls contained in the toolbox. The tasks include the following:

- Adding a combo box to a design

- Adding a frame to a design

- Adding check boxes to a design

- Adding a list box to a design

- Setting the tab order in a design

- Disabling a control

- Formatting a set of controls

- Adding a menu bar to a design

- Writing menu procedures

- Adding scroll bars to a design

Chapter Objectives

The objectives for this chapter involve working with additional controls in the toolbox; however, the discussion is framed in terms of a short (and rather silly) problem. In solving the problem, you should think visually about how a form should look before you begin to add controls to that design. The objectives are as follows:

1. Thinking about a problem

2. Using design-time and runtime properties to manipulate list boxes and combo boxes

3. Using format commands to align and lock a set of controls

4. Using frame controls to improve user-interface design

5. Controlling the tab order in a design

6. Learning to enable and disable a control

7. Creating a menu bar and writing code for menu procedures

8. Adding a scroll bar to a design

The following are the specific controls introduced in this chapter:

Combo boxes

List boxes

Option buttons

Check boxes

Scroll bars

This set completes the standard Windows controls.

Objective 4.1   Thinking About a Problem

Visual interfaces are easy to create if you are handed the problem and the interface. They are most difficult when you are facing an actual ill-defined problem and when you have no knowledge of the type of interface that is required. As a way of simulating the design process, you can step through a problem, taking the role of both the program designer and the user.

Better yet, ask a colleague to assume the role of the user while you act as the designer, and employ role playing to arrive at a solution using the hypothetical scenario described in the following sections.

4.1.1   Role 1: The User

"I need a way of entering personal information about our students," mutters the admissions officer. "People in data processing are telling me about their newfound capability to solve computing problems faster than in the past, but I'm still suspicious. I just don't know enough about the computer to tell smoke from fire."

"What I want is a simple system," continues the admissions officer. "The system should permit me to enter into the computer a person's name and sex, the student's year in school, some special category if applicable (we have several), and what the student thinks of himself or herself. Because I hate typing, I want a system that is as simple to use as possible. I also do not want to move too fast."

"I would like to review the design to be used in entering one student into the system. I want to display a student's name and gender; determine whether the student is a freshman, sophomore, junior, or senior; and conduct a self-image survey, which asks the student whether or not he or she is wise, kind, cute, or sturdy. The student should check all that apply."

4.1.2   Role 2: The Program Designer

"I wish I had some idea of what the admissions officer wants," the designer contemplates. "Perhaps after my meeting today, I will have something to go on. I guess I'd better write down some questions to ask."

4.1.3   The Meeting

Read this section after role playing in the preceding scenario or thinking about the topics of conversation that might take place at a meeting.

In speaking with the admissions officer, the program designer should ask questions to determine the nature of the problem, and determine the types of input to be entered into processing and the types of output to expect. Assume that a tape recording was made of the meeting between the admissions officer and the program designer, and the following is a transcription of that tape.

Adm. officer:	Good morning. Glad you could make it.
Designer:	My pleasure. Are you ready to begin?
Adm. officer:	Yup. Go ahead.
Designer:	Perhaps you could tell me what type of application you are interested in.
Adm. officer:	I would like a small student admissions system limited to four or five types of information. I need to record the name and sex of the student, his or her year in school, and the student's self-image assessment.
Designer:	Do you want the student's full name?
Adm. officer:	Yes.
Designer:	Will you have to type in the name, or can you pull this information from another computer file?
Adm. officer:	We'll have to type in the name, I'm afraid. This information is to be used for gaining insight about the self-image of our students. If possible, we would like to enter all the information when speaking with each student.
Designer:	Okay. I just wanted to know how you intended to collect the data.
	Let me ask another question. Can we limit the student's choices of year in school to freshman, sophomore, junior, and senior?

Adm. officer:	For 90 percent of our students, the answer is yes; however, we have other categories, such as *adult special.*
Designer:	Does that mean you want to be able to enter the name of the category or add the word *other* as a choice?
Adm. officer:	Let's use *other.*
Designer:	How do you plan to collect the self-image information of a student?
Adm. officer:	For now, we want to ask each student to choose *wise, kind, cute,* or *sturdy* in a survey question.
Designer:	Only these four choices?
Adm. officer:	We might add others later, but for now we only want to check off these four.
	One more thing: We don't want to get in too deep to begin with. Would it be possible for you to show me a design that handles only one student? This would help us determine how we want to move ahead and what we want from a larger system.
Designer:	Seems simple enough. Let me get back to you later today.

4.1.4   Arriving at a Solution

After reading the preceding conversation, can you picture in your mind what type of application the admissions officer needs? Can you picture a possible form and the types of controls needed on this form? If you can, you are beginning to think visually.

More difficult to determine is the exact nature of the problem the admissions officer is attempting to solve. If you get the impression that the admission's staff is not very sure of their requirements, you are correct. The staff wants some type of system to support the study of student profiles, but the specifics of such a system are still quite vague.

Objective 4.2   Using Design-Time and Runtime Properties to Manipulate List Boxes and Combo Boxes

Before you continue the case study, you need to learn about two of the controls that you might choose for your admissions design. These are *list boxes* and *combo boxes.* Both controls are designed to provide a list of choices, but in different ways. A list box is limited to a list of choices. From this list, a user can make one or several choices. A combo box restricts the user to one choice or entry. It is called a combo box because it is a combination of a list box (used for selecting items from a list) and a text box (used for entering text).

4.2.1   List Box Properties

Add a list box to a blank Visual Basic form to study the properties of this control. Besides the normal font and size properties, four properties of particular interest at this time are the MultiSelect property, Sorted property, List property, and Style property.

The *MultiSelect* List Box Property

The MultiSelect property enables the user to make more than one selection from a list. The syntax for this property is as follows:

```
[form.] {filelistbox ¦ listbox}.MultiSelect = {0 ¦ 1 ¦ 2}
```

Table 4.1 shows the settings of the MultiSelect property.

TABLE 4.1   *MultiSelect* Settings

Setting	Description
0	Multiple selections are not allowed (the default).
1	Simple multiple selection. Clicking the mouse or pressing the spacebar selects or deselects an item in a list.
2	Extended multiple selection. Shift+click or Shift+arrow key (up or down depending on where you are in the list) extends the selection to allow a block of items to be selected. Ctrl+click selects or deselects an item from the list.

Returning to the admissions project, can you determine which setting is needed for that design?

The *Sorted* List Box Property

The Sorted property allows items added to the list box to be displayed in alphabetical order.

```
{listBox ¦ combobox}.Sorted = {True ¦ False}
```

Table 4.2 shows the settings of the Sorted property.

TABLE 4.2   *Sorted* Settings

Setting	Description
True	List items are sorted by character code.
False	List items aren't sorted alphabetically.

The *List* Property

The List property is the grouping of strings held by a list or combo box. To specify an individual string item in the control, an index value must be specified. The syntax is as follows:

```
object.List(index) [= string]
```

The first item in the List always has a value of zero. To change the second item in a list box named lstItems, the code might read as follows:

```
lstItems.List(1) = "My new item"
```

The Style List Box Property

A list box features two styles: Standard and Checkbox. With the Standard style, the list box displays a list of text items. One or more items can be selected from this list, as determined by the MultiSelect setting. With the Checkbox style the ListBox control displays with a check box next to each text item. Multiple items in the ListBox can be selected by checking the checkbox beside them.

4.2.2   The Combo Box *Style* Property

Combo box properties are similar, but certainly not identical, to list box properties. An important combo box property is the Style property. Also, you need to use the AddItem method and the Form_Load() procedure to describe how a combo box or list box is filled with data and displayed.

There are three styles of combo boxes (see Figure 4.1). The following list contains a description of each:

Figure 4.1   *The three combo box styles provide flexibility in using space on a form.*

■ **Style 0**—A drop-down combo box. The user clicks the detached arrow to open (and drop down) the list of choices. Selecting one of the choices places it in the text portion of the combo box. Use Style 0 when you want the user to select from a list and you want to conserve screen space. This style of combo box enables a user to type in a choice that doesn't appear on the list.

- **Style 1**—A simple combo box. Observe that the detached arrow is missing from this combo box. This leads to the display of all items, provided there is space. If additional space is required, a vertical scroll bar is automatically inserted. Similar to Style 0, this style of combo box enables a user to type in a choice that doesn't appear on the list.

- **Style 2**—A drop-down list box. Like the drop-down combo box, a drop-down list box requires the user to click an arrow (attached, not detached) to open the list. Selecting one of the choices places it in the text portion of the combo box. This style saves space, but *does not* enable the user to enter text. The user can make list selections only.

4.2.3   The *AddItem* Method

Adding data to a combo box or list box is not as obvious as you might expect. To add items to a combo box or list box, use the `AddItem` method. The syntax for this method is as follows:

```
{ComboBox ¦ ListBox}.AddItem item [, index]
```

Table 4.3 explains the components of the `AddItem` syntax.

TABLE 4.3   Syntax of the *AddItem* Method

Component	Description
AddItem	A built-in Visual Basic method.
item	The string expression to add to the list. If the expression is a literal string, it must be enclosed in quotation marks.
index	Indicates the placement of the item in the list (and is optional). An index of 0 represents the first position.

As an example, if you want to add the word *Freshman* to `cboMyCombo` and to the first position in the list, you would type the following:

```
cboMyCombo.AddItem "Freshman", 0
```

If an index is not added, the `AddItem` method adds items in the order indicated by the code.

4.2.4   The *Form_Load()* Event

A `Form_Load()` event occurs when a form is loaded into memory. Among other functions, this event is used to fill combo boxes and list boxes with data. When the form is loaded at runtime, the code in the `Form_Load()` event populates list boxes and combo boxes with list items. As an example, examine the following procedure:

```
Private Sub Form_Load()
    lstSport.AddItem "Pool"
    lstSport.AddItem "Basketball"
    lstSport.AddItem "Soccer"
    lstSport.AddItem "Darts"
End Sub
```

This procedure fills the list box lstSport with the words *Pool, Basketball, Soccer,* and *Darts* when the form is loaded at runtime. Because the index is not indicated, the list will be loaded as entered.

4.2.5   Manipulating Items in a List Box or Combo Box

After items have been added to a list box or combo box, they can be sorted by setting the Sorted property, or removed one at a time using the RemoveItem method. There is also a Clear method to clear a list box or combo box, removing all items with a single instruction.

Sorting a List Box or Combo Box

If you want items sorted in a list box or combo box, set the Sorted property to True, omitting the index. This sorts the list in alphabetical order, in ascending order (A–Z). Because the order is not case sensitive, the words "Darts" and "darts" will be treated the same.

Removing Items from a List Box or Combo Box

Removing an item from a combo box or list box uses the built-in RemoveItem method. The syntax for this method is as follows:

```
{ListBox | ComboBox}.RemoveItem index
```

For example, the following instruction would remove "Pool" from the list box shown earlier in section 4.2.4, "The Form_Load() Event."

```
lstSport.RemoveItem 0
```

Clearing Items from a List Box or Combo Box

Clearing all items from a combo box or list box requires the Clear method. The syntax in this instance is as follows:

```
{ListBox | ComboBox}.Clear
```

The following instruction, for example, clears all the items from lstSport (see section 4.2.4, "The Form_Load() Event").

```
lstSport.Clear
```

4.2.6   Using Runtime Properties to Manipulate List Boxes or Combo Boxes

Not all the properties of List or Combo Box controls are available during design time. Like other controls, some are only available at runtime and are known as *runtime properties.* Some of these runtime properties are read-only. That means that only the property's value can be retrieved during runtime. You can't assign it a value with code. Runtime properties that can be assigned values are known as *read/write properties.* That means that their values can be both retrieved and assigned with code.

Both list boxes and combo boxes have a runtime property called `ListCount`, which is read-only. It returns the number of items in a list box or combo box. You will not see the property in the Properties window during design time, nor can you assign it a value during runtime. Its value changes as items are added or removed from a list box or combo box. Although it is read-only, the `ListCount` value can be retrieved and displayed. For example, to learn the number of items in the `lstSport` example (see section 4.2.4), you might write the following code fragment:

```
Print lstSport.ListCount
```

Assuming that nothing had been added or deleted after the `Form_Load()` procedure, the number `4` would be printed on the form. Because lists always start with `0`, the index value of the last item in a list is not equal to the `ListCount`. Instead, it is equal to `ListCount -1`.

List boxes and combo boxes have two other runtime properties named `List` and `ListIndex`. The `List` property, which is read/write, retrieves or assigns the expression in the list box or combo box. (This differs from the `AddItem` method, which populates the list box or combo box.)

If you wanted to print the fourth item in a combo box, you might enter the following code fragment:

```
Print cboProducts.List(3)
```

If the fourth item was `"men's gloves"` and you wanted to change it to `"women's gloves"`, you would enter the following code fragment:

```
cboProducts.List(3) = "women's gloves"
```

The `ListIndex` property, a read/write property, indicates the index value of the currently selected item in a list box or combo box. It is frequently used to ensure that the first item in a list box is displayed. The following code fragment indicates that the first item is displayed in a combo box rather than an empty line:

```
cboProducts.ListIndex = 0
```

If you wanted to have the tenth item in a 20-item combo box displayed, enter the following code:

```
cboProducts.ListIndex = 9
```

To go to the last item in a list or combo box, enter the following code:

```
cboProducts.ListIndex = cboProducts.ListCount -1
```

Finally, the list box has a runtime `Text` property that assigns or reads the string at the current ListIndex location. You learn more about list and combo boxes in Chapter 14, "Lists and Arrays."

Exercise 4.1   Adding a List Box to a Form

With your beginning knowledge of how combo and list boxes work, you'll add a list box to a form and fill it with data in this exercise. To continue with the admissions project in Objective 4.1, "Thinking About a Problem," you will provide an initial design for the admissions officer. After you find out more about what the admissions staff wants, you will add features to your design. Figure 4.2 illustrates the design this exercise asks you to complete.

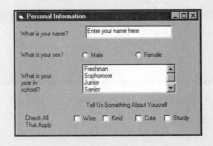

Figure 4.2   *The initial student profile display features three new controls: option buttons, a list box, and check boxes.*

Is this the design you visualized? Does it contain a text box, option buttons, a list box (or combo box), check boxes, and labels?

1. Begin a new project.

2. Change the caption of the form to **Personal Information**.

3. Add a `txtName` text box, as shown in Figure 4.2.

4. Add two option buttons, as shown in Figure 4.2. Type the captions **Male** and **Female**. Use the names `optMale` and `optFemale`.

5. Add a list box, as shown in Figure 4.2. Name the list `lstSchoolYr`.

6. Add four check boxes: `chkWise`, `chkKind`, `chkCute`, and `chkSturdy`. Type the captions **Wise**, **Kind**, **Cute**, and **Sturdy**.

7. Add the following five labels:

    What is your name?

    What is your sex?

    What is your year in school?

    Tell Us Something About Yourself.

    Check All That Apply.

8. Fill the list with item information. Place the item information in the `Sub Form_Load()` event procedure, as follows:

```
Private Sub Form_Load()
    'Warning:  A list box begins with the lowercase letter L,
    'not the number 1
    lstSchoolYr.AddItem "Freshman"
    lstSchoolYr.AddItem "Sophomore"
    lstSchoolYr.AddItem "Junior"
    lstSchoolYr.AddItem "Senior"
    lstSchoolYr.AddItem "Other"
End Sub
```

9. Close the code window, and run the program. The list box should show the five items as entered. Use the Tab key to move from one control to another. If the tab order is not correct, don't worry: You learn how to change it in Exercise 4.3.

10. Save this project for use with the next exercise.

Objective 4.3   Using Format Commands to Align and Lock a Set of Controls

You may have noticed in the next exercise that it sometimes is difficult to properly align a set of controls so they are even in both horizontal and vertical directions. Then, too, once you have spent time working on a detailed design, it would be nice if you could lock controls, making them impossible to move as long as the lock remains. Fortunately, there are several format commands designed to help you align the controls on a form and to lock them once you are satisfied with a design.

4.3.1   Format Commands

There are seven format commands designed to help you in the design of a form. These are explained in the following sections.

Format Align

The Format, Align command provides seven different alignment options: Left, Center, Right, Top, Middle, Bottom, to Grid. If you have a set of option buttons you want to align to the left, press the Shift key and select each button. After you select the set of controls, Format, Align, Left will align the entire set to the left.

Format Make Same Size

This command makes two controls the same size; however, it does not align them. The size options that are possible are to make two or more controls the same in Width, Height, or Both (both width and height).

Format Size to Grid

A Visual Basic form contains a grid that helps to control the alignment of controls. If you want to place a control exactly on the gridlines, however, select the Format, Size to Grid command.

Format Horizontal Spacing

This command is used to make equal, increase, decrease, or remove horizontal spacing between commands. If you want to make the spacing equal, for example, select Format, Horizontal Spacing, Make Equal.

Format Vertical Spacing

Like the previous command, this format command is used to make equal, increase, decrease, or remove vertical space between commands.

Format Center in Form

The Format, Center in Form command is used to center controls either Horizontally or Vertically. Like the other Format command, select the commands to center using the Shift key. After you select several, you can center them on the form.

Format Order

This final format command enables you to Bring to Front or Send to Back controls that overlap. If Command1 lies on top of Command2, click on Command2 and select Format, Send to Back. This will place Command1 in front of Command2.

4.3.2   Lock Controls

A special format command is Format, Lock Controls. This command locks the controls on a form, while in design made, making them impossible to move. When controls are locked, the normal blue boxes that frame the control change to the color white (see Figure 4.3).

Figure 4.3   *The sizing handles on a control change from blue to white when that control is locked.*

Objective 4.4   Using Frame Controls to Improve User-Interface Design

Exercise 4.1 might have helped you to discover that frames were needed for the option buttons, if you did not add them to your design in sequence. As a test, place two option buttons on a form, followed by a check box and another set of option buttons. You will discover that only one option can be selected when you want to enable the user to make two selections.

Frames are used to define a group of options. Stated in a broader context, the Frame control provides a visual and functional container for a set of other controls, such as option buttons and check boxes.

Adding a frame to a form is somewhat difficult when you want to place other controls inside the frame. The important lesson to remember when adding a frame to a form is to add the frame first, then drag (not double-click) or cut and paste the controls to be contained onto the frame. Perform the following steps:

1. Create the frame.

2. Select the control to be added in the toolbox and then "draw" the control in the frame or cut existing controls and, with the frame having the focus, paste the controls into the frame.

Exercise 4.2   Adding Frames to a Form

For this exercise, you add two frames to the admissions form designed in Exercise 4.1 and replace the list box with a Style 2 combo box. Figure 4.4 shows the revised design.

Figure 4.4   *This design adds two frames and replaces the list box with a combo box.*

1. Open the project and add a frame to your design. Attempt to drag the two option buttons into the frame. What happens?

2. Try again. Cut and, with the frame having the focus, paste the two option buttons into the frame. After pasting the buttons, adjust the frame as needed.

continues

Exercise 4.2   continued

3. Draw a third option button inside the frame.

4. Add the caption **Gender** to `Frame1`. Name the frame `fraGender`.

5. Add the captions **Male**, **Female**, and **Don't Care** to the three option buttons. (Sorry for the last category. We're just trying to keep you awake.)

6. Cut and paste into a second frame the four check boxes from your design, and add the label **Tell Us Something About Yourself**. Name the frame `fraTellUs`.

7. Replace the list box with a Style 2 combo box. Name the box `cboSchoolYr`. Change the `Form_Load()` procedure to load the combo box using this name.

8. Align all controls using the Format commands. After you are satisfied with your design, lock all controls.

9. Test your design and write down what you feel is wrong with your design. What purpose does the frame placed around `Gender` serve? What purpose is served by the frame placed around `Tell Us Something About Yourself`?

10. Save this project for use with the next exercise.

Objective 4.5   Controlling the Tab Order in a Design

When designing a form, such as the one for the admissions officer, you can view such a form as a *record* for one student. The record, in turn, contains *fields,* such as student name, sex, year in school, and self-evaluation scores. When placing information on this form, users want to begin in the upper left-hand corner of the form (the first field), enter information at that point, and then press Tab on the keyboard to jump to the next field (either the field to the immediate right or the field on the next line). If you try this with your design, one of the problems you might discover is that the tab order is incorrect. When you press Tab after making an entry, you do not jump to the next field (to the right or down), as you would like.

The initial tab order is based on the sequence you followed in adding controls to a form. In the admissions example, if you added the text box first followed by an option button, the text box should have the focus first. The Tab key then moves the focus from the text box to the first option button.

4.5.1   The *TabIndex* Property

If some controls are deleted on a form and others added, the tab order you desire might be lost. To regain this order, set the `TabIndex` property for a control. The syntax for this change is as follows:

```
control.TabIndex = value
```

A value of 0 indicates the starting point of the order. This is followed by the values 1, 2, and so on.

When the tab index for one control is changed, all others are adjusted automatically, with following controls adjusted upward. Suppose that you have the following tab order in your design:

```
chk1    TabIndex = 0

chk2    TabIndex = 1

chk3    TabIndex = 2
```

Changing the tab index for chk3 from 2 to 0 leads to the following order:

```
chk1    TabIndex = 1

chk2    TabIndex = 2

chk3    TabIndex = 0
```

4.5.2   The *TabStop* Property

Besides changing the tab order, it also is possible to remove a control from the tab order. To do this, set the TabStop property to False, as in the following example:

```
control.TabStop = False
```

Once set to False, the tab order is maintained; however, the control is skipped when the user cycles through the order.

The TabStop property explains how a set of option buttons is able to work when contained by a frame. When the user makes a selection, the TabStop property is set to True, as in the following example:

```
Option1.TabStop = True
```

However, once set to True, all other option buttons are set to False:

```
Option2.TabStop = False
Option3.TabStop = False
```

This leads to skipping the remaining options within the frame. To move among option buttons in a frame, use the arrow keys.

Exercise 4.3   Controlling the Tab Order

In this exercise, you will control the tab order for the admissions office application.

1. Open the project, and check the tab order in your design.

2. Change the tab index property of the last check box. Set the TabIndex to 0 for chkSturdy, and run the program. What happens?

continues

Exercise 4.3   continued

3. Return to design mode and set the TabIndex to 0 for chkWise.

4. Continue to move up the design, always setting the next control in the tab order to 0. In so doing, you will move up the design, moving from right to left and bottom to top.

5. Test your design. What happens when you make one sex choice and press Tab?

6. Save your project at this time for use with the next exercise.

Objective 4.6   Learning to Enable and Disable a Control

Controls in Visual Basic can be enabled or disabled by setting the Enabled property to True or False, respectively. The syntax for this property is as follows:

```
[form.][control.]Enabled [= Boolean]
```

The Boolean value is either True or False. The following expression enables the object to respond to events:

```
option3.Enabled = True
```

The following expression prevents the object from responding to events:

```
option3.Enabled = False
```

Disabling an option button dims (grays) the color of the button to indicate that the button cannot be used.

Exercise 4.4   Disabling an Option Button

In this exercise, you will disable the option button for the sex choice shown as Don't Care.

1. Open the project and move to the Don't Care button.

2. Press F4 to open the Properties window.

3. Change the Enabled property to False.

4. Run and test your design. What happens when you try to click the Don't Care option?

Objective 4.7   Creating a Menu Bar and Writing Code for Menu Procedures

Visual Basic provides a menu bar builder, which enables the Visual Basic programmer to create a menu for an application at design time. Menus are a different type of control. They are used to provide an application design with a set of commands that is easy to find and to use. They have the advantage of adding functionality to a program without sacrificing much screen "real estate." The ease with which a developer can add a menu bar to a Visual Basic application is one of the language's strongest features.

4.7.1   The Menu Design Command

To add a menu bar to a design, give the form focus and choose Tools, Menu Editor, or click the Menu Design button on the toolbar. The dialog box shown in Figure 4.5 opens.

Figure 4.5   *The Menu Editor serves as a tool for adding menu selections to the top of a form.*

The two most important properties for the Menu control are the first and second text boxes. Use these two boxes as follows:

1. Add the caption for the control in the Caption text box. The caption is the text that will appear on the menu bar. For example, type &File. (The purpose of the ampersand is described in the next set of steps.) Observe that the word *File* appears both in the caption text box and as the first entry in the Menu control list box. When you run the program, the word *File* will appear as the first name on the menu bar.

2. Press Tab and enter the name of the Menu control. This is the name you use to refer to the control from code. For example, type the name mnuFile.

After the menu caption and name have been entered, it is possible to add the subordinate command to fall under the command category. To add a subordinate command, do the following:

1. Click <u>N</u>ext to advance the list box to the next entry, clear the caption and name boxes, and advance to the next line.

2. Enter the caption for the control in the Caption text box. For example, enter the caption &End.

3. Following the entry of this name, click the right arrow. The list box should look as follows:

```
&File
....&End
```

This indicates that the command End is subordinate to the File command. The ampersand in front of both menu commands enables standard Windows keyboard navigation to menu choices. Placing the ampersand in front of the letter *F* enables the user to press Alt+F to access File menu choices.

4. Enter the name of the command. For example, enter the name mnuFileEnd (which means the End choice under the File menu).

5. Tab to <u>S</u>hortcut to set the shortcut key. Open the combo box to select Ctrl+E as the shortcut key combination. By pressing the Ctrl+E on the keyboard, the End command is triggered. Alternatively, the user could use Alt+F and then press the E key to execute the mnuFileEnd instruction.

6. Click OK if you have completed building the menu bar.

You will return to the menu bar in other applications. For now, you should become familiar with adding just the File, End command sequence to an application.

4.7.2 Writing Code for a Menu Control

Adding the word *File* to the menu bar and the word *End* to the list of File commands does little more than add the captions to the menu bar. The next step is to write a Click() event procedure for a command. When the user chooses a Menu control, a Click() event triggers the menu event procedure. This event procedure is one that the Visual Basic programmer must write.

Writing the code for a Menu control is done in the same way as writing the code for other controls.

1. Click the form to open the code window.

2. Find the name of the menu command in the Object list.

3. Find the Click procedure in the procedure list.

4. Add the instructions for the Click() event. To end a program, for example, type the word End. The completed procedure is as follows:

```
Private Sub mnuFileEnd_Click()
    End
End Sub
```

Exercise 4.5 Adding Menu Commands to Your Application

In this exercise, you add a File menu and End command to the admissions office application. Figure 4.6 shows the modified display.

Figure 4.6 *When opened, this menu bar will reveal the End command.*

1. Open the project and choose Tools, Menu Editor Design (or click the Menu Design icon on the toolbar).

2. Type &File for the command Caption and mnuFile for the Name.

3. Click Next.

4. Type &End for the command Caption and mnuFileEnd for the Name. Add a shortcut key of Ctrl+E. Click the right arrow key to make this command subordinate to the File command.

5. Click OK to close the dialog box.

6. Choose File, End to add the following mnuFileEnd procedure:

```
Private Sub mnuFileEnd_Click()
    End
End Sub
```

7. Test your design. Test the different keyboard methods for ending your application. Press Ctrl+E (the shortcut) or Alt+F and then the E key (standard Windows keyboard navigation) to end the application.

Objective 4.8 Adding a Scroll Bar to a Design

Before concluding this chapter, you should visualize a second design situation. It's time to move away from the admissions project and begin working on a new problem. Consider the following scenario.

4.8.1 Designing a Demonstration Scroll Bar

"I want a simple application to explain to my students how a scroll box works. Named Measuring Speed, the application should have a minimum range of 0 miles per hour (mph) and a maximum range of 120mph. As a student uses the scroll bar, it should be possible to click the ends of the bar or the middle to demonstrate a slow and a fast scroll. Some kind of Help system should be provided to explain the technique to follow in a fast and a slow scroll. The user should also be able to click to stop the application."

Given only this information, make a sketch of how your design will look.

4.8.2 Scroll Bar Basics

Whether you know it or not, you are quite familiar with scroll bars, having worked in a Windows environment. In the Visual Basic toolbox, you'll find a Vertical Scroll Bar control and a Horizontal Scroll Bar control. As shown by Figure 4.7, each scroll bar contains a scroll arrow at the ends and a scroll box that moves from end to end when you drag it using the mouse. The scroll box is used to indicate the current value specified by the bar.

Scroll Box   Scroll Shaft   Scroll Arrow

Figure 4.7 *A scroll bar requires two procedures: one for the scroll box and another for the scroll shaft and scroll arrows.*

Different mouse actions determine how rapidly values change on a scroll bar. Click the arrow to move an incremental unit toward the end. Use the scroll box to drag through a range of values. Click the scroll shaft between the arrow and the scroll box to move a larger increment between the scroll box and the end.

The five most important properties of the scroll bar are those that set the upper and lower range values (Max and Min), the large and the small change values (LargeChange and SmallChange), and the value (Value). Table 4.4 explains these properties.

TABLE 4.4   Scroll Bar Properties

Property	Description
Max	Sets the maximum value for a scroll bar. For example, the maximum for a temperature scroll bar might be 212.
Min	Sets the minimum value for a scroll bar. For example, the minimum for a temperature scroll bar might be −32.
LargeChange	Determines the amount of change to the value property when the user clicks the space between the scroll box and the scroll arrow.
SmallChange	Determines the amount of change to the value property when the user clicks a scroll arrow.
Value	Specifies the return value represented by the current position of the scroll bar.

By default, LargeChange and SmallChange are set to 1; however, it is possible to change this setting to a number from 1 to 32767 (inclusive). The default settings for Max and Min are 32767 and 0, respectively. The possible range for these settings is from -32768 to 32767. Max and Min determine maximum and minimum values, respectively; the actual value depends upon the position of the scroll box.

4.8.3   The *Scroll()* and *Change()* Event Procedures

Two event procedures are associated with the design of a scroll bar: the Change() event and the Scroll() event. The Change() event occurs whenever the Value property changes. The code associated with the Change() event might read as follows:

```
Private Sub HScroll1_Change()
    lblValue.Caption = HScroll1.Value
End Sub
```

The purpose of this procedure is to report the change whenever the value changes. That is, whenever the user clicks the space between the scroll box and the scroll arrow or selects the scroll arrow, the new value of the scroll bar is displayed in the label named lblValue.

The Scroll() event is unique to scroll bars. Even so, the code associated with the Scroll() event is similar to the code for the Change() event:

```
Private Sub HScroll1_Scroll()
    lblValue.Caption  = Hscroll1.Value
End Sub
```

The Scroll() event occurs whenever the user drags the scroll box. Like the Change() event, this procedure immediately displays the changed value of HScroll1 as the user drags the scroll box.

You might consider the difference between the two events as a jump in values, say from 0 to 30, with the Change() event, and a continuous updating of the value while the scroll bar is being dragged with the Scroll() event.

Exercise 4.6   Using Scroll Bars in an Application

In this exercise, you design the speed-measuring application you were asked to visualize in section 4.7.1, "Designing a Demonstration Scroll Bar."

1. Open a new project and change the form caption to **Measuring Speed**.

2. Add a text box and remove the text caption. Change the name to **txtSpeed**.

3. Add the Horizontal Scroll Bar control. Name it **hsbSpeed**.

4. Set the following properties for the scroll bar:

   ```
   Max = 120
   Min = 0
   LargeChange = 10
   SmallChange = 1
   ```

5. Add a command button, change the caption to **Stop**, change the name to **cmdStop**, and write an End() event procedure.

6. Add a second command button, change the caption to **Help**, and change the name to **cmdHelp**.

7. Write the following code for the cmdHelp button:

   ```
   Private Sub cmdHelp_Click()
       Dim Message as String
       Dim Title as String
       Message = "Click the ends to make a small change or the
   ↪middle to make a large change."
       Title = "Help with the scroll bar"
       MsgBox Message, , Title
   End Sub
   ```

8. Double-click the scroll bar to open the code window and enter the following code:

   ```
   Private Sub hsbSpeed_Change()
       txtSpeed.Text = hsbSpeed.Value & " mph"
   End Sub
   ```

9. Write the Scroll() procedure for the scroll bar. This code is as follows:

   ```
   Private Sub hsbSpeed_Scroll()
       txtSpeed.Text = hsbSpeed.Value & " mph"
   End Sub
   ```

10. Test your design. Experiment by changing the Max and Min values and the LargeChange and SmallChange values.

This exercise included some code statements with which you are unfamiliar. Don't worry. It will become clearer when we review how to assign values to variables, and the syntax and usage of the MsgBox statement. For now, think of how far you have come!

Chapter Summary

The objectives of this chapter were developed to help you think visually in the design of a Visual Basic program, and to instill in your mind the process followed in design. You should think about the problem and visualize in your mind the design requested by the user. In doing this, you might recognize that different types of text boxes and buttons become important, as do frames and the tab order. Placing commands on a menu bar is another possibility. Scroll bars add still another form of functionality to a design.

List boxes and combo boxes present to the user a list of items. With a list box, the `MultiSelect` property permits more than one selection. A list box can also have multiple columns. A combo box is a combination of a text box and list box. The `Style` property determines the type of combo box. Currently, there are three styles.

Methods are required to add, delete, or clear items from a list or combo box. The `AddItem` method serves to add items; the `RemoveItem` method is used to delete an item. The `Clear` method removes all items from a list. The `Sorted` list box and combo box property lists items alphabetically.

Items can be loaded into a list box or combo box using the `Form_Load()` procedure.

Frames are used to store a set of option buttons and other types of controls. When enclosed by a frame, only one option button can be selected within the frame. Option buttons placed outside the frame are not affected.

The tab order of a design is controlled by the `TabIndex` setting. An index value of `0` determines the first tab in a tab-order sequence. The `TabStop` property is used to skip a control in a tab order sequence.

You use the Menu Editor to build a menu for a design. Each item placed on a menu must have a caption and a menu name. You determine a menu hierarchy by placing subordinate menu items to the right of a menu name. After the menu bar is built, procedures must be written for each menu command.

In the design of an interface, scroll bars provide an interesting visual picture. The `Value` property determines the return value represented by the current position of the scroll bar. The range of returned values is set by the `Min` and `Max` properties. The speed with which values change is determined by the `SmallChange` and `LargeChange` properties.

`Change()` and `Scroll()` event procedures are both required with scroll bars. The `Change()` event occurs whenever the user clicks a scroll arrow or the space between the scroll box and the scroll arrow. The `Scroll()` event occurs whenever the user drags the scroll box.

Skill-Building Exercises

This set of exercises asks you to work with combo and list boxes, option buttons and frames, and scroll bars. In addition, you are asked to practice using the Format commands to improve your layout of controls. The last two exercises make use of AddItem and RemoveItem methods.

1. Test the differences between the three styles of combo boxes. Place all three combo boxes on the screen (see Figure 4.1). Place the list items **Pool**, **Basketball**, **Soccer**, and **Darts** in each combo box. Use styles 0, 1, and 2. Remove the text from the styles. Add the labels Combo Box - Style 0, Combo Box - Style 1, and Combo Box - Style 2. Test your design. What conclusions can you draw?

2. Extend the last exercise by adding the two list box styles to your design. Place the same list items in each list box. Add the labels List Box - Style 0 and List Box - Style 1. Test your design. What is the difference between the two list box styles?

3. Format the last exercise as follows, redesigning as needed:

   ■ Place all combo boxes on the left and all list boxes on the right.

   ■ Left-align all combo boxes and make them the same size.

   ■ Left-align all list boxes and make them the same size.

   ■ Lock all controls when you have completed this design.

4. Design a form which asks the user the following question: Which combo box style does not permit a user to enter text? Provide these possible answers: Standard combo box, drop-down combo box, checkbox list box, drop-down list box, and simple combo box. Use option buttons for all possible answers. Place these buttons with a frame. Align all buttons. Finally, when the user runs this application, show the correct answer.

5. Create horizontal and vertical scroll bars. Set the scroll bar range for both bars for values between 1 and 45. Set the SmallChange value to 1 and the LargeChange value to 5. Use a label to display the scroll bar value. Change the background color (Backcolor) for the label and the form. Change the caption on the form. Write both Change() and Scroll() procedures. In writing these procedures, add the following instructions, changing the name of the Label1 to Hscroll1 and Vscroll1 as necessary:

   ```
   Label1.Caption = {H | V}scroll1.Value
   ```

6. Place a Style 2 combo box on a form. Add a text box, a label, and a command button. Write a Form_Load() procedure that adds the following cities to the combo box: **New York**, **Los Angeles**, **Chicago**, **San Francisco**, **Atlanta**, and **Houston**. Place the label over the text box, and change its caption to read **Enter Additional City**. In the command button with the caption **Add City**, add a procedure that appends whatever city the user enters into the text box to the top position of the combo box.

7. Extend Exercise 4.4 by adding two more command buttons. Make **Clear** the caption for one command button, and write a procedure in that button's `Click()` event to clear all items in the combo box. Make **Delete** the caption of the other command button, and write a procedure that will delete the currently selected item.

INTRODUCTION TO THE GRAPHIC CONTROLS AND GRAPHIC METHODS OF VISUAL BASIC

Windows owes its tremendous popularity, in part, to the appeal of its interface. As with other graphical user interfaces (GUIs), users quickly come to appreciate the visual cues that Windows provides to guide them through a program. They especially like interface colors, shapes, and images. If given a choice, most users prefer to click a mouse button to enter instructions rather than type commands. Standard GUI features, such as buttons, pull-down list boxes, sizable forms, and drag-and-drop functionality, have greatly eased the introduction of computing to millions of new users.

This chapter introduces several controls that can assist you in adding visual interest and definition to your program. These graphic controls—the Line control, Shape control, and Image control—provide flexible ways to enhance the visual appeal of an application. By exploiting the graphic richness of Windows, these controls enable you to easily add geometric shapes, colors, and images to the user interface. The Label control, which you have already used, is also a graphic control.

This chapter introduces several of Visual Basic's graphic methods, which are coded instructions that directly "draw" upon a Visual Basic form, picture box, or `Printer` object. Graphic methods differ from graphic controls by performing operations at a lower level. A good illustration of the difference between the two is to compare using the `Print` method (a graphic method) on a form and assigning a new caption to a label that has been placed on a form. Both actions produce text output, but the `Print` method operates directly on the form. Assigning a new caption to a Label control triggers code assigned to the Label control, which then "draws" the text. The differences will become clearer as you work through the exercises in this chapter, which show you how to do the following:

- Manipulate the Line control in design-time and runtime
- Add a Shape control to a project and manipulate its properties in code

- Learn to adjust layering for graphic controls, including the Label control, in design-time and runtime

- Add images to the Image control in both design-time and runtime

- Work with the `Line`, `PSet`, and `Print` graphic methods

Chapter Objectives

This chapter addresses all of the Visual Basic graphic controls (other than the Label control): the Line control, Shape control, and Image control. The objectives are as follows:

1. Learning the basics of the Visual Basic coordinate system

2. Manipulating the Line and Shape controls in design-time and runtime

3. Layering controls in design-time and runtime

4. Using the design-time and runtime properties of the Image control

5. Introducing the Visual Basic graphic methods

Objective 5.1   Learning the Basics of the Visual Basic Coordinate System

Before you use graphic controls, it is important to understand how these controls differ from other Visual Basic controls and how the coordinate system works. The coordinate system is used in the precise placement of controls on a form or within a container, such as a frame or a picture box.

5.1.1   How Graphic Controls Differ from Other Visual Basic Controls

The graphic controls are added to a form like other controls: you can double-click the toolbox or select the control in the toolbox and then "draw" it on the form. Two of these controls, the Line control and Shape control, have no events associated with them. Their properties can be adjusted with code, but they cannot, for example, recognize a mouse click. In the code window under the Object combo box, the line or shape objects are not listed because they have no events to code. Internally, Windows treats the Line and Shape controls as part of the form.

The Image control—which can display a bitmap image—can recognize mouse events, such as clicking, double-clicking, or being dragged over with the mouse. The Image control, like the Line and Shape controls, however, cannot receive focus. Although an event can be triggered by clicking an Image control, the Image control does not then retain the focus the way a command or option button does. The

Label control has similar behavior: it can receive mouse events, but it cannot retain focus. (You will work with the Image control's mouse events in Chapter 12, "Programming User Events.")

5.1.2 The Relationship of Graphic Controls to a Form

Every form has a coordinate system. No matter where a control is on a form, its location can be described by x and y coordinates of the form. These coordinates are expressed in the Left (x) and Top (y) properties of controls. The Width and Height properties of controls measure, appropriately enough, the value of the controls' width and height relative to the coordinate system of the form. The x coordinate of the right side of a control, therefore, would be approximately the value of the control's Left property plus the value of the control's Width Property. This will become clearer as you work with the controls' locations.

Like other x,y coordinate systems, Visual Basic's coordinate system is a two-dimensional grid. In Figure 5.1, you see highlighting where the x- and y-axes values begin for a form. By default, the 0 values of the x-axis (horizontal) and the y-axis (vertical) are in the extreme upper-left corner.

Figure 5.1   *The Visual Basic coordinate system is applied to a form and containers placed on a form.*

Unlike the coordinate system typically used in graphs, the value for the y-axis increases as you approach the bottom of a form. As Figure 5.1 shows, a separate coordinate system is maintained for Visual Basic's two container controls: the Frame control and the Picture Box control. You have used the Frame control to group option buttons, and you will briefly read about the Picture Box control in this chapter. Remember, a control's Left and Top properties are determined by the coordinate system for the container in which the control is placed. Therefore, the Left (x-axis value) and Top (y-axis value) properties of an option button within a frame are determined by the coordinate system of the frame, not the form.

The default scale mode of forms and controls is twips. How do twips relate to a measurement system you can understand? A twip is 1/20 of a printer's point. There are 72 points per inch and, therefore, 1440 twips, which makes a twips-to-inches association somewhat difficult. You will eventually become used to twips notation. For example, examine the Top, Left, Width, and Height properties of a blank form. Their values are expressed in twips.

Objective 5.2   Manipulating the Line and Shape Controls in Design-Time and Runtime

This section examines the Line and the Shape controls and how their properties can be set during design-time or runtime. Both controls are found on the toolbox; as such, they contain sets of easy-to-find properties. Before starting this section, find both controls on the toolbox.

5.2.1   The Line Control Properties

The Line control actually is one of the few controls that does not have Left, Top, Width, or Height properties. Instead, it has four properties to locate it on a form or inside a container control: X1, X2, Y1, and Y2. The coordinates X1 and Y1 define one endpoint of the line, and the coordinates X2 and Y2 define the other endpoint. The Line control also has three border properties: BorderColor, BorderStyle, and BorderWidth.

Exercise 5.1   Manipulating the Line Control in Design-Time and Runtime

In this exercise, you use the Line control to set properties in design-time and during runtime. You begin with design-time property changes and observe the change after each new property setting.

Part 1: Design-Time Changes

1. Open a new project and double-click the Line control.

2. In the Property window for Line1, add **1000** to the current value of the X2 property of Line1.

3. Add **1000** to the value of the Y2 property of Line1.

4. Change the Line1.BorderWidth property to 20.

5. In the BorderColor property, select a new color from the color options.

Part 2: Experiment with Runtime Changes

1. Open a new project, and add two lines approximately one-half inch long near the upper-left corner of the form. Keep the lines separate and drag them into position. Position Line1 horizontally and Line2 vertically with their ends touching.

2. Make sure that the X1 point of Line1 (the horizontal line) and the Y1 point of Line2 (the vertical line) are at the intersection of the lines.

---

3. In the `Form_Click()` event, add the following code:

```
Private Sub Form_Click()
    Line1.BorderWidth = 4
    Line2.BorderWidth = 4
    Line1.X2 = Line1.X2 + 500
    Line2.Y2 = Line2.Y2 + 500
End Sub
```

4. Run and test the program. Click the form more than once. With each mouse click on the form, the horizontal and vertical lines should increase their sizes by 500 twips as you add to the `Line1.X2` and `Line2.Y2` property values.

5.2.2   The Shape Control Properties

The Shape control is even more flexible than the Line control. A single control can be made into one of six shapes: a rectangle, a square, an oval, a circle, a rounded rectangle, or a rounded square (see Figure 5.2).

Figure 5.2   *You can change the size of each of the shape selections to meet the needs of your application.*

These shapes are controlled by the Shape control's `Shape` property and can be set in either design-time or runtime. The Shape control is positioned and sized on a form or inside a container control with the familiar `Left`, `Top`, `Width`, and `Height` properties. Its other properties are similar to that of the Line control, except it also has `FillStyle` and `FillColor` properties. By clicking `FillColor` in the Property window, a color palette appears for your selection. The appearance of the interior of a shape depends on the `FillStyle` setting. The eight `FillStyle` settings are `solid`, `transparent`, `horizontal`, `vertical`, `upward`, `downward`, `cross`, and `diagonal` (see Figure 5.3).

Figure 5.3   *The* `FillStyle` *property is used to distinguish one shape from another.*

The interior appearance is also affected by the Shape control's `BackStyle` and `BackColor` properties. If the `BackStyle` is set to `Transparent(0)`, the color of the object behind the shape, such as a form, will be the shape's `BackColor`. If `BackStyle` is set to `Opaque`, the `BackColor` will be that set by the `BackColor` property.

103

By mixing `BackColor`, `FillColor`, and `FillStyle`, a wide variety of pleasing visual effects can be achieved.

You can employ the Shape control to perform numerous functions. You can use it as a marquee border, in simple animation, or to give the user visual feedback of the processing status. One of the best ways to get to know the Shape control is to simply experiment with its properties during design-time. All entered property changes are immediately reflected on the Shape control on the form.

Exercise 5.2   Changing the Shape Control's Properties During Runtime

This exercise is similar to the last one. It changes the Shape control during runtime to demonstrate the flexibility available to you by simply changing object properties. Figure 5.4 shows the design that you are to create.

Figure 5.4   *The Change My Shape button will change the shape from an oval to a rectangle.*

1. Open a new project, and add a Shape control and a command button to the form.

2. Change the Form's caption to **I'm a blue oval**.

3. Name the command button **cmdChangeMe**, and change its caption to **Change My Shape**.

4. Change the Shape control's properties so that it appears as a royal blue oval with the following properties:

   ```
   FillStyle = Solid
   Shape     = Oval
   FillColor = royal blue
   ```

5. In the `cmdChangeMe_Click()` event, add the following code:

   ```
   Private Sub cmdChangeMe_Click()
       ShpTest.Shape = 0 ' rectangle
       ShpTest.FillColor = vbRed ' bright red
       ShpTest.Width = 1500
       ShpTest.Height = 3500
       Form1.Caption = "Now, I'm a Red Rectangle!"
   End Sub
   ```

   In this code, `vbRed` is a constant built-in to Visual Basic. (Constants, both built-in or defined by you, are discussed in Chapter 6, "Variables and Constants.")

6. Run and test the program. The `Click()` event should generate a red vertical rectangle.

Objective 5.3   Layering Controls in Design-Time and Runtime

You may have noticed that Visual Basic has different graphic layers. A command button, for example, always appears in front of a graphic control, as does an option button or a combo box. The output of the Print command also appears behind a windowed control.

5.3.1   The Design-Time Layering of Controls

If two controls of the same graphic level overlap, it is necessary to designate which control appears in front. This can be set in either design-time or runtime. Labels, the Line control, and the Shape control are all in the middle graphic level. If you want a label to overlap a Shape control, you must place it on top of the Shape control. In design-time, you can accomplish this in one of two ways:

- You can place the controls on the form in the order that you want them to appear, placing the bottom control first. Any subsequent control goes on top of the one that preceded it within its graphic level.

- You can determine the placement of the controls by choosing Format, Order (also available by right-clicking), and selecting either Bring to Front or Send to Back. By selecting controls and using these Format, Order menu commands, you can arrange the layering of controls within a graphic level as you want.

Exercise 5.3   Welcoming the Shape Control

In this exercise, you design an interface to explore the graphic layers. Figure 5.5 shows the interface during design-time; Figure 5.6 shows the interface during runtime.

Figure 5.5   *Use a rectangle with a small label placed on top of it.*

continues

Figure 5.6   *The Label control in this design represents the topmost graphical layer, while the shape control represents the middle graphical layer.*

1. Create the interface you see in Figure 5.5. Draw the rectangle first and then place the small Label you see on top of it. Name the command button **cmdWelcome** and the Label **lblWelcome**.

2. Set the following lblWelcome properties:

   ```
   Alignment = Center
   BackStyle = Transparent
   ForeColor = White
   AutoSize = True
   WordWrap = True
   ```

3. Select the Label, choose F̲ormat, O̲rder, and select S̲end to Back. (Alternatively, select the label and right-click your mouse. The B̲ring to Front and S̲end to Back menu choices should be available to you.) Now bring the Label to the front again by choosing F̲ormat, O̲rder, and selecting B̲ring to Front.

4. In the cmdWelcome_Click() event, enter the following code:

   ```
   ShpTest.Shape = 4 ' rounded rectangle
   ShpTest.Top = 200
   ShpTest.Left = 200
   ShpTest.Width = 4000
   ShpTest.Height = 3000
   ShpTest.BorderWidth = 6
   lblWelcome.Caption = "Welcome to the Shape Control!!"
   lblWelcome.FontSize = 24
   lblWelcome.BorderStyle = 0 ' set to no border
   lblWelcome.Top = ShpTest.Top + ShpTest.Height / 8
   lblWelcome.Left = ShpTest.Width / 4
   ```

5. Run and test the program. It should produce an image similar to that in Figure 5.6 (note the alignment).

This code is a little more complicated than that in previous exercises. The last two lines of the procedure might be difficult to understand at first. You set the top and left position of lblWelcome by making reference to ShpTest properties. The next-to-last line of code positions the top of lblWelcome 1/8 of the way from the top of ShpTest.

Do you understand how this is done? First, take the top of ShpTest and then add to it 1/8 of the value of ShpTest.Height (remembering that the y axis increases as you approach the bottom of a form). Similarly, the left value of lblWelcome is set one quarter of the way in from the left side of ShpTest.

5.3.2 The *ZOrder* Method

Runtime control of the graphic layers is more complex than control during design-time. In runtime, you can designate the order of controls and forms by using the ZOrder method. It is called ZOrder because it controls placement of controls in the Z dimension. The syntax of this method is as follows:

```
[object.]ZOrder [position]
```

The object component can be any form or control except the timer or menu, and position can be either 0 or 1. If no position argument is specified, 0 is assumed, and the control is brought to the topmost position. If the position argument is 1, then the control is sent to the rear of the ZOrder.

Exercise 5.4   Toggling *ZOrder*

In this exercise, you use the ZOrder method to manipulate the z dimension position of two command buttons and two Shape controls. Figure 5.7 shows the interface during design-time.

Figure 5.7   *You use the* ZOrder *method to arrange the control and the order of shapes within the same graphical layer.*

1. Create the interface you see in Figure 5.7. Add two command buttons, **Command1** and **Command2**, to a form. Choose Format, Order, and make sure that Command1 has the topmost position.

2. Add two Shape controls, **Shape1** and **Shape2**, to a form. Make sure Shape1, a red oval, has the topmost position and that Shape2, a blue, rounded rectangle, has the bottom-most position.

3. In the Command1_Click() event, add the following code:

```
Command1.ZOrder 1
Shape1.ZOrder 1
```

4. In the Command2_Click() event, add the following code:

```
Command2.ZOrder 1
Shape2.ZOrder 1
```

5. Run and test the program. Observe the toggling of the ZOrder as Command1 and Command2 are clicked.

Objective 5.4   Using the Design-Time and Runtime Properties of the Image Control

The Image control displays bitmap images in a flexible, resource-efficient way. Unlike the Picture Box control, which is a container control for storing controls and images and receiving graphics method commands, the purpose of the Image control is solely to display images. This makes it much less taxing on system resources than the Picture Box control. If you need to display an image and do not need the added functionality of the Picture Box control, use the Image control.

5.4.1   The Image Control's Special Properties

The Image control is simple and powerful. Having most of the properties of the other graphic controls, it also has the Picture and the Stretch properties.

The *Picture* Property

One of the most powerful properties is the Picture property. If you simply designate the path of the bitmap image to be displayed, the Image control will, by default, display the image in its original size. You can either enter the path, or, by double-clicking the Picture property in the property box, you can browse and select an appropriate image file in the dialog box that appears. The image file must have a .BMP, .JPG, .GIF, .DIB, .WMF (Windows Metafile Format), or .ICO (icon format) extension.

The *Stretch* Property

The Image control also has a Stretch property. Its default value is False, which means that the Image control will take on the size of the image that is loaded into it. If you change the size of the image after loading it, the image will be cropped. By setting the Stretch property to True, you make the size of the image conform to whatever size you set the Image control.

Exercise 5.5   Experimenting with the Image Control

In this exercise, you experiment with the Image control during design-time and during runtime. In part one, you experiment with the Stretch property; in part two you add a Click() event to an image box.

Part 1: Changing Image Control Properties

1. Open a new project and add an Image control to your form. Name it **imgTest**.

2. Open the Properties window and double-click the Picture property. The Load Picture dialog box should appear. Select an image on your hard disk. If you have no files with the .BMP or .WMF extensions, you can find small icon images with the .ICO extension in the \icons subdirectory under your Visual Basic directory.

---

3. Leaving the `Stretch` property of `imgTest` to its default value of `False`, select the Image control and then change its size with the newly loaded image. If you shrink the image, you will see the image cropped. If you enlarge the image, transparent space is added.

4. Change the `Stretch` property to `True`, and experiment with changing the size of the image.

5. Change the `imgTest Stretch` property back to `False`, and reload your image by double-clicking in the `imgTest.Picture` property and selecting your image again.

Part 2: Coding an Image `Click()` Event

1. Add two command buttons to your form. Name one **cmdShow** and the other **cmdHide**. Add the following code to cmdShow() event:imgTest.Visible = True

   Add the following code to the cmdHide() event:

   ```
   imgTest.Visible = False
   ```

2. Add the following code to the `imgTest_Click()` event.

   ```
   MsgBox "You clicked the image"
   ```

3. Run and test the program. Notice that the `Click()` event triggers a `msgBox`, but the program's focus remains with whatever command button had focus before the `Click()` event.

5.4.2   Using the *LoadPicture* Function During Runtime

So far, you have manipulated the design-time property settings. With the `LoadPicture` function, you can load a new image into the Image control during runtime, or clear it. The syntax for the `LoadPicture` function is straightforward:

```
LoadPicture([stringexpression])
```

The `stringexpression` is the path to the image file. The following is an example:

```
Image1.Picture = LoadPicture("C:\images\City.BMP")
```

If the image was in the root directory of the application, only the image file name would need to be used as an argument.

```
Image1.Picture = LoadPicture("City.BMP")
```

To clear an image from an Image control, simply assign a null string to the `LoadPicture` function argument:

```
Image1.Picture = LoadPicture("")
```

You can use the LoadPicture function to assign values to Picture properties dynamically. Besides images, forms have Picture properties that will load a bitmap image into the form's background. Picture boxes also have a Picture property.

Exercise 5.6   Using the *LoadPicture* Function

In this short exercise, you design three Click() events: two to load different icon files (.ICO) in an image box and one to clear the image box.

1. Open a new project, and draw the interface you see in Figure 5.8.

Figure 5.8   *This display uses the* LoadPicture *function to place an image in the image box.*

2. Name the Image control **imgLoad**. Name the command buttons **cmdRocket**, **cmdBicycle**, and **cmdClear**. The bicycle image is bicycle.ico, found under the vb\icons\industry subdirectory (and on the student disk).

3. In the cmdRocket_Click() event, enter the following code:

    ```
    Dim Path As String
    Path = "C:\vb\icons\industry\"  ' change path as necessary
    imgLoad.Picture = LoadPicture(Path & "Rocket.ico")
    ```

    If the path to the Visual Basic subdirectories is different, make the necessary changes when assigning an expression to the Path variable.

4. In the cmdBicycle_Click() event, enter the following:

    ```
    Dim Path As String
    Path = "C:\vb\icons\industry\"
    imgLoad.Picture = LoadPicture(Path & "Bicycle.ico")
    ```

5. In the cmdClear_Click() event, enter the following:

    ```
    imgLoad.Picture = LoadPicture("")
    ```

6. Run and test the program.

As a rule, it is unwise to code a specific Path statement; instead, you should try to determine at runtime the location of your application. Visual Basic provides the App system object, which has a Path property that can be read. (The App object and its Path property are addressed in Chapter 18, "Sequential File Processing and Error Trapping.")

Objective 5.5 Introducing the Visual Basic Graphic Methods

Graphic methods, such as the Print, Line, and Circle methods, can be said to "draw" on the bottom layer of forms and picture boxes. Graphic methods give you great flexibility and are very efficient in keeping file sizes small. Their flexibility comes from their being much more closely linked than graphic controls to the rich graphic capabilities inherent in the Windows operating system. To their disadvantage, graphic methods typically take longer to code than graphic controls: They require a more complex syntax than the code required to manipulate graphic control properties.

As with most things, the best way to learn the Visual Basic graphic methods is to experiment with them. The more you practice with graphic methods, the more fun you will have with them.

5.5.1 *CurrentX* and *CurrentY* Runtime Properties

When using graphic methods, such as the Print method, you can designate where the drawing operation begins by designating the CurrentX and CurrentY properties. These properties set the x and y values on a form, picture box, or Printer object. By setting these properties immediately before invoking the Print or some other graphic method, you can specify where on a form or picture box you want drawn output to appear.

CurrentX and CurrentY are runtime properties. They do not appear in the properties window during design-time and can be specified only with coded instructions.

Exercise 5.7 Using *CurrentX* and *CurrentY* for Printing

In this exercise, you use the Picture Box control and CurrentX and CurrentY to display a message on a form and inside a picture box at a specified location. Figure 5.9 shows the design you are asked to create.

Figure 5.9 *CurrentX and* CurrentY *properties specify where graphics methods, such as* Print, *begin.*

continues

---

1. Design the interface. Name the picture box **pic1**, the command button **cmdPrintIt**, and set the form caption to **Using CurrentX, CurrentY with the Print method**. Add the caption **Print Message** to the command button. Make sure the form `ScaleMode` for the form is set to twips. Set the `Form.Height` property to **3000** and the `Form.Width` property to **5000**.

2. In the `cmdPrintIt_Click()` event, enter the following code:

```
Private Sub cmdPrintIt_Click()
    Dim message As String
    message="I'm placing this message where I wanted!"
    frmDisplay.Font.Bold = True
    frmDisplay.CurrentX = 400
    frmDisplay.CurrentY = 2200
    frmDisplay.Print message    'This prints at the bottom of the
➥form
    Pic1.Font.Bold = True
    Pic1.CurrentX = 400
    Pic1.CurrentY = 200
    Pic1.Print message    'This prints the message inside the
➥picture box
End Sub
```

3. Run and test the program. Notice that the 0,0 starting point is unique for each container, whether it's a form or a picture box.

5.5.2 The *Line* Method

The `Line` method is one of the more useful, if somewhat complicated, graphic methods to use. It can be used to draw either lines or rectangles. It can control the color of a line as well as the fill, if any, of a rectangle. The complete syntax of this method is as follows:

```
[object.] Line[[Step](x1,y1)]-[Step](x2,y2),[color][,B[F]]]
```

Table 5.1 explains the components of the `Line` method syntax.

TABLE 5.1 Syntax of the *Line* Method

Component	Description
object	Object on which the line or rectangle is drawn.
Step	Keyword that specifies that the starting points are relative to the current graphics position, given by `CurrentX` and `CurrentY`.
x1,y1	Values (single-precision) indicating the coordinates of the starting point for the line or rectangle. The unit of measurement is determined by the `ScaleMode` of the object. If omitted, the line begins at the position indicated by `CurrentX` and `CurrentY`.
Step	Keyword that specifies that the endpoint coordinates are relative to the line starting point.

Component	Description
x2,y2	Values (single-precision) indicating the coordinates of the end-point of the line to draw.
color	Long integer value indicating the RGB color used to draw the line. If omitted, the ForeColor property is used. You can use the RGB function or QBColor function to specify the color.
B	Option that causes a box (rectangle) to be drawn using the xl,yl and x2,y2 coordinates to specify opposite corners of the box.
F	If the B option is used, the F option specifies that the box is filled with the same color used to draw the box. You cannot use F without B. If B is used without F, the box is filled with the current FillColor and FillStyle; the default value for FillStyle is transparent.

This is a complicated syntax, but it should become clearer when you move to the following examples. Remember the following additional key points:

- The width of the line is controlled by the DrawWidth property of the object (Form, PictureBox, or Printer) upon which the drawing occurs. The setting of the DrawMode and DrawStyle affects the way the line is drawn on the background.

- When the Line method executes, CurrentX and CurrentY are set to the endpoint specified by the x2,y2 arguments. When drawing lines that are connected, subsequent lines should have as their starting point the endpoint of the previous line.

- The DrawMode determines the "pen" of the drawing. There are 16 different settings, some of which can be quite complex. (Refer to Visual Basic Help for more information about DrawMode properties.)

Exercise 5.8   Drawing a Triangle with the *Line* Method

Look again at the syntax of the Line method. If you delete the X1,Y1 coordinates from the method, the line will be drawn from the CurrentX and CurrentY position to the endpoints. The Step keyword enables you to describe the length of the line drawing. This exercise asks you to draw a simple triangle using this method.

1. Add a button named **cmdDraw** to a form.

2. Set the ScaleMode of the form to pixels. This helps insure that most line drawings with angles, such as triangles, do not have small gaps at line intersections.

continues

113

Exercise 5.8   continued

3. In the `cmdDraw_Click()` event, enter the following code:

```
Private Sub cmdDraw_Click()
    DrawWidth = 2
    CurrentX = 150
    CurrentY = 175
    Line -Step(300, 0)    ' draw the base line
    Line -Step(-150, -150) ' draw the right side of the triangle
    Line -Step(-150, 150)  ' draw the left side
End Sub
```

4. Run and test the program.

`CurrentX` and `CurrentY` change when each `Line` method is executed. In this instance, you drew a triangle in a counter-clockwise direction. If you were drawing the triangle in a picture box, the object would have to be referenced, as in the instruction `Pic1.Line-Step (300,0)`.

Exercise 5.9   Using the *Line* Method with the *B* and *F* Arguments

The `B` and `F` options of the `Line` method enable the developer to construct rectangles with different `ForeColor`, `FillColor`, and `FillStyle` attributes (see Figure 5.10). An endless combination of rectangles can be created. This exercise provides a simple demonstration of these methods. Before you begin, review the syntax of the `Line` method to remind yourself how the `B` and `F` arguments work together and in conjunction with the `FillColor`, `ForeColor`, and `FillStyle` properties. This exercise demonstrates the interaction of these properties.

Figure 5.10   *You also can use the* `Line` *method to draw rectangular shapes.*

1. Draw the interface you see in Figure 5.10. Set the `Width` property of the form to 5000 twips and the `Height` property to 4000 twips. Add a command button, `cmdDraw`, and place it at the bottom of the form.

2. In the cmdDraw_Click() event, enter the following code:

```
Private Sub cmdDraw_Click()
    frmDisplay.DrawWidth = 4
    frmDisplay.FillStyle = vbFSTransparent
    frmDisplay.ForeColor = vbBlack
    frmDisplay.Line (100, 100)-(2700, 800), , B
    frmDisplay.FillStyle = vbFSSolid
    frmDisplay.ForeColor = vbBlue
    frmDisplay.FillColor = vbYellow
    frmDisplay.Line (1500, 1500)-(2900, 2900), , BF
    frmDisplay.ForeColor = vbRed
    frmDisplay.FillColor = vbBlue
    frmDisplay.FillStyle = vbCross
    frmDisplay.Line (3100, 100)-(4000, 3000), , B
End Sub
```

3. Run and test the program. You should see output similar to that in Figure 5.10.

The FillStyle, ForeColor, and FillColor properties and the B and F arguments determine the appearance of each of the rectangles. These properties are set before the Line method is invoked.

The first rectangle has a transparent FillStyle and a black ForeColor. The second has its FillColor set to yellow, but observe that the F argument overrides this assignment. The rectangle is blue, taking on the color of the specified ForeColor property. The last rectangle has different ForeColor and FillColor property settings. A blue cross pattern is drawn inside a rectangle with a red border color.

Experiment with this exercise. You will be surprised by the wide variety of effects that can be created!

5.5.3   The *PSet* Method

With the PSet method, you can paint individual pixels on your screen with a color you specify. It is very flexible, and is particularly useful for coloring irregularly shaped objects or groups of pixel points. The size of the points you draw with the PSet method depends on the DrawWidth property of the object upon which you are drawing. As with other graphic methods, CurrentX and CurrentY are set when PSet is executed. The syntax is as follows:

```
[object.]PSet[Step](x,y)[,color]
```

Table 5.2 explains the components of the PSet method syntax.

TABLE 5.2   Syntax of the *Pset* Method

Component	Description
object	Object on which the point is to be drawn.
Step	Keyword specifying that the coordinates are relative to the current graphics position given by CurrentX and CurrentY.
x,y	Values (single-precision) indicating coordinates, which depend on the unit of measurement of the Scale properties of the object.
color	Color specified for a point. If omitted, current ForeColor is used. RGB or QBColor functions can be used.

Exercise 5.10   Making Confetti

This exercise draws 1,000 pieces of "confetti" on a form using the PSet method (see Figure 5.11). The program draws colors in four-pixel squares, and the procedure stops when 1,000 pieces of "confetti" have been drawn. The code uses several more advanced features of the Visual Basic language:

- It uses a built-in Visual Basic function, the Rnd function, to randomly generate numbers. These numbers are used to specify CurrentX and CurrentY locations and to specify colors for drawing the "confetti."

- Colors are specified by the QBColor function, which can generate 16 standard Windows colors.

- A loop is used, which causes code to be repeatedly executed until a certain condition is met. Loops are introduced in Chapter 11, "Working with Loops." Nevertheless, this code illustrates the importance of a loop structure, and it illustrates how the PSet method can be used.

Figure 5.11   *You can use the* PSet *method to draw one pixel at a time on the form.*

1. Draw the interface you see in Figure 5.11. The interface consists of a single form (frmDisplay) and a command button (cmdConfetti).

2. In the cmdConfetti_Click() event, enter the following code:

```
Private Sub cmdConfetti_Click()
    Dim XPos As Single
    Dim YPos As Single
    Dim counter As Integer
    Dim color As Integer
    frmDisplay.DrawWidth = 4
    Do    'Beginning of the loop
      XPos = Rnd * frmDisplay.ScaleWidth
      YPos = Rnd * frmDisplay.ScaleHeight
      color = Rnd * 15       'Random number function
      PSet (XPos, YPos), QBColor(color)
      counter = counter + 1
    Loop Until counter >= 1000  'end of the loop
End Sub
```

3. Run and test the program.

Observe that three numeric values are determined by using the Rnd function: the x position and y position for the PSet method, and the color. These three values are then used by the PSet method to draw a four-pixel point. All of this code is placed inside a loop that executes 1,000 times, thereby generating 1,000 pieces of "confetti."

5.5.4   The *RGB* Color Function

In the previous exercise, you used the QBColor function. This function is a holdover from earlier versions of Basic, and was used extensively when most color monitors handled just 16 colors. Until a few years ago, 16-color VGA was the default resolution and color mode for Windows. More powerful hardware, especially improved video systems, has made 65,000 colors or even 16 million colors standard on new Windows machines, although 256 colors is still considered to be somewhat "standard."

Visual Basic takes advantage of this video capability with the RGB function, which enables the programmer to specify each of the color combinations—red, green, and blue—to designate a color.

The function has the following simple syntax:

```
RGB(red, green, blue)
```

You assign values between 0 and 255 for each of the colors with 255 designating the most intensity. If the function reads RGB (0,0,0), it will return black. The expression RGB(255,255,255) would return white. Red, green, and blue colors have 255 in one argument with the other two values set to 0, as in RGB(255,0, 0). The expression RGB(255,255,0) returns yellow. Assuming your computer has the graphics capability, it is possible to designate 16,777,216 colors using the RGB Color Function (256*256*256), as shown in Figure 5.12.

Figure 5.12   *This design enables you to test the RGB method to examine over 16 million colors.*

Exercise 5.11   Surveying RGB Mixtures

This application replicates some of the functionality in a standard Windows Color dialog box.

1. Draw the interface you see in Figure 5.12. The interface includes three scroll bars (**hsbRed, hsbGreen, hsbBlue**), a picture box (**picColor**), and three labels (**lblRed, lblGreen,** and **lblBlue**).

2. Set the Min value for the scroll bars to **0** and the Max value at **255**.

3. Declare Red as Integer, Blue as Integer, Green as Integer in the Code window under (General), as follows:

```
Option Explicit
Dim Red As Integer
Dim Green As Integer
Dim Blue As Integer
```

   You are not declaring the variables in a procedure; instead, you are declaring them at the module level. This kind of declaration is addressed in Chapter 10, "Defining the Scope of Variables and Procedures."

4. In the hsbRed_Change() event, enter the following code:

```
Private Sub hsbRed_Change()
  Red = hsbRed.Value
  Green = hsbGreen.Value
  Blue = hsbBlue.Value
  picColor.BackColor = RGB(Red, Green, Blue)
  lblRed.Caption = "Red " & hsbRed.Value
End Sub
```

5. Copy this code, and paste it into the Change and Scroll events of all the scroll bars. Change the assignments to the caption properties of the appropriate label.

6. Run the program and experiment with the color mixtures. Depending upon your video driver settings, the patterning of non-solid colors in the picture box will vary.

5.5.5   Topics for Further Study

The preceding exercises have illustrated the differences between graphic controls and graphic methods. Consider Exercise 5.8, for which you drew a triangle with the Line method. Similar output could also have been achieved by using three Line controls. By using graphic methods, however, your program had less impact on system resources.

Taking full advantage of the Windows rich graphic environment with Visual Basic requires becoming familiar with a broad and deep body of knowledge. Your working through the exercises of this chapter made a good "down payment" on gaining that knowledge; however, space limitations prevent exploring the topic in greater depth. As a guide to your future study, the following are some important topics to review on your own:

- **ScaleMode property**—You have worked mainly in twips, but Visual Basic allows you to set other scale modes for the interior dimensions of a form. You also can customize the scale mode for a picture box. A form's Top, Left, Width, and Height properties are always expressed in twips, but the interior portion of the form—that is, the space inside the form border—takes on the scale specified in the form's ScaleMode property. The scale might be in pixels, centimeters, or inches, or can even be user-defined.

- **There are four additional scale properties**—ScaleTop, ScaleLeft, ScaleWidth, and ScaleHeight, which express the values of the form's interior dimensions. Controls placed on a form take on the ScaleMode of the form. The same is true for controls placed inside a picture box. For example, if the ScaleMode is set to pixels, a command button's Width property would be expressed in pixels rather than twips.

- **Circle method**—To draw circles, ovals and arcs, you can use the Circle method on either a form or picture box. The syntax of the Circle method is somewhat complex, but the method is very flexible. See the Visual Basic online Help for details.

- **Persistent graphics**—When using graphics methods, there are two primary ways of creating persistent graphic output:

  1. You can place the code for the graphic output in a form's Paint event. This means the code will execute every time the form refreshes itself. A form refreshes, or repaints, itself every time a window in front of it is moved away, a window is moved or its size changed, or the Refresh method of the form is invoked in code.

  2. You can set the Form's AutoRedraw property to True. A persistent bitmap of the form is created in memory, and graphic methods generate output on this persistent bitmap. When the form refreshes itself, it uses this persistent bitmap. Consult the Visual Basic online Help for more information.

Chapter Summary

Visual Basic's graphic controls include the Line control, Shape control, Image control, and Label control. Graphic controls differ from other Visual Basic controls in that they cannot receive focus. The Image control and the Label control, however, can receive events, such as `Click()` events.

Graphic controls, like all Visual Basic controls, have positioning properties, such as `Top`, `Left`, `Width`, and `Height`, and, in the case of the Line control, `X1`, `Y1`, `X2`, and `Y2`. The positioning properties are determined by the coordinate system of the container in which the graphic control is placed. Containers can be a form, picture box, or frame. The coordinate system for all containers starts at the x,y coordinate 0,0 in the upper-left corner of the container. To specify the point for a `Print` method to begin, you can designate the exact `CurrentX` and `CurrentY` position for a form or picture box.

Graphic controls exist in a middle graphic layer between the background of the container in which they are placed and other non-graphic controls, such as command buttons. The layering of graphic controls within their layer can be adjusted in design-time by the <u>B</u>ring to Front and <u>S</u>end to Back commands. The `ZOrder` method can be used to reorder the layering of controls during runtime.

The Image control enables bitmaps (.BMP, .GIF, .DIB, .ICO), JPEG compressed image files (.JPG) and Windows Metafile Format files (.WMF) to be displayed in your application without the high resource requirements of a picture box or an additional form. Images can be loaded into the Image control in design-time by double-clicking the `Picture` property of the Image control and assigning the path of the bitmap to the control. During runtime, bitmaps can be loaded into an Image control using the `LoadPicture` function. The size of the control can be changed to fit the image, or the image resized to fit the control.

Besides `Print`, graphic methods include the `Line`, `Pset`, and `Circle` methods. The `Line` method is used for drawing both lines and rectangles. The `Circle` method is used for drawing circles, ovals, and arcs. The `PSet` method draws individual pixels. All three of these graphic methods include arguments for determining the color of graphic output.

Color arguments in graphic methods can take the result of two color functions: `QColor` or `RGB`. The `QColor` function returns one of 16 colors, while the `RGB` function, depending upon the computer's video system, can return up to 16 million colors.

Skill-Building Exercises

These exercises ask you to work with shapes and lines to construct different patterns on a form. You will be asked to work more with image boxes, picture boxes, shapes, and the line control.

1. Place a rectangle on a form. Draw two diagonal lines on the rectangle. One line should appear in the top-left corner and extend to the bottom-right corner; the second should appear in the top-right corner and extend to the bottom-left corner. Add the title **Shapes** and **Lines** to this form.

2. This exercise is an extension of the first exercise. Once again, place a rectangle on a form, two lines, and a command button with the caption **Resize me**. When the user clicks the button, have the rectangle move to a different position on a form, along with the two diagonal lines, running from the top-left to bottom-right corners of the form and from the top-right to the bottom-left corners of the form. Name this form **Resizing Lines** and a Shape. To solve this exercise, assign edges of the shape and the x,y coordinates of the lines during runtime.

3. Place a circle on a form and a label on top of the circle. Add a label `Click()` event. When the user clicks the label, have it display on more than one line the following:

   ```
   I am the sun, and I am bright.
   ```

   Name this form **Make the Sun Shine**.

4. Add three ovals to a form and place labels over each oval. Name the labels **lblGreen**, **lblRed**, and **lblYellow**. Add a command button named **Stop Lights**. When the user clicks the button, display `GO` on the green label, `BRAKE` on the yellow label, and `STOP` on the red label. Add the appropriate colors to each oval (red, yellow, and green). Name the form **What are the colors?**

5. Place two picture boxes on a form. In the top picture box, place an image box. Display a picture of a bell in this image box. Set the `Stretch` property to `True` to make a good-looking bell. In the bottom picture box, add a label. Finally, add an image `Click()` event. When the user clicks the bell, use the label to display the following:

   ```
   Ding!   Dong!   Ding!
   ```

6. Using the `Line` method, write a program that creates three empty squares that are diagonally arranged from the top left of a form to the bottom right.

7. Change the preceding exercise so that the border colors of the three squares are different and none are black. Give the middle square has a blue interior color.

PROGRAMMING

VARIABLES AND CONSTANTS

When you first begin to write programs in Visual Basic, it becomes important that you learn the difference between a variable and a constant and how each is used in an application. Computers store computation results and data in variables or constants. Variables require locations in memory that can assume any value. The information stored in a variable can be recalled in another part of an event procedure by using the variable name associated with it. The information stored in a constant is data that remains the same throughout the program. It cannot be altered during the running of a program.

In this chapter, you learn about the type of data assigned to either a variable or a constant, and how to do the following:

- Declare a constant
- Name a variable
- Make variable declarations explicit
- Use fixed- and variable-length strings
- Work with integer variables
- Work with Boolean variables
- Work with floating-point variables
- Work with variables of type Currency
- Work with variables of type Date
- Work with variables of type Variant and the VarType and TypeName functions
- Work with Time, Date, Now, and DateDiff functions

Chapter Objectives

The objectives for this chapter are the following:

1. Learning the difference between a variable and a constant

2. Declaring a variable using a data type

3. Declaring and using the five types of numeric variables

4. Working with fixed- and variable-length string variables

5. Using functions for testing variables, including type `Variant`

6. Declaring and using variables of type `Date`

Objective 6.1   Learning the Difference Between a Variable and a Constant

When first starting to learn to program, the meaning of a variable as opposed to a constant can be troublesome. To keep matters simple, think of a value that does not change over time, such as the date of your birth. Because this date will not change, it is called a constant. When programming, use constants to store values that do not change over the course of the program. Table 6.1 shows the types of constants.

TABLE 6.1   Constant Types

Type	Example
Literal number	`1 + 2 * 5` (or expression)
String	`"This is a happy day"`
Symbolic constant	`Const PI = 3.141592654` (used with Const)

6.1.1   Declaring a Constant

When assigned to a symbolic name, a constant must be declared using the keyword `Const`. Suppose that the following is placed at the top of a procedure:

```
Const HEADING = "Paper 6201"
```

Later in the procedure, the instruction

```
Print HEADING
```

would produce the message:

```
Paper 6201
```

The new version of Visual Basic has numerous additional constants to make programming tasks easier. Most of these constants contain the `vb` prefix. Table 6.2 shows some of the color constants in Visual Basic.

TABLE 6.2   Color Constants

Constant	Value	Description
vbBlack	0x0	Black
vbRed	0xFF	Red
vbGreen	0xFF00	Green
vbYellow	0xFFFF	Yellow
vbBlue	0xFF0000	Blue
vbMagenta	0xFF00FF	Magenta
vbCyan	0xFFFF00	Cyan
vbWhite	0xFFFFFF	White

In addition, there are numerous system colors specified by user choices in the Windows Control Panel. These also have constant designations, such as vbDeskTop that represents the user's choice for desktop color. These constants are easily accessible in Visual Basic's online Help file.

Other built-in constants are too numerous to include in this text, but you can examine them in the online Help file. For example, one can use integers to specify a form's WindowState, but using the built-in constants is easier and makes your code much more readable. Table 6.3 shows the WindowState constants and their meanings.

TABLE 6.3   *WindowState* Constants

Constant	Value	Description
vbNormal	0	Normal
vbMinimized	1	Minimized
vbMaximized	2	Maximized

Among the most frequently used constants are True and False for assigning values to Boolean data types. For example, the value for the MaxButton on a form is either True or False. If set to True, the Maximum button will appear on the form. If set to False, the Maximum button will not appear.

6.1.2   A Variable

A variable contains a value that is expected to change, hence the name. An example is your age. Whether you like it or not, your age is variable. With every day, the number of days since your birth changes. In programming, use variables to store values that are expected to change over the course of the program.

In the code thus far, you have assigned values to object properties, such as label.caption and textbox.text. In doing this, you have assigned a value to a variable. In Visual Basic, object properties are variables because they can take on more than one value.

Objective 6.2   Declaring a Variable Using a Data Type

A data type specifies the type of data assigned to a variable or a constant. Data type declarations specify the data required by the program. Before you use a variable in Visual Basic, you must declare it, provided Option Explicit is turned on. (See section 6.2.2, "Option Explicit Declaration," later in this chapter for more information.) It also is good programming practice to specify the type of data to be stored for a variable. The data types supported by Visual Basic, along with the associated type-declaration suffix, storage size, and range, are shown in Table 6.4.

TABLE 6.4   Visual Basic Data Types

Data Type	Suffix	Storage Size	Range
Byte	none	1 byte	0 to 255
Boolean	none	2 bytes	True or False
Integer	%	2 bytes	–32,768 to 32,767
Long (long integer)	&	4 bytes	–2,147,483,648 to 2,147,483,647
Single (single-precision, floating-point)	!	4 bytes	–3.402823E38 to –1.401298E–45 for negative values; 1.401298E–45 to 3.402823E38 for positive values
Double (double-precision, floating-point)	#	8 bytes	–1.79769313486232E308 to –4.94065645841247E–324 for negative values; 4.94065645841247E–324 to 1.79769313486232E308 for positive values
Currency (scaled integer)	@	8 bytes	–922,337,203,685,477.5807 to 922,337,203,085,477.5808
Decimal	none	14 bytes	+/–7.9228162514264 to 337,593,543,950,335
Date	none	8 bytes	January 1, 100 to December 31, 9999
Object	none	4 bytes	Any object reference
String (variable-length)	$	10 bytes + string length	0 to approximately 2 billion (65,400 for Microsoft Windows version 3.1 and earlier)

Data Type	Suffix	Storage Size	Range
String (fixed-length)	$	Length of string	1 to approximately 65,400
Variant (with numbers)	none	16 bytes	Any numeric value up to the range of a Double
Variant (with characters)	none	22 bytes + string length	Same range as for variable-length String
User-defined (using Type structure)	none	Number required by elements	The range of each element is the same as the range of its data type

As shown in Table 6.4, 8 of these 15 data types are used with numbers, including the data types Byte and Boolean; two are used with strings; one is of type Date; and one is of type Object. The type Variant is a combination data type. It can contain numeric, string, date, and object types. However, it cannot contain a user-defined type, which is typically a mixture of different standard data types. The Decimal data type can only be used within type Variant.

For now, study these data types, but do not worry if you have questions because you will return to most of them. Some, such as the Object reference data type, will not be discussed until you deal with Object variables. Do observe, however, the number of bytes required by each type of variable. A long integer requires twice as much memory as a short integer. Double-precision and currency require four times as much memory as an integer. The type declaration characters placed alongside some of the standard types can be substituted for the data type name shown when declaring a variable. They are added as suffixes. For example, the following declarations mean the same thing:

```
Dim number As Integer
Dim number%
```

6.2.1   Naming a Variable

When naming a variable (or a symbolic constant), choose a meaningful name that reflects the type of data to be stored. This improves the readability of the program and makes changes to the program easier. With Visual Basic,

- Each variable must have a unique variable name.

- Variable names must be limited to 255 characters.

- Variable names must begin with an alpha character.

- Variable names cannot contain an embedded period.

- Variables must be unique within the same scope.

The following are valid variable names:

```
NameScreen
HighValue
```

However, the following examples are invalid variable names:

Name	Reason the Name Is Invalid
5High	The name begins with a digit.
Form	This name is not unique.
Happy day	Blank spaces are not allowed.
Good.day	An embedded period is not allowed.

6.2.2   The *Option Explicit* Declaration

If the Require Variable Declaration property is set to Yes (by selecting the check box), all variables in Visual Basic must then be declared. To set this property, choose Tools, Options, and select the Editor tab (see Figure 6.1). By default, all variables in Visual Basic are of type Variant unless explicitly typecast in the variable declaration. In this book, other than in a few circumstances, variables are explicitly declared as specific data types. This is called *declaring a variable*. Variable declaration makes your code execute faster and easier to read.

Figure 6.1   *Selecting the Require Variable Declaration check box means you must explicitly declare each variable in your program.*

Once checked, the following statement appears in the Declarations section of a module:

```
Option Explicit
```

When you use Option Explicit, all variables in a module must be explicitly declared before they can be used.

The following statement declares the variable message as a variable of type String:

```
Dim message As String
```

The following statement declares the variable count as a variable of type Integer:

```
Dim count As Integer
```

In the programs that follow, you will declare all variables before they are used. This will help you to recognize the different types of variables. It also will help you to avoid mixing types, such as trying to assign a string to a numeric variable. If a variable is not declared, a syntax error will occur.

Objective 6.3   Declaring and Using the Five Types of Numeric Variables

There are five types of numeric variables:

- Type Integer and Type Long (long integer) are used in declaring whole numbers (those without a decimal point).

- Type Single (single precision) and Type Double (double precision) are used in declaring floating point numbers (those with a decimal point).

- Type Currency is used in declaring monetary numbers.

In this section, you briefly examine each type.

6.3.1   Integer Variables

Integer variables are stored as 16-bit numbers ranging in value from −32,768 to 32,767. They are used when integer numbers (numbers with no decimal places) are required in a Visual Basic program. When working with numbers with no decimal point, you must determine whether the number will be less than or greater than the appropriate range of values for type Integer to be used. If the number is outside that range, type Long is necessary.

Exercise 6.1   Working with Integers

In this exercise, you enter a person's age, height in inches, and weight in pounds. Figure 6.2 shows the completed solution to this exercise.

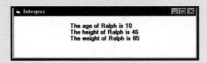

The age of Ralph is 10
The height of Ralph is 46
The weight of Ralph is 85

Figure 6.2   *This display enables you to show three strings followed by three integer values.*

continues

Exercise 6.1   continued

1. Start a new project.

2. Change the Caption property of the form to **Integers** and the Name property to **frmInt**.

3. Write the following procedure:

```
Private Sub Form_Click()
    'Program with three integer variables
    'Declare all variables
    Dim person As String
    Dim age As Integer
    Dim height As Integer
    Dim weight As Integer

    'Assign values to all variables
    person$ = "Ralph"
    age = 10
    height = 46
    weight = 85

    'Display the results
    Print
    Print Spc(20); "The age of "; person$ " is"; age
    Print Spc(20); "The height of "; person$ " is"; height
    Print Spc(20); "The weight of "; person$ " is"; weight
End Sub
```

4. Run the program. Test to determine whether the suffix notation works. Change the declarations as follows, and run your program again.

```
Dim person$
Dim age%
Dim height%
Dim weight%
```

6.3.2   Long Integer Variables

Long integer variables are stored as signed 32-bit numbers ranging in value from −2,147,483,648 to 2,147,483,647, or about plus or minus two billion. This type must be used whenever a number exceeds the range of type Integer. Consider a zip code, such as 97405. Because this is larger than 32,767, type Long is required. A string could also be used, and would be required for postal codes that contain letters of the alphabet (such as Canadian postal codes).

Exercise 6.2   Adding a Long Integer

This exercise asks you to display a person's name and address. It requires the use of a long integer.

1. Begin a new project.

2. Change the Caption property to **Using a Long Integer** and the Name property to **frmLongInt**.

3. Write the following procedure:

```
Private Sub Form_Click()
    'Program to display a name and address
    'Declare all variables
    Dim person As String
    Dim street As String
    Dim city As String
    Dim state As String
    Dim zip As Long

    'Assign values to all variables
    person$ = "A.B. Waxworth"
    street$ = "1234 Mittlebox Canyon"
    city$ = "Lost Canyon"
    state$ = "OR"
    zip = 97405          'This number is greater than 32767

    'Display the results
    Print Tab(5); person$
    Print Tab(5); street$
    Print Tab(5); city$
    'Place state and zip on the same line
    Print Tab(5); state$; zip
End Sub
```

4. Test this program. Use type Integer rather than type Long for the zip code to observe the error.

6.3.3   Single-Precision Variables

Single-precision variables are used to store values containing decimal places. Type Single (which stands for single precision) represents a rational number that has both a whole and a fractional part. Due to this fractional part, this type is used to store a floating point number.

The following are examples of floating point numbers:

```
50.33435     5.5     -503.88865
```

A floating point number provides greater precision than an integer. This precision is indicated by the number of significant digits that can be represented in storage. A calculation using type Single might return a value of 23.25. The same calculation using a variable of type Integer would truncate (cut off) the fractional portion and return a value of 23. As another example, type Single might return the value 23.5, whereas type Integer would round the value (.5 and above), and return 24. The next exercise demonstrates this concept.

Exercise 6.3 Using a Single-Precision Variable

This short exercise asks you to study how rounding a number works.

1. Start a new project.

2. Change the Caption property to **Single Precision** and the Name property to **frmSPrec**.

3. Write the following procedure:

```
Private Sub Form_Click()
    'Program to compare single precision to an integer

    'Declare all variables
    Dim precise As Single
    Dim truncated As Integer
    Dim rounded As Integer

    'Make the first set of assignments
    precise = 50.33435
    truncated = 50.33435

    'Display them
    Print Tab(5); precise
    Print Tab(5); truncated

    'Make the second set of assignments
    precise = 5.5
    rounded = 5.5
    'Display them
    Print Tab(5); precise
    Print Tab(5); rounded

    'Make the third set of assignments
    precise = -503.88865
    rounded = -503.88865
    'Display them
    Print Tab(5); precise
    Print Tab(5); rounded
End Sub
```

In this program, a variable (such as precise) can be assigned different values. The first assignment sets the value of precise to 50.33435. After this value is printed, a second value can be assigned to precise and printed. Could this second value be assigned before the first value is printed? It could, but the first assigned value would be lost and could not be printed.

6.3.4   Double-Precision Variables

Double-precision variables store larger floating point numbers, but require twice as many bytes of storage compared to type `Single`. Type `Double` is used for very large or very small numbers (a number with 308 places to the right using scientific notation).

In choosing between type `Single` and type `Double`, use type `Single` unless the calculation requires greater precision. Besides needing greater storage, type `Double` requires more time to run than type `Single`.

Exercise 6.4   Comparing Single- and Double-Precision Variables

This brief exercise asks you to compare a single-precision variable to a double-precision variable.

1. Place a command button on a form, named **cmdDivide**, and add the `Caption` property **Print 1/3**. Add the form caption **Test of Precision**.

2. Write the following `cmdDivide_Click()` procedure:

```
Private Sub cmdDivide_Click()
    Dim test1 As Single
    Dim test2 As Double
    'Enter 15 number 3s

    test1 = .333333333333333
    test2 = .333333333333333
    Print "Single precision is = "; test1
    Print "Double precision is = "; test2
End Sub
```

3. Run and test the program. You will see the different degrees of precision in the displayed results.

6.3.5   Currency Variables

Currency variables are used for calculations involving money and for fixed-point calculations in which accuracy is very important. Type `Currency` variables are stored as 64-bit numbers (eight bytes) and are scaled by 10,000 to provide a fixed-point number with 15 digits to the left of the decimal and 4 digits to the right.

Exercise 6.5   Using Currency Variables

This short exercise helps to clarify why currency variables are needed.

1. Place a command button on a form, named **cmdLoan**, and add the Caption property **Show Loan**. Add the form caption **Test of Currency**.

2. Write the following cmdLoan_Click() procedure:

```
Private Sub cmdLoan_Click()
  Dim Amount As Currency
  'Try this one next.  Comment out the above statement
  'Dim Amount As Single
  Dim IntRate As Single
  Dim SimpleInt As Currency

  Amount = 100000000
  IntRate = .08
  SimpleInt = 8000000

  Print "The amount of the loan is $"; Amount
  Print "The interest rate is "; IntRate; "%"
  Print "The simple interest for 1 year is $"; SimpleInt
End Sub
```

3. Run and test this program, using 100,000,000 (one-hundred million) as the loan amount. In testing, change the data type for the variable Amount from type Currency to type Single, and run the program again. Observe the results.

6.3.6   Boolean Variables

Boolean data types can be used in circumstances for which you simply want to determine whether a variable or condition is True or False. It is frequently used in logical tests and with If...Then statements (which are covered in Chapter 8, "If...Then...Else Logic and the Select Case Statement"). For now, you should know Boolean variables can act like a switch, becoming either True or False.

Exercise 6.6   Using the *Boolean* Data Type

This short exercise asks you to set to True and to False a variable of type Boolean. Figure 6.3 shows the interface you are asked to create.

1. Create the interface as shown in the figure. Name the label on the left **lblWrap**, and set its WordWrap property to True.

2. Name the label on the right **lblNoWrap**, and make sure its WordWrap property is also set to True.

3. Enter the following code in the `cmdTest_Click()` event:

```
Private Sub cmdTest_Click()
    Dim wraptest As Boolean
    wraptest = lblWrap.WordWrap
    lblWrap.Caption = "WordWarp is " & wraptest
    lblNoWrap.WordWrap = False
    wraptest = lblNoWrap.WordWrap
    lblNoWrap.Caption = "WordWrap is " & wraptest
End Sub
```

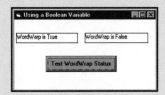

Figure 6.3   *This interface requires the use of Boolean variables.*

In this last procedure, the variable `wraptest` takes on two values within a single procedure. Initially, it is assigned the Boolean value for the `WordWrap` property in `lblWrap`, which is the value `True`. After its `True` value is displayed, `wraptest` is assigned the value of the `False` property. This value is displayed in the `lblNoWrap` label.

Objective 6.4   Working with Fixed- and Variable-Length String Variables

A string variable can hold any character, word, or phrase that the keyboard can produce. In Visual Basic, there are two types of string variables:

- **Variable-length**—Strings in which the number of characters in the string is not specified in advance. The maximum length of a string in 32-bit Windows operating systems is nearly two billion characters. In 16-bit Windows, it is around 65,500 characters. In a variable-length string, each character requires 1 byte of storage, and there is an additional 10 bytes of string information in 32-bit Windows.

- **Fixed-length**—Strings in which the number of characters in the string is specified in advance.

A string variable is defined as type `String`. Consider the following declaration:

```
Dim YourName As String
```

This instruction declares `YourName` as a variable of type `String`. The `String` suffix `$` cannot be used in this declaration. For example, the following returns an error:

```
Dim YourName$ As String
```

However, the following does not return an error:

```
Dim YourName$
```

Consider the following code:

```
Private Sub cmdStart_Click()
  'The Start command is used to display a message
  Dim message As String
  Print
  message$ = "Welcome to Visual Basic"
  Print Spc(30); message$
End Sub
```

Why use a string variable when the following instruction would display the same thing?

```
Print "Welcome to Visual Basic"
```

String variables are advised when a string is to be used several times in a program, or when the contents of the string need to be manipulated. Visual Basic provides a large number of string functions and statements designed to join strings, compare strings, use strings with variants, or convert strings to numbers, for example. See Chapter 17 "String Functions" for more information.

6.4.1   String Variables

String variables can be assigned a series of characters or a null string. In addition, the value of a string can be assigned to another string variable.

A null string is a string without characters. It is written as follows:

```
Person$ = ""
```

This specifies a string of zero length. A text box or label is cleared with a null string. The following instruction clears the text from the text box:

```
txtName.Text = ""
```

The following instruction clears the text from the label caption:

```
lblName.Caption = ""
```

6.4.2   Assigning One String to Another

Assigning one string to another is a common practice. The following instructions illustrate this type of assignment:

```
MyName$ = "Marvelous"
Person$ = MyName$
```

In this example, the string `MyName` and the string `Person` both store the name `Marvelous`.

6.4.3   String Concatenation

The ampersand (&) can be used with strings to combine one string with another. This is called string concatenation, and the ampersand is called the string concatenation operator. Consider the following code:

```
First$ = "Robert"
Last$ = "Rogers"
MyName$ = First$  &  " " &  Last$
Print MyName$
```

This leads to the following display:

```
Robert Rogers
```

Observe the middle portion of the `MyName$` instruction. The " " is a string that contains a single blank space. Lacking the space, `Print MyName$` would display the following:

```
RobertRogers
```

Likewise, the code

```
First$ = "Robert"
Last$ = "Rogers"
MyName$ = Last$  &  ", " &  First$
Print MyName$
```

leads to the display

```
Rogers, Robert
```

In older versions of Visual Basic, string concatenation could be performed with either the + operator or the & operator. Visual Basic 6, however, refers to string concatenation with the & operator. This makes code easier to read and doesn't confuse string concatenation with arithmetic operations.

In displaying string values, a string variable can be concatenated with itself, as the following example illustrates:

```
MyName$ = "Robert"
MyName$ = MyName$ & "Rogers"
Print MyName$
```

This works if you add spacing, as the next exercise demonstrates.

Exercise 6.7   Entering Variable String Data on a Form

This exercise asks you to design a form to record your first name, middle initial, and last name, and to display your name after all values have been entered. Use text boxes for all data entry. Display the name on the form, not in a text box (see Figure 6.4).

Figure 6.4   *This application features three strings to display a person's name.*

1. Add three text boxes and two command buttons. Name the text boxes **txtFirst**, **txtMiddle**, and **txtLast**. Name the command buttons **cmdDisplay** and **cmdQuit**. Add three labels: **First Name**, **Middle Initial**, and **Last Name**.

2. Double-click the Line tool to place a line on the form. Click the edge of the line to position the endpoint on the screen.

3. Write a cmdDisplay_Click() procedure as follows, leaving Form1 as the name of the form:

```
Private Sub cmdDisplay_Click()
  Dim MyName As String

  MyName = txtFirst.Text
  MyName = MyName & " " & txtMiddle.Text
  MyName = MyName & " " & txtLast.Text
  Form1.CurrentX = Line1.X1
  Form1.CurrentY = Line1.Y1 + 150
  Form1.Print "      Your name is: "; MyName
End Sub
```

4. Write a cmdQuit_Click() procedure, and name the form **Entering a Name**.

5. Run and test your program.

Exercise 6.8   Displaying a Name in a Different Order

Modify Exercise 6.7 to display your last name, followed by your first and middle initial. To do this, change only the Print statements used to control the way in which your name is printed. Change the form caption to **Entering a Name II**. Run and test your modified program.

6.4.4   Fixed-Length String Variables

Fixed-length string variables hold a string to a specified size. A fixed-length string is declared using the following syntax:

```
String * size
```

For example:

```
Dim YourName As String * 50
```

Exercise 6.9   Using Fixed-Length Strings

Modify Exercise 6.7 to use fixed-length strings: 10 for the first name, 1 for the middle initial, and 15 for the last name. Using Figure 6.5 as a guide, do the following:

Figure 6.5   *This application features fixed-length strings rather than variable-length strings.*

1. Change the three declaration statements to show all three strings as fixed-length, and name the strings **first**, **middle**, and **last**, as follows:

```
Dim first As String * 10
Dim middle As String * 1
Dim last As String * 15
```

2. Modify the code so that the Print statement displays the first, middle, and last strings:

```
first = txtFirst.text
middle = txtMiddle.text
last = txtLast.text
```

continues

141

Exercise 6.9   continued

```
Form1.CurrentX = Line1.X1
Form1.CurrentY = Line1.Y1 + 150
Form1.Print "       Your name is ";
Form1.Print "    " & first & " " & middle & " " & last
```

In this code, the $ is not used for the three strings. Remember that the $ is optional for all strings, both fixed- and variable-length strings.

3. Run and test your design. In testing, add a name larger than the fixed-length size. Also, examine the output. How do fixed-length strings affect the way in which output is displayed?

Objective 6.5   Using Functions for Testing Variables, Including Type *Variant*

Type Variant is the default in Visual Basic (the type that all variables become if they are not explicitly declared). You can, for example, simply declare a variable without a specific data type, such as in the declaration Dim x. The variable x could then be assigned any data type, and Visual Basic would assess the assignment and make its own determination of data type.

You also can declare a variable as type Variant, such as in the declaration Dim x As Variant. As such, it can contain numeric, string, date, Boolean, empty, and null values.

6.5.1   The *VarType* Function

The VarType function serves to test how Visual Basic has determined a variable assignment. The function returns a value to indicate the type of data stored. The return values of the VarType function are shown in Table 6.5.

TABLE 6.5   Return Values of the *VarType* Function

Constant	Value	Description
vbEmpty	0	Empty (uninitialized)
vbNull	1	Null (no valid data)
vbInteger	2	Integer
vbLong	3	Long integer
vbSingle	4	Single-precision, floating-point number
vbDouble	5	Double-precision, floating-point number
vbCurrency	6	Currency
vbDate	7	Date

Constant	Value	Description
vbString	8	String
vbObject	9	Object
vbError	10	Error
vbBoolean	11	Boolean
vbVariant	12	Variant (used only with arrays of Variants)
vbDataObject	13	Data-access object
vbDecimal	14	Decimal
vbByte	17	Byte
vbUserDefinedType	36	Variant that contains user-defined type
vbArray	8192	Array)

As indicated, Empty and Null do not mean the same thing. Empty means the variable has not been initialized (and hence the value of the variable is not known). This would be the case if you had declared the variable without an explicit type declaration, as in the simple declaration Dim x. Null means the variable has been initialized, but contains no valid data.

Although the Variant data type is flexible and can accommodate many programming needs, it is the largest data type you can use, so it can impose a marked performance penalty. Code can be more difficult to debug if type mismatches are encountered. By defining variables explicitly, code is easier to follow, program speed improves, and less memory is required.

Type Variant, as a rule, should be avoided. On a few occasions, functions will return values that you are uncertain of; you can use a Variant data type and then test for the return value using the VarType function. The Variant data type also must be used in applications that use object linking and embedding, referred to as OLE. (For more information about OLE, see Chapter 26, "Working with Objects from Microsoft Office.") If you are called upon to maintain code that has used Variant data types, you will also want to be able to employ the VarType function.

Exercise 6.10   Using the *VarType* Function

This short exercise asks you to determine the return values of variables when they are declared to be of type Variant. The design consists of a list box (lstDisplay) and a single command button (cmdTest).

1. On a form, add a list box named **lstDisplay** and a command button named **cmdTest**.

2. In the cmdTest_Click() event, add the following code:)

```
Dim sVar As Variant 'Will be used to store a string
Dim iVar As Variant 'Will be used to store an integer
```

continues

Exercise 6.10   continued

```
Dim lVar As Variant 'Will be used to store a long integer
Dim dVar As Variant 'Will be used to store type double
Dim ret As Variant

sVar = "Using the VarType Function"
iVar = 980
lVar = 1000000
dVar = 0.09878654321

ret = VarType(sVar)
lstDisplay.AddItem ret
ret = VarType(iVar)
lstDisplay.AddItem ret
ret = VarType(lVar)
lstDisplay.AddItem ret
ret = VarType(dVar)
lstDisplay.AddItem ret
```

3. Run and test the program. In the list box, you should see a listing of the integer values consistent with the return type values shown in Table 6.5.

6.5.2   The *TypeName* Function

Visual Basic also includes a function named TypeName, which returns a string describing the variable used as an argument in the function. Like the VarType function, TypeName has the simple syntax of TypeName(variablename) in which variablename is of any type except a user-defined type.

Exercise 6.11   Using the *TypeName* Function with the *VarType* Function

This exercise asks you to extend the previous one. The design is limited to a list box and a single command button.

1. Extend the previous exercise by changing the relevant section of code in the cmdTest_Click() event to read as follows:)

```
ret = VarType(sVar) & "   " & TypeName(sVar)
lstDisplay.AddItem ret
ret = VarType(iVar) & "   " & TypeName(iVar)
lstDisplay.AddItem ret
ret = VarType(lVar) & "   " & TypeName(lVar)
lstDisplay.AddItem ret
ret = VarType(dVar) & "   " & TypeName(dVar)
lstDisplay.AddItem ret
```

2. Run and test the program. The string expression of the variable type is returned by the TypeName function and displayed in the list box.

Objective 6.6   Declaring and Using Variables of Type *Date*

The Date data type is used for both dates and times, and is employed with Visual Basic's versatile and extensive Time and Date functions.

6.6.1   The *Time* Function

A function commonly used with type Date is the Time function. Time returns the time as found on your computer's clock. The syntax is simply the following:

```
Time
```

This function returns a Variant of Type 7 (see Table 6.5). Time returns an eight-character string, formatted as hh:mm:ss, where hh is the hour, mm is the minute, and ss is the second.

6.6.2   The *Date* Function

A second function commonly used with type Variant is the Date function. Date returns the system clock date. The syntax is simply as follows:

```
Date
```

This function also returns a Variant of Type 7.

6.6.3   The *Now* Function

The Now function combines the time and date, and uses the Date variant. Now returns the date and time as found on the computer's clock. The syntax is simply the following:

```
Now
```

This function returns a Variant of Type 7. It is a double-precision number used to represent a date between January 1, 100 through December 31, 9999.

Exercise 6.12   Displaying the *Time* and *Date* of the System Clock

This short exercise asks you to use type Date to display the time and date found on the system clock (the clock maintained by your computer). It uses the Time, Date, and Now functions. If the time and date are not correct, you might want to change them, using the time and date DOS commands or changing the time and date in the Windows Control Panel. Figure 6.6 shows the interface that you are to create.

continues

Figure 6.6   *This application illustrates the use of the* Date *function, the* Time *function, and the* Now *function.*

1. Add three labels, **lblDate**, **lblTime**, and **lblNow**, and a single command button named **cmdShowTime**. Place a Caption property of **Time & Date** on cmdShowTime.

2. Write the following cmdShowTime_Click() procedure:

```
Private Sub cmdShowTime_Click()
   Dim Today As Date
   Today = Date
   lblDate.Caption = Today
   Today = Time
   lblTime.Caption = Today
   Today = Now
   lblNow = Today
End Sub
```

In this procedure, you could have simplified the code to assign the returns of the different functions directly to the label. However, this procedure illustrates how Time and Date function returns can be assigned to a variable.

3. Run and test your program. Declare Time and Today as variables other than type Date or type Variant, and observe what happens.

6.6.4   The *DateDiff* Function

If you explore Visual Basic to any extent, you will discover that it contains a large number of functions that simplify the handling of dates. One of these functions is DateDiff. (Additional functions are discussed in Chapter 16, "Numeric Functions.") This function returns a numeric data type containing the number of intervals between two dates.

The syntax is as follows:

```
DateDiff(interval, date1, date2[, firstdayofweek[, firstweekofyear]])
```

The following list explains the elements of the syntax:

interval is a string expression representing the interval between the dates.

The settings are year ("yyyy"), quarter ("q"), month ("m"), day of year ("y"), day ("d"), weekday ("w"), week ("ww"), hour ("h"), minute ("n"), and second ("s").

date1, date2 are the two dates you want to compare.

firstdayofweek is a constant that specifies the first day of the week.

firstweekofyear is the first week of the year. If not specified, Sunday is assumed to be the first day of the week, and the week in which January 1 occurs is assumed to be the first week.

The firstdayofweek argument has the settings shown in Table 6.6.

TABLE 6.6   Settings for the *firstdayofweek* Constant

Constant	Value	Description
vbUseSystem	0	Use application setting if one exists; otherwise, use NLS API setting
vbSunday	1	Sunday (default)
vbMonday	2	Monday
vbTuesday	3	Tuesday
vbWednesday	4	Wednesday
vbThursday	5	Thursday
vbFriday	6	Friday
vbSaturday	7	Saturday

The firstweekofyear argument has the settings shown in Table 6.7.

TABLE 6.7   Settings for the *firstweekofyear* Constant

Constant	Value	Description
vbUseSystem	0	Uses the application setting if one exists; otherwise, uses NLS API setting
vbFirstJan1	1	Starts with the week in which January 1 occurs (default)
vbFirstFourDays	2	Starts with the first week that has at least four days in the new year
vbFirstFullWeek	3	Starts with the first full week of the year

For example, if you want to find the number of days between today and a date entered into processing, you could write the following (in which Tomorrow is a variable of type Date):

```
DateDiff("d", Date, Tomorrow)
```

Exercise 6.13   Finding the Number of Shopping Days Until Christmas

In this short exercise, you determine the number of shopping days between today and December 25. Figure 6.7 illustrates the interface.

Figure 6.7   *This application uses the* DateDiff *function to determine the number of shopping days between today's date and 12/25/97.*

1. Add two command buttons, **cmdTellMe** and **cmdEnd**, and two labels (not text boxes), **lblToday** and **lblDays**. Add the form caption and the two descriptive labels, as shown in Figure 6.7. Write the cmdEnd procedure.

2. Write the following cmdTellMe procedure, changing Date2 as necessary:

```
Sub cmdTellMe_Click()
  Dim Date2 As Date
  Date2 = "12/25/98" 'Change to fit the year
  lblToday.Caption = Date
  lblDays.Caption = DateDiff("d", Date, Date2)
End Sub
```

3. Run and test your program. Determine what happens if you add a string constant for Date2.

Chapter Summary

The purpose of this chapter is to introduce you to the different data types permitted by Visual Basic. By now, you should have a good understanding of the data types: type Integer, Long, Single, Double, Currency, String (fixed- and variable-length strings), Date, and Variant.

You also should have a good understanding of the difference between a constant and a variable. A constant stores values that are not expected to change over the course of a program. Contrary to that, a variable stores values that are expected to change. Object properties represent variables because they can be changed.

When naming variables, use a unique name of 255 characters or less that begins with an alpha character and contains no embedded periods. Variable names must be unique within the same scope.

To force the declaration of variables, select Require Variable Declaration. This will add Option Explicit in the environment options settings.

Remember that type Integer and type Long are used for declaring whole numbers, and type Single and type Double are used for floating point numbers. Use type Currency when dealing with dollars and cents. This avoids scientific notation.

String variables can be of variable length (the default) or of fixed length. To declare a fixed-length string, add the size of the string, as shown in the following example:

```
Dim YourName As String * 50
```

Type Variant is the default in Visual Basic when a variable is not declared. This type can contain numeric, string, date, empty, and null values. When writing procedures, type Date variables should be used to store date and time values.

There are a large number of date and time functions used with date variables. The functions described in this chapter are Date, Time, Now, DateDiff, and two special functions, VarType and TypeName. VarType returns the type of variant represented by a variable, and TypeName returns a string that names the variable.

Skill-Building Exercises

These exercises ask you to further experiment with common data types, including both numeric and string types. In addition, you are asked to use common date and time functions, including the DateDiff function.

1. Create a display such that when the user clicks a button named Now Is, a time and date stamp appears in one label, and the following message appears in a second label (using two lines):

   ```
   The Date is <insert the current date here>
   The Time is <insert the current time here>
   ```

2. Use option buttons to confine user input to clicking either The sun is how many miles from the earth or The moon is how many miles from the earth. When the user makes a choice, use one of two labels to display the result. For the sun, the label should display the following:

   ```
   The sun is 9.3E+07 miles from the earth.
   ```

   For the moon, the label should read as follows:

   ```
   The moon is 238000 miles from the earth.
   ```

3. Modify the fixed-string exercise. Create a display for the entry of a first name, middle name, and last name; however, display only the last name followed by the initials of the first and middle names. Place a comma after the last name, and add one period each after the first and middle initials, as in the following example:

   ```
   Fox, P. E.
   ```

4. Place a frame on the screen, and add eight option buttons. Use the following table to add a caption to each button and to determine the distance of each planet from the earth:

Planet	Distance from Earth
Mercury	53,000,000
Venus	25,000,000
Mars	35,000,000
Jupiter	390,000,000
Saturn	793,000,000
Uranus	1,700,000,000
Neptune	2,678,000,000
Pluto	2,700,000,000

Use a label to display the distance from the earth when the user clicks a planet. Use constants for the first three planets; use variables for the remaining planets. Do not use scientific notation, but rather show the entire number without commas.

5. Create a design that asks the user to input his or her name in one text box and city of birth in another. When the user clicks a button, display the sentence "[Username] was born in [City]" on a label control.

6. This somewhat morbid project asks you to determine the number of days you have left on earth. The only date to be entered into processing is your birthday (use txtBirthdate). In writing the cmdBadNews event, declare a constant as follows:

```
Const ITSOVER = 27375          '75 years times 365 days
```

This assumes that you will live until you are 75 years old. Determine the number of days you have lived so far, and display the results in the label named lbluhoh. After this, determine the days you have left to live to display the following:

```
Print "If you live to age 75 you have "; OhNo; " days left."
```

Calculating one's own demise is sobering, isn't it?

7. Extend this last exercise so that the program calculates the exact number of days between your birthday and your 75 birthday, taking into account leap years.

CHAPTER 7

MATH OPERATORS AND FORMULAS

In Visual Basic, you can use mathematics and formulas when writing instructions. If you are wondering how all this works, consider how you perform mathematics using a calculator: You enter a number, tell the calculator what to do with the number (add, subtract, multiply, or divide), and enter a second number. After the second number is entered, the operation (addition, subtraction, multiplication, or division) is performed.

This chapter explains how mathematical expressions are written using Visual Basic. Much like using a calculator, you enter a number, a mathematical operator, and a second number. In Visual Basic, there are three types of mathematical operators: arithmetic, unary, and assignment. When you complete this chapter, you will know how to perform the following tasks:

- Use the seven arithmetic operators

- Write arithmetic expressions

- Arrange an arithmetic expression using operator precedence

- Use single and nested sets of parentheses

- Use a unary operator

- Use the assignment operator

- Work with the Val() and Str() functions

Chapter Objectives

The objectives of this chapter are derived from the skills outlined in the preceding list, as follows:

1. Understanding the seven arithmetic operators

2. Writing arithmetic expressions using arithmetic operators

3. Understanding the unary and assignment operators

4. Converting strings to numbers and numbers to strings

151

Objective 7.1   Understanding the Seven Arithmetic Operators

Many types of programming problems require the manipulation of numbers. For example, in computing the interest on a loan, you multiply the daily interest rate by the principal amount and then by the number of days. Still, other uses of arithmetic include taking the power of a number, such as 4 raised to the fourth power, or finding the remainder of 10 divided by 3.

7.1.1   Operators and Operands

Operators and operands are troublesome terms, but you need to understand them. An *operator* is a symbol used to designate an action performed on two numbers. Arithmetic operators specify a mathematical action, such as addition, subtraction, multiplication, and division. Arithmetic operators manipulate two operands placed one on each side of the operator. An *operand* is a constant, such as the number 5; a variable, such as var1; or an expression, such as (5x + y), for which the expression is enclosed by parentheses. Remember the following relationship:

```
<Operand1> operator <Operand2>
```

An operator is used to join two operands.

7.1.2   The Seven Types of Operators

In Visual Basic, there are seven types of arithmetic operators. Table 7.1 lists each operator, its symbol, and an example of its use.

TABLE 7.1   Binary Mathematical Operators

Operator	Symbol	Example	Result
Addition	+	4 + 5	9
Subtraction	–	9 - 6	3
Multiplication	*	3 * 4	12
Division	/	8 / 2	4
Exponentiation	^	2 ^ 3	8
Integer division	\	5 \ 2	2
Modulus	Mod	5 Mod 2	1

Besides the familiar addition and subtraction operator symbols (+ and –, respectively), the symbol for multiplication (*) differs from the familiar symbol (×), and division (/) is not shown by the more familiar sign. The following are examples of these four operators (refer to Table 7.1):

```
4 + 5 =  9
9 - 6 =  3
3 * 4 = 12
8 / 2 =  4
```

The exponentiation operator (^) is used to raise a number to a power. The following example shows 2 raised to the 3rd power:

```
2 ^ 3 = 8
```

Integer division generally is performed along with the modulus operator. With integer division, no remainder is provided. Instead, the difference is truncated (that is, the remainder is simply chopped off), as follows:

```
5 \ 2 = 2
```

The modulus operator then is used to compute the remainder. By using the preceding example but substituting the modulus operator for integer division, the remainder of the difference is computed:

```
5 Mod 2 = 1
```

If the modulus operator finds no remainder, as would be the case with 5 Mod 5, the result of the operation is 0.

With Visual Basic, addition, subtraction, multiplication, division, and exponentiation can all be used with Integer, Long (long integer), Single (single precision), Double (double precision), and Currency data types. Addition and subtraction can be used with the Date data type. Integer division and modulus can only be used with Integer and Long.

Exercise 7.1   Computing the Interest on a Loan

This short exercise asks you to compute the balance and the interest on a loan, and indicate the interest a person must pay. Use a daily interest rate of 0.002328, a principal of $5,000, and 50 days as the number of days since taking out the loan.

1. Write the following Form_Click() procedure:

```
Private Sub Form_Click()
    'Program to compute the new balance on a loan
    Dim days As Integer
    Dim principal As Integer
    Dim dailyInterest As Single
    Dim interest As Single
    Dim balance As Single

    days = 50
    principal = 5000
    dailyInterest = .002328

    interest = principal * dailyInterest * days
    balance = principal + interest
    Print "The balance you owe is "; balance
    Print "The interest you must pay is "; interest
End Sub
```

2. Run and test your program. Find out what happens when you use (×) to multiply instead of (*).

Exercise 7.2   Computing Exponentiation

This initial exercise asks you to write a program to compute the number 2 raised to the 32nd power.

1. Start a new project, and write the following Form_Click() procedure:

```
Private Sub Form_Click()
    'Program to raise the power of a number
    Print "2 to the 32 power is"
    Print (2 ^ 32)
End Sub
```

2. Test your program. Try other relationships, such as 32 ^ 2.

Exercise 7.3   Using Integer Division and the Modulus Operator

This short program asks you to divide 5,000 by 12 and to display the integer result and the remainder.

1. Write a Form_Click() procedure as follows:

```
Private Sub Form_Click()
    'Program to demonstrate integer division and modulus
    Dim sum As Integer
    Dim result As Integer
    Dim remainder As Integer

    sum = 5000
    result = sum \ 12
    remainder = sum Mod 12
    Print "The result is "; result;
    Print " and the remainder is "; remainder
End Sub
```

2. Run and test your program. In testing, divide 5,000 by 5,000 to observe what happens when there is no remainder.

Objective 7.2   Writing Arithmetic Expressions Using Arithmetic Operators

An arithmetic expression is two or more operands connected by arithmetic operators. An arithmetic expression is written to return a value. The following is an example of an arithmetic expression:

```
x + y * 2 ^ 3
```

With an expression such as the preceding, each operator links two operands to form a binary linking (an operator is placed between two operands). In processing this expression, Visual Basic examines the type of action to be performed and processes the one with the highest order or the highest precedence first. In Visual Basic, the precedence for the seven binary operators and the negation operator (discussed in the next section) is shown in Table 7.2.

TABLE 7.2   Order of Precedence of the Mathematical Operators

Order	Operator	Symbol
1	Exponentiation	^
2	Negation	–
3	Multiplication and division	*, /
4	Integer division	\
5	Modulus	Mod
6	Addition and subtraction	+, –

7.2.1   Operator Precedence

What is meant by precedence and how does it work? Precedence provides a priority (or order of importance) to the different types of arithmetic actions. If an expression contains operators of different types, the operator with the highest precedence (or rank order) is performed first. In the following expression, exponentiation is performed first:

```
x  +  y  *  2  ^  3
```

Why? Exponentiation has a higher precedence than either addition or multiplication. After this action, the expression would be reduced to read as follows:

```
x  +  y  *  8
```

Suppose that you know that y = 5. If processing continues, multiplication would be performed next because that operator has higher precedence than addition. The expression would be reduced to read as follows:

```
x  +  40
```

Finally, if you know that x = 3, then the value of the completed expression can be resolved. That is, 3 + 40 = 43.

If an expression contains operators with the same order of precedence, then left-to-right processing occurs. In the following expression, multiplication and division have the same precedence:

```
5  +  4  *  15  /  3
```

Thus, the expression would be reduced to the following:

```
5  +  60  /  3
```

Next, division is performed because division has a higher precedence than addition. The reduced expression would read as follows:

```
5  +  20
```

Finally, the value of 25 could be determined by addition.

7.2.2   Use of Parentheses

The order of precedence can be overruled by using parentheses, as follows:

```
(5  +  4)  *  (15  /  3)
```

Because the expressions inside the parentheses are resolved before the symbol to multiply is reached, this example is reduced to the following:

```
9  *  5
```

The final operation produces 45. What this suggests is that you make good use of parentheses to leave nothing to chance. It also makes debugging your program much easier.

Exercise 7.4   Computing an Average of Three Numbers

This simple exercise asks you to compute the average of the following numbers: 150.10, 175.20, and 200.30. All values are of type `Currency`.

1. Write a `Form_Click()` procedure as follows:

```
Private Sub Form_Click()
    'Program to demonstrate the need for parentheses
    'Computing an average
    Dim amount1 As Currency
    Dim amount2 As Currency
    Dim amount3 As Currency
    amount1 = 150.1
    amount2 = 175.2
    amount3 = 200.3
    Print "The average is "; (amount1 + amount2 + amount3) / 3
End Sub
```

2. Run and test your program. In your testing, remove the parentheses and inspect the results. Are you surprised? Also observe that the three values of type `Currency` are divided by an integer; however, the result is of type `Currency`. Visual Basic converts the result into the larger type. Because type `Currency` is larger than type `Integer`, the result is type `Currency`.

7.2.3   Nested Parentheses

Parentheses can be nested; that is, one set of parentheses placed inside another:

```
(5  + (4  *  15)) / 3
```

The innermost set of parentheses is evaluated first, in this instance leading to the following reduced expression:

```
(5  +  60) / 3
```

After this, the values within the remaining set of parentheses are evaluated, leading to

```
65 / 3
```

7.2.4   Adding an Arithmetic Expression to a Print Statement

An arithmetic expression need not always be assigned to a variable. Instead, if all values are known, they can be used directly in an instruction, such as a Print instruction. The instruction

```
Print (5 + (4  *  15)) / 3
```

leads to the display

```
21.66667
```

Objective 7.3   Understanding the Unary and Assignment Operators

Numeric operators (besides arithmetic operators) include the unary operator and the assignment operator. These operators are easy to understand because they require only a single operand.

7.3.1   The Unary Operator

Arithmetic operators are binary and require two operands. The Visual Basic language also features a unary operator, which requires a single operand. As shown in Table 7.2, this operator is called negation. It acts to change a value from positive to negative or negative to positive.

For example, if TestNum is equal to 5, the following expression changes the value of 5 from +5 to –5:

```
- TestNum
```

Likewise, if TestNum is equal to –5, the following expression changes the value of –5 to +5:

```
- TestNum
```

7.3.2   The Assignment Operator

The assignment operator is a binary operator that assigns or copies the value of the right operand to the left operand. It moves the value of an expression into a memory location. You employed this operator in Chapter 3, "Adding Controls and Event Procedures to Form Modules," using the following syntax:

```
variable = expression
```

Visual Basic uses the equal sign operator in making these right-to-left assignments. The following expression assigns the value of 11 to the variable y and stores this value in memory:

```
y = 5  +  (3  *  2)
```

The assignment operator is used to copy the value of a constant, a variable, an arithmetic expression, or a function, as shown in the following table:

Expression	Type
high_mark = 98	Constant
weight = measure1	Variable
cost = price * quantity	Arithmetic expression
miles = travel(time)	Function

7.3.3   A Counter Variable

An assignment instruction becomes more meaningful with an instruction such as the following:

```
count  = count  + 1
```

From mathematics, you would say that this equation is invalid because the two instances of count cancel each other out. In programming, however, an assignment is made rather than the determination of equality. In the preceding example, the value of count + 1 (the expression) is assigned to the variable count. If the old count is 5, the expression count + 1 leads to a new count of 6. A count increment occurs when a variable is increased by a constant, such as 1. A count decrement occurs when a variable is reduced by a constant amount, as in the following instruction:

```
count = count - 1
```

7.3.4   Adding the Object Name to the Variable Name

The left-hand side of an assignment instruction can be altered using the following syntax:

```
object.property = expression
```

For example, the following instruction assigns the constant value vbBlue (&HFF0000) to the BackColor property of Form1.

```
Form1.BackColor = vbBlue
```

Exercise 7.5   Fahrenheit to Celsius Conversion

In this exercise you are asked to write a program to convert degrees Fahrenheit into degrees Celsius and Celsius into Fahrenheit, for which Fahrenheit is equal to 32 degrees and Celsius is equal to 0 degrees. The formulas to remember are as follows:

- Subtract 32 from degrees Fahrenheit, and multiply by 5/9 to determine degrees Celsius.

- Multiply degrees Celsius by 9/5, and add 32 to determine degrees Fahrenheit.

CHAPTER 7   MATH OPERATORS AND FORMULAS

1. Open a new project and write the following `FormClick()` procedure:

```
Private Sub Form_Click()
    'Program to convert Fahrenheit to Celsius
    'and Celsius to Fahrenheit

    Dim Celsius As Single
    Dim Fahrenheit As Single
    Fahrenheit = 32
    Celsius = (Fahrenheit - 32) * (5 / 9)
    Print Fahrenheit; "degrees Fahrenheit equals "; Celsius;
➡"degrees Celsius"
    Print

    Celsius = 0
    Fahrenheit = (9/5 * Celsius) + 32
    Print Celsius; "degrees Celsius equals "; Fahrenheit;
➡"degrees Fahrenheit"
End Sub
```

2. Run and test your program. As one test, try running this program without parentheses.

Exercise 7.6   The Money Exchange

You are asked to create an application titled Money Exchange. The application must be able to convert dollars into deutschemarks. The relative value of currency continuously fluctuates, so for this exercise, one dollar is equal to 1.667 deutschemarks, and one deutschemark is equal to 0.6 dollars.

Figure 7.1 shows the display you are asked to create. During runtime, however, the display does not work as shown; rather, when the user enters a dollar amount, the Calculate Dollars command button disappears, leaving only the Calculate Deutschemarks button visible. Likewise, when the user enters a deutschemark amount, the Calculate Deutschemarks command button disappears, leaving only the Calculate Dollars button visible.

Figure 7.1   *You can use the Money Exchange display to convert currency.*

continues

Exercise 7.6   continued

1. Design the form as shown in Figure 7.1. Use two text boxes and two command buttons. Add the three labels: **Please Enter Amount in Deutschemarks or Dollars**, **Deutschemarks**, and **Dollars**. Add the form caption **Money Exchange**. Add the captions **Calculate Dollars** and **Calculate Deutschemarks** to the two command buttons (one is invisible).

2. Name the Deutschemarks text box **txtMarks**; name the Dollars text box **txtDollars.**

3. Name the Deutschemarks command button **cmdMarks**; name the Dollars command button **cmdDollar.**

4. Set both buttons to invisible and disabled.

5. Write the cmdDollar_Click() procedure as follows:

```
Private Sub cmdDollar_Click()
    Dim marks As Currency
    Dim dollars As Currency
    marks = txtMarks.Text
    dollars = marks * .6
    txtDollars.Text = dollars
End Sub
```

6. Write the cmdMarks_Click() procedure as follows:

```
Private Sub cmdMarks_Click()
    Dim marks As Currency
    Dim dollars As Currency
    dollars = txtDollars.Text
    marks = dollars * 1.666667
    txtMarks.Text = marks
End Sub
```

7. Write a txtDollars_KeyDown() procedure. When text is entered in the Dollars text box, remove all text from the Deutschemarks text box. In addition, set Calculate Deutschemarks visible and enabled; set Calculate Dollars invisible.

```
Private Sub txtDollars_KeyDown (KeyCode As Integer, Shift As
Integer)
    txtMarks.Text = ""
    cmdMarks.Visible = True
    cmdMarks.Enabled = True
    cmdDollar.Visible = False
    cmdDollar.Enabled = False
End Sub
```

Observe what the assignments in this procedure do. The first assignment clears the txtMarks text box. The next four assignments make the cmdMarks button visible and enabled and the cmdDollar button invisible and disabled.

8. Write a `txtMarks_KeyDown()` procedure. When text is entered into the Deutschemarks text box, make the `Calculate Dollars` command button visible and enabled.

```
Private Sub txtMarks_KeyDown (KeyCode As Integer, Shift As
Integer)
    txtDollars.Text = ""
    cmdDollar.Visible = True
    cmdDollar.Enabled = True
    cmdMarks.Visible = False
    cmdMarks.Enabled = False
End Sub
```

This procedure is the reverse of the previous one. The assignments clear text from `txtDollars`, make the dollar button visible and enabled, and make the marks button invisible and disabled.

9. Run and test your revised program.

Objective 7.4   Converting Strings to Numbers and Numbers to Strings

Exercise 7.6 might have revealed a problem between numbers and strings. When entering a number in a text box, it must be entered as a string (because it is text). If you enter an alpha character (a character from the alphabet), Visual Basic generates a type mismatch error. Similarly, when displaying a number in a text box, or a label, the number must be displayed as a string. Assigning a number directly to a `Label Caption` property or a `TextBox Text` property generally doesn't generate an error because Visual Basic will convert it. It is good programming practice, however, to explicitly assign strings to object properties expecting them.

How can you convert one data type, such as a string, to another data type, such as a number? Visual Basic contains two broad functions to ensure that a string is represented as a number and a number represented as a string: the `Val()` and `Str()` functions. Visual Basic also contains numerous other functions for converting data types, which are covered in Chapter 16, "Numeric Functions," and Chapter 17, "String Functions." For now, you will use only the `Val()` and `Str()` functions.

7.4.1   The *Val()* Function

The `Val()` function is used to convert a string to a number. The syntax for this function is as follows:

```
Val(stringexpression)
```

The following is an example:

```
Val("600")
```

The `Val()` function evaluates string expressions from left to right, and it stops reading the string once it encounters an alpha character.

7.4.2 The *Str()* Function

The `Str()` function converts a number to a string. The syntax is as follows:

```
Str(number)
```

The following is an example:

```
Str(600)
```

When a number is converted to a string, a leading space is always reserved for its sign.

7.4.3 Revising the Money Exchange Example

The `Val()` and `Str()` functions should be used in the previous money exchange exercise. The revised `cmdDollar_Click()` procedure would be written as follows:

```
Private Sub cmdDollar_Click()
    Dim marks As Currency
    Dim dollars As Currency

    marks = Val(txtMarks.Text)
    dollars = marks * .6
    txtDollars.Text = Str(dollars)
End Sub
```

In this revised procedure, the marks entered into the program as text are converted to a number before they are assigned to the variable marks. After dollars are calculated, they must be displayed. In the revised procedure, the dollar amount is converted to a string before it is displayed in the text box. The `cmdMarks_Click()` procedure should be changed in a similar fashion.

Exercise 7.7 Using the *Val()* and *Str()* Functions

This exercise asks you to design a program to enter a value into a text box for either Fahrenheit or Celsius (see Figure 7.2). If Celsius is selected, the temperature is converted from degrees Fahrenheit to degrees Celsius. If Fahrenheit is selected, the temperature is converted from degrees Celsius to degrees Fahrenheit. Use a text box, txtTemp, to enter the temperature and a label, lblTemp, to display the output.

Figure 7.2 *The Temperature Conversion application enables you to enter a temperature and convert it to degrees Fahrenheit or degrees Celsius.*

---

1. Add the single text box, the three labels, and the two command buttons. Name the buttons **cmdFahren** and **cmdCelsius**. Name the form **Temperature Conversion**.

2. Write a cmdFahren_Click() procedure to convert degrees to Fahrenheit. Use the Val() and the Str() functions. The procedure is written as follows:

```
Private Sub cmdFahren_Click()
    'Convert to degrees Fahrenheit
    Dim DegreesF As Integer
    Dim DegreesC As Integer

    DegreesC = Val(txtTemp.Text)
    DegreesF = (DegreesC * 9/5) + 32
    lblTemp.Caption = Str(DegreesF)
End Sub
```

3. Write a cmdCelsius_Click() procedure to convert degrees to Celsius. Use the Val() and Str() functions. Write the procedure as follows:

```
Private Sub cmdCelsius_Click()
    'Convert to degrees Celsius
    Dim DegreesF As Integer
    Dim DegreesC As Integer

    DegreesF = Val(txtTemp.Text)
    DegreesC = (DegreesF  - 32 ) *  5/9
    lblTemp.Caption = Str(DegreesC)
End Sub
```

4. Run and test the program. In testing, enter a letter instead of a number for the temperature.

Exercise 7.8   Displaying Your Taxes

This exercise also asks you to use the Val() and Str() functions. You are asked to enter your income and display the tax you owe. Figure 7.3 shows the interface you are asked to create.

Figure 7.3   *The Display Taxes form shows the amount of tax you will pay for a given income.*

continues

Exercise 7.8   continued

1. Add a text box (**txtSalary**), a label (**lblTax**), and a command button (**cmdTaxes**). Add the form caption **Display Taxes**. Add the caption **Taxes at 28%** to the command button.

2. Write the `cmdTaxes_Click()` procedure as follows:

```
Private Sub cmdTaxes_Click()
    Dim salary As Currency
    Dim tax As Currency
    tax = .28
    salary = Val(txtSalary.Text)
    lblTax.Caption = Str(tax * salary)
End Sub
```

3. Run and test your program. Enter a null value and click the Taxes at 28% button. Add 0 and click the button. With the Val() function, lblTax will display a zero when a null value or zero value is entered.

Chapter Summary

In Visual Basic, there are eight arithmetic operators when the negation operator is counted. These operators and their precedence are as follows:

Order	Operator	Symbol
1	Exponentiation	^
2	Negation	–
3	Multiplication and division	*, /
4	Integer division	\
5	Modulus	Mod
6	Addition and subtraction	+, –

Remember that an operator is the symbol used to designate an action to be performed on two operands (to form a binary linking), or on a single operand in the case of the negation operator. Also remember that integer division and the modulus operator can be used only on data of type Integer and type Long (long integer).

The order of precedence shown in the preceding table can be overruled through the use of parentheses, including nested parentheses.

An arithmetic expression is two or more operands connected by an arithmetic operator. This expression can be added directly to a Print statement, as follows:

```
Print (5 + (4 * 15)) /3
```

Or, it can be assigned to a variable:

```
y = (5 + (4 * 15)) /3
```

The unary operator requires a single operand, while the assignment operator is a binary operator. The assignment operator copies the value of the right operand to the left operand. The left operand can be a counter variable, such as the following:

```
count = count + 1
```

It also can be the property of an object.

Visual Basic contains two functions to ensure that a string and a number are represented properly. The Val() function converts a string to a number; the Str() function converts a number to a string. Because numbers are often entered in a program by using a text box (which enters a string), the string should be converted to a number before it is used in a program.

Skill-Building Exercises

This set of exercises asks you to select the correct data types to work with. The first exercise, for example, deals with large numbers. Experiment with different data types to determine the results. Other exercises ask you to place formula in your code. You will discover how easy it is to use formulas when writing Visual Basic code.

1. The speed of light is 186,000 miles per second. Use four Print statements to display the following on a form titled LightSpeed:

   ```
   The speed of light in miles per second is <enter computed value>
   The speed of light in feet per second is <enter computed value>
   The speed of light in miles per minute is <enter computed value>
   The speed of light in miles per second squared is <enter computed value>
   ```

   Write a Form_Click() procedure, and declare light as a variable of type Long.

2. Design a program to determine a person's total pay. You know the following:

   ■ The rate of pay is $6 per hour.

   ■ A person works 50 hours, and is paid 1.5 times the rate for hours greater than 40.

   Design a Click() event to display the person's regular pay, overtime pay, and total pay.

3. Place three circles on a display, as follows:

   ■ Radius 250, color red

   ■ Radius 500, color blue

   ■ Radius 750, color yellow

   Control the radius using code. Add three labels to display the area of each circle. The formula is pi times the square of the radius. Pi is equal to 3.14159.

4. Create an application which asks the use to input the number of at bats of a baseball player and the number of hits. Display the player's batting average.

5. Extend the previous exercise to add walks and another category (For example, struck by pitch) and calculate the player's total on-base average.

6. You receive a commission on sales according to the following formula:

   ■ First $1,000: seven percent

   ■ From $1,001 to $10,000: four percent

   ■ From $10,001 to $50,000: three percent

   ■ Over $50,000: two percent

   Compute your commission for a sale of $150,000. Use five labels to show the sale amount, the commission earned at each level, and the total commission earned.

7. Design an application that converts meters into miles and miles into meters. From road races, you know that 10,000 meters is equal to 6.2 miles. Build your application to make it foolproof. When the user enters meters, set the text for miles equal to zero, the command button for miles visible, and the command button for meters invisible. Do the opposite if miles are entered by the user.

IF...THEN...ELSE LOGIC AND THE SELECT CASE STATEMENT

One of the most common logical structures in any computer language is the If...Then... Else structure. This structure allows a condition to be tested, with action taken based upon the evaluation of that condition. With simple If...Then logic, action is taken when a test condition evaluates to True. With If...Then...Else logic, one action is taken if the test condition is True; another is taken if the test condition is False.

Like the If...Then logical construct, the Select Case structure evaluates a test expression to determine if it is satisfied. However, Select Case functions in the same way as a set of If statements. Using Select Case is advantageous when you create a set of multiple-choice options. If the Case option matches the Case test expression, code is executed for that option.

In this chapter, you work with many If...Then, If...Then...Else, and nested If...Then...ElseIf...Else structures, as well as the Select Case structure. When you complete this chapter, you will be able to perform the following tasks:

- Use relational operators
- Write an If...Then...Else logical construct
- Use logical operators
- Use the ElseIf statement
- Use the complete operator precedence
- Use the Select Case structure
- Write different types of Select Case test expressions

Chapter Objectives

The objectives in this chapter are considerable. Besides working with If…Then…Else logic, you are expected to use both relational and logical operators. The objectives are as follows:

1. Understanding the relational operators

2. Knowing the different forms of the If…Then…Else syntax

3. Understanding the logical operators

4. Using nested If…Then…Else logic

5. Using If…Then logic to manipulate objects

6. Understanding and using the Select Case syntax

Objective 8.1   Understanding the Relational Operators

Before examining If…Then…Else structures, consider two important concepts: relational operators and the logic that follows from the use of this type of operator.

8.1.1   Relational Operators

The relational operators and their meanings are shown in Table 8.1.

TABLE 8.1   The Relational Operators

Operator	Description
=	Equality
>	Greater than
<	Less than
<>	Not equal to (no equality)
>=	Greater than or equal to
<=	Less than or equal to

Relational operators differ from arithmetic operators by returning a value for True (-1) or False (0). They are sometimes referred to as comparison operators because they are used to compare one value with another. For example, the following comparisons are all true:

```
5 < 6
7 = 7
1 <= 3
2 <> 4
```

Likewise, the following comparisons are false:

```
6 > 8
7 = 12
5 <= 2
2 <> 2
```

The syntax of these relational operators should be familiar. The only one that differs from standard mathematical notation is not equal to, shown as <>.

8.1.2   Relational Operators and Logic

Relational comparisons are used to express logic. For example, in English, you might state:

```
If (Is it raining?) Then
    "Open your umbrella"
Else
    "Carry your umbrella"
End If
```

This structured English (as it is called because it reads like a special form of English) begins with a question: Is it raining? If it is (the answer is yes or true), then do the first action specified: Open your umbrella. If it is not (the answer is no or false), then do the alternative action specified: Carry your umbrella. It is this form of English that is carried over to the Visual Basic syntax.

Objective 8.2   Knowing the Different Forms of the *If...Then...Else* Syntax

The If...Then...Else procedure always features a relational comparison as part of its test condition. However, the structure has three forms:

- **Form 1**—The first form can be placed on one line.

  ```
  If (test condition) Then (do this if condition is True) [Else (do
  this if condition is False)]
  ```

- **Form 2**—This second form is indented such that If...Else...End If are aligned. Statement blocks are always indented to make the structure easier to read.

  ```
  If test condition Then
    [statement block 1]
  [Else]
    [statement block-2]
  End If
  ```

- **Form 3**—The third form features a nested If...ElseIf...Else...End If alignment. Statement blocks are indented, as in the second form.

  ```
  If test condition 1 Then
    [statement block 1]
  [ElseIf condition 2 Then
    [statement block 2]]
  [Else]
    [statement block-n]
  End If
  ```

8.2.1 *If...Then* Syntax

The first form is the clearest. It avoids the use of the keywords `ElseIf` (one word) and `End If` (two words). As an example, consider the following code:

```
If (age >= 7) Then Print "Go to school"
```

With this form, the test condition is based on the value of the variable age. It is enclosed in parentheses, even though these are not required, to aid in reading. The code reads as follows: If a child's age is seven or more, the `Then` portion of the instruction is invoked, and the message `Go to school` is displayed. After the display, the next instruction in the program will be executed. If the child's age is less than seven, no message will appear. Instead, the program flow of control will immediately move to the next instruction in the program.

When using this form, the entire statement must be placed on one line. The following code would lead to an error:

```
If (age >= 7) Then
    Print "Go to school"
```

Fortunately, if you make this error, it will be easy to identify. The Visual Basic editor will inform you that it expects the `End If` keywords.

8.2.2 The *If...Then...Else* Format

The `If…Then…Else` syntax is more common to Visual Basic programs. With this form, the action that follows a `True` condition can be placed on a separate line, provided the `End If` statement is used. For example, the following code would not lead to an error:

```
If (age >= 7) Then
    Print "Go to school"
End If
```

Remember the following two rules when writing this code:

- The keyword `Then` must be on the same line as the keyword `If`.

- The `End If` statement is required.

With this syntax, it is possible to place more than one instruction between `If` and `End If`. Placing several instructions together forms what is called a *block of statements*. With a block, the `If` statement marks the beginning of the block, and the `End If` statement marks the end of the block. Suppose that you had a computer-based, multiple-choice test, and you had declared the variable `Answer` for the requested user input and `Correct` as the variable to track total correct answers. Part of the procedure to track scoring might look like the following:

```
If Val(Answer) = 12 Then
    lblFeedBack.Caption = "Problem 15 is correct"
    Correct = Correct + 1      ' increment the correct answer total
End If
```

In this example, if the value stored in the variable Answer is equal to 12 (the test is True), the block of statements placed between the If and End If keywords is executed.

The keyword Else is optional with this form; however, this keyword is required when an alternative response is needed. Consider the following code:

```
If Val(Answer) = 12 Then
    lblFeedBack.Caption  = "Problem 15 is correct"
    Correct  = Correct + 1     ' increment the correct answer total
Else
    lblFeedBack.Caption = "Problem 15 is incorrect"
    Incorrect = Incorrect + 1  ' increment the incorrect answer total
End If
```

This code is read as follows:

> When the answer is not 12 (the test is False), skip the statements that follow If, and jump to the Else portion of the structure. Execute the instructions placed under the Else until reaching End If.

Program style is important when writing If...Then...Else instructions. The Then keyword must be placed to the right of the test condition. In addition, the block of instructions that follow should be indented to aid in their reading. The keywords If, Else, and End If are left justified to improve the readability and maintenance of the code.

Exercise 8.1   Using *If* Statements to Check the Value of a Number

This exercise asks you to enter a number from 1 to 10 and to use If...Then statements to determine whether the number is within this range. Figure 8.1 shows the interface you should create.

Figure 8.1 *In this example, If...Then logic is used to determine whether a number falls within the range of 1 to 10.*

1. Add two labels, one text box, and the **cmdEnd** command button. Change the caption of the form and write the End procedure.

2. Use a label to show the results. Name the label **lblResult**.

3. Use the text box to accept user input. Name the text box **txtAnswer**.

continues

171

Exercise 8.1   continued

4. Use a `LostFocus()` procedure for the text box. With a `LostFocus()` event, user input is evaluated after it is entered into the text box and focus has shifted to another control. The code is written as follows:

```
Private Sub txtAnswer_LostFocus()
    Dim Amt As Integer
    Amt = Val(txtAnswer.Text)
    If (Amt > 0) Then
        lblResult.Caption = "Number is OK"
    End If
    If (Amt > 10) Then
        lblResult.Caption = "Number is too high"
    End If
    If (Amt <= 0) Then
        lblResult.Caption = "Number is too low"
    End If
End Sub
```

Observe how indentation improves the readability of this code. Because there are no `Else` statements, each `If` statement could have been placed on a single line.

5. Run and test your code. Test values of –1, 0, 1, 9, 10, and 11.

8.2.3   The *If...Then...ElseIf...Else* Format

The third form of the `If…Then…Else` structure features what are known as nested or multiple `If…Then` tests. It reads as follows:

```
If (this is True) Then
    Do action 1
ElseIf (this is True) Then
    Do action 2
Else
    Do action 3
End If
```

With this form, it is possible to conduct more than one test to find a `True` condition. In this example, three actions are possible. But multiple `If…Then` tests are not limited to three. Multiple `ElseIf` conditional tests can follow an initial `If` test. This example could easily contain five conditional tests, which is called a nested `If…Then` structure. You will return to it after you are more familiar with the first two forms.

Objective 8.3   Understanding the Logical Operators

The logical operators and their meanings are shown in Table 8.2.

TABLE 8.2   Logical Operators

Operator	Description
And	Conjunction
Or	Disjunction (inclusive Or)
Xor	Exclusive Or
Not	Complement
Eqv	Equivalence
Imp	Implication

These operators also return a True (−1) or False (0) value. They are sometimes referred to as compound operators because they are used to compare the results of two test conditions. Because these operators are more difficult to understand than the relational operators, consider each one carefully.

8.3.1   The *And* Logical Operator

Perhaps it would be best to start with an example. Consider the following code:

```
If (Money > 5000) And (Bills <= 5000) Then
    Print "I can actually pay off some of my debts"
End If
```

In this instance, both test conditions must be True: Money must be greater than 5000 and Bills less than or equal to 5000 for the condition to be True. When it is True, the message I can actually pay off some of my debts is displayed. If Money was greater than 5000, but Bills was 5100, the message would not be displayed. Likewise, if Money was less than 5000 and Bills was less than 5000, the message would not be displayed.

The rule for the And logical operator is as follows: Both test condition1 and test condition2 must be True for the expression as a whole to be True.

8.3.2   The *Or* Logical Operator

The rule for the Or logical operator is as follows: At least one test condition must be True for the expression as a whole to be True.

The structure is as follows:

```
If (Money > 5000) Or (Bills <= 5000) Then
    Print "I can actually pay off some of my debts"
End If
```

With this code, if Money was greater than 5000 or Bills was 5000 or less, the message I can actually pay off some of my debts would be displayed. Note that this example would be troublesome in real life. If Bills was less than 5000, but Money was 1000, you could still pay off some of your debts.

Consider a more realistic example by returning to the test-answer code. Suppose that you asked the user for a number that could be evenly divided by four, and the possible numbers were in the range from 11 to 21. The correct answer could be 12, 16, or 20. To test for a correct answer, you would need to check these three possibilities. The If…Then statement might look like the following:

```
dblInput = Val(Text1.Text)

If dblInput  = 12 Or dblInput = 16 Or dblInput = 20 Then
    Answer = "The answer is correct"
    Correct = Correct + 1
Else
    Answer = "Sorry, the answer is incorrect"
    Incorrect = Incorrect + 1
End If
```

As indicated, the keyword If is used only once. If dblInput = 12 Or dblInput = 16, Or dblInput = 20, the statement as a whole would be correct. And, if the numbers are not 12, 16, or 20, the answer is incorrect.

8.3.3   The *Xor* Logical Operator

The rule for the Xor logical operator is as follows: One test condition, and only one test condition, must be True for the expression as a whole to be True.

Consider the same structure:

```
If (Money > 5000) Xor (Bills <= 5000) Then
    Print "I can actually pay off some of my debts"
End If
```

If Money was greater than 5000 and Bills was less than 5000, the expression would be False. Why? Because more than one expression would be True. This is why the Xor operator is exclusive while the Or operator is inclusive. With Or, both sides can be True for the expression to be True. With Xor, only one side can be True-not both.

8.3.4   The *Not* Logical Operator

The Not operator can be confusing and often is discouraged when writing Visual Basic code. The rule for the Not operator is as follows: if the expression is True, the result is False. If the expression is False, the result is True.

The code is as follows:

```
If (Not (Money <= 5000)) And  (Bills <= 5000) Then
    Print "I can actually pay off some of my debts"
End If
```

This code reads as follows:

> If `Money` is not less than or equal to `5000` and `Bills` is less than or equal to `5000`, then print the message. Thus, if `Money` was greater than `5000` (not less than or equal to `5000`) and `Bills` was less than `5000`, the expression would evaluate to `True`.

8.3.5   The *Eqv* Logical Operator

The `Eqv` (equivalence) logical operator uses the following syntax:

```
result = expression1 Eqv expression2
```

The results table from this operator is as follows:

If Expression 1 Is	And Expression 2 Is	The Result Is
True	True	True
True	False	False
False	True	False
False	False	True

The rule for the `Eqv` operator is as follows: both test conditions must be `True` or both test conditions must be `False` for the expression as a whole to be `True`.

This operator is not commonly used in Visual Basic; however, you need to know that it exists.

8.3.6   The *Imp* Logical Operator

The `Imp` (implication) operator is the most difficult of all. Fortunately, it is also little used. The syntax for this operator is as follows:

```
result = expression 1 Imp expression 2
```

The results table from this operator is as follows:

If Expression 1 Is	And Expression 2 Is	The Result Is
True	True	True
True	False	False
True	Null	Null
False	True	True
False	False	True
False	Null	True
Null	True	True
Null	False	Null
Null	Null	Null

In addition to `True` plus `True` is `True`, and `False` plus `False` is `True`, three other `True` results occur: when the first test is `False` and the second is `True` or `Null`, or when the first test is `Null` and the second is `True`.

8.3.7   The Expanded Operator Precedence

The addition of relational and logical operators expands the table of operator precedence. As shown in Table 8.3, there are 14 precedence levels in Visual Basic. Relational operators have a lower precedence than arithmetic operators; logical operators have a lower precedence than relational operators.

TABLE 8.3   Order of Precedence of Operators

Level	Operator	Name
1	^	Exponentiation
2	-	Negation
3	*, /	Multiplication and division
4	\	Integer division
5	Mod	Modulo arithmetic
6	+, -	Addition and subtraction
7	&	String concatenation
8	+, >, <, <>, >=, <=	Relational operators
9	Not	Logical negation
10	And	Conjunctive
11	Or	Inclusive Or
12	Xor	Exclusive Or
13	Eqv	Equivalence
14	Imp	Implication

Precedence explains how such an expression as the following works:

```
If Money > 5000 And Bills <= 5000 Then
```

Before the logical `And` operator is used, the two relational operators are used to test the stated conditions. This sequence occurs because the relational operators have a higher precedence than the `And` operator. If the reverse were true, the expression would have to be rewritten with parentheses to override precedence, as follows:

```
If (Money > 5000) And (Bills <= 5000) Then
```

For readability and code maintenance, logical expressions should be placed inside parentheses even if they are not required.

Objective 8.4   Using Nested *If...Then...Else* Logic

Visual Basic extends the usefulness of If...Then...Else logic by including the capability to test for multiple conditions with the ElseIf keyword. This enables you to write nested logic. Review the syntax of the third form:

```
If test condition1 Then
    [statement block 1]
[ElseIf condition 2 Then
    [statement block 2]]
[Else]
    [statement block-n]
End If
```

With this logic, more than one condition (condition 1, 2, and 3) can be tested to determine whether the result is True or False.

Suppose that you write a program that asks the user to quickly estimate in whole numbers (integers) the total of a seven-item grocery list. Further, suppose that you want to give immediate feedback on an estimate. You might have the person enter the amount in a text box and have a procedure compare the answer to different values and provide feedback accordingly. If the grocery list totaled $23.78, you might write the code for the event as follows:

```
dblInput = Val(Text1.Text)

If (dblInput = 23) Or (dblInput = 24) Then
    MsgBox "You're almost on the money; it's 23.78. Good estimate!"
ElseIf (dblInput =  21) Or (dblInput = 22) Then
    MsgBox "You're just a little low"
ElseIf (dblInput = 25) Or (dblInput = 26) Then
    MsgBox "You're just a little high"
Else
    MsgBox "Try again"
End If
```

Are you beginning to understand how nested logic works? If the first test is False (the answer is neither 23 nor 24), try the second test. If the second test is False (the answer is neither 21 nor 22), try the third test. If the third test is False (the answer is neither 25 nor 26), then move to the Else portion of the structure. This portion provides the default message when all tests are False.

You can place logical operators in condition statements to test for ranges of values, but here you must be careful because Or will not work the way you might expect. Use And instead. Visual Basic tests each condition from left to right, so ranges should be listed in either ascending or descending order, as in the following example:

```
dblInput = Val(Text1.Text)
If (dblInput >= 21)  And (dblInput < 23) Then
    MsgBox "You're just a little low"
ElseIf  (dblInput  >= 23)  And (dblInput <= 24) Then
    MsgBox "You're almost on the money; it's 23.78. Good estimate!"
ElseIf (dblInput > 24) And (dblInput <= 26) Then
    MsgBox "You're just a little high"
Else
    MsgBox "Try again"      'handles all values under 21 and over 26
End If
```

Do you understand why Or would not work in this code? If the user entered 12, the first condition would be True because the 12 is less than 23, and only one condition needs to be True for the test condition as a whole to be True.

Exercise 8.2   Using *If...Then...ElseIf* to Check the Value of a Number

This exercise uses the same interface as Exercise 8.1. Use If…Then…ElseIf to check the value of a number between 1 and 10.

1. Rewrite the Lost_Focus() procedure to read as follows:

```
Private Sub txtAnswer_LostFocus()
    Dim Amt As Integer
    Amt = Val(txtAnswer.Text)
    If (Amt > 10) Then
        lblResult.Caption = "Number is too high"
    ElseIf (Amt <= 0) Then
        lblResult.Caption = "Number is too low"
    Else
        lblResult.Caption = "Number is OK"
    End If
End Sub
```

2. Run and test this code. Use –1, 0, 1, 9, 10, and 11 as test values.

Objective 8.5   Using *If...Then* Logic to Manipulate Objects

The previous sections have been limited to programmed instructions, with little emphasis given to objects. In this section, which begins with changing the properties of command buttons, consider how If…Then logic is used with objects.

8.5.1   Using *If...Then* to Change the Properties of Command Buttons

Imagine a button that constantly shifts between two messages: one says push me, and the other says push me again. How might you design a form so that when the button is pushed, the second message appears requesting to be pushed again? When the button is pushed again, the first message reappears requesting to be pushed, and so on, in endless succession. You can accomplish this by changing the property of an object (such as a button) based on the results of a conditional test.

Exercise 8.3   Push My Button

This exercise asks you to design a form to toggle between two button captions. Figure 8.2 shows this simple interface.

Figure 8.2   *If...Then logic is used to create a toggle button.*

A program requirement that toggles between two states (True or False), suggests that a Boolean data type be used. In this instance, you are switching between two messages that are displayed as button captions. You can use If...Then logic to test which state you are in and execute code based on the results of the test.

1. Draw a button (**cmdPushMe**), and in the Property box, change its caption in plain bold font to **push me**.

2. Change the Style property of cmdPushMe to 1-Graphical.

3. In the Picture property of cmdPushMe select the Face.ico icon placed on the student disk, or select Face.ico from the Misc. folder in the Graphics sub-directory of Visual Basic. This icon is also placed in this chapter folder on the companion disk.

4. In the DownPicture property, select Face3.ico. This icon is also in the Graphics subdirectory of Visual Basic and is placed in this chapter folder on the companion disk.

5. Now write a procedure for the button so that its caption toggles back and forth. The code for the command button is as follows:

```
Private Sub cmdPushMe_Click()
    Static urgent As Boolean
```

continues

Exercise 8.3   continued

```
        If urgent = False Then
          cmdPushMe.Font.Italic = True
          cmdPushMe.Caption = "push me again!"
          urgent = True
        Else
          cmdPushMe.Font.Italic = False
          cmdPushMe.Caption = "push me"
          urgent = False
        End If
    End Sub
```

Notice that you want to retain information about the state you are in, so declare the Boolean variable with the keyword Static. This method of declaring variables is discussed in Chapter 10, "Defining the Scope of Variables and Procedures."

6. Test and run the program and then continue with the next exercise.

Exercise 8.4   Buttons to Push, Again

The last design won't win any computer game contests, but dress it up as much as you can. Suppose that you have a message after every sixth push that states, Thanks, that feels much better! (see Figure 8.3). It's still pretty boring, but at least you get some gratitude for slavishly pushing buttons.

Figure 8.3   *The button toggle exercise is extended to display a message using a message box.*

1. Enter the following code into the `cmdPushMe_Click()` event:

```
Static urgent As Boolean
Static counter As Integer
Dim ans As Integer
Dim Msg As String

If urgent = False Then
   cmdPushMe.Font.Italic = True
   cmdPushMe.Caption = "push me again!"
   urgent = True
Else
   cmdPushMe.Font.Italic = False
   cmdPushMe.Caption = "push me"
   urgent = False
End If

Msg = "Thanks, that feels much better!"
counter = counter + 1
If counter = 6 Or counter = 12 Or counter = 18 Then
   ans = MsgBox(Msg, , "Thanks")
End If
```

Did you notice that you can have more than one If...Then structure in the same procedure? The message box function used in this exercise is discussed in Chapter 9, "Inputting Values and Formatting Output."

2. Run and test the program.

Exercise 8.5 Push Me: The Final Episode

Continue the last example. Suppose that you decide to be a bit obsessive—you really like clicking buttons. After 18 clicks, you decide that this has to stop. Here's a way to address the concerns of the "button obsessed." The procedure employs the Mod operator. The message appears after every six clicks for as long as the user keeps pressing the button. Now you can also use the Not operator to toggle the value of Urgent rather than directly assign the value in code.

1. At the `cmdPushMe_Click()` event, write the following:

```
Static urgent As Boolean
Static counter As Integer
Dim ans As Integer
Dim Msg As String

If urgent = False Then
   cmdPushMe.Font.Italic = True
   cmdPushMe.Caption = "push me again!"
Else
   cmdPushMe.Font.Italic = False
```

continues

181

```
        cmdPushMe.Caption = "push me"
    End If

    Msg = "Thanks, that feels much better!"
    counter = counter + 1
    If counter Mod 6 = 0 Then
        ans = MsgBox(Msg, , "Thanks")
    End If

    urgent = Not urgent   ' this instruction toggles the value of
    ➥urgent
```

2. Try it. What happened? A message is not displayed every time cmdPushMe is pushed.

Take a look at how the variable Counter is used. When the result of the test condition counter Mod 6 is 0 (that is, after each sixth button click), control is passed to the message box to display the message. Also notice that because you are dealing with a Boolean data type, you can use the Not operator to toggle its value in the procedure's last instruction.

8.5.2   Using *If…Then* to Check Scroll Bar Values

You can use If…Then structures to change the properties of all types of controls. As this next exercise shows, you can use If…Then to check the position of a scroll bar and to display different messages depending on that position.

Exercise 8.6   Using *If…Then* to Control Messages for a Scroll Bar

Draw a three-inch horizontal scroll bar and a label of approximately the same width just above it (see Figure 8.4). Using If…Then…Else logic, have the label display the scroll bar position at the beginning, middle, or end. When the scroll button reaches the end, display a message box stating that you have reached it, and have the scroll button automatically reset itself to the beginning. At the starting position, have the label caption urge the user to move the scroll bar.

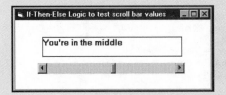

Figure 8.4   *Use* If…ElseIf…Else…End If *statements to control messages displayed on a label.*

1. Add the scroll bar and label, as shown in Figure 8.4. Set the Min value for the scroll bar to 0 and the Max value to 60.

2. Write the following HScroll1_Change() procedure:

```
Private Sub HScroll1_Change()
   Dim Msg1 As String
   Msg1$ = "You've reached the end!"
   If Hscroll1.Value = 0 Then
      lblResult.Caption = "Move the Scroll Bar!"
   ElseIf Hscroll1.Value = 1 Then
      lblResult.Caption = "This is the beginning"
   ElseIf Hscroll1.Value = 30 Then
      lblResult.Caption = "You're in the middle"
   ElseIf Hscroll1.Value = 50 Then
      lblResult.Caption = "You're nearing the end"
   ElseIf Hscroll1.Value = 60 Then
      MsgBox Msg1$, , "You did it!"
      Hscroll1.Value = 0
   End If
End Sub
```

3. Write the same procedure for the HScroll1_Scroll() event. Remember that with a scroll bar, the Scroll() event is needed to control the scroll box.

4. Write the following Hscroll1_GotFocus() event:

```
Private Sub HScroll1_GotFocus()
   HScroll1.Value = 0
   lblResult.Caption = "Move the scroll bar!"
End Sub
```

5. Run and test your program. Why doesn't the HScroll1_Scroll() procedure work the same way as the HScroll1_Change() procedure?

Objective 8.6   Understanding and Using the *Select Case* Syntax

The Select Case structure derives its name from the selection of one case from a set of cases. This structure is advisable when there are several possible selections. It tends to be easier to read than a long series of If...Then expressions.

8.6.1   The *Select Case* Syntax

The syntax for the Select Case structure is less complex than it might initially appear. The words Select Case mark the beginning of the structure, and the words End Select mark the end. The complete syntax is as follows:

```
Select Case testexpression
   [Case expressionlist1
      [statementblock1]]
   [Case expressionlist2
      [statementblock2] ]
   Case Else
      [statementblock - n]]
End Select
```

Table 8.4 explains the components of the Select Case syntax:

TABLE 8.4   The Syntax of the *Select Case* Statement

Component	Description
testexpression	Any numeric or string expression
expressionlist	A comma delimited list of an expression, a range expression (using To), or a condition expression (using Is)

Consider the following example:

```
Name$ = "Ted"
Select Case Name$
   Case "Ted"
      Print "Hello Ted"
   Case "Jane"
      Print "Hello Jane"
   Case "B. J."
      Print "Hello B.J."
   Case Else
      Print "Hello!  Anyone home?"
End Select
```

In this example, the test expression must match one of the three literal string expressions: "Ted", "Jane", or "B.J.". If it does, then the appropriate message is printed. If no match is made, then the Case Else portion of the statement is executed, leading to the message, "Hello! Anyone home?" Because "Ted" matches the value assigned to the test expression Name$, the message "Hello Ted" is displayed.

As this example illustrates, the Select Case statement looks for a match between the testexpression and an expressionlist. When a match is found, the statement block of the expressionlist is executed. Following execution, control is passed to the statement immediately following End Select. If more than one of the expressionlist statements match the testexpression, then the statement block of the first expressionlist is executed, and all others are skipped.

`Case Else` indicates which statement block to execute if no match is found between the `testexpression` and the `expressionlist`. If there is no `Case Else`, and no `expressionlist` matches the `testexpression`, control passes to the statement following `End Select`. `Case Else` is advised when it is important to specify that no test expression match was made. For example, notice what happens if you rewrite the previous code to read as follows:

```
Name$ = "Roger"
Select Case Name$
   Case "Ted"  : Print "Hello Ted"
   Case "Jane" : Print "Hello Jane"
   Case "B. J." : Print "Hello B.J."
   Case Else : Print "Hello!  Anyone home?"
End Select
```

Because no match is made, the message `Hello! Anyone home?` is displayed. Notice that with the use of a colon, the statement block can be placed on the same line as the `expressionlist`.

8.6.2   Variations of *expressionlist* and *testexpression*

You can write the `expressionlist` for a case or the `testexpression` itself in several ways. This section discusses three possibilities.

Comma Delimited Multiple *expressionlist*

The `expressionlist` can contain comma delimited multiple expressions. For example, the following would be a valid `expressionlist`:

```
Case 0, 5, 8, 11, 13
```

With this test, a case is selected if the `testexpression` matches one of these values.

Range Delimited Expression

The `expressionlist` can also cover a range of values by using the keyword `To`, as in

```
Case 21 To 27
```

or by employing a comparison operator with the keyword `Is`, as in the following:

```
Case Is >= 20
```

In this second example, the `Is` keyword used in `Case` statements is not the same as the `Is` comparison operator. In the preceding test expression, a `testexpression` value of `20` or greater would provide a match between the test and the expression.

Object Property *testexpression*

A `testexpression` can be the value of a control property, such as the value of a scroll bar. Consider the following code:

```
Select Case HScroll1.Value
```

The `testexpression` is the value of the scroll bar. It must search the various cases for a match of this value. In the next set of exercises, you draw heavily on this type of `testexpression`.

Many Visual Basic programmers prefer to use the `Select Case` statement in place of a complex `If…ElseIf…Else` statement because it is easier to read. It also tends to execute faster because multiple conditional tests need not be made. Exercise 8.7 demonstrates this concept. Compare this code to that written for Exercise 8.6.

Exercise 8.7   Moving the Scroll Bar

As in Exercise 8.6, place a horizontal scroll bar on a form in order to display different messages that depend on the position of the scroll box. Use Figure 8.4 once again for the visual layout.

1. Draw the interface shown in Figure 8.4, adding a scroll bar and a label. Set the scroll bar's Min value to **0** and the Max value to **45**.

2. Write the `Hscroll1_Change()` and the `Hscroll1_Scroll()` event procedures as follows:

```
Private Sub HScroll1_Change()
    Dim ans As Integer
    Select Case HScroll1.Value
        Case 0
            Label1.Caption = "Move the scroll bar!"
        Case 1 To 10
            Label1.Caption = "You're near the beginning"
        Case 11 To 35
            Label1.Caption = "You're in the middle"
        Case 36 To 44
            Label1.Caption = "You're near the end"
        Case 45
            ans = MsgBox("You're at the end!", 0, "Time to Quit")
            HScroll1.Value = 0  ' reset the scroll bar value
    End Select
End Sub

Private Sub HScroll1_Scroll()
    Dim ans As Integer
    Select Case HScroll1.Value
        Case 0
            Label1.Caption = "Move the scroll bar!"
        Case 1 To 10
            Label1.Caption = "You're near the beginning"
        Case 11 To 35
            Label1.Caption = "You're in the middle"
```

```
            Case 36 To 44
               Label1.Caption = "You're near the end"
            Case 45
                ans = MsgBox("You're at the end!", 0, "Time to
        ➥Quit")
                HScroll1.Value = 0   ' reset the scroll bar value
        End Select
    End Sub
```

Notice that the test expression HScroll1.Value is matched by the values of the expression lists in the Case statements. If you excluded the Case statement for the value 45, you could have entered Case Is >= 35. The keyword Is is demonstrated in Exercise 8.8.

3. Add the following code to display an opening message:

```
Sub Form_Load()
    Call HScroll1_Change ' displays opening message
    Call Hscroll1_Scroll
End Sub
```

Exercise 8.8   Extracting Salary Requirements and Giving the User Feedback

This exercise asks you to display a message box message following the entry of the salary a person thinks he or she deserves. This exercise uses the InputBox function to retrieve user input. This function is explained in detail in Chapter 9, "Inputting Values and Formatting Output." Figure 8.5 shows this simple interface.

Figure 8.5   *This design features a* Select Case *structure to determine various salary requirements.*

1. Create the interface shown in Figure 8.5, adding the two command buttons **cmdSalary** and **cmdEnd**, their captions, and the form caption. Write the cmdEnd_Click() procedure.

continues

2. In the cmdSalary_Click() event, enter the following code:

```
Private Sub cmdSalary_Click()
   Dim ans As Integer
   Dim Msg As String
   Msg$ = "Please enter your salary requirements in round
dollar amounts(no commas)"

   Select Case Val(InputBox(Msg$))
      Case Is < 10000
         ans = MsgBox("This is probably not the right position
for you.", 0, "Sorry")
      Case 10000 To 15000
         ans = MsgBox("You're underestimating your value. We
need positive thinkers here!", 0, "Sorry")
      Case 15001 To 25000
         ans = MsgBox("You're an attractive candidate. Can we
talk?", 0, "We're Interested")
      Case 25001 To 40000
         ans = MsgBox("You're within range. Let's negotiate.",
0, "We're Interested")
     Case 40001 To 50000
         ans = MsgBox("You obviously think well of yourself.
Let's talk to see if you're worth it.", 0, "Perhaps")
      Case Is > 50000
         ans = MsgBox("We are not sure this position offers you
enough opportunity.", 0, "Sorry")
   End Select
End Sub
```

It often is difficult to determine just what your test expression should be. In this example, you take the numeric value of a string. With numeric values, you can cover all possible responses with numeric ranges. The test expression need not be complex. The simplest and perhaps most common testexpression tests for the index value of an object placed in a control array.

Exercise 8.9   Identifying World Capitals

This exercise uses the List Index property of a list box in combination with the Select Case statement (see Figure 8.6).

Figure 8.6   *Click a capital city to identify its country.*

1. Create the form shown in Figure 8.6. Add the necessary code to the Form_Load() event so that the capital cities appear when the program is run. Name the list **lstCapital**. A label named **lblCountry** occupies the space above the Clear and End buttons. Write the cmdEnd_Click() procedure.

2. Set the MultiSelect property of lstCapital to **0** (None).

3. In the lstCapital_Click() event, enter the following code:

```
Private Sub lstCapital_Click()
    Select Case lstCapital.ListIndex
        Case 0
            lblCountry.Caption = "Paris is the capital of France"
        Case 1
            lblCountry.Caption = "London is the capital of the
United Kingdom"
        Case 2
            lblCountry.Caption = "Kuala Lumpur is the capital of
Malaysia"
        Case 3
            lblCountry.Caption = "La Paz is the capital of
Bolivia"
    End Select
End Sub
```

Notice that list boxes (combo boxes as well) have built-in index properties. Select Case structures are used extensively when working with list and combo boxes.

4. In addition to the ListIndex property, list and combo boxes have a ListCount property that can be read at runtime. The ListCount property returns the number of items in the list. Because all array items in Visual Basic start with zero unless otherwise specified, the last ListIndex item is one fewer than ListCount. The total numbers of items in the list in the preceding example is 4, but the largest ListIndex number is 3. There are two ways to code the Clear button. Following is one way to simply reference the exact ListIndex numbers:

```
Private Sub cmdClear_Click()
    lblCountry.Caption = ""
    lstCapital.Selected(0) = False
    lstCapital.Selected(1) = False
    lstCapital.Selected(2) = False
    lstCapital.Selected(3) = False
End Sub
```

This works, but what if the number of list items changes? Suppose that the program has the user add items to the list? How do you program it so that the Clear button works, no matter what the user does to it? You can handle this by referencing the ListCount property within a loop and remembering that it is different from the largest ListIndex number.

Exercise 8.9   continued

```
Private Sub cmdClear_Click()
    Dim n As Integer
    lblCountry.Caption = ""
    For n = 0 To lstCapital.ListCount - 1
        lstCapital.Selected(n) = False
    Next n
End Sub
```

The loop in this code will probably not be clear to you until you read Chapter 11, "Working with Loops." It is used to illustrate that a loop can be employed when the number of items in a list is subject to change.

Exercise 8.10   Checking Text-Box Input for Correct Names

This exercise introduces the Asc() function to check whether users have put their names in the correct text box. It uses one Select Case structure embedded in another. Figure 8.7 shows the interface you are to create.

Figure 8.7   *This design uses the* Select Case *structure to determine whether the user has entered his or her last name in the correct text box.*

1. Draw the interface shown in Figure 8.7. There are two text boxes (**txtNameAtoL** and **txtNameMtoZ**). The instruction and alphabet range identifiers are labels.

2. Notice that you do not have a button on this form. Instead, use the KeyDown() event to execute your code. The user's natural tendency to press Return after entering input will be used to trigger code execution.

3. Enter the following code into the txtNameAtoL_KeyDown() event of the top text box:

```
Private Sub txtNameAtoL_KeyDown (Keycode As Integer, Shift As
Integer)
    Select Case Keycode
       Case vbKeyReturn
          Select Case Asc(txtNameAtoL.Text)
             Case 65 To 76
                MsgBox "Thank you!",0,"You did it!"
             Case 97 To 108
                MsgBox "Please enter the first letter in
uppercase",0, "Comprehend?"
             Case Else
                MsgBox "Please enter your name in the
appropriate box",0,"Please"
                txtNameAtoL.Text  = ""
       End Select
    End Select
End Sub
```

4. Enter the following code into the KeyDown() event of the bottom text box:

```
Private Sub txtNameMtoZ_KeyDown (Keycode As Integer, Shift As
Integer)
    Select Case Keycode
       Case vbKeyReturn
          Select Case Asc(txtNameMtoZ.Text)
             Case 77 To 90
                MsgBox "Thank you!",0,"You did it!"
             Case 109 To 122
                MsgBox "Please enter the first letter in
uppercase",0, "Comprehend?"
             Case Else
                MsgBox "Please enter your name in the
appropriate box", 0, "Please"
                txtNameMtoZ.Text  = ""
       End Select
    End Select
End Sub
```

By referencing the built-in constant for the Return key, you can trigger code execution whenever the user presses the Return key after entering text. The keyword To is used in the Case expression list to set the ranges of the ANSI values (see Appendix A, "The ANSI Character Set"). These values are returned by the Asc() function applied to the text box input. For example, the number 109 returns the letter m. The Select Case structure is an efficient way to test for letters of the alphabet.

Chapter Summary

This chapter introduced the three forms of the If…Then…Else logical structure as well as relational and logical operators. Both types of operators are needed in writing useful If…Then…Else structures.

The three forms of the syntax should be more than familiar by now. In review, the complete syntax is as follows:

Form 1

```
If (test condition) Then (do this if condition is True) [Else (do this
➥if condition is False)]
```

Form 2

```
If test condition Then
   [statement block 1]
[Else]
   [statement block-2]
End If
```

Form 3

```
If test condition 1 Then
   [statement block 1]
[ElseIf condition 2 Then
   [statement block 2]]
[Else]
   [statement block-n]
End If
```

In practice, the second and third forms are used most frequently.

Visual Basic has six relational operators and six logical operators. The relational operators all have the same precedence. All relational operators have a higher precedence than the logical operators.

Table 8.5 lists specific rules for the most frequently used logical operators.

TABLE 8.5   Rules for Logical Operators

Operator	Rule
And	Both test conditions must be True for the expression as a whole to be True.
Or	At least one test condition must be True for the expression as a whole to be True.
XOr	Only one test condition can be True for the expression as a whole to be True.
Not	If the expression is True, the result is False; if the expression is False, the result is True.

You use the ElseIf (one word) statement to write nested If…Then structures. By using ElseIf, you can test a series of conditions to determine whether one evaluates to True.

If...Then logical structures are especially useful when changing the properties of objects based on test conditions. As illustrated in this chapter, you can use If...Then to change the properties of command buttons or to display different messages that depend on the value setting on a scroll bar.

The Select Case syntax, which is not complex, should be remembered. The syntax is as follows:

```
Select Case testexpression
    [Case expressionlist1
        [statementblock1]]
    [Case expressionlist2
        [statementblock2] ]
    Case Else
        [statementblock - n]]
End Select
```

The most difficult part of this syntax is the expression list, which can take several forms. These forms include an expression list, a range (using To), or a condition (using Is). The test condition can either be an assigned value or the value of an object's property.

Many Visual Basic programmers prefer to use Select Case rather than a series of If...ElseIf statements because of its readability and flexibility.

Skill-Building Exercises

This set of exercises asks you to gain more experience in working with If...Then...Else logic and the Select Case statement. Use If...Then...Else logic for the first three exercises plus exercise 5, and the Select Case statement for exercises 4, 6, and 7.

1. Create an interface that contains a shape, a label, and a command button. Begin with a rectangle. When the user presses the command button the first time, display I'm a Rectangle in the label. When the user presses the command button the second time, change the shape and display I'm a square. Keep pressing the command button to change the shape and to display I'm an oval, I'm a Circle, I'm a Rounded Rectangle, and I'm a Rounded Square. After running out of shapes, display No more shapes on the last click. Use If...Then statements in your solution.

2. Create a limited expert system using If...Then statements. Ask the user whether the temperature is greater than, or equal to, 60 degrees and to click Yes or No. Use option buttons to ask the user whether it is raining and to click Yes or No. Have the user click a command button to analyze the responses to these questions. Display the evaluation of user input by using a label that displays the following possible messages:

Temp >= 60 degrees	Raining	Message
Yes	Yes	Bring umbrella
No	Yes	Bring coat and umbrella
Yes	No	No coat or umbrella is needed
No	No	Bring coat only

If the user fails to check Yes or No to both questions, display the following message:

```
Need to check both conditions.
```

3. Write a program to compute a person's grade on an examination. Ask the user to enter a score and press the Return key. If the score is 90-100, assign an A; 80-89, assign a B; 70-79, assign a C; 60-69, assign a D; and below 60, tell the student to meet with you. Use a Select Case statement to display one of the following messages after the student enters a score:

```
Your grade is A. Well done!

Your grade is B. Good job!

Your grade is C. You passed!

Your grade is D. Do you need help?

Your performance was not acceptable. Please meet with me.
```

If the person enters an invalid score (below 0 or above 100), display Your score must be between 0 and 100.

4. Place a set of option buttons inside a frame, naming the control array **optFood**. Label the buttons **Veggies**, **Dairy**, **Fruits**, **Meat**, **Junk Food**, and **Beverages**. Use a Select Case statement to display one of the following messages, depending on the user's selection:

```
Veggies are good for you.

Meat will make you beefy.

Dairy products will give you strong bones.

Junk food! Are you serious?

Fruits are easy to digest.

Beverages provide the body with fluid.
```

5. Extend Exercise 8.10 so that the program uses an If-Then conditional key for testing whether or not the user has depressed the Enter key.

6. Lake County has instituted an income tax based upon a 2% surcharge of the adjusted gross income of the Federal income tax return. The rules of the county tax are that no household making less than $15,000 is taxed. Every household is entitled to a $150 tax credit for each household member. Create a simple interface for calculating the Lake County tax. Display that no tax is owed for those whose tax is less than or equal to zero.

7. Here is the interface for the Pseudo Personality Test (see Figure 8.8). The shapes appear when the check box buttons are selected. Thus, more than one check box can be indicated. Based on the selections, the Evaluate button displays a personality evaluation of the user in the label.

Figure 8.8   *The design interface for the personality evaluation displays the shape that is checked and the text of its meaning.*

1. Draw the interface and then write the code for it. No shape should appear on the screen when beginning a test. When the user makes a selection, the shape will appear.

2. Cover all possible test selections by using If...Then...Else logic: a user can select a single shape or all three.

3. Make up your own evaluation messages for display in the label. There should be a total of eight combinations. Possible messages to display are as follows:

Shape Section	Response
Rectangle only	You're traditional, but harbor a wild streak.
Oval only	You have a tendency to be hedonistic, but inside you are deeply spiritual and artistic.
Square only	Ossified is the term that comes to mind.
Rectangle and oval	Harness your raging passions to a higher end, and you'll go far.
Rectangle and square	You're not totally rigid, but rigor mortis is a constant threat.
Oval and square	Your contradictions bedevil you.
Rectangle, oval,	Some might think you're well-rounded, but square and indecisive sum it up nicely.
No selection	Please restart by selecting one or more shapes.

4. Be sure that the test can be played more than once in succession. Add a Clear button to clear the shape selection check boxes, the shapes themselves, label output, and variable values so that a new test can be conducted.

5. After the Evaluate button is clicked, make it invisible and make the Clear button visible. After the Clear button is clicked, reverse this process.

INPUTTING VALUES AND FORMATTING OUTPUT

This chapter takes a close look at the way in which you can use Visual Basic to enter data into processing, display it onscreen, and print it with a printer. Besides using text boxes, common ways of entering data into processing include the use of input and message boxes. The pop-up menu is another vehicle for enabling the user to make selections.

A second topic concerns how numbers, dates, and times can be formatted with Visual Basic. This chapter describes methods that you can use to display and print results in different ways. A typical design practice is to use one form to enter data and a second to display it. The results from the second form are then printed.

In this chapter, you learn several new tasks, including how to do the following:

- Use the `InputBox()` function
- Use the `MessageBox()` function
- Design a pop-up menu
- Format numbers, dates, and time
- Use the `PrintForm` method

Chapter Objectives

The objectives for this chapter focus on ways of entering data and displaying or printing processed results, as follows:

1. Understanding the uses of an input box
2. Understanding the uses of a message box
3. Learning how to add a pop-up menu
4. Learning how to format numbers, dates, and time
5. Understanding the `PrintForm` method

Objective 9.1   Understanding the Uses of an Input Box

An input box is a dialog box that opens and waits for the user to enter information or click a button. It differs from a message box, which only displays a message for the user to read. This chapter begins with the concept of the InputBox() function.

9.1.1   The *InputBox()* Function

A function differs from a procedure. A procedure does not return a value, while a function must return one and only one value. For example, in Chapter 6, "Variables and Constants," the Date function is used, which returns the current date from the system clock. If a value is to be returned, a function rather than a procedure must be written.

You can recognize a function by the way in which it is written. A function call is written as follows:

```
returnvalue = FunctionName (argumentlist)
```

On the other hand, the following example shows the way a procedure is written:

```
ProcedureName (argumentlist)
```

The InputBox() function is written as follows:

```
age = InputBox (argumentlist)
```

In this instruction, the InputBox() function returns one and only one value and assigns it to the variable age.

9.1.2   The Syntax of the *InputBox()* Function

The syntax for the InputBox() function is the following:

```
InputBox(prompt [,title][,default][,xpos] [,ypos][,helpfile,context])
```

Table 9.1 describes the components of the InputBox() function syntax.

TABLE 9.1   Syntax of the *InputBox()* Function

Component	Description
prompt	A string expression displayed as a message in a dialog box.
title	The title of the input box shown in the title bar.
default	The response if no other input is provided.
xpos	The horizontal distance between the left edge of the dialog box and the left edge of the display screen.
ypos	The vertical distance between the upper edge of the dialog box and the top of the display screen.

Component	Description
helpfile	A string expression that identifies the Help file that you use to provide context-sensitive help for the dialog box. If help-file is provided, context must also be provided.
context	A numeric expression that is the Help context number that the Help author assigned to the appropriate Help topic. If context is provided, helpfile must also be provided.

You cannot change the size of an input box; you can alter only its position onscreen. Nonetheless, you can add a considerable amount of information to an input box, as Exercise 9.1 illustrates.

Exercise 9.1   Using an Input Box for Data Entry

Use an input box, rather than a form or a text box, to enter information for processing. Figure 9.1 shows the input box you are asked to create.

Figure 9.1   *The input box enables you to collect additional information, such as the user's height in inches.*

1. Open a new project and add the form caption **Input Box Data Entry**.

2. Add three labels and their captions. Add three text boxes named **txtAge**, **txtHeight**, and **txtPounds**.

3. Add the **Quit** command button and the cmdQuit procedure to end the program.

4. Add the following Form_Load() procedure:

   ```
   form1.Show
   txtAge.SetFocus
   ```

   If you try to set the focus without the form1.Show instruction, an error will result. The form must be seen before the focus can be set.

continues

Exercise 9.1   continued

5. Add a `txtAge_GotFocus()` procedure. The procedure should get age, height, and weight from three input boxes-one value at a time. It should be written as follows:

```
Private Sub txtAge_GotFocus()
    'Program to get string values from the user
    'and convert them to integers
    Dim age As String
    Dim height As String
    Dim weight As String
    Dim answer As Integer

    'Get age and convert the string to a number
    age = InputBox("What is your age in years:", "Age", , 40,
2400)
    txtAge.Text = Val(age)

    'Get height and convert to a number
    height = InputBox("What is your height in inches", "Inches",
, 40, 2400)
    txtHeight.Text = Val(height)

    'Get weight and convert to a number
    weight = InputBox("What is your weight in pounds", "Pounds",
, 40, 2400)
    txtPounds.Text = Val(weight)
    answer = MsgBox("You're lying!!", 0, "Weight Detector")

    ' set focus to another text box to avoid regenerating the
event
    txtHeight.SetFocus
End Sub
```

6. Test your completed program.

Notice that the input boxes appear as soon as the program is run because you set the focus to `txtAge` in the `Form_Load()` event (after showing the form) and have the code trigger the `txtAge_GotFocus()` event.

Objective 9.2   Understanding the Uses of a Message Box

In Exercise 9.1, you used a `MessageBox()` function to display an opinion about the truthfulness of the user. A `MessageBox()` function displays a message in a dialog box and waits for the user to respond. This response is limited to clicking the appropriate command button.

9.2.1   The Syntax of the *MessageBox()* Function

The syntax of the `MessageBox()` function is somewhat simpler and more limited than an input box. It consists of the following:

```
MsgBox(prompt[, buttons][, title][, helpfile, context])
```

Table 9.2 describes the components of the MessageBox() function syntax.

TABLE 9.2   Syntax of the *MessageBox()* Function

Component	Description
prompt	A string expression displayed as the message in the dialog box. The maximum length of a prompt is approximately 1,024 characters, depending on the width of the characters used. If prompt consists of more than one line, you can separate the lines by using either a carriage return character (Chr(13)), a linefeed character (Chr(10)), or a combination of the two (Chr(13) & Chr(10)) between each line.
buttons	A numeric expression that is the sum of values specifying the number and type of buttons to display, the icon style to use, the identity of the default button, and the modality of the message box. If omitted, the default value for buttons is 0.
title	A string expression displayed in the title bar of the dialog box. If you omit title, the application name is placed in the title bar.
helpfile	A string expression that identifies the Help file to use to provide context-sensitive help for the dialog box. If helpfile is provided, context also must be provided.
context	A numeric expression that is the Help context number the Help author assigned to the appropriate Help topic. If context is provided, helpfile also must be provided.

The buttons argument can lead to some complexity. Besides more than a dozen types, more than one type can be specified for a single message box. Consider the following code:

```
Private Sub Form_Click()
    Dim mbtype As Integer
    Dim Ans As Integer
    Dim Msg As String
    Dim Title As String
    Msg = "Are you OK?"
    Title = "Message Box Title"
    mbtype = vbYESNO + vbQuestion + vbDefaultButton1
    Ans = MsgBox(Msg, mbtype, Title)
End Sub
```

This procedure will display a message box with Yes and No as the choices. The default button will be Yes. A question mark icon will appear before the message "Are you OK?" because you are using the vbQuestion message box (see Figure 9.2).

Figure 9.2   *This message box displays a warning query and has yes and no as choices, with yes as the default.*

There are many button argument types. Their built-in symbolic constants, integer values, and meanings are described in Table 9.3.

TABLE 9.3   Button Arguments

Constant	Value	Description
vbOKOnly	0	Displays OK button only.
vbOKCancel	1	Displays OK and Cancel buttons.
vbAbortRetryIgnore	2	Displays Abort, Retry, and Ignore buttons.
vbYesNoCancel	3	Displays Yes, No, and Cancel buttons.
vbYesNo	4	Displays Yes and No buttons.
vbRetryCancel	5	Displays Retry and Cancel buttons.
vbCritical	16	Displays Critical Message icon.
vbQuestion	32	Displays Warning Query icon.
vbExclamation	48	Displays Warning Message icon.
vbInformation	64	Displays Information Message icon.
vbDefaultButton1	0	Makes the first button the default.
vbDefaultButton2	256	Makes the second button the default.
vbDefaultButton3	512	Makes the third button the default.
vbDefaultButton4	768	Makes the fourth button the default.
vbApplicationModal	0	Application modal: The user must respond to the message box before continuing work in the current application.
vbSystemModal	4096	System modal: All applications are suspended until the user responds to the message box.
vbMsgBoxHelpButton	16384	Adds Help button to the message box.
vbMsgBoxSetForeground	65536	Specifies the message box window as the foreground window.
vbMsgBoxRight	524288	Right justifies the text.
vbMsgBoxRtlReading	1048576	Specifies that text is to be read from right to left on Hebrew and Arabic systems.

Not counting the Quit button, Figure 9.3 shows 12 different types of message boxes as button captions. Of the 12, the first column uses single message box types, while the second introduces message boxes with icons. The last column shows message boxes with combined types.

Figure 9.3   *The different types of message boxes enable you to fulfill a variety of input and output needs in your programs.*

1. Open a new project and change the caption to Message Boxes.

2. Place the command buttons on the form, and change the captions as shown in Figure 9.3. Add a cmdQuit_Click() procedure to end the program.

3. Declare the following variables at the form level:

```
Dim Ans As Integer
Dim title As String
Dim msg As String
```

4. Write the cmdOK_Click() procedure, as follows:

```
Private Sub cmdOK_Click()
    msg = "With this style the user can only click OK"
    title = "OK Message Box"
    Ans = MsgBox(msg, vbOKOnly, title)
End Sub
```

5. Test your design after adding this code.

6. Place the other command buttons (or as many as you find necessary) on the form. The messages (msg), titles (title), and answers (Ans) are as follows:

   ■ OK-CANCEL message box

```
msg = "With this style the user can only click OK or Cancel"
title = "OK-CANCEL Message Box"
Ans = MsgBox(msg, vbOKCancel, title)
```

continues

Exercise 9.2   continued

- **YES-NO-CANCEL** message box

```
msg  = "With this style the user can only click Yes, No, or
➥Cancel"
title = "Yes-No-Cancel Message Box"
Ans = MsgBox (msg, vbYesNoCancel, title)
```

- **RETRY-CANCEL** message box

```
msg  = "With this style Retry and Cancel are possible"
title = "Retry-Cancel Message Box"
Ans = MsgBox (msg, vbRetryCancel, title)
```

- **CRITICAL** message box

```
msg  = "With this style the Critical icon is presented"
title = "Critical Message Box"
Ans = MsgBox (msg, vbCritical, title)
```

- **QUESTION** message box

```
msg  = "With this style the Question icon is presented"
title = "Question Message Box"
Ans = MsgBox (msg, vbQuestion, title)
```

- **EXCLAMATION** message box

```
msg  = "With this style the Exclamation icon is presented"
title = "Exclamation Message Box"
Ans = MsgBox (msg, vbExclamation, title)
```

- **INFORMATION** message box

```
msg  = "With this style the Information icon is presented"
title = "Information Message Box"
Ans = MsgBox (msg, vbInformation, title)
```

- **YES-NO-INFORMATION** message box

```
msg  = "The Information icon is presented with Yes-No Choices"
title = "Combination Message Box"
Ans = MsgBox (msg, vbYesNo + vbInformation, title)
```

- **YES-NO-QUESTION** message box

```
msg  = "Do you want to continue?"
title = "Yes-No-Question Message Box"
Ans = MsgBox (msg, vbYesNo+ vbQuestion, title)
```

- **NO-SET-AS-DEFAULT** message box

```
msg  = "No is set as the default"
title = "Combination Message Box"
Ans = MsgBox (msg, vbYesNo + vbInformation + vbDefaultButton2,
➥title)
```

- **YES-SET-AS-DEFAULT** message box

```
msg  = "Yes set as the default"
title = "Yes-No-Cancel Message Box"
Ans = MsgBox (msg, vbYesNoCancel +vbDefaultButton1, title)
```

7. Run and test all message boxes.

Message boxes are used to prompt the user to make choices or to provide the user with information that is critical to further processing of the program. Two of the button integer values you can use to customize a message box have no effect on buttons at all. These two values are `vbApplicationModal` (the default) or `vbSystemModal`. As a general rule, you should leave your message boxes to the default value of `vbApplicationModal`, and reserve the use of `vbSystemModal` for those situations in which there is a risk of your application destabilizing the current computer session.

9.2.2   The Return Values of the *MessageBox()* Function

The most critical part of employing message boxes is ascertaining user response so that the processing of your program can proceed according to the user's choices. In Exercise 9.2, all `MessageBox()` function return values are assigned to the integer variable `Ans`. Table 9.4 presents the values of possible user choices and their constant names.

TABLE 9.4   Return Values of the *MessageBox()* Function

Constant	Value	Button
vbOK	1	OK
vbCancel	2	Cancel
vbAbort	3	Abort
vbRetry	4	Retry
vbIgnore	5	Ignore
vbYes	6	Yes
vbNo	7	No

In Exercise 9.2, the value returned to `Ans` changes depending on a user's selection. You might want to extend the exercise by adding instructions so that the values of the variable `Ans` are printed on the form.

Objective 9.3   Learning How to Add a Pop-Up Menu

In Chapter 4, "Learning to Think Visually," you learned how to add a menu bar to a design. However, there are times when it is more convenient to open a pop-up menu, namely, one that is displayed on a form. The syntax for a pop-up menu is as follows:

```
object.PopupMenu menuname, flags, x, y, boldcommand
```

Table 9.5 explains the components of the pop-up menu syntax.

TABLE 9.5   Pop-Up Menu Syntax

Component	Description
object	Optional. An object expression that evaluates to an object in the Applies To list. If object is omitted, the form with the focus is assumed to be an object.
menuname	Required. The name of the pop-up menu to be displayed. The specified menu must have at least one submenu.
flags	Optional. A value or constant that specifies the location and behavior of a pop-up menu, as described in Settings.
x	Optional. Specifies the x-coordinate where the pop-up menu is displayed. If omitted, the mouse coordinate is used.
y	Optional. Specifies the y-coordinate where the pop-up menu is displayed. If omitted, the mouse coordinate is used.
boldcommand	Optional. Specifies the name of a menu control in the pop-up menu to display its caption in bold face. If omitted, no controls in the pop-up menu appear in bold.

The optional flags argument affects the location and behavior of the pop-up menu. This argument works only for applications running under Windows 95. The application will ignore this argument when running under 16-bit versions of Windows or Windows NT 3.51 and earlier. These settings are shown in Table 9.6.

TABLE 9.6   Settings for the *Flags* Argument

Constant	Value	Description
		Location
vbPopupMenuLeftAlign	0	The default. Places the left side of the pop-up menu at x.
vbPopupMenuCenterAlign	4	Centers the pop-up menu at x.
vbPopupMenuRightAlign	8	Places the right side of the pop-up menu at x.
		Behavior
vbPopupMenuLeftButton	0	The default. Causes an item on the pop-up menu to react to a mouse click only when the left mouse button is used.
vbPopupMenuRightButton	2	Causes an item on the pop-up menu to react to a mouse click when either the right or the left mouse button is used.

As in the MessageBox() function, you can combine these constants to customize pop-up menu properties.

9.3.1   Building a Pop-Up Menu

Building a pop-up menu follows the same procedure as building a menu that appears on the menu bar, with one exception: The Visible property of the topmost menu name is turned off, making the menu invisible. An event, such as a mouse click, then makes the menu appear. Exercise 9.3 illustrates how this is done.

Exercise 9.3   Creating a Pop-Up Menu to Display Different Greetings

This exercise asks you to create a pop-up menu. When the user clicks the mouse on the form, the menu appears. From the menu, the user can select Greeting1, Greeting2, Greeting3, or End the program.

1. Create a new project, adding the caption **Pop-Up Menu** to the form.

2. Choose Tools, Menu Editor and build the following menu (leaving all items visible for the moment):

    ```
    Caption             "Message"
    Name                mnuMessage
    ......Caption       "Greeting1"
    ......Name          mnuGreeting1
    ......Caption       "Greeting2"
    ......Name          mnuGreeting2

    ......Caption       "Greeting3"
    ......Name          mnuGreeting3
    ........Caption     "End"
    ........Name        mnuEnd
    ```

    In this menu, mnuGreeting1, mnuGreeting2, and mnuGreeting3 are subordinate to mnuMessage; mnuEnd is subordinate to mnuGreeting3.

3. Write the following Form_Click() procedure:

    ```
    Private Sub Form_Click()
        PopupMenu mnuMessage, 4, 1400, 1400
    End Sub
    ```

4. Write the following menu procedures:

    ```
    Private Sub mnuGreeting1_Click()
        Print "Good morning!"
    End Sub

    Private Sub mnuGreeting2_Click()
        Print "How are you today?"
    End Sub

    Private Sub mnuGreeting3_Click()
        Print "Feeling great, you say!"
    End Sub

    Private Sub mnuEnd_Click()
        Print "Sorry.  Have to run."
        End
    End Sub
    ```

5. Now for the important point: Return to the menu builder and check off the Visible check mark for mnuMessage.

6. Run your program. Click the form to make the pop-up menu appear.

9.3.2   Using a Pop-Up Menu

The question of when to use a pop-up menu is an interesting one. Some designers use pop-up menus when users need to refer to a menu often. A simple click of a command button or a mouse click opens the menu. One disadvantage of a pop-up menu is that only one can be displayed at a time; thus, calls to a pop-up menu are ignored if one is already displayed. Calls are also ignored if a pull-down menu is active.

In the newer version of Windows, context menus appear with the click of the right mouse button. This behavior is built in, for example, with the Visual Basic Text Box control. If you want to build context menus for your applications, use the `vbPopupMenuRightButton` flag when building pop-up menus.

Objective 9.4   Learning How to Format Numbers, Dates, and Time

An important part of displaying or transmitting results is formatting them in a familiar form. This especially is important when converting numerical values to strings or to currency. Without formatting, the currency representing the numerical value might appear quite different from what the designer expected.

9.4.1   The *Format()* Function

The `Format()` function formats any expression according to a set of string instructions that you specify. Formatting, for example, allows a string to appear as currency, with a specified number of leading or trailing zeros and with commas separating thousands. Format instructions can be either named or written in a user-defined format.

The syntax of the `Format()` function is as follows:

```
Format(expression[, format[, firstdayofweek[, firstweekofyear]]])
```

Table 9.7 explains the components of the `Format()` function syntax, while Table 9.8 and Table 9.9 show the settings of the function's `firstdayofweek` and `firstweekofyear` arguments, respectively.

TABLE 9.7   *Format()* Function Syntax.

Component	Description
expression	Any valid expression
format	A valid named or user-defined format expression
firstdayofweek	A constant that specifies the first day of the week (see Table 9.8 for the settings)
firstweekofyear	A constant that specifies the first week of the year (see Table 9.9 for the settings)

TABLE 9.8   *firstdayofweek* Settings

Constant	Value	Description
vbUseSystem	0	Uses NLS API setting
vbSunday	1	Sunday (default)
vbMonday	2	Monday
vbTuesday	3	Tuesday
vbWednesday	4	Wednesday
vbThursday	5	Thursday
vbFriday	6	Friday
vbSaturday	7	Saturday

TABLE 9.9   *firstweekofyear* Settings

Constant	Value	Description
vbUseSystem	0	Uses NLS API setting
vbFirstJan1	1	Starts with the week in which January 1 occurs (default)
vbFirstFourDays	2	Starts with the first week that has at least four days in the year
vbFirstFullWeek	3	Starts with the first full week of the year

9.4.2   Using Named and User-Defined Formats with Numbers

The easiest way to format an expression is to use one of the named formats. Table 9.10 shows the available format names.

TABLE 9.10   Named Formats

Format	Description
General Number	Displays number with no thousands separator.
Currency	Displays number with thousands separator, if appropriate; displays two digits to the right of the decimal separator. Output is based on system locale settings.
Fixed	Displays at least one digit to the left and two digits to the right of the decimal separator.
Standard	Displays number with thousands separator, at least one digit to the left and two digits to the right of the decimal separator.

continues

TABLE 9.10   continued

Format	Description
Percent	Displays number multiplied by 100 with a percent sign (%) appended to the right; always displays two digits to the right of the decimal separator.
Scientific	Uses standard scientific notation.
Yes/No	Displays No if number is 0; otherwise, displays Yes.
True/False	Displays False if number is 0; otherwise, displays True.
On/Off	Displays Off if number is 0; otherwise, displays On.

A full description of these named formats is available in Visual Basic's online Help. A standard number, for example, displays the number with a thousands separator, at least one digit to the left and two digits to the right of the decimal separator. Therefore, the return from the Format() function call Format(1234, "Standard") would return 1,234.00.

Examine the return from the Format(8450, "Currency") function call:

```
$8,450.00
```

In this example, using a named format simplifies the more difficult task of adding a dollar sign, pound signs, and leading and trailing zeros.

To create a user-defined numeric format, you can use one or more of the symbolic constants shown in Table 9.11.

TABLE 9.11   User-Defined Numeric Format Constants

Symbol	Description
0	Prints a trailing or a leading zero in the format position if appropriate.
#	Never prints trailing or leading zeros.
.	Decimal place holder.
,	Thousands separator.
%	The expression is multiplied by 100. The percent sign (%) is inserted in the position where it appears in the format string.
-+$()	Literal character: displays a character as typed.

Examine the return values from the following Format() function calls:

Return	Format Function
$600.75	Format(600.75, "$###.##")
8,450	Format(8450, "#,#00")
$1	Format(0.5, "$#,##0")
300.00%	Format(3, "0.00%")
50E+03	Format(50000, "00E+00")

As you can see, using one of the named formats is much easier, but by using these symbolic constants, you can customize your output to appear exactly as you want. Remember that when writing format statements, you must place both named and user-defined formatting patterns in quotation marks.

Exercise 9.4   Entering and Displaying Numeric Data

This exercise asks you to enter payroll data on one form and display it on a second form. Figure 9.4 shows the forms you are asked to complete.

Figure 9.4   *This data entry display asks you to enter the data needed to calculate and display gross pay, taxes paid, and net pay, using the format function.*

1. Open a new project, name the form **frmInput**, and then add the caption **Payroll Input**.

2. Add the two command buttons and change the names to **cmdCalculate** and **cmdEnd**. Add the captions and write the cmdEnd_Click() procedure.

3. Add the five text boxes and the five labels. Name the text boxes as follows: **txtName**, **txtRate**, **txtTax**, **txtRegHrs**, and **txtOverHrs**. Add all label captions.

4. Add a second form and name the form **frmRegister**. Change the caption to **Payroll Register**.

5. Place a command button on this form and name it **cmdReturn**. Return, in this context, means return to the first form.

6. Write the event procedure for the cmdReturn button. The code should read as follows:

```
Private Sub cmdReturn_Click()
    frmInput.Show
    frmRegister.Hide
End Sub
```

continues

Exercise 9.4   continued

7. Return to frmInput, and write the Calculate Pay procedure. Your code should read as follows:

```
Private Sub cmdCalculate_Click()
    Dim GrossPay As Currency
    Dim TaxPay As Currency

    Dim TaxRate As Single
    Dim PayRate As Currency
    Dim Regular As Integer
    Dim Overtime As Integer
    Dim NetPay As Currency

    PayRate = Val(frmInput.txtRate.Text)
    TaxRate = Val(frmInput.txtTax.Text)
    Regular = Val(frmInput.txtRegHrs.Text)
    Overtime = Val(frmInput.txtOverHrs.Text)

    GrossPay = (PayRate * Regular) + (1.5 * PayRate * Overtime)
    TaxPay = GrossPay * TaxRate
    NetPay = GrossPay - TaxPay

    'Show second form
    Load frmRegister
    frmRegister.Show

    frmRegister.Print
    frmRegister.Print
    frmRegister.Print "     Gross pay is :"; Format$(GrossPay,
"Currency")
    frmRegister.Print "     Taxes are    :"; Format$(TaxPay,
"Currency")
    frmRegister.Print "     Net pay is   :"; Format$(NetPay,
"Currency")
End Sub
```

In this procedure, named formats are used in place of symbols.

8. Test your design with the following data: a person is paid $8.00 per hour, has a tax rate of 0.25, and works 40 regular hours and 10 overtime hours.

9.4.3   Using Named and User-Defined Date and Time Formats

You also can use the Format() function with dates and times. Named date and time formats are much easier to use than user-defined date and time formats. An extensive set of symbolic constants for dates and times can be employed in user-defined formats to obtain the exact output you want. The symbolic constants are available in Visual Basic's online Help. The named date and time formats are defined by the International section of the Control panel. The format names and descriptions are shown in Table 9.12.

TABLE 9.12   Date and Time Formats

Format	Description
General Date	Displays a date and/or time. For real numbers, displays a date and time (for example, 4/3/99 05:34 PM); if there is no fractional part, displays only a date (for example, 4/3/99); if there is no integer part, displays the time only (for example, 05:34 PM). The date display is determined by your system settings.
Long Date	Displays a date according to your system's Long Date format.
Medium Date	Displays a date using the Medium Date format appropriate for the language version of Visual Basic.
Short Date	Displays a date using your system's Short Date format.
Long Time	Displays a time using your system's Long Time format. It includes hours, minutes, and seconds.
Medium Time	Displays a time in 12-hour format using hours and minutes and the AM/PM designator.
Short Time	Displays a time in 24-hour format (for example, 17:45).

Because the symbolic constants for user-defined dates and times are so extensive, they are not listed here. Press the F1 key and consult Visual Basic's online Help. Examples of user-defined dates and times are listed in the following table. In the examples, the slash (/) is used as the date separator and the colon (:) as the time separator.

Format Syntax	Result
m/d/yy	5/16/99
dddd,mmmm dd,yyyy	Monday, May 16, 1999
d-mmmm	16-May
mmmm-yy	May-99
hh:mm AM/PM	09:30 AM
h:mm:ss a/p	9:30:12 a
d-mmmm h:mm	15-May 9:30

Exercise 9.5   Exploring the Use of Date Formats

This short exercise asks you to use named formats and user-defined formats. Figure 9.5 shows the output that you are asked to create.

Figure 9.5   *This display shows the four named date formats and four user-defined formats.*

1. Open a project and change the form caption to **Date Formats**.

2. Write a `Form_Click()` procedure to format the `Now` function. Use all named date formats and user-defined formats. The procedure is written as follows:

```
Private Sub Form_Click()
    'Using named formats
    Print "               This set uses named formats"
    Print
    Print "  Today's date is "; Format(Now, "General Date")
    Print
    Print "  Today's date is "; Format(Now, "Long Date")
    Print
    Print "  Today's date is "; Format(Now, "Medium Date")
    Print
    Print "  Today's date is "; Format(Now, "Short Date")

    Print
    'User defined format symbols
    Print "               This set shows date variations"
    Print
    Print "  Today's date is "; Format(Now, "m/yy")
    Print
    Print "  Today's date is "; Format(Now, "dddd,mmmm,yyyy")
    Print
    Print "  Today's date is "; Format(Now, "d-mmmm")
    Print
    Print "  Today's date is "; Format(Now, "mmmm,yy")
End Sub
```

3. Run and test your program.

Exercise 9.6   Exploring the Use of Time Formats

This exercise is much like the last. It asks you to use both named time formats and special, symbolic formats. Figure 9.6 shows the output for this exercise.

Figure 9.6   *This display shows the three named time formats and three user-defined formats.*

1. Begin a project, changing the form caption to **Time Formats**.

2. Write a Form_Click() procedure to format the Now function. Use all named time formats and user-defined formats. The Form_Click() procedure is written as follows:

```
Private Sub Form_Click()
    'Using named formats
    Print "              This set uses named formats"
    Print
    Print "  The time is "; Format(Now, "Long Time")
    Print
    Print "  The time is "; Format(Now, "Medium Time")
    Print
    Print "  The time is "; Format(Now, "Short Time")

    Print
    'User defined format symbols
    Print "              This set shows time variations"
    Print
    Print "  The time is "; Format(Now, "hh:mmmm AM/PM")
    Print
    Print "  The time is "; Format(Now, "h:mm:ss a/p")
    Print
    Print "  The time is "; Format(Now, "d-mmmm h:mm")
End Sub
```

3. Run and test your program.

Objective 9.5   Understanding the *PrintForm* Method

Besides displaying processed results on the computer screen, results can be printed by using a computer printer. There are two alternatives for sending information to a printer. The first uses the PrintForm method. The second uses Printer methods for which the Printer object is accessed with the keyword Printer.

9.5.1   The *PrintForm* Method

To print a form as it appears onscreen, insert the word PrintForm in an event procedure. This directs the computer to print, bit by bit, the image shown on the screen. The syntax for this method is as follows:

```
[form.]PrintForm
```

That's it!

Exercise 9.7   Printing a Form

This exercise asks you to design a simple interface and print it. Do the following:

1. Open a new project and change the form caption to **NotePad.**

2. Add a text box and two command buttons. For the text box, change the name to **txtNotes.** The text box should accept multiple lines.

3. Write the cmdEnd_Click() procedure.

4. Write the cmdPrint_Click() procedure as follows:

   ```
   Private Sub cmdPrint_Click()
       PrintForm
   End Sub
   ```

5. Test your design. Enter some text into the text box and click Print to print the text on the computer printer.

9.5.2   The *Printer* Object

Although the PrintForm method is simple, there are times when you do not want to print the entire form. You might, for example, only want to print the text inside a text box. Additionally, you might want to change the font and configure the display page to better fit the printed page. The Printer object is required to accomplish such specific tasks.

The resolution of the PrintForm method is not nearly as fine as can be obtained by using the Printer object. To fully utilize the Printer object, however, you are required to use graphic methods.

Chapter Summary

This chapter considers several alternatives to using labels and text boxes for processing and displaying information.

The InputBox() function is used to display a dialog box for entering values into processing. The syntax is as follows:

```
InputBox(prompt [,title][,default][,xpos] [,ypos][,helpfile,context])
```

With an input box, a dialog box appears asking the user for information, and disappears after the user clicks OK.

The MsgBox() function is used to display a message or warning. The syntax is as follows:

```
MsgBox(prompt[, buttons][, title][, helpfile, context])
```

With a message box, a dialog box appears providing the user with information. It disappears after the user clicks an option, such as OK.

With a pop-up menu, a series of choices are presented to the user. These choices can range from opening an input screen to displaying a report. The advantage of a pop-up menu is that it can be opened quickly and placed on any position of the screen. It disappears after the user makes a choice.

The Format() function is used to change the appearance of numbers, dates, and times. Named formats exist for all three, and simplify the formatting process. Flexibility is added by allowing for the use of user-defined format symbols.

The PrintForm method directs the computer to print, bit by bit, the image shown on the display screen.

Skill-Building Exercises

This set of exercises asks you to work more with time and date functions, formatting functions, the input box function and the Printer object. You also are asked to convert a menu bar to a pop-up menu. Collectively, these exercises should help you to gain skill in entering values into processing and formatting them.

1. Design a form with five labels to display the following:

    - Current hour and minutes (for example, 9:41)

    - Morning or evening (for example, AM)

    - Month (for example, January)

    - Day (for example, 15)

    - Year (for example, 19xx)

    Add a Click() event to display The time is and The date is, formatted as stated here.

217

2. This exercise consists of the following two parts:

   - Design a form placing **Date** and **End** on the menu bar. When the user clicks Date, display an InputBox() to enable the user to enter the date if it differs from the default (use a Short Date as the default). Display the date using a label.

   - Using the same form, remove Date and End from the menu bar, placing both on a pop-up menu instead. Use the pop-up menu to allow the user to enter a date if it differs from the default, or to end the program.

3. Modify the payroll program in Exercise 9.4 by formatting the data to be displayed on the payroll register. When you have completed the exercise, GrossPay, TaxPay, and NetPay totals should be aligned as follows:

   $2,000.00

   $0,200.00

   $1,800.00

4. Modify the payroll program in Exercise 9.4 by adding a CheckTax() procedure. If the user enters a tax rate in excess of 1 (such as 15), call the procedure. Within the procedure, use a message box to tell the user The tax rate must be less than 1. Make **Check tax rate** the title of the message box.

   After displaying the message, set the focus to allow the user to enter an acceptable tax rate. Only when the rate is acceptable should the payroll register be displayed.

5. Large sheet products in construction are often priced in fractional cents per square foot (for example, 2.5 cents per square foot). Write an application that has the user input a total bid price and the total square footage for a job. Calculate and display the unit cost per square foot to one hundredths of a cent (four decimal places).

6. Using the InputBox function, ask the user to input their date of birth. Using the prompt argument of the InputBox function, indicate to the user they are to enter it in short date format (m/d/y). Using the Format function, inform the user which day of the week they were born.

7. Modify Exercise 9.7 by printing the text inside the text box rather than the entire form. To complete this exercise, you will need to use the following methods with the Printer object:

Printer.Print	Prints the specified text or a blank line
Printer.EndDoc	Indicates the end of the document and releases the printer

   To set the font, use the following statement:

   ```
   Printer.FontSize = <set the font size here>
   ```

CHAPTER 10

DEFINING THE SCOPE OF VARIABLES AND PROCEDURES

Thus far, you have worked with constants and numeric and string variables, giving little attention to how or where variables and constants are declared. In Visual Basic, the placement of the variable declaration together with keywords used to make the declaration determine the variable's scope, which describes how variables and constants can be seen by various parts of a program. Stated another way, scope determines the life of a variable.

In Visual Basic, variable scope is determined by where the variable is declared. A variable declaration can occur at the procedure, module, or global level. Variable scope is also determined by how the variable is declared with certain keywords. Variable declaration keywords include `Dim`, `Static`, and `Public`.

Procedures also have scope. Some procedures are available to the entire program, while others are only available to other procedures within the module in which they reside. Keywords that determine procedure scope include `Private`, `Public`, and `Static`.

The scope of variables and procedures has particular importance in programs that contain more than one module, as most applications do. How can a variable be seen, for example, between two forms? If data needs to be shared by two modules, how is this accomplished? Can data be shared without using variables that can be seen by the entire application? This chapter addresses these questions.

This chapter also introduces user-defined data types: a data type created by the grouping of other data types. User-defined data types are the beginning of objects, and make objects easier to understand.

In this chapter, you learn many terms and several tasks, including how to do the following:

- Declare procedure-, module-, and global-level variables
- Create and use a code module

- Make a procedure call

- Pass data and objects from one procedure to another

- Define and use a user-defined data type

- Use more than one form in a program

- Call procedures on other forms

- Declare a static variable

- Write a `Sub Main()` procedure to initiate a program

Chapter Objectives

The objectives for this chapter address the different ways of declaring variables in a Visual Basic program, as follows:

1. Understanding the differences in scope among procedure, module, and global variables

2. Understanding static scope

3. Understanding the scope of procedures

4. Working with multiple forms in an application

5. Declaring and using a user-defined data type

6. Understanding procedures as object methods

Objective 10.1   Understanding the Differences in Scope Among Local, Module, and Global Variables

The scope of variables determines how and where a variable is declared in a program and the other parts of a program that can read a value from that variable or assign a value to it. The three levels are defined as follows:

- **Procedure-level scope**—The variable is exposed only while a procedure is executing. Only code within the procedure itself can read or assign a value to the variable. The variable is declared as Private.

- **Module-level scope**—The variable is exposed to the entire module, whether the module is a form, a code .BAS file, or a class module. Any procedure within the form or code module can read or assign a value to the variable. The variable is declared as Private.

- **Global-level scope**—The variable is exposed to the entire program. Any procedure within the program can read or assign a value to the variable. The variable is declared as Public.

Before moving to specific examples of variable scope, it is important to understand how, why, when, and where variables are declared in a Visual Basic program. Within a procedure, form, or module, most variables are declared using the Dim statement, using the following syntax:

```
Dim variablename [As type]
```

In Visual Basic, variable declarations are not required before a variable is used and, in fact, are not required at all. Visual Basic automatically declares a variable with the name you use and assigns it type Variant, which is the default. This practice is not recommended, however, as it can slow down program execution speed, easily lead to errors, and make code extremely difficult to debug and maintain.

To avoid the problem of Visual Basic automatically assigning a type, place the following statement in the declaration section of a form or a standard module:

```
Option Explicit
```

This statement will recognize any variable that has not been declared in advance and display an error whenever such a variable is found. Most Visual Basic programmers always work with Option Explicit turned on. This can be set by typing in Option Explicit yourself or by selecting the Require Variable Declaration check box in the Editor tab options after choosing Tools, Options (see Figure 10.1).

Figure 10.1   *The second checkbox, Require Variable Declaration, requires you explicitly declare all variables in your code.*

10.1.1   Placement of the *Dim* Statement

You can place Dim statements at the procedure or module level of a Visual Basic program. The module level includes those variables and procedures declared under the (General) object in the code window of a form, code, or class module.

When placing Dim inside a procedure, the declared variables are defined only within the procedure. This will become important when the procedure scope is examined and demonstrated (see section 10.1.4, "Procedure Scope and Local Variables"). A good programming practice is to place all Dim statements at the beginning of a procedure, rather than placing them throughout a procedure. This makes a program easier to read and helps to ensure that the variable has been defined before it is used.

10.1.2   Global Declaration with the *Public* Keyword

Another way of declaring a variable is by using the `Public` statement. The syntax is the same as `Dim` with the exception that the word `Public` replaces the word `Dim`, as follows:

```
Public variablename [As type]
```

The keyword `Public` means that the variable can be seen and used by every procedure in every module in a Visual Basic program. This knowledge will become important when you consider the concept of global scope (see section 10.1.6, "Global Scope and Global Variables"). The placement of global declarations of variables is especially important. If you want variables or constants to be seen by the entire application, they must be made in the declarations section of a standard module (or .BAS file). If placed at the module level of form and class modules, the declared variable is available only if the form or class modules are loaded into memory.

Figure 10.2 shows the General Declarations section of a standard code module. All standard modules have this General section. The Declarations drop-down menu is used to reveal all declarations that are general to the module. A standard module contains Visual Basic code and only code. A standard code module is created by clicking the drop-down Module icon on the tool bar or by selecting Project, Add Module (see Figure 10.3). This icon is the second from the left. A standard code module has a .BAS suffix.

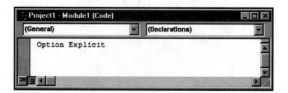

Figure 10.2   *The (General) section of a standard module contains the* `Option Explicit` *statement.*

Figure 10.3   *The Declarations drop-down menu enables you to add a code module your project.*

10.1.3 The *Static* Declaration

A third way of declaring a variable is by using the `Static` statement. A `Static` variable can be used at the procedure level only. `Static` declares a variable that will retain its value when multiple calls are made to a procedure.

The syntax for a `Static` variable is similar to `Dim` and `Public`:

```
Static variablename [As type]
```

10.1.4 Procedure Scope and Local Variables

A local variable is recognized only within the procedure in which it is declared. The following instructions declare `Cat` as a local variable of type `String` within a procedure:

```
Private Sub cmdLocal_Click()
    Dim Cat As String
    Cat =  "Night Eyes"
    Print "The name of my cat is :"; Cat
End Sub
```

The variable, `Cat`, can only be seen and used by this `cmdLocal_Click()` procedure. When the procedure ends, the value assigned to `Cat` is cleared from memory. As a general rule, always declare variables as locally as possible. This reduces the chance that a variable will be assigned an errant value and reduces the size of your application's persistent memory footprint.

Exercise 10.1   Demonstrating Procedure Scope

This exercise demonstrates the concept of procedure scope. You are asked to write two procedures with the same variable name used in both. Because the life of the variable ends when the procedure ends, declaring two variables with the same name poses no problems. Figure 10.4 shows the interface you are asked to create. The following code segments show that the variable `Cat3` is declared twice–once within each procedure.

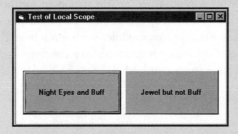

Figure 10.4 *This design enables you to declare a variable with the same name in two different procedures to reveal different values.*

continues

---

1. Create the interface as shown in Figure 10.4. Name the first command button **cmdCats1** and the second command button **cmdCats2**. Add the caption **Test of Procedure Scope** to the form.

2. Write the cmdCats1_Click() procedure as follows:

```
Private Sub cmdCats1_Click()
    Dim Cat1 As String
    Dim Cat3 As String

    Cat1 = "Night Eyes"
    Print "The name of my first cat is "; Cat1
    Cat3 = "Buff"
    Print "The name of my third cat is "; Cat3
End Sub
```

3. Write the cmdCats2 Click() procedure as follows:

```
Private Sub cmdCats2_Click()
    'Cat1 is the same variable name as used in the
    'first procedure
    Dim Cat1 As String
    Dim Cat3 As String
    Cat1 = "Jewel"
    Print "The name of my second cat is "; Cat1
    'Display this message without assigning a value
    Print "The name of my third cat is "; Cat3
End Sub
```

4. Run and test your procedure. Observe what happens when you try to display the name of Cat3 in the second procedure. The assignment in the first procedure is local to that procedure and does not carry over to the second procedure.

5. Save this project so that you can use it in the next exercises.

10.1.5   Module Scope and Module-Level Variables

Besides being used in a procedure, the Dim statement can be used in the General Declarations section of a form or code module. The variable can then be accessed by any procedure written for that module. With module-level scope, the life of the variable ends when the module is removed from memory. For a form module, this would occur when the form is unloaded.

Exercise 10.2   Illustrating Module-Level Scope

This exercise is like the last and uses the same interface (refer to Figure 10.4). The difference lies in the placement of the variable declarations. The following code segments define the variable Cat3 within the General section of the module level.

1. Modify the interface shown in Figure 10.4 to make the caption of the second button read **Jewel and Buff**. This time, "Buff" the cat will be displayed. Change the caption of the form to read **Test of Module Scope**.

2. Modify the cmdCats1_Click() procedure as follows:

```
Private Sub cmdCats1_Click()
    Dim Cat1 As String
    Cat1 = "Night Eyes"
    Print "The name of my first cat is "; Cat1
    Cat3 = "Buff"
    Print "The name of my third cat is "; Cat3
End Sub
```

Observe that Cat3 is not declared.

3. Modify the cmdCats2_Click() as follows:

```
Private Sub cmdCats2_Click()
    'Cat1 is the same variable name as used in the first
procedure
    Dim Cat1 As String
    Cat1 = "Jewel"
    Print "The name of my second cat is "; Cat1
    Print "The name of my third cat is "; Cat3
End Sub
```

Once again, Cat3 is not declared.

4. Declare Cat3 in the General section of the form module. This code reads as follows:

```
Option Explicit
Dim Cat3 As String
```

5. Run and test your program.

"Buff" the cat should be displayed by using either procedure. This behavior holds not only for form modules, but for standard modules as well (.BAS files). Declaring a variable with the keyword Dim in the General declarations section of a standard module makes that variable accessible to all procedures written for that standard module.

10.1.6   Global Scope and Global Variables

Global variables can only be declared in the General declarations section of a standard module. They are declared with the keyword `Public`. Once declared, global variables can be assigned or read by procedures in the entire application—including event procedures and all forms or general procedures written within all standard modules.

Before declaring a global variable, a wise practice is to add a standard code module (.BAS file) to your project. This places all global variables in one place and makes it easy to check them later. To add such a file, click the Module icon on the tool bar (see Figure 10.3), or choose Project, Add Module. A dialog box will appear with two tabs: one to assign an entirely new code module and one to add an existing code module. Select the tab to add a new code module. A module with the default file name `Module1.Bas` will be added to the Project Explorer Window. This new module has a `Name` property. As with a form, changing the name does not change the filename.

Exercise 10.3   Illustrating Global Scope

This exercise is similar to Exercise 10.2 and uses the same interface. The difference lies in the placement of the variable declarations and in the addition of a standard (.BAS) module, where `Cat3` is declared as a `Public` variable (see Figure 10.5).

Figure 10.5   *Declare global variables inside a standard code module.*

1. Change the caption of the form to read **Using a Global Declaration**.

2. Neither the `cmdCats1 Click()` or `cmdCats2 Click()` procedure needs to be changed from Exercise 10.2. However, remove the declaration of `Cat3` from the General section of the form module.

3. Add a standard code module file and declare `Cat3` as follows:

   ```
   Option Explicit
   Public Cat3 As String
   ```

4. Test your program. Change `Public` to `Dim` and determine what happens.

10.1.7   Overriding Scope Declarations

Procedure scope always takes priority over higher-level scope declarations. For example, if you declare a variable as global as in

```
Public Cat3 As String
```

followed by the same declaration in a procedure, written as

```
Dim Cat3 As String
```

the Procedure declaration will take priority, and no error will be reported.

Exercise 10.4   Overriding a Scope Declaration

Use the same interface as that in Exercise 10.3.

1. Change the form caption to read **Overriding a Global and Module Declaration**. Change the caption for cmdCats2 Click() to read **Jewel and Pansy**.

2. At the form module level, write the following:

```
Option Explicit
Dim Cat3 As String
```

This code should now appear in two places: in the Form1.frm module level and as a global variable in Module1.Bas.

3. Revise cmdCats2_Click() to read as follows:

```
Private Sub cmdCats2_Click()
    'Cat1 is the same variable name as used in the
    'first procedure
    Dim Cat1 As String
    Dim Cat3 As String
    Cat1 = "Jewel"
    Print "The name of my second cat is "; Cat1

    'Cat3 is a global variable in a .BAS file
    Cat3 = "Pansy"
    Print "The name of my third cat is "; Cat3
End Sub
```

4. Run and test your program. Jewel and Pansy should be displayed, not Jewel and Buff.

Objective 10.2   Understanding Static Scope

With static scope, the value of a locally declared variable is retained in memory after the procedure in which the variable is declared ends. So in this sense, the variable behaves like a module-level variable. Unlike module level variables, however, static variables expose themselves only to the local procedures in which they are declared. They persist as long as the module in which they are declared is in memory, but limit themselves to being assigned a value or read only when the procedure in which they are declared executes.

A classic use of a static variable is as a variable that serves to keep a count. Suppose that you want to know how often an event procedure, such as a button click, is called. A static variable enables you to keep track of this number inside the procedure itself. The following code illustrates the use of such a counter variable:

```
Public Sub First()
    Static Num As Integer
    Num = Num + 1    'Increment Num by 1
End Sub
```

In this code, Num is incremented by 1 each time the procedure is processed. The first time the procedure is processed, the value of Num is set to 1. The second time the procedure is processed, the value of Num is set to 2. Remember that static variables cannot be used at the module level.

You can also use the Static keyword in a procedure declaration as in Private Static Command1_Click(). With this type of static declaration, all local variables within this button click procedure would retain their values between button clicks, even if declared with the Dim statement.

Objective 10.3   Understanding the Scope of Procedures

So far we have discussed variable scope, a concept that determines which part of a program can assign values to, or read values from, a variable. In object-oriented terms, another way of describing scope is to say that objects expose themselves to other objects. They can expose themselves in either expansive or limited ways. A variable declared locally only exposes itself to other variables in that procedure. A variable declared at the module level exposes itself to all procedures in that module, whether it is a form module or a standard module (.BAS file). Global variables are exposed to the entire application.

Procedures can also expose themselves. Because Visual Basic adds event procedures for you automatically inside the code editor, it is easy to forget that procedures, like variables, are declared. With variables, you use such keywords as Dim and Public. For procedures you use the keyword Sub. Functions are declared with the keyword Function. The Sub and Function statements declare the procedure or function, but they don't specify to what other objects the procedure or function should be exposed. This requires other keywords.

10.3.1   Adding and Calling a Procedure in a Form Module

By default, all built-in event procedures (such as Form_MouseMove) in form modules are declared so that they are exposed only to other procedures on the form. This scope for standard event procedures is achieved by having the default keyword Private placed in the procedure declaration.

You also can add your own procedures to a form module. These procedures are sometimes referred to as general procedures to distinguish them from the event procedures associated with forms and controls. When you add your own procedures, you must decide how you want it exposed or scoped. By declaring a procedure with the Private keyword, you limit the exposure of the procedure to the module in which the procedure is declared.

To call a procedure, simply place the procedure name in code. The alternative is to use the optional Call statement. The following is the syntax for this statement:

```
[Call] name [(argumentlist)]
```

Table 10.1 describes the components of the Call statement.

TABLE 10.1   Syntax of the Call Statement

Component	Description
Call	An optional keyword used to signify the transfer of program control to another procedure
name	The name of the procedure to pass control to
argumentlist	The variables or expression to pass to another procedure

In this book, you are always asked to use the keyword Call when calling another procedure. This makes Call statements easier to identify and procedures easier to follow.

To add your own procedure to a form module, select Tools, Add Procedure, and the dialog box you see in Figure 10.6 will appear. By default, the procedure you add is a Sub routine with Public scope.

Figure 10.6   *The Add Procedure dialog box is used to add a procedure (Sub) or a function (Function) to a project and to give it either* **Public** *or* **Private** *scope.*

Exercise 10.5   Adding a General Procedure in a Form Module

In this exercise, you code an event procedure that calls a general procedure placed in a form module. Figure 10.7 illustrates the output for this exercise. The interface consists of two labels, lblPrompt and lblDisplay, and a text box, txtInput.

Figure 10.7   *This interface tests the use of a general procedure added to a form module using the Add Procedure command.*

1. Place the controls on the form as shown. The **lblPrompt** control is above **txtInput** and **lblDisplay** is below it. Change the caption of lblPrompt to **Please input your name and press the Enter key**. The lblDisplay control has its BorderStyle set to Single.

2. Add the following txtInput_KeyPress() procedure:

    ```
    Private Sub txtInput_KeyPress(KeyAscii As Integer)
        If KeyAscii = vbKeyReturn Then
            Call DisplayName
        End If
    End Sub
    ```

3. Add a new procedure and name it DisplayName(). With the code window open, choose Tools, Add Procedure, and set the scope to Private.

4. Write the following code:

    ```
    Private Sub DisplayName()
        Dim username As String
        Dim msg As String
        username = txtInput.Text
        msg = "Hello " & username & " !"
        lblDisplay.Caption = msg
    End Sub
    ```

5. Run and test your design.

The general procedure you added is called by the KeyPress() event procedure. As your programs become larger, code placed in the user event is often quite short. The code serves to call procedures in either a form or standard code module. We consider adding procedures to a standard code module next.

10.3.2   Adding and Calling a Procedure in a Standard Module

Adding a procedure to a standard code module is similar to adding a procedure to a form module. As before, choose Tools, Add Procedure from the menu; the dialog box will appear. The default scope of the procedure is set to Public. This permits the procedure to be seen and called by any other module.

An important difference between a general procedure in a standard module and one in a form module is that a form must be explicitly loaded into memory before a public procedure in the form can be called by another module. Visual Basic handles the loading of standard code modules automatically. Any publicly scoped procedure in a standard code module can be called.

Another difference between general procedures placed in a form module and procedures placed in a standard code module is that control names need to be explicitly referenced. General procedures placed in a form module usually refer to controls on the form. Because standard code modules do not contain controls, any reference to them must include the form that contains the control. For example, rather than referring to a text box as simply txtInput, refer to it by its complete name, such as Form1.txtInput.

Exercise 10.6   Calling a Procedure in a Standard Code Module

This exercise is an extension of the earlier exercise. Rather than calling a general procedure on the form, however, you will add a procedure to a code module and call the procedure from a form.

1. Save the form and project created in Exercise 10.5 under new names (for example, **f10-6.frm** and **p10-6.vbp**). Keep the name of the form as **Form1**.

2. Add a standard code module to the project (choose Project, Add Module), and save the module as **m10-6.bas**. If you want, you may also name the module (for example, **M10_6**).

3. Important: remove the DisplayName() procedure from the form. (You can use Edit, Cut, to place the code in the Windows Clipboard for use in Step 4.)

4. Add a new procedure to the code module. With the code window having the focus, choose Tools, Add Procedure, and set the scope of the procedure to Public. Add the code so that it reads as follows:

```
Public Sub DisplayName()
    Dim username As String
    Dim msg As String
    username = Form1.txtInput.Text
    msg = "Hello " & username & " !"
    Form1.lblDisplay.Caption = msg
End Sub
```

continues

Exercise 10.6   continued

5. The code in the txtInput_KeyPress() event is the same as that in Exercise 10.5.

6. Run and test the program.

Notice the difference in the DisplayName() procedure written for the standard code module. In the following statements, the references to the controls on Form1 must include the form reference:

```
username = Form1.txtInput.Text
Form1.lblDisplay.Caption = msg
```

Because the controls are in a separate module, the DisplayName() procedure must know which module contains txtInput and lblDisplay.

The coding of a module reference is unwieldy and inflexible. Assume that you want to have a generic procedure that could display the string Hello on any form that contained a label named lblDisplay. Even better would be a procedure that could display any message on any label on any form. Next, you will learn how such procedures are written.

10.3.3   Passing a Variable to a Procedure

In Exercise 10.5 and Exercise 10.6, you executed code in general procedures, one in a form module and one in a standard code module, respectively. Both procedures referred to specific controls on a specific form and displayed an identical message.

General procedures can be made more flexible if they are written to contain arguments, which are variables that are placed in the procedure declaration. These variable values are then passed to the procedure when the procedure is called. Reexamine the DisplayName() procedure in Exercise 10.5:

```
Private Sub DisplayName()
    Dim username As String
    Dim msg As String
    username = txtInput.Text
    msg = "Hello " & username & " !"
    lblDisplay.Caption = msg
End Sub
```

This procedure reads the value from the text box txtInput. A more flexible way of writing the procedure would be to have the procedure that called DisplayName(), the txtInput_KeyPress() event, pass the string expression in the txtInput text box to the DisplayName() procedure:

```
Private Sub DisplayName(username as string)
   Dim msg As String
   msg = "Hello " & username & " !"
   lblDisplay.Caption = msg
End Sub

Private Sub txtInput_KeyPress(KeyAscii As Integer)
   Dim person as string
   If KeyAscii = vbKeyReturn Then
      person = txtInput.text
      Call DisplayName(person)
   End If
End Sub
```

The declaration of `DisplayName()` now contains an argument. Whenever the `DisplayName()` procedure is called, it expects to receive a string expression. An error will now occur if the procedure is called without an argument. You may have observed that some of Visual Basic's built-in event procedure declarations contain arguments. Examine, for example, the `txtInput_Keypress()` event. The procedure is designed to pass the ASCII value (an integer value) of the key that is pressed. A `MouseDown()` procedure contains even more arguments:

```
Private Sub Form_MouseDown(Button As Integer, Shift As Integer, X As
➥Single, Y As Single)
```

In this case, the procedure is passed the mouse button the user has clicked (`Button` argument), the status of the Shift, Alt, and Ctrl keys (the `Shift` argument), and the location of the mouse cursor (the `X` and `Y` arguments).

Exercise 10.7   Passing Primitive Data Types to a Procedure

In this exercise, you pass the `DisplayName()` procedure two primitive `Data` type arguments, a string expression, and an integer. Figure 10.8 illustrates the output for this exercise. The interface consists of three labels, `lblPrompt1`, `lblPrompt2`, and `lblDisplay`, two text boxes, `txtNameInput` and `txtAgeInput`, and a command button `cmdOK`.

Figure 10.8   *In this design, a person's name and age are passed to a procedure.*

1. Place the controls on the form as shown in Figure 10.8. The `lblPrompt1` control is to the left of `txtNameInput` (caption of **Enter name:**) the `lblPrompt2` is to the left of `txtAgeInput` (caption of **Enter age:**). The `lblDisplay` control (at the bottom) has its `BorderStyle` set to `Single`.

continues

2. Add the following `cmdOK_Click()` procedure:

```
Private Sub cmdOK_Click()
    Dim person As String
    Dim age As Integer
    person = txtNameInput.Text
    age = Val(txtAgeInput.Text)
    Call DisplayName(person, age)
End Sub
```

3. Add the `DisplayName()` procedure to the form module. With the code window open, choose <u>T</u>ools, Add <u>P</u>rocedure and set the scope to `Private`. Write the following code:

```
Private Sub DisplayName(username As String, userage As Integer)
    Dim msg As String
    msg = "Hello " & username & "! You are " & userage & " years
➥old."
    lblDisplay.Caption = msg
End Sub
```

4. Run and test your design.

5. Save this project. You will be asked to use it for the next exercise.

The `cmdOK_Click()` procedure reads the values from the two text boxes, assigns them to the variables, and then passes the variables to the `DisplayName()` procedure. Observe the error that occurs if you remove one of the arguments from the instruction that calls `DisplayName()` (for example, `Call DisplayName(person)`).

When you call procedures and pass values, what really is being passed is the memory addresses of the passed variable. In Exercise 10.7, this method of passing values (called passing by reference) enables the `DisplayName()` procedure to access the values and create the displayed message. Visual Basic also enables you to pass copies of the variable rather than pass the address with the `By Val` statement. This difference in passing values to procedures and functions is covered in Chapter 21, "Modular Design."

10.3.4   Passing a Control Object to a Procedure

Visual Basic is made even more flexible with its capability to pass complex data types, such as objects, to procedures. You have worked with objects, mainly in the Visual Basic toolbox, when you've added visible controls to a form. You have manipulated these objects by changing their properties and invoking their methods in code.

For now, assume that you want to write a generic procedure that receives values from passed arguments and then, after manipulating them, displays them in a specified label control. The label itself (really its address) can be passed to a procedure along with the primitive data types. Such a procedure can be placed in a standard code module and be made available to the entire application.

Exercise 10.8   Passing an Object to a Procedure

In this exercise, you extend Exercise 10.7 by adding the label as an argument in the DisplayName() procedure and place the DisplayName() procedure in a standard code module. The interface remains the same as that in the preceding exercise, but you now include a code module.

1. Open Exercise 10.7 and save the form under a new name (for example, save f10-7.frm as **f10-8.frm**). Save the project under a separate name as well (for example, save p10-7.vbp as **p10-8.vbp**). Rename the project in the project's Name property.

2. Add a code module to the project, and save it as **m10-8.bas**. Important: Remove the DisplayName() procedure from Form1 (you may want to cut it for use below), and place the DisplayName() procedure in the m8-8 code module. Change the scope of the procedure to Public, and add the third argument to the procedure. The code reads as follows:

```
Public Sub DisplayName(username As String, userage As Integer,
➥dlabel As Label)
    Dim msg As String
    msg = "Hello " & username & "! You are " & userage & " years
➥old."
    dlabel.Caption = msg
End Sub
```

3. Change the cmdOK_Click() procedure as follows:

```
Private Sub cmdOK_Click()
    Dim person As String
    Dim age As Integer
    person = txtNameInput.Text
    age = Val(txtAgeInput.Text)
    Call DisplayName(person, age, Form1.lblDisplay)
End Sub
```

4. Run and test your design.

Notice the differences from the previous program. Because the scope of DisplayName() is now Public, you can see it from outside the code module. The procedure declaration contains the declaration of a Label data type as an argument. This kind of declaration, a declaration of an object, is covered in detail in Chapter 19, "Object Types, Variables, and Collections." For now, you should know that this type of declaration and usage is common in Visual Basic.

The procedure that calls DisplayName(), the cmdOK_Click() event, passes the full reference of the Label control (Form1.lblDisplay) so that the code in the standard module can resolve where lblDisplay resides.

In Exercise 10.8, you passed a control to a procedure in a standard code module along with two primitive data types. By passing data via procedure arguments, data can be shared between two modules without using global variables. All of the variables in the exercise are local. Remember that variables should always be declared as locally as possible. Using procedure arguments helps you keep variables local and restricts the use of global variables.

You also can pass data between form modules by using only local variables. This often is accomplished by passing locally declared variables along with a form reference to code in a standard module. The standard code module, in turn, can show the value of the form variable. Demonstrating this, however, requires that you first learn about working with more than one form in a program, which is discussed in the following section.

Objective 10.4   Working with Multiple Forms in an Application

Most Visual Basic applications require the use of multiple forms. With Visual Basic, you can have as many forms as you need for a project; however, only one form is loaded and displayed at project startup. Loading more than one form requires the Load statement and the Show method.

10.4.1   The *Load* Statement

The Load statement loads a form (or controls that are elements of a control array) into memory. At startup, Visual Basic only loads one form: the startup form that you designate. To examine which form is the startup form, select the Project Properties dialog box by choosing Project, [name of project], and selecting Properties. Under the General tab, you will see a combo box for the startup object (see Figure 10.9). The forms designed for the project and Sub Main() are displayed. You can select one and only one of these choices as the startup object. If you select Sub Main(), you must add a module that is called Main(). Visual Basic then starts from this procedure rather than from a form.

Figure 10.9   *Specify the Startup Object using the General tab of the Project Properties box.*

The `Load` statement permits more than one form (or control) to be loaded at startup. The syntax is as follows:

```
Load object
```

For example, the following instruction loads the second form, provided `frmMain` is the startup form:

```
Load frmDisplay
```

10.4.2 The *Show* Method

The `Show` method displays a form. The following syntax is used to show a form stored in memory:

```
[form.]Show [style]
```

The following are the two style options for this method:

- **Modal (a style of 1)**—A window or dialog box that requires the user to take an action before your application can proceed

- **Modeless (a style of 0)**—A window or dialog box that does not require the user to take an action

What happens if you fail to load a form before you show it? During program execution, Visual Basic checks to determine whether the form has been loaded. If not, the `Show` method loads an unloaded form automatically. However, the reverse is not true. If you load a form into memory and fail to show it, it will remain hidden, but its `Public` procedures will be available to be called. Even so, you should normally load forms explicitly. This makes your code easier for you and others to read.

Exercise 10.9 Working with More than One Form

This exercise introduces working with more than one form. It asks you to receive input on one form, pass the data to a procedure in a standard code module, then display the data on another form. Figure 10.10 shows how your finished design should appear onscreen.

Figure 10.10 *Working with more than one form requires using the* `Load()` *statement and the* `Show` *method.*

continues

237

Exercise 10.9   continued

1. Begin a new Standard EXE project. Save the default form as **f10-9A**, and name it **frmMain**. Add another form to the project (select Project, Add Form), save it as **f10-9B** and name it **frmDisplay**. Add a code module to the project and save it as **m10-9.bas**. Name the project **P10_9.vbp**, and save it to disk as **p10-9.vbp**.

2. Change the caption of frmMain to **Main Form**. As in the two previous exercises, the two text boxes are named **txtNameInput** and **txtAgeInput**, and the name of the command button is **cmdOK**.

3. The name of the label on frmDisplay is **lblDisplay**. Its BorderStyle is set to Single, and its WordWrap property is set to True.

4. Add the following Form_Load() procedure to frmMain:

```
Private Sub Form_Load()
    'Position startup form
    frmMain.Left = 500
    frmMain.Top = 500
End Sub
```

5. Add the following cmdOK_Click() procedure to frmMain:

```
Private Sub cmdOK_Click()
    Dim person As String
    Dim age As Integer
    person = txtNameInput.Text
    age = Val(txtAgeInput.Text)
    Call DisplayMessage(person, age)
End Sub
```

6. Choose Tools, Add Procedure to add a publicly scoped procedure named DisplayMessage() to the m10-9 standard code module:

```
Public Sub DisplayMessage(username As String, userage As
➥Integer)
    Dim msg As String
    Dim nextBDay As Integer
    nextBDay = userage + 1
    msg = "At your next birthday, " & username & ", you will be"
    msg = msg & nextBDay & " years old."
    Load frmDisplay
    frmDisplay.Left = frmMain.Left + frmMain.Width + 100
➥' position left
    frmDisplay.Top = frmMain.Top ' position top
    frmDisplay.lblDisplay.Caption = msg
    frmDisplay.Show
End Sub
```

7. Choose Project, P10_9 Properties to ensure that the startup object is frmMain.

8. Run and test your program.

Notice how the label again must be fully referenced inside the code module. You also could have passed a form reference and a label reference to the `DisplayMessage()` procedure. You are asked to do this in the "Skill-Building Exercises" section at the end of the chapter.

10.4.3   Using a *Main()* Procedure to Start an Application

Besides using a form at startup, you can specify that a procedure—always named `Main()` and placed in the standard code module—be the startup object. In most

---

Exercise 10.10   *Sub Main()*: Starting Your Program with Code Rather than Form

programs, a `Main()` procedure is used to check environmental parameters and to load program constants and other frequently called data into memory.

This exercise asks you to use the same interface as Exercise 10.9 and make several minor adjustments to the code.

1. Save each of the elements from Exercise 10.9 as new elements in a new project. Save f10-9a.frm as **f10-10a.frm**, f10-9b.frm as **f10-10b.frm**, m10-9.bas as **m10-10.bas**, and the whole project as **p10-10.Vbp**. Rename the project **P10_10.vbp**.

2. By choosing <u>T</u>ools, Add <u>P</u>rocedure, add a publicly scoped procedure named Main to the standard code module. Using the cut and paste features of the Windows Clipboard, remove the code from the `frmMain_Load()` event and place it in the `Sub Main()` procedure. Also move the relevant code from the `DisplayMessage()` procedure so that the code reads as follows:

```
Public Sub Main()
    Load frmMain
    frmMain.Left = 2000
    frmMain.Top = 2000
    Load frmDisplay
    frmDisplay.Left = frmMain.Left + frmMain.Width + 100
    frmDisplay.Top = frmMain.Top
    frmMain.Show
    frmDisplay.Show
End Sub

Public Sub DisplayMessage(username As String, userage As
➥Integer)
    Dim msg As String
    Dim nextBDay As Integer
    nextBDay = userage + 1
    msg = "At your next birthday, " & username & ", you will be"
    msg = msg & nextBDay & " years old."
    frmDisplay.lblDisplay.Caption = msg
End Sub
```

continues

Exercise 10.10   continued

3. Choose Project, P10_10 Properties, and make Sub Main() the startup object on the General tab of the Project Properties dialog box.

4. Run and test your code. Both forms should appear at project startup. The capability to pass values to the DisplayMessage() procedure should remain.

10.4.4   Benefits of *Sub Main()* Code and General Procedures in Standard Modules

Some Visual Basic programmers stress the importance of placing code in a Main procedure. A Sub Main() procedure enables an application to do error checking before launching the program. If you had a graphics-oriented application, for example, you might check the user's screen resolution and adjust the size of your forms and controls accordingly. A Sub Main() procedure is a good place to perform such system checking routines.

Should most of your procedures be placed on forms or in standard modules? Placing most of your procedures in standard modules makes some sense. The reasoning is quite straightforward. Code that is tied to a form is bound to the form. This does not permit code to be edited unless the form is opened. If the form is deleted, the code attached to it is also deleted. Code placed in a standard module is saved in a separate .BAS file. This code can be edited without opening a form. If a form is deleted, the code can be revised to reflect this occurrence; however, the code is not lost.

User interface events often are small procedures that call lengthier procedures in standard module files. For example, when writing a cmdButton_Click() procedure, the code necessarily is tied to the button and the form. When the button is deleted, the code associated with this button also should be deleted. Suppose that the button called a procedure in an existing .BAS file. Deleting the button still allows another event, such as a menu-item click, to call the same code. Developing your programs in this way enables you to quickly make changes to the user interface without requiring a lot of new coding.

Objective 10.5   Declaring and Using a User-Defined Data Type

This chapter emphasizes declaring the scope of variables. As you have seen, these variables can be either primitive (sometimes called simple) data types or complex object data types, such as components (including controls). Visual Basic includes an object type that can be considered half-way between a primitive data type and a full-fledge software component in its complexity: a user-defined type.

User-defined types combine variables of several different data types to form a single variable. Usually the variables making up the user defined type are primitive or simple data types. A user defined type is sometimes called a structure (in the C programming language), or a record (in the Pascal programming language). A user-defined type requires the Type statement.

10.5.1 Declaring a User-Defined Data Type

The syntax for a user-defined type begins with the keyword Type and ends with the keyword End Type. The complete syntax is as follows:

```
[Private ¦ Public] Type varname
    elementname [(subscripts)] As type
    [elementname [(subscripts)] As type
End Type
```

Table 10.2 describes the components of the syntax.

TABLE 10.2 Syntax of the User-Defined Data Type

Component	Description
Private ¦ Public	Indicates the scope of the user-defined type. If declared Private, it is only available to other procedures in the module in which it is declared. The default is Public.
Type	Indicates the beginning of a user-defined type.
varname	The variable name assigned by the user to the type declaration.
elementname	The name of an element of the user-defined type.
type	One of the following: Integer, Long, Single, Double, Currency, Boolean, String (fixed-length or variable), Date, Object (reference), another user-defined type, Variant, or an object type (such as an Excel spreadsheet OLE object).
End Type	Indicates the ending of the definition.

The preceding syntax helps to explain what a user-defined type means. The type can consist of more than one element, and the elements can be of different types. A user-defined type can also contain another user-defined type as one of its types.

A user-defined type must be declared at the module level of a code module; however, this placement does not lead to an allocation of memory. Memory is reserved once a user-defined type is declared.

Consider the following example:

```
Public Type Asset
    Name As String * 20
    Location As Integer
    Value As Currency
End Type
```

This definition indicates that type Asset contains three members: one of type String, a second of type Integer, and a third of type Currency. The declaration using this type, then, might be the following (which declares the variable Inventory as being of type Asset):

```
Dim Inventory As Asset
```

After a user-defined type has been defined, it can be declared as a single variable or, more commonly, is placed into an array, which is a group of variables that share the same name. (Control arrays are introduced in Chapter 11 "Working with Loops," and variable arrays are addressed in Chapter 14, "Lists and Arrays," and Chapter 15, "Multidimensional Arrays, Tables, Arrays of User-Defined Types, and the MSFlexGrid Control.") For now you will work with only single variables of user-defined types.

10.5.2   Using a User-Defined Data Type and Referencing Its Elements

Loading a structure with data requires a simple assignment statement, much like other variables; however, this is where the concept of a record begins to take on meaning. The following statement assigns the name Laser Printer to the first element of the user-defined type:

```
Inventory.Name = "Laser Printer"
```

Displaying the value stored in an element of a structure requires the structure variable name and the element to be displayed. The following statement prints the value stored in the first element of the user-defined type:

```
Print Inventory.Name
```

Exercise 10.11   Creating and Displaying Values Stored in a User-Defined Data Type

In this exercise, you define a product record, store the value for a single record, and display the contents of the record. Figure 10.11 shows the display you are asked to create.

Figure 10.11   *The user-defined type in this example is used to define a product record.*

1. Add the command button (cmdShow) as shown in Figure 10.11, and change the form caption. Change the font for the form to bold.

2. Add a new standard (.BAS) code module, and write the following type definition:

```
Public Type Product
    Name As String * 20
    Price As Currency
    Cost As Currency
    OnHand As Integer
End Type
```

3. Write the Show Records procedure as follows:

```
Private Sub cmdShow_Click()
    Dim inventory As Product
    inventory.Name = "Laser Printer"
    inventory.Price = 599.99
    inventory.Cost = 378.5
    inventory.OnHand = 32

    CurrentX = 1000
    CurrentY = 200
    Print "Product: ", inventory.Name
    CurrentX = 1000
    CurrentY = 400
    Print "Price:", Format(inventory.Price, "Currency")
    CurrentX = 1000
    CurrentY = 600
    Print "Cost:", Format(inventory.Cost, "Currency")
    CurrentX = 1000
    CurrentY = 800
    Print "OnHand:", inventory.OnHand
End Sub
```

4. Run and test your program.

This procedure initially declares Inventory as a variable of type Product. Following this, values for the four elements of the variable are assigned. Once assigned, all that remains is to display the contents of the variable.

Objective 10.6   Understanding Procedures as Object Methods

You might have noticed that a user-defined type can be employed to hold information about real things in the world, such as persons, places, or things. In short, user-defined types can hold information about any object. You can consider user-defined types as the beginning of object-oriented programming. You have seen how objects possess properties. Object properties are held in data structures that are very similar to user-defined type data structures.

Objects have two key differences from user-defined types, as follows:

- The scope of their individual elements (members) can be either public or private. The public members become part of the object's interface; the private members are used only by the object itself.

- An object contains code that works on the data held by the object. This code is an object method.

You have already worked with object methods, such as the Clear method of a list box or the Print method of a form. Believe it or not, you have already created your own object methods. In Visual Basic, every time you add a procedure to a form module, such as an event procedure or a general procedure, you are declaring and coding an object method.

Procedures that are publicly declared on a form module can be called from another module, as long as the form is loaded into memory. When you call the procedure, you follow a syntax that is quite familiar:

```
object.method [argument]
```

By default, event procedures on forms, such as button clicks, are scoped to be Private to the form module in which they are declared; however, you can change the scope of these event procedures to Public. They then can be called from any other module. Exercise 10.12 illustrates this principle.

Exercise 10.12   Creating and Calling a *Public* Procedure on a Form

In this exercise, you set the scope of a procedure on a form to Public and then call it from another form module.

1. Start a new project and add two forms. Name one form **frmRequest** and the other **frmRespond**. Save frmRequest as **f10-12a** and frmRespond as **f10-12b**. Name the project **p10_12**.

2. On frmRequest, add a command button named **cmdRequest**. On frmRespond add a command button named **cmdRespond** and a label named **lblDisplay** (see Figure 10.12).

Figure 10.12   *This design requires two forms such that a request on one form can be sent as a message to the second form.*

---

3. In the `cmdRespond_Click()` event, set the scope by changing the keyword `Private` to `Public`, and add the following code:

```
Public Sub cmdRespond_Click()
    frmRespond.lblDisplay.Caption = "I'm accessible to anyone."
End Sub
```

4. Add the following code in the `cmdRequest_Click()` procedure:

```
Private Sub cmdRequest_Click()
    frmRespond.Top = frmRequest.Top
    frmRespond.Left = frmRequest.Left + frmRequest.Width + 200
    frmRespond.Show
    frmRespond.cmdRespond_Click
End Sub
```

5. Make `frmRequest` the startup object in the dialog box that appears when you choose Project, Properties.

6. Run and test the program.

Notice the syntax used in this exercise. You dropped the use of the optional `Call` keyword. Because a `Click()` event has no arguments, you simply invoked a method of the `frmRespond` object, `frmRespond.cmdRespond_Click`.

A more accurate description of this exercise is to say that you invoked a method of the `frmRespond` object, which was an instance of the `frmRespond` class. A more complete explanation is provided in Chapter 19, "Object Types, Variables, and Collections," and Chapter 20, "Class Modules." For now, you should know that the procedures you write for forms are really object methods!

Chapter Summary

Defining scope is determined, primarily, by the placement of `Dim` statements, which can be placed at the procedure and module level of a program. `Dim` statements at the procedure level define scope, which is local to the procedure. `Dim` statements placed at the form module level define scope local to the form and all procedures written for that form. `Dim` statements placed at the module level define scope local to the module and all forms and procedures associated with that module.

A global declaration using the `Public` statement extends the scope of a variable to all modules, forms, and procedures.

A `Static` declaration is used at the procedure level only. Static scope extends throughout the life of a variable. It remains local, but the value of the variable is retained in memory between procedure calls. A common static variable is a counter variable.

Higher scope declarations can be overridden by lower scope declarations. If a variable is defined as a global variable, the same variable name can be used in a declaration statement in a procedure. The local declaration takes priority over the global declaration.

The concept of scope can be difficult to master. As a general rule, keep the scope of variables as local as possible by using as few module levels as possible and avoiding global variables. Why this rule? Because the life of a local variable ends when a procedure ends; it cannot create errors in several places throughout a program. This is in sharp contrast to a global variable, which can affect each procedure in a program.

Procedures also have scope. They can be private to the module in which they are declared, or they can be made public. Public procedures in standard code modules are available to the entire application. Public procedures in form modules are available only if the form is loaded into memory.

The `Call` statement is used to call another procedure. To call a procedure, the name of the procedure and the arguments to be passed, if any, must be indicated.

Primitive (simple) and complex variables and objects can be passed to procedures. By default, the address of these variables are passed—not their actual values.

Variable scope becomes especially important in multimodule projects. In applications with more than one form, the `Load` statement and the `Show` method are used to load forms into memory and to make them visible. Because only one form or module is loaded at project startup, additional forms must be loaded by using the `Load` statement and must be shown by using the `Show` method.

A `Sub Main()` procedure can be used at startup in place of a form. A main benefit of a `Sub Main()` procedure is that code that must be executed before loading a form can be executed in this procedure. Placing most of your code in standard modules allows it to be saved as a file, independent of forms that it might require in processing.

Visual Basic enables the creation of user-defined types: unique data types that are a grouping of other data types, most often primitive data types. The variables that make up a user-defined type are called members.

Skill-Building Exercises

These exercises ask you to work with more than one form, to pass object variable to procedures, create and work with user-defined types, and expand a public procedure.

1. This project asks you to use four forms and a standard code module. Each form should be designed to display a different color. Name the forms **frmColor1**, **frmColor2**, **frmColor3**, and **frmColor4**, but change no other properties.

   Use a standard code module to declare and write a `Main()` procedure to call four procedures: `color1`, `color2`, `color3`, and `color4`. Within each procedure, load and show the form, change the form caption, and change the form background color.

2. This project also asks you to use four forms, named **frmBlue**, **frmRed**, **frmYellow**, and **frmGreen**. When the program runs, only frmBlue should be visible. Click frmBlue to show frmRed. Click frmRed to show frmYellow. Click frmYellow to show frmGreen. Click frmGreen to print text on each of the forms as indicated by the following table:

Text	Form
THIS	**frmBlue**
IS	**frmRed**
A GREAT	**frmYellow**
DAY	**frmGreen**

3. Extend Exercise 10.8. Request the user's city of residence, pass the variable along to the DisplayName() procedure, and add the city name to the message displayed.

4. Extend Exercise 10.9. Pass the form on which the message is to be displayed as well as the label that should display the message to the DisplayName() procedure. All form and label references in the procedure should then use the passed object arguments.

5. Write a program that defines an employee user-defined data type. Include the employee number, first name, last name, pay rate, and date hired as elements in the data type definition. Create a button-click procedure that assigns values to this data type and then displays the values on the form.

6. Extend the preceding exercise. Add a form module general procedure that assigns values to the elements of the user-defined type and then passes the variable to a procedure that increases the pay rate of the employee by five percent. Display the results of processing on the form.

7. Modify Exercise 10.12 by expanding the cmdRespond_Click() event. Add code that displays a caption on a new label added to frmRequest. The caption should read "**Thanks, I received your message.**"

8. Create a project comprised of two forms (Form1 and Form2) and one code module. In the code module, define a user defined type called "Student" containing two elements: Name and Number. Declare a global variable of type Student. In a Main procedure assign values to the elements of the global Student variable and display these values in the captions of Form1 and Form2.

CHAPTER 11

WORKING WITH LOOPS

Now that you understand variable and procedure scope and the `If...Then...Else` construct (having worked through Chapter 6, "Variables and Constants," and Chapter 8, "`If...Then...Else` Logic and the `Select Case` Statement," respectively), it is time to move to a more fascinating topic: loops. The loop logical structures provide the Visual Basic designer with enormous flexibility.

Loops enable code to be repeatedly executed under a variety of conditions. This is why loops are associated with the term iteration (literally, repetition). This chapter first addresses three types of loops. The first type is known as a `For-Next` loop (which has a syntax that looks more difficult than it really is). It executes a fixed number of times until a condition is met. The second and third types are `Do` and `While` loops, respectively. These loops continue to execute while or until a specified condition is satisfied.

You also are introduced to the concept of a control array, which is nothing more than a set of like objects with the same name. Following this, you are introduced to the `Do` loop syntax—which, as you will discover, takes multiple forms—and the easier-to-understand `While` loop syntax.

You will learn several tasks in this chapter, including how to perform the following tasks:

- Code a simple `For-Next` loop structure
- Use a control array
- Increment and decrement a loop
- Code a nested `For-Next` loop
- Use the `DoEvents` statement
- Move shapes with a loop
- Use the `Do-Loop Until` and `Do-Loop While` structures
- Use a nested `Do-Loop Until` structure
- Set the Timer control
- Use a `While-Wend` structure

Chapter Objectives

The six objectives for this chapter focus on learning to write programs using the variety of loop structures in Visual Basic 6, as follows:

1. Understanding the `For-Next` loop syntax

2. Using a control array in a program

3. Using a nested `For-Next` loop in a program

4. Understanding how `Do` loops work

5. Understanding how `While-Wend` loops work

6. Adding the Timer control to a project

Objective 11.1   Understanding the *For-Next* Loop Syntax

With loops, code executes in cycles. It starts at the top of the loop clause, goes through the body of the loop, and continues to cycle until a condition is met. Certain loops can cycle indefinitely, or until the user decides to interrupt them. As an example, the snooze button on your alarm clock can be used to demonstrate a loop structure. Consider the following pseudocode:

```
Beginning of Loop:    For three times, when the alarm goes off, then

Body of Loop:         Press the snooze button.
                         Sleep a few more minutes.

Ending of Loop:       Return to the beginning of the loop.
```

As this loop indicates, you press the snooze button three times. After that, you must get up when the alarm goes off.

11.1.1   The *For-Next* Loop Syntax

A `For-Next` loop works the same way as the alarm clock example except that the maximum number of times you intend to press the snooze button is set. For example, you will press it exactly three times. When executing a known (designer designated) number of cycles, the logical structure recommended is the `For-Next` structure. The structure sets the maximum number of cycles executed by using a counter variable, which changes with each iteration of the cycle. The syntax of a `For-Next` loop is as follows:

```
For counter = start To end [Step step]
    [statements block 1]
    [Exit For]
    [statements block 2]
Next [counter]
```

Table 11.1 explains the components of the For-Next loop syntax.

TABLE 11.1   Syntax of the *For-Next* Loop

Component	Description
For	The beginning of the For-Loop structure. The word For must appear at the start of the loop.
counter	A numeric variable of type Integer or type Long.
start	The initial value of counter.
To	The keyword to separate the start from the end value.
end	The final value of counter.
Step	The keyword to indicate that an increment (or decrement) value will be given.
step	The value by which the loop counter is incremented (or decremented). The default is +1.
statements	The instructions placed within the loop. It also is referred to as the loop body.
Exit For	An alternative way to exit the loop.
Next	The end of the For-Next loop structure. It causes the Step increment to be added to, or subtracted from, counter.

Does this syntax seem complex? It is until you work through some examples. Consider the following code fragment:

```
For SumIt = 10 to 20 Step 5
    Print SumIt
Next
```

This code could also be written as

```
For SumIt = 10 to 20 Step 5
    Print SumIt
Next SumIt
```

This code runs slower, but does indicate where a loop ends. As an alternative, you can write

```
For SumIt = 10 to 20 Step 5
    Print SumIt
Next 'SumIt
```

In this code, SumIt is treated as a comment.

Can you determine how the values will be displayed? The values will be the following:

```
10    15    20
```

Consider what happens. The first time through the loop, the variable SumIt is set to 10. This value is printed. The second time through the loop, SumIt is incremented by the step increment, which changes 10 to 15. This value is printed. The final time through the loop, SumIt is incremented again by 5, which is added to 15. The value 20 is printed.

As a beginning rule, call the counter variable something recognizable and relevant to the procedure. To sum a set of numbers, for example, you might well call the counter variable SumIt, as in the preceding code fragment. Frequently used counter variables are i, j, k and l. Avoid such names as X, Y, or Foo.

Another important rule is to indent the body of the loop and align the For with the Next statement, as shown in the following code:

```
For SumIt = 10 to 20 Step 5
    Print SumIt
Next
```

As you will soon appreciate, indenting becomes very important when the loop body contains many instructions, or when one loop is placed inside another loop.

Exercise 11.1   Displaying the Iterations of a Loop

In this simple example, you explore how the option Step works in For-Next logical structures. Figure 11.1 shows the form you are asked to design.

Figure 11.1   These For-Next loops run from 0 to 100 in steps of 10 and steps of 5.

1. On a tall, narrow form, draw three buttons near the upper-right corner, one underneath the other. Add a Picture Box control to this form. Add the caption **Tracker**.

2. Add the captions **For-Next 10**, **For-Next 5**, and **Clear**.

3. On the top button's Click() event, enter the following code:

```
Private Sub cmdForNext10_Click()
    Dim Tracker As Integer
    For Tracker = 0 To 100 Step 10
      Form1.Print Tracker * 10
      Picture1.Print Tracker / 10
    Next Tracker
End Sub
```

4. On the second button, enter the same code, but change the step value to 5 so that the loop condition reads as follows:

```
For Tracker = 0 To 100 Step 5.
```

5. On the last button's `Click()` event, enter `Form1.Cls` and `Picture1.Cls` to clear the form and the picture. This code reads as follows:

```
Private Sub cmdClear_Click()
    Form1.Cls
    Picture1.Cls
End Sub
```

6. Run and test the program. Figure 11.1 shows the results of clicking the top-most button.

How does this program work? With the `Step` value of the top button set at `10`, the procedure takes every tenth value of the range `Tracker` and multiplies it by 10 (displaying it on the form) and divides it by 10 (displaying it in the picture box). With the `Step` value set to `5`, the middle button's procedure takes every fifth value of the `Tracker` range and multiplies and divides it by 5. The middle button's procedure cycles twice as many times as the first, and displays twice as many return values.

Adding `Step` to a `For-Next` procedure is optional. If it isn't added, the loop's default increment is `1`.

11.1.2 *Step* Increment and Decrement

The `step` increment in a `For-Next` loop can be positive or negative. Consider the following code fragment:

```
For num = 100 To 5 Step -5
    Print num
Next num
```

Can you guess what will be printed? The first value will be `100`, the second `95`, and so on. Looking in a backward direction is useful for creating interesting patterns. When the `Step` increment is negative, the term decrement takes on importance. Remember that when the `Step` increment is positive, you increment the counter; when it is negative, you decrement the counter. To decrement, you must use the `Step` keyword, even if you are decrementing by one.

Objective 11.2 Using a Control Array in a Program

A control array is a group of like objects with the same name. This might seem confusing at first, but it's not difficult once you write a few programs. Consider the following code fragment:

```
Private Sub cmdMoney_Click()
    Dim arraynum as integer
    Dim NewPrice as Currency
    For arraynum = 0 To 4
        NewPrice = Val((txtPrice(arraynum).Text) * 1.075)
        txtPrice(arraynum).Text = NewPrice    ' a control array
    Next                                       ' next loop iteration
End Sub
```

This code is somewhat different from the code you have seen before. In this example, five text boxes are specified, with each one given the name txtPrice. The first object of the array is txtPrice(0), while the last is txtPrice(4). A control array is advised when like objects have similar code events. They are distinguished from one another by their index numbers (0, 1, 2, 3, and 4).

It is easy to make a control array. First, design the first object and assign it a name. Then, select and copy the object (Ctrl+C or choose Edit, Copy), and paste it (Ctrl+V or choose Edit, Paste). When you paste the new control, a dialog box asks whether you want to create a control array (see Figure 11.2). If you do, select Yes. The Index property of the second object is changed from 0 to 1, thus providing the second object with a unique identifier, but with the same object name as the first object.

Figure 11.2 *When you copy and paste a control on a form, you are asked whether you want to create a control array.*

11.2.1   The Counter Variable and Control Arrays

The counter variable is important in several ways in a loop structure. In the preceding For-Next example, arraynum is declared as the counter variable. It then is used twice to refer to the index of the txtPrice control array. The linking the first time through the loop can be read as follows (with 0 indicating the value of arraynum):

```
NewPrice = Val(txtPrice(0).Text) * 1.075
txtPrice(0).Text = NewPrice
```

The second time through the loop, the index value is changed from 0 to 1. The new code reads as follows:

```
NewPrice = Val(txtPrice1(1).Text) * 1.075
txtPrice(1).Text = NewPrice
```

11.2.2   Why Use Control Arrays?

Now do you have a better understanding about the value of control arrays? The preceding code could have been designed with five different text boxes, such as txtPrice1, txtPrice2, and so on; however, that design would not have allowed you to use a loop to change prices. It would have required five separate sets of coded instructions. Five might not seem like a large number, but imagine an online wholesale ordering system for which individually ordered items are displayed in labels and then marked up by the order taker. Suppose that 80 items have been ordered. With a control array and a loop, all those item prices could be changed with the same code.

Exercise 11.2   Showing Fill Styles

Loops are very useful for dealing with lists of values, including object property values. The FillStyle property of a shape, for example, has eight styles (0 through 7). Using a loop, it is easy to display these eight fill styles for Visual Basic Shape controls. Figure 11.3 shows the design you are asked to create.

Figure 11.3   *This display features a control array of eight shapes, each assigned a different fill style.*

1. Draw a shape (a circle) on a form and set its Visible property to False. Set the form background color and the shape fill color to contrasting colors.

2. Copy and paste the shape, responding <u>Y</u>es to whether you want to create a control array.

3. Create an eight-member array of identical shapes on the form.

4. Add a button and the caption **Show Fill Styles**, and add the following code for the button Click() event:

```
Private Sub cmdShow_Click()
  Dim FillNum As Integer
  For FillNum = 0 To 7
      Shape1(FillNum).FillStyle = FillNum  'FillNum is used
➥twice here
      Shape1(FillNum).Visible = True
  Next
End Sub
```

5. Run and test the program. As one test, change the loop from 1 to 8, and observe the problem.

Objective 11.3   Using a Nested *For-Next* Loop in a Program

Multiple For-Next loops, with one set of For-Next statements placed inside a second, lead to a nested For-Next loop. With a nested loop, the innermost loop must finish its execution before the outside loop is incremented or decremented.

11.3.1   The Nested Loop Syntax

The following is the syntax for a nested For-Next loop, with one For-Next loop placed inside an outer For-Next loop:

```
For counter1 = start To end [Step step]
   [statements block 1]
   For counter2  = start To end [Step step]
      [statements block 2]
   Next [counter2]
   [statements block 1 continued]
Next [counter1]
```

This indentation used in writing a nested For-Next loop is important. It enables the eye to separate the outer loop from the inner loop.

To illustrate how a nested loop works, consider the following code fragment:

```
Dim outer, inner As Integer
   For outer = 10 to 20 Step 5
      For inner = 1 to 5
         Print inner * outer
      Next inner
   Next outer
```

Can you determine how the values will be displayed? The following is the first set of values displayed:

```
1 * 10 = 10     2 * 10 = 20     3 * 10 = 30     4 * 10 = 40     5 * 10
➡= 50
```

This completes the processing of the inner loop, at which point the outer loop is incremented by five. The following is the second set of values:

```
1 * 15 = 15     2 * 15 = 30     3 * 15 = 45     4 * 15 = 60     5 * 15
➡= 75
```

This completes the processing of the inner loop once again. Control is passed by the instruction Next outer, which increments the outer loop by five one more time. The following is the third set of values:

```
1 * 20 = 20     2 * 20 = 40     3 * 20 = 60     4 * 20 = 80     5 * 20
➡= 100
```

11.3.2   The *DoEvents* Statement

The DoEvents statement passes control to Windows. In other words, it forces Visual Basic to yield execution to Windows so that Windows can process all messages in the operating system message queue before being asked to process additional code.

As illustrated by Exercise 11.3, numeric calculations in the processor execute far more rapidly than the video system can repaint the screen. Without the DoEvents statement, most computer graphic systems simply freeze until all the numeric calculations are completed. Following this, the results are displayed. By using DoEvents, you ensure that screen redraws are completed and calculated values displayed in the list box before beginning another inner loop cycle.

You will use DoEvents in programs in which it is essential to control the sequencing of events, especially as it affects graphical output.

Exercise 11.3   Using Nested Loops and List Boxes

This exercise asks you to use a nested loop and to place the results of processing into one of five list boxes. It also contains an inner loop with a DoEvents statement. This statement ensures that a number is fully displayed before the next display instruction is reached. Figure 11.4 shows the display that you are asked to create.

Figure 11.4   *This display shows the results of using an outer loop to designate list boxes and an inner loop to populate each list box.*

1. Create a control array of five list boxes, add the two command buttons, and add the captions to the command buttons and to the form. Use a lowercase L (that is, **l**) in naming the list boxes **lstNum()**. Make sure that it is not the numeral 1, which looks similar to an l, but is illegal as the first letter of an object name. Make the list boxes different colors to clearly separate the boxes on the screen.

continues

Exercise 11.3   continued

2. Write the cmdTryIt_Click() procedure as follows:

```
Private Sub cmdTryIt_Click()
   Dim inner As Integer
   Dim outer As Integer
   Dim item As String
   Dim sleep As Long

   For outer = 0 To 4
      lstNum(outer).Visible = True
      For inner = 1 To 10
         DoEvents
         item = Str((outer + 1) * inner)
         lstNum(outer).AddItem(item)
            For sleep = 1 To 100000
            Next sleep
      Next inner
   Next outer
End Sub
```

Within the second loop (loop inner), the value of outer times inner (adding 1 where necessary) is computed. The result is assigned to the variable item. The AddItem method is used, making the assignment of the item to the list. Following this, a third nested loop is indicated. This loop acts to delay the display of numbers on the display screen.

3. Run and test your program. As one of your tests, comment out the DoEvents statement. This will help you to better understand the function provided by this statement.

11.3.3   The *Exit For* Statement

With nested loops, it sometimes becomes necessary to exit from a loop structure before the loop completes all iterations. Consider the following code sample:

```
For sleep = 1 To 100000
   If sleep > 35000 Then Exit For
Next sleep
```

This code reduces the number of iterations from 100,000 to 35,000. When 35,000 is reached, the innermost loop ends; however, the entire nested loop does not end. Instead, control is transferred to the statement that immediately follows the Next sleep instruction, which in Exercise 11.3 was the Next inner instruction. To escape this loop, a second Exit For statement is required.

11.3.4   Moving Shapes with *For-Next* Loops

For-Next loops are especially useful for manipulating shapes and other types of visual objects by relying on the Visual Basic coordinate system. As an example, consider the following code fragment:

```
For Position = 1 To 50
   Shape1.Left = Shape1.Left + 60
Next Position
```

In this example, Shape1.Left refers to the movement of the shape to the left. Shape1.Left + 60 indicates that each iteration of the loop moves Shape1 60 twips to the right. This is equivalent to 1/24 of an inch with each loop iteration.

Exercise 11.4   Moving a Shape to Make the Moon Rise

This example asks you to move a shape by making the moon rise in the sky. Figure 11.5 shows the form you are asked to design, which places the moon at its highest position in the sky. At that point, a message appears.

Figure 11.5   *A* For-Next *loop is used to make the moon rise from the lower-left corner of the form to the position illustrated.*

1. On the form, set the WindowState property to Maximize (2) and the BackGroundColor property to a dark blue. Title the form **Moonrise**.

2. Place a Shape control in the bottom-left corner, and change its properties so that it is a one-inch yellow circle.

3. Set the circle's Left property to 250 and its Top property to 5800. (This assumes a 640 by 480 resolution, and that the form ScaleMode is in its default mode of Twips).

4. At the bottom of the page, draw a command button wide enough to hold the caption **Watch the moon rise**. This caption will change to **Watch the moon fall** when the dialog box appears. Add a second command button, **End moonwatch**. Write the End procedure.

continues

259

Exercise 11.4   continued

5. Add the following code to the cmdRise_Click() command button:

```
Private Sub cmdRise_Click()
  Dim Position As Integer
  Dim ans As Integer

  For Position = 1 To 100
     Shape1.Left = Shape1.Left + 30
     Shape1.Top = Shape1.Top - 40   ' ascend
  Next

  ans = MsgBox("Howoooool!", 0, "Moonrise")

  Shape1.Left = 250
  Shape1.Top = 5800
End Sub
```

Note that the coordinates of a Visual Basic form begin with 0,0 (left, top). To make the moon rise, you need to subtract from the Top property value. After the moon reaches the highest point, the message box appears.

6. Run and test this code. Save the project, but leave it open. The next exercise asks you to write additional code to make the moon fall.

Exercise 11.5   The Moon Descending

Suppose that you wanted to watch the moon also descend from the night sky. It would be a simple matter of having the moon begin to descend when it reaches the uppermost position in its path. To make the moon descend, however, you must add to the Top property value. When the moon reaches its highest point, you will change the caption on the command button to Watch the moon fall. When the message box button is clicked, the moon will descend.

1. Change the cmdRise() procedure to work as follows:

```
Private Sub cmdRise_Click()
  Dim Position As Integer
  Dim ans As Integer

  For Position = 0 To 100
    Shape1.Left = Shape1.Left + 30
    Shape1.Top = Shape1.Top - 40    ' ascend
  Next Position

  cmdRise.Caption = "Watch the moon fall"
  ans = MsgBox("Howoooool!", 0, "Moonrise")

  For Position = 0 To 100
    Shape1.Left = Shape1.Left + 30
    Shape1.Top = Shape1.Top + 40   'descend
  Next Position

  Shape1.Left = 250
  Shape1.Top = 5800
  cmdRise.Caption = "Watch the moon rise"
End Sub
```

In the second loop, the moon continues to travel to the right of the screen while it descends. Instead of subtracting, twips must be added for this movement to take place.

2   Run the modified program. Because the message box suspends operation, clicking it starts execution again, and the moon descends.

By changing the number of loop iterations and the amount of the movement of Shape1.Left and Shape1.Top in each cycle iteration in Exercise 11.4 and Exercise 11.5, you can adjust the speed and distance of the moon's movement. Experiment to get the results you like.

Objective 11.4   Understanding How *Do* Loops Work

Do loops continue to execute code within a loop while a condition is True or until a condition becomes True. They especially are useful when dealing with situations in which the exact number of iterations required (loops) cannot be determined in advance. In designing a Do loop, a conditional test is used. The test returns a value of True or False, and works in the same way as the If...Then conditional test.

11.4.1   The Do-Loop Syntax

The syntax of the Do-Loop is complex. As shown in the following examples, you can place the conditional test of the loop either at the beginning or the end of the loop construct. The two options are as follows:

- **Option 1**—In the following code, the conditional test is at the beginning of the Do-Loop structure:

```
Do [{While | Until} condition]
    [statements block 1]
    [Exit Do]
    [statements block 2]
Loop
```

- **Option 2**—In the following code, the conditional test is at the end of the Do-Loop structure:

```
Do
    [statements block 1]
    [Exit Do]
    [statements block 2]
Loop [{While | Until} condition]
```

Both the Option 1 syntax and Option 2 syntax permit the following four types of Do loops to be written:

- The Do-While Loop structure:

```
Do While(this condition is True)
    [statements]
Loop
```

- The Do-Until Loop structure:

```
Do Until(this condition is True)
    [statements]
Loop
```

- The Do-Loop While structure:

```
Do
    [statements]
Loop While(this condition is True)
```

- The Do-Loop Until structure:

```
Do
  . [statements]
Loop Until(this condition is This)
```

In this syntax, every keyword is optional except the keywords Do and Loop. Even so, be careful! If you make a construct with only Do and Loop (without While or Until) with no conditional test, you can easily create an infinite loop and suspend your computer's operation within an unending cycle. You might then have to exit Visual Basic, lose all unsaved work, and launch the program again. You will read about this in detail later in section 11.4.4, "Overflow Errors and Infinite Loops," but first look at the different Do-Loop structures.

11.4.2   Working with the Four *Do-Loop* Styles

In this section, you further examine the four Do-Loop styles. You should remember that with Do-While Loop and Do-Until Loop, it is possible to completely avoid the loop body. With Do-Loop While and Do-Loop Until, you must execute the loop body at least once.

Do-While Loop

Do-While Loop, the first of these four forms, performs a relational test at the top of the loop and tests for a positive condition. The loop continues to execute while the relational test remains True. Consider the following pseudocode example:

```
Do While("You are hungry")
    Eat
Loop
```

In this loop, you will continue to eat while you are hungry.

Do-Loop While

Do-Loop While is similar to the Do-While Loop except that the test condition is placed at the bottom of the loop. This ensures that the loop executes at least once. This is particularly useful when you want a user to enter a value and test after data entry. Continuing the last example:

```
Do
    Eat
Loop While("You are hungry")
```

In this loop, you would eat first before checking to determine whether you are hungry. (It's easy to gain weight with this practice, isn't it?)

Do-Until Loop

The Do-Until Loop acts like the Do-While Loop except that it tests for the negation of the While condition. Consider how the previous example needs to be reworded with Do-Until, as in the following:

```
Do Until("You are Not hungry.")
    Eat
Loop
```

As stated, you would continue to eat until you are not hungry, which is the negation of you are hungry.

Do-Loop Until

Do-Loop Until also tests for the negation of the While condition, after executing the loop body at least once. The following syntax continues with the example:

```
Do
    Eat
Loop Until("You are Not hungry.")
```

In this instance, you would eat at least once before deciding that you were not hungry.

Exercise 11.6   Using *Do-Loop Until*

To survey the different ways Do loops can be constructed, use the form shown in Figure 11.6. The code of the cmdDoLoop_Click() event (top button) will display the products of 4 from 1 to 60.

Figure 11.6   *This example is similar to Exercise 11.1, but uses* Do *loops rather than* For-Next *loops.*

continues

Exercise 11.6   continued

1. Draw the picture box and three buttons (**cmdDoLoop**, **cmdClear**, and **cmdEnd**) on a form as shown, and add the appropriate captions.

2. For the **Clear** button, enter Form1.Cls and Picture1.Cls instructions.

3. For the **Do-Loop Until** button, enter the following code:

```
Private Sub cmdDoLoop_Click()
  'program to display products of 4 from 1 through 60

  Dim increment As Integer
  Dim result As Integer
  increment = 1
  Do
    'multiply the increment variable by 4
    result = increment * 4
    Form1.Print result
    Picture1.Print result
    'increment the variable
    increment = increment + 1
  Loop Until result >= 60
End Sub
```

4. Run the program.

Similar to the tracker exercise using For-Next loops (see Exercise 11.1), this code displays an increment of the products of four. The counter variable (entitled increment), however, must be incremented in the body of the loop. Alternatively, you could move the conditional clause to the top of the construct so that the code would read Do Until result >= 60, and the bottom of the construct would simply read Loop.

Exercise 11.7   Using *Do-Loop While*

How would you need to change the preceding code if you used While rather than Until? In this case, you would need to change the relational operator (from >= to <), so that the code fragment would read Loop While result < 60.

1. Use the same form as the one designed for Exercise 11.6, or create a new one.

2. Insert the following Do-Loop While instructions:

```
Do
  result = increment  *  4     ' multiply the increment variable
➥by 4
  Form1.Print result
  Picture1.Print result
  increment = increment + 1        ' increment the variable
Loop While result < 60
```

3. Run the program.

Like the Do-Until Loop, the While keyword can be placed at the top of the construct with the single word Loop placed at the bottom of the loop structure.

11.4.3   The *Exit-Do* Statement

The `Exit-Do` statement is an optional statement. It provides another way to exit a `Do` loop. The syntax for this statement is as follows:

```
Exit {Do ¦ For ¦ Function ¦ Sub}
```

When this statement is reached in a `Do` loop, control is transferred from the loop body to the statement that follows the `Loop` statement.

As a general rule, `Exit Do` always should be used with an `If` statement, as in the following example:

```
If Value >= 50000 Then
    Exit Do
End If
```

If the test condition in this example is `True` and the value is greater than `50000`, it leads to an exit from the `Do` loop.

If `Do` loops are nested, as in the following structure, then the `Exit Do` statement in the innermost `Do` loop transfers control to the statement `y = y + 1`, which follows `Loop Until x > 10`. `Exit Do` does not terminate the entire nested loop.

```
Do                              'Beginning of outer loop
   Do                           'Beginning of inner loop
      Exit Do                   'Exit from inner loop
   Loop Until x > 10            'End of inner loop
   y = y + 1
Loop Until y > 15               'End of outer loop
```

You can use `Exit Do` as a statement without qualification, or you can make it the `Then` branch of an `If...Then` statement. As an example, the code you have been writing can be changed to read:

```
Do
    result = increment  *  4  'multiply the increment variable by 4
    Form1.Print result
    Picture1.Print result
    increment = increment + 1 'increment the variable
    If result >= 60 Then
       Exit Do
    End If
Loop
```

Although this code works, be careful. Think of what would happen if you changed the code to read as follows:

```
Do
    If result <= 60 Then
       Exit Do
    End If
    result = increment * 4  ' multiply the increment variable by 4
    Form1.Print result
    Picture1.Print result
    increment = increment + 1 ' increment the variable
Loop
```

Because no result has been determined, the code does not know how to make the relational test. Nothing would be displayed, and the loop would end.

11.4.4   Overflow Errors and Infinite Loops

When working with loops, an incorrect setting of the test condition can lead to overflow errors. An uncontrolled loop in which the conditional test cannot be met will eventually reach some limit. For example, an integer counter variable might run past 32,767, and you will encounter an overflow error. Suppose that you changed the loop in Exercise 11.7 to read as follows:

```
Do
    result = increment * 4    ' multiply the increment variable by 4
    Form1.Print result
    Picture1.Print result
    increment = increment + 1 ' increment the variable
Loop While result >=  0
```

With this code, an overflow message is produced because the loop would eventually run past 32,767. With other data types, you might encounter a stack overflow error because you simply run out of memory. Depending on the size of your computer's memory and the speed of its processor, the time will vary before you get the overflow message.

Remember the following rule when working with Do loops: Make sure that you have an out. In writing the loop, write a statement that moves a condition closer and closer to meeting the requirements of the test condition.

Stack and variable overflows are one type of problem; an infinite loop is another. While writing loop constructs, you can write an infinite loop for which there is no exit other than using Ctrl+Break keys on the keyboard to escape. At times, you might even have to exit the application and lose unsaved work. So be certain that your loop contains a statement that will satisfy the test condition. For example, suppose that you thought you would use a loop to test repeatedly whether an inputted value is correct. You might, at first, write a procedure like the following in which Reply represents the input:

```
Do
    Reply = Val(Text1.text)
    If Reply > 1 And Reply < 10 Then
      MsgBox "Thank you"
      Exit Do
    Else MsgBox "That's incorrect"
    End If
Loop
```

What happens? If Reply is correct (the return value is True), then there is no problem. If the user enters an incorrect answer, however, you get the message box with the message That's incorrect. And you get it again, and again, and again. Eventually, you might need to reboot your computer because you can't escape the loop. As a rule, just stick with an If...Then...Else conditional test, rather than a Do loop.

11.4.5   Converting *For-Next* Loops to *Do* Loops

For-Next loops are good points of departure for practicing coding Do loops. Most For-Next loops can readily be converted to a Do-Loop structure; however, the counter variable found in the For-Next structure will have to be rewritten. The For-Next code used earlier in Exercise 11.2 looks like the following:

```
Private Sub cmdShow_Click()
   Dim FillNum As Integer

   For FillNum = 0 To 7
      Shape1(FillNum).FillStyle = FillNum
      Shape1(FillNum).Visible = True
   Next FillNum
End Sub
```

To convert this code to a Do-Loop structure, you must add your own increment instruction and place this instruction inside the loop, as follows:

```
Private Sub cmdShow_Click()
   Dim FillNum As Integer
   FillNum = 0
   Do
      Shape1(FillNum).FillStyle = FillNum
      Shape1(FillNum).Visible = True
      FillNum = FillNum + 1     'increment the variable
   Loop While FillNum <= 7
End Sub
```

Exercise 11.8   Changing a *For-Next* Structure to a *Do-Loop* Structure

The result is the same. Try it.

In this exercise, you convert a For-Next structure to a Do-Loop structure.

1. Add the array of shapes as shown in Figure 11.7.

2. Add the command buttons (**cmdShow**, **cmdEnd**), and add the captions shown in Figure 11.7. Write the cmdEnd_Click() event procedure.

3. Write the cmdShow_Click() procedure:

```
Private Sub cmdShow_Click()
   Dim FillNum As Integer
   FillNum = 0
   Do
      Shape1(FillNum).FillStyle = FillNum
      Shape1(FillNum).Visible = True
      FillNum = FillNum + 1     'increment the variable
   Loop While FillNum <= 7
End Sub
```

continues

Figure 11.7   *Display fill styles with a* Do-Loop.

4. Run and test your design.

What is different between this code and the previous code? The counter variable is incremented inside the loop body. With a For-Next loop, the counter variable is incremented when it reaches the Next FillNum statement.

Exercise 11.9   Using Nested *Do* Loops to Create the Mercury 1 Commemorative Launch

The first American in space, Alan Shepard, didn't orbit Earth. He just went up into space and splashed down into the Caribbean. To commemorate the flight, code an image of a rocket going into space and then floating down with a parachute attached. Use two Do loops with the inner loop nested inside the other. Figure 11.8 shows the form you are asked to create.

1. Use Paint, the bitmap editing software bundled with Windows. Under the Image menu, set the Attributes so that the image is 0.4 inches wide and one inch long.

2. Draw a rocket with the nose touching the top of the image frame at the center. Set the background color to a light blue.

3. Save the image twice in your Visual Basic subdirectory: once as **rocket.bmp** and again as **para.bmp**. Now edit para.bmp to add a parachute canopy with the parachute cords converging at the bottom of the image at the center. Use the same background color as rocket.bmp. Save the revised image.

Figure 11.8   *The Mercury 1 Commemorative Launch contains a rocket ready to launch and a parachute (hidden) that will return the rocket to the Earth.*

4. Return to Visual Basic, start a new project, and set the form properties to `Form1.Top = 0`, `Form1.Height = 7260`, and `Form1.Width = 6200`. Set the form background color the same as in your .BMP images.

5. Place two image controls on the form, each with a height of `1440` and a width of `570`. Name one **imgRocket** and the other **imgChute**.

6. In `imgRocket`, load the rocket.bmp image. (Double-click the `Picture` property on the property window.)

7. In `imgChute`, load the para.bmp image.

8. Set the `imgRocket.Left` property to `2760` and the `imgRocket.Top` property to `5520`.

9. Set the `imgChute.Left` property also to `2760` and its `Top` property to `-8800`. (It will disappear from the form but don't worry—it's still there.) Set the `imgChute.Visible` property to `False`.

10. Draw a button to the right of the rocket image, and add the caption **Launch and Return**.

continues

Exercise 11.9   continued

11. Write the following code for the cmdLaunch_Click() event:

```
Private Sub cmdLaunch_Click()
  Dim counter As Integer
  cmdLaunch.Enabled = False      ' prevent multiple launches
  counter = 0
  Do
     Do
        imgRocket.Top = imgRocket.Top - 2 ' ascend at rapid
➥rate
        Loop Until imgRocket.Top <= -7360     ' top of imgRocket is
➥at the
                                              ' bottom of imgChute
                                              ' -8800(imgChute.Top)
+
' 1440(height of images)

        imgChute.Visible = True                ' show the parachute

        Do
         imgChute.Top = imgChute.Top + 1
         imgRocket.Top = imgRocket.Top + 1 ' descend at a slower
➥rate
        Loop Until imgRocket.Top >= 5520       ' stop when rocket
➥lands at
                                               ' original position

        imgChute.Visible = False            ' make parachute
➥disappear
        imgChute.Top = -8800                ' move it back off of
➥form
        counter = counter + 1               ' increment the counter
     Loop Until counter = 1              ' limit loop to 1 iteration,
                                         ' reset if you like

     cmdLaunch.Enabled = True               ' permit another launch
  End Sub
```

Review what you coded. This is very similar to the Moonrise, except that this time you have two Do-Loop inner structures nested within an outer Do-Loop structure. When cmdLaunch is clicked, you disable it. This prevents the user from clicking multiple times and relaunching the code. The first loop is executed, and imgRocket ascends at a rate of 2 twips per cycle. The loop is exited, and the Visible property of imgChute switched to True.

You enter the second loop, at which point imgRocket and imgChute descend at a slow rate because with every cycle they only descend by 1 twip. Once the rocket lands, the imgChute Visible property is switched to False and reset to its original position. The command button, cmdLaunch, is enabled to permit the user to relaunch.

Both inner loops are placed within a larger loop with a counter to provide for several launchings of the rocket. If you only wanted Alan Shepard to go into space once, you would remove this outer loop.

12. Run the program. Depending on your computer's processor and graphics system, the rocket will ascend or descend at different speeds. Adjust the code to suit your machine.

13. Save the program because you will come back to it in Exercise 11.11.

Objective 11.5 Understanding How *While-Wend* Loops Work

Besides the four forms of the Do loop, Visual Basic supports a While-Wend statement. The syntax for this statement is as follows:

```
While condition
   [statements]
Wend
```

This format is sometimes favored in place of the Do-While Loop statement; however, the latter does provide more flexibility. There is no corresponding Exit While to permit an immediate exit from the loop. As an example of this syntax, consider the following code:

```
count = 0
While count < 20
   Print "Hello! How are you today?"
   count = count + 1
Wend
```

Like Do-While Loop structures, the counter variable should be initialized prior to entry into the loop body. Within the loop body, the counter variable is incremented (or decremented) in order to eventually satisfy the test condition.

Objective 11.6 Adding the Timer Control to a Project

Visual Basic has a built-in control that cycles repetitively named the Timer control, which can sometimes be used instead of a loop logical structure, especially when you want to control precisely the timing of the executed code.

The important thing to remember about the Timer control is that it is periodic. The code placed in the Timer() event will continue to execute until the control is disabled. The Timer control doesn't appear during runtime, so don't worry about its placement on the form.

11.6.1 The *Interval* Property

If you inspect the properties of the Timer control, you will discover that there are very few. You will generally adjust the Interval property, for which the syntax is as follows:

```
[form.]timer.Interval [= milliseconds]
```

Table 11.2 shows the settings for milliseconds.

TABLE 11.2 *Milliseconds* Settings

Setting	Description
0	Disables the Timer (the default).
1 to 65535	Sets the number of milliseconds between calls to the Timer. 10,000 milliseconds equals 10 seconds.

Thus, the following instruction tells the Timer to fire every 10 seconds:

```
Timer.Interval = 10000
```

The Timer continues to fire until it is disabled, as discussed next.

11.6.2   The *Enabled* Property

The second property of great importance to the Timer control is the Enabled property. The Timer is disabled by the setting:

```
Timer.Enabled = False
```

This action suspends the countdown set by the Interval property. Changing the setting to True resumes the countdown set by the Interval property, as follows:

```
Timer.Enabled = True
```

Exercise 11.10   Setting the Timer

Before adding a timer to the Mercury 1 Commemorative Launch, use the Timer control. Figure 11.9 shows the form you are asked to design.

Figure 11.9   *For this exercise, the timer will keep running until it is disabled.*

1. Draw a form with a picture box and the two command buttons (**cmdTime** and **cmdClear**). Add a caption to the form and to all buttons.

2. Double-click the Timer control to add the timer to the form.

3. Go to the Timer1 property box. Set the Enabled property to False, which turns the timer off.

4. The Interval property determines at what frequency the code in the Timer() event will be executed. The interval is divided into thousandths of a second. To have the Timer() event execute the code every second, set the Interval property to 1000.

5. Enter the following in the Click() event for the cmdClear button:

```
Private Sub cmdClear_Click()
  Picture1.Cls
  '  timer1.Enabled = False  ' be sure this line is commented
out at first
End Sub
```

6. Enter the following in the Click() event for the cmdTime button:

```
Private Sub cmdTime_Click()
  timer1.Enabled = True
End Sub
```

In this code the timer is turned on. It remains on until it is disabled.

7. Double-click the Timer control, and the Timer1_Timer() event will appear. Enter the following:

```
Private Sub Timer1_Timer()
  Picture1.Print "The timer control has fired"
End Sub
```

8. Run the program.

9. Now change the Clear button's Click() event code to disable the timer. The revised code is as follows:

```
Private Sub cmdClear_Click()
  Picture1.Cls
  timer1.Enabled = False  ' instruction is no longer commented
out
End Sub
```

10. Run the program again. You should now have a greater feeling of control.

When using the Timer control, you will usually set its Enabled property to False during design-time, and enable it or disable it with code.

Remember that conditional loops do not affect underlying property assignments. Consider the following code:

```
Private Sub cmdTime_Click()
Dim count as integer
count = 1
While count < 20
timer1.Enabled = True
count = count + 1
Wend
End Sub
```

When you first look at this code, you might think that the Enabled property for the timer will be True only while the count variable is < 20. But object properties are only changed by direct assignments, such as the assignment timer1.Enabled = False in the cmdClear_Click() event.

Now use a `Timer()` event so Mercury 1 can get a proper countdown and blastoff.
Figure 11.10 shows the form you are asked to design.

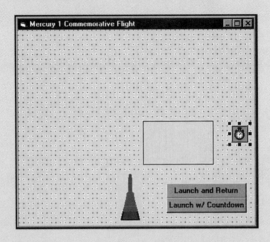

Figure 11.10   *This revised Mercury 1 launch design contains a* Timer *control that displays a
countdown before launching.*

1. Add a `Timer` control to the form, and add a second button below the
   `Launch and Return` button with the caption **Launch w/ Countdown**.

2. Add a label about 1.5 inches wide above the buttons. This area will display the countdown messages. Name the label **lblCountDown**.

3. Place a border around the label, and give it the same background color as
   the form.

4. Because the label display will be controlled by the `Timer()` event, set its
   `Visible` property to `False`. You will make it visible when you need to display the countdown, and make it invisible when you don't.

5. Set the `Enabled` property of the `Timer` control to `False`. Set the `Interval`
   property to one second (enter `1000`).

6. You will need an additional variable. Call it `Countdown`, and declare it at
   the module level. Enter the following in the General declarations window
   of the form module:

   ```
   Dim Countdown as Integer
   ```

7. Enter the following code in the `Timer1_Timer()` event:

```
Private Sub Timer1_Timer()
    lblCountDown.Visible = True        ' make countdown display visible
    lblCountDown.Caption = 10 - Countdown

    If Countdown = 10 Then
        lblCountDown.Caption = 10 - Countdown & " WE HAVE IGNITION!"
    ElseIf Countdown = 11 Then
        lblCountDown.Caption = "Blastoff!"
    ElseIf Countdown = 12 Then
        lblCountDown.Visible = False   ' make countdown display
        ➥invisible
        lblCountDown.Caption = ""          ' clear display for subsequent
                                           ' launches
        Timer1.Enabled = False     ' turn off the timer event
        Call cmdLaunch_Click()     ' call the procedure to launch
        ➥rocket
    End If

    Countdown = Countdown + 1          ' increment variable
End Sub
```

Examine these instructions. Once per second the `Timer1_Timer()` event occurs, and `lblCountDown` displays the difference of `10 - Countdown`. Once per second the `Countdown` variable value is also increased by 1. When `Countdown` reaches 10, `lblCountDown` displays 0 (`10 - Countdown`) and adds an encouraging message. When `Countdown` reaches 11, `Blastoff` is displayed (instead of -1). When `Countdown` reaches 12, `lblCountDown` is made invisible and the caption cleared. `Timer1` is disabled and the launch procedure is initiated by calling the `cmdLaunch_Click()` event.

8. So what do you need to add to the Countdown button `Click()` event? Only the following two instructions:

```
Private Sub cmdCount_Click()
    Countdown = 0
    Timer1.Enabled = True
End Sub
```

Remember that after the first launch, the `Countdown` variable now equals 12. By setting it to 0 every time the Countdown button is pushed, you ensure that the `Timer1_Timer()` event will start the countdown at 10.

continues

9. Next, for consistency's sake, disable both launch buttons when the Countdown button is clicked, and enable them both after the rocket has landed. Modify the cmdCount_Click() procedure to read as follows:

```
Private Sub cmdCount_Click()
   cmdLaunch.Enabled = False
   cmdCount.Enabled = False
   Countdown = 0
   Timer1.Enabled = True
End Sub
```

10. The following code should be added to the cmdLaunch_Click() event right below where cmdLaunch itself is enabled again:

```
cmdCount.Enabled = True
```

Examine the earlier code to determine this position.

Chapter Summary

This chapter addresses several topics critical to the study of Visual Basic. It discusses the meaning of a loop and demonstrates how code can be written to execute in cycles. To perform this type of processing, the For-Next syntax must be understood. In review, this syntax is as follows:

```
For counter = start To end [Step step]
    [statements block 1]
    [Exit For]
    [statements block 2]
Next [counter]
```

Besides a counter variable, the syntax must include start and end values and the keyword Next, which signals the end of the loop. Observe that the entire statement block is optional. When you wrote the sleep loop to slow the program, no statements appeared within the body of the loop. Remember that a loop counter can be incremented or decremented. To decrement a counter, begin with the highest value, and subtract from this value using a negative step increment.

The concept of a control array is perhaps the most difficult conceptual topic presented. Keep this concept in the back of your mind: *a control array is nothing more than a group of objects with the same name.* To help you, Visual Basic provides the index number for each object within the group. You can place more than one control array on a design. For example, you might have a control array of text boxes and another control array of list boxes.

A nested For-Next loop is nothing more than one For-Next loop placed inside another. Even so, remember how iteration works. The innermost loop must complete its entire execution before control is passed to the next outer loop. There is no limit on the number of nested loops that you can use; however, going beyond three might make your code difficult to read.

The DoEvents statement enables an event to be completed before the next event is started. The DoEvents statement passes control to Windows and enables windows messages to be processed before executing the next line of code.

The Exit-For statement is used to exit a loop before all iterations have been completed. Most often, a test condition is written to determine if it is time to exit a loop. The exit itself is for the immediate loop only.

The coordinate system in Visual Basic defines x and y positions on the display screen, with x = 0 and y = 0 set as the defaults in the upper-left corner of the display screen. Objects are moved using a unit of measurement called a twip (1,440 twips equals one inch). The Left and Top properties are used to move an object.

The two syntax options for Do loops are as follows:

- **Option 1**—In the following code, the conditional test is at the beginning of the Do-Loop structure:

```
Do [{While ¦ Until} condition]
    [statements block 1]
    [Exit Do]
    [statements block 2]
Loop
```

- **Option 2**—In the following code, the conditional test is at the end of the Do-Loop structure:

```
Do
    [statements block 1]
    [Exit Do]
    [statements block 2]
Loop [{While ¦ Until} condition]
```

With the first option, the body of the loop need not be executed at all if the test condition is False to begin with (using the Do-While Loop), or if the test condition is True to begin with (using the Do-Until Loop). With Do-Loop While or Do-Loop Until, the body of the loop is executed at least once.

The While-Wend loop is another type of loop structure. The loop body of this structure continues to be executed until the test condition becomes False.

The Timer control is sometimes used instead of a loop structure. The Timer control is periodic: It fires during a specified interval and is turned on and off by the Timer.Enabled property or by setting the Interval property to 0. The Timer_Timer() procedure (see Exercise 11.10) is often used to control the actions taken each time the timer is fired.

Skill-Building Exercises

This set of skill-building exercises asks you to expand on a number of problems presented in the chapter. Some of the exercises ask you to convert from a Do-Loop to For-Next structures, while others combine graphics methods from Chapter 5 with loops. Skill-Building Exercise 5 asks you to extend the Mercury 1 Commemorative Launch program by adding scroll bars to control the speed of the launch.

1. Write a program to rotate the fill shapes that are shown earlier in this chapter in Figure 11.3. Make three rounds in all, visiting each fill style three times. Do the following:

   a. Make each shape style visible, and keep it visible using a go-to-sleep loop.

   b. Make each shape style invisible, and keep it invisible using a go-to-sleep loop.

   c. Use `DoEvents` to enable completion of each nested loop.

2. Modify Exercise 11.3 to display the following pattern:

   ```
   10    8    6    4    2
   10    8    6    4
   10    8    6
   10    8
   10
   ```

   In your design, use five list boxes. Use nested loops in your solution. Add a `DoEvents` instruction.

3. Write a program using `Do` loops that displays numbers from 1 to 10 raised to the second power. The output should look as follows:

   ```
   Number raised
   to the 2nd power is

   1                                          2
   2                                          4
   ```

   Continue this pattern to number 10. Display the numbers on the form and the results in a picture box.

4. Change the code in the Moonrise program so that it uses a `Do-Loop` structure rather than a `For-Next` structure.

5. Using a combination of `Do` loops and `If...Then` logic, add two scroll bar controls to the Mercury 1 Commemorative Launch program that enable the users to control the speed of ascent and descent. Also add a check box or option button that enables them to control how many times the rocket will launch. (You will need to add several extra variables.)

6. Place a 3000 x 3000 twip picture box on a form. In a button click event use the PSet graphic method (see Chapter 5) and nested `Do loops` to create a grid of dots on the picture box. Each dot should be separated by 200 twips. The effect should be similar to that of the positioning grid of a Visual Basic form during design time. Also add a button click event to clear the graphic output on the picture box.

7. Using the same interface as in the previous skill building exercise, use a `Do Loop` and the `Line` method to create a button click event which causes two 4 pixel wide lines (see `DrawWidth` property) to be drawn on the picture box simultaneously (refer to Chapter 5, "Introduction to the Graphic Controls and Graphic Methods of Visual Basic"). One line (in Blue) should start in the upper-left corner and be drawn to the lower-right corner. The other line (in Red) should

PROGRAMMING USER EVENTS

Thus far, you have used a small number of user events, mostly the clicking of buttons, selecting from list box and combo box items, and selecting from menu commands. Visual Basic makes available an assortment of other user events, including keyboard actions and mouse events, such as dragging and dropping icons. Many users prefer highly graphical environments and the visual cues such environments provide. This chapter explores how to better exploit this environment by introducing several new types of user events.

The following sections concentrate on new keyboard and mouse events—the principal actions for receiving user input. New keyboard events include `KeyUp()`, `KeyDown()`, and `KeyPress()`. New mouse events include `MouseDown()`, `MouseUp()`, `MouseMove()`, `DragOver()`, and `DragDrop()`. These keyboard and mouse events are shared by many controls, and their differences are discussed here.

The tasks in this chapter involve employing various user events in your programming. By the end of this chapter, you will be able to do the following:

- Know how to trap individual keys using the `KeyUp()`, `KeyDown()`, and `KeyPress()` events

- Know how to trap key combinations, such as Ctrl+F12 or Alt+Y

- Understand the different built-in mouse procedure arguments

- Know how to use `MouseDown()`, `MouseUp()`, and `MouseMove()` events

- Understand and use the `Drag` method

- Understand and use the `DragOver()` event

- Understand and use the `DragDrop()` event

Chapter Objectives

The objectives for this chapter address the three sets of user events: keyboard events and two types of mouse events.

Common mouse events involve clicking the mouse button and moving the mouse, which lead to MouseDown(), MouseUp(), and MouseMove(), respectively. More advanced and interesting mouse events include DragOver(), when you drag the mouse over an object, and DragDrop(), when you drag the mouse to an object and release the mouse button. These issues and others are addressed in the following three objectives for this chapter:

1. Understanding KeyPress(), KeyUp(), and KeyDown() events

2. Working with mouse events

3. Understanding Drag() and DragDrop() events

Objective 12.1   Understanding *KeyPress()*, *KeyUp()*, and *KeyDown()* Events

The keyboard events in Visual Basic enable you to capture just about any single key or key combination. In the Windows development environment, it is standard design practice to provide the user with a variety of methods for performing the same action. Frequently used menu commands should be provided with keyboard actions known as *shortcut keys*. Some applications also should provide the user with a toolbar of icons to perform frequently used functions. This section shows you how to capture keyboard events that are not provided by shortcut keys designated in the Menu Editor.

12.1.1   The Form *KeyPreview* Property

The different key events can be confusing at first, but they share one thing in common: They work only on the object that has the current focus. The object of focus for keyboard events is usually a control, such as a text box or a combo box. A form, in general, can only have the focus if it is either blank or all controls are disabled. If you want to add a key event for a form, you need to set the form's KeyPreview property to True. The form then will receive keyboard events before any control on the form control does. This is especially useful if you want to have certain keys perform the same action, no matter which control has the current focus. Such keys might be F10 for saving a file, or the key combination Alt+X for exiting a program. This does not, however, apply if you have used these keys as shortcut keys in the Menu Editor window.

12.1.2   *KeyPress()* Versus *KeyDown()* and *KeyUp()* Events

Two types of events that are similar are KeyPress() and KeyDown() (or KeyUp()). A KeyPress() occurs when a key corresponding to an ASCII character is pressed. Use

Visual Basic Help to inspect this character set. KeyDown() and KeyUp() events occur as any key on the keyboard is pressed and released. The following difference between these two types of events is subtle, but important:

- A KeyPress() event supplies a generated character when a key is pressed and an event is triggered when that character is recognized in code.

- KeyDown() and KeyUp() events are triggered by the physical key on the keyboard itself, not by an ASCII generated character. To interpret the event, you must supply the code to do it.

KeyDown() and KeyUp() events have two arguments: KeyCode and Shift. If you press an uppercase K or a lowercase k, the KeyDown() event would get the same KeyCode. The event indicates that it was the physical key itself that was pressed. The argument Shift provides the Shift key state. By examining it, the computer can determine which shift key (Shift, Crtl, Alt) was depressed simultaneously with the key represented by the KeyCode argument.

KeyUp() and KeyDown() can capture more keys of the keyboard than a KeyPress() event because the ASCII code is limited by a 0 to 127 character set. By using the built-in KeyCode constants, however, there is little that you cannot capture. There are over 90 KeyCode constants, with the full list of constants provided in Visual Basic's online Help. KeyCode constants are provided for special keys on the keyboard, all numeric keys, all letters of the alphabet, all keys on the numeric keypad, and all function keys. Table 12.1 shows examples of KeyCode constants.

TABLE 12.1   Examples of *KeyCode* Constants

Constant	Value	Description
vbKeyBack	8	Backspace key
vbKeyTab	9	Tab key
vbKeyClear	12	Clear key
vbKeyReturn	13	Enter key
vbKeyShift	16	Shift key
vbKeyCapital	20	Caps Lock key
vbKeyEscape	27	Esc key
vbKeySpace	32	Spacebar key
vbKeyDelete	46	Del key
vbKeyA	65	The letter A key (same as ASCII)
vbKey0	48	The number 0 key (same as ASCII)
vbKey1	49	The number 1 key (same as ASCII)
vbKeyNumpad4	100	The 4 key on the numeric pad
vbKeyMultiply	106	Multiplication (*) key on the numeric pad
vbKeyF1	112	F1 key
vbKeyF2	113	F2 key

The KeyPress() event has only one argument: KeyAscii. For example, the code for a command button KeyPress() event would read as follows:

```
Command1_KeyPress(KeyAscii As Integer)
```

It treats an uppercase K and a lowercase k as two separate characters. It can handle all number and letter keys, punctuation keys, and a few special keys, such as the Esc key (unless a command button has the Cancel property set to True), the Backspace key, and the Enter key (unless there is a command button with Default set to True).

Which event should you use? The obvious answer is to use KeyDown() and KeyUp() for handling keys the KeyPress() event can't. These include arrow (directional) keys, Page Up and Page Down, numeric keypad keys, and function keys not used by the menu commands. You can also use KeyDown() and KeyUp() if you want to know when a key is being held down and when it is released, such as in certain graphics programs.

One way to become familiar with the difference between the two events is to simply enter the following code in the KeyPress() event and experiment with different keys, as in the following:

```
Print Chr(KeyAscii)
```

Next, comment out the code in the KeyPress() event, enter the following code in the KeyDown() event, and continue the experiment with the following:

```
Print Chr(KeyCode)
```

Compare how upper- and lowercase keys are handled by the two events.

Exercise 12.1 Using the Return Key

The Return key has the ASCII value 13 and is used to trigger events in text-based controls after the user has completed input. Filling out an online data entry form, for example, frequently requires this type of event. A benefit of using the vbKeyReturn event is that it avoids the need for a command button to trigger an event.

1. Place a text box and a label on a form (see Figure 12.1). Name the text box **txtKeyPress** and the label **lblKeyPress**. Set the text MultiLine value to True.

2. In the txtKeyPress_KeyPress() event, enter the following code:
   ```
   If KeyAscii = vbKeyReturn Then
       lblKeyPress.Caption = txtKeyPress.Text
   End If
   ```

3. Place some sample text in the text box and press the Enter key.

4. Add a command button to the form and set its Default property to True. Write no code for this control.

5. Run the program by typing in text and pressing the Enter key. Surprised? The text will not be displayed. When the button is set to True, it becomes the default Command button.

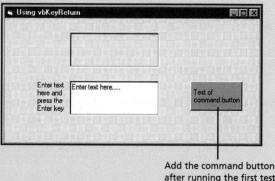

Add the command button
after running the first test.

Figure 12.1 *The* vbKeyReturn *constant enables the user to press the Enter key to place text on the label.*

6. Change the Default property of the command button back to False, type in text a third time and press Enter. Note the difference in program behavior.

Exercise 12.2   Using a Function Key as a Menu Shortcut Key

This exercise is similar to the preceding one, but demonstrates the use of a function key coupled with the KeyDown() event.

1. With the form from Exercise 12.1 still onscreen, change the KeyPreview property of the form to True.

2. In the Form_KeyDown() event, enter the following code:

```
Private Sub Form_KeyDown (Keycode As Integer, Shift As Integer)
   If Keycode = vbKeyF12 Then End
End Sub
```

3. Start the program, enter some text into the text box, press Enter, and then press F12. You exit the program.

4. In Design mode, change the form's KeyPreview property back to False, and try it. This time it doesn't work because txtKeyPress has the focus and the program can't read F12.

5. Run and test your program.

Objective 12.2   Working with Mouse Events

Mouse events provide the Visual Basic developer enormous flexibility in making an application easy to use. Forms and certain controls, such as picture boxes and images, can detect the position and state of the mouse button.

12.2.1   The Mouse Events

A form recognizes a mouse event when the pointer is over a part of the form with no controls. Most controls can recognize a mouse event when the pointer is over the control. Other than drag-and-drop events (which are addressed later in Objective 12.3, "Understanding *Drag()* and *DragDrop()* Events"), the mouse has the following three events:

- **MouseMove()**—Occurs whenever the mouse pointer is moved to a new point onscreen.

- **MouseUp()**—Occurs when the user releases any mouse button.

- **MouseDown()**—Occurs when the user presses any mouse button.

These mouse events have four arguments: Button, Shift, X, and Y (see Table 12.2). The syntax reads as follows:

```
Command1_MouseDown(Button As Integer, Shift As Integer, X As Single, Y
➥As Single)
```

TABLE 12.2   Mouse Event Arguments

Component	Description
Button	Refers to the specific mouse button pressed (left, right, or middle)
Shift	Refers to the state of the Shift, Alt, and Ctrl keys
X and Y	Refer to the coordinates of the form or control to which the mouse pointer is pointing

A MouseMove() event over a control does not trigger a simultaneous MouseMove() event on the underlying form.

Exercise 12.3   Using the Move Method with a *MouseDown()* Event

In this exercise, you move an image placed on a form, using the mouse Move method. Figure 12.2 shows the interface.

1. Embed an icon, such as that of a small house, in an image control placed on a form. Name the control **imgHouse**.

2. Enter the following code into the `Form_MouseDown()` event:

```
Private Sub Form_MouseDown(Button As Integer, Shift As Integer,
➡X As Single, Y As Single)
    Dim xadjust, yadjust As Integer
    xadjust = imgHouse.Width \ 2
    yadjust = imgHouse.Height \ 2
    imgHouse.Move X - xadjust, Y - yadjust
End Sub
```

Figure 12.2   *An icon image is placed on the form and moved from one location to another using the mouse.*

3. Run the program. By this simple reference to the mouse pointer's x and y coordinates, you can position a control anywhere you want on the form. Because the `Move` method places the upper-left corner of the control at the x and y coordinates, you can center the image by employing the adjustment variables you see in the procedure.

Exercise 12.4   Using the *MouseMove()* Event

This exercise asks you to create a design that continues to trigger a continuous event as the mouse is moved. Figure 12.3 shows the design interface.

Figure 12.3   *The* `MouseMove()` *event enables the user to draw on the form.*

continues

Exercise 12.4   continued

1. Place a shape on the form and enter the following code into the `Form_MouseMove()` event:

```
Private Sub Form_MouseMove (Button As Integer, Shift As
Integer, X As Single, Y  As Single)
   shp1.Left = X + 500
   shp1.Top = Y - 500
End Sub
```

2. Run the program to watch the `MouseMove()` event operate continuously as the mouse is moved. This means that the computer is recognizing many separate events in quick succession. It is prudent to avoid this event for something that requires a great deal of computing time.

3. Add the following line of code to the preceding `Form_MouseMove()` event:

```
Form1.Circle (X,Y), 40
```

This code fragment employs the graphic method `Circle` and illustrates the frequency with which circles are drawn by the `MouseMove()` event. Experiment by moving the mouse pointer both quickly and slowly.

12.2.2   The *Button* Argument with Mouse Events

As shown earlier in Table 12.2, the `Button` argument in mouse events refers to the left, middle, or right mouse buttons. These buttons can be identified by referencing the built-in constants in the `Button` argument shown in Table 12.3.

TABLE 12.3   *Button* Argument Constants

Constant	Value	Description
vbKeyLButton	0x1	Left mouse button
vbKeyRButton	0x2	Right mouse button
vbKeyMButton	0x4	Middle mouse button

In `MouseUp()` and `MouseDown()` events, you can only test for one button at a time. In `MouseMove()` events, however, you can test to see whether more than one button is being used.

Exercise 12.5   Coding a *MouseUp()* Event

This short exercise asks you to experiment with the MouseUp() event.

1. On a new form, enter the following code for Form_MouseUp() event:

```
Select Case Button
    Case vbKeyLButton
      Print "You released the left mouse button"
    Case vbKeyRButton
      Print "You released the right mouse button"
End Select
```

2. Run the program.

3. If you press more than one button, Visual Basic interprets it as two events. Try it.

Continue with the next exercise.

Exercise 12.6   Coding a *MouseMove()* Event

Use the same interface as in Exercise 12.5, but replace the MouseUp() event with a MouseMove() event. The three built-in constants for the mouse buttons are as before:

Left mouse button = 1

Right mouse button = 2

Middle mouse button = 4

If you want to test for mouse buttons depressed simultaneously, you can add these constants. If the left and right buttons were depressed at the same time, for example, you could test for the button value 3.

1. Comment out the code in the MouseUp() event provided for the last exercise.

2. Enter the following code into the Form_MouseMove() event:

```
Private Sub Form_MouseMove(Button As Integer, Shift As Integer,
➥X As Single, Y As Single)
    Select Case Button
        Case vbKeyLButton
            Circle (X, Y), 40
        Case vbKeyRButton
            Circle (X, Y), 80
        Case vbKeyLButton + vbKeyRButton
            Circle (X, Y), 120
    End Select
End Sub
```

3. Run the program. Unlike MouseUp() and MouseDown() events, pressing the left and right buttons together causes a separate event.

Objective 12.3 Understanding *Drag()* and *DragDrop()* Events

In program design, you can drag controls in Visual Basic; that is, the user can hold the mouse button down and move (drag) a control. When the mouse button is released, the control is dropped.

Drag-and-drop events have both a source and a target. The source is the control that is being dragged. The target is the form (or control) over which the source is being dragged or upon which the source is being dropped.

12.3.1 Drag-and-Drop Elements

Properties, events, and methods control drag-and-drop operations, as shown in Table 12.4.

TABLE 12.4 Drag-and-Drop Elements

Element	Description
Properties	
DragMode	Enables automatic or manual dragging of an icon
DragIcon	Identifies which icon is displayed when the control is dragged
Events	
DragDrop()	Recognizes when a control is dropped onto an object (a target event)
DragOver()	Recognizes when a control is dragged over an object (a target event)
Method	
Drag	Starts or stops manual dragging (typically a Source method)

The easiest way to enable dragging is to set the Source control's DragMode property to Automatic in the Property Manager window. This indicates that the Source control can always be dragged. However, it does not mean that the control's position will be permanently moved: A move has to be coded separately.

12.3.2 The *DragOver()* Event

The DragOver() event is a target event. It is coded for objects over which you expect to be dragging other objects. The DragOver() event has the following syntax:

```
Command1_DragOver(Source As Control, X As Single, Y As Single, State As
➥Integer)
```

Table 12.5 explains the components of the DragOver() event syntax.

TABLE 12.5 *DragOver()* Event Syntax

Component	Description
Control	The generic object reference used by the Source argument. Visual Basic passes the control that is being dragged over the target object.
State	Refers to the status of the source object.
X and Y	Refer to the current mouse pointer position over the target object.

The State argument has the values shown in Table 12.6.

TABLE 12.6 *State* Argument Values

Constant	Value	Description
vbEnter	0	Source control dragged into target
vbLeave	1	Source control dragged out of target
vbOver	2	Source control dragged from one position in target to another

Exercise 12.7   Coding a *DragOver()* Event

This exercise and the next ask you to use the same display form (see Figure 12.4). Objects on the form include three image controls and a command button. Their names are **imgCloud**, **imgCat**, **imgSun**, and **cmdReset**, respectively.

Figure 12.4   *Drag the cloud or the sun over the cat to reveal a message.*

continues

1. In the cmdReset_Click() event, enter the following code:

```
imgCat.Visible = True
imgCloud.Visible = True
imgSun.Visible = True
Form1.Cls
```

2. Set the DragMode property in imgSun and imgCloud to Automatic.

3. In the imgCat_DragOver() event, enter the following code:

```
Private Sub imgCat_DragOver(Source As Control, X As Single,
➥Y As Single, State As Integer)
"
   Const ENTER = 0
   Const LEAVE = 1

   Select Case Source
      Case imgCloud
         If State = ENTER Then
            Print "Meow, Yuk, It's rain!"
            'Make sun disappear
            imgSun.Visible = False
         ElseIf State = LEAVE Then
            'Make sun reappear"
            imgSun.Visible = True
            Print "Meow, Ah there's the sun!"
         End If

      Case imgSun
         If State = ENTER Then
            Print "Meow, It's getting warm; I need water!"
            'Make cloud disappear
            imgCloud.Visible = False
         ElseIf State = LEAVE Then
            'Make cloud reappear"
            imgCloud.Visible = True
            Print "Meow, Ah there's a cloud!"
         End If
   End Select
End Sub
```

4. Run and test the program. Save it: It will be used in the next exercise.

12.3.3   The *DragDrop()* Event

The DragDrop() event also is a target event and is generated when one object is dropped on another. It is triggered when the user drags an object with the mouse button depressed and then drops it by releasing the mouse button. The syntax is as follows:

```
Image1_DragDrop(Source As Control, X As Single, Y As Single)
```

The Source and X and Y arguments for this event are the same as those for the DragOver() event (refer to Table 12.5).

Exercise 12.8   Coding a *DragDrop()* Event

In this exercise, you are asked to drag an object over another object and release the mouse button to give the impression that the object has been dropped into a container of some type. The container object might be a trash can icon, a file icon, or a mailbox icon. Use the same design interface as in Exercise 12.7.

1. In the `imgCat_DragDrop()` event, enter the following code:

```
Select Case Source
    Case imgCloud
        Print "I'm wet, this cat's going to scat"
        imgCat.Visible = False
    Case imgSun
        Print "Ouch, That's hot! This cat's going to scat"
        imgCat.Visible = False
End Select
```

2. Run and test the program.

12.3.4   Using the *Drag* Method

To have more precise control over when you can drag a control, you can change the `DragMode` property setting to Manual. Dragging the control then needs to be explicitly enabled by employing the `Drag` method. The syntax for the method is as follows:

```
object.Drag action
```

Object is a control that you can drag, and action is a method argument that specifies the action to perform. If action is omitted, the default is to begin dragging the object. The `.Drag` action settings are described in Table 12.7.

TABLE 12.7   Drag Action Settings

Constant	Value	Description
vbCancel	0	Cancels drag operation
vbBeginDrag	1	Begins dragging control
vbEndDrag	2	Drops control

Exercise 12.9   Using the *Drag* Method

This exercise illustrates use of the Drag method. Create the interface shown in Figure 12.5. The interface includes a list box named lstDocs, an image with a trash can icon embedded in it named imgTrash, and a label aligned with the bottom of the form named lblStatus.

Figure 12.5   *This exercise enables you to drag an item from the list box and drop it into the trash can.*

1. In the Drag icon property for lstDocs, embed an image similar to that shown in Figure 12.6.

Figure 12.6   *The Drag icon image appears when you drag an item to the trash can.*

2. Set the DragMode property of lstDocs to Manual.

3. In the Form_Load() event, add the following code:

```
Private Sub Form_Load()
   Dim n As Integer
   For n = 1 To 10
      lstDocs.AddItem "Draft" & Str$(n) & ".doc"
   Next
End Sub
```

4. In the lstDocs_MouseMove() event, enter the following code:

```
Private Sub lstDocs_MouseMove(Button As Integer, Shift As
➥Integer, X As Single, Y As Single)
   Select Case Button
     Case vbKeyLButton
        If X > (lstDocs.Width - 100) Then lstDocs.Drag
vbBeginDrag
   End Select
End Sub
```

5. In the lstDocs_MouseUp() event, enter the following code:

```
lstDocs.Drag vbEndDrag
```

6. In the `imgTrash_DragDrop()` event, enter the following code:

```
Private Sub imgTrash_DragDrop(Source As Control, X As Single,
➥Y As Single)
    If TypeOf Source Is ListBox Then
    lblStatus.Caption = Source.List(Source.ListIndex) & " has been
➥removed"
        Source.RemoveItem (Source.ListIndex)
    Else
        lblStatus.Caption = "Unrecognized control."
    End If
    lstDocs.Drag vbEndDrag
End Sub
```

7. Run and test the program.

Two sections of this code merit special comment. In the `Mouse_Move()` event for `lstDocs`, the code tests to see whether the left mouse button is depressed. If this test evaluates to `True` and the mouse pointer comes within 100 twips of the right edge of the list box, dragging is enabled.

In the `imgTrash_DragDrop()` event, the generic object reference `Control` is used. Visual Basic passes to the `DragDrop()` event the control that is being dropped. The `TypeOf` argument in an `If...Then` statement tests for object type.

Chapter Summary

In this chapter, you worked with a broader range of user events than you have in earlier chapters. These included capturing individual keys with `KeyPress()`, `KeyUp()`, and `KeyDown()` events and exploiting the rich variety of mouse events built into Visual Basic.

The `KeyPress()` event captures ASCII generated characters, while `KeyDown()` and `KeyUp()` events capture the physical key itself. `KeyUp()` and `KeyDown()` events capture more keyboard keys than the `KeyPress()` event, which is limited to keyboard keys that generate ASCII characters. To add a shortcut key to your application that is not on the form menu bar, set the form's `KeyPreview` property to `True`. On data entry forms, you can capture the user pressing the Return key by using the `KeyPress()` event and the `vbKeyReturn` key constant. When doing this, make sure that no command button on the form has its `Default` property set to `True`.

Mouse events in Visual Basic include `MouseDown()`, `MouseUp()`, and `MouseMove()`. These events have four built-in arguments: `Button`, `Shift`, `X`, and `Y`. They enable a wide range of mouse actions to be coded, including mouse button clicks in combination with `Shift` arguments (Shift, Ctrl, and Alt keys) and mouse clicks in defined areas using `X` and `Y` arguments.

Drag events include the `DragOver()` and `DragDrop()` events. These events include both a source and a target and also have built-in arguments. The `DragOver()` event arguments include Source, X, Y, and State. These enable you to detect which specific control is being dragged over a target, the location of the mouse pointer as the control is being dragged, and the point at which the mouse pointer enters the target, is over the target, and is leaving the target.

The DragDrop() event's three arguments—Source, X, and Y—enable detection of which control is being dropped upon a target and the position of the mouse pointer as a control is dropped. To have explicit control over when Source controls can be dragged, the program designer can set the Source control's DragMode properties to Manual and then explicitly enable and disable dragging with the Drag method. When a Source control that has been enabled with the Drag method is released, it generates a DragDrop() event on the target.

Skill-Building Exercises

This set of exercises asks you to experiment with a variety of user events including key events and mouse events, including MouseMove() and DragOver() and DragDrop(). In Exercise 5, you are asked to use the Line method discussed in Chapter 5.

1. Write a procedure that asks whether the user wants to exit the program when the Esc key is pressed. If the answer is yes, end the program; otherwise, continue.

2. Place a label control at the bottom of the form. Code a Mouse_Move event that constantly displays in the label the X and Y position of the mouse cursor.

3. Extend the previous exercise by adding a large command button to the form. Code the Mouse_Move events for both the form and the button so that the name of the object and its X and Y mouse cursor values are displayed in the label caption.

4. Add a 3000 x 3000 twip picture box to a form. Using the Line method (refer to Chapter 5), permit the user to create a rectangle in the picture box by defining one corner of the rectangle (depress the left mouse button) and the opposite corner of the rectangle (depress the right mouse button). Add a button click event to clear the picture box.

5. Extend the previous exercise by adding a label below the picture box. In the picture box's Mouse_Move() event, code a procedure that alerts the user through four individual messages displayed in the label when the mouse pointer is less than 200 twips from the left, right, top, or bottom of the picture box.

6. Use the TypeOf statement to test controls in a DragDrop() event. Add a picture box on the right-hand side of a form and a label, an option button, a check box, and an image on the left. Code a drag-and-drop procedure using a TypeOf statement so that when the control on the left is dropped on the picture box, a message appears on the picture box identifying what type of control was dropped (see Figure 12.7).

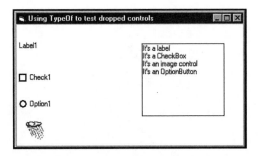

Figure 12.7   *You can drag and drop all four controls on this display into the image box.*

7. Alter the preceding exercise so that when a control is dragged over the picture box, its type is displayed in the picture box. Have the message display once, and when the dragged control leaves the picture box, have the message erased.

INTRODUCTION TO DEBUGGING

Debugging is the process of diagnosing and fixing errors in your code. Visual Basic provides a set of tools to assist you in debugging, which this chapter introduces. As you write code to handle a greater variety of tasks and your applications become larger, Visual Basic's debugging capabilities will prove increasingly useful.

The debugging tools in Visual Basic represent the capabilities of the Debug system object. This object is essentially a spy on the computer's memory. It retrieves values from memory that you request. The Debug object also will execute coded instructions if the objects and variables of the instructions are within the scope of the procedure being examined.

One of the most important facts to remember about Visual Basic's debugging tools is that you can use them for much more than just fixing mistakes: They also enable you to observe how well code works. Observing variables change value during a procedure or seeing program control switch from one procedure to another, for example, teaches you a lot about how a program has been put together. Visual Basic's debugging tools enable these kinds of observations and many more. In this chapter, you examine Visual Basic's debugging tools by observing how they are used with functioning code. When you complete this chapter, you will be able to do the following:

- Discern some of the different types of errors that you can encounter

- Set a breakpoint in your code and perform both Step Into and Step Over code execution while in break mode

- Employ the debugging tools of the Visual Basic Debug toolbar and menu

- Add a watch expression

- Use Quick Watch

- Use the Debug object's Locals window

- Set a breakpoint on expressions when they become True

- Query the Debug object with the Immediate window

- Query the Debug object using the Print method during runtime

Chapter Objectives

The objectives of this chapter teach you about different types of programming errors, the use of the debugging commands, and the use of the Debug object and its Print method, as follows:

1. Understanding the different types of programming errors

2. Working with Visual Basic's third mode: Break

3. Working with watch expressions

4. Understanding the Debug object and its Print method

5. Use the Debug Object's Assert method

Objective 13.1   Understanding the Different Types of Programming Errors

Programming errors generally break down into two types: syntax errors and logic errors. Syntax errors generally can be prevented by choosing Tools, Options and checking the Auto Syntax Check box on the Editor Tab. During design-time, if you enter code with syntax errors, you are prompted with a message informing you of the nature of the error. Color coding provided by the Visual Basic editor also helps you to catch this type of error.

Logic errors are more troublesome. With this type, code seems to execute correctly, but produces incorrect results. Visual Basic's analytic debugging tools can assist you in tracking down errors of logic by letting you observe code as it executes step by step.

There is another general category of errors called runtime errors. These occur if code attempts to execute an instruction that is impossible to carry out. If you try to save a file to a disk that is not formatted or attempt to divide by zero, for example, a runtime error message will be generated. Many of these errors occur when you first attempt to run code and can be corrected immediately, such as by correcting a variable type mismatch error. They most often represent a logic error in that you forgot to do something or wrote code that could not be executed.

You can trap these runtime errors and handle them with a message to the user. You will work more with error trapping in later chapters, which deal with file input/output and database applications, beginning with Chapter 18, "Sequential File Processing and Error Trapping."

Objective 13.2   Working with Visual Basic's Third Mode: Break

So far you have worked in two modes in Visual Basic: design-time and runtime. Visual Basic provides another mode known as *break mode*. During break mode, Visual Basic's debugging tools are available to help analyze and fix your code. You can easily tell which mode you are in by looking at the designation in the brackets to the right of "Microsoft Visual Basic" on the Visual Basic title bar.

You might have noticed, and already used, the buttons on the Visual Basic Standard toolbar for testing and stopping execution of your code during design-time (see Figure 13.1). They look like the play, pause, and stop controls on a compact disc player.

Figure 13.1 *The buttons on the Standard toolbar run a program, end execution, or place the program in break mode.*

These same buttons are available on the Debug toolbar, which is shown in Figure 13.2. To make the Debug toolbar visible, choose View, Toolbars, and select Debug. Like other toolbars, you can add the Debug toolbar to the toolbars underneath the Visual Basic title and menu bar. You also can make it "free floating" by dragging it onto the desktop.

Figure 13.2 *The buttons on the Debug toolbar enable you to run, break, and stop program execution, to step through code, and to watch code values using special debug windows.*

During code execution, clicking the Break button on the Debug toolbar puts a program into break mode. When you press it, the Start and End debugging buttons immediately to the right on the toolbar are enabled, as are the Step Over and Step Into buttons, the Locals, Immediate, and Watch Windows. The other debugging buttons are disabled. These buttons and the available corresponding keyboard shortcuts are illustrated in Figure 13.2.

The first step in debugging is to set a breakpoint in code. Although you can press the Break button next to the Run button, typically you set the breakpoint by selecting a code statement where you would like program execution to stop. While in the code window with your cursor on the line where you would like the break to begin, simply press F9 or click the Toggle Breakpoint button. When the code is next executed, operation is suspended immediately before the breakpoint. After a breakpoint is reached, you can step through your code. Begin with a simple exercise.

Exercise 13.1   Setting a Breakpoint and Stepping Through a Procedure

For this exercise, you will use a modified version of Exercise 11.4, "Moving a Shape to Make the Moon Rise," from Chapter 11, "Working with Loops." For all exercises, place the floating Debug toolbar onscreen.

1. Open project p13-1.vbp, which is stored on the disk packaged with the book.

2. Press the Run button. Once in runtime mode, press the Break button immediately to the right of the Run button. You should see that the Visual Basic title bar indicates you are in break mode.

3. Press the Immediate Window button (or press Ctrl+G). The Immediate window should now appear and have focus. This window is the one you will work with most frequently in debugging operations. It provides an immediate "view" into memory. In the Immediate window, type **Print Form1.Caption**. You should see the caption of the form displayed. Next, type **Print Form1.Left**. These two instructions invoke the Print method of the Debug object.

4. Change the focus back to the Moon Rise window and press the button captioned "Watch the moon rise." Nothing happens, right? That's because you placed the program in break mode, suspending its operation before the command button was pressed. To continue program execution, press the Run button again (or press F5).

5. In general, it is better to set a breakpoint within the code window itself, so that you know exactly where code is suspended and can continue debugging from there. You do that next.

In the `cmdRise_Click()` event of p13-1.vbp, you should have the following code:

```
Private Sub cmdRise_Click()
   Do While shpMoon.Top >= 200   'SET BREAKPOINT HERE
      shpMoon.Left = shpMoon.Left + 60
      shpMoon.Top = shpMoon.Top - 80    ' ascend
   Loop
   MsgBox " Howwooooooooool!", 0, "MoonRise"
   Do
      shpMoon.Left = shpMoon.Left + 60
      shpMoon.Top = shpMoon.Top + 80   'descend
   Loop While shpMoon.Top <= 4200
   shpMoon.Left = 120
   shpMoon.Top = 4300
   cmdRise.Caption = "Watch the moon rise"
End Sub
```

Set your cursor on the line of the code fragment Do While shpMoon.Top >= 200 at the beginning of the procedure. To set a breakpoint in the code window, you have three options: simply press F9; press the Toggle Breakpoint button (the hand icon) on the Debug toolbar; or select Debug, Toggle Breakpoint. The entire line of code should be highlighted with a color. (The color can be changed in the Editor Format dialog box by choosing Tools, Options.)

6. Run the program and press the Watch the Moon Rise button. Immediately, the code window appears with a rectangle around the code you have selected as the breakpoint. You are now in break mode. The rectangle represents the code that will be executed next as you step through the procedure.

7. To step through the code, simply press F8 or click the button with the single footstep (the Step Into button) on the Debug toolbar. Arrange the different windows onscreen so that you can see the code window as well as the Moon Rise application. As you step through each iteration of the ascending loop, you should see the moon's position change slightly.

Exercise 13.2   Stepping Over a Procedure

You used the single step procedure (Step Into) in Exercise 13.1 by pressing the F8 key. This time, you will use Step Over to avoid looking at code stored in a procedure. Step Over code is identical to Step Into code, except when the code contains a call to a procedure. A single step will step into the called procedure. Step Over executes the called procedure and then stops at the next statement immediately following the procedure call. Sound confusing? This exercise should make it clear.

1. Open p13-2.vbp on your disk.

continues

2. The code is almost identical to the previous exercise except the loop that controls the moon's descent is contained in a separate procedure (Descend). In addition, two variables—msg and loopcounter—have been added. The cmdRise_Click() event and the Descend() procedures are as follows:

```
Private Sub cmdRise_Click()
    Dim msg As String
    Dim loopcounter As Integer
    msg = " Howwoooooooooool!"
    Do While shpMoon.Top >= 200
      shpMoon.Left = shpMoon.Left + 60
      shpMoon.Top = shpMoon.Top - 80   ' ascend
      loopcounter = loopcounter + 1
    Loop

    cmdRise.Caption = "Watch the moon fall"
    MsgBox msg, 0, " Moonrise"
    loopcounter = 0
    Call Descend 'SET BREAKPOINT HERE
    shpMoon.Left = 120
    shpMoon.Top = 4300
    cmdRise.Caption = "Watch the moon rise"
End Sub
Private Sub Descend()
    Dim loopcounter As Integer
    Do
      shpMoon.Left = shpMoon.Left + 60
      shpMoon.Top = shpMoon.Top + 80     'descend
      loopcounter = loopcounter + 1
    Loop While shpMoon.Top <= 4200
End Sub
```

3. Put a breakpoint on the line (shown in bold) Call Descend.

4. Run the program. When you get to the breakpoint, try single stepping through the code first. Notice how you move into the Descend procedure?

5. Exit the program and restart. When you get to the breakpoint, click the Step Over button or press Shift+F8. This time, the called procedure (Descend) should execute and the step rectangle should proceed to the next line of code in cmdRise_Click(): shpMoon.Left = 120.

13.2.1   Clearing Breakpoints

A breakpoint remains in your code until you clear it. You clear it by pressing F9 or the clicking Toggle Breakpoint button when the cursor is on the breakpoint. Alternatively, you can clear one or more breakpoints in your code by selecting Debug, Clear All Breakpoints or by pressing Ctrl+Shift+F9.

Exercise 13.3   Stepping Out of a Procedure

If you discover you are inside a called procedure and want the called procedure to continue executing, you can step out of a procedure. Program execution will continue by passing control to the next line of code immediately following the call to the procedure. This exercise illustrates how this debugging feature works.

1. Open p13-2.vbp on your disk, or if it is open already, make sure that all breakpoints have been cleared.

2. In the Descend procedure, place a breakpoint on the single word instruction Do at the beginning of the loop (shown in bold):

```
Private Sub Descend()
   Dim loopcounter As Integer
   Do
      shpMoon.Left = shpMoon.Left + 60
      shpMoon.Top = shpMoon.Top + 80     'descend
      loopcounter = loopcounter + 1
   Loop While shpMoon.Top <= 4200
End Sub
```

3. Run the program. When the program hits the breakpoint, single step through several iterations of the loop. Then press the Step Out button on the Debug toolbar (or press Ctrl+Shift+F8). The program will continue executing until the Descend procedure is complete and program control has returned to the cmdRise_Click() event. You should see the code execution rectangle now over the instruction shpMoon.Left = 120 in that event.

13.2.2   The Locals Window

Besides an Immediate window, the Debug object includes a Locals window, which shows the values of all locally declared variables within the procedure being examined by the Debug object. You can examine these values and even change them from the Locals window. The Locals window can greatly accelerate diagnosing errors in your code. A quick scan of variable values often indicates the source of a problem.

Exercise 13.4   Using the Locals Window

In this exercise, you will employ the Locals window to examine the value of locally declared variables and then change the value of the variable.

1. Open p13-2.vbp on your disk, or if it is open already, make sure all breakpoints have been cleared.

continues

Exercise 13.4   continued

2. In the `cmdRise_Click()` procedure, place a breakpoint at the instruction `MsgBox msg, 0, "Moonrise"` (shown in bold):

```
Private Sub cmdRise_Click()
    Dim msg As String
    Dim loopcounter As Integer
    msg = " Howwooooooooooool!"
    Do While shpMoon.Top >= 200
      shpMoon.Left = shpMoon.Left + 60
      shpMoon.Top = shpMoon.Top - 80   ' ascend
      loopcounter = loopcounter + 1
    Loop

    cmdRise.Caption = " Watch the moon fall"
    MsgBox msg, 0, " Moonrise" ' SET BREAKPOINT HERE
    loopcounter = 0
    Call Descend
    shpMoon.Left = 120
    shpMoon.Top = 4300
    cmdRise.Caption = " Watch the moon rise"
End Sub
```

3. Run the program until you hit the breakpoint. Click the Locals Window button on the Debug toolbar. You should see the window, as illustrated in Figure 13.3.

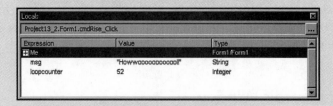

Figure 13.3   *The Locals window displays the values of local variables and the objects of the Form module.*

The Locals window shows the two variables—`msg` and `loopcounter`—and the implicit variable `Me`, referring to the form module.

4. In the Locals window, select the value for `msg`. After the value column has focus, a cursor should appear. Change the value of `msg` from " Howwooooooooooool!" to some other value.

5. Press the Step Into button or press F8. You should see the `MsgBox` statement display the newly assigned value.

Objective 13.3   Working with Watch Expressions

Setting a breakpoint and stepping through code is one pillar of debugging in Visual Basic. The other is setting a watch expression for values. With a watch expression, you can monitor an expression or variable as it changes or reaches a value that you define. This is especially useful, for example, if something goes wrong within a long loop procedure when values reach a certain range. By defining the range for the watch expression, you can avoid tedious repetitions of the loop and focus on where you think the problem begins.

Another advantage of watch expressions is that you can add them at design-time or in break mode. You can even instruct Visual Basic to enter break mode when an expression reaches a certain value.

Exercise 13.5   Adding a Watch Expression at Design-Time and Using Quick Watch

This exercise asks you to set two types of watch expressions: a regular watch and a quick watch. A regular watch enables you to watch how the value of an expression changes when you are in break mode. Regular watch selections appear in a Watches window. A quick watch also enables you to check the value of a variable while in break mode; however, the watch is not retained in the Watches window.

1. Open p13-2.vbp and make sure that all breakpoints have been cleared.

2. Select Debug, Add Watch (alternatively, right-click within the code window and then select Add Watch). You will see the dialog box for adding a watch expression. Change the dialog box so that it conforms to the one presented in Figure 13.4. You will watch the loopcounter variable.

Figure 13.4   *You use the Add Watch dialog box to define the variable or expression that you want to watch.*

continues

3. Notice that you have set the context to the procedure cmdRise_Click() placed on Form1 for Project p13_2. The context sets the scope of variables watched in the expression. Because the variable loopcounter is declared locally, you set its context to the procedure in which it is declared.

The context setting would be set to All Procedures for a variable declared at the module level. When you press the OK button on the Add Watch dialog box, the Watches window appears with the variable value that you intend to watch (see Figure 13.5).

Figure 13.5   *The Watches window shows the value, type, and context for each selected expression.*

4. Add another watch expression for the loopcounter variable in the Descend procedure.

5. Set a breakpoint at the following instruction:

```
MsgBox msg, 0, " Moonrise"
```

6. Run the program.

7. When the program enters break mode, change the focus to the Watches window. The watch pane should display the value of loopcounter for the cmdRise_Click() procedure. Now step into (F8) the next line of code. After clicking the OK button on the message box, continue single stepping through the Descend procedure for several loop iterations.

You should see the value of the loopcounter for cmdRise_Click() remain at zero. The loopcounter variable for the Descend procedure, while at first out of context, will begin to increment in value with each loop iteration.

8. Stay within the Descend procedure and use your pointer to select the expression shpMoon.Top. Click the Quick Watch button on the toolbar (the eyeglasses icon) or press Shift+F9.

9. A dialog box displays the integer value of shpMoon.Top and provides a choice of Add Watch or Cancel. Note the value of shpMoon.Top and then select Cancel.

10. Step through another two iterations of the Descend loop and select shpMoon.Top again. Press the Quick Watch button or press Shift+F9. How has the value changed?

11. Leave this program open so you can continue to use it for the next exercise.

   One feature of Visual Basic's debugging tools is that there is nearly always more than one way of accomplishing the same thing. All these values could have been examined in the Locals window as well as in the Watches window. You also could have selected the Immediate window and entered the following:

```
Print shpMoon.Top
```

Exercise 13.6   Setting a Break When a Watch Expression Becomes True

An added advantage of watch expressions is that you can use them to set breaks. By assigning a value or using a comparison operator in an expression, you can have the code break when a variable or expression reaches a certain value.

1. Go back to design mode. Clear all breakpoints by selecting Debug, Clear All Breakpoints (or Ctrl+Shift+F9). Remove all watch expressions by selecting them in the Watches window and pressing the Delete key.

2. Select Debug, Add Watch. The dialog box that was shown in Figure 13.4 appears.

3. In the expression box, enter shpMoon.Left >= 2000. Be sure the context is set to the cmdRise_Click() procedure. Under Watch Type, select the Break When Value Is True option button (see Figure 13.6).

Figure 13.6   *The Add Watch window offers you three types of watches: a regular watch expression, create a breakpoint when the value is true, and create a breakpoint when the value changes.*

continues

> **Exercise 13.6   continued**
>
> 4. Run the program. When it breaks, change the focus to the Watches window. The watch pane tells you the expression is now True.
>
> 5. To get the precise value of shpMoon.Left, select it and take a quick watch (Shift+F9) of its value or examine its value in the Locals window.
>
> When adding and editing watch expressions, you must select the right expression to evaluate. If you choose to watch an entire assignment, you often will receive a message in the watch pane that evaluates to False. If you select the entire expression shpMoon.Top = shpMoon.Top - 80, for example, the Debug window will work, but consistently return a value of False.
>
> What you might really want to know is the value of shpMoon1.Top as it goes through the loop. Simply set shpMoon.Top as the expression to evaluate, or use a comparison operator so the program will break where you want, as in the following:
>
> ```
>     shpMoon.Top >= 2000
> ```

Objective 13.4   Understanding the *Debug* Object and Its *Print* Method

Visual Basic treats the Debug window as a separate object named, appropriately enough, Debug. You have already used its one method—Print—which can prove extremely useful. With the Debug.Print method, the Immediate window can display values of expressions and variables at points you designate in your code. You can also query the immediate pane itself. You can even enter a Debug.Print request directly into your code and then remove it later when you are ready to make an executable file.

> **Exercise 13.7   Using the *Debug.Print* Method in Code**
>
> This exercise asks you to insert Debug.Print expressions in your code and to observe the results in the Immediate window.
>
> 1. Go back to p13-2.vbp and clear all watch expressions and breakpoints.
>
> 2. Insert a Debug.Print instruction at the sixth line (which is set in bold) in the CmdRise_Click() event:

```
Private Sub cmdRise_Click()
    Dim msg As String
    Dim loopcounter As Integer
    msg = " Howwoooooooooool!"
      Do While shpMoon.Top >= 200
        Debug.Print shpMoon.Left; shpMoon.Top; loopcounter
        shpMoon.Left = shpMoon.Left + 60
        shpMoon.Top = shpMoon.Top - 80  ' ascend
        loopcounter = loopcounter + 1
    Loop

      cmdRise.Caption = " Watch the moon fall"
      MsgBox msg, 0, " Moonrise"
      loopcounter = 0
    Call Descend
    shpMoon.Left = 120
    shpMoon.Top = 4300
    cmdRise.Caption = " Watch the moon rise"
End Sub
```

3. Run the program, but, before clicking Watch the Moon Rise, position the Immediate window to the side so you can observe it. Click the command button.

Observe the Immediate window. Visual Basic's performance slows as it prints the values for each iteration of the ascending loop, but it's a good way to observe how code is working! Using the Print method in code is especially useful with very troublesome procedures for which you are having difficulty determining the problem.

Objective 13.5   Use the *Debug* Object's *Assert* Method

The Debug object has one more method which can prove very useful when developing an application, the Assert method. The Assert method makes an assumption about your code and goes into break mode when that assumption proves false. The syntax for the Assert method is as follows:

```
Debug.Assert (boolean expression)
```

Consider the following:

```
Debug.Assert (CityName = "Portland")
```

In this case, if the CityName variable isn't Portland, the application will enter break mode. You can use the Assert method liberally throughput your code because as with all Debug object methods, it isn't added to the final compiled application by the compiler. The Assert method is especially useful for testing return values from functions.

Exercise 13.8 Using the *Debug.Assert* Method in Code

This exercise asks you to insert a Debug.Assert expression in your code and to observe the results when a function returns an incorrect value.

1. Place a button (**cmdTest**) and a label (**lblDisplay**) on a form.

2. Insert a Debug.Assert instruction in the cmdTest_click event, as follows:

```
Private Sub cmdTest_Click()
    Dim strAnswer As String

    strAnswer = InputBox("Please enter the site of the 2000
➥Summer Olympics.", _
                "Testing the Assert method")
    Debug.Assert (strAnswer = "Sydney")
    lblDisplay.Caption = strAnswer
```

3. Observe the result if the user does not enter " Sydney."

Chapter Summary

In this chapter, you became familiar with Visual Basic's debugging tools. Debugging tools are especially helpful in large, complex projects in which the source of undesired program behavior is not readily apparent. Debugging tools also can help examine the functionality of unfamiliar code. Visual Basic's debugging tools are not difficult to use, but they are so flexible that it can be difficult to decide which tool is best for examining your code. There are always several ways of accomplishing the same thing.

One pillar of debugging is setting a breakpoint and stepping through code. You can single step through code, one instruction at a time. You also can step over procedures, which is useful for ignoring procedure calls you are confident work properly. As you step through code, you can examine expression values by using the Immediate Watch window.

The other pillar of debugging is setting and observing watch expressions. When regular watch expressions are added, they can be seen in the Watches window. Watch expressions can be added either during Design-time or in break mode. A quick watch enables you to check the value of a variable while in break mode.

These two pillars of debugging are combined when a watch expression is added that causes the program to break when an expression becomes True or a value changes. Using these powerful features, you can have your program break when your code approaches an expression value that is proving troublesome. From there, you can step through your code and examine possible sources of difficulty using the Immediate Watch window.

The Debug object has one method: Print. You can use this method on a query basis in the immediate pane when the program is in break mode. You also can place Debug.Print instructions in your code so that expression values will be outputted to the Immediate window for examination after the code has stopped executing.

The Assert method goes into break mode whenever the assert statement is reached and returns a value of false. This method is especially useful for testing return values from functions.

Skill-Building Exercises

The exercises in this section ask you to modify programs that you wrote in Chapter 11, "Working with Loops."

1. The debugging tools are most useful with complex applications with multiple forms in which values are passed from one procedure to another. You will use the debugging tools later, as you develop more complex applications. To review the debugging tools, it is best to start by setting breakpoints and watch expressions on code you are familiar with. Take Exercise 11.11, "Adding a Timer Countdown to the Mercury 1 Commemorative Launch," and practice using Visual Basic's debugging tools on it.

2. Return to Exercise 11.3, "Using Nested Loops and List Boxes," in Chapter 11, which introduced nested loops. Set a breakpoint so that the program breaks every time you are about to exit the inner loop and return to the outer loop.

3. In Exercise 11.3, set a breakpoint that places the program in break mode when the variable item becomes equal to, or greater than, 26.

4. In Exercise 11.3, set a breakpoint that places the program in break mode when the variable sleep becomes equal to, or greater than, 99999. Then, single step through the program until you reach the sleep loop again.

5. Change the code in Exercise 11.3 so that the value of sleep on every 10,000 iterations of the sleep loop is displayed in the Immediate window. (Hint: Use a Mod operator.)

6. In Exercise 11.11, use the Assert method on the imgChute Top property to break program execution when the rocket begins its descent.

7. Use the Assert method to break execution of Exercise 13.2 when the loopcounter variable reaches a value of 15 as the moon ascends.

LISTS AND ARRAYS

This chapter introduces you to the concept of the variable array. In Chapter 11, "Working with Loops," you learned about the concept of the control array. With a control array, like objects are given the same name. A variable array works in a similar way: It is a list of more than one variable with the same name and the same data type. This chapter begins with the subject of lists because lists help illustrate a one-dimensional array. This chapter also provides more practice in working with list and combo boxes.

Several new concepts are presented in this chapter, while other concepts that were touched on only briefly in previous chapters are discussed in detail. When you complete this chapter, you will be able to perform the following tasks:

- Select and assign an item from a list

- Add an item to a list during runtime

- Remove an item from a list during runtime

- Move items from one list to a second list

- Declare a variable array in more than one way

- Use both a control and a variable array in an instruction

- Use the array functions LBound and Ubound to determine the range of an array

Chapter Objectives

The first three objectives for this chapter tackle list boxes and combo boxes. The last two then deal with declaring and working with one-dimensional arrays. The objectives are as follows:

1. Selecting an element from a list box

2. Selecting an element from a combo box

3. Selecting multiple items from a list

4. Understanding one-dimensional variable arrays

5. Working with control and variable arrays

Objective 14.1   Selecting an Element from a List Box

A list is an array, provided the variables are of the same data type. With Visual Basic, lists are commonly associated with List Box and Combo Box controls. Both List Box and Combo Box controls feature one-dimensional arrays because all values are placed in a single column.

In Chapter 4, "Learning to Think Visually," you were asked to design a list box, but were not asked to select an element from the list for use elsewhere. In this section, you gain additional experience in working with list boxes. You will work more extensively with list box and combo box runtime properties.

Before a list box can be utilized by a program, it must be loaded. This is accomplished with the `AddItem` method. In review, the syntax for the `AddItem` method when loading a list is as follows:

```
listname.AddItem item [,index]
```

Table 14.1 explains the components of the `AddItem` method.

TABLE 14.1   Syntax of the *AddItem* Method

Component	Description
listname	The name of the control
item	The string expression to add to the control
index	The position of the item in the control when the index begins with 0

If an index is omitted and you want the list to be sorted, set the control `Sorted` property to `True`.

14.1.1   The *Selected* Property

After you place the items in a list, a specific item can be selected. Although selection is usually made by the user, a selection can be made within Visual Basic using the `Selected` property. The syntax for this property is as follows:

```
[form.]{filelistbox ¦ listbox}.Selected(index)[= {True ¦ False}]
```

The `Selected` property settings are Boolean (`True` or `False`). When an item is selected, the `Selected` property becomes `True`. For other items in the list, the `Selected` property remains `False`, unless multiple selections are permitted. What might not be apparent is that the `Selected` property is not available to you in design-time. It can only be read or assigned during runtime.

14.1.2   The *ListCount* and *ListIndex* Properties

Determining the selected item from a list requires knowledge of the following two additional properties:

- **ListCount**—Determines the number of items in the list box.

- **ListIndex**—Determines the index of the selected item in a list.

This information is known after a list has been loaded at runtime, making both properties runtime properties. The ListIndex settings are shown in Table 14.2.

TABLE 14.2   *ListIndex* Settings

Setting	Description
-1	No item is currently selected.
N	The nth item in the list has been selected. N varies from 0 to the last element in the list (the number of elements minus one).

The following expression returns the string of the selected item:

```
list1.List (ListIndex)
```

Exercise 14.1   Selecting Items from a List

This silly little exercise asks you to create a list of fruit (you can add nuts as well if you like), select one from the list, and display the selected fruit using a label. Figure 14.1 shows how the form is to be designed.

Figure 14.1   *Double-clicking an item in the list on the left places it on the label.*

1. Design the form as shown, adding a list box (**lstFruit**) and three labels (**lblFruit** and two descriptive labels). Set the caption of this form to **Fruit Market**.

continues

Exercise 14.1   continued

2. Write a `Form_Load()` procedure to load the list at runtime. Use `AddItem` to add the strings to the list, as follows:

```
Private Sub Form_Load()
    lstFruit.AddItem "Oranges"
    lstFruit.AddItem "Apples"
    lstFruit.AddItem "Grapes"
    lstFruit.AddItem "Pears"
End Sub
```

3. Write a `lstFruit_DblClick()` procedure to take a list box selection and display it as a caption. Write the following:

```
Private Sub lstFruit_DblClick()
    Dim item As Integer
    'Search the entire list to determine which item is selected

    For item = 0 To (lstFruit.ListCount - 1)
        If lstFruit.Selected(item) = True Then
            lblFruit.Caption = lstFruit.List(item)
            Exit For
        End If
    Next item
End Sub
```

The tricky parts of this procedure involve the `item` counter variable, the upper boundary of which is only known at runtime. You determine how many iterations of the loop should be made by making reference to the `ListCount` property. In this example, `ListCount` equals 4 because four fruit are contained in the list.

Because items in list boxes are part of arrays that begin at 0, subtract 1 from `ListCount` to determine the number of loop iterations to execute. The item counter variable runs from 0 to 3 (`ListCount - 1`). The loop checks to determine which of the list items has been selected—the `Selected(item)` property is `True`. When the `True` element is found, it is assigned to the label caption.

Because you are selecting only one item at a time from the list box, it is possible to reference the `ListIndex` property without using a loop. Every time an item is selected by the user, the `ListIndex` property changes, so you could write the following single line of code for the `DblClick()` event, and get the same behavior:

```
lblFruit.Caption = lstFruit.Text
```

Note, however, that this code would not work if you wanted to select multiple items before updating the label. This is illustrated in Exercise 14.4.

14.1.3   The *AddItem* and *RemoveItem* Methods

After items are added to a list, the list need not remain unchanged. You can add additional items to a list in a procedure using the `AddItem` method. You also can remove items from a list using the `RemoveItem` method. The syntax for `RemoveItem` is as follows:

```
listname.RemoveItem index
```

The component index represents the position of the item within the list, and must be specified with this method.

Exercise 14.2   Adding and Removing Items from a List

This exercise expands Exercise 14.1. As shown in Figure 14.2, you are asked to add command buttons for adding an item to the list (**Add Element**) and removing an item from the list (**Delete Element**). In addition, you are asked to keep track of the number of elements in the list (**No. of Elements**).

Figure 14.2   *With this design, you can select fruit from the list, add fruit, or delete fruit from the list.*

1. Add the additional command buttons (**cmdAdd** and **cmdRemove**) and two labels (**lblNum** and one descriptive label), as shown in Figure 14.2.

2. Modify the Form_Load() procedure to display the number of items in the list following the loading of all items. The new procedure should read as follows:

```
Private Sub Form_Load()
    lstFruit.AddItem "Oranges"
    lstFruit.AddItem "Apples"
    lstFruit.AddItem "Grapes"
    lstFruit.AddItem "Pears"
    lblNum.Caption = Str$(lstFruit.ListCount)
End Sub
```

In this procedure, the ListCount property determines the number of items in the list (which is four).

3. Write a cmdAdd_Click() procedure to add an item to the list. Add the fruit **Bananas**. Remember to revise the number of items in the text box. The code reads as follows:

```
Private Sub cmdAdd_Click()
    lstFruit.AddItem "Bananas"
    lblNum.Caption = Str$(lstFruit.ListCount)
End Sub
```

continues

Observe how the AddItem method is used in this instance. Besides the Form_Load() procedure, you can place AddItem in a command click procedure.

4. Write a second cmdRemove_Click() procedure to remove an item from the list. After a list item is selected, it can be removed. Do the following:

```
Private Sub cmdRemove_Click()
    Dim item As Integer

    For item =(lstFruit.ListCount · 1) To 0 Step ·1
        If lstFruit.Selected(item) = True Then
            lstFruit.RemoveItem item
                Exit For
        End If
    Next item

    lblNum.Caption = Str$(lstFruit.ListCount )
End Sub
```

In this procedure, the ListCount property is again used. The ListCount property changes as items are added or removed from the list. By decrementing from the end of the list to the beginning when removing multiple items, you avoid generating index errors. You can refresh the lblNum.Caption by reassigning the ListCount property after each addition or deletion.

You also could reference the ListIndex property to remove items. The cmdRemove_Click() procedure could be written as follows:

```
lstFruit.RemoveItem(lstFruit.ListIndex)
lblNum.Caption = Str$(lstFruit.ListCount)
```

But again, this would work only if you want to remove one item at a time from a list.

Objective 14.2   Selecting an Element from a Combo Box

Working with lists is complicated by the requirement of placing a loop within a procedure to determine which list element or elements have been selected. With a combo box, this requirement does not hold.

Transferring a selection from a Combo Box control is much easier than using a List Box control. After a combo box is filled with data, using a Form_Load() procedure, you can assign the combo box selection to another control using the following syntax:

```
control.Text = combo1.Text
```

Because a selected item appears in the text box, a search using loops is not required to identify the item.

Exercise 14.3   Transferring Information from Combo Boxes to a Text Box

This short exercise asks you to select a pet and ship the pet to a city. Figure 14.3 shows two combo boxes and a text box: The selection in the first combo box is combined with the city in the second combo box.

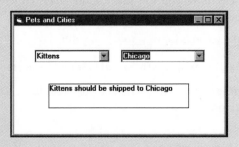

Figure 14.3   *Pull down the first combo box to select a pet and the second to select a city.*

1. Create the design showing two combo boxes (**cboPets** and **cboCities**) and one label with borders (**lblOutput**). Change the name of the form to **Pets and Cities**.

2. Write a Form_Load() procedure to add **Fish**, **Kittens**, **Snakes**, and **Mice** to the first combo box, and **Boston**, **Chicago**, **New York**, and **Atlanta** to the second combo box. The procedure is as follows:

```
Private Sub Form_Load()
    cboPets.AddItem "Fish"
    cboPets.AddItem "Kittens"
    cboPets.AddItem "Snakes"
    cboPets.AddItem "Mice"

    cboCities.AddItem "Boston"
    cboCities.AddItem "Chicago"
    cboCities.AddItem "New York"
    cboCities.AddItem "Atlanta"
End Sub
```

3. Write a cboPets_Click() procedure to assign the pet selection to lblOutput caption.

```
Private Sub cboPets_Click()
    lblOutput.Caption = cboPets.Text
End Sub
```

Observe how simple this procedure is compared to the procedure for the list box.

4. Write a cboCities_Click() procedure to assign the city selection and to complete the sentence.

```
Private Sub cboCities_Click()
 lblOutput.Caption = cboPets.Text & " should be shipped to" &
➥cboCities.Text
End Sub
```

319

Objective 14.3   Selecting Multiple Items from a List

Thus far, you have considered only single selections from a list box. To work with multiple selections from a list (not a combo box), use the MultiSelect property. With multiple selections, you can make more than one choice. This provides a unique advantage to the use of lists over combo boxes.

The syntax for the MultiSelect property is as follows:

```
[form.]{filelistbox ¦ listbox}.MultiSelect = Setting
```

Either a filelistbox or a listbox are control candidates. Table 14.3 explains the MultiSelect settings.

TABLE 14.3   *MultiSelect* Settings

Setting	Description
0	Multiple selection is not allowed (the default).
1	Simple multiple selection. Clicking the mouse or pressing the spacebar selects an item in the list.
2	Extended multiple selection. Shift+click or Shift+arrow key extends the selection from the previous selected item to the current item.

Exercise 14.4   Making Multiple Selections

This exercise asks you to make several selections from a list of birthday supplies and assign them to a second list. Figure 14.4 shows the completed design.

Figure 14.4   *Selecting from the Available list box places items in the Selected list box.*

1. Add the two list boxes (**lstAvailable** and **lstSelected**), the labels, and the command button (**cmdOrder**) shown in Figure 14.4. Label the form **Birthday Supplies**.

2. Set the MultiSelect property to Simple for the list on the left-hand side (lstAvailable).

3. Write the Form_Load() procedure to add the items shown in the lstAvailable, as follows:

```
Private Sub Form_Load()
    lstAvailable.AddItem "Balloons"
    lstAvailable.AddItem "Streamers"
    lstAvailable.AddItem "Punch"
    lstAvailable.AddItem "Cookies"
    lstAvailable.AddItem "Clown"
    lstAvailable.AddItem "Cake"
    lstAvailable.AddItem "Candles"
End Sub
```

4. Write the cmdOrder_Click() procedure to find the highlighted items on the Available list and assign them to the Selected list. In the assignment, use the AddItem method and the ListIndex property.

```
Private Sub cmdOrder_Click()
    Dim item As Integer
    'Loop searches entire list to determine which
    'items to move to the second list
    For item = 0 To (lstAvailable.ListCount - 1)
        If lstAvailable.Selected(item) = True Then
            lstSelected.AddItem lstAvailable.List(item)
        End If
    Next item
End Sub
```

If an element in the first list is selected (is True), it is added to the second list. In multiple selections, a loop is mandatory to iterate through the list to determine which list elements have been selected. You cannot simply reference the current ListIndex or text properties as you can with single selection situations.

5. Run and test your program.

Objective 14.4   Understanding One-Dimensional Variable Arrays

With a better understanding of lists and combo box selections firm in your mind, it's time to move to the subject of one-dimensional variable arrays. A *one-dimensional variable array* is a list of more than one variable with the same name. (Multidimensional arrays are discussed in Chapter 15, "Multidimensional Arrays, Tables, Arrays of User-Defined Types, and the MSFlexGrid Control.")

14.4.1   The Purpose of Arrays

You use arrays in programming to avoid the cumbersome ordeal of having to invent unique names for every variable in a program. As an example, suppose that you have five friends and want to assign them their names. You could use a single variable for each friend, as follows:

```
Dim friend1 As String
Dim friend2 As String
Dim friend3 As String
Dim friend4 As String
Dim friend5 As String
```

However, an easier way of writing this is to use a one-dimensional variable array. This reduces the preceding individual statements to the following:

```
Dim friend(1 to 5) As String
```

The `friend` component is the name of the variable array, and `1 to 5` specifies the number of array elements.

14.4.2   Declaring Array Variables

Although not difficult, the declaring of an array is troublesome in that arrays, like other variables, have scope. They can be declared in several ways: at the procedure level, at the module level, and globally. The scope rules for declaring an array should be familiar (refer to Chapter 10, "Defining the Scope of Variables and Procedures"):

- **Global array**—Place the `Public` statement in the Declarations section of a standard code module to declare the array. No further declarations are needed.

- **Module-level array**—Place the `DIM` statement in the General Declarations section of a form module or standard module. No further declarations are needed.

- **Array with local scope**—Use one of the following within a procedure, preferably at the beginning:

  `Static` scope for the array

  `Static` scope for the entire procedure and `DIM` for the array

  `ReDim` for the array

As these rules indicate, changing the scope of an array variable changes the way in which it is declared. The first item of "Skill-Building Exercises" at the end of this chapter asks you to write several procedures to test the different ways of declaring an array. Before you do this, however, you need to consider the differences between the keywords `Dim` and `ReDim`, and between array elements and array subscripts.

Dim and ReDim

When working with variable arrays, the difference between `Dim` and `ReDim` becomes important. The `Dim` statement declares variables and allocates storage space. However, when you write a statement at the procedure level, such as the following, you cannot resize the array at a later time:

```
Dim friends(1 to 5) As String
```

Instead, use ReDim as in the following statement:

```
ReDim friends(1 to 5) As String
```

With ReDim, you can dynamically control or redimension the size of the array. For example, assume that the amount of your friends increases from five to eight. You can write the following code to dynamically increase the size of the array from five to eight array elements:

```
Size = 8
ReDim friends(1 to Size)
```

Dynamic allocation is important for the following several reasons:

- It enables the size of an array to be changed as items are added or deleted from a list. In many programs, the size of a list will not be known in advance. ReDim allows the size of a list to be kept flexible.

- ReDim enables an array to be declared at the procedure level. As a rule, define all variables, including array variables, at the lowest level or scope possible. ReDim provides this capability.

- It is possible to release the memory allocated for an array. By reducing the size of an array to zero, all memory is released, as in the following instruction:

  ```
  ReDim Friends(0)
  ```

You also can declare an array as follows:

```
Dim Codes() As Integer
```

The number of Codes() is not specified. This permits use of the following statement later in the program for dynamic allocation of memory:

```
ReDim Codes(5) As Integer
```

Variable Array Elements and Subscripts

One of the most confusing concepts of working with arrays is distinguishing between the number of array elements and the use of array subscripts. Consider the following declaration:

```
ReDim days(6) As String
```

This declaration indicates that the variable days actually contains seven elements because, by default, all arrays in Visual Basic are zero-based. The numeric value in the array declaration specifies the upper index value of the array. What it does not tell you is how to reference a specific day, such as the first of the six days. A specific day is referenced as follows: days(0), days(1), days(2), days(3), days(4), days(5), days(6). The values 0, 1, 2, 3, 4, 5, and 6 are called subscripts. To determine the value of the first element of the array, a subscript of 0 is used.

You might ask, "Can array elements and subscripts be numbered beginning with the number 1?" Fortunately, you can accomplish this in two ways. The first is to insert an `Option Base` statement in the Declarations section of a module. Consider the following statement:

```
Option Base 1
```

This specifies a subscript of 1 rather than 0 for the first element.

A second way—the one favored by the authors—is to use the keyword `To` in the declaration of an array. The following statement specifies the beginning and the ending subscript numbers:

```
ReDim days(1 To 7) As String
```

14.4.3 Assigning a Value to an Array Element

Given this initial understanding of how arrays are declared, you might question next how values are assigned to array elements. Assigning a value to an array element is accomplished using an assignment statement, such as the following:

```
friend(0) = "B. J. McGathering"
friend(1) = "M. H. Pickel"
```

Continue until your assignments are finished. The expression on the right-hand side is assigned to the array variable. A loop represents another way of assigning an expression to an array element, as in the following example:

```
For Inside = 1 to 10
    num(Inside) = Inside
Next Inside
```

In this example, `num(1)` to `num(10)` contain the values of 1 through 10.

14.4.4 Displaying the Contents of an Array

The quickest way of displaying the contents of an array is to use a `For...Next` loop when the number of array elements is known. Consider the following code:

```
For OfMine = 0 To 4 Step 1
    Print Spc(25) ; Friend(OfMine)
Next OfMine
```

In this example, the first value displayed would be the value stored in `Friend(0)`.

Exercise 14.5   Assigning Values to an Array

This simple exercise asks you to assign the days of the week to an array named days and to print out the contents of the array once all assignments have been made. Figure 14.5 shows the output of this design.

Figure 14.5   *This form displays the contents of the variable array named* days(1 to 7).

1. Place a single command button (**cmdShowMe**) on the form, and change the form title to **Days of the Week**.

2. Write a cmdShowMe_Click() procedure as follows:

```
Sub cmdShowMe_Click()
    ReDim days(1 To 7)  As String
    Dim index As Integer

    days(1) = "Sunday"
    days(2) = "Monday"
    days(3) = "Tuesday"
    days(4) = "Wednesday"
    days(5) = "Thursday"
    days(6) = "Friday"
    days(7) = "Saturday"

    Print
    Print
    Print Spc(20); "The days of the week are:"
    Print

    For index = 1 To 7
        Print Spc(25); days(index)
    Next index
End Sub
```

You can declare this array in one of four ways. The first is shown in the preceding code: It uses ReDim. The four ways are as follows:

continues

A. Sub cmdShowMe_Click()

    ReDim days(1 To 7) As String

B. Sub cmdShowMe_Click()

    Dim days(1 To 7) As String

C. Sub cmdShowMe_Click()

    Static days(1 To 7) As String

D. Static Sub cmdShowMe_Click()

    Dim days(1 To 7) As String

With the fourth alternative, the entire procedure is declared as type Static. This means that the contents of the array days will not be lost if the procedure is called more than once.

3. Run and test your program, trying all four ways of declaring the array.

14.4.5   Using the *LBound* and *UBound* Functions

The LBound and UBound functions enable you to test the upper and lower boundaries of an array when they are unknown to you. The syntax is as follows:

```
LBound(arrayname[, dimension])
UBound(arrayname[, dimension])
```

The components of the syntax are explained in Table 14.4.

TABLE 14.4   Syntax of the *LBound* and *Ubound* Functions

Component	Description
arrayname	Name of the array variable. It follows standard variable naming conventions.
dimension	A whole number indicating which dimension's lower or upper boundary is returned. (Multidimensional arrays are discussed in Chapter 15.")

Exercise 14.6   Using the *LBound* and *Ubound* Functions

This brief exercise shows how to test for the upper and lower boundaries of an array. Figure 14.6 shows the interface that you are to create.

Figure 14.6   *This display indicates that the upper and lower boundaries of the array are changed by the program.*

1. Start a new project, and add a command button named **cmdTest**.

2. In the cmdTest_Click() event, enter the following code:

```
Private Sub cmdTest_Click()
    ReDim arraynum(1 To 200) As Integer
    Cls
    Print
    Print
    Print Spc(15); "Upper bound is: " & Str$(UBound(arraynum))
    Print Spc(15); "Lower bound is: " & Str$(LBound(arraynum))

    ReDim arraynum(1 To 50)
    Print Spc(15); "Upper bound is now : " &
Str$(UBound(arraynum))
    Print Spc(15); "Lower bound is now : " &
Str$(LBound(arraynum))
End Sub
```

The values returned from the UBound and LBound functions can be used in For...Next loops, which iterate through arrays that are dynamically changed during runtime.

3. Run and test your code.

Objective 14.5   Working with Control and Variable Arrays

Sometimes it is necessary to combine controls with variable arrays. Consider the following statement:

```
txtText(element).Text = arrayVariable(element)
```

This assignment statement assigns the value of the variable array element to a text box within an array of text boxes. Using both control arrays and variable arrays in a single instruction is common and useful. Exercise 14.7 and Exercise 14.8 demonstrate this technique.

Exercise 14.7   Working with a Control and a Variable Array

This exercise asks you to modify the last exercise by placing the names of the week into seven labels (see Figure 14.7).

Figure 14.7   *The names of the week are presented by a control array of seven labels.*

1. Add the control array of seven labels to your design, using the name **lblDays**.

2. Rewrite the cmdShowMe_Click() procedure to assign the seven elements of the variable array days to the seven text boxes, as follows:

```
Private Sub cmdShowMe_Click()
ReDim days(0 To 6)  As String  ' need to change because
➥control arrays ' are zero based
  Dim index As Integer

  days(0) = "Sunday"
  days(1) = "Monday"
  days(2) = "Tuesday"
  days(3) = "Wednesday"
  days(4) = "Thursday"
  days(5) = "Friday"
```

```
      days(6) = "Saturday"
      For index = 0 To 6
         lblDays(index).Caption = days(index)
      Next index
   End Sub
```

In this code, the index references each member in the control array and each element in the variable array. This single line of code should help clarify the similarity between a control and a variable array. Both require an index or subscript. More importantly, the value of the elements of a variable array can be assigned as a property value to a member of a control array.

3. Run and test your code.

Exercise 14.8   Creating an Application with Variable Arrays

Suppose that you are responsible for informing people on vacation about possible side trips and their costs. A side trip can be chosen from a list, causing the price of the trip to appear. After all side trips are scheduled, a total price is calculated. When customers change their minds, the add-on trip listing can be cleared, and the customer can start again. Figure 14.8 shows a layout for this design. You are working with the following prices:

```
Tyrolean Weekend          $455.55
Rhine River Cruise         630.75
Personal Louvre Guide      120.35
Milan Fashion Tour         330.33
Schwartzwald Spa Weekend   765.45
```

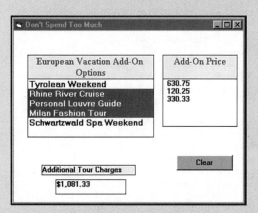

Figure 14.8   *The Don't Spend Too Much application enables you to determine the cost of each side trip and the total cost of your selections.*

continues

1. Add the two list boxes (**lstOptions** and **lstPrice**), the a command button (**cmdClear,**), and the label (**lblTotal**), as shown in Figure 14.8. The Additional tour charge box is a Label control, not a Text Box control. Change the form caption to "**Don't Spend Too Much**." An alternative title is "**Go Ahead; Spend. You Only Live Once!**"

2. At the module level declare an array:

```
Dim AddPrice(0 To 4)   As Currency
```

3. Write the Form_Load() procedure to add the five list items to lstOptions and populate the AddPrice array:

```
Private Sub Form_Load()
   lstOptions.AddItem "Tyrolean Weekend"
   lstOptions.AddItem "Rhine River Cruise"
   lstOptions.AddItem "Personal Louvre Guide"
   lstOptions.AddItem "Milan Fashion Tour"
   lstOptions.AddItem "Schwartzwald Spa Weekend"
   AddPrice(0) = 455.55
   AddPrice(1) = 630.75
   AddPrice(2) = 120.25
   AddPrice(3) = 330.33
   AddPrice(4) = 765.45
End Sub4. Write the lstOptions_Click() multi-select procedure.
➥If an item is selected, add the item to the second lstPrice,
➥and keep a running total.Private Sub lstOptions_Click()
   Dim i As Integer
   Dim RunTotal As Currency

   Select Case lstOptions.ListIndex
      Case 0
         lstPrice.AddItem "455.55"
      Case 1
         lstPrice.AddItem "630.75"
      Case 2
         lstPrice.AddItem "120.25"
      Case 3
         lstPrice.AddItem "330.33"
      Case 4
         lstPrice.AddItem "765.45"
   End Select

'Add prices to array

   lstPrice.Clear
   'Loop to get choices
   For i = 0 To 4
      If lstOptions.Selected(i) = True Then
         lstPrice.AddItem Str$(AddPrice(i))
         RunTotal = RunTotal + AddPrice(i)
      End If
   Next

   lblTotal.Caption = Format(Str$(RunTotal), "Currency")

End Sub
```

Because there is a one-to-one correspondence between the array declared at the module level and the vacation options displayed in lstOptions list box, you can use a single For loop to determine whether an item is selected and to retrieve that item's price. Another means of associating a number with a string in a ListBox is to use the ListBox ItemData property. The associated number must be an integer. Examine this property in Visual Basic's online help. An end of chapter exercise asks you to revamp this exercise by changing the prices to integer values and using the ItemData property.

5. Write the cmdClear_Click() procedure to clear the list. Use a For...Next loop to iterate through the list box.

```
Private Sub cmdClear_Click()

    Dim i As Integer
    'Turn off previous choices
    For i = 0 To 4
        lstOptions.Selected(i) = False
    Next

    'Clear price list
    lstPrice.Clear

    'Clear totals box
    lblTotal.Caption = ""
End Sub
```

6. Run and test your code.

14.5.1   Dynamically Sizing Global Arrays

The capability to dynamically size arrays is one of Visual Basic's greatest strengths. Frequently, a global declaration of an array is made with no elements defined, such as the declaration in a standard module:

```
Public friend() As String
```

You then can dynamically resize this array within procedures, as in the following instruction:

```
ReDim friend (1 to 5) As String
```

Once done working with an array, you can clear memory by simply redimensioning it, as follows:

```
ReDim friend(0) As String
```

Alternatively, you can use the Erase statement, which deallocates the memory, as in the following:

```
Erase friend
```

14.5.2   The *Preserve* Keyword

How do you manage an array that has had values assigned that you want to preserve as it is resized? In this case, use the keyword Preserve. Suppose that you had first made the declaration ReDim friends(1 to 3) As String and assigned the values "Bob", "Jean", and "Bill" to friends(1), friends(2), and friends(3), respectively. You could preserve those values when resizing the array with the declaration:

```
ReDim Preserve friends(1 to 4)
```

You could assign a value to the new array element friends(4), and previous assignments to other array elements would be preserved. If you had resized the array with the following statement, all previous assigned values would be lost:

```
ReDim friends (1 to 4)
```

Exercise 14.9   Demonstrating the *Preserve* Keyword

This exercise shows how values can be retained by using the keyword Preserve when an array is resized. You are asked to create the display shown in Figure 14.9.

FIGURE 14.9   *This display shows the effect of both using and not using the keyword* Preserve.

1. Create a new project, and add a single command button to the form named **cmdTestPreserve**.

2. In the `cmdTestPreserve_Click()` event, enter the following code:

```
Private Sub cmdTestPreserve_Click()
    Font.Bold = True
    Dim i As Integer
    ReDim pet(1 To 3) As String    ' dimension array

    pet(1) = "cats"          ' assign values
    pet(2) = "dogs"
    pet(3) = "birds"

    Print
    Print
    'display them
    Print "Array has been declared: ReDim pet (1 to 3) As
➥String"

    For i = LBound(pet) To UBound(pet)
        Print Spc(5); pet(i)
    Next
    Print
    Print

       ReDim Preserve pet(1 To 4) As String    ' redimension
                                               ➥array and
                                               ' preserve
                                               ➥previous values

    ' display them and the string length of array elements
    Print "Array has been resized to four elements and has been
➥preserved."
    Print "Declaration: ReDim Preserve pet(1 To 4) As String "

    For i = LBound(pet) To UBound(pet)
        Print Spc(5); pet(i) & " string length is " & Len(pet(i))
    Next
    Print
    Print

       ReDim pet(1 To 4) As String   ' redimension array without
                                     ➥preserving
                                     ' previously assigned values

    ' display them and the string length of array elements
    Print "Array has been resized to four elements but
➥NOT preserved:"
    Print "Declaration: ReDim pet(1 To 4) As String"

    For i = LBound(pet) To UBound(pet)
        Print Spc(5); pet(i) & "string length is " & Len(pet(i))
    Next
End Sub
```

Remember to use the `Preserve` keyword in order to save values to arrays if you resize them dynamically.

3. Run and test your code.

Chapter Summary

This chapter begins with lists and combo boxes as examples of one-dimensional lists of items. When only one item can be selected from a list, one `Selected` property will be set to `True`; for all other items, the `Selected` property will be set to `False`. When multiple items can be selected from a list, each item must be tested (using a loop) to determine which selected properties are set to `True`.

With a combo box, determining which item has been selected is much easier because it always appears in the combo text box.

The largest section of this chapter—Objective 14.4, "Understanding `One-Dimensional` Variable Arrays"—addresses the description and use of one-dimensional variable arrays. A one-dimensional array is a list of more than one variable with the same name.

You can declare variable arrays in several ways. The preferred way generally is the use of `ReDim`, as in the following example:

```
ReDim friend(5) As String
```

`ReDim` permits the size of an array to be dynamically controlled, keeps the variable declaration at the procedure level, and permits memory to be released by reducing the size of the array to zero.

Besides `ReDim`, it is possible to declare a global array, to declare an array at the form level, or to create a local array with `Static` scope (for the array or for all variables in the procedure).

Array subscripts often begin with zero. In the preceding declaration, the array `friends()` contains six elements: the subscript of the first item is (`0`), and the subscript of the sixth item is (`5`). To begin subscripts and elements with the number 1, declare an array using `Option Base 1` or the `To` keyword, as in the following example:

```
ReDim friend (1 To 6) As String
```

You assign values to array variables in the same manner as you make assignments to non-array variables. The following, for example, is a valid assignment:

```
friend(1) = "Hank"
```

You perform the manipulation of an array using loops. Displaying the contents of the preceding array declared is done as follows:

```
For OfMine = 1 to 6
Print friend(OfMine)
Next OfMine
```

Variable and control arrays are often combined. The following instruction assigns the value stored in a variable array to a property of a control array:

```
lblFriends(index).Caption = friend(index)
```

You can test the upper and lower boundaries of arrays with the UBound and LBound functions. To ensure that values previously assigned to an array are not lost when the array is redimensioned, use the Preserve keyword. If you had made an original declaration of ReDim cities(1 to 5) As String and then assigned the values "Seattle", "Portland", "Chicago", "Boston", and "St. Louis" to the array, you could retain these values when you redimension the array to add "Phoenix" with the following declaration:

```
ReDim Preserve cities (1 to 6) As String.
```

Skill-Building Exercises

This skill-building exercise set differs from several others by asking you to design a rather large application at the beginning. You are asked to experiment with the different ways of declaring an array. Besides additional practice with declarations, you are asked to use LBound and UBound functions, the Preserve keyword, and to modify the European Vacation Option exercise.

1. This project consists of several parts. It asks you to use different rules for declaring an array. Figure 14.10 illustrates an array testing program that displays the test results in a text box. See section 14.4.2, "Declaring Array Variables," earlier in this chapter for the rules for declaring arrays in this exercise.

Figure 14.10   *Five array tests are used to show the different ways of dimensioning an array.*

A. Declare sweets() at the procedure level. The array contains: **Cakes**, **Cookies**, **Ice Cream**, **Jelly Rolls**, and **Gum**. Complete the following procedure:

```
Private Sub cmdTest1_Click()
    'Declare sweets as a static array of type string
    Static sweets(1 to 5) As String
    Dim i As Integer
    'Clear the results box
    'Load the array
    'Clear the text box
    'Display the array
End Sub
```

B. Declare yums() at the procedure level. The array contains: **Cakes**, **Cookies**, **Ice Cream**, **Jelly Rolls**, and **Gum** (the same as the last array). Complete the following procedure:

```
Private Sub cmdTest2_Click()
   'This procedure declares yums()
   'as array of type string
   ReDim yums(1 To 5)  As String
   Dim I As Integer
   'Load the array
   (Use the code from Step 1 to complete this procedure.)
End Sub
```

C. Declare goodies() at the form module level to allow the same array to contain different things.

```
option Explicit
```

Write a procedure to call two other procedures, named some() and more(). Complete the following procedure:

```
Private Sub cmdTest3_Click()
   Dim i As Integer
   'Goodies is dimensioned at the form level
   'Call the two procedures
End Sub
```

Complete the some() procedure. Goodies contains the same items as before: **Cakes**, **Cookies**, **Ice Cream**, **Jelly Rolls**, and **Gum**.

```
Private Sub some()
   Dim i As Integer
   'Clear the text box
   'Load the Goodies array
   'Display the array
End Sub
```

Complete the more() procedure. The contents of Goodies is **More Cakes**, **More Cookies**, **More Ice Cream**, **More Jelly Rolls**, and **More Gum**:

```
Private Sub more()
   Dim i As Integer
   'Load the Goodies array
   'Clear the text box
   'Display the array
End Sub
```

D. Declare the procedure as type Static. More_sweets contains the same items as Goodies. Complete the following procedure:

```
Private Static Sub cmdTest4_Click()
   'The word static is placed in the definition of the
➥procedure
   Dim i As Integer
   Dim More_sweets(1 To 5)  As String
   'Load the More_sweets array
   (add code to complete)
End Sub
```

E. Declare the global array `More_Sweets` within a standard code module (a .BAS file):

```
Option Explicit
```

Complete the procedure:

```
Private Sub cmdTest5_Click()
    Dim i As Integer
    (add code to complete)
End Sub
```

What conclusions can you draw from these five tests?

2. Write a procedure that declares an array that contains the names of ten of your favorite cities or towns, assigns values to the array, and displays them in a list box with a loop that uses the `LBound` and `UBound` functions. Extend this exercise so that when one of the cities is clicked, the message `"[city name] is a great place to visit!"` is displayed.

3. Write a program that lists 10 of your favorite movies in a list box. Using a text box or other means (for example, the `InputBox` function), permit the user to add to the list. Also provide a way for the user to remove items from the list.

4. Extend the preceding exercise by globally declaring an unassigned array of your 10 favorite movies. Change the selection property of the list box so that the user can make multiple selections. Write a procedure so that, depending upon user selections, the global array is redimensioned to the number of user selections, selected movies are assigned to the global array, and the array (using `LBound` and `UBound` functions) is printed on a display label. At the end of the procedure, clear the array from memory.

5. Experiment with the preceding exercise using the `Preserve` keyword in the array declaration and removing code that clears the array from memory. What changes do you notice in program behavior?

6. Write a procedure which populates a 26 member array with the capital letters of the alphabet and prints the array on a form. (**Hint:** Examine the ANSI values in Appendix A and use the `Chr$` function).

7. Revamp Exercise 14.8, the European vacation option, by using the `ItemData` property of the `listbox`. This exercise will require no separate array and will require you to change vacation option prices to integer values. Consult the Visual Basic online help for information on this property.

15

MULTIDIMENSIONAL ARRAYS, TABLES, ARRAYS OF USER-DEFINED TYPES, AND THE *MSFLEXGRID* CONTROL

Besides one-dimensional arrays and lists, Visual Basic provides several ways of creating two-dimensional arrays or tables, as well as even larger dimensioned arrays. This chapter begins with the concept of multidimensional arrays, followed by the MSFlexGrid custom control and user-defined data types. This chapter concludes with a more complex type of array, known as an array of structures.

This chapter presents several new and important concepts. When you complete this chapter, you will be able to perform the following tasks:

- Declare a multidimensional array
- Use a table look-up procedure
- Transfer items from a multi-column list
- Use the `MSFlexGrid` control
- Employ an array of user-defined types

Chapter Objectives

The objectives of this chapter each address a different topic. It begins with multidimensional arrays, moves to tables (multidimensional lists and an `MSFlexGrid`), and ends with user-defined types. The following are the four objectives:

1. Declaring and using multidimensional arrays
2. Designing a multi-column list
3. Using the `MSFlexGrid` control
4. Employing an array of user-defined types

Objective 15.1   Declaring and Using Multidimensional Arrays

Besides one-dimensional arrays, Visual Basic allows for multidimensional arrays. Although most multidimensional arrays are limited to two or three dimensions, you can declare arrays of up to 60 dimensions with Visual Basic, provided that you can visualize beyond three dimensions and have the memory to handle it. Consider the following examples of two-dimensional array declarations:

```
ReDim MyTable (9, 9) As Integer
ReDim MyTable(1 To 10, 1 To 10) As Integer
```

The array named `MyTable` consists of 10 rows, 10 columns, and stores 100 elements. A three-dimensional array declaration is similar. It might be as follows:

```
Static MyTable (1 To 10, 1 To 10, 1 To 10) As Integer
```

This array would store 1,000 elements (10×10×10).

15.1.1   Declaring a Multidimensional Array

Like one-dimensional arrays, static and dynamic multidimensional arrays are permitted. To create a dynamic array, declare the array with a `Public` statement or a `Dim` statement at the module level, or a `Static` or `Dim` statement in a procedure, as in the following example:

```
Static MyTable() As Integer
```

Use `ReDim()` in a procedure to allocate the number of array elements:

```
ReDim MyTable (1 to 10, 1 to 10) As Integer
```

This instruction allocates memory for a 10×10 array.

15.1.2   Writing a Table Look-Up Procedure

Multidimensional arrays especially are useful whenever two or more array values are required to determine a value. Table look-up provides an excellent example of how this works. A value checked using the first column of a two-dimensional array leads to a value stored in the second column of the array.

Exercise 15.1   A Table Look-Up to Compute Taxes

A favorite table look-up exercise involves determining a person's income and, based on that income, looking up the percentage of tax the person must pay. After the percentage is known, the person's tax can be computed. Figure 15.1 shows the simple interface required for this exercise.

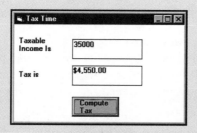

Figure 15.1 *Enter your taxable income, and click Compute Tax to determine your income tax.*

1. Create the interface as shown in Figure 15.1, adding one text box and three labels (the one to display the tax is named **lblTax**). Add the command button (**cmdCompute**), and change the form caption.

2. Write the cmdCompute_Click() procedure as follows:

```
Private Sub cmdCompute_Click()
    Static taxrate(4, 1) As Single
    Dim income As Currency
    Dim tax As Currency
    Dim flag As Boolean
    Dim i As Integer

    taxrate(0, 0) = 10000
    taxrate(1, 0) = 20000
    taxrate(2, 0) = 30000
    taxrate(3, 0) = 40000
    taxrate(4, 0) = 50000

    taxrate(0, 1) = .09
    taxrate(1, 1) = .12
    taxrate(2, 1) = .13
    taxrate(3, 1) = .14
    taxrate(4, 1) = .16

    income = Val(txtIncome.Text)
    flag = False
    For i = 4 To 0 Step -1
      If income >= taxrate(i, 0) Then
        tax = taxrate(i, 1) * income
        lblTax.Caption = Format(Str$(tax), "Currency")
        flag = True
        Exit For
      End If
    Next i
    If flag = False Then
      If income >= 0 Then
        lblTax.Caption = Format("0", "Currency")
      Else
        lblTax.Caption = "Income must be positive"
      End If
    End If
End Sub
```

3. Run and test your program.

continues

Do you understand from this procedure how table look-up works? First a person's income level is checked to determine how many thousands of dollars are earned. After this is known, the tax percentage can be found. The tax percentage multiplied by the income determines the total amount of tax the person owes.

This program must include steps for low income or negative income. With negative income, the message "Income must be positive" is displayed. You might want to change this to $0.00.

Exercise 15.2   A Table Look-Up to Compute Taxes Based on Marital Status

This exercise adds further complexity to the problem of looking up the tax a person is required to pay. Figure 15.2 illustrates that a person's marital status affects tax liability (compare Figure 15.1 to Figure 15.2).

Figure 15.2   *A single person's income tax is higher than a married person's income tax.*

1. Change the interface by adding a marital status frame and two option buttons: one for Married (**optMarried**) and one for Single (**optSingle**).

2. Declare the array **taxrate** at the general level. This will make it global to all procedures. This statement should read as follows:

   ```
   Dim taxrate(4, 1) As Single
   ```

3. Revise the **cmdCompute_Click()** procedure to call the function **taxrate1** if a person is married, and **taxrate2** if a person is single. The code in this procedure is limited to the following statements:

   ```
   Private Sub cmdCompute_Click()
      Dim married As Integer
      If (optMarried.Value = True) Then
         Call taxrate1
      Else
         Call taxrate2
      End If
   End Sub
   ```

4. Use a tax look-up procedure in `taxrate1()` to determine a married person's tax. This procedure reads as follows:

```
Private Sub taxrate1()
    Dim income As Currency
    Dim tax As Currency
    Dim flag As Boolean
    Dim i as Integer

    taxrate(0, 0) = 10000
    taxrate(1, 0) = 20000
    taxrate(2, 0) = 30000
    taxrate(3, 0) = 40000
    taxrate(4, 0) = 50000

    taxrate(0, 1) = .09
    taxrate(1, 1) = .12
    taxrate(2, 1) = .13
    taxrate(3, 1) = .14
    taxrate(4, 1) = .16

    income = Val(txtIncome.Text)

    flag = False
    For i = 4 To 0 Step -1
      If income >= taxrate(i, 0) Then
        tax = taxrate(i, 1) * income
        lblTax.Caption = Format(Str$(tax), "Currency")
        flag = True
        Exit For
      End If
    Next i
    If flag = False Then
      If income >= 0 Then
        lblTax.Caption = Format("0", "Currency")
      Else
        lblTax.Caption = "Income must be positive"
      End If
    End If
End Sub
```

5. Use a tax look-up procedure in `taxrate2()` to determine a single person's tax. The tax rates are as follows:

```
taxrate(0, 0) = 10000
taxrate(1, 0) = 20000
taxrate(2, 0) = 30000
taxrate(3, 0) = 40000
taxrate(4, 0) = 50000

taxrate(0, 1) = .11
taxrate(1, 1) = .14
taxrate(2, 1) = .17
taxrate(3, 1) = .2
taxrate(4, 1) = .22
```

Complete the rest of this procedure on your own.

6. Run and test your program. Whose taxes are higher: taxes for single people or taxes for married people?

Objective 15.2   Designing a Multi-Column List

Besides multidimensional arrays, you can design multi-column lists to look like tables, even though they function like simple lists. To create a multi-column list, change two properties: `Listbox.Columns` and `Listbox.MultiSelect`. Change the number of columns from one to the number desired, and change the `MultiSelect` property to allow for more than one item to be selected.

Exercise 15.3   Creating a Multi-Column List for Making Multiple Selections

This short exercise asks you to create a multi-column list that allows for multiple selections. Figure 15.3 illustrates the two list box designs.

Figure 15.3   *A multi-column list enables the user to select from a table of items.*

1. Create the design shown in Figure 15.3, adding two list boxes (**lstSale** and **lstBuyMe**), the command button (**cmdIWant**), two labels, and all captions.

2. For each list box, change the number of columns to 3 and `MultiSelect` to 1.

3. Write the `Form_Load()` procedure to add the items to `lstSale`:

```
Private Sub Form_Load()
    lstSale.AddItem "Kittens"
    lstSale.AddItem "Dogs"
    lstSale.AddItem "Snakes"
    lstSale.AddItem "Bunnies"
    lstSale.AddItem "Mice"
    lstSale.AddItem "Hamsters"
    lstSale.AddItem "Fish"
    lstSale.AddItem "Birds"
    lstSale.AddItem "Rats"
    lstSale.AddItem "Turtles"
    lstSale.AddItem "Worms"
    lstSale.AddItem "Bugs"
End Sub
```

4. Write the `cmdIWant_Click()` procedure, as follows:

```
Private Sub cmdIWant_Click()
    'n is the number in the list
    Dim n As Integer

    lstBuyMe.Clear
    For n = 0 To (lstSale.ListCount - 1)
        If lstSale.Selected(n) = True Then
            lstBuyMe.AddItem lstSale.List(n)
        End If
    Next
End Sub
```

5. Run and test your program.

This procedure initially clears the Buy Me list. It then loops through the For Sale list to determine which items are selected. The `AddItem` method is used to display the selected items on the Buy Me list. Although the list box has multiple columns, the items in the list merely wrap from one column to the next. To specify that certain tabular data be displayed in certain columns or rows, it's much easier to use a control other than the built-in list box. These include either controls bound to an underlying database or the `MSFlexGrid` control.

Chapter 23, "Accessing and Manipulating Databases with Visual Basic," and Chapter 24, "Using Data Access Objects" turns to databases and data-bound controls. Next, you learn about the `MSFlexGrid` control.

Objective 15.3   Using the *MSFlexGrid* Control

A third way to work with tables in Visual Basic is to utilize the MSFLXGRD.OCX component. This component displays an `MSFlexGrid` on screen and enables you to display information in rows and columns. The control itself looks like a table or spreadsheet. If the `MSFlexGrid` control is not already added to your toolbox, you can add it by choosing Project, Components, and selecting the Controls tab (see Figure 15.4). Like other controls, select the check box to add the `MSFlexGrid` to your toolbox.

Figure 15.4   *The Components Controls tab allows you to add .OCX components to your toolbox.*

Table 15.1 shows four properties of the MSFlexGrid control that are especially important.

TABLE 15.1   *MSFlexGrid* Control Properties

Property	*Description*
Rows	Sets the total number of fixed and nonfixed rows in the MSFlexGrid.
Cols	Sets the total number of fixed and nonfixed columns in the MSFlexGrid.
FixedRows	Sets the number of fixed rows in the MSFlexGrid.
FixedCols	Sets the number of fixed columns in the MSFlexGrid.

What is the difference between fixed and nonfixed rows and columns? A fixed row or column is used for adding row and column descriptions to the MSFlexGrid. These rows and columns do not scroll when scroll bars are added to the MSFlexGrid and are shaded gray on the MSFlexGrid. A nonfixed row or column is used to store MSFlexGrid values. These rows and columns scroll when necessary. They are not shaded and are shown in white.

Each intersection of a row and column forms an `MSFlexGrid` location called a cell. An individual cell location can be set by using an assignment statement to the `Row` and `Col` (singular) properties. For example, the following sets the cell nonfixed location at `Grid1(1,1)`:

```
Grid1.Row = 1
Grid1.Col = 1
```

After the cell has been identified, you can change the individual cell properties. Table 15.2 shows the cell properties.

TABLE 15.2   Cell Properties

Property	Description
Text	Returns or sets the text contents of a cell.
CellPicture	Returns or sets an image to be displayed in the current cell. These images are often icons.
CellFont	This group of properties sets the font characteristics of cells containing text: CellFontName, CellFontSize, CellFontBold, CellFontItalic, and so on.
ColSel, RowSel	Returns or sets the starting or ending row or column for a range of cells. These properties enable you to select a region of the MSFlexGrid control and change that region's appearance.
BackColor, BackColorBkg, BackColorFixed, BackColorSel	Returns or sets the background color of various elements of the MSFlexGrid. By using the ColSel and RowSel properties, a region can be created.
ColWidth, RowHeight	Returns or sets the width of the specified column or row in twips.

The `MSFlexGrid` has many more properties than those listed here. Consult the Visual Basic online Help for full documentation. The following exercises will give you a sense of the more prominent properties.

You can add text to an individual cell of the `MSFlexGrid` by identifying the cell with the `Row` and `Col` properties and then assigning a value to the control's `Text` property. You also can add text one row at a time, using the `AddItem` method. A string expression that is the argument of the `AddItem` method must then be delimited between cells by the tab character (ASCII value 9). The next exercise demonstrates these two methods of adding string data to cells.

Exercise 15.4   Entering Numbers into the *MSFlexGrid*

Perhaps the best way to learn how to use the MSFlexGrid control is through an example. Figure 15.5 shows the table of numbers you are asked to create.

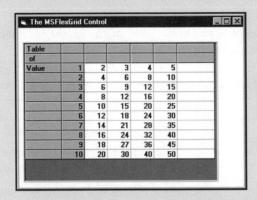

Figure 15.5   *The* MSFlexGrid *control creates a two-dimensional table for you to work with.*

1. Double-click the MSFlexGrid control to place the grid onscreen. Add the form caption.

2. Open the MSFlexGrid control's property box, and set the following:

   ```
   Cols = 5
   Rows = 3
   ```

3. Write the following Form_Load() procedure:

   ```
   Private Sub Form_Load()
      Dim Row As Integer
      Dim Col As Integer
      Dim TK As String
      Dim temp As String

      Grid1.Cols = 7
      TK = Chr$(9)  ' Tab
      For Row = 0 To 9      'Fill each row one at a time
         temp = "" & TK
         For Col = 0 To 4
            temp = temp & ((Row + 1) * (Col + 1)) & TK
         Next Col
         Grid1.AddItem temp      'Add entire row
      Next Row

      Grid1.FixedRows = 2     'Grid property
      Grid1.FixedCols = 2     'Grid property

      Grid1.Col = 0
      Grid1.Row = 0
      Grid1.Text = "Table"
      Grid1.Col = 0
      Grid1.Row = 1
      Grid1.Text = " of "
      Grid1.Col = 0
      Grid1.Row = 2
      Grid1.Text = "Value"
   End Sub
   ```

In this code, the first two statements set the number of rows and columns. Following this, text is added to selected cells. The AddItem method adds rows, so in design-time you set the number of rows to 3 and add them dynamically in a For...Next loop.

4. Test your program. Change the number of FixedRows and FixedCols to 1 to observe some interesting differences.

Exercise 15.5   Entering Items from Text Boxes into an *MSFlexGrid*

Besides adding numbers to an MSFlexGrid using a Form_Load() procedure, it is possible to add values to an MSFlexGrid, row by row or column by column. Figure 15.6 shows the next grid interface that you are to complete. This interface works as follows: After entering the name of the student and the student's scores, click Add to add the names to the grid; click Next to clear the text boxes to allow the next student's name and scores to be added to the grid.

Figure 15.6   *The MSFlexGrid enables you to create a spreadsheet of values.*

1. Create the form shown in Figure 15.6, adding the MSFlexGrid, the two command buttons (**cmdAdd** and **cmdNext**), the name text box (**txtName**), and a control array of five text boxes (**txtScore**) to hold student scores. Add the labels and the form caption.

2. Set the Column property of the grid (Cols) to 6. Leave the Row property set to 1.

continues

3. Write the `cmdAdd_Click()` procedure as follows:

```
Private Sub cmdAdd_Click()
    Dim temp1 As String
    Dim temp2 As String
    Dim score As Integer
    Static row As Integer

    row = row + 1
    grid1.Rows = row
    temp1 = txtName.Text & Chr$(9)

    For score = 0 To 4
        temp2 = temp2 & txtScore(score) & Chr$(9)
    Next score
    grid1.AddItem temp1 & temp2
End Sub
```

In this procedure, two temporary strings are declared: one to store the student's name and one to store the student's scores. The variable row is declared as type Static. This allows it to be incremented by 1 as each new student is added to the grid.

Within the procedure, temp1 stores the student's name, and temp2 stores the student's scores. A Tab key (Chr$(9)) is required to place a score in a different cell on the grid.

4. Write the `cmdNext_Click()` procedure as follows:

```
Private Sub cmdNext_Click()
    Dim i As Integer

    txtName = " "
    For i = 0 To 4
        txtScore(i) = " "
    Next
    txtName.SetFocus
End Sub
```

This procedure first clears the student's name and then continues to clear all student scores. The SetFocus instruction places the cursor in the txtName text box.

5. Run and test your program.

Objective 15.4   Employing an Array of User-Defined Types

You were briefly exposed to user-defined types in Chapter 10, "Defining the Scope of Variables and Procedures." User-defined types provide a way to add a table to a design without employing a multidimensional array, which requires that all elements and all dimensions of the array be of the same data type. User-defined types, on the other hand, combine variables of several different data types to form a single variable.

When an array of these variables is created, a table of mixed data types can be created. This type of array provides a program designer with an enormously useful tool in a wide variety of programming tasks. It allows related data to be held together without defining an entire class.

15.4.1   Declaration of a User-Defined Type

You will recall that a user-defined type must be defined in a standard code module with the Type statement:

```
[Private ¦ Public] Type UserType
    elementname [(subscripts)] As typename
    [elementname [(subscripts)] As typename
End Type
```

You then can use this new data type in variable declarations, such as the following:

```
Dim MyType As UserType
```

Consider the following example. Type Asset contains three members: one member of type String, a second of type Integer, and a third of type Currency.

```
Type Asset
    Name As String * 20
    Location As Integer
    Value As Currency
End Type
```

The declaration using this type then might be as follows:

```
Dim Inventory As Asset
```

This declares the variable Inventory as being of type Asset.

15.4.2   A User-Defined Variable Array

After a user-defined type has been defined, it can be declared as a single variable or as an array. The following declares the variable Part as type Asset:

```
Dim Part As Asset
```

The following declares Inventory to be an array of 100 items, all of which are type Asset:

```
Dim Inventory(1 To 100) As Asset
```

This type of array is called an array of structures because each element in the array contains a complex data type or structure.

Exercise 15.6   Extending Options Using an Array of User-Defined Type

In the European vacation program created in Exercise 14.8, "Creating an Application with Variable Arrays," in Chapter 14, you displayed prices of vacation options, but did not display the option along with the price. A better design would hold vacation information together, displaying both the option description and its price.

Employing a user-defined type is one means to gain such functionality. You could create a type called VacationOption that would hold data about the vacation add-on amount and its current selection status. You could place the following declaration in a standard code module:

```
Public Type VacationOption
   Description as String
   Amount as Currency
   SelStatus as Boolean
End Type
```

This data structure will be used to help track the selection status of vacation add-on options.

1. Open Exercise 14.8 if you have completed it, and save it and its files under a new name, such as **p15-6.vbp**. (Otherwise, complete Exercise 14.8 first.) Increase the width of the listPrice listbox to accommodate both the vacation option description and price.

2. Add a standard module to the program, and make the declaration for the VacationOption user-defined type shown above.

3. Change the declaration at the form module level to the following:

   ```
   Dim EuroChoice(0 To 4) As VacationOption
   ```

4. Change the code in the Form_Load() event to populate the list box and add data to the EuroChoice array.

   ```
   Private Sub Form_Load()

       lstOptions.AddItem "Tyrolean Weekend"
       lstOptions.AddItem "Rhine River Cruise"
       lstOptions.AddItem "Personal Louvre Guide"
       lstOptions.AddItem "Milan Fashion Tour"
       lstOptions.AddItem "Schwartzwald Spa Weekend"

       EuroChoice(0).Description = "Tyrolean Weekend"
       EuroChoice(0).Amount = 455.55
       EuroChoice(0).SelStatus = False

       EuroChoice(1).Description = "Rhine River Cruise"
       EuroChoice(1).Amount = 630.75
       EuroChoice(1).SelStatus = False

       EuroChoice(2).Description = "Personal Louvre Guide"
       EuroChoice(2).Amount = 120.25
       EuroChoice(2).SelStatus = False
   ```

```
            EuroChoice(3).Description = "Milan Fashion Tour"
            EuroChoice(3).Amount = 330.33
            EuroChoice(3).SelStatus = False

            EuroChoice(4).Description = "Schwartzwald Spa Weekend"
            EuroChoice(4).Amount = 765.45
            EuroChoice(4).SelStatus = False

        End Sub
```

5. In the lstOptions_Click event, change the code so that it toggles the selection status of the vacation option and then loops through the array to retrieve the information to display and calculate the add-on total, as in the following:

```
        Private Sub lstOptions_Click()
            Dim amt As Currency
            Dim i As Integer
            Dim SelItem As Integer
            Dim RunTotal As Currency

            ' clear the list box
            lstPrice.Clear

            ' retrieve lstoptions.listindex
            SelItem = lstOptions.ListIndex
            'toggle the selection status
            EuroChoice(SelItem).SelStatus = Not
➥EuroChoice(SelItem).SelStatus

            For i = LBound(EuroChoice) To UBound(EuroChoice)
                If EuroChoice(i).SelStatus = True Then
                    RunTotal = RunTotal + EuroChoice(i).Amount
                    lstPrice.AddItem EuroChoice(i).Description & " - " &
➥EuroChoice(i).Amount
                End If
            Next
            lblTotal.Caption = Format(RunTotal, "Currency")

        End Sub
```

Observe that because there is a one-to-one correspondence between the indexes of the Eurochoice array and the index of the lstOptions listbox, you can use the ListIndex property of lstOptions to reference the array when toggling the SelStaus element value.

6. Change the cmdClear_Click event to use a single loop to set the SelStatus element of the EuroChoice array to False and to clear the selection status of listbox items:

```
        Private Sub cmdClear_Click()
          Dim i As Integer
          'Turn off previous choices
          For i = 0 To 4
            EuroChoice(i).SelStatus = False
            lstOptions.Selected(i) = False
          Next
          'Clear price list
          lstPrice.Clear
```

continues

```
        'Clear totals box
        lblTotal.Caption = ""
    End Sub
```
7. Run and test the program.

Chapter Summary

An array with more than one dimension is called a multidimensional array. Declare a multidimensional array by placing a comma between the dimensions, as follows:

```
ReDim MyTable (1 to 10,1 to 10) As Integer
```

A multi-column list resembles a two-dimensional array; however, it functions like a simple list. To create this type of list, change the number of columns to the number desired.

The MSFlexGrid control places a two-dimensional array onscreen and looks like a table or a spreadsheet. When using the MSFlexGrid control, fixed rows and columns are used for adding grid headings; nonfixed rows and columns are used to store grid data. You can add string data to cells in the following two ways:

- Identified individual cells with the Cell and Row properties; then, the Text property can be assigned a new value or read.

- Add tab-delimited strings to the MSFlexGrid control with the AddItem method. The ColSel and RowSel properties allow a range of cells to be selected.

User-defined types can be placed in arrays with declarations, such as the following:

```
Dim Inventory(1 To 100) As Asset
```

This allows a table of mixed data types to be created, providing the programmer a very useful tool for maintaining related data together without creating a class.

Skill-Building Exercises

This set of exercises asks you to practice using two-dimensional arrays, the MSFlexGrid control, and user-defined types. The last two exercises are especially challenging. You are asked to build and then extend a race car speedway. When the designs are complete, you should be able to use a grid to display the results of the race, as well as set the octane levels of the cars.

1. Use a nested loop and a two-dimensional array to display the following pattern on the screen after a `Form_click()` procedure:

   ```
   0 1 0 0 0
   0 1 1 0 0
   0 1 1 1 0
   0 1 1 1 1
   0 1 1 1 1
   ```

   Name the array `num()`. Use row and column array values in your solution.

2. Use a two-dimensional array named `scores()` to store the bowling team scores for four players. Assign the following scores to each player:

	Player			
Round	1	2	3	4
No. 1	140	150	220	160
No. 2	160	220	230	120
No. 3	165	200	230	140
Avg.	155	190	226	140

   Use a nested loop to produce the table, including the average score for each player. Use a `Form_click()` procedure to display the results. Do not store the average in the array.

3. Modify the preceding exercise by using an `MSFlexGrid` to record player scores. In your design, add the words **Round 1**, **Round 2**, **Round 3**, and **Average** to a set of fixed rows; add **Player 1**, **Player 2**, **Player 3**, and **Player 4** to a set of fixed columns. Write a `Grid1_MouseDown()` event that will enable you to use the right mouse button to enter player scores. When the user right-clicks, open an input box asking the user to enter a score. After all scores have been entered, compute the average score for each player.

4. Define a user-defined type for Employees that holds the name of the employee, his or her employee ID number, hire date, and his or her paygrade (grades range from 1 to 7). Declare an array of five employees, assign data to the array and display the employee name and paygrade in a listbox.

5. Extend the previous exercise by adding a textbox to the form in which the user can enter hours worked. When users click on a name in the listbox, calculate their total pay. Pay for paygrade level 1 is 12.50 per hour and rises in 1.25 increments through paygrade level 7.

6. This and the next exercise ask you to design a race car speedway. This initial exercise asks you to race two cars by setting the octane mixtures for each car by using two scroll bars. A start button begins the race. The first car runs the length of the track, and the time of the run is displayed. The second car then runs the length of the track, and its time is displayed. A checkered flag appears for the car with the winning time.

   In your design, use a picture box for the track, a Line control to separate the two lanes on the track, pictures of cars, and a checkered flag embedded in Image controls. Use `DoEvents` to ensure that each car completes a race before the second car starts.

7. Attach an `MSFlexGrid` to the race car speedway of the preceding exercise to illustrate the time of each car, whether the time for the car represents the driver's best, the course record, and the number of races won by a car. If a car beats the course record, display this fact with a message box.

NUMERIC FUNCTIONS

Besides event and general procedures—namely those that begin with such statements as `Private Sub` and end with `End Sub`—it also is possible to write function procedures and to use built-in functions supplied by Visual Basic. Both function and built-in function procedures return a single value. They differ from general procedures that do not return a value.

Function procedures are written by the Visual Basic designer, much like general procedures. Numeric built-in functions deal with ways of manipulating and converting numbers. The built-in `Abs()` function, for example, is provided to return the absolute value of a number.

This chapter shows you how to write a Visual Basic function procedure, and introduces a number of built-in numeric functions. (The next chapter examines string functions.) Functions often simplify the writing of a Visual Basic program. Instead of writing a procedure, the Visual Basic programmer is able to use a numeric function to compute a value using one or more mathematical formulas and return the value of that computation. When you complete this chapter, you will be able to perform the following tasks:

- Call a numeric function
- Write a numeric function procedure
- Write a recursive function procedure
- Use the built-in numeric conversion functions
- Use the built-in mathematical functions
- Use the built-in financial functions

Chapter Objectives

The objectives of this chapter address how numeric functions work. To begin, you learn how to create a function, and you discover how a function differs from a procedure. You then are introduced to a special type of function called a *recursive function.* This is a function that calls itself. Finally, you examine the use of built-in numeric functions. These are provided by the Visual Basic language. The four chapter objectives are as follows:

1. Understanding how numeric functions work

2. Writing numeric function procedures

3. Writing a recursive function

4. Using built-in numeric functions

Objective 16.1   Understanding How Numeric Functions Work

The syntax for a Visual Basic function is similar to the syntax for a Visual Basic procedure. The following is the simplified syntax:

```
[Public | Private] [Static] Function functionname (arguments)
➡[As type]
    function statements
End Function
```

Following are the differences between a function and a general procedure:

■ The Function keyword identifies the beginning of the function; the End Function keywords mark the end of the function.

■ Arguments typically are required by a function. These argument values most often are passed from a procedure to a function.

■ The [As type] part of the declaration syntax specifies the type of data to be returned by a function. If a function returns a value of type Integer, this type should be indicated.

As an example, consider the following event procedure:

```
Private Sub Form_Click()
    Dim Length As Integer
    Dim Width As Integer
    Dim Height As Integer
    Length = 4
    Width = 6
    Height = 5
    Label1.Caption = cubeIt(Length, Width, Height)
End Sub
```

The cubeIt(Length, Width, Height) statement represents a function call. It calls a function with the same name of cubeIt(). The function call passes the function three values: a value for the length, a value for the width, and a value for the height. Each argument is separated by a comma.

The function cubeIt() is written as follows:

```
Public Function cubeIt(Length, Width, Height) As Integer
    cubeIt = Length * Width * Height
End Function
```

The function computes the cube as 120 and returns this integer value to the general procedure. The returned value is assigned to Label1.Caption.

Why write a function as simple as cubeIt() and add it to a program? A function such as this will simplify a program if the function cubeIt() is called at different times in several places in a program, or if the function simplifies the writing of the procedure.

16.1.1   Common Mistakes

A common mistake is to write the preceding procedure as follows:

```
Private Sub Form_Click()
  Dim Length As Integer
  Dim Width As Integer
  Dim Height As Integer
  Length = 4
  Width = 6
  Height = 5
  cubeIt(Length, Width, Height)
  Label1.Caption = cubeIt
End Sub
```

This leads to a syntax error. The function call, because it returns a value, must assign that value to a variable in the program, as in the following code:

```
Label1.Caption = cubeIt(Length, Width, Height)
```

Another common mistake is to write the calling statement as follows:

```
Label1.Caption = cubeIt(Length * Width * Height)
```

This will lead to an argument-count-mismatch error because the addition of the multiplication operators (instead of the commas) shows one value being passed to the function instead of three.

A third mistake is to write a function call to a procedure rather than a function:

```
Public Sub cubeIt(Length, Width, Height)
  cubeIt = Length * Width * Height
End Sub
```

This procedure will lead to a compiler error because the function call statement specifies a call to a function, not a procedure:

```
Label1.Caption = cubeIt(Length, Width, Height)
```

16.1.2   The Expanded *Function* Syntax

The initial Function syntax described at the beginning of this objective is actually an abbreviated one. The expanded syntax is as follows:

```
[Public | Private] [Static] Function functionname (argument list)
➡[As type]
  [statement block]
  [functionname = expression]
  [Exit Function]
  [statement block]
  [functionname = expression]
End Function
```

The argument list can be expanded to read as follows:

```
[ByVal]variable[()][As type] [,[ByVal]variable[()] [As type]]
```

Table 16.1 explains the new terms in this syntax.

TABLE 16.1   The Expanded Function Syntax

Term	Description
Static	Signifies that the function's local values are retained between function calls.
Private	Indicates that the Function procedure is accessible only to other procedures in the module in which it exists.
Public	Indicates that the Function procedure is accessible to procedures in other modules.
Exit Function	Causes an immediate exit from the procedure.
ByVal	Indicates that the argument is passed by value rather than by reference. Passed by value means that a copy of the value is passed rather than the address (in memory) of the value. Use of the ByVal keyword is reviewed in Chapter 21, "Modular Design."

Although As type in this syntax is optional, a good programming practice is to specify the type, as in the following example:

```
Public Function cubeIt(Length As Integer, Width As Integer, Height As
➥Integer) As Integer
```

This revised declaration indicates that the function will receive three values, all type Integer, and return a single value of type Integer.

Objective 16.2   Writing Numeric Function Procedures

Visual Basic contains a number of built-in functions, and you also can purchase libraries of functions. Even so, there will be times when function procedures are written by a programmer.

A common use of function procedures is to conduct an analysis of a set of numbers to return a computed value or to determine a characteristic of the set. In Exercise 16.1, for example, you are asked to use a function to return a runner's pace in minutes per mile. Following this, you are asked to write functions to determine the highest and lowest values in a set of numbers.

Exercise 16.1 Writing a Simple Function Procedure

Design a program called **Convert Race Results**, as shown in Figure 16.1. The program requires you to check either a 10 kilometer run/walk or an 8 kilometer run/walk. You then are asked to enter the time required to complete the run/walk in minutes and seconds. Given this information, the program computes your pace in minutes per mile.

Figure 16.1 *This design asks the user to click the type of race and enter the time in minutes.*

1. Add the option buttons (place in a frame), the labels, the text box, and the command button on a form.

2. Add a `txtTime_KeyPress()` procedure. Get the time from the text box and call a function, named `mph()`, to compute and return the pace of the walker/runner. Display this pace. This code is as follows:

```
Private Sub txtTime_KeyPress (KeyAscii As Integer)
    Dim result As Single
    Dim newTime As Single
    If KeyAscii = vbKeyReturn Then
        newTime = CSng(txtTime.Text)
        result = mph(newTime)
        lblPace.Caption = Str$(result)
    Else
        Exit Sub
    End If
End Sub
```

With this code, you must press the Enter key on the keyboard to compute the pace of the runner (walker). The function `mph()` is called, and the computed value is assigned to the variable result.

3. Write the function `mph()`. This function receives the time required to walk or run the distance, and checks to determine whether the run/walk was 8 kilometers or 10 kilometers and greater than 0.

continues

Exercise 16.1   continued

```
Function mph (newTime as Single) as Single
   If (opt10K = True And newTime > 0) Then
      mph = CSng(newTime / 6.2)
   ElseIf (opt8K = True And newTime > 0) Then
      mph = CSng(newTime / 5.1)
   End If
   txtTime.SetFocus
End Function
```

This function determines whether the choice is 10 kilometers or 8 kilometers and whether the time is greater than 0. If it is, then the miles per hour is computed and returned to the calling procedure.

4. Write a `cmdClear()` procedure that enables you to try again before deciding to end.

```
Private Sub cmdClear_Click()
   lblPace.Caption = ""
   txtTime.Text = ""
   txtTime.SetFocus
End Sub
```

5. Test this procedure. Select the type of race you want to run and indicate your time in minutes to complete the race.

Exercise 16.2   Returning the Highest and Lowest Values

This exercise asks you to create an array and to search the array for the highest and lowest values. Two functions are utilized in performing this search. One function searches the array for the highest value. After it is found, this value is returned. A second function searches the array for the lowest value. After it is found, this value is returned. Figure 16.2 shows the form to create.

Figure 16.2   *Enter all team scores in the array before pressing the Get High And Low Scores button.*

1. Write a program that allows you to enter 15 scores for three teams. Design the interface, using an array of text boxes. Press the Tab key to move from one cell to the next in the table. This will allow you to enter scores one row at a time.

2. Write a cmdScores() procedure. This procedure (which follows) contains two function calls: one to a function named High_Score(), which computes and returns the highest of all scores, and another to a function named Low_Score(), which computes and returns the lowest of all scores.

```
Private Sub cmdScores_Click()
    Static score(0 To 14) As Integer
    Dim num As Integer
    Dim High As Integer
    Dim Low As Integer
    For num = 0 To 14
        score(num) = Val(txtScore(num).Text)
    Next num
    High = High_Score(score(), num - 1)
    lblHigh.Caption = Str$(High)
    Low = Low_Score(score(), num - 1)
    lblLow.Caption = Str$(Low)
End Sub
```

3. Write a High_Score() function. This function searches the array of scores to determine and return the highest value:

```
Private Function High_Score (score() As Integer, num As
➥Integer)
    Dim max As Integer
    Dim High As Integer
    High = 0
    For max = 0 To num
        If (score(max) > High) Then
            High = score(max)
        End If
    Next max
    High_Score = High
End Function
```

4. Write a Low_Score() function. This function is similar to the High_Score() function, but returns the following low score:

```
Private Function Low_Score (score() As Integer, num As Integer)
    Dim min As Integer
    Dim Low As Integer
    Low = 1000
    For min = 0 To num
        If (score(min) < Low) Then
            Low = score(min)
        End If
    Next min
    Low_Score = Low
End Function
```

5. Run and test your design. As one test, have duplicate high and low scores. Does this lead to problems?

continues

Several features of this exercise merit special emphasis. First, examine the function declarations. Function arguments that expect to receive an array must be declared with a set of parentheses. Procedures that pass an array to the function must also pass them with a set of parentheses.

Second, observe that along with the array, the array's upper bound also is passed. This permits the Low_Score() and High_Score() functions to know how many iterations of the For loop to execute. In this case, you use the counter variable num. Notice that the upper bound of the array is passed as num-1. This is because the last iteration of the For...Next loop in cmdScores_Click() increments the num counter variable so that it equals 15 at the end of the loop execution. By decrementing it by 1, you can pass along the upper bound of the array.

Alternatively, you could have passed the score array to the High function with the following assignment expression:

```
High = High_Score(score(), UBound(score)).
```

Notice also how the variables High and Low are initialized in the High_Score() and Low_Score() functions. They are each assigned an absurd value. High is assigned the value 0, and Low is assigned the value 1000. These values are replaced in the first assignment in the execution of the function For loops. At the end of the loop's execution, the high and low values in the array are respectively determined.

Objective 16.3   Writing a Recursive Function

In the preceding exercises, you saw procedures call functions. Functions can also call other functions. Functions can even call themselves. This is known as *recursion*. Recursive functions provide elegant solutions to several kinds of computing problems, including complex sorting algorithms.

Some computer languages, such as Prolog, are designed to use recursion extensively. Recursive functions, however, can be difficult to debug. This chapter demonstrates a recursive function to determine the factorial of a number. You are asked to write this example in the first exercise in the "Skill-Building Exercises" section at the end of this chapter.

In the following procedure, the function call statement is Label1.Caption = fact(n).

```
Private Sub Form_Click()
   'Program to determine the factorial of a number using
   'recursion
   Dim n As Integer
   n = 4
   Label1.Caption = fact(n)
End Sub
```

The corresponding Function procedure is passed the value of n, and is written as follows:

```
Public Function fact(n As Integer) As Integer
  If (n <= 1) Then
    fact = 1
  Else
    fact = n * fact(n - 1)       ' fact() calls itself
  End If
End Function
```

The calling statement passes control to the function fact(). The function uses a test condition to determine whether n is equal to 1. This condition will eventually end the recursion. In the preceding example, because n is equal to 4, the else portion of the statement executes with the following result:

```
fact = 4 * fact(3)
```

To evaluate this statement, fact() is called again, leading to the following statement:

```
fact = 3 * fact(2)
```

This is followed by

```
fact = 2 * fact(1)
```

At this point, n is equal to 1, and the recursive calls stop. However, the calls must then be resolved. The following are the unresolved calls:

```
(a)  fact = 4 * fact(3)
(b)  fact = 3 * fact(2)
(c)  fact = 2 * fact(1)
```

Knowing that fact(1) is equal to 1 and remembering that a function has static scope, this stack of unresolved calls can be resolved as follows:

```
fact(1) = 1
fact(2) = 2
fact(3) = 6
```

This leads to the answer 24, which is determined by the expanded equations:

```
(a)  fact = 2 * 1 =  2
(b)  fact = 3 * 2 =  6
(c)  fact = 4 * 6 = 24
```

This is the same as 4! (four factorial).

Objective 16.4   Using Built-In Numeric Functions

Visual Basic contains a number of built-in numeric and string functions. (The latter are addressed in Chapter 17, "String Functions.") The three types of numeric functions discussed in the remainder of this chapter are as follows:

■ Numerical conversion

■ Mathematical

■ Financial

16.4.1   Numeric Conversion Functions

Numeric conversion functions convert one numeric data type to another (see Table 16.2).

TABLE 16.2   Numeric Conversion Functions

Function	Description
Int()	Returns the integer value of the number entered as the argument. With a negative number, it returns the first integer less than or equal to the number.
Fix()	Returns the integer value of the number entered as the argument. With a negative number, it returns the first integer greater than or equal to the number.
Round()	Returns the number rounded to a specified number of decimal places.
CInt()	Returns the rounded integer closest to the value of the argument.
CLng()	Returns the rounded long integer closest to the value of the argument.
CSng()	Converts the argument to a single-precision number.
CDbl()	Converts the argument to a double-precision number.
CCur()	Converts the argument to a number of type Currency.
CStr()	Converts the argument to a string.
CVar()	Converts the argument to a value of type Variant.

As an example of the first two numerical conversion functions, if the argument is −8.6, Int() will return −9, while Fix() will return −8.

Of the seven remaining types, CCur() is a most useful function when a value computed as type Double or Single needs to be expressed as type Currency. The following statements explicitly state that a value of type Currency is to be assigned to the variable SalesTax:

```
TaxRate = 0.082
SalesTax = CCur(Cus_Sale * TaxRate)
```

At times, this process of transforming data explicitly is known as *casting the data to a type*. The CCur() function in the preceding example casts the product of Cus_Sale and TaxRate to type Currency.

The Round function takes an argument specifying the number of decimal places to perform the rounding. Following are the instructions:

```
Print Round(123.456, 1)
Print Round(123.456, 2)
Print Round(123.456, 3)
```

which produces the following output:

```
123.5
123.46
123.456
```

16.4.2   Mathematical Functions

Other, perhaps more common, mathematical functions provided with Visual Basic are in Table 16.3. These differ from the previously described numeric functions, which are designed to handle rounding of numbers or casting to an explicit data type.

TABLE 16.3   Mathematical Functions

Function	Description
Exp()	Returns the base of the natural logarithm of the argument raised to a specified power.
Log()	Returns the natural logarithm of the argument.
Sqr()	Returns the square root of the argument.
Randomize()	Seeds all random numbers by using the number entered as the argument.
Rnd()	Returns a random number determined by the computer.
Abs()	Returns the absolute value of the argument.
Sgn()	Returns the sign of the value of the argument.
Atn()	Returns the arctangent of the argument in radians.
Cos()	Returns the cosine of the argument in radians.
Sin()	Returns the sine of the argument in radians.
Tan()	Returns the tangent of the argument in radians.

Exercise 16.3   Taking the Square of a Number and Casting It to Type Integer

This brief exercise asks you to enter a number and take the square root of it, and then cast the number as an integer before it is displayed. Figure 16.3 shows the form to create.

1. Add the labels and the text box as shown.

Figure 16.3   *The square root of a number makes use of the* Sqr() *function.*

continues

Exercise 16.3   continued

2. Write a txtNumber_Change() procedure. Compute the square of a number entered in txtNumber.Text. Following this, use CLng() to cast the number to type long. Display the number in lblSquare.

```
Private Sub txtNumber_Change()
    Dim number As Long
    'After taking the square root, cast the number as type long
    number = CLng(Sqr(Val(txtNumber.Text)))
    lblSquare.Caption = number
End Sub
```

3. Run and test your program.

16.4.3   Generating Random Numbers

Although most of the mathematical functions are easy to understand, two of them—Rnd() and Randomize()—are somewhat unusual and require additional clarification. In many situations, these two functions are used in pairs. The syntax for Rnd() is as follows:

```
Num = Rnd [(number)]
```

Rnd() returns a number of type Single between 0 and 1, and the value for number determines how Rnd() generates the random number. The relationship between number and the value returned is as follows:

Value of number	Value Returned
< 0	The same value every time, as determined by number
> 0	The next random number value in the sequence
= 0	The value most recently generated

To have the program generate a different random number every time a procedure is run, use the Randomize statement without an argument. Simply write the following:

```
Randomize       'Place this before Rnd()
```

This will initialize the random number generator before Rnd() is called.

Because the random number generator returns a value between 0 and 1, it is often necessary to convert this number to a larger or smaller number. To convert the number to a range of integers, such as 1 to 6, write the following statement:

```
Int((Rnd * 6) + 1)
```

This converts the random number to one of six integers (1, 2, 3, 4, 5, or 6).

Exercise 16.4   Using the Randomize Statement to Roll a Die

This exercise asks you to design a program to roll a die and show the result using a picture of a die. Figure 16.4 shows the form with which you are asked to work. With this picture box and seven circles, you can display the die markers 1, 2, 3, 4, 5, and 6.

Figure 16.4   *A single die can be used to display the numbers 1–6.*

1. Design the form as shown in Figure 16.4. Use a picture box and create an array of circle shapes, numbered from 0–6.

2. Initialize the die to make all shapes invisible to begin. This code is as follows:

```
Private Sub initialize()
    'Make the die invisible
    pic1.Visible = False
    'Make the die markings invisible
    shape1(0).Visible = False
    shape1(1).Visible = False
    shape1(2).Visible = False
    shape1(3).Visible = False
    shape1(4).Visible = False
    shape1(5).Visible = False
    shape1(6).Visible = False
End Sub
```

3. Write the cmdRoll_Click() procedure.

```
Sub cmdRoll_Click()
    Dim die1 As Integer
    'Set seed
    Randomize
    die1 = Int((Rnd * 6) + 1)
    Print die1
    Call initialize
    pic1.Visible = True
    Select Case die1
        Case 1
            shape1(3).Visible = True
        Case 2
            shape1(0).Visible = True
            shape1(6).Visible = True
        Case 3
            shape1(0).Visible = True
            shape1(3).Visible = True
            shape1(6).Visible = True
```

continues

Exercise 16.4   continued

```
            Case 4
                shape1(0).Visible = True
                shape1(2).Visible = True
                shape1(4).Visible = True
                shape1(6).Visible = True
            Case 5
                shape1(0).Visible = True
                shape1(2).Visible = True
                shape1(3).Visible = True
                shape1(4).Visible = True
                shape1(6).Visible = True
            Case 6
                shape1(0).Visible = True
                shape1(1).Visible = True
                shape1(2).Visible = True
                shape1(4).Visible = True
                shape1(5).Visible = True
                shape1(6).Visible = True
        End Select
    End Sub
```

4. Test this design. Run the exercise several times to determine whether the program displays the same or a different set of random numbers.

Exercise 16.5   Generating a Set of Random Numbers and Displaying Them on a Grid

This exercise asks you to use the MSFlexGrid control to create a table of rows and columns and to fill the rows and columns with random numbers in the range of 1–50. Create the interface shown in Figure 16.5.

Figure 16.5   *This grid displays a different set of random numbers each time the program is run.*

1. For the Grid property dialog box, set the number of rows and columns at 5, turn off scroll bars, and set the number of fixed rows and fixed columns to 0. Name the grid **Grid1**.

2. Write the cmdShow_Click() procedure, and use a nested For...Next loop. Within the inner loop, get the first row value. Then, get a random number and assign it to the first row and column intersection, and then assign it to Result. Use the following code:

```
Private Sub cmdShow_Click()
    Static Result(0 To 4) As Integer
    Dim Row As Integer
    Dim Column As Integer
    For Row = 0 To 4                'Start at top row
        Grid1.Row = Row
        For Column = 0 To 4
            Randomize
            Result(Column) = Int(50 * Rnd + 1)
            Grid1.Col = Column
            Grid1.Text = Result(Column)
        Next Column
    Next Row
End Sub
```

3. Run and test this design. As one test, generate a different set of random numbers, such as from 1–40.

16.4.4 Financial Functions

Besides common numerical functions, Visual Basic provides a set of specialized financial functions. These are most useful when working with interest and its effect on the value of money. Table 16.4 shows financial functions. The first six are used when working with annuities, and the last four deal with cash flow.

TABLE 16.4 Financial Functions

Function	Description
FV()	Returns the future value of an annuity based on periodic, constant payments and a constant interest rate over a specified period.
IPmt()	Returns the interest payment for a given period of an annuity based on periodic, constant payments and a constant interest rate over a specified period.
NPer()	Returns the number of periods for an annuity based on periodic, constant payments and a constant interest rate.
Pmt()	Returns the payment for an annuity based on periodic, constant payments and a constant interest rate over a specified period.
PPmt()	Returns the principle payment for an annuity based on periodic, constant payments and a constant interest rate over a specified period.
Rate()	Returns the interest rate per period for an annuity.

continues

TABLE 16.4   continued

Function	Description
NPV()	Returns the net present value of an investment based on periodic and variable cash flows (payments and receipts) and a discount rate. This function requires an array of cash flows.
PV()	Returns the present value of an investment based on a periodic and constant cash flow (payments and receipts) and a discount rate.
IRR()	Returns the internal rate of return for a series of periodic cash flow (payments and receipts).
MIRR()	Returns the modified internal rate of return for a series of periodic cash flow (payments and receipts).

The financial functions all require several arguments. The arguments and their meanings are found by using the Visual Basic online Help under the heading "Financial Functions." In computing the payment for a house, for example, the payment function is needed. The syntax for this function is as follows:

```
Pmt (rate, nper, pv, fv, type)
```

Table 16.5 shows the components of the syntax.

TABLE 16.5   *Pmt()* Function Syntax

Component	Description
rate	The interest rate per period. If an annual rate is specified, such as 6 %, the percentage must be divided by 100 (to make it .06) and by 12 (to reduce it to .005). This reflects the monthly payment percentage.
nper	The number of payments. If years are specified, this number must be multiplied by 12 to determine the number of months.
pv	The present value of the loan. If you want to borrow $50,000 today, the present value is −50000 (a negative number).
fv	The future value of the loan. Because you want to pay off your home (eventually), the fv is 0.
type	When the payment is due. Use 1 for the beginning of a month and 0 for the end of the month. End of month payments are assumed.

Exercise 16.6   Using Financial Functions to Determine Your New House Payment

Suppose that you want a simple design to show you how large your house payments will be. Create the design shown in Figure 16.6.

Figure 16.6   *Add the amount of the loan, the interest rate, and the life of the loan to compute the monthly payment.*

1. Add the three text boxes and labels (including one for the computed result), as shown in Figure 16.6. Name the text boxes **txtBorrow**, **txtRate**, and **txtYears**. Name the results label **lblPayment**, and add a border to it. Add the command button, **cmdCompute**.

2. Write the cmdCompute() procedure as follows:

```
Private Sub cmdCompute_Click()
    Dim yearIRate As Single
    Dim nperiods As Integer
    Dim borrow As Currency
    Dim payment As Currency
    yearIRate = CSng(txtRate.Text) / (12 * 100)
    nperiods = CInt(txtYears.Text) * 12
    borrow = CCur(txtBorrow.Text)
    payment = Pmt(yearIRate, nperiods, -borrow, 0, 0)
    lblPayment.Caption = Format(payment, "Currency")
End Sub
```

3. Run and test your program. Get the amount you want to borrow, the yearly interest rate, and the number of years of the loan. Compute the monthly payment.

Chapter Summary

This chapter describes the use of functions. Unlike procedures, a function must return only one value. The following is the expanded function syntax:

```
[Public | Private] [Static] Function functionname (argument list)
➥[As type]
  [statement block]
  [functionname = expression]
  [Exit Function]
  [statement block]
  [functionname = expression]
End Function
```

When writing a function, the function call must reference the function name and contain the same number of arguments as the argument list of the function. The following code is a function call, containing three arguments:

```
Label1.Caption = cubeIt(Length, Width, Height)
```

The function would be written as follows:

```
Function cubeIt(Length, Width, Height) As Integer
```

As shown, the argument list is the same; the function returns a value of type Integer. The return instruction is placed within the body of the function, as in the following code:

```
cubeIt = Length * Width * Length
```

This value is assigned to cubeIt(), which in turn assigns the value to the caption in the calling statement.

Certain categories of functions can call themselves. These are known as recursive functions. They call themselves repeatedly until a condition is met; then, the multiple calls to the function are resolved.

Visual Basic contains a number of built-in functions. These include numeric conversion functions, mathematical functions, and financial functions. Numeric conversion functions enable the transforming of data explicitly. This is known as casting to a type. For example, CCur() will cast a value to type Currency.

Mathematical functions include Rnd() and Randomize(), the two functions needed in creating a unique set of random numbers. To create such a set, place the Randomize statement in front of the Rnd() function.

Financial functions provide specialized ways of analyzing money. Six financial functions are available when working with annuity problems, and four are available for use with cash-flow problems.

Skill-Building Exercises

This set of exercises asks you to work with a recursive function, the random number functions, the round function, and the built-in numeric functions. Experiment with the last two exercises using different levels of interest and rates of inflation.

1. Write a program to test the cubeIt() and fact() functions discussed in Objective 16.1, "Understanding How Numeric Functions Work," and Objective 16.3, "Writing a Recursive Function," respectively.

2. Write a program to call a function to compute a set of 10 random numbers between 1–100. After these are displayed, call the function a second time to compute a second and different set of 10 random numbers from 1–100.

3. Create a design to allow the user to enter a number from 2–8 and to click one of the following to raise the number to a power: square, cube, fourth, fifth, sixth, seventh, or eighth. Display the result using a label. As an example, the user should be able to display "2 raised to the 8th power."

4. Place a combo box on a form and set its style property to 1 (simple combo) and extend the list portion of the combo box so that it can handle up to 10 numbers. Instruct the user to input decimal values into the text portion of the combo box. When the user presses the Enter key, round the inputted numbers taking the ListCount property of the combo box as the degrees of precision to employ. Display the result in the list portion of the combo box.

5. Extend the previous exercise by displaying the sum of values in the combo box in a label placed on the form.

6. This exercise asks you to use a built-in numeric function to determine what your savings will be if you decide to deposit a fixed amount of money each month. You must enter the amount you want to save each month, the expected rate of interest, and the number of years you plan to save. Display the result using a label.

7. You have just won the lottery! Enter the amount you will be paid each year, the number of years you are to be paid, the yearly rate of inflation. Then, determine what that amount would be worth if you were paid a lump-sum amount today. Use a built-in numeric function. Display your result using a label.

STRING FUNCTIONS

String functions deal with ways of manipulating and converting strings. The Val() function, for example, is used to translate a string into a number, while the Str$() function converts a number into a string. The Format$() function is used to format numbers, dates, and times.

This chapter considers several other types of string functions besides Val(), Str$(), and Format$(). Because strings are used so often in Visual Basic programming, it is important to know how they can be inspected, converted, manipulated, and compared. Built-in string functions are used for this purpose.

You learn many tasks in this chapter, after which you will be able to perform the following tasks:

- Determine the length of a string
- Convert a string from upper- to lowercase and lower- to uppercase
- Convert a string to its numeric code, or an ANSI code (formerly ASCII code) to a character
- Convert a string to a specified data type
- Work with functions that return part of a string
- Use statements to modify strings
- Return a substring from a larger string
- Compare strings with the Like operator
- Use the string compare function
- Sort strings in ascending order
- Use the String() and the Space() functions

Chapter Objectives

The objectives for this chapter are based on the different categories used to inspect, convert, manipulate, and compare strings, as follows:

1. Determining the length of a string

2. Understanding string conversion categories

3. Manipulating strings

4. Modifying strings

5. Comparing and sorting strings

6. Working with string array functions

7. Constructing strings

Objective 17.1   Determining the Length of a String

It often is necessary to inspect a string to determine its length. The function for doing this is the Len() function. The syntax for Len() is simply the following:

```
Len (string)
```

The following instructions display a value of 5:

```
First$ = "Smith"
Print Len(First$)
```

The Len() function is often used to test whether string variables or object properties have been assigned values. Testing for the length of a string, for example, is one way to determine whether the user has entered data into a text box. Consider the following procedure:

```
Private Sub txtState_LostFocus
   Dim answer As String
   Const strDefault = "OR"
   If Len(txtInput.Text) Then
     answer = txtInput.Text
     Call testanswer(answer) ' procedure to test user input
   Else
     txtState.Text = strDefault
   End If
End Sub
```

By using a simple test of string length, this code helps ensure that required data input is received before processing continues. The Len() function, combined with other string functions, can help make your application less subject to user input errors.

Objective 17.2 Understanding String Conversion Categories

String conversion categories serve to convert a string from one form to another. There are several categories of string conversion, including the following:

- Converting the case of a string from upper- to lowercase and lower- to uppercase. This is known as *converting the case of a string*.

- Converting a string to its numeric code or converting a numeric code to a string. This often is known as *converting a character to an ANSI number or an ANSI code to a character*.

- Converting a string to a specified data type.

In Visual Basic, there are often two versions of functions that return strings: one version returns a Variant of type string; the other adds a dollar sign ($) suffix to the function and explicitly returns a string. We usually employ functions that append the dollar sign. Using this version is more resource efficient, and it makes certain that data string conversions are taking place.

A list of functions that return strings and can carry a dollar sign follows. Some you have encountered before; many you will learn about in this chapter. These functions have the same usage and syntax as their variant versions without the dollar sign.

Chr$()	CurDir$()	Date$()	Dir$()
Error$()	Format$()	Hex$()	Input$()
LCase$()	Left$()	LTrim$()	Mid$()
Oct$()	Right$()	RTrim$()	Space$()
Str$()	String$()	Time$()	Trim$()
UCase$()			

17.2.1 Converting the Case of a String

Three functions are used in converting the case of a string: LCase(), UCase(), StrConv(). The following is the syntax for these functions:

```
LCase$ (strexpr)
UCase$ (strexpr)
StrConv (strexpr, conversion)
```

The component strexpr is the string expression to be converted, and conversion is the value specifying the type of conversion to perform. Table 17.1 shows the three conversion argument settings for the StrConv() function.

TABLE 17.1 *Conversion* Argument Settings for *StrConv()*

Constant	Value	Description
vbUpperCase	1	Converts the string to uppercase characters
vbLowerCase	2	Converts the string to lowercase characters
vbProperCase	3	Converts the first letter of every word in the string to uppercase

The following instructions

```
Name$ = "Sally sue"
Print Name$
Print UCase$(Name$)
Print LCase$(Name$)
Print StrConv(Name$, vbProperCase)
```

lead to the following output:

```
Sally sue
SALLY SUE
sally sue
Sally Sue
```

17.2.2   Converting Strings to ANSI Code

Every string character is represented by an ANSI (American National Standards Institute) code that ranges from 65 to 90 for uppercase letters and 97 to 122 for lowercase letters. The entire ANSI code range is from 0 to 255. (See Visual Basic Help for the entire table of values, or see Appendix A, "The ANSI Character Set.") The two ANSI conversion functions are Asc() and Chr$(). Asc() returns the ANSI code for a string expression, while Chr$() returns an ANSI character. The syntax for these two functions is as follows:

```
Asc (strexpr)
```

```
Chr$ (ANSIcode)
```

As an example of the Asc() function, consider the following instructions:

```
Print Asc("A")
Print Asc("a")
```

These would display the following:

```
65
97
```

As an example of the Chr$() function, consider the following instructions:

```
Print Chr$(65)
Print Chr$(97)
```

These would display the following:

```
A
a
```

How is this latter function used in a Visual Basic program? A common need is to create a tab character for tab-delimited text or a variable that combines a linefeed with a carriage return. Consider the following instruction:

```
NewLine = Chr$(13) & Chr$(10)
```

NewLine starts on a new line because the ANSI code for 13 represents a carriage return, and the code for 10 is a linefeed. Visual Basic also provides constants for these characters (for example, vbTab, vbCr, vbLf, vbCrLf, and vbNewLine).

Consider the use of the vbNewLine constant in an instruction, such as the following:

```
FName$ = "Roger" & vbNewLine & vbNewLine
LName$ = "Rabbit"
Name$ = FName$ & LName$
MsgBox Name$
```

In the message box, the following output would appear:

```
Roger
'space'
'space'
Rabbit
```

In database applications using Structured Query Language(SQL), single quotes are used to designate strings. This character may be generated by using the Chr$(39) function call, as in the following example:

```
strWhereClause = "WHERE City = " & Chr$(39) & "Portland" & Chr$(39)
```

17.2.3   Converting Strings to Numbers and Numbers to Strings

Several functions convert strings to numbers and numbers to strings. Table 17.2 lists the 10 types and their meanings.

TABLE 17.2   Functions for String/Number Conversion

Function	Description
Val()	Converts a string to a number
Str$()	Converts a number to a string
Hex$()	Converts a number to a hexadecimal string
Oct$()	Converts a number to an octal string
CDate()	Converts a string to type Date
CInt()	Converts a string to type Integer
CLng()	Converts a string to type Long
CSng()	Converts a string to type Single
CDbl()	Converts a string to type Double
CCur()	Converts a string to type Currency

Of these 10 functions, types Val() and Str$() are of the most importance because text boxes and combo boxes are used so often in getting and displaying values.

The middle two functions, Hex$() and Oct$() serve a special purpose. These often are used when manipulating memory addresses and byte values.

The last six conversion functions—CDate(),CInt(),CLng(),CSng(),CDbl(), and CCur()—are the same as those described in Chapter 16, "Numeric Functions." These cast functions are more explicit than Val(). If Val() cannot return a numeric value, it returns a 0. The following instructions would display 0:

```
Number$ = "Ten"
Print Val(Number$)
```

The following instructions would generate the error Type mismatch because "Ten" is not a number:

```
Number$ = "Ten"
Print CCur(Number$)
```

Objective 17.3   Manipulating Strings

The more difficult string functions to work with are the six functions that return part of a string. Table 17.3 lists these six functions and their meanings.

TABLE 17.3   Functions for Returning Part of a String

Function	Description
Left$()	Returns a substring from far left
Right$()	Returns a substring from far right
Mid$()	Returns a substring
LTrim$()	Strips the blanks from the far left
RTrim$()	Strips the blanks from the far right
Trim$()	Strips the blanks from both ends of a string
StrReverse()	Returns a string in which the character order of a specified string is reversed
Replace()	Returns a string in which a specified substring has been replaced with another substring a specified number of times

Each of these functions contains arguments, which explains why these functions are complex.

17.3.1 The *Left$()*, *Right$()*, and *Mid$()* Functions

The syntax for the `Left$()` is as follows:

```
Left[$](strexpr, n)
```

The `strexpr` component is the string from which the substring is returned, and `n` is the number of characters to return.

The following function call, for example, returns the first four characters, `What`:

```
Left$("What is your name?", 4)
```

The syntax for `Right$()` is the same as `Left$()`, with a change in the keyword:

```
Right[$](strexpr, n)
```

The following function call returns the last five characters, `name?`:

```
Right$("What is your name?", 5)
```

The syntax for `Mid$()` contains three arguments (see Table 17.4):

```
Mid[$](strexpr, start [,n])
```

TABLE 17.4 Arguments for *Mid$()*

Component	Description
strexpr	The string from which the substring is returned
start	The character position where the substring begins
n	The length of the substring

The following function call returns the sixth and seventh characters (2 in total), beginning at the sixth character and displaying the word `is`:

```
Mid$("What is your name?", 6, 2)
```

If the length of the string (`n`) to return is omitted or if there are fewer than `n` characters in the text (including the character at start), all characters from the start position to the end of the string are returned. For example, consider the following statement:

```
Mid$("What is your name?", 6)
```

It will return the following:

```
is your name?
```

The beginning is the sixth character, and the last character is the last character in the string.

17.3.2   The *LTrim$()*, *RTrim$()*, and *Trim$()* Functions

The three trim functions, `LTrim$()`, `RTrim$()`, and `Trim$()`, are easy to understand. These remove the blanks from a string. The syntax for these functions are as follows:

```
LTrim[$](strexpr)
RTrim[$](strexpr)
Trim[$](strexpr)
```

As an example, consider the following code fragment:

```
message = "             This is a test."
text = Ltrim$(message)
Print text
```

It displays the following:

```
This is a test.
```

The `LTrim$()`, `RTrim$()`, and `Trim$()` functions strip blank space that is input by users. You could, for example, extend the earlier example (from Objective 17.1, "Determining the Length of a String") to test user input:

```
Private Sub txtState_LostFocusDim answer As String
    Const strDefault = "OR"
    If Len(Trim$(txtInput.Text)) <> 0 Then
      answer = txtInput.Text
      Call testanswer(answer) ' procedure to test user input
    Else
      txtState.Text = strDefault
    End If
End Sub
```

17.3.3   The *StrReverse* and *Replace* Functions

The `StrReverse` function returns a string in which the character order of a specified string is reversed. The syntax is simple:

StrReverse(string1)The following code instructions:

```
ret = StrReverse("abcde")
Print ret
```

would generate the following output:

```
Edcba
```

The Replace function has a more complex syntax and the return values can vary. The function replaces a substring with another substring a specified number of times. The following syntax is somewhat complex:

TABLE 17.5 Syntax of the *Replace* Function

Part	Description
expression	Required. String expression containing substring to replace
find	Required. Substring being searched for
replacewith	Required. Replacement substring
start	Optional. Position within expression where substring search is to begin. If omitted, 1 is assumed
count	Optional. Number of substring substitutions to perform. If omitted, the default value is –1, which means make all possible substitutions
compare	Optional. Numeric value indicating the kind of comparison to use when evaluating substrings. See "Settings" section for values

Settings for the *compare* Argument

Constant	Value	Description
vbUseCompareOption	–1	Performs a comparison using the setting of the Option Compare statement
vbBinaryCompare	0	Performs a binary comparison
vbTextCompare	1	Performs a textual comparison
vbDatabaseCompare	2	Microsoft Access only. Performs a comparison based on information in your database

Return Values

Replace returns the following values under the described syntax:

1. If expression is zero length, the return value is a zero length string.

2. If expression is Null, an error is returned.

3. If find is zero-length, a copy of expression is returned.

4. If replacewith with is zero length, a copy of the expression is returned with all occurrences of find removed.

5. If Len(expression)> Len(expression) argument>start > Len(expression), a zero-length string is returned.

6. If count is 0, a copy of the expression is returned.

```
Consider the following code expression:Dim s1 As String
Dim ret As String

s1 = "With five sad faces on the wall, the five Sad campers felt
➥sad about their day."
ret = Replace(s1, "sad", "happy", 1, 1)
Print ret
ret = Replace(s1, "sad", "happy", 1, 2)
Print ret
ret = Replace(s1, "sad", "happy", 1, 2, vbTextCompare)
```

```
Print ret
ret = Replace(s1, "sad", "happy", 1, 3, vbTextCompare)
Print ret
```

This would produce the following output:

```
With five happy faces on the wall, the five Sad campers felt sad about
their day.
With five happy faces on the wall, the five Sad campers felt happy
about their day.
With five happy faces on the wall, the five happy campers felt sad
about their day.
```

With five happy faces on the wall, the five happy campers felt happy about their day. Observe that the default setting uses a direct binary comparison, so return values will not include replacements where there is a difference in case unless the comparison argument includes the vbTextCompare constant setting.

Exercise 17.1   Entering Strings and Printing Initials

This exercise asks you to enter a person's name and display the person's initials. Figure 17.1 shows how the completed form should look.

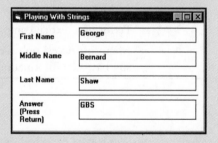

Figure 17.1   *This exercise uses the* Left$() *function to display the first letter in a string.*

1. Open a new project and change the Form1 caption to **Playing with Strings**; add the four text boxes and the four labels; and use the Line tool to place a line on the form. Name the controls **txtFirst**, **txtMiddle**, **txtLast**, and **txtInitials**.

2. Write a KeyPress() procedure to extract the first letter from each name and add the three letters to the fourth text box.

```
Private Sub txtInitials_KeyPress (Key Ascii As Integer)
    Dim first As String
    Dim middle As String
    Dim last As String

    first = Left$(txtFirst.text, 1)
    middle = Left$(txtMiddle.text, 1)
    last = Left$(txtLast.text, 1)
    txtInitials.text = first & middle & last
End Sub
```

As indicated, Left$() is used to extract the first letter from each string.

3. Test your design and save this project.

Exercise 17.2   Testing Input and Displaying It in Uppercase

This exercise asks you to employ several of the newly introduced string functions. User input is tested for length and converted to uppercase for display. Figure 17.2 shows the display that you are to create.

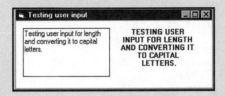

Figure 17.2   *All letters typed will appear in uppercase within the label placed on the right-hand side.*

1. Open a new project and change the Form1 caption to **Testing user input**. Add a text box (**txtInput**) and a label (**lblDisplay**). Change the MultiLine property for txtInput to True, and the WordWrap property of lblDisplay to True.

2. Write a KeyPress() procedure for txtInput, as in the following:

```
Private Sub txtInput_KeyPress(KeyAscii As Integer)
    Dim s1 As String
    If KeyAscii = vbKeyReturn Then
        s1 = txtInput.Text
        If Trim(Len(s1)) <> 0 Then
            s1 = UCase(Trim(s1))
            lblDisplay.Caption = s1
        Else
            lblDisplay.Caption = "Please input data"
            Exit Sub
        End If
    End If
End Sub
```

3. Test your program. What happens if you remove Trim() from your code and type in blank spaces before and after the typed text?

This exercise asks you to employ the Replace function in a program which substitutes a comma for a dash character in a string.

1. Place a label (**lblDisplay**) and a command button (**cmdReplace**) on a form.

2. In the Form_Load event, assign a string to the label caption that has city names separated by a dash character:

```
Private Sub Form_Load()
    lblDisplay.Caption = "Atlanta-Boston-New York-Seattle-
Portland-Chicago"
End Sub
```

3. In the cmdReplace_Click event, write code to replace the dash character with a comma, as in the following:

```
Private Sub cmdReplace_Click()
    Dim strReturn As String
    Dim strEvaluate As String
    strEvaluate = lblDisplay.Caption
    strReturn = Replace(strEvaluate, "-", ",")
    lblDisplay.Caption = strReturn
End Sub
```

4. Run and test the program.

Objective 17.4   Modifying Strings

Three statements (not functions) are available to modify strings, as shown in Table 17.6.

TABLE 17.6   Statements for Modifying Strings

Name	Description
LSet	Used to left justify a string
RSet	Used to right justify a string
Mid	Used to merge one string with another

These statements are similar in that they all require string variables or buffers to be allocated before they can be used. They are used to replace part of one string with another. These functions have purposes other than just alignment. The LSet statement, for example, can be used to prepare a string before it is saved to disk in a fixed length or random access record. This type of input/output operation is addressed in the chapters dealing with files: Chapter 18, "Sequential File-Processing and Error Trapping." These functions also are used in advanced Visual Basic to work with string addresses in calls to Windows API functions.

17.4.1   The *LSet* and *RSet* Statements

To left justify and right justify text inside a string variable, you can use `LSet` and `RSet`, respectively. The statement syntax is as follows:

```
LSet stringvar = stringexpr
RSet stringvar = stringexpr
```

The component `stringvar` is the name of a string variable, and `stringexpr` is the string expression.

As mentioned, the variable must have space allocated to handle the string expression. The following code fragment, for example, would not display the word `"Test"` with three leading spaces:

```
Dim s1 as String
LSet s1 = "   Test"
Print s1
```

Although declared, no space has been allocated. The following code examples would display the value of s1:

```
Dim s1 as String
s1 = "0123456789"
LSet s1 = "   Test"
Print s1
Dim s1 as String * 10
LSet s1 = "   Test"
Print s1
```

Observe that after using the `LSet` or `RSet` statement, text occupying the variable is replaced entirely by the newly aligned string. The leading spaces of s1 could be removed from the display by using the `Trim()` or `LTrim()` functions.

17.4.2   The *Mid* Statement

The `Mid` statement differs from the `Mid$()` function. The `Mid$()` function, which is described in section 17.3.1, "The `Left$()`, `Right$()`, and `Mid$()` Functions," returns part of a string specified in the function arguments. The `Mid` statement replaces part of a string with another string. Like the `LSet` and `RSet` statements, space must first be allocated. The syntax for the `Mid` statement is similar to that of the `Mid$()` function:

```
Mid[$](stringvar, start [,n]) = stringexpr
```

Table 17.7 explains the syntax.

TABLE 17.7   Syntax of the *Mid* Statement

Component	Description
stringvar	Name of the string variable to modify.
start	Character position in `stringvar` where the replacement of text begins.
n	Number of characters to replace. If omitted, all of the string is used.
stringexpr	The string expression that replaces part of `stringvar`.

Consider the following code fragment:

```
message = "Rolling down the river      "
Mid$(message, 18) = "highway."
Print message
```

This displays the following:

```
Rolling down the highway.
```

Notice that without the extra space allocated, the preceding code would be displayed as follows:

```
Rolling down the highw
```

Exercise 17.4   Illustrating the *LSet* Statement

In this exercise, the LSet statement is used to load text into a variable string buffer. The ANSI values of the loaded string are then displayed to illustrate the use of the LSet statement. (See Appendix A, "The ANSI Character Set," for the ANSI code.) Create the design shown in Figure 17.3.

Figure 17.3   *The* LSet *statement places blank spaces (ANSI 32) into the array when the text is less than the array length.*

1. Change the caption to **Illustrating the LSet Statement**. Add a text box (**txtInput**) and two labels (**lblDeclared** and **lblAssigned**). Add a label with its caption set to Input text of fewer than 25 characters and press Return.

2. Write a KeyPress() procedure for txtInput:

```
Private Sub txtInput_KeyPress(KeyAscii As Integer)
    Dim s1 As String * 25
    Dim s2 As String
    Dim n As Integer
    If KeyAscii = vbKeyReturn Then
        For n = 1 To Len(s1)
            s2 = s2 & Str$(Asc(Mid(s1, n, 1)))
        Next
        lblDeclared.Caption = "Ascii values of String variable s1
➥declared: "& vbCrLf & s2
        s2 = ""
        LSet s1 = Trim(txtInput.Text)
        For n = 1 To Len(s1)
            s2 = s2 & Str$(Asc(Mid(s1, n, 1)))
```

```
        Next
        lblAssigned.Caption = "Ascii values of String variable s1
➥assigned: "& vbCrLf & s2
    End If
End Sub
```

3. Run and test the program.

In this exercise, two strings are declared: s1, a fixed length string of 25 characters, and s2, a variable length string that holds the ANSI values for characters in
s1. Two For...Next loops are used to iterate through s2, which has been
assigned string conversions of the ANSI values of the individual characters in s1.

In the first For...Next loop, all characters are 0 because s1 has only been declared.
In the second For...Next loop, you see the results of the LSet statement. All characters in s1 have been replaced with either the inputted text from txtInput or with
a space character (ANSI value of 32).

Exercise 17.5   Displaying Names in the Proper Case

This exercise combines many of the string functions that have been introduced
to enable you to display names in the proper case, while accommodating those
of Celtic ancestry. It is a bit longer than others and somewhat complex, but illustrates how string functions can be used to check and correct user input. Figure
17.4 shows the interface.

Figure 17.4 *This application displays the name* McDonald *spelled with a capital* D *(instead of* Mcdonald).

1. Create the interface shown in Figure 17.4. It is the same as the one in
Exercise 17.1, except for the addition of a frame with the option buttons.
The option buttons are part of a three-member control array named
optStatus().

continues

391

2. Add the following GotFocus() procedure for the bottom text box (txtFormat):

```
Private Sub txtFormat_GotFocus()
    Dim first As String * 20
    Dim middle As String * 2
    Dim last As String * 25
    Dim display As String * 50
    Dim i As Integer

    first = txtFirst.Text
    first = TestString(first)
    middle = Trim(txtMiddle.Text)
    middle = StrConv(Left(middle, 1) & ".", vbProperCase)
    last = txtLast.Text
    last = TestString(last)
    For i = 0 To 2
        If optStatus(i).Value = True Then
            RSet display = optStatus(i).Caption & ":   " &
➥Trim(first) & " " & middle & " " & Trim(last)
            Exit For
        End If
    Next
    txtFormat.Text = display
End Sub
```

This procedure executes when the user inputs a name and then tabs to the txtFocus text box, which generates a GotFocus() event. In this event, the user's first and last names are passed to the TestString() function and displayed, along with his or her status, near the middle of txtFormat using the RSet function.

3. Add the TestString() function at the form module level, as in the following:

```
Public Function TestString(pass As String) As String
    Dim i As Integer
    Dim CapCount As Integer
    pass = Trim(pass)

    If Len(pass) <> 0 Then       ' test for empty inputs
        If Left(pass, 2) = "Mc" Or Left(pass, 3) = "Mac" Then
➥' test for Celts
            For i = 1 To Len(pass)    ' count number of capital
➥letters
                If Asc(Mid$(pass, i, 1)) >= 65 And Asc(Mid$(pass, i,
➥1)) <= 90 Then
                    CapCount= CapCount + 1
                End If
            Next
            If CapCount <= 2 Then ' permit no more than 2 capital
➥letters
                TestString = pass
            Else
                TestString = Trim(StrConv(pass, vbProperCase))
            End If
```

```
            Else
                  TestString = Trim(StrConv(pass, vbProperCase))
            End If
        Else
            TestString = ""
        End If
    End Function
```

The `TestString()` function permits those with last names starting with Mc or Mac to have a second capital letter placed in the name. Those who, by mistake, enter more than two capital letters have their input placed in proper case with the `StrConv()` function.

17.4.3   The *InStr()* Function

A unique string function is `InStr()`, which returns the numerical starting position of a substring within a larger string. The syntax has the following two forms:

```
InStr([start,], strexpr1, strexpr2)

InStr(start, strexpr1, strexpr2 [,compare])
```

Table 17.8 explains the components of the syntax.

TABLE 17.8   Syntax of the *InStr()* Function

Component	Description
start	Indicates the position at which the search should begin.
strexpr1	The string expression to be searched.
strexpr2	The string expression to be searched for.
compare	Specifies the string `Compare` method for which the two compare arguments are 0 and 1. With 0, the comparison is case sensitive. With 1, the comparison is not case-sensitive.

Consider the following code fragment:

```
message = "Rolling down the river"
newmess = InStr(message, "river")
Print newmess
```

This would display 18.

The number indicates the position in the string where the word `river` begins. The following code fragment would not find the substring `"river"`:

```
message = "Rolling down the liver"
newmess = InStr(message, "river")
Print newmess
```

In this case, the function returns 0. Likewise, the following code will return 0 because the compare argument makes the comparison case-sensitive:

```
message = "Rolling down the River, 0"
newmess = InStr(message, "river")
Print newmess
```

Objective 17.5   Comparing and Sorting Strings

There are two ways to compare strings: using relational operations, including the Like operator, and using the string compare function.

17.5.1 The *Like* Operator

The Like operator returns a Boolean value of True or False. The following is the syntax for an instruction that contains the Like operator:

```
strexpr Like pattern
```

The component pattern can include the wild cards ?, *, #, [charlist], and [!charlist], as explained in Table 17.9.

TABLE 17.9   Wild Cards for Pattern

Character	Description
?	Any one character
*	Any group of characters
#	Any digit
[charlist]	Any one character in a list of characters
[!charlist]	Any one character not in a list of characters

As examples, the following comparisons would all return True:

```
"Cat" Like "?at"
"Cat" Like "C*"
"12 Rounders" Like "1# Rounders"
"12 Rounders" Like "12 [BHR]ounders"
"12 Rounders" Like "12 [!ABCDEFG]ounders"
```

17.5.2   The *StrComp()* Function

The string compare function, StrComp(), is designed to compare one string with another. The syntax for this function is as follows:

```
StrComp(strexpr1, strexpr2 [,compare])
```

This is very similar to the second form of the InStr() function. As with InStr(), compare options are 0 or 1, with 0 indicating the string is not case-sensitive and 1 indicating it is case-sensitive. Table 17.10 lists the return values of this function and their comparisons.

TABLE 17.10   Return Values of the *InStr()* Function

Return	Comparison
−1	strexpr1 < strexpr2
0	strexpr1 = strexpr2
1	strexpr1 > strexpr2
NULL	strexpr1 = NULL or strexpr2 = NULL

Consider the following code fragment:

```
message1 = "Rolling down the river"
message2 = "Rolling down the highway"
num = StrComp(message1, message2)
Print num
```

This code would display the value 1. Why 1? Because the r in the word river is greater than the h in the word highway.

17.5.3   The *Option Compare* Statement

The Option Compare statement is an alternative way of setting case sensitivity. The syntax is as follows:

```
Option Compare { Binary | Text }
```

Placing the following statement in the declarations section of a form indicates that string (text) comparisons are no longer case-sensitive:

```
Option Compare Text
```

17.5.4   Sorting Strings

The easiest way to sort a list of strings is to use a list box or combo box and set the Sorted property to True. This will place added items in alphabetical order. Many third-party products provide libraries (DLLs) to which you can pass an array, even very large arrays, and the libraries' functions will sort them for you. For small arrays, however, do not hesitate to sort them yourself.

Exercise 17.6   Sorting Strings

One of the easiest sort algorithms is a *bubble sort*. It is not the fastest sort algorithm, but for small arrays or arrays that are nearly sorted, it is quite suitable. It is also one of the easiest to code. The best way to learn about a bubble sort is to use it. Create the interface shown in Figure 17.5.

Figure 17.5   *This display shows the list before and after the bubble sort procedure.*

1. Add a list box (lstElements) to the right- and left-hand sides, and a large label with its WordWrap property set to True.

2. In the Form_Load() event, add the following code:

```
Private Sub Form_Load()
    lstElements.AddItem "Lee's Restaurant"
    lstElements.AddItem "AAA  Detective Service"
    lstElements.AddItem "Zee's Restaurant"
    lstElements.AddItem "AAAAA Detective Service"
    lstElements.AddItem "AAAA  Detective Service"
    lstElements.AddItem "Dee's Restaurant"
    lstElements.AddItem "AAAAAA Detective Service"
    lstElements.AddItem "AA  Detective Service"
    lstElements.AddItem "Bee's Restaurant"
    lstElements.AddItem "A Detective Service"
End Sub
```

3. In the cmdSort_Click() event, enter the following code:

```
Private Sub cmdSort_Click()
    Dim i As Integer
    Dim topindex As Integer
    Dim test As Integer
    Dim Temp As String
    Dim NextItem As Integer
    Dim loopcount As Integer

    ReDim sortarray(lstElements.ListCount - 1) As String

    'assign array elements
    For i = 0 To lstElements.ListCount - 1
        sortarray(i) = lstElements.List(i)
    Next

    'perform bubble sort
```

```
            NextItem = 0
            Do While NextItem < UBound(sortarray)
                topindex = UBound(sortarray)
                Do While topindex > NextItem
                    test = StrComp(sortarray(topindex), sortarray(topindex
➡- 1), 1)
                    If test = -1 Then
                        Temp = sortarray(topindex)
                        sortarray(topindex) = sortarray(topindex - 1)
                        sortarray(topindex - 1) = Temp
                    End If
                    topindex = topindex - 1
                Loop
                NextItem = NextItem + 1
            Loop

            'display results
            lblDisplay.Caption = ""
            Temp = ""
            For i = LBound(sortarray) To UBound(sortarray)
                Temp = Temp & sortarray(i) & Chr(13) & Chr(10)
            Next
            lblDisplay.Caption = Temp
        End Sub
```

4. Run and test the program. Check the sort algorithm by setting the list box `Sorted` property to `True`.

As you study this code, its operation should become clear to you. Almost all sort algorithms are based on nested loops. Data is successively looped through, tested, and then placed.

In the bubble sort, two nested loops are used. A counter variable (`NextItem`) is used so the outer loop iteration is equal to the remaining number of elements in the array (`Sortarray`). In the inner loop, the variable `topindex` is at first equal to the top element of the array. It is then compared (using the `StrComp` function) to the element immediately below it.

If `topindex` encounters an array element with a value less than its own (closer to the front of the alphabet), it swaps places with it. This new element is compared to array elements; if it also encounters a value lower than its own, they swap places. By the completion of the first iteration of the outer loop, the lowest array element (closest to the front of the alphabet) has been identified and placed at the beginning of the array.

The second outer loop iteration only processes array elements from the second position from the end of the array. By completion of the second outer loop iteration, the second lowest array element has been identified. This process continues until the last loop is only comparing the last and next-to-last element of the array. These successively smaller loops "bubble" highest values to the top of the array.

Objective 17.6   Working with String Array Functions

Visual Basic 6.0 introduces several functions for working with strings and arrays. Typically, the strings are delimited, meaning that the string is split apart by a delimiter such as a space character (ANSI value 32), comma, or tab character. The string array functions are shown in Table 17.11.

TABLE 17.11   String Array Functions

Function	Description
Split	Returns a zero-based, one-dimensional array containing a specified number of substrings
Join	Returns a string created by joining a number of substrings contained in an array
Filter	Returns a zero-based array containing a subset of a string array based on a specified filter criteria

17.6.1   The *Split* and *Join* Functions

The first two functions are mirrors of each other. You can use the Split function to process data stored in sequential files. Usually, this type of data is delimited. The Split function easily allows this data to be placed in an array for examination and processing, such as sorting. Sequential files are discussed in Chapter 18, "Sequential File Processing and Error Trapping." The Join function places a single dimensional string array into a single string expression.

The Split function has the following syntax shown in Table 17.12:

```
Split(expression[, delimiter[, count[, compare]]])
```

TABLE 17.12   Syntax of the *Split* Function

Part	Description
expression	Required. String expression containing substrings and delimiters. If expression is a zero-length string(""), Split returns an empty array; that is, an array with no elements and no data.
delimiter	Optional. String character used to identify substring limits. If omitted, the space character (" ") is assumed to be the delimiter. If delimiter is a zero-length string, a single-element array containing the entire expression string is returned.
count	Optional. Number of substrings to be returned; −1 indicates that all substrings are returned.
compare	Optional. Numeric value indicating the kind of comparison to use when evaluating substrings. The setting are the same as for the Replace function in Table 17.5.

The Join function syntax is simpler than the Split function syntax:

The Join function syntax is displayed in Table 17.13:

TABLE 17.13 *Join* Function Syntax

Part	Description
list	Required. One-dimensional array containing substrings to be joined.
delimiter	Optional. String character used to separate the substrings in the returned string. If omitted, the space character (" ") is used. If delimiter is a zero-length string (""), all items in the list are concatenated with no delimiters.

Exercise 17.7   Using the *Split* and *Join* Functions

This exercise uses the Split and Join functions to manipulate a list of city names. The user may choose the delimiting character and add different city names to the list. Figure 17.6 shows the interface for the project.

Figure 17.6   *This display shows the interface for testing the* Split *and* Join *functions.*

1. Draw the interface shown in Figure 17.6. The form includes a text box for inputting city names (**txtInput**), a combo box for selecting a delimiting character (**cboDelimiter**), a listbox for displaying the array returned by the Split function (lstCities), a command button (**cmdTestSplit**) and a label at the bottom of the form (**lblDisplayCities**) for displaying the return value from the Join function.

2. The combo box should have its Style property set to 1 - Simple Combo. Add two labels and set the Caption values prompting user input for the text box and combo box.

continues

3. In the Form_Load event, add code to populate the delimiter combo box and provide default values for the cities list in txtInput:

```
Private Sub Form_Load()
    Dim strCity As String

    strCity = "Atlanta Boston Seattle"
    txtInput.Text = strCity

    With cboDelimiter
      .AddItem "[Space]"
      .AddItem ","
      .AddItem "/"
      .AddItem "|"
      .ListIndex = 0
    End With
End Sub
```

4. In the cmdTestSplit_Click event, enter code to create an array using the Split function and to return the array to a single string with the Join function:

```
Private Sub cmdTestSplit_Click()
    Dim retString() As String
    Dim strDisplay As String
    Dim strSplit As String
    Dim i As Long
    Dim strDelimiter As String

    ' test for space character selection
    If cboDelimiter.Text = "[Space]" Or Trim(cboDelimiter.Text) _
= "" Then
        strDelimiter = Chr$(32)
    Else
        strDelimiter = cboDelimiter.Text
    End If

    If Len(Trim(txtInput.Text)) <> 0 Then
        lstCities.Clear
        strSplit = txtInput.Text
        ' get the array
        retString = Split(strSplit, strDelimiter)
        ' display the array's values
        For i = LBound(retString) To UBound(retString)
            lstCities.AddItem Trim(retString(i))
        Next
        ' return the array to a single string and display it
        strDisplay = Join(retString)
        lblDisplayCities.Caption = strDisplay
    End If

End Sub
```

5. Run and test the program.

Note the necessity of using something other than a space character to delimit city names such as New York and San Francisco.

17.6.2   The *Filter* Function

The Filter function is a specialized function for working with string arrays. The function returns an array from a larger string array based upon filter criteria. The filter criteria specifies a substring of any the larger array elements. The syntax for the Filter function is indicated in Table 17.14:

```
Filter(InputStrings, Value[, Include[, Compare]])
```

TABLE 17.14   *Filter* Function Syntax

Part	Description
InputStrings	Required. One-dimensional array of strings to be searched.
Value	Required. String to search for.
Include	Optional. Boolean value indicating whether to return substrings that include or exclude Value. If Include is True, Filter returns the subset of the array that contains Value as a substring. If Include is False, Filter returns the subset of the array that does not contain Value as a substring.
Compare	Optional. Numeric value indicating the kind of string comparison to use. See Table 17.5 (Replace function) for values.

Exercise 17.8   Using the *Filter* Function

This exercise uses the Filter function to return a string array from a larger array of product codes. The subarray returned if filtered by a product prefix. Observe that only a substring contained by each of the InputStrings in the Filter function syntax is required. Figure 17.7 shows the interface for this exercise.

Figure 17.7   *The* Filter *function returns a string array from a larger array based upon filter criteria.*

continues

1. Place two list boxes on a form. Name the left hand listbox **lstProducts** and the right hand listbox **lstFiltered**.

2. At the module level of the form, make the following array declaration:

```
Dim plist(1 To 30) As String
```

3. In the Form_Load event, add code to populate this array and the list box with product codes. Have three different prefixes and numeric root values ranging from 1001 to 1010. For example, AA-1001, AB-1001, and AC-1001.

```
Private Sub Form_Load()
    Dim i As Long
    Dim strPrefix As String
    Dim intProductRoot As Integer
    Dim strProduct As String
    strPrefix = "AA-"
    intProductRoot = 1001
    For i = 1 To 30
        strProduct = strPrefix & intProductRoot
        plist(i) = strProduct
        lstProducts.AddItem strProduct
        intProductRoot = intProductRoot + 1
        If i Mod 10 = 0 Then
            If i < 20 Then strPrefix = "AB-"
            If i >= 20 Then strPrefix = "AC-"
            intProductRoot = 1001
        End If
    Next
End Sub
```

4. In the lstProducts_Click event, use the Filter function to return all products having the same prefix as the product clicked on by the user. Display these values in the lstFiltered listbox.

```
Private Sub lstProducts_Click()
    Dim product As String
    Dim ret() As String
    Dim i As Long

    product = Left(lstProducts.Text, 3)
    ret = Filter(plist, product, True)
    lstFiltered.Clear

    For i = LBound(ret) To UBound(ret)
        lstFiltered.AddItem ret(i)
    Next
End Sub
```

5. Run and test the program.

Objective 17.7   Constructing Strings

Finally, two functions are designed to construct strings: the String$() function and the Space$() function. The syntax for the String$() function consists of the following two formats:

```
String[$](number, charcode)
String[$](number, string)
```

Table 17.15 explains the syntax.

TABLE 17.15   *String$() Function Syntax*

Component	Description
number	Indicates the length of the string
charcode	Indicates the ANSI code
string	Indicates the first character to place in the return string

The Space$() function, in contrast to the String$() function, returns a string of blank spaces. The syntax is as follows:

```
Space[$](number)
```

The number component is the number of blank spaces to return.

As an example of these final two functions, consider the following code fragment:

```
Print String$(10, "*") + Space$(10) + String$(10, "*")
```

This will display the following:

```
**********          **********
```

The String$() function has special use in advanced Visual Basic. It frequently is employed to create a string buffer and address in memory so that values from Windows API functions can be returned.

Chapter Summary

String functions deal with ways of manipulating and converting strings. Determining the length of a string is accomplished using the Len(string) function.

A more complex set of string functions deals with converting a string from one form to another. Converting the case of a string is accomplished using LCase$(), UCase$(), and StrConv(). Converting a character to its ANSI value is accomplished using Asc(). Converting an ANSI value to a character is accomplished using Chr$(). Ten functions convert strings to numbers and numbers to strings: Val(), Str$(); Hex$(), Oct$(), CDate(), CInt(), CLng(), CSng(), CDbl(), and CCur().

Ways of manipulating strings also feature a number of different functions. Left$(), Right$(), and Mid$() return part of a string. LTrim$(), RTrim$(), and Trim$() remove blank spaces from a string. The Replace$() function replaces substrings within a larger string with a specified value.

Ways to justify the display of a string are to use two statements (not functions). These are LSet and RSet. The Mid statement is used to merge one string with another.

A unique string function is InStr(). This function returns the position of a substring within a larger string.

The Like operator and the StrComp() function are two ways to compare strings. The StrComp() function is especially useful for sorting sets of strings. The return values from this function are as follows:

Return	*Comparison*
-1	strexpr1 < strexpr2
0	strexpr1 = strexpr2
1	strexpr1 > strexpr2
NULL	strexpr1 = NULL or strexpr2 = NULL

If a sort requires ignoring case sensitivity, place Option Compare {Binary|Text} in your code.

Three functions assist with the manipulation of string arrays: Split(), Join(), and Filter(). The Split() and Join() functions mirror each other. The Split() function places a delimited string within a single dimension string array. The Join() function takes a single dimension string array and return a single string with the array elements joined. The Filter() function returns a subarray from within a larger array based upon a specified criteria.

Finally, String$() and Space$() represent two ways of constructing strings. String$() displays a string of characters; Space$() displays a string of blank spaces.

Skill-Building Exercises

These skill-building exercises give more practice in working with string functions. You are asked to use the Len(), Instr(), Left$(), and Mid$() functions, the LSet statement, and the Replace(), Spit(), and Filter() functions. You also are asked to sort a list of strings.

1. For this exercise, use the same form as the one used for Exercise 17.1. The purpose of this exercise is to determine if a name is too long. Check the length of each part of the person's name:

- If the first name is greater than 10 characters, print "The first name is too long."

- If the middle name is greater than two characters, print "The middle initial is too long."

- If the last name is greater than 15 characters, print "The last name is too long."

    Use an If...Then or Select Case structure in your procedure. Do not use a GOTO statement to exit the structure. Instead, set a flag to 1, and change it to 0 if a name is found to be too long.

2. The App.Path property is a string property that can be read to determine where your application resides. Write a procedure that examines the passed string of the App.Path and then prints out "Drive: [drive letter]" on one line and "Path: [application path minus drive]" on the line below. In your procedure, use the Len(), Instr(), Left$(), and Mid$() functions. For a challenge, extend this exercise to accommodate network drives that have double-slash path identifiers (for example, M:\\).

3. Create a string of 20 characters using the String$() function. Then, using the LSet statement, place the string expression "Testing" within it. Finally, use the Instr() function to display the position where you first encounter an empty space. (*Hint:* the ANSI value for a space is 32.)

4. Write a single function that places the following string expressions in the order of first name, middle initial, and last name, and in the correct case.

```
Jones, Amos Borden
McDonald, Angus Stewart
Miller, Lewis Allen
```

5. Write a routine that examines a string and sorts the letters into ascending order by their ANSI values.

6. When working with databases and the SQL language, single apostrophes in names (e.g. O'Hara) can create problems. The Replace() function makes dealing with such strings much easier. Write a routine which replaces the apostrophes with space characters in the following string:

```
"O'Hara, O'Malley, de L'Orme, O'Shaunnesy"
```

7. Using the Trim(), Split(), and Filter() functions, write a routine which, depending upon user selection, returns cities having multiple word in their names (New York, for example) or those comprised of single words (Portland, for example). Examine the following string to test the routine:

```
"Miami, New York, Chicago, Seattle, Boston, San Franciso, San
Diego, Los Angeles, Austin"
```

SEQUENTIAL FILE PROCESSING AND ERROR TRAPPING

If the data needed by a program is to be saved, it must be stored on a disk. Typically, users must deal with the following two types of files:

- **Program files**—Contain executable programs, usually with an .EXE extension.

- **Data files**—Contain the data to read to and from program files. These files may include files with many different types of extensions. The Microsoft Word executable program (Winword.EXE) edits and manages files with (.DOC) extensions. Text editors manage files which frequently have (.TXT) file extensions.

With Visual Basic, you can create program files that open, alter, and save data files. Because Visual Basic is frequently used for the development of database-oriented applications, the language's capability to manage low level file input/output (file I/O) often is neglected. In fact, Visual Basic offers some of the most flexible and capable means of writing data to and reading data from permanent storage of any Windows development environment.

Visual Basic offers the following three types of native data file processing:

- **Binary**—The most adaptable, if code intensive, means of storing data. Binary files can hold any form of data, including bitmap images, sound files, and executable files. When storing records, binary files typically require a lookup file to specify the starting byte position and length of an individual record in order to identify and retrieve specific data.

- **Random Access**—Data is stored and retrieved as identically sized records. The record is defined by a User Defined Type, where every string is declared of fixed length. While necessarily wasting some storage space with unfilled data in records, the identically sized records greatly ease the management and retrieval of records.

■ **Sequential**—Data is managed as one continuous sequential stream of characters. Typically used for storing text and log files. Files often are processed line-by-line, with carriage return and linefeed characters punctuating the sequential file stream and identifying individual lines.

This chapter covers sequential files and the important topic of error trapping. Sequential files are often used in conjunction with database management systems, especially in logging results. Even though they are important for a variety of applications, binary and random-access files are not covered in this book.

This chapter guides you through many tasks associated with file processing. It begins with an introduction to the following four file-processing controls:

■ Drive List Box control

■ Directory List Box control

■ File List Box control

■ Common Dialog control

It then addresses how to write to and read from a sequential file. It also includes how to incorporate error trapping into your programs, which is an important aspect of all computer programs, especially programs that manage file input and output operations.

When you complete this chapter, you will be able to perform the following tasks:

■ Add drive, directory, and file list boxes to a design

■ Use the Common Dialog control

■ Set the path for the drive and directory

■ Use the App object and its properties

■ Incorporate file error-handling instructions in a design

■ Understand the difference between the Common Dialog control's Filter, FilterIndex, and Action properties

■ Write to and read from a file of sequential records

■ Know how to open and close a file

■ Understand the difference between Input # and Line Input #

■ Design and use a sequential record

■ Write the instructions to kill (delete) a file

Chapter Objectives

The preceding lengthy list of tasks is distilled into the following four objectives. The first introduces you to the three file controls, as well as the `Common Dialog` control. The final following three objectives explore sequential file processing, including the tasks of error trapping, creating a sequential file, and removing a sequential file when it is no longer needed:

1. Using built-in Visual Basic file-processing controls

2. Adding error-handling procedures to file processing

3. Understanding design concepts of sequential file records

4. Writing, reading, or appending to a sequential file

Objective 18.1   Using Built-In Visual Basic File-Processing Controls

Many Visual Basic applications require information about the current disk drive (to determine which drive is open), the directories stored on the disk placed in the current drive, and the files stored within a directory or placed on the disk. This drive-directory file system helps to explain why Visual Basic places three controls on the toolbox to deal with file processing. These are the *Drive List Box*, the *Directory List Box*, the *File List Box*. Visual Basic also includes the `Common Dialog` controls custom control for adding common file management features to your programs.

18.1.1   The Three Individual File System Controls

Three file-system controls stored in the Visual Basic toolbox are designed to provide specific file-system information. Each tool, shown as a separate icon on the Visual Basic toolbox, serves a special purpose:

- **Drive List Box control**—Displays available disk drives on a computer. This includes mapped network drives. Click the down arrow to reveal the available drives.

- **Directory List Box control**—Displays the directories created for a disk placed in a disk drive. Click a folder to reveal the contents of a particular directory.

- **File List Box control**—Displays the files stored within the directories, including the root directory. The scroll bar appears when the number of stored files is large.

These tools tell you which files (the file list box) are stored on a specific drive (the drive list box) within the named directory (the directory list box). As shown in Figure 18.1, the folder named VB is on drive C. It contains a number of files, beginning with ADDSCCUS.DLL.

Drive list box

Directory list box   File list box

Figure 18.1 *The three file controls enable you to examine the contents of a drive, the directories of a drive, and the files within a directory.*

Exercise 18.1   Using Drive, Directory, and File List Boxes

This exercise asks you to design your own unique file-processing system by using the drive, directory, and file list boxes. Figure 18.2 shows the form that you are to create. With this design, you can change the disk drive, open directories on the drive, and view files stored in a directory.

Figure 18.2 *This interface shows the folders and files stored on drive C, the files stored for Chapt18, and the file that is selected.*

1. Create the interface, as shown in Figure 18.2. Add a drive list box, a directory list box, and a file list box. Add a label with a border to store the file selected (lblFile). These are three new controls. All are located on the Tool Box.

2. Write the following Form_Load() procedure:

```
Private Sub Form_Load()
    'Return the current path for the current drive
    'Set the path of the drive
    Drive1.Drive = CurDir$
    'Set the path of the directory
    Dir1.Path = CurDir$
    'Set the path of the file
```

```
        File1.Path = CurDir$
        'Set the file filter pattern
        File1.Pattern = "*.*"
    End Sub
```

This procedure is difficult to follow. The keyword CurDir$[("drive")] returns the path for the specified drive. If no drive is specified, CurDir$ returns a string for the current drive. In the example, the directory and file path are set for the current directory. Observe that Drive1, Dir1, and File1 are controls placed on the design. The *.* wild card indicates that all files with this pattern are to be selected.

3. Write the Drive1_Change() procedure to control a change in a disk drive.

```
    Private Sub Drive1_Change()
        Dim Msg As String
        Dim answer As Integer
        'set error handling
        On Error GoTo Drive1_ChangeErr

        Dir1.Path = Drive1.Drive

    Exit Sub
    Drive1_ChangeErr:
        Msg = "Error " & Err.Number & ": " & Err.Description
        answer = MsgBox(Msg, vbOKCancel, "Error in setting path")
        If answer = vbOK Then
            Resume
        Else
            Drive1.Drive = Dir1.Path
            Err.Clear
            Exit Sub
        End If

    End Sub
```

In this code, the following instruction sets the path of the directory to the current drive:

```
    Dir1.Path = Drive1.Drive
```

The remaining instructions deal with the handling of errors. For example, an error will result if drive A is selected and there is no diskette in the drive. Objective 18.2, "Adding Error-Handling Procedures to File Processing," addresses the writing of error-handling instructions. For now, do not worry if you do not understand how error-handling works.

4. Write the Dir1_Change() procedure to control a change in the directory.

```
    Private Sub Dir1_Change()
        'Code to determine the files in a directory
        File1.Path = Dir1.Path
        If File1.FileName <> "" Then
            lblFile.Caption = File1.FileName
        Else
            lblFile.Caption = File1.Pattern
        End If
    End Sub
```

continues

411

In this code, the following instruction sets the path of the file to the path of the current directory:

```
File1.Path = Dir1.Path
```

If there is no filename, the text displayed is either a specific file name or a file pattern.

5. Write the File1_Click() procedure to display in the text box a file selected in the file list box. This procedure is limited to a single instruction:

```
Private Sub File1_Click()
   'Click to select and display the file
   lblFile.Caption = File1.FileName
End Sub
```

This instruction tells the user to click the file name to display it in the label caption.

6. Run and test your design. Study what you have done. The three key instructions are as follows:

```
Dir1.Path = Drive1.Drive   'Set the path of the directory from
➥the drive
File1.Path = Dir1.Path     'Set the path of the file from the
➥directory
lblFile.Caption = File1.FileName  ' Select the file
```

Each time you change the path of one control, you change the path of the next control in the control hierarchy. Changing the Drive property on the Drive control requires a change in the Path property of the Directory control. Changing the Path property of the Directory control requires a change to the Path property of the File control, changing the list of files displayed.

18.1.2   The *Common Dialog* Control

A fourth control when working with files is the Common Dialog control. As shown in Figure 18.3, this control opens the standard Windows dialog box that integrates the drive, directory, and file list boxes. It permits the designer to control the types of files (in the Files of Type list) to display. In the example in Figure 18.3, the file box filter is set to list files of type icons (.ICO).

Figure 18.3   *The* Common Dialog *control adds a common look and feel to Windows file operations.*

The Common Dialog control encapsulates functions built into Windows itself. These functions present a common user interface for opening and saving files, making color and font selections, and printing documents. Use of the Common Dialog control is encouraged because the end user encounters interfaces seen in other Windows programs. The Common Dialog control exposes properties and methods for customizing the appearance and behavior of these dialog boxes.

Key properties for the Common Dialog control include the Filter, FilterIndex, DialogTitle, and Filename properties. Key methods include the different "Show" methods, as described in Table 18.1.

TABLE 18.1   *Common Dialog* Control Dialog Boxes

Method	Description
ShowOpen	Displays the Open dialog box
ShowSave	Displays the Save As dialog box
ShowColor	Displays the Color dialog box
ShowFont	Displays the Font dialog box
ShowPrinter	Displays the Print or Print Options dialog box
ShowHelp	Invokes the Windows Help engine

The *Filter* Property

The Filter property for the Common Dialog control specifies the types of files that are to be displayed in the dialog box's file list box. In Exercise 18.2 you will provide the user the choice of viewing all files, only text files, or only icon files. The Filter property has the following syntax:

```
[form.]CMDialog.Filter [ = description1|filter1|description2|filter2...]
```

Both a description and filter arguments are required, with a pipe (|) separating the two, as follows:

Description	Separator Filter	Arguments
Text Files (.TXT)	|	.TXT

The following string assignment, for example, will show all files, or only text files, or only icon files:

```
cmDialog1.Filter = _
"All Files (*.*)|*.* |Text Files (*.txt)|*.txt|icons (*.ico)|*.ico"
```

When writing this instruction, don't include spaces before or after the pipe. If you do, these spaces will be included in the description and filter values.

The *FilterIndex* Property

The `FilterIndex` property specifies the default filter. When writing the `FilterIndex` property, the index for the first defined filter is 1, the second is 2, and so on. To set the default to the third filter, use the following code:

```
[form.]CmDialog.FilterIndex = 3
```

This example indicates that `icon(*.ico)|*.ico` files should be displayed as the default.

Exercise 18.2   Using the *Common Dialog* Control

Design an application that allows you to open a file, inspect icons stored in the c:\vb\samples directory, and load an icon on your display using an image box. (There are also several icon files stored on your disk.) Figure 18.4 illustrates how the dialog box is represented on the form. Figure 18.5 shows the use of the completed design.

Figure 18.4   *The* Common Dialog *control is invisible at runtime and can be placed at any position on a form.*

Figure 18.5   *The interface opens the* Common Dialog *control to allow an icon to be displayed on the image box.*

1. Select the Common Dialog control from the Component dialog box (Project|Components|Microsoft Common Dialog Control 6.0). Add the control to your form and name it **dlgDemo**. Like the Timer control, this control will be invisible when you run the application.

2. Add the command buttons (**cmdShow**) and an image box (**Image1**) to the form. Figure 18.4 shows this form (with the dialog box added). Change the caption of the form.

3. Write the Form_Load() procedure as follows:

```
Private Sub Form_Load()
   'This statement changes the drive to the path
   'of the application. App is an object, with
   'properties, but no methods
   ChDrive App.Path
   'Changes the directory to the path of the application.
   ChDir App.Path
End Sub
```

The meaning of this code is explained in section 18.1.4 "Working with the *App* Object."

4. Write the Show Icons (cmdShow_Click()) procedure:

```
Private Sub cmdShow_Click()
   Dim Msg As String
   Dim answer As Integer

   On Error GoTo cmdShowClickErr

   With dlgDemo
      .Filter = "All Files (*.*) | *.* |Text Files (*.txt) |
*.txt¦icons (*.ico) | *.ico"
      .FilterIndex = 3
      .DialogTitle = "Select Icon to Display"
      .ShowOpen
   End With
   If dlgDemo.FileName <> "" Then
```

continues

```
            Image1.Picture = LoadPicture(dlgDemo.FileName)
        End If

    Exit Sub
    cmdShowClickErr:
        Msg = "Error " & Err.Number & ": " & Err.Description
        answer = MsgBox(Msg, vbOKCancel, "Error in selecting file")
        If answer = vbOK Then
          Resume Next
        Else
          Err.Clear
          Exit Sub
        End If

    End Sub
```

5. Run your design. When you click Show Icons, the Common Dialog control should appear, prompting you to indicate the icon file that you want to inspect. Click the file and then click OK to remove the dialog box and to display the icon.

18.1.3   Working with the *Flags* Property of the *Common Dialog* Control

For full control of the Common Dialog control, you must use the Flags property. Flags are integer constants that are added together, similar to the Button argument of the MsgBox function you worked with in Chapter 9, "Inputting Values and Formatting Output." The Flags property constants customize the appearance and behavior of the dialog box, depending on which Show method you are invoking. The following instruction, for example, would hide the read-only check box on the Open File dialog box and would ensure that a file existed before being opened:

```
dlgDemo.flags = cdlOFNHideReadOnly + cdlOFNFileMustExist
```

The number of Flag constants is far too numerous to enumerate here. Consult Visual Basic's online help for a full listing. The next exercise will give you a flavor for the use of these constants.

Exercise 18.3   Using the *Common Dialog* Control *Flag* Property

In this exercise, you experiment with some of the Flag property constants for five different Common Dialog Control Show methods. Figure 18.6 illustrates the interface for working with this control property. On the left is a frame control with a control array of five option buttons. The interface also features a command button and a label control.

Figure 18.6 · *The* Flag *property enables the developer to customize the appearance and behavior of the* Common Dialog *control.*

1. Select the Common Dialog control from the Component dialog box (Project|Components|Microsoft Common Dialog Control 6.0). Add the control to your form and name it dlgDemo.

2. Add the command button (cmdOK), a label control (lblDisplay) with its BorderStyle property set to 1-Fixed Single.

3. Add a frame (fraShowOptions) to the design and change its caption as depicted in Figure 18.6. Inside the frame place a control array of five option buttons (optShow) with their Caption properties set as shown.

4. Write the cmdOK_Click() procedure as follows:

```
Private Sub cmdOK_Click()
  Dim i As Integer

  With dlgDemo
  For i = optShow.LBound To optShow.UBound
    If optShow(i).Value = True Then
      Select Case optShow(i).Caption
        Case "ShowOpen"
          .Filter = "Text Files (*.txt)|*.txt"
          .FilterIndex = 1
          .DialogTitle = "Open text file"
          .flags = cdlOFNHideReadOnly + cdlOFNFileMustExist
          .ShowOpen
          If .FileName <> "" Then lblDisplay.Caption =
➡.FileName
        Case "ShowSave"
          .Filter = "Text Files (*.txt)|*.txt"
          .FilterIndex = 1
          .DialogTitle = "Save text file"
          .flags = cdlOFNHideReadOnly + cdlOFNCreatePrompt + …
─
              cdlOFNOverwritePrompt
          .ShowSave
          If .FileName <> "" Then lblDisplay.Caption =
➡.FileName
        Case "ShowColor"
          .flags = cdlCCFullOpen
```

continues

417

Exercise 18.3   continued

```
                        .ShowColor
                        lblDisplay.BackColor = .Color
                    Case "ShowFont"

                        .flags = cdlCFBoth
                        .ShowFont
                        lblDisplay.Caption = "Hello World"
                        lblDisplay.FontName = .FontName
                        lblDisplay.FontSize = .FontSize
                        lblDisplay.FontBold = .FontBold
                        lblDisplay.FontItalic = .FontItalic
                    Case "ShowPrinter"
                        .flags = cdlPDDisablePrintToFile +
  ➥cdlPDNoPageNums
                        .ShowPrinter
                End Select
                Exit For
            End If
        Next
    End With
End Sub
```

5. Run and test the program.

This exercise only names files and displays them with the ShowOpen and ShowSave methods. In Objective 18.4, "Writing, Reading, or Appending to a Sequential file," you will open and save sequential files using the Common Dialog control to supply the file names.

Some Show methods require prior setting of Flag property constants. Without specifying the fonts to show (dlgDemo.flags = cdlCFBoth, for example), the ShowFont method will indicate that no fonts are installed on the user's machine.

18.1.4   Working with the *App* Object

The App object (short for application) is a global object available at runtime. It is used to determine or specify information about the title of the application, its path, and the name of its executable and Help files. When working with files, the App object often is paired with the ChDir and ChDrive statements.

You use ChDir to change the default directory on a specific drive. The syntax is limited to the following:

```
ChDir path
```

The path component is a string expression written to identify which directory becomes the default directory.

You use ChDrive to specify a default (disk) drive. The syntax is as follows:

```
ChDrive drive
```

The drive component is a string expression to identify the default drive.

Consider how ChDrive and ChDir are used with the App object. The following instructions set the default of the drive and the directory:

```
ChDrive App.Path
ChDir App.Path
```

The first instruction sets the default drive to the same drive that stores the application. The second instruction sets the default directory to the same directory that stores the application.

You also can use ChDrive and ChDir to set a specific path, such as in the following code:

```
ChDrive "b:\"
ChDir "b:\ch22\"
```

Objective 18.2   Adding Error-Handling Procedures to File Processing

In Exercises 18.1 and 18.2, error-handling code was added to key routines. As you begin to create larger programs, and especially as you begin to develop file I/O routines, error-handling code *should be added to nearly every procedure.*

Why is error handling so important? When a compiled Visual Basic program encounters an error and no code exists to handle the error runs, the error is fatal and the program simply crashes! For example, a procedure might require that data be written to drive A on the computer, which presupposes that a diskette has been placed in the drive and is ready to receive data. However, what happens if a diskette has not been inserted? Without error-handling instructions, you have angered some very unhappy users.

Error-handling code was not added to Exercise 18.3. The Common Dialog control has some built in error handling itself. If you save a file without naming it, for example, nothing happens. The Common Dialog control ignores it, but not all errors are handled, and the cmdOK_Click event in Exercise 18.3 should have error handling added to it. In the next brief exercise, you will observe the result of that omission.

Exercise 18.4   Observing Unhandled Errors

In this exercise, you comment out the assignment of Flags constants before the ShowFont method in Exercise 18.3. You then compile the program and observe the result of an unhandled error.

1. Save the files for Exercise 18.3 as Exercise 18.4 (for example, **f18-4.frm**, **P18_4.vbp**). Rename the Project to **P18_4**.

continues

Exercise 18.4   continued

2. Change the code in the cmdOK_Click procedure so that the assignment of the Flag constant is commented out for the ShowFont block. The code should read as follows:

```
Case "ShowFont"
'    .Flags = cdlCFBoth
    .ShowFont
    lblDisplay.Caption = "Hello World"
    lblDisplay.FontName = .FontName
    lblDisplay.FontSize = .FontSize
    lblDisplay.FontBold = .FontBold
    lblDisplay.FontItalic = .FontItalic
```

3. Compile the program (File|Make P18_4.exe).

4. Run the program and observe the result when you attempt to select a font. Irritating, isn't it?

18.2.1   Error Handling with the *Err* Object and *On Error* Statement

Whenever an error is encountered, an Err object is created. The Err object is a global, intrinsic object in Visual Basic and need not be created explicitly in code. Instead, Visual Basic itself assigns values to the properties of the Err object, which assist you in handling an error. The Err object is available for you to as long as you have enabled error handling with an On Error statement.

The combination of the On Error statement with the Err object can be a little confusing, so the following section examines them in turn. Observe how error handling is accomplished in practice.

18.2.2   The *Err* Object

The Err object has three key properties and two methods listed in Table 18.2.

TABLE 18.2   *Err Object* Properties and Methods

Attribute	Description
Number	The number of the error raised
Description	A text description of the error
Source	A string specifying the object or application generating the error
Clear method	Clears all property settings of the Err object
Raise method	Generates a runtime error with a number of a description that you specify

Re-examine the error-handling code in Exercise 18.2. You will see that the Number and Description properties were used to build a general error-handling message.

18.2.3   The *On Error* Statement

The On Error statement specifies where program control should go when a runtime error is encountered and enables an error-handling routine or section of the code where error-handling is treated.

The three forms of this statement are as follows:

```
On Error Resume Next
On Error GoTo 0
On Error GoTo line
```

The *On Error Resume Next* Syntax

The On Error Resume Next statement indicates that when a runtime error occurs, control should be transferred to the statement that follows the error:

```
On Error Resume Next
```

In other words, the program is allowed to continue even though it contains a runtime error.

The *On Error GoTo 0* Syntax

In contrast to On Error Resume Next, the On Error GoTo 0 statement (zero, not capital O) is easier to understand:

```
On Error GoTo 0      'zero, not capital O
```

This statement disables any enabled error handler. It is used to turn off error trapping.

The *On Error GoTo Line* Syntax

This syntax is the most useful because it neither instructs the computer to continue executing code if an error is encountered or turns off error handling. The On Error GoTo line statement specifies that when an error is discovered by Visual Basic, the program will go to a line number or to a line label where, presumably, an error handler has been placed. In this book, a line label always is used to identify error-handling code sections. A *line label* is a string identifier followed by a colon.

The error-handling section usually enumerates the numbers of the errors it wants specifically to handle and also includes a generic handler for unanticipated errors. Where do these error numbers come from? The list of error numbers and their meanings are found using Visual Basic Help under the heading "Trappable Errors." They include messages such as "File not found" (53) and "Disk not ready" (71). When writing code, select the error message to report which type of error will most likely occur, with the explanation given through use of the message box.

Examine the following code shown. This command button click assigns the value 35 to an array index the user has entered into a text box (txtInput). The array ranges from 1 to 10. Two probable errors you would want to trap include an out of range error (the user enters a value outside the range of the array) or a type mismatch error (the user enters a non-numeric value). The code instructs that when an error is discovered, the On Error statement will enable an error-handling routine and go to (or jump to) the statement that begins with the label cmdTestErr:

```
Private Sub cmdTest_Click()
  Dim msg As String
  Dim answer As Integer
  Dim test(1 To 10) As Integer
  Dim i As Integer

  On Error GoTo cmdTestErr
  i = CInt(txtInput.Text)

  test(i) = 35
  Print test(i)

  Exit Sub
cmdTestErr:
  Select Case Err.Number
    Case 9  ' out of range
      msg = "Error 9: " & Err.Description & _
    ". Please enter a number beween 1 and 10."
      answer = MsgBox(msg, vbOK, "Testing input")
      txtInput.SetFocus
      Exit Sub
    Case 13 ' type mismatch
      msg = "Error 13: " & Err.Description & ". Please enter a
➥numeric value."
      answer = MsgBox(msg, vbOK, "Testing input")
      txtInput.SetFocus
      Exit Sub
    Case Else
      msg = "Error : " & Err.Description
      answer = MsgBox(msg, vbOK, "Testing input")
      Exit Sub

  End Select

End Sub
```

Observe that an Exit Sub statement is placed immediately *before* the cmdTestErr: label. Without this Exit statement, the code would fall into the error handler if no error was encountered. This itself would generate an error.

The On Error GoTo statement means that the flow of program control has passed to the error handler section. Once in the error handler section, the program designer must decide where the program will flow next. In the preceding example, you exit the program so that the user may correct the input. Alternatively, if the error was fixed within the error handler, program control might flow back to the point in the program where the error occurred. Resume statements indicate where you want to re-enter the routine.

The *Resume* Statement

The `Resume` statement does not require the `On Error` statement; however, it must appear within the error-handling routine (or an error will occur). The syntax for this statement contains the following three forms:

```
Resume [0]
Resume Next
Resume line
```

Table 18.3 explains the syntax.

TABLE 18.3 *Resume* **Statement Syntax**

Component	Description
0	Indicates that program execution is to resume with the statement that caused the error
Next	Indicates that program execution is to resume with the statement immediately following the statement that caused the error
line	Indicates that program execution is to resume at a designated line label or line number

Exercise 18.5 Adding Error Handling to the Common Dialog Program

In this exercise, you add error handling to Exercise 18.4.

1. Save the files for Exercise 18.4 as Exercise 18.5 (for example, **f18-5.frm**, **P18_5.vbp**). Rename the Project to **P18_5**.

2. Change the `cmdOK_Click` event to read as follows:

```
Private Sub cmdOK_Click()
    Dim i As Integer
    Dim msg As String
    Dim answer As Integer
      On Error GoTo cmdOK_ClickErr:
    With dlgDemo
    For i = optShow.LBound To optShow.UBound
      If optShow(i).Value = True Then
        Select Case optShow(i).Caption
          Case "ShowOpen"
             .Filter = "Text Files (*.txt)¦*.txt"
             .FilterIndex = 1
             .DialogTitle = "Open text file"
             .Flags = cdlOFNHideReadOnly + cdlOFNFileMustExist
             .ShowOpen
             If .FileName <> "" Then lblDisplay.Caption =
➡.FileName
          Case "ShowSave"
             .Filter = "Text Files (*.txt)¦*.txt"
             .FilterIndex = 1
             .DialogTitle = "Save text file"
             .Flags = cdlOFNHideReadOnly + cdlOFNCreatePrompt _
+ cdlOFNOverwritePrompt
```

continues

Exercise 18.5   continued

```
                    .ShowSave
                    If .FileName <> "" Then lblDisplay.Caption =
➥.FileName
               Case "ShowColor"
                    .Flags = cdlCCFullOpen
                    .ShowColor
                    lblDisplay.BackColor = .Color
               Case "ShowFont"
                    .Flags = cdlCFBoth
                    .ShowFont
                    lblDisplay.Caption = "Hello World"
                    lblDisplay.FontName = .FontName
                    lblDisplay.FontSize = .FontSize
                    lblDisplay.FontBold = .FontBold
                    lblDisplay.FontItalic = .FontItalic

               Case "ShowPrinter"
                    .Flags = cdlPDDisablePrintToFile + cdlPDNoPageNums
                    .ShowPrinter
          End Select
          Exit For
     End If
  Next
  End With

  Exit Sub
  cmdOK_ClickErr:
     msg = "Error " & Err.Number & ": " & Err.Description
     answer = MsgBox(msg, vbOKCancel, "Error in dialog box.")
     If answer = vbOK Then
        Resume Next
     Else
        Err.Clear
        Exit Sub
     End If

  End Sub
```

3. Compile and test the executable program. As one test, drive to read from a drive on your computer, but to not insert a disk. An error will be reported.

Objective 18.3   Understanding Design Concepts of Sequential File Records

Although Visual Basic provides four controls for providing information about disk drives, directories, and files, it does not provide a specific control for storing data on files. Program instructions are required to do all of this. As mentioned in the chapter introduction, file access can be done in three ways in Visual Basic: random, sequential, and binary, with random being the default.

All three types feature the processing of records. A *record* is the unit of data to be processed by the computer at one time. Perhaps the best way of understanding the makeup of a record is by examining a user-defined type. Consider the following structure of a patient record in a hospital.

```
Type Patient
   PatientID     String * 9
   LastName      String * 15
   FirstName     String * 15
   Ward          Integer
   DoctorID      Integer
End Type
```

In this example, each element of the record type is called a *field*. Thus, `PatientID` is a field. The collection of data for all fields for one person represents a *single record*. The collection of data for all fields for all persons then represents a *data file*.

18.3.1   Sequential File Access

Sequential file access is especially useful for text files in which each character in the file represents either a character (including blank spaces) or a text formatting character (such as a new line).

Text processing is limited to reading and writing strings of text rather than sets of records. With sequential access, two files are typically required: one from which to read data and one to write data to. It is not possible to read from, and write to, the same sequential file at the same time. If, for example, you want to insert a record into a sequential file, it is necessary to read from one file and write to a second file until the desired file location is reached, at which time a new record is inserted and written to the second file (not the first). After this is done, all remaining records must be read from the first file and written to the second.

Another method is to load the file completely into memory and then insert a record at the correct position or add records to the end of the file, and write the entire file to disk. With larger memories now standard on desktop computers and the capability of Visual Basic string to handle a little over two billion characters, this is more practical than it once was.

Although designed for text files, sequential access also can be used in processing records. In this instance, the fields of the record must be defined and placed in read and write instructions.

Functions and Statements

The functions and statements shown in Table 18.4 and Table 18.5, respectively, are used in sequential file processing.

TABLE 18.4   Functions for Sequential File Processing

Function	Description
Dir, Dir$	Returns the name of the file or directory that matches a specific pattern
EOF	Returns a value to indicate whether the end-of-file (EOF) has been reached
FileCopy	Copies a file
FileDateTime	Returns a string that indicates when the file was created or last modified
FileLen	Returns the length of a file in bytes. Used with unopened files
FreeFile	Returns an available file number for file access
GetAttr	Returns an integer that indicates the attributes of a file, directory, or volume label
Input	Returns a specified number of characters read from a sequential file
Loc	Returns the current position within an open file
LOF	Returns the size of an open file in bytes
Seek	Sets the position in a file for the next read or write
SetAttr	Sets the attribute information for a file

TABLE 18.5   Statements for Sequential File Processing

Statement	Description
Open	Enables input or output to a file
Close	Closes input or output to a file
Reset	Closes all files opened with the Open statement and writes the contents of all file buffers to disk
Input #	Reads characters from a sequential file and assigns data to variables
Line Input #	Reads a line from a sequential file into a String or Variant variable
Print #	Writes display-formatted data to a sequential file
Write #	Writes raw delimited data to a sequential file

Many of the functions and statements can be understood by reading their descriptions in Table 18.4 and Table 18.5, respectively. Others require some clarification. The following sections help you become familiar with many of the functions and statements used in sequential file processing.

The *Open* Statement

Before a file can be used, it must be opened. The syntax for the Open statement is as follows:

```
Open file For[ mode] [Access access][lock] As [#]filenumber[Len =
➥reclength]
```

Table 18.6 explains the components of the syntax.

TABLE 18.6   Syntax for the *Open* Statement

Component	Description
file	The filename or path plus the filename.
mode	One of the following: Append, Binary, Input, Output, or Random.
Access	One of the following: Read, Write, or Read Write.
lock	Specifies which file operations are permitted: Shared, Lock Read, Lock Write, or Lock Read Write.
filenumber	An integer from 1 to 511, inclusive. A file number is required.
reclength	The record length, which for sequential files is the number of characters buffered.

The purpose of the Open statement is twofold: to create a new file and to open a file. If the file exists, the statement opens it; if the files does not exist, the Open statement creates it. After opened, one of the following operations can be performed:

- Input (read) characters from a file
- Output (write) characters to a file
- Append (write) characters to an existing file

Remember: You must open a file first before any I/O operations can be performed on it.

18.3.2   Writing Text to a File

Before writing data to a file, the data must be in a form ready for output, and a file must be opened for outputting or appending. Only then can the Print # or Write # statements be used.

The question arises as to which approach is best. With Write #, Visual Basic separates each value (number and string) with a comma and puts quotation marks around string expressions. The Write # statement is more typically used when writing a sequential record to a file. The formatting of the Write # statement also makes it readily importable by other desktop applications, such as spreadsheets and databases.

The `Print #` statement does add comma delimiters. It typically is used in tandem with the `Line Input #` statement and the `Input` function. For this reason, use `Write #` when you want to write comma-delimited sequential records to a file, which then can be read with the `Input #` statement later on.

The *Write* # Statement

The syntax of the `Write #` statement is as follows:

```
Write # filenumber [,expression list]
```

The component `filenumber` is the number used in the `Open` statement, and `expression list` lists the fields of the record to be written to a file.

For example, a `Write #` instruction must be written as follows:

```
Write #1, FirstName$, LastName$, JobRank%, Start%
```

In this instance, each record consists of four fields.

The *Print* # Statement

The syntax of the `Print #` statement is as follows:

```
Print # filenumber, [[{Spc(n) | Tab(n)}][expression][{;|,}]
```

The component `filenumber` is the number used with the `Open` statement, and `expression` is the numeric or string expressions to be written to a file.

If you are writing to a file using text placed in a text box, a `Print #` instruction might be written as follows:

```
Print #1, Text1.Text
```

18.3.3   Reading Data from a File

Data placed on a sequential file can be read using the `Input #` and `Line Input #` statements or the `Input` function. The `Input #` statement reads a list of numeric or string expressions from a file. This statement is used when the exact type of data is known in advance. This is in contrast to the `Line Input #` statement, which reads a text file one line at a time, reading all characters up to a carriage return and line feed combination. In reading the file, it does not retain the carriage return and line feed. The `Input` function reads a specified number of characters into a string. When returning characters, it returns everything including carriage return and line feed characters. It often is used to place an entire text file into a single string.

The syntax for the `Input #` statement is as follows:

```
Input # filenumber, variable list
```

The component `filenumber` is the number used in the `Open` statement, and variable `list` is a comma-delimited list of the assigned variable values read from the file.

As an example, an `Input #` statement must be written as follows:

```
Input #1, FirstName$, LastName$, JobRank%, Start%
```

The *Line Input* # Statement

The syntax for the `Line Input #` statement is as follows:

```
Line Input # filenumber, variablename
```

The component `filenumber` is the number used in the `Open` statement, and `variablename` is the name of the variable used to receive a line of text from the file.

As an example, a `Line Input #` instruction might read as follows:

```
Line Input #1, TextLine
```

`TextLine` represents one line of text.

The *Input* Function

The syntax for the `Input` function is:

```
Input(number, [#]filenumber)
```

Both arguments are required. The number specifies the number of characters to return. The filenumber must be any valid file number. The following instruction

```
strReturn = Input(LOF(1), 1)
```

would place the entire contents of the file opened as #1 into the `strReturn` variable.

The *Close* Statement

After all records have been read from, or written to, a file, the file should be closed. The `Close` statement is simply as follows:

```
Close [[#] filenumber] [,[#] filenumber]...
```

If no arguments are provided, the statement closes all open files. To close a single file, such as file #1, write the following:

```
Close #1
```

To close all open files, type the following instruction:

```
Close
```

Exercise 18.6   Using The *Input* Function and the *Print* Statement to Design a File Note Pad

Design a file note pad that enables you to write notes and save them on a disk. For this exercise, you use the Input function and the Print statements and the enable and disable commands to disallow reading from a file until a note has been created and written to the file.

1. Add the text box and the three command buttons, as illustrated (see Figure 18.7). Add all captions and write the End procedure. If the files are to be placed on a specific drive, set ChDrive and ChDir in the Form_Load procedure.

Figure 18.7 *This design allows text to be entered, written to a disk, and read back from the disk.*

2. Allow the text box to accept multiple lines.

3. Disable the **Read** command button.

4. Write the cmdWrite_Click() procedure (changing the file path as necessary) as follows:

```
Private Sub cmdWrite_Click()

    Dim Msg As String
    On Error GoTo ErrorWrite

    Open "notes.txt" For Output As #1
    Print #1, txtNotes.Text
    Close #1
    txtNotes.Text = ""
    cmdRead.Enabled = True
    cmdWrite.Enabled = False

    Exit Sub
ErrorWrite:
    Msg = "Error: " & Err.Number & " " & Err.Description
    MsgBox Msg, vbOKCancel, "Error in writing file"
    Exit Sub

End Sub
```

When writing this code, do not forget to add the Exit Sub instruction prior to the error-handling code. If you do not add this statement, a run-time error will be indicated because the label (in our case, ErrorWrite:) is reached, but not called.

5. Write the cmdRead_Click() procedure (changing the file path as necessary). The instructions for this program are as follows:

```
Private Sub cmdRead_Click()
    Dim fnum As Integer
    Dim strDisplay As String
    Dim Msg As String

    On Error GoTo ErrorRead

    fnum = FreeFile
    Open "notes.txt" For Input As #fnum

    strDisplay = Input(LOF(fnum), fnum)
    txtNotes.Text = strDisplay

    Close #fnum

    cmdWrite.Enabled = True
    cmdRead.Enabled = False

    Exit Sub
ErrorRead:
    Msg = "Error: " & Err.Number & " " & Err.Description

    MsgBox Msg, vbOKCancel, "Error in reading file"
    Exit Sub

End Sub
```

In this procedure, the Input function reads the entire file into the strDisplay string variable.

6. Run and test the program. Add the text shown in Figure 18.7, or any text you want.

Exercise 18.7   Using the *Line Input* # Statement

Modify the note pad program to enable it to accept line input. Use line input when you want to read individual lines from a note pad, include blank lines in your text, or write in outline form. Figure 18.8 shows the user interface for this design (and the preceding sentence rendered as separate lines).

Figure 18.8   *The* Line Input *# statement reads lines of text as they are written to disk.*

1. Modify the cmdRead_Click() procedure written for Exercise 18.6 as follows:

```
Private Sub cmdRead_Click()
    Dim fnum As Integer
    Dim strDisplay As String
    Dim strhold As String
    Dim Msg As String

    On Error GoTo ErrorRead

    fnum = FreeFile
    Open "notes.txt" For Input As #fnum

    Do While Not EOF(fnum)
        Line Input #fnum, strhold
        strDisplay = strDisplay & strhold & vbCrLf
    Loop

    txtNotes.Text = strDisplay

    Close #fnum

    cmdWrite.Enabled = True
    cmdRead.Enabled = False

    Exit Sub
ErrorRead:
    Msg = "Error: " & Err.Number & " " & Err.Description

    MsgBox Msg, vbOKCancel, "Error in reading file"
    Exit Sub

End Sub
```

2. Modify the `cmdWrite_Click()` procedure to create the notes2.txt file:

```
Private Sub cmdWrite_Click()

    Dim Msg As String
    On Error GoTo ErrorWrite

    Open "notes.txt" For Output As #1
    Print #1, txtNotes.Text
    Close #1
    txtNotes.Text = ""
    cmdRead.Enabled = True
    cmdWrite.Enabled = False

    Exit Sub
ErrorWrite:
    Msg = "Error: " & Err.Number & " " & Err.Description
    MsgBox Msg, vbOKCancel, "Error in writing file"
    Exit Sub

End Sub
```

3. Run and test this design. Add the text shown in Figure 18.8 or add your own lines of text.

Objective 18.4   Writing, Reading, or Appending to a Sequential File

Although random and binary often are preferred methods of working with records, sequential files can and should be used for such tasks as creating a log of time series data or a written record of processing. In design, the fields important to a record must be identified. This is followed by the design of a data-input interface that allows for the entry of data for a record, and the design of a report that lists the data entered.

To delete a file from a disk, use the Kill statement (terrible name, I agree). The following is the syntax for this statement:

```
Kill filespec
```

The component `filespec` is the name of the file to delete.

Observe the following rule: Kill will not work with an open file. A file must be closed before the Kill statement can be applied.

The Kill statement is used in Exercise 18.9.

Exercise 18.8   Writing and Reading Records Using a Sequential File

Design an input screen for entering inventory information and for writing inventory records to a sequential file. After records are placed on a file, they can be read and displayed.

Figure 18.9 shows the data-entry screen used for capturing records. Each inventory record contains four fields: product name (Prod Name), product price (Prod Price), product cost (Prod Cost), and product inventory (Prod. Inventory). After a record has been entered, it is written to a file. Figure 18.10 shows the report produced after all records have been entered into processing (four records in the example).

Figure 18.9   *For this application, add the name of the product and its price, cost, and quantity in inventory.*

Figure 18.10   *This Inventory Register is produced from the records stored on the sequential file.*

1. Create the interface shown in Figure 18.9. Add four text boxes, four labels, and four command buttons. Add the captions for all. Write the End procedure, but not the Kill procedure (which is described in Exercise 18.9). Add a Close statement to the End procedure. Name the form **frmDataEntry**.

2. Write the cmdWrite_Click() procedure as follows:

```
Private Sub cmdWrite_Click()
    'These instructions create a program entitled prod.tex
    Static count As Integer
    Dim Msg As String
    On Error GoTo ErrorWrite

    txtProductName.SetFocus
    If txtProductName.Text = "" Then
        Close #1
        Exit Sub
    End If

    count = count + 1
    If count <= 1 Then
        Open "prod.txt" For Append As #1
    End If

    Write #1, txtProductName.Text, Val(txtProductPrice.Text), _
    Val(txtProductCost.Text), Val(txtProductInv.Text)
    txtProductName.Text = ""
    txtProductPrice.Text = ""
    txtProductCost.Text = ""
    txtProductInv.Text = ""

    Exit Sub
ErrorWrite:
    Msg = "Error: " & Err.Number & " " & Err.Description

    MsgBox Msg, vbOKCancel, "Error in writing file"
    Exit Sub

End Sub
```

In this procedure, the file is opened only once and is not closed. This allows more than one record to be appended to the file. The file is opened in Append mode to allow for one record after another to be added to the file. After a record has been added to the file, all text fields are cleared.

3. Add a second form, **frmReport** (see Figure 18.10), and write the End procedure for this form. Return to the first form.

4. Write the cmdRead_Click() procedure:

```
Private Sub cmdRead_Click()
    Dim pname As String
    Dim price As Currency
    Dim cost As Currency
    Dim pinventory As Long
    Dim Msg As String

    On Error GoTo ErrorRead
    frmReport.Cls
    frmReport.Show
    Close
    frmReport.Print "Product Inventory"
```

continues

```
            frmReport.Print "Name", "Price", "Cost", "Inventory"
            frmReport.Print

            Open "prod.txt" For Input As #2

            Do Until EOF(2)
               Input #2, pname, price, cost, pinventory
               frmReport.Print pname, Format(price, "$#,###.00"), _
               Format(cost, "$#,###.00"), Format(pinventory, "#######")

            Loop
            Close
            Exit Sub

        ErrorRead:
            Msg = "Error: " & Err.Number & " " & Err.Description

            MsgBox Msg, vbOKCancel, "Error in reading file"
            Exit Sub

        End Sub
```

5. Write the following `Form_Load()` procedure to set the focus on the data-entry form:

```
Private Sub Form_Load()
   ChDrive App.Path
   ChDir App.Path
   txtProductName.SetFocus
End Sub
```

6. Run and test your design. The next exercise asks you to use the same design, but to add the `Kill` procedure code.

This exercise illustrates how to write a `Kill` procedure to delete a file from disk. Use the design interface shown in Figure 18.9, but add a new button between the Write button and the End button named Kill (**cmdKill**).

1. Add a common dialog control to your project (Project|Components| Microsoft Common Dialog Control 6.0).

2. Add the control to the interface for Exercise 18.8 and name the control `dlgGetFile`.

3. Add a `cmdKill_Click()` procedure to your previous design:

```
Private Sub cmdKill_Click()
    Dim Msg As String
    Dim FileName As String
    Dim Ans As Integer

    On Error GoTo Errhandler

    With dlgGetFile
        .Filter = "Text Files (.txt)|*.txt"
        .FilterIndex = 1
        .DialogTitle = "Select file for deletion"
        .Flags = cdlOFNFileMustExist + cdlOFNHideReadOnly
        .ShowOpen

        If .FileName <> "" Then
            FileName = .FileName
        Else
            Exit Sub
        End If
    End With

    Ans = MsgBox("Sure you want to delete " & FileName & "?", 4)
        If Ans = vbYes Then
            Kill FileName
        End If

    Exit Sub

Errhandler:
  If Err.Number = 53 Then
     Msg = "Sorry, file could not be found"
  Else
     Msg = "Sorry, unable to delete file"
  End If
  Resume Next
End Sub
```

4. Run and test your design. Be sure to avoid deleting necessary text files on your machine.

Chapter Summary

This file processing chapter was written to introduce you to the drive-directory-file sequence used by Visual Basic, as well as the four toolbox controls designed to allow you to add file selection functionality to your applications. The first three tools are individual file controls, and the fourth integrates the three file controls:

- Drive List Box control

- Directory List Box control

- File List Box control

- Common Dialog control

The App object is a global object available at runtime. This object is used, in part, to set the default drive and directory. The following instruction sets the default drive to be the same as the path of the application:

```
ChDrive App.Path
```

Error handling is added to file processing code to trap errors, such as when a drive does not respond to a request, or when a file does not exist. Visual Basic contains a large number of trappable errors. The following instruction

```
On Error GoTo ErrorSection
```

must be matched with the following label

```
ErrorSection:
```

found later in the code.

The Err object's Number, Description, and Source properties are assigned new values whenever an error is encountered. These properties may be used in reporting errors in the error-handling section of code.

Common Dialog control properties include the Filter property (which determines how files are displayed), the FilterIndex property (which determines the default files), and the Action property (which displays one of the six types of dialog boxes of the Common Dialog control).

Sequential access files are especially useful for reading and writing text files. Before a file can be used, it must be opened. Once opened, it is possible to read or write to a file. To write to a sequential file, use the Write # or the Print # statements; to read from a sequential file, use the Input # or Line Input # statements (the pound sign (#) is followed by the number of the file). You also use the Input function.

After using a file, close it with the Close statement.

Besides text, records can be written to, or read from, a file. Writing records to a file features the use of the Append mode. When reading from a file, individual fields must be read.

Deleting a file from a disk requires the Kill statement. Kill will not work unless a file is closed.

Skill-Building Exercises

This set of exercises provides additional practice in working with the Common Dialog control, sequential files, and error-trapping. You will be required to modify file exercises contained in the chapter and to work with new sequential files.

1. Place a Common Dialog control on a form and use the ShowColor method to display the Color dialog box after a command button Click() event. When the dialog box appears, select a color to change the background color of the form. Use the following statement:

```
Form1.Backcolor = cmDialog1.Color
```

2. Place a `Common Dialog` control, a text box, and three command buttons—
   cmdRead, **cmdWrite**, and **cmdEnd**—on a form. Before starting this exercise,
   make a copy of the original file so you can return and restart; then, perform
   the following steps:

   a. When the user clicks `cmdRead`, call a procedure named `OpenMe()` that displays text boxes to open as the `FilterIndex` default. Open notes.txt, the
   file created in this chapter, display the stored data in the text box, and
   close the file. Disable the `Read` and enable the `Write`.

   b. Change the text in the text box.

   c. When the user clicks `cmdWrite`, call a second procedure named
   `CloseMe()`. Open a second file, write the revised file to Notes1.txt, and
   close the file. Enable the `Read` and disable the `Write`.

   d. Test your design. Open Notes1.txt to determine if your revision was
   changed.

3. Create a program to read the file layout.txt stored on your disk. Use a `Common
   Dialog` control to open this file. Read the contents of the file, line-by-line, to
   display in a list box the fields of the file. Data that corresponds to this layout
   is found in cities1.txt. (You will use this second file in the final exercise.)

   Allow the user to display the contents of this layout, but not to change the
   contents of the file. **Warning:** Make copies of the layout.txt file in case it is
   destroyed.

4. Modify Exercise 18.8 to allow you to display the records stored in prod.txt
   and to append new records to the file. (Remember to make a backup copy of
   this file.) Use a `Common Dialog` control to open a file and to display the records
   currently stored on it. Add the following record to the file:

   ```
   Light        $6.50          $4.50              300
   ```

   Write this new record to the file. As a test, display the contents of the revised
   file.

5. Alter the previous exercise by displaying the contents of prod.txt in an
   `MSFlexGridControl` on frmReport.

6. Extend the previous exercise by allowing the user to delete a selected row of
   data on the grid by clicking on a row with a right mouse button click (Use
   the `Mouse_Down` event and set `SelectionMode` to `SelectionByRow`). Allow the
   user to save any changes to prod.txt to disk.

7. Design a program that displays three types of information stored in the
   cities1.txt file. (Remember to make a backup copy of this file.) These fields
   are the area name (name of the city, for example, Portland), the name of the
   state, and the 7/1/94 Resident All-Age Population Estimate. The layout of
   this file is shown in the file layout.txt.

To complete this exercise, you will have to read the file line-by-line, followed by the use of the `Instr()` and `Mid$()` functions. These functions will enable you to parse the file to extract the desired information. Place your output on a grid, containing three columns and 215 rows. Use column widths of 2,000, 1,500, and 1,200.

As a test, the following should be the first line of output displayed on the grid:

```
New York city          NY                  7333253
```

OBJECT TYPES, VARIABLES, AND COLLECTIONS

When building a Visual Basic application, you always work with objects. These objects include forms, controls, and software components made available to you by other applications or software components you create. As described in Chapter 1, "Running a Visual Basic Program," Visual Basic 6 is much more object-oriented than earlier versions.

Because forms and controls are visible, it is difficult to think of them as data types; however, they are data types of a special kind. They are *object data types*. They differ from user-defined types because they hold both data (properties) and code (methods), and they receive events.

Object variables are declared as object data types, just as you would declare a variable as a primitive data type or as a user-defined data type. Whenever you add a form to a project, Visual Basic automatically declares it as a global form, using the name assigned. This gives it an Object variable declaration.

Using Object variables, much like string and numeric variables, it becomes possible to manipulate forms, controls, and other complex data structures. As an example, it is possible to create new instances of forms during runtime. Using a control array, it is possible to create new instances of Visual Basic controls. Finally, you can create your own objects in Visual Basic. These objects contain code to be used by your own application or exposed and used by other applications. In advanced Visual Basic, you can even create your own controls.

The tasks you will learn in this chapter include the runtime use of built-in Visual Basic objects as well as the creation of new instances of forms and controls. Although the practical, real-world use of this chapter's exercises might not be readily apparent, the exercises introduce the syntax for manipulation of objects that will be useful as you progress through this book. This includes the modules you create using class modules in Chapter 20, "Class Modules," and especially the objects made available by the DAO and ADO data access libraries (Chapter 24, "Using Data Access Objects" and Chapter 25, "ActiveX Data Objects." In this chapter, you will learn how to accomplish the following tasks:

- Declare an Object variable
- Learn the scope and life of Object variables
- Use the TypeName function
- Use a specific object type
- Use the Set, Nothing, and New keywords
- Change the property of an object created at runtime
- Use the forms and controls collections with the For Each...Next structure
- Dynamically load elements of control arrays

Chapter Objectives

All the tasks for this chapter are condensed into five objectives, as follows:

1. Understanding the makeup of Object variables
2. Knowing the difference between generic and specific object types
3. Working with multiple instances of forms
4. Understanding forms and controls collection
5. Dynamically loading a control array

Objective 19.1   Understanding the Makeup of *Object* Variables

An Object variable is declared similarly to a string or numeric variable: Use Dim, Static, or Public keywords to declare an Object variable. There are, however, several critical differences between an Object variable and a variable of a primitive data type. First and foremost, objects are instances of classes. Second, Object variables are *references* to objects, not the objects themselves.

When you declare an Object variable, you are creating a reference to that object. The object cannot be manipulated until it is bound to the variable using the Set keyword. How objects are bound to Object variables is addressed in detail in this section, but first you need to review classes and object references so that these concepts are clear.

19.1.1   Objects as Class Instances

When you add a control to a form, you are in fact creating an instance of that specific control's class. Think of a class as a cookie cutter or a template. Each instance of the class gets its shape and behavior from the cookie cutter. The class defines the properties of the object (data), the methods of the object (the code), and the events to which the class will respond. When you add a control to a form, it "knows" the events to which it might be asked to respond.

Using a cookie cutter or a template is the essence of encapsulation. You, as a programmer, can use control objects (software components) and not have to be aware of their inner workings. You work with the objects' public interface: the properties, methods, and events the designer of the control has made available to you. However, you never are required to examine the computer code used in the creation of the class.

Visual Basic provides a function that can be used to determine an `Object` variable's class: the `TypeName` function. Although the function also works with simple data types, its main use is to return a string expression describing the class membership of a variable. The following is the syntax for the `TypeName` function:

```
TypeName(varname)
```

The `varname` argument contains any variable except a user-defined type variable.

Exercise 19.1   Using the *TypeName* Function to Read Object Classes

This initial exercise shows the use of the `TypeName` function, and unveils the classes behind the Visual Basic controls and objects with which you have already worked.

1. Create the interface shown in Figure 19.1. Name the form **frmTest** and add five controls: **Image1**, **Label1**, **Command1**, **Shape1**, and **Vscroll1**. Add the list box and name it **lstType**. Observe that we are mixing the format in defining these objects.

Figure 19.1   *This interface will allow you to use the* `TypeName` *function to determine class membership of each control placed on the form.*

2. In the `Command1_Click()` event, enter the following code:

```
lstType.AddItem TypeName(lstType)
lstType.AddItem TypeName(Command1)
lstType.AddItem TypeName(Shape1)
lstType.AddItem TypeName(Image1)
lstType.AddItem TypeName(VScroll1)
lstType.AddItem TypeName(Label1)
lstType.AddItem TypeName(frmTest)
```

3. Run and test the program. You should see the class names of all the control objects, as shown in Figure 19.1.

In section 19.4.2, "Using the For Each...Next Structure to Work with Collections," you are introduced to the For Each...Next syntax, which enables you to loop through all the controls on the form, and display their type names and hence their class membership. As the output in the list box illustrates, each time you add a control to a form you are creating an instance of its class. If you place two labels on this form, for example, you create two instances of the label class.

Notice the difference for the form named frmTest. Its class name is frmTest, not Form. When you add a form module to a Visual Basic project and add code to it, you are not adding an object to your program; you are defining a class. When you run the project and load the form, you create an instance (object) of that class definition.

How is this possible? Think again about what makes an object: properties, methods, and events that are defined for the class. Every time you add an event procedure or a general procedure to the form, you are defining a class method. Forms have predefined properties that make up their class properties. Even so, Visual Basic enables you to add your own properties to a form. In advanced Visual Basic, you can even create your own events for a form.

Visual Basic provides a specific module designed for creating your own classes: the class module (which is addressed in Chapter 20, "Class Modules"). Whether you realize it or not, by starting with a form, you have already been defining classes. After a class is defined, multiple instances (objects) of these classes can be created.

19.1.2   *Object* Variables as References to Objects

Object variables refer to an object, but they are not the object itself. Any object occupies more than 4 bytes in memory, but if you look up the size of Object variables, you will see that they occupy 4 bytes. With 8 bits to a byte, that makes 32 bits, which not coincidentally is the size of a memory register in a 32-bit operating system, such as Windows. Object variables hold the memory address of the object. In other computer languages, such a variable is called a *pointer variable*. In Visual Basic, Object variables have some properties of pointers, but not all of them.

Examine some instructions that bind an Object variable to an object you recognize: a command button. Consider the following code for a form that contains a command button named Command1:

```
Dim objectref as CommandButton
Set objectref = Command1
objectref.caption = "I have a new caption"
```

The first instruction declares objectref as an object of type CommandButton. The second uses the Set statement to bind the Object variable to the Command1 command button. The syntax for this statement is as follows:

```
Set objectvar = {[New] objectexpression | Nothing}
```

The keywords New and Nothing are optional. The third instruction changes the caption of Command1.

Rather than using a reference to a command button, you could, of course, simply assign a new value to the command button's caption property. In most instances, you would do that because a command button is a software component defined for you as a control. As a control, an instance of a command button is created for you when you add it to a form.

Visual Basic also allows you to use software components other than controls. These objects are created during runtime and are defined in class modules. To create an object during runtime, you create an instance of the class. This is done by declaring an Object variable and then binding the variable with the Set keyword. There are several ways of making these Object variable declarations. The discussion turns to this subject next.

Objective 19.2   Knowing the Difference Between Generic and Specific Object Types

The preceding example used a specific object data type, a CommandButton, to declare an Object variable. This variable then was bound to a Visual Basic component: a Command Button control. It is possible, however, to use the generic word Object as your Object variable type. You thus could make an Object variable declaration for a command button with the following instruction:

```
Dim mycmd as Object
```

The generic object types are as follows:

- Form—Any form in an application

- Control—Any control in an application

- MDI Form—The MDI form in the application (if one exists)

- Object—Any object

There are many more specific object types built into Visual Basic—mainly the software components contained in the toolbox. These include the following:

CheckBox	Frame	OLE
ComboBox	Grid	OptionButton
CommandButton	HScrollBar	PictureBox
CommonDialog	Image	Shape
Data	Label	TextBox
DirListBox	Line	Timer
DriveListBox	ListBox	VScrollBar
FileListBox	Menu	

As a rule, use a specific object type whenever possible. This makes it easier for Visual Basic to determine how to resolve references to objects and makes your application run much faster. It also makes your Visual Basic code much easier to read.

The difference in speed depends on whether Object variables in your code are early-bound (the fastest) or late-bound (slowest). A variable is bound when Visual Basic can resolve to which kind of object a variable refers. If Visual Basic can resolve the Object variable when your application is compiled, which specific Object variable declarations allow it to do, then Visual Basic knows where to retrieve information about the class when it encounters the variable in code.

If the Object variable declaration is generic, however, Visual Basic must first make inquiries during runtime to resolve to which class the object belongs. It then must retrieve the class information. This adds considerable overhead. Thus, as a general rule, remember to always declare Object variables as specifically as possible.

Exercise 19.2   Using Generic and Specific Object Declarations

This short exercise illustrates how a generic type object declaration differs from a specific type object declaration.

1. Create the interface shown in Figure 19.2.

Figure 19.2   *This interface shows how generic and specific object variables can be bound to controls.*

2. In the Command1_click() event, enter the following code:

```
Private Sub Command1_Click()
    Dim genobj As Control        'A generic declaration
    Dim sobj As VScrollBar       'A specific declaration

    Set genobj = Text1     'Set first generic variable
    genobj.Left = 200

    Set genobj = Shape1    'Set second generic variable
    genobj.Left = 200

    Set genobj = Command1   'Set third generic variable
    genobj.Left = 200

    Set sobj = VScroll1    'Set specific Object variable
    sobj.Left = Form1.ScaleWidth - sobj.Width
End Sub
```

3. Run and test the program.

In this exercise, you use the generic object type Control and the specific object type VScrollBar. You successively bind controls to the variable genobj with the Set statement. The specific Object variable, sobj, is bound to Vscroll1. Observe the results if you attempt to bind the Object variable sobj to one of the other controls, such as Command1.

Objective 19.3   Working with Multiple Instances of Forms

Designing a form in Visual Basic actually is the creation of a new class. As a class instance, individual forms are instantiated when you use the Load statement. You usually only create one instance of a form; however, it is possible to create many instances of a single form. Sound strange? Exercise 19.3 will demonstrate this concept.

19.3.1   The *New* Keyword

To create multiple instances of objects from classes, you can use the New keyword. This book uses the New keyword to create multiple instances of the same form, multiple instances of components we create with class modules, and software components exposed to our applications by other applications.

The following instruction declares the variable NextForm as a new instance of Form1:

```
Dim NextForm As New Form1
```

Initially, the new instance is an exact copy of the original form as it exists at design-time. The shape and contents of the new form are the same as the original form.

To inspect the new form, write the following:

```
NextForm.Show
```

19.3.2   The *Move* Method

When you create a new instance of a form, it becomes an exact copy and completely covers the original. To separate the new instance from the original, it must be moved. The Move method does this with the following syntax:

```
[object.]Move left[,top[,width[,height]]]
```

Table 19.1 explains the components of the Move syntax.

TABLE 19.1   Syntax of the *Move* Method

Component	Description
object	The form or control to move
left	The value for the left edge of the object
top	The value for the top edge of the object
width	The new width of the object
height	The new height of the object

Although the left argument is the only argument required (right does not appear in the syntax), you cannot specify width or height unless previous arguments are used. Width, for example, cannot be used without specifying left and top. Height cannot be used without specifying left, top, and width.

Exercise 19.3   Creating a New Instance of a Form

This brief exercise asks you to create multiple instances of a form. Figure 19.3 illustrates the form you are asked to create and how multiple instances appear.

Figure 19.3   *These forms are all identical and represent instances of a class defined by a form module.*

1. Create the visible form shown in Figure 19.3. Name the form **frmDemoClassInstance**. Add a text box (**txtMessage**) and two command buttons (**cmdNew** and **cmdEnd**). Write the cmdEnd procedure.

2. Write the cmdNew_Click() procedure as follows:

```
Private Sub cmdNew_Click()
    'Declare a new form object
    Dim F As New frmDemoClassInstance

    F.Show
    F.Move Me.Left + (Me.Width \ 10), Me.Top + (Me.Height \ 10)
End Sub
```

3. Run and test your program. Observe that the F.Move method is needed to separate the new form from the original.

The optional keyword New always ensures that a new instance of a form is created at runtime. You cannot, however, use the keyword New with a generic form class. It can be used only with a specific form class, such as frmDemoClassInstance or frmMain, not simply Form. The following statement, for example, is not allowed because Form is generic:

```
Dim MyForm As New Form
```

You cannot use the New keyword to create runtime instances of controls. Controls must be created during design-time. Visual Basic does permit you to dynamically add and remove controls from control arrays. You will dynamically load and unload control arrays in Objective 19.5, "Dynamically Loading a Control Array," later in this chapter. The following instruction is not allowed, for example, because New cannot be used with a control:

```
Dim MyText As New Text1
```

19.3.3   Using the *Me* Implicit Object Variable

In Exercise 19.3, you used the Me implicit object variable. The Me variable refers to the *currently executing* class instance. Every time you click cmdNew, you employ the size and position properties of the current class instance to create a new object. The Me implicit variable refers to the current object. Other languages often use the word *this* to refer to the current class instance. Visual Basic uses the word Me.

19.3.4   *Set* and *New* with the Keyword *Nothing*

In Exercise 19.3, you used the keyword New in the declaration of the Object variable. This binds the Object variable to the object in one statement. You then used the Show method to display the new form instance. In practice, the New keyword generally is used in combination with the Set keyword. The following is the syntax for the declaration of the Object variable and its binding:

```
Set objectvar = New objecttype
```

The following statements

```
Dim MyForm As frmMain
Set MyForm = New frmMain
```

appear equivalent to the statement

```
Dim MyForm As New frmMain
```

They are not quite the same, however. When the following statement

```
Set MyForm = New frmMain
```

is used, you can use the keyword Nothing to make the following assignment

```
Set MyForm = Nothing
```

This allows the Object variable to be dereferenced, indicating that an Object variable does not refer or point to any object. When an Object variable is set to Nothing, Visual Basic will not attempt to create another class instance the next time you attempt to use the variable. Consider the following code:

```
Dim MyForm As frmMain
Set MyForm = New frmMain
MyForm.Show
Set MyForm = Nothing
If MyForm Is Nothing Then
  [do the following because Nothing will always be true]
End If
```

Using the Nothing keyword allows the memory referenced by the Object variable, MyForm, to be reclaimed.

The other difference between these two methods is the manner by which the object is actually created. Consider again the two instructions:

```
Dim MyForm As frmMain
Set MyForm = New frmMain
```

In this case, MyForm is created when the Set statement executes. The developer knows explicitly when the object is created. In the following alternative form of declaration

```
Dim MyForm As New frmMain
```

a new instance of the frmMain class isn't created until a reference to a property or method of MyForm is made. Based on different program conditions, the object creation might occur at any number of places in program execution.

19.3.5   Changing Properties of Form Instances

When you use the New keyword with a form, Visual Basic creates a new instance of a form. Each instance originally retains the properties of the original class definition, making it an exact clone. You can, however, change the properties of a new instance of a form at runtime; for example, you can change the caption, messages placed in text boxes, labels, colors, and so forth, as the next exercise demonstrates.

Exercise 19.4   Changing *Object* Variable Properties

This exercise asks you to use the same form as the last exercise, but to change the caption of the new form instance, the caption on the command button, and the message in the text box. In addition, you are asked to change the message in the text box on the original form and to disable the New Instance command buttons on both the original and the copy of the original form. Figure 19.4 shows how the new form instance will appear.

1. Write the cmdNew_Click() procedure as follows:

```
Private Sub cmdNew_Click()
    Dim F As frmDemoClassInstance
    Set F = New frmDemoClassInstance
    F.Show
    F.Move Me.Left + (Me.Width \ 10), Me.Top + (Me.Height \ 10)
    F.Caption = "My Caption my Caption"

    'New notation to separate object from property
    F.txtMessage.Text = "Finally, a new message"
    F.cmdNew.Caption = "Don't press"
    F.cmdNew.Enabled = False
    Me.cmdNew.Enabled = False
    Me.txtMessage.Text = "That's all folks!"
End Sub
```

Figure 19.4   *In this display, you create a new form instance and change the properties of controls on both forms, independent of each other.*

In this code, two forms can be referenced as F and frmDemoClassInstance because F is created as an instance of the frmDemoClassInstance class. Once created, you can change the properties of F and frmDemoClassInstance because each represents an independent entity.

2. Run and test your procedure. Click both forms to determine whether they were changed as desired.

Objective 19.4   Understanding Forms and Controls Collection

Visual Basic provides collections to make it possible to access all the forms in an application or the controls placed on a form. For each application, there is a forms and a controls collection. These collections are declared globally with the predefined keywords Forms and Controls. Visual Basic contains several types of collections. In advanced Visual Basic, you can even create your own objects and your own object collections.

19.4.1   Collection Syntax

The following is the syntax for a forms collection in which index is a numerical expression:

```
Forms(index)
```

The following statement unloads all loaded form instances in a program:

```
For i = 0 to Forms.Count -1
   Unload Forms(i)
Next i
```

Observe that the index of the forms collections begins with 0.

Exercise 19.5   Unloading an Instance of an Object

This exercise asks you to load and unload instances of an object. As shown in Figure 19.5, a Remove Instance command button has been added to the earlier design.

Figure 19.5   *Besides adding a form instance, you also can remove any instance created using coded statements.*

1. Create a new project and save the form from Exercise 19.3 as a new form named **f19-5.frm**. Add the **Remove Instance** command button and change the form and button captions.

2. Add the following code to the cmdRemove_Click() event:

```
Private Sub cmdRemove_Click()
   Dim i As Integer
   If (forms.Count > 1) Then
        Unload forms(forms.Count - 1)
   Else
        cmdRemove.Enabled = False
   End If
   forms(forms.Count - 1).Print forms.Count
End Sub
```

Observe that all forms will be unloaded until only one form remains because the form index begins with 0. To reference the last member of the forms collection, you can use the expression Forms(Forms.Count - 1). In the cmdRemove_Click() event, as each form is unloaded, the count of the forms collection is printed on the last member of the collection until Count equals 1.

3. Add the `cmdNew_Click()` code:

```
Private Sub cmdNew_Click()
    Dim F As New frmDemoClassInstance
    F.Show

    F.Move Me.Left + (Me.Width \ 10), Me.Top + (Me.Height \ 10)
    F.Print Forms.Count
End Sub
```

4. Run and test your program.

19.4.2   Using the *For Each...Next* Structure to Work with Collections

To work with collections, use the `For Each...Next` structure. The syntax for this loop structure is as follows:

```
For Each element In group
    [statements]
    [Exit For]
    [statements]
Next [element]
```

Table 19.2 explains the components of the `For Each...Next` structure.

TABLE 19.2   *For Each...Next* Syntax

Component	Description
element	A variable used to iterate through the elements of the collection. For collections, `element` can only be of type `Variant`, a generic object, or any specific OLE automation object variable.
group	The name of an object collection.
statements	One or more instructions that are executed on each item in the group.

As an example, when working with the forms collection, the statements read as follows:

```
Dim frmNew as Form
For Each frmNew In Forms
    [statements]
    [Exit For]
    [statements]
Next [element]
```

Observe that `Form` is singular and `Forms` is plural. `Forms` is a collection, whereas `Form` is an element of the collection.

Exercise 19.6   Iterating Through the Forms and Controls Collections

This exercise iterates through the controls collection of two identical forms and illustrates use of the For Each...Next statement to list each control. Figure 19.6 shows the interface you are asked to create.

Figure 19.6   *Place several controls on a form, add a list box to show the results, and use the* For Each...Next *statement to list all controls assigned to each instance of a form.*

1. Build the two forms. The forms contain a list box, picture box, OLE control, frame, combo box, command button, and scroll bars. Name one **Form1** and the other **Form2**. Save the forms as **f19-6A.frm** and **f19-6B.frm**. Save the project as **p19-6.vbp**.

2. Make Form1 the startup object, and put the following code in its Form_Load() event:

   ```
   Load Form2
   Caption = Caption & "  -  " & Name
   ```

   This places both forms in memory.

3. Set the Visible property of one or two of the controls to False.

4. Enter the following code for the command button on Form1 named cmdTest with the caption List controls:

   ```
   Private Sub cmdTest_Click()
     Dim ctrl As Control
     Dim tstForm As Form
     Dim item As String
     For Each tstForm In Forms
       For Each ctrl In tstForm.Controls
         item = tstForm.Name & "    " & ctrl.Name & "    " &
   ctrl.Visible
         List1.AddItem item
       Next
     Next
   End Sub
   ```

5. Run and test this exercise.

Each element in the For Each...Next syntax must be an object of the same type as that in the group. In this instance, you declare the variable ctrl as a generic Control object and tstForm as a generic Form object. The nested loops iterate through the collection hierarchy. Each element of the Forms collection is first selected, and all controls contained within that form (Form1) are listed. Following this, all the controls contained on the second element in the Forms collection (Form2) are listed.

Also observe that Form2 is loaded into memory, but it is not shown. Even so, the controls placed on this form can be listed. If the form had not been loaded into memory, it would not have been considered part of the forms and controls collections.

Objective 19.5   Dynamically Loading a Control Array

Although elements of a control array are not treated as Object variables, they can be loaded and unloaded at runtime. In this manner, they behave like Object variables. By adding an element to a control array, a new "instance" can be created.

Two properties, LBound and UBound, make working with dynamic control arrays easy. Read at runtime, they return the lowest and highest elements, respectively, in the control array. This enables you to write a single loop procedure to process values in the control array event as its size is dynamically changed.

Suppose that you developed an application for online ordering. As users make selections, an invoice could be created, adding one label at a time. After the order is completed, the total could be calculated with code similar to the following:

```
Private Sub Calculate()
  Dim  as Integer
  Dim RunTotal as Currency
  RunTotal=0
  For  n = lblOrderitem.LBound to  lblOrderItem.UBound
    RunTotal = Runtotal + Val(lblOrderItem(n).Caption)
  Next
    ' code to display RunTotal
End Sub
```

Exercise 19.7   Using a Dynamic Control Array

This exercise asks you to dynamically load a control array of shapes on the display screen. The interface is very simple (see Figure 19.7).

Figure 19.7   *This design interface consisting of shapes and labels is dynamically changed during runtime.*

1. Build the interface shown in Figure 19.7. It contains two unmarked controls: a shape and a label. Each has its Index property set to 0. Set their Visible properties to False. The display also contains two command buttons (**cmdNew** and **cmdAlter**).

2. Write the cmdNew_Click() procedure.

```
Private Sub cmdNew_Click()
    Static  i As Integer
    Dim hgt As Integer
    hgt = CInt(Shape1(0).Height / 2)
    Label1(0).BorderStyle = 0
    If Label1.UBound <> 6 Then
        For i = 1 To 6
          Load Shape1(i)
          Load Label1(i)
          Shape1(i).Shape = i - 1
          Label1(i).Caption = Shape1(i).Index
          Shape1(i).Top = Shape1(i - 1).Top + Shape1(i 1).Height
          Label1(i).Top = Shape1(i).Top + hgt
          Shape1(i).Visible = True
          Label1(i).Visible = True
        Next
    Else
        Exit Sub
    End If
End Sub
```

By changing the BorderStyle property of the original control, Label1(0), before loading new control array elements, the appearance of each subsequent array member is changed. Each individual array member can now be referenced and have its properties changed.

3. Add a new command button to the form and name it **cmdAlter**. Write the following code:

```
Private Sub cmdAlter_Click()
    Dim i As Integer
    For i = Label1.LBound To Label1.UBound
        Label1(i).BorderStyle = 1
        Label1(i).Font.Size = 10
    Next
End Sub
```

By employing the LBound and UBound properties of the Label1 control array, you can change every element of the array without knowing how many elements were contained within it.

4. On your own, add a procedure that unloads the related Shape control element every time a Label control is clicked.

5. Run and test this exercise.

Chapter Summary

This chapter introduced the use of Object variables. Object variables can be declared like other variables. Their scope is also similar to other variables. They differ, however, in that they are references to objects. These object references are not assigned to an object until the Set statement is used. You can declare an Object variable by using the generic objects of Object, Form, or Control; or, preferably, by using specific object references. For controls, these specific object references could be included in such declarations as the following:

```
Dim X as TextBox
Dim Y as Label
Dim Z as CommandButton
```

Object variables that refer to specific forms and objects can be declared by using the New keyword. If declared in conjunction with the Set statement, object references to forms can be cleared from memory using the Nothing keyword. The properties of each instance of the form can be changed, as well as the properties of the controls that the form contains. The Me implicit variable refers to the currently executing class instance.

Visual Basic maintains a forms collection for the entire application and a controls collection for each form. You can iterate through these collections by using the For Each...Next structure. For form and control collections, the Object variable that refers to each collection member can be declared with generic variables, as shown in the following example:

```
Dim f as Form
For Each f in Forms
  [Add statements here]
Next

Dim fControl as Control
For Each fcontrol in Controls
  [Add statements here]
Next
```

You can dynamically load and unload controls, provided they are elements of a control array. The LBound and UBound runtime properties of the arrays refer to the last and first elements, respectively, of the control array. These are altered dynamically as the size of the array changes.

Skill-Building Exercises

These skill-building exercises ask you to declare and use object variables and to work with the Forms property and the controls collection. You also are asked to work with a number of statements described in the chapter, including the Set statement. Note that you should be able to work through this set of exercises before moving to the next chapter, which draws on the concept presented in this chapter.

1. Add a check box and a command button to a form. In the command button's Click() event, enter code that declares a specific Object variable for a check box, binds the variable to the check box on the form, and then changes the variables Caption, BackColor, Left, and Top properties.

2. Using the Forms collection Count property, modify Exercise 19.5 so that the width of newly created forms is incrementally increased by 10%. (Hint: The most recently created form can be referenced as Forms (Forms.Count - 1.)

3. Place a command button and a shape control on a form. During design-time, make the shape a blue circle. Write a program so that in the button Click() event, a specific Object variable is declared, the shape control is bound to this variable, and the variable is then passed to a form-level procedure.

   The form-level procedure should change the shape's BackColor to red and increase its Height and Width properties by a factor of 3. In the procedure, assign the shape's Name to the shape's Tag property and then print the new Tag property value on the form.

4. Add a label, a picture box, an option button, a check box, a shape control (with BackStyle set to Opaque), a list box, and a command button on a form. Set them randomly on the form. In the command button, write a procedure that, using the controls collection, passes the controls and their controls collection index to a procedure. In the procedure, align the controls across the top of the form, change their BackColor properties to red, and assign the control's name to the control's Tag property.

Before exiting the button `Click()` event, list the control's Tag properties in the list box. (*Hint:* To align the controls, test the index number. If it isn't zero, then you can reference the previous index number to set the control's position.)

5. Write a program that enables the user to enter price data into a text box. Every time the user presses the Enter key, the price is displayed in a label that is dynamically loaded and then shown. The program should also include a means of summing the prices and displaying the results. (Hint: Use the `KeyPress()` event, and check if `KeyAscii = vbKeyReturn`.) Also, use the control array `LBound` and `UBound` properties. Remember, if you add a new control, `Load lblPrice(lblPrice.Ubound + 1)`, it becomes `lblPrice(lblPrice.Ubound)`.

6. Add three labels and three command buttons to a form. When you click on a label or command button, pass the control to a general procedure that tests for the class membership of the control. If the control is a label, change the caption of the control to "Acceptable." If the control is a command button, change the caption of the button to "Unacceptable."

7. By using a `Set` statement, it is possible to pass the picture contained within an image control to the cell of an `MSFlexGridControl` (for example, `Set Grid1.CellPicture = imgEarth.Picture`). Place an image control and an `MSFlexGrid` control on a form. Select an icon and display it in the image control. By clicking on the image control, display five copies of the icon in the third row of the grid. (*Hint:* To ensure the image can be seen, specify row height by reading the `Height` property of the image control.)

CLASS MODULES

This chapter introduces you to building your own objects in Visual Basic by defining classes. You already have defined classes, methods, and properties. Every time you add a procedure to a form, you define a class method. Every time you declare a `Public` variable at the module level, you, in essence, create a form property. Visual Basic permits you to explicitly define your own form properties with special procedures called `Property` procedures.

Visual Basic forms can be used as software components by being deployed in multiple Visual Basic projects. Developers more typically, however, build software components with class modules, which enable the developer to define classes explicitly. They encourage a deliberate object-oriented approach to application development. Like forms, class modules have their own properties, methods, and events. Class modules differ from forms, principally by not having a visual interface.

Class modules contain only code, but the code differs from that held in standard code modules. Code in a class module defines the properties, methods, and events for objects created from that class. Class modules hold their data and code together. Another way of describing this is to say that classes encapsulate data and code in a way that makes objects created from the class easy to manipulate. Standard code modules, by contrast, contain procedures, which vary widely in their functions; standard code modules do not explicitly hold data and code together. As important, code in class modules can be compiled to become an ActiveX DLL, ActiveX EXE, and, in advanced Visual Basic, an ActiveX control. Other applications can then create objects from the class that you have defined.

Class modules were built into Visual Basic to allow for the design of robust and reusable components. Components that are to be used by many applications need to contain code that is well-tested and as error-free as possible. This chapter addresses some of the fundamental ways in which class modules are designed to make code more robust. Creating procedures for class modules is a more involved process than writing procedures for standard code modules or forms. It takes forethought and careful analysis before the first line of code is written. The tradeoff is code that tends to be reliable and easy to maintain.

In this chapter, you learn to perform the following tasks:

- Define your own property for a form
- Add `Property Let` and `Property Get` procedures to a form
- Add a class module to a project
- Define class properties and class methods
- Instantiate objects from the class you create
- Use class `Initialize()` and `Terminate()` events
- Add objects you have defined to an instance of the `Collection` class

Chapter Objectives

Because this chapter focuses on the definition and use of classes, it first reviews the fundamental features of objects and introduces the mechanics of creating several simple classes. It reviews the way instances of classes (objects) can be placed in collections. This chapter concludes with some guidelines on creating class modules. The objectives of this chapter are as follows:

1. Reviewing object features
2. Adding a class module to a project
3. Adding objects to a collection
4. Employing good programming practices when creating class modules

Objective 20.1   Reviewing Object Features

Objects are instances of classes. Objects possess properties, contain methods, and can handle events. *Properties* hold data that describe the object; methods tell the object what to do; events are actions the object undertakes when it receives a particular message. Properties and methods of the class are referred to as *class members*. Review each of these features of objects in more detail.

20.1.1   Object Properties

Properties hold data that describe an object. You already have worked with the properties of forms as well as some of the properties of Visual Basic's system objects, such as the `Screen` or `App` object. The `Caption` property of a form, for example, describes the string expression displayed on the form's title bar. This property can be read as

```
strVariable$ = Form1.Caption
```

or it can be assigned a new value (written to)

```
Form1.Caption = "I have a new caption!"
```

Some properties are read-only. The `ListCount` property of a list box, for example, is a read-only property.

The properties of an object that can be read or written to are part of the object's interface. That is, code that seeks to manipulate or read object properties "sees" only those properties the object exposes. It does not see data that the object does not expose.

How does this work in practice? Because you have already worked with forms, let's start with form properties.

Exercise 20.1   *Public* and *Private* Module Level Declarations

In this exercise, you experiment with the scoping of module-level variables and review concepts introduced in Chapter 10, "Defining the Scope of Variables and Procedures." You work with two forms (see Figure 20.1). One form launches a second form. The first form assigns a value to, and reads a value from, variables declared at the module level of the second form. One of the variables is declared as `Public` and the other is declared as `Private`.

Figure 20.1   *Create two forms to test private and public scope.*

1. Create two forms, as illustrated in Figure 20.1. The form on the left is named **frmMain**, and the form on the right is named **frmTest**. Change the captions as shown. Save these two forms to disk, respectively, as **f-20A.frm** and **f-20B.frm**. Save the project as **p20_1.vbp**.

2. On `frmMain`, add two command buttons named **cmdTestPublic** (upper button) and **cmdTestPrivate** (lower button). The label control is named **lblDisplay** and has its `BorderStyle` property set to 1 (fixed single).

3. On `frmTest`, make the two following declarations at the module level and add the `Form_Load()` event:

```
Public PublicProperty As Integer
Private PrivateProperty As String

Private Sub Form_Load()
    PublicProperty = 67
    PrivateProperty = "I am a string"
End Sub
```

continues

Exercise 20.1   continued

4. On frmMain, add the following code to the button Click() events and the
Form_Load() event:

```
Private Sub cmdTestPublic_Click()
    'This can be displayed since PublicProperty is declared
    ' as type public
    lblDisplay.Caption = Str$(frmTest.PublicProperty)
End Sub

Private Sub cmdTestPrivate_Click()
    'This cannot be displayed since PrivateProperty is declared
    ' as type private
    cmdTestPrivate.Caption = frmTest.PrivateProperty
End Sub

Private Sub Form_Load()
    frmTest.Top = frmMain.Top      ' position frmTest
    frmTest.Left = frmMain.Left + frmMain.Width + 200
    frmTest.Show
End Sub
```

5. Specify frmMain as the startup object and then run and test the program.

When you click the top button, the cmdTestPublic_Click() event assigns a value
to the publicly declared variable on frmTest and then reads that value and displays it on the label lblDisplay. The cmdTestPrivate_Click() event, however,
should generate an error message like that shown in Figure 20.2.

Figure 20.2   *This dialog box displays a compile error stating that a method or data member
was not found.*

The message generated in Exercise 20.1 states, Method or data member not found.
As far as Visual Basic is concerned, a publicly declared variable is a data member or
property of the form. Because the PrivateProperty variable was declared with the
Private statement, its scope was limited to the frmTest module. It was not part of
the public interface for the frmTest class. The variable PublicProperty, however,
did become part of the class interface. It could be assigned a value and that value
could be read. Also observe how the variable PublicProperty was read in the
cmdTestPublic_Click() event. It was referred to with the same object.property
notation you have used with other objects.

The PublicProperty variable in frmTest can be assigned any integer value. If
assigned a string expression, an error occurs. Suppose that you want to create a variable that can only take positive integer values. A publicly declared integer variable

at the module level might be assigned an errant value and introduce errors into processing. Visual Basic provides special procedures to cover this contingency. They are called Property procedures, and they are executed when an object property is assigned a value or read. Property procedures act as a buffer between the direct assignment or reading of object property values.

20.1.2 *Property* Procedures and Data Hiding

Although a publicly declared variable in a module acts like a property of a class and is assigned new values and read with the object.property syntax, class properties are properly defined with Property procedures. Property procedures allow variables that are defined as Private in a module to be assigned new values and read from outside the object. They promote one of the central tenets of object-oriented programming: the encapsulation of data into hidden data members. These terms will become clear as you work with Property procedures. Creating a class property in Visual Basic that can be both assigned new values and read is usually a three-step process:

1. Declare a Private variable at the module level of a form or class module.

2. Create a Property Let procedure to assign new values to the object property.

3. Use a Property Get procedure to read the object property value.

A read-only property has only a Property Get procedure. Values returned by the Property Get procedure can be assigned or determined only from within the object. The following exercise takes you through the mechanics of creating a Property procedure.

Exercise 20.2   Hiding Class Data

Like Exercise 20.1, this exercise contains two forms: frmMain and frmTest (see Figure 20.3). The second form, frmTest, contains the variable declarations and the Property procedures. This exercise demonstrates the way data members of a class stay hidden and are accessed only with Property procedures.

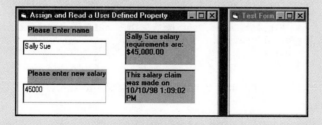

Figure 20.3 *Create two forms to test the hiding of class data.*

continues

Exercise 20.2 continued

1. Create the two forms that you see illustrated in Figure 20.3. The first form, **frmMain**, has two text boxes on the left: **txtName** in the upper position and **txtSalary** in the lower position. Above each text box are labels that prompt the user to enter data. Set the TabIndex property for txtName to 0 and the TabIndex for txtSalary to 1.

2. On the right side of frmMain are two larger labels with their BorderStyle properties set to 1 (fixed single). The upper label is named **lblSalary**, and the lower label is named **lblTimeStamp**. Both of these labels have their WordWrap properties set to True.

3. Change the captions for the forms as shown.

4. Save frmMain to disk as **20-2A.frm** and frmTest as **20-2B.frm**. Save the project as **p20_2.vbp**.

5. In the frmMain Form_Load() event, enter the following code to position frmTest and make it visible:

```
Private Sub Form_Load()
    frmTest.Top = frmMain.Top
    frmTest.Left = frmMain.Left + frmMain.Width + 200
    frmTest.Show
End Sub
```

6. Add the following procedures to the txtName_KeyPress() and txtSalary_KeyPress() events:

```
Private Sub txtName_KeyPress(KeyAscii As Integer)
    If KeyAscii = vbKeyReturn Then
      frmTest.EmployeeName = txtName.Text
      txtSalary.SetFocus
    End If
End Sub

Private Sub txtSalary_KeyPress(KeyAscii As Integer)
    If KeyAscii = vbKeyReturn Then
        frmTest.Salary = Val(txtSalary.Text)
        lblSalary.Caption = frmTest.EmployeeName &   "salary
requirements are: "& Format$(frmTest.Salary, "Currency")

        lblTimeStamp.Caption = "This salary claim was made on " &
frmTest.TimeStamp
    End If
End Sub
```

7. For safety's sake, add the two lines of code to the txtName_LostFocus() event:

```
Private Sub txtName_LostFocus()
  frmTest.EmployeeName = txtName.Text
  txtSalary.SetFocus
End Sub
```

8. At the module level of frmTest, declare the following variables to complete the first step of the three-step class Property procedure:

```
Option Explicit
'The lowercase m notation stands for a private data class
member
Private m_EmployeeName As String
Private m_Salary As Double
Private m_TimeStamp As Date
```

These module-level variables are declared, and will have their values read and assigned by Property procedures.

9. Add code to the Form_Load() event to the frmTest form to initialize these variables:

```
Private Sub Form_Load()
    ' initialize object property values
    m_Salary = 0
    m_TimeStamp = Now
    m_EmployeeName = "Employee"
End Sub
```

10. With the code window of frmTest having the focus, choose Tools, Add Procedure from the Visual Basic menu bar. You should see the dialog box in Figure 20.4. Select the Property option button, make sure the scope of the procedure is Public, and name the procedure Salary.

Figure 20.4   *The Add Procedure dialog box provides space for a name and allows you to set the type and the scope.*

11. Click OK in the Add Procedure dialog box and you will immediately see two procedure declarations added to the code window:

```
Public Property Get Salary() As Variant
End Property

Public Property Let Salary(ByVal vNewValue As Variant)
End Property
```

continues

Visual Basic adds these procedures automatically to the code window. The Let procedure assigns values to a variable; the Get procedure reads values. By default, the object property is a Variant data type. Data types for Property Let and Property Get procedures must match. Because the Salary property will return a Double numeric value, change the procedure declarations to read as follows:

```
Public Property Get Salary() As Double
End Property

Public Property Let Salary(ByVal dNewValue As Double)
End Property
```

12. Add the following code for the salary Let and Get procedures:

```
Public Property Let Salary(ByVal dNewValue As Double)

    Select Case dNewValue
        Case Is <= 0
            MsgBox "Sorry, salary must be a positive value."
        Case Else
            m_Salary = dNewValue
    End Select
        m_TimeStamp = Now
End Property

Public Property Get Salary() As Double
    Salary = m_Salary
End Property
```

Observe that values for salary must be greater than zero. The m_TimeStamp variable also is assigned a value when a new salary is assigned.

13. Add a second class Property procedure to frmTest for the EmployeeName property (remembering to change the data types to String!):

```
Public Property Get EmployeeName() As String
    EmployeeName = m_EmployeeName
End Property

Public Property Let EmployeeName(ByVal sNewValue As String)
    m_EmployeeName = sNewValue
End Property
```

14. Add a third TimeStamp class property, which is a read-only property of type Date. (Delete the Property Let procedure when it is inserted by the Add Procedure dialog box.)

```
Public Property Get TimeStamp() As Date
    TimeStamp = m_TimeStamp
End Property
```

15. Make sure that frmMain is the startup object and then run and test the program.

This is a lot of code to accomplish what could be accomplished more easily by standard coding procedures. But observe the increased flexibility of encapsulating data into class properties. Visual Basic, for example, provides no signed numeric data types. It is, therefore, impossible to restrict `Integer`, `Single`, or `Double` numeric data types to positive values unless input is checked each time, such as in a text box `KeyPress()` event.

By placing this value as an object property, the value can be checked in the `Property Let` procedure of a class. This was done in the case of the `Salary` property. The `Let Salary` procedure also might check to see whether an employee has been identified before a salary value can be assigned.

Encapsulation of data into class properties allows multiple forms to use the same data-validation procedure and can easily be updated as conditions change. Although data placed into class properties is more time-consuming than simply using publicly declared variables, class data promotes code reuse, shortening software development projects in the long term.

Observe also that the data held by the object is now hidden. All the newly added data members of `frmTest` were declared privately. The only way to alter their values or read them is through the `Property Let` and `Property Get` procedures. This data hiding is central to robust, object-oriented programming. These kinds of procedures are sometimes referred to as *class mutator methods* (a `Property Let` procedure) or *accessor methods* (a `Property Get` procedure).

20.1.3   Object Methods

In Exercise 20.1 and Exercise 20.2, you extended the class definition of a form named `frmTest`. Just as you can assign data to class properties, you also can place in class methods code to operate on that data. Methods can be private to the object or made part of the object's interface by declaring the procedure as type `Public`.

Consider, for example, a `ListBox` class. One of the public procedures of the `ListBox` class is `Clear`. This method now is available to you as a class method. How the `ListBox` class implements the `Clear` method is hidden from you. All you know is that it works. The `ListBox` class therefore encapsulates the `Clear` method. The `ListBox` class also has privately scoped procedures that are not accessible. For example, how does the `ListBox` class reorder `ItemIndex` numbers when an item is deleted? It presumably invokes a method internally, but this method is not made available to you through the `ListBox` interface.

When adding class methods, you need to determine whether the method will become part of the class interface or hidden from the user.

Exercise 20.3   Adding a *Class* Method

This exercise extends Exercise 20.2 by adding a method that calculates a 4.7% increase above the new salary. (We're getting greedy!) The user now can select a check box to calculate such a raise (see Figure 20.5). Because this option works solely on the calculation of the Salary property itself and is not invoked separately as an object calculation, the method need not be Public. It simply can be used internally by the object to calculate the requested value.

Figure 20.5   *The check box determines whether the method to increase a person's salary is to be executed.*

1. Save the files from the previous exercise under new names (such as, f20-2A.frm as **f20-3A.frm**, f20-2B.frm as **f20-3B.frm**, and p20-2.vbp as **p20-3.vbp**). Remember to change the Name property of the project to **p20_3**.

2. Add the check box **chkRaise** and the command button **cmdOK** to frmMain. Position frmMain and frmTest, as illustrated in Figure 20.5.

3. Add the following code to the chkRaise_Click() event:

```
Private Sub chkRaise_Click()
   If chkRaise.Value = 1 Then
      frmTest.Raise = True
   Else
      frmTest.Raise = False
   End If
End Sub
```

4. Erase (or cut) the code from the txtSalary_KeyPress() event, and place or paste the following code in the cmdOK_Click() event:

```
Private Sub cmdOK_Click()
   frmTest.salary = Val(txtSalary.Text)
   lblSalary.Caption = frmTest.EmployeeName &  " salary
requirements are: " & Format$(frmTest.salary, "Currency")
   lblTimeStamp.Caption = "This salary claim was made on " &
   frmTest.TimeStamp
End Sub
```

5. Add an additional declaration for the `Raise` property in the General declarations section of the `frmTest` module:

```
Private m_Raise As Boolean
```

The module now contains four class property variables: `m_EmployeeName`, `m_Salary`, `m_TimeStamp`, and `m_Raise`.

6. As with the other class properties, add the `accessor` and `mutator` methods for the `Raise` object property:

```
Public Property Get Raise() As Boolean
    Raise = m_Raise
End Property

Public Property Let Raise(ByVal vNewValue As Boolean)
    m_Raise = bNewValue
End Property
```

7. Add the following line of code to the `frmTest_Load()` event to initialize this new data member:

```
m_Raise = False
```

8. Add the following method to the `frmTest` module, which calculates the new salary with a 4.7% increase:

```
Private Function AddRaise(salary As Double)
    AddRaise = (salary * 0.047)
End Function
```

9. Finally, change the `Property Let Salary` procedure so that the user can calculate a new salary with or without a 4.7% increase:

```
Public Property Let salary(ByVal dNewValue As Double)
    Select Case dNewValue
        Case Is <= 0
            MsgBox "Sorry, salary must be a positive value."
        Case Else
            If m_Raise = True Then
                m_Salary = dNewValue + AddRaise(dNewValue)
            Else
                m_Salary = dNewValue
            End If
    End Select
    m_TimeStamp = Now
End Property
```

10. Run and test the program.

20.1.4 Object Events

Objects also can contain events. Most of the code you have written so far is procedures that respond to user events, such as a button click or the press of a key on the keyboard. These events are triggered when the object receives an operating system message. When you click a mouse button on a form, for example, an operating system message is sent to the object (a window); and if the form's `Click()` event has code in it, the code is fired.

Visual Basic enables you to create your own events for objects, but it is rare that you will need to add them. The visual interface for your program can almost always be handled by the events provided by Visual Basic, and the standard and custom controls provided in the different Visual Basic versions. Additionally, a rich market of third-party controls exists for Visual Basic.

The capability to design events for objects is used primarily in advanced Visual Basic when creating ActiveX controls and advanced data controls. This often requires use of the Windows API, a topic beyond the scope of this book. The software components that you create will not require custom events. Most will be invisible components created from class modules. That objective is discussed next.

Objective 20.2   Adding a Class Module to a Project

In the preceding exercises, you added your own properties and methods to forms. You, in effect, extended the definition of classes named frmTest. Custom properties for forms were introduced first because you are already familiar with forms, but the frmTest classes were not especially efficient. They contained a lot of extra data and a visual interface that was not needed to work with salary calculations for employees.

The frmTest Property procedures that you added in the preceding two exercises are part of the code that you might use to define an object called Employee. This object would contain data about an Employee (object properties) and make certain calculations with that data (object methods). As you can see, a full-blown Employee class definition might contain quite a bit of code.

Data that you might want to hold about the employee include the employee's name, social security number, company ID number, date of birth, date of hiring, pay grade, and emergency information. Methods to operate on that data might include not only payroll calculations (including local taxes, state taxes, federal taxes, payroll savings matching plans, and automatic charitable contribution deductions), but also benefit calculations based upon years of service.

Think of another, simpler, object: a customer order entry. An order entry usually includes the product name, the quantity ordered, the unit price of the item, and the total amount of the order entry. Although in most online ordering applications you would want to have this information displayed, you can think of an order entry item as a discrete object. Such an object can be described in a class module.

20.2.1   Inserting Class Modules into a Project

Adding a class module to a project is very similar to adding a form module or standard code module to a project. Choose Project, Add Class Module from the Visual Basic menu bar. A standard dialog box will appear with tabs named New and Existing. You can choose to insert a new module or an existing module.

Like forms and standard modules, class modules have a Name property (press F4). It is important that you do not accept the default name provided. Instead, immediately give the class module a meaningful name. Like form and standard code modules, class modules are saved to disk under a separate file name. Class modules saved to disk have a .CLS file extension.

When you examine a class module, the code window is nearly identical to that of a standard module. There is a General Declaration section and a *Class* object (click the left drop-down combo box). The *Class* object has two events listed: Initialize and Terminate (click the right drop-down combo box). The first event is easy to understand. It fires whenever an object of that class is instantiated with the Set statement, or declared with the New keyword and then referenced in code. The Terminate() event is less obvious. It executes when the last variable reference to the object leaves memory. This will become clear when you write code for the Initialize() and Terminate() events in sections 20.2.3, "The Initialize() Event," and 20.2.4, "The Terminate() Event," respectively.

20.2.2 Creating an *OrderItem* Class

Creating a new class with a class module should seem straightforward to you. You already have worked with Property Let and Property Get procedures and coded general methods for form classes. The main difference is that when it comes time to create (instantiate) an object from the class, you must bind an object variable with the Set statement or declare an object variable with the New keyword.

Exercise 20.4   Creating and Using an *OrderItem* Class

In this exercise, you will use a class module to create an OrderItem class. You will instantiate the class as needed as the user makes order selections. In this case, imagine that you have a limited list of tools from which the user can select (see Figure 20.6). The exercise consists of a single form module, named frmOrder, and a single class module, named OrderItem.

Figure 20.6   *This order form enables you to select the quantity of an item and display the ordered items by product number.*

continues

---

1. Start a project and create the form shown in Figure 20.6. Name the form **frmOrder** and save it to disk as **f20-4.frm**. Name the project **p20_4** and save it to disk as **p20-4.vbp**.

2. On the form is a combo box (**cboQuantity**), and two list boxes: **lstProducts** (in the middle) and **lstOrder** (on the right). Change the form caption, as shown, and add the labels identifying the controls.

3. In the Form_Load() event, add code to populate the cboQuantity and lstProduct with data:

```
Private Sub Form_Load()
   Dim i As Integer

      ' populate the combo box with quantity choices
      For i = 1 To 10
         cboQuantity.AddItem Str$(i)
      Next
      ' display the first item
      cboQuantity.ListIndex = 0

      ' populate the list box with products
      With lstProducts
         .AddItem "Saw"
         .AddItem "Hammer"
         .AddItem "Socket Set"
         .AddItem "Circular Saw"
         .AddItem "Cordless Drill - 1/4 in."
         .AddItem "Cordless Screw Driver"
      End With
End Sub
```

The design enables the user to make a quantity selection and then, by clicking the lstProducts list box, have the order line item displayed in the lstOrder list box. You need to define the OrderItem class before you can code the lstProducts_Click() event.

4. Add a class module to your project. Press F4 and change the Name property of the class module to OrderItem. Save it to disk as **cls20-4.cls**.

In this imaginary store, tools are priced by taking a markup from cost. The standard markup is 45 %. (In retailing, markup is measured from the retail price. So an item bought wholesale for $50.00 and sold at retail for $100.00 is said to have a 50 % markup. A $50.00 item sold for $90.00 has a 40% markup: $50.00 + (.8 * 50).) This calculation requires that you know the unit cost and the quantity ordered. In addition, the OrderItem class holds data on the product name, a line item number, and the item total.

5. Declare the following private data members at the General Declaration level of the OrderItem class:

```
Option Explicit

Private m_OrderNum As Integer
Private m_ProductName As String
Private m_Quantity As Double
Private m_UnitCost As Currency
Private m_ItemTotal As Currency
Private Const Markup = 0.9
```

6. Add the mutator and accessor methods (property procedures) for the class data members:

```
Public Property Get orderNum() As Integer
    orderNum = m_OrderNum
End Property

Public Property Let orderNum(ByVal nNewValue As Integer)
    m_OrderNum = nNewValue
End Property

Public Property Get ProductName() As String
    ProductName = m_ProductName
End Property

Public Property Let ProductName(ByVal sNewValue As String)
    m_ProductName = sNewValue
End Property

Public Property Get quantity() As Double
    quantity = m_Quantity
End Property

Public Property Let quantity(ByVal dNewValue As Double)
    m_Quantity = dNewValue
End Property

Public Property Get UnitCost() As Currency
    UnitCost = m_UnitCost
End Property

Public Property Let UnitCost(ByVal cNewValue As Currency)
    m_UnitCost = cNewValue
End Property
```

You have yet to add all the data validation checking that normally would be present in the Property Let methods.

7. Add a read-only property that returns the order item total:

```
Public Property Get ItemTotal() As Currency
    m_ItemTotal = (m_UnitCost + (m_UnitCost * Markup)) *
m_Quantity
    ItemTotal = m_ItemTotal
End Property
```

continues

8. On `frmOrder`, add the following code to the `lstProducts_Click()` event:

```
Private Sub lstProducts_Click()
    Dim toolorder As OrderItem
    Static ordernumber As Integer
    Dim quantity As Integer
    Dim product As String
    Dim itemtotal As Currency
    Dim strDisplay As String

    Set toolorder = New OrderItem
    product = lstProducts.Text
    ordernumber = ordernumber + 1
    quantity = Val(cboQuantity.Text)

    ' ascertain the unit cost
    Select Case product
        Case "Saw"
            toolorder.UnitCost = 7.99
        Case "Hammer"
            toolorder.UnitCost = 6.99
        Case "Socket Set"
            toolorder.UnitCost = 14.99
        Case "Circular Saw"
            toolorder.UnitCost = 29.49
        Case "Cordless Drill -1/4 in."
            toolorder.UnitCost = 24.95
        Case "Cordless Screw Driver"
            toolorder.UnitCost = 11.95
    End Select

    With toolorder
        .orderNum = 1000 + ordernumber
        .ProductName = product
        .quantity = quantity
    End With
    'display the order

    strDisplay = toolorder.orderNum & "   "
    strDisplay = strDisplay & toolorder.quantity & "   "
    strDisplay = strDisplay & toolorder.ProductName & "   "
    strDisplay = strDisplay & Format(toolorder.ItemTotal,
    ➥"Currency")

    lstOrder.AddItem strDisplay
End Sub
```

9. Run and test the program.

The `lstProducts_Click()` event merits further explanation. Every time the user clicks the `lstProduct` list box, a new instance of the `OrderItem` class is created by the instruction `Set toolorder as New OrderItem`. Unlike a form, which is instantiated when a form instance is created with the `Load` statement, classes defined in class modules need to be instantiated with object variables. The object variable `toolorder` is now ready to have values assigned to its properties.

Values are read from the combo box for quantity of the order line item and from the list box for the product name. The unit cost is determined by the product name and assigned. The orderNum property is determined by arbitrarily incrementing a Static variable. Finally, when all the properties are set, the order line item can be displayed in the lstOrder list box with the ItemTotal property read from the OrderItem class.

Should the calculation of the line item total be encapsulated in the read-only ItemTotal property or should it, instead, have been placed in a class method, perhaps a CalculateLineItem method? Making these kinds of determinations is sometimes a close call—or even a matter of taste.

20.2.3   The *Initialize()* Event

In Exercise 20.4, you could count on the fact that the application using the OrderItem class assigned values to the Product Name, Quantity, and Unit Cost properties before the ItemTotal property was read. This, however, is a dangerous assumption, particularly if the class is to be used in multiple applications. It is the responsibility of the class module to ensure that interdependent properties are managed so as to avoid errors, not the responsibility of other applications or applications that instantiate objects from the class.

Suppose that you tracked average order item sizes. This calculation would require a division operation, and you would have to ensure that the class did not attempt to divide by zero. A class member with a Date data type that had to be within a certain range would need data validation code added to the mutator (Property Let) method. A ShipDate property, for example, might not be allowed to have a date prior to the OrderDate property.

You can minimize these kinds of errors by assigning default values to class properties every time the class is instantiated. This will not prevent all errors, but will ensure that default values are assigned and that the user is presented with non-null values when accessing an object property.

As discussed earlier, Visual Basic class modules have two built-in events: the Initialize() event and the Terminate() event. The Initialize() event fires every time a class instance (object) is created. In this event, all data members of the class should be initialized and assigned default values. You can complete the code for Exercise 20.4 by adding the following code to the OrderItem class module:

```
Private Sub Class_Initialize()
    m_ProductName = "Product"
    m_UnitCost = 0
    m_Quantity = 0
    m_OrderNum = 1001
End Sub
```

Remember that you can find the Initialize() event by selecting the implicit Class object under the General Declarations item in the left-hand combo box in the class module code window.

20.2.4   The *Terminate()* Event

Terminate() events are used to execute cleanup code. Such cleanup code usually involves memory-management tasks, such as setting object variable references to Nothing or reclaiming memory allocated to large arrays. (Arrays were addressed in Chapter 14, "Lists and Arrays.")

The Terminate() event fires when the last reference to the class instance is removed from memory by falling out of scope or by having all of the variables that refer to that object set to Nothing. It is possible to have multiple object variables refer to the same class instance. It is only when all of these variable references are removed from memory that the Terminate() event fires.

Exercise 20.5   Demonstrating the *Terminate()* Event

In this short exercise, you learn how multiple object variables can refer to the same object and the effect this has on the Terminate() event. Figure 20.7 shows the form you are asked to create.

Figure 20.7   *This design displays a dialog box to verify that the* Terminate() *event has executed properly.*

1. Save cls20-4.cls as **cls20-5.cls** on disk.

2. Create a new project and save it as **p20-5.vbp**. Name the project **p20_5**.

3. Add cls20-5.cls to the project.

4. Name the form **frmTestTerminate**, and save it to disk as **f20-5.frm**. Name the buttons **cmdRemove1** and **cmdRemove2**. Change the captions of the buttons and the form as illustrated.

5. Add the following code in the Terminate() event of the OrderItem class:

```
Private Sub Class_Terminate()
  MsgBox "I am gone!", 0, "Terminate Event fired"
End Sub
```

6. Make the following object variable declarations at the module level of `frmTerminate`:

```
Dim Reference1 As OrderItem
Dim Reference2 As OrderItem
```

7. In the `Form_Load()` event, bind the `Reference1` variable to a new class instance and then set the `Reference2` variable to the same object:

```
Private Sub Form_Load()
   Set Reference1 = New OrderItem
   Set Reference2 = Reference1
End Sub
```

8. Finally, add code to set these object variables to `Nothing` in the button click procedures:

```
Private Sub cmdRemove1_Click()
   Set Reference1 = Nothing
End Sub

Private Sub cmdRemove2_Click()
   Set Reference2 = Nothing
End Sub
```

9. Run and test the program. First click Remove `Reference1` and then click Remove `Reference2`. The `Terminate()` event does not fire until the last reference to the object is removed from memory.

20.2.5   Examining the *OrderItem* Class with the Class Browser

In Chapter 1, "Running a Visual Basic Program," you were briefly introduced to the Object Browser. Just as you can use the Object Browser to observe classes in the Visual Basic libraries, the Object Browser permits you to examine classes that you have defined for individual projects.

You have a choice in how broadly you want to expose classes defined in class libraries. If they are confined to an individual project, the code is compiled into the .EXE, and the class is not exposed for others to use. If, however, you compile classes defined in class modules into an ActiveX .DLL or ActiveX .EXE, the class can be used by other applications. These choices are examined in Chapter 22, "Creating an ActiveX DLL."

To observe the members of your project's classes, you need only press the F2 key. This launches Object Browser. Alternatively, you can choose View, Object Browser from the Visual Basic menu bar. For the `OrderItem` class defined in Project p20_5, Object Browser should look like that illustrated in Figure 20.8.

Figure 20.8   *The Object Browser displays the members and events of a class.*

By selecting any one of the class members in the list box on the right side of the Object Browser, information about that class member is revealed at the bottom of the Object Browser. The data types for data members are displayed. Arguments for class methods can be displayed, as can the exposure of class properties. For example, select the ItemTotal property for the OrderItem class. The Object Browser indicates it is read-only. Select the Markup constant. The Object Browser displays its numeric value. Double-click the Markup constant to view the code.

As the classes you create become larger and as you begin to share class modules among projects, you will become quite familiar with the Object Browser. It is a handy way to remind yourself of the private data members, as well as the public interface the object provides for use by other modules.

Objective 20.3   Adding Objects to a Collection

As illustrated by the OrderItem class, an individual object is created every time the user places an order for an individual item at a certain quantity. It would be convenient if you could group these objects together. Fortunately, Visual Basic provides you with a generic Collection object for just this purpose. Although the objects need not be of the same class, you will find it convenient to place members of the same class into a Collection.

You will recall that you worked with the built-in forms and controls collection in Chapter 19, "Object Types, Variables, and Collections." You iterated through the collection by using For Each...Next syntax. Now that you can create you own objects, you look at the Collection object with a little more specificity.

As an object, the `Collection` must first be declared and bound with an object variable. The following instructions declare the `Tools` object variable as a `Collection` and bind it to a new class instance:

```
Dim Tools as Collection
Set Tools = New Collection
```

After a collection has been created, objects can be added to it. An important difference between the `Collection` object and the `Forms` and `Controls` collections is that instances of the `Collection` object follow a one-based index. That means the index value of the first member of the collection is `1`, not `0`, as with the `Forms` and `Controls` collection. Iteration through the collection can be accomplished in the following two ways:

■ Using a standard `For...Next` loop you could write the following instructions:

```
Dim i as integer
For i = 1 to Tools.Count
   ' execute code here
Next
```

■ If the members of the `Collection` were all of the `OrderItem` class, you could write the instructions as follows:

```
Dim counter as OrderItem
For Each counter in Tools
   ' execute code here
Next
```

As an object, the `Collection` object has its own properties and methods. Fortunately, these are very few, but very useful. The `Collection` object has a single property: `Count`. This is a read-only property that returns the number of objects in a collection. The `Collection` object has three methods, as explained in Table 20.1.

TABLE 20.1 *Collection* Object Methods

Method	*Description*
`Add`	Adds an object to a collection
`Remove`	Removes an item from a collection
`Item`	Returns an item from a collection by its index or by its key

The following sections discuss these methods.

20.3.1   The *Add* Method of the *Collection* Object

You add objects to a collection with the `Add` method. When objects are added, they can also be given a numeric index or a unique string expression to identify them. This allows them to be more easily retrieved with the `Item` method. The key, however, is optional. The complete syntax for the method is as follows:

```
object.Add item, key, before, after
```

Table 20.2 explains the components of the Add method syntax.

TABLE 20.2   Syntax of the *Add* Method

Component	Description
object	Required. A Collection object that has been instantiated.
item	Required. An expression of any type that specifies the member to add to the collection.
key	Optional. A unique string expression that specifies a key string that can be used, instead of a position index, to access a member of the collection.
before	Optional. An expression that specifies a relative position in the collection. The member to be added is placed in the collection before the member identified by the before argument.
	For a numeric expression, before must be a number from 1 to the value of the collection's Count property.
	For a string expression, before must correspond to the key specified when the member being referred to was added to the collection. You can specify a before position or an after position, but not both.
after	Optional. An expression that specifies a relative position in the collection. The member to be added is placed in the collection after the member identified by the after argument.
	If numeric, after must be a number from 1 to the value of the collection's Count property.
	If a string, after must correspond to the key specified when the member referred to was added to the collection. You can specify a before position or an after position, but not both.

Keys, whether numeric or a string key, cannot be duplicated. Suppose that you had an object variable, toolorder, that represented an instance of the OrderItem class. The following instruction would add the object to the collection:

```
Tools.Add toolorder
```

The following instruction would add the item with the ProductName as the unique string identifier:

```
Tools.Add toolorder, toolorder.ProductName
```

20.3.2   The *Remove* Method of the *Collection* Object

The Remove method removes items from the collection. You identify the numeric or string index expression when the item was first added to the collection. The syntax is straight-forward:

```
object.Remove index
```

Table 20.3 explains the components of the Remove method syntax.

TABLE 20.3   Syntax of the *Remove* Method

Component	Description
object	Required. A Collection object
index	Required. An expression that specifies the position of a member of the collection
	If a numeric expression, index must be a number from 1 to the value of the collection's Count property
	If a string expression, index must correspond to the key argument specified when the member referred to was added to the collection

20.3.3   The *Item* Method of the *Collection* Object

The Item method returns an item from a collection by the index or key used when the object was added to the Collection. The syntax for the method is as follows:

```
object.Item(index)
```

Table 20.4 explains the components of the Item method syntax.

TABLE 20.4   Syntax of the *Item* Method

Component	Description
object	A Collection object
index	Required. An expression that specifies the position of a member of the collection
	If a numeric expression, index must be a number from 1 to the value of the collection's Count property
	If a string expression, index must correspond to the key argument specified when the member referred to was added to the collection

Exercise 20.6   Using a *Collection* Object

In this somewhat lengthy exercise, you substitute individual labels in control arrays for the lstOrder list box used in Exercise 20.4. This allows order items to be aligned (see Figure 20.9). You also add a Collection object to your program that you use to calculate an ongoing order total.

1. Open Exercise 20.4 and save f20-4.frm to disk as **f20-6.frm**, save cls20-4.cls as **cls20-6.cls**, and save p20-4.vbp as **p20-6.vbp**. Change the Name property of the project to **p20_6**.

2. Important! Comment out the Terminate() event code for the OrderItem class.

Figure 20.9   *This application expands the previous exercise by creating and displaying label control arrays.*

3. Add a MSFlexGrid control to the project by selecting it under the Components dialog box (Project|Components).

4. Alter frmOrder so that it appears as displayed in Figure 20.9. It will need to be made wider to accommodate the MSFlexGrid control that will substitute for lstOrder. Remove lstOrder from the form, and add the MSFlexGrid, naming it grdOrder and setting its Width property to 4500 twips.

5. In the bottom right corner of the form, add a label named **lblTotal**, and remove any text from the Caption property.

6. At the module level of frmOrder, make the following declaration:

```
Dim purchase As Collection
```

7. In the `Form_Load()` event, add code that instantiates the purchase `Collection` object, initializes the quantity combo box and product list box with data, and calls a procedure to set initial grid properties:

```
Private Sub Form_Load()
    Dim i As Integer

    ' populate the combo box with quantity
    For i = 1 To 10
        cboQuantity.AddItem Str$(i)
    Next
    ' display the first item
    cboQuantity.ListIndex = 0

    ' populate the list box with products
    With lstProducts
        .AddItem "Saw"
        .AddItem "Hammer"
        .AddItem "Socket Set"
        .AddItem "Circular Saw"
        .AddItem "Cordless Drill - 1/4 in"
        .AddItem "Cordless Screw Driver"
    End With

    Call PrepGrid(grdOrder)

    Set purchase = New Collection
End Sub
```

8. Add the following `PrepGrid` procedure:

```
Private Sub PrepGrid(grid As MSFlexGrid)

    With grid
        .FixedRows = 1
        .FixedCols = 1
        .ScrollBars = flexScrollBarBoth
        .Rows = 2
        .Cols = 5
        .AllowUserResizing = flexResizeColumns

        ' set headers
        .Row = 0
        .Col = 0
        .Text = ""
        .Row = 0
        .Col = 1
        .Text = "Order#"
        .CellFontBold = True
        .Row = 0
        .Col = 2
        .Text = "Qty."
        .CellFontBold = True
```

continues

Exercise 20.6   continued

```
                    .Row = 0
                    .Col = 3
                    .Text = "Product"
                    .CellFontBold = True
                    .Row = 0
                    .Col = 4
                    .Text = "Item Price"
                    .CellFontBold = True


                    ' set column widths
                    .ColWidth(0) = 350
                    .ColWidth(1) = 550
                    .ColWidth(2) = 550
                    .ColWidth(3) = 2000
                    .ColWidth(4) = 1000
             End With
      End Sub
```

9. Change the lstProducts_Click() event so that it will create a new
   OrderItem object, assign it data, display the data in the grid control, add
   the object to the purchase collection, and iterate through the collection to
   ascertain the order total.

```
      Private Sub lstProducts_Click()

          Dim toolorder As OrderItem
          Dim Counter As OrderItem
          Dim product As String
          Static ordernumber As Integer
          Dim quantity As Integer, i As Integer
          Dim total As Currency
          Dim strDisplay As String
          Dim rownum As Long

          Set toolorder = New OrderItem


          product = lstProducts.Text
          ordernumber = ordernumber + 1
          quantity = Val(cboQuantity.Text)

          Select Case product
            Case "Saw"
              toolorder.UnitCost = 7.99
            Case "Hammer"
              toolorder.UnitCost = 6.99
            Case "Socket Set"
              toolorder.UnitCost = 14.99
            Case "Circular Saw"
              toolorder.UnitCost = 29.49
            Case "Cordless Drill - 1/4 in"
              toolorder.UnitCost = 24.95
            Case "Cordless Screw Driver"
              toolorder.UnitCost = 11.95
          End Select

          With toolorder
            .orderNum = 1000 + ordernumber
```

```
            .ProductName = product
            .quantity = quantity
        End With

        strDisplay = ""

        strDisplay = Str$(grdOrder.Rows - 1) & vbTab &
        ➥Str$(toolorder.orderNum) & _
        vbTab & Str$(toolorder.quantity) & vbTab & _
        toolorder.ProductName & vbTab & _
        Format$(toolorder.ItemTotal, "Currency")
        rownum = grdOrder.Rows - 1
        grdOrder.AddItem strDisplay, rownum

        purchase.Add toolorder          ' add item to collection

        total = 0                       ' initialize variable

        For Each Counter In purchase    ' calculate total
            total = total + Counter.ItemTotal
        Next
        ' display total
        lblTotal.Caption = "Total: " & Format$(total, "Currency")

    End Sub
```

10. Run and test the program.

A lot is going on in this procedure. Most of the code adds property values to new instances of the OrderItem class and builds the string for adding to the grdOrder MSFlexGrid control. The heart of the new code is near the end of the procedure. The toolorder object is added to the purchase collection and then the collection is iterated through to calculate a running order total.

No changes were made to the OrderItem class itself other than commenting out the Terminate() event code. You are beginning to see code reused!

Notice that you did not use an index or key when adding the OrderItem objects to the purchase collection. Because this code only adds and totals ordered items, you did not need to retrieve individual Collection members with the Item method, so you did not use the index or key arguments.

Suppose that you want to extend the functionality of the program in Exercise 20.6 so that users could remove ordered items before finally committing to a final purchase, or at least change the quantity of an individual order item. It also might be nice to have sales tax automatically calculated. In addition, you might need to have differential pricing: one price for retail customers and another for wholesale customers. Which of these functions should be handled by the OrderItem class and which should be handled by a hypothetical Order class?

As you work with classes and extend their functionality, issues about which class should handle which function quickly become central concerns of the developer. In fact, you should not begin to create a class until you have a very good idea about the function of the class and its relationship to other classes.

The Collection object provides a lot of the functionality central to an Order class, but not all of it. How, for example, should the individual order numbers for each line item be renumbered if an item is deleted? This would presumably be a function of an Order class, but it could not be handled by a Collection object alone. In fact, wrapping a Collection object inside a class makes a lot of sense.

Objective 20.4   Employing Good Programming Practices when Creating Class Modules

You now have been exposed to the object-oriented nature of Visual Basic. If your head is swimming, don't worry. The longer you work with class modules, the more natural "object-oriented thinking" becomes. Although there is much still to learn about class modules, you have been exposed to the heart of it. The following are some critical issues to remember:

- Data members of class modules should (almost) always be private to the module rather than declared publicly. Even if you think it isn't possible that an errant value could be assigned to the variable, as the class definition evolves, you will see a need to put a data-validation procedure in place. Yes, all those Property Let and Property Get procedures can become tedious, but it is worth it in the long run.

- Use a naming convention for class data members and their associated Property procedures that is easy to work with. Using an m_ prefix for class data members is one standard practice. The associated Property Let and Property Get procedures have the prefix removed.

- All data members should be initialized with default values.

- When designing a class, remember that you are aiming for robust and reusable code.

- Properties often are described as an attribute of an object and methods as actions that work on an object. It often is difficult to distinguish between what is properly a property and what is a method. The distinction is less important than making sure the code is reliable; and, when made part of the class interface, readily understandable to other users of the class.

- Collections created from the Collection class are one-based, not zero-based.

- As your classes begin to take on significant size, don't forget the Object Browser. It's a handy tool!

Chapter Summary

This chapter introduced you to class modules. Like form and standard code modules, class modules can be added to the project, named, and saved to disk as a file. Class modules are designed to promote object-oriented design in Visual Basic programs.

Class modules promote the encapsulation of data by allowing privately scoped module-level variables to be accessed through `Property Let` and `Property Get` procedures. Other names for these procedures are mutator (`Property Let`) methods and accessor (`Property Get`) methods. Methods for class modules can be created by creating publicly scoped procedures in the class module.

Objects are instantiated from class modules by the use of object variables. Object variables can be declared with the `New` keyword, as in `Dim toolorder as New OrderItem`. The object will be instantiated when the first reference is made to the new variable in code, as in `toolorder.ProductName = Saw`. Alternatively, the object variable can be simply declared and then instantiated with the `Set` statement and the `New` keyword, as in the following example:

```
Dim toolorder as OrderItem
Set toolorder = New OrderItem
```

Class modules have two built-in events: `Initialize()` and `Terminate()`. The `Initialize()` event can be used to assign default values to class data members. The `Terminate()` event is used to execute cleanup code. The `Terminate()` event fires when the last variable reference to the object is removed from memory by the `Nothing` statement or by falling out of scope.

Objects can be placed into collections by the use of the `Collection` object. The lowest index number of a collection created from the `Collection` object is 1. `Collection` objects have three main methods: `Add`, `Remove`, and `Item`. Either a numeric index or a string key can be used when adding an object to the collection. The index is used to retrieve the object with the `Item` method or delete the object with the `Remove` method.

Visual Basic's object-oriented emphasis places special demand on designing classes well. Key concepts to remember when designing classes are as follows:

- Keep data members private.

- Use an easily workable naming convention.

- Initialize all data members.

Skill-Building Exercises

These exercises ask you to modify a class by adding or modifying properties. In addition, you are asked to create a new class called Vehicle for Exercises 20.3 and 20.4. Finally, you are asked to modify Exercise 20.6 to provide both a new interface and added functionality.

1. Extend Exercise 20.4 by adding a `TimeStamp` property to the `OrderItem` class. Display the property in the `lstOrder` list box when it is selected. Be sure that all data members of the class are properly initialized.

2. Using the program you created in the preceding exercise, add a `WholeSale` property to the `OrderItem` class. Set this as a Boolean value. Change the `Property Get ItemTotal` procedure to accommodate this new property. Wholesale prices have a 25% markup. Change the interface for `frmOrder` to accommodate the changes you have made. (*Hint:* Use a check box.)

3. Create a small class of your own called **Vehicle**, which holds information on the make and model of the vehicle, the year it was manufactured, and its useful life. For cars manufactured before 1991, the useful life is seven years; for vehicles manufactured after 1991, the useful life is eight years. (*Hint:* Use the `Year` function to determine the current year.) Make sure the class uses `CarYear` for the year of manufacture, not `Year` to avoid name conflicts.

4. Create an interface to use the class that you created in the preceding skill-building exercise. On the left side of a form, place a combo box to let the user select a year between 1980 and the current model year. Include a list box or combo box so the user can select one of four manufacturers: **Ford**, **General Motors**, **Chrysler**, or **Honda**. Supply a text box so that the user can input model type. Finally, add a command button captioned **OK,** which will instantiate the class object and assign it property values and display those values in another list box.

5. Extend the preceding skill-building exercise by adding a class method (function) called `DisplayUsefulLife`. This method returns the useful life that the vehicle still has left from the current year, or how many years past its useful life the vehicle has enjoyed. Display this information in the second list box. As users enter data on the form and click the command button, add these objects to a collection. In a separate label, display the average year of the vehicles in the collection as automobiles are added.

6. Change the interface of Exercise 20.6 so that the grid displays a column for indicating whether an item in the grid is taxable. When the user clicks on a cell under the taxable column, place a red "X" in the cell that is center aligned (see the `CellAlignment` property). Toggle off the X if it already exists in the cell.

7. *Challenge:* Extend the previous skill-building exercise so that when the user clicks on the grid to indicate an item is taxable, the total tax amount for the order is incremented or decremented. The tax rate is 15%. Display the subtotal for items ordered, the total tax amount for the order, and the total amount (subtotal + tax amount). (*Hints:* Change the `OrderItem` class so it has a `Taxable` property and a read-only `AmountTax` property. Use the string representation of the row number for the key argument when adding `toolorder` items to the purchase Collection.) Items then can be retrieved from the Collection with the `Item` method to change the `Taxable` property.

APPLICATIONS

CHAPTER

21

MODULAR DESIGN

When developing Visual Basic applications, modular design is encouraged through the use of a hierarchy of forms and careful segmentation of application functionality into code and class modules. Applications often are constructed in layers. The different Visual Basic module types are then used to build these layered Visual Basic applications.

This chapter includes exercises that review the use of multiple forms in a larger application. It also clarifies the passing of values between procedures and between procedures and functions. Specifically addressed are the differences between call by reference (by address) and call by value. A "traditional" approach to a sample application is compared and examined with a new, more object-oriented approach.

You learn many tasks in this chapter. After you work through the exercises, you will be able to perform the following:

- Create a login window
- Add password control to a design
- Design a visual chart of a Visual Basic application
- Show, hide, load, and unload forms
- Use call by reference
- Pass an array to a procedure
- Use call by value
- Work with arrays of user-defined types
- Work with an object collection
- Use the MSFlexGrid control to display the results of processing
- Segment an application using standard code modules
- Segment an application using class modules

493

Chapter Objectives

This chapter condenses the preceding lengthy list of tasks into four objectives that address the use of modules and layers in program design:

1. Understanding the significance of modular design

2. Understanding the difference between call by reference and call by value

3. Using code modules in the processing/business-rule and data layers

4. Using class modules in the processing/business-rule and data layers

Objective 21.1 Understanding the Significance of Modular Design

Modular design is the breaking down of a computer program into recognizable, functional components, as opposed to creating one long application. The complexity of building applications for graphic-oriented operating systems, such as Windows, places a premium on employing reusable software modules. Ideally, these components can be used to rapidly deploy software that is reliable and readily understandable to those who must maintain it. Needless to say, software development often falls short of this ideal. Adhering to modular design principles, however, makes the chances of meeting this ideal much greater. The benefits of modular design include making it easier to perform the following tasks:

- Define the solution to the design problem

- Communicate to others the internal construction (or organization) of the design

- Specify the functionality of a coded procedure by designing each procedure (or function) to accomplish a specific task

- Assign programming tasks to a group of people

- Write computer instructions (leading to more rapid development of computer applications)

- Isolate problems better during program design and testing

- Maintain computer programs when errors occur

Perhaps the most important benefit is the third: specifying the functionality of a coded procedure. When designing a Visual Basic program, use a form to convey a specific function, write procedures or functions to perform one and only one task, and use standard and class modules to clarify the importance of application specifics and where they are defined. With a modular design, it is possible to clearly specify the functions and organization of an application.

21.1.1   The Layers of an Application

One frequently used approach to software development is to think about an application as being composed of several layers, such as the following:

- **User-interface layer**—The user interface layer refers to the forms and visual components by which the user navigates through the program and executes the program's functions. This layer ideally is easily learned, logical, and obvious in the execution of the program's core functionality. It retrieves user input and displays the results of processing.

- **Processing- or business-rule layer**—This layer comprises the modules that retrieve and write persistent data on a disk, maintain program security, and perform calculations on data. It is called the business-rule layer, because it is here that the policies of the enterprise are often implemented in code. One rule might specify the difference between the markups for wholesale and retail customers. Another rule might state that prompt payment of invoices entitles the customer to a discount. These rules often are encapsulated in this middle layer.

- **Data layer**—Consisting of the application's persistent (stored) data, the data layer often is represented by a relational database. (Databases are covered in Chapter 23, "Accessing and Manipulating Databases with Visual Basic," and Chapter 24, "Using Data Access Objects.")

There is no hard and fast rule for employing these layers. It is better to think of them as a logical architecture, not a preordained model that must be followed. Business rules, for example, are frequently handled at the data layer as stored procedures in the database. Speed requirements might necessitate bypassing a business-rule module to access data directly.

This chapter is organized around the concept of layers to help you become familiar with this idea. Although a layered approach often is explicitly used in developing client/server applications, this design approach is not limited to client/server database programs. Multimedia, game, and even standalone applications can employ similar modular design.

21.1.2   Using Form Modules to Build the Interface Layer

Because a Visual Basic application can be designed using numerous forms, the organization of the forms collection needs to be understood by others. A forms-based structure chart provides such a picture. As shown in Figure 21.1, one way of depicting the interface layer of a design is by tracing the design hierarchy. In the example, only two symbols are used: one to depict forms and one to depict code segments. As illustrated, this application begins with a Welcome window (which is a login window) and proceeds to the Main Menu window. From the Main Menu window, it is possible to search by name, category, or keyword, and to obtain help. Selecting any of these four choices leads to another form. (The link to Help is indicated by the encircled 1s in the diagram.)

Figure 21.1   *A forms-based structure chart shows how the various forms of a design are related.*

21.1.3   A Login Window and a Main Window

Most multiple-form designs feature a login window and a main window. The login window is added to provide security of access to a design. Unless the user knows the correct login name and password, access to a design is denied. The main window serves as the "home base" in a design. This window illustrates the various ways to navigate through a design. With many designs, a return-to-main-window option is provided to always allow the user to return to this "home base."

Exercise 21.1   Creating a Login Window

Create a login window to screen users from access to an application. The login name is assigned within the code; however, a search of a file of login names is more typical in practice. Figure 21.2 and Figure 21.3 show the login window and the Main Menu window, respectively.

Figure 21.2   *The login window requires the user to enter a user name and coded password.*

Figure 21.3   *A correct password opens the Main Menu window.*

1. Create the forms **frmLogin** and **frmMain** (see Figures 21.2 and 21.3).
2. Write the following code for the OK command button.

```
Private Sub cmdOK_Click()
    Dim message1 As String
    Dim message2 As String
    Dim message3 As String
    Dim options As Integer

    'Password is Open
    message1$ = "Please enter your password"
    message2$ = "Login name not found, please try again"
    message3$ = "Login error"

    If txtPassWord.Text = "" Then
      Beep
      MsgBox message1, 1, message3
       txtPassWord.SetFocus
    ElseIf (txtPassWord.Text = "Open") Or (txtPassWord.Text =
➥"open") Then
        frmLogin.Hide
        frmMain.Show
    Else
```

continues

497

```
        MsgBox message2, 1, message3
      End If
   End Sub
```

In this procedure, an error allows the user to try again; however, the user must enter the password—the word Open or open—to gain access to frmMain. After an error, focus is given to the text box where the error occurred.

3. Write a Form_Load() procedure to display empty text in the text boxes when frmLogin appears. This code is as follows:

```
Private Sub Form_Load()
   txtLogin.Text = ""
   txtPassWord.Text = ""
End Sub
```

4. Write the following cmdReturn_Click() procedure for frmMain.

```
Private Sub cmdReturn_Click()
   frmMain.Hide
   frmLogin.Show
End Sub
```

Once again, the visible form is hidden before the new form appears. Making the password invisible requires a change to a single property: PasswordChar.

5. Go to the password text box. Change the PasswordChar property on frmLogin to an asterisk (*).

6. Test your modified design. Use a different PasswordChar.

21.1.4   Building a User Interface Prototype

Visual Basic graphical design tools, properly used, can dramatically improve the communication between the end user and the developer. An application's visual interface may be rapidly built to receive end user response and input. This process leads to clarification of application requirements, often affecting the design of the business rule and data layers of an application. If used in an iterative fashion until the application specification is complete, Visual Basic's tools help the end user and developer share a combined vision of the deliverable application.

Prototyping the user interface layer in this manner requires that the user be able to navigate through an application's multiple forms. You already have used most of the available methods and statements to control forms and their displays. As a review, Table 21.1 lists these methods and statements and their meanings.

Table 21.1   Methods and Statements for Controlling Forms

Method/Statement	Description
Hide method	Hides a form but does not unload it.
Show method	Shows a hidden form. If the form is not loaded, the Show method loads the form into memory and displays it.
Load statement	Loads a form (or control) into memory.
Unload statement	Unloads a form (or control) from memory.

Recall that the Load statement adds a form to memory, while Unload removes a form from memory. To ensure that a form is totally removed from memory, you can set the form instance to nothing as in Set Form1 = Nothing.

If a form is used more than once during runtime, it is wise to hide, but not unload, the form following its use. This improves program performance. If a form is used infrequently, it is best to unload it from memory because this saves memory.

Exercise 21.2   Prototyping an Application User Interface

In this somewhat lengthy exercise, you build a user interface prototype of a university course registration system. The hypothetical university is Einstein University. As lengthy as this exercise may be, it necessarily leaves out many portions of what would be required in a real world registration system.

This exercise asks you to work with five forms. Included is frmMain. the form that serves as the "homebase" of the application. In addition, there are three forms for user input: frmNewStudent, frmNewCourse, and frmRegistration. Finally, there is a form for displaying reports, frmReports.

In this exercise, you construct an application's user interface. You add enough code to permit an end user to navigate through the application, observe the core functionality to be included in the program, and get the application's "look and feel."

Figure 21.4 shows the navigational relationship among the various forms. You will use this exercise again in Chapter 23, "Accessing and Manipulating Databases with Visual Basic," and add the data and business logic layers to the application.

continues

Exercise 21.2   continued

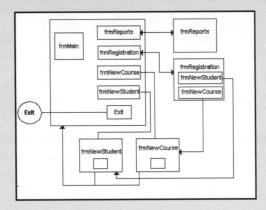

Figure 21.4   *From* frmMain, *you can move to any form, and all forms navigate back to* frmMain. *You also can move to* frmNewStudent *and* frmNewCourse *from* frmRegistration.

1. Open project P21-2.vbp on the companion disc. Observe that frmMain has been set as the Project start-up object. The interface for frmMain is shown in Figure 21.5A. The form is characterized by two Frame controls containing option buttons and command buttons. The functionality of these frames is replicated by menu choices. The frame on the left with the caption "Add New" indicates where the user can navigate in the application to enter new data in the system. The frame on the right with the caption "Reports," lists the reports the user may see. Examine the form and become familiar with the names of the various controls on the form.

Figure 21.5A   *This form serves as the application's main "homebase."*

2. Add the following event procedures for frmMain:

```
' declared at the module level
Dim wid As Single
Dim hgt As Single

Private Sub cmdOK_Click()
  If optStudent.Value = True Then
      frmNewStudent.Show vbModal
  ElseIf optCourse.Value = True Then
     frmNewCourse.Show vbModal
  ElseIf optRegister = True Then
     frmRegistration.Show
  End If


End Sub

Private Sub cmdOKReport_Click()
  Dim i As Integer

  If frmReports Is Nothing Then Load frmReports
  For i = optReport.lbound To optReport.UBound
     If optReport(i).Value = True Then
        frmReports.ReportName = optReport(i).Caption
        Exit For
     End If
  Next
  frmReports.Show
End Sub

Private Sub Form_Load()
  wid = Screen.TwipsPerPixelX
  hgt = Screen.TwipsPerPixelY
  Me.Width = 600 * wid
  Me.Height = 250 * hgt
End Sub

Private Sub Form_Unload(Cancel As Integer)
  Dim i As Long
  For i = Forms.Count - 1 To 0 Step -1
    Unload Forms(i)
  Next
End Sub

Private Sub mnuALL_R_Click()
  optReport(3).Value = True
  Call cmdOKReport_Click
End Sub

Private Sub mnuCourseS_Click()
  optReport(0).Value = True
  Call cmdOKReport_Click
End Sub

Private Sub mnuCourseSizes_Click()
  optReport(2).Value = True
  Call cmdOKReport_Click
End Sub
```

continues

501

Exercise 21.2   continued

```
          Private Sub mnuExit_Click()
            End
          End Sub

          Private Sub mnuMakeReg_Click()
             frmRegistration.Show
          End Sub

          Private Sub mnuNewCourse_Click()
             frmNewCourse.Show vbModal
          End Sub

          Private Sub mnuNewStudent_Click()
             frmNewStudent.Show vbModal
          End Sub

          Private Sub mnuSR_Click()
            optReport(1).Value = True
            Call cmdOKReport_Click
          End Sub
```

The core application navigation code is in the `cmdOK_Click` and `cmdOKReport_Click` events. The option buttons on the left are named individually and an `If…Then` statement is used to identify which option button the user has selected. The option buttons on the right are placed in a control array and a loop is used to identify which option is selected. The caption of the selected option then is assigned to a Property held by `frmReports`.

The `frmNewStudent` and `frmNewCourse` are shown modally while `frmRegistration` and `frmReports` are shown in the default non-modal manner. The capability of the user to return to `frmMain` from `frmRegistration` and `frmReports` without unloading either form necessitates the code seen in the `frmMain_Unload` event. By looping through the implicit Forms collection, the developer can ensure that all other application forms are unloaded should the user close `frmMain`.

3. The form, `frmAddStudent`, as shown in Figure 21.5B, presents text boxes for data the user must input and combo boxes for user data selection. Major areas of study and expected years of graduation are data likely to be placed in permanent storage and thus available for user selection.

Figure 21.5B   *This data entry forms allows new student data to be entered for permanent storage.*

4. Add the code for frmNewStudent:

```
Private Sub cmdCancel_Click()
    Unload Me
End Sub

Private Sub cmdOK_Click()
    Unload Me
End Sub
```

Because you are only prototyping navigation through the application, the form is unloaded with either button click.

5. The form frmNewCourse is similar to frmNewStudent (see Figure 21.5C).

Figure 21.5C   *This data entry form allows new course data to be entered for permanent storage.*

6. The prototype navigation code for frmNewCourse is identical to that of frmNewStudent, as in the following:

```
Private Sub cmdCancel_Click()
    Unload Me
End Sub

Private Sub cmdOK_Click()
    Unload Me
End Sub
```

7. The form frmRegistration uses the data in permanent storage so that the user need only make selections. It also enables the user to navigate to the two other data entry forms, frmNewStudent and frmNewCourse, via the submenus under the top menu captioned Add New (see Figure 21.5D).

continues

Figure 21.5D *This data entry form allows course registrations to be made from user selections from combo boxes.*

8. Add the prototype navigation code for `frmRegistration`, as in the following:

```
Private Sub cmdCancel_Click()
   Unload Me
End Sub

Private Sub cmdOK_Click()
   Unload Me
End Sub

Private Sub mnuMainForm_Click()
   Unload Me
   frmMain.Show
   frmMain.WindowState = vbNormal
   frmMain.SetFocus
End Sub

Private Sub mnuNewCourse_Click()
   frmNewCourse.Show vbModal
End Sub

Private Sub mnuNewStudent_Click()
    frmNewStudent.Show vbModal
End Sub
```

9. The report form `frmReports` contains an `MSFlexGridControl`, where all reports in the application will be displayed. The form has a property added to it named `ReportName` with `accessor` and `mutator` Property procedures. This passes the report to be displayed to `frmReports`. In this prototype, it is expected that some reports will require some user selection before being created. In anticipation of this need, an identifying label and combo box are added above the grid control. A line control separates the two form areas (see Figure 21.5E).

Figure 21.5E   *This report form uses a* MSFlexGrid *control to present a wide variety of reports to the user.*

10. Add navigation and grid formatting code for frmReports, as in the following:

```
' at module level
Option Explicit
Private m_ReportName As String

Private Sub Form_Load()
    Me.Width = Screen.TwipsPerPixelX * 600
    Me.Height = Screen.TwipsPerPixelY * 400
    With grdReport
       .FixedRows = 1
       .FixedCols = 0
       .Rows = 2
       .Left = 200
       .Top = Line1.Y1 + 150
       .Width = Me.ScaleWidth - 400
        Line1.X1 = .Left
        Line1.X2 = .Width
       .ColWidth(0) = 2000

    End With
End Sub

Public Property Get ReportName() As String
    ReportName = m_ReportName
End Property

Public Property Let ReportName(ByVal sNewValue As String)
     m_ReportName = sNewValue
End Property

Private Sub Form_Paint()
    lblPrompt.Caption = m_ReportName
End Sub

Private Sub Form_Unload(Cancel As Integer)
    Set frmReports = Nothing
End Sub

Private Sub mnuMain_Click()
    Unload Me
```

continues

505

```
              frmMain.Show
              frmMain.WindowState = vbNormal
              frmMain.SetFocus
          End Sub
```

For prototyping purposes, the ReportName property is displayed in the prompt label so that the user gets some response for launching a report during user-interface prototype testing. The use of a highly adaptable control such as the MSFlexGrid control to handle all data for read-only reports takes an explicitly modular approach to application design. One form is designed to handle a multitude of requests for presentation of data from permanent storage.

11. Run and test the program.

Objective 21.2   Understanding the Difference Between Call by Reference and Call by Value

Central to modular design is the built-in capability to create procedures and functions, which are, in turn, called by a procedure or function. In this way, the modules that make up an application are able to interact and pass data among themselves. The Call statement serves to call a procedure. With either procedures or functions, arguments can be passed from the calling statement. For procedures, following is the syntax for the Call statement:

```
[Call] name [(argumentlist)]
```

The component argumentlist is optional.

The argument list is received by the called procedure and follows another syntax. The complete syntax for a procedure is as follows:

```
[Private ¦ Public] [Static] Sub name [(arglist)]
   [statements]
   [Exit Sub]
   [statements]
End Sub
```

The argument list (arglist) must be used when the call to the procedure contains arguments. This arglist must contain the same number of arguments as those found in the calling statement.

The complete syntax for a Function is only slightly more complex, with the As type clause added to the syntax:

```
[Public ¦ Private] [Static] Function name [(arglist)] [As type]
   [statements]
   [name = expression]
   [Exit Function]
   [statements]
   [name = expression]
End Function
```

As with procedures, if the call to the function contains arguments, the called function also must contain the same number of arguments in the `arglist` as those found in the calling statement. The `As type` clause specifies the type of data returned by the function. Why is this `As type` clause used? With a procedure, no values are returned following processing. With a function, one and only one value is returned. The `As type` clause indicates the type of data being returned.

When passing arguments to a procedure or a function, you can pass arguments by reference or by value.

21.2.1   Call by Reference

Call by reference, the default, means that a copy of the address of the variable (not its value) is passed to the receiving procedure or function. Argument values passed by address can be directly altered by the procedure or function.

Exercise 21.3   Passing Values by Address

This exercise asks you to pass three values to a function named `calc_max`; the purpose of the function is to find the highest number and return it to the calling procedure. Figure 21.6 shows the data-entry screen for entering the numbers, while Figure 21.7 shows the highest value entered.

Figure 21.6   *Enter three numbers, and when you are satisfied, click Yes in the section labeled* `Are numbers correct?`.

Figure 21.7   *The function examines all three numbers and returns the highest value.*

continues

1. Create the forms **frmResults** and **frmDataEntry**. The text boxes on frmDataEntry represent a control array named txtNum(0 to 3). Place the option buttons (**optYes**, **optNo**, and **optChoice**) in a frame. Write the End procedure (shown as Stop) for frmResults.

2. Write the following cmdGetNum_Click() procedure in the frmResults module:

```
Private Sub cmdGetNum_Click()
    frmResults.Hide
    frmDataEntry.Show
    frmDataEntry!optChoice.SetFocus
End Sub
```

3. Write the optYes_Click() and optNo_Click() procedures in the frmDataEntry module:

```
Private Sub optYes_Click()
    Dim num1, num2, num3 As Integer
    Dim max As Integer

    num1 = CInt(txtNum(0).text)
    num2 = CInt(txtNum(1).text)
    num3 = CInt(txtNum(2).text)

    max = calc_max(num1, num2, num3)

    frmDataEntry.Hide
    frmResults.Show
    frmResults.lblResult.Caption = "The highest value is " &
➥Str$(max)
End Sub
```

This first procedure reveals a function call with three values passed to a function named calc_max(). When the maximum value is returned, it is displayed on frmResults (not frmDataEntry).

```
Private Sub optNo_Click()
    Dim i As Integer
    For i = 0 To 2
        txtNum(i).text = ""
    Next i

    txtNum(0).SetFocus
    optChoice.SetFocus
End Sub
```

This second procedure clears all text boxes, and allows the user to start again.

4. Write the optChoice_Click() procedure:

```
Private Sub optChoice_Click()
    txtNum(0).SetFocus
    txtNum(0).text = 0
    txtNum(1).text = 0
    txtNum(2).text = 0
End Sub
```

This code sets all values in the text box to zero and gives the topmost text box the focus.

5. Write the calc_max() function in the frmDataEntry module as follows:

```
Private Function calc_max (num1, num2, num3)
If num1 > num2 And num1 > num3 Then
calc_max = num1
ElseIf num2 > num3 Then
calc_max = num2
Else
calc_max = num3
End If
End Function
```

6. Run and test your program.

In this function, the three numbers are compared to one another to determine which number is the largest. This number is returned to the calling procedure.

Exercise 21.4 Passing an Array to a Procedure

Arrays can be passed to a procedure, much like a single variable, using call by reference. With arrays, you must remember the following two style changes:

- The array name in the calling statement must be followed by empty parentheses.

- The called procedure must specify the array name.

In this exercise, you will pass an array to a procedure where it is filled with letters. Following this, you will pass the filled array to a second procedure where the stored values are printed (see Figure 21.8).

Figure 21.8 *The Get Characters* Click() *event calls two procedures: one to fill an array with letters and a second to display the array of letters on the form.*

1. Add the two command buttons, **cmdGetChar** and **cmdEnd**, and write the End procedure.

continues

2. Write the following `cmdGetChar` procedure:

```
Private Sub cmdGetChar_Click()
    Static letters(0 To 25) As String * 1
    Call fun1(letters())
    Call fun2(letters())
End Sub
```

3. Write the following `fun1()` and `fun2()` procedures:

```
Private Sub fun1 (letters() As String * 1)
    'This procedure fills the array with letters
    Dim i As Integer
    For i = 0 To 25
      letters(i) = Chr$(i + 65)
    Next i
End Sub

Private Sub fun2 (letters() As String * 1)
    'This procedure prints the filled array of letters
    Dim i As Integer
    For i = 0 To 25
      Print letters(i) & " ";
    Next i
End Sub
```

4. Run and test your program.

The `fun1` procedure fills the array with letters and returns control to the calling function, `cmdGetChar`. The `fun2` procedure displays the array of letters and returns control to the calling function.

21.2.2   Call by Value

Call by value means that a copy of the variable (not its address) is passed to the receiving procedure or function. Arguments passed by value cannot be altered by the procedure or function. Instead, only the copy can be altered.

To pass an argument by value, two special rules are required:

- In the calling statement, insert parentheses around the argument in the call statement, as in the following example:

```
Call Reverse ((my_age), my_name)
```

In this example, the variable `my_age` (placed within parentheses) is passed by value; the variable `my_name` is passed by address.

- The second special rule is found in the called function. With call by value, the `ByVal` keyword is placed in the procedure's parameter list, as in the following example:

```
Private Sub Reverse (ByVal my_age, my_name)
```

This clearly indicates that `my_age` is an argument passed by value. As before, `my_name` is an argument passed by reference.

Exercise 21.5   Passing Arguments by Value

Make a call to a procedure, named Reverse, that changes your entered name, but not your entered age. Figure 21.9 shows the interface to create.

Figure 21.9 *With pass by value, your age is copied before it is passed, which leads to multiple values.*

1. Create the interface shown in Figure 21.9. The top row contains two text boxes (**txtAge1** and **txtName1**); the bottom row contains two labels (**lblAge2** and **lblName2**).

2. Write the following cmdPassIt_Click() procedure:

```
Private Sub cmdPassIt_Click()
    Dim my_age As Integer
    Dim my_name As String
    'Assign the initial values of age and name
    my_age = Val(txtAge1.Text)
    my_name = txtName1.Text

    'Pass my_age by value
    'Pass my_name by address
    Call Reverse((my_age), my_name)
    txtAge1.Text = Str$(my_age)
    txtName1.Text = my_name
End Sub
```

3. Write the following Reverse() procedure:

```
Private Sub Reverse (ByVal my_age, my_name)
    'Add ByVal in the parameter list to indicate
    'passing by value
    'Passing by address requires no special reference
    'My_age will have an initial and an after value
    my_age = my_age + 1
    'Sorry!  You're name will always be Freddy the frog
    my_name = "Freddy the frog"

    lblAge2.Caption = my_age
    lblName2.Caption = my_name
End Sub
```

4. Run the program. Observe that after the procedure is called, the new values of txtAge1 and txtName1 are displayed, using the labels. Only one of these will retain the original value passed to the function named Reverse. Test this program by reversing the argument passed by value and the argument passed by address.

21.2.3   Choosing the Best Method

The decision to use call by value or call by reference is sometimes determined in advance for you. When making Windows API (application program interface) calls, for example, the ByVal designation is typically required. As another example, you typically avoid passing large arrays by value in order to conserve memory. Instead, large arrays usually are passed by reference.

In addition to saving memory, passing by reference is faster because variables need not be copied. For these reasons, passing by reference is the most common calling convention, and it is the Visual Basic default.

Objective 21.3   Using Code Modules in the Processing/Business-Rule and Data Layers

You have worked with forms and employed statements and methods to navigate through a multiple-form application. This section presents the use of a standard code module to perform the business-rule services typically found in the processing or business-rule layer of an application. This layer of an application performs the following tasks:

- Retrieves information from the user

- Makes calculations

- Reads and writes persistent data to and from a database or file

- Returns the results of processing to the user interface layer

21.3.1   Placement of Code in Standard Code Modules

With single forms, references to objects do not require the full reference, which includes the form name. This differs from a multiple-module application. In that environment, references to objects in other modules—such as controls placed on a form module—require a full reference to the object. You might, for example, want to pass a control as a parameter to a procedure in a standard code module. Or, you might simply want to assign a new value to one of the control's properties. Any reference to the control requires that the module in which it resides be referenced.

Changing the caption property of a label named lblDisplay on a form module named frmInvoice, for example, would require the full reference when the assignment statement came from another module:

```
frmInvoice.lblDisplay.Caption = "New order!"
```

Assume that the label is to be passed to a public procedure in another module:

```
Public Sub ChangeCaption(DisplayLabel as Label, NewCaption as String)
    DisplayLabel.Caption = NewCaption
End Sub
```

The call to the procedure would require a full reference, as in the following:

```
Call ChangeCaption(frmInvoice.lblDisplay, "New Order!")
```

21.3.2   Segmenting an Application with Standard Code Modules

Until the recent advent of object-oriented software development, modular design meant short procedures with precise functions that readily could be documented and maintained. All data validation procedures might be placed together in one group of procedures, data access procedures in another group, and data presentation procedures in yet another. In Visual Basic, the use of a set of standard modules is still seen in a majority of applications.

Building your own class modules within Visual Basic is a relatively new feature. Class modules existed in Visual Basic 4.0, but the advanced class design capabilities of Visual Basic 6.0 have moved the language much closer to a genuine object-oriented language.

Exercise 21.6   Using Forms and a Standard Module to Create a Ski Rental Shop Application

Using standard code modules to segment an application into a logical, layered design remains the heart of most Visual Basic programs. This exercise demonstrates how standard code modules can be used for this purpose.

The ski rental application is composed of two forms and one standard module. One form is as an order form for ski rental equipment, and the other form, the invoice form, displays the ordered rental items and a total. The invoice form uses the MSFlexGrid control. Because of space limitations, the data layer in this application is represented by a global array of user-defined types rather than a random-access file. The data layer in most applications is represented by the stored tables of a relational database.

In this somewhat lengthy exercise, you use a standard code module as the primary means to build the processing/business-rule layer of an application. The user may select ski items to rent, and if desired, provide the customer a standard 15 percent discount. Figure 21.10 and Figure 21.11 show the two forms for this application.

continues

Exercise 21.6   continued

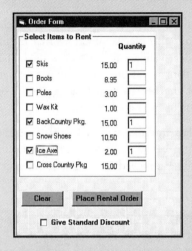

Figure 21.10   *The ski rental order form provides a selection of rental items.*

Figure 21.11   *The ski rental invoice shows the items that were selected and their total cost.*

1. Add the two forms (**frmOrder** and **frmInvoice**) to a project. Save these as **f21-6A.frm** and **f21-6B.frm**, respectively.

2. Place a frame on frmOrder, and change the caption to **Select Items to Rent**.

3. On frmOrder, place three control arrays inside the frame: an array of check boxes named **chkItem()**, an array of labels without borders named **lblPrice()**, and an array of text boxes named **txtQuantity()**. All three control arrays have a subscript range of 0 to 7 running from top to bottom.

4. Add the two command buttons, **cmdClear** and **cmdOrder**. Change the captions as shown.

5. Add a final check box to the form below the two command buttons. Name the check box **chkDiscount**, and change the caption as shown.

6. Place an MSFlexGrid control on frmInvoice, and name the grid control InvGrid. (Remember that to add the MSFleaxGrid control to your toolbox, select Project, Components and make the selection from the Custom Controls tab.)

7. Add a standard code module to your project and save it to disk as **m21-6.BAS**.

8. In the declaration section of the standard code module, make the following declarations:

```
Type orderitem
    description As String
    quantity As .Integer
    fee As Currency
    Linetotal As Currency
End Type

Public skirental() As orderitem
Private Const StdDiscount = 0.85
```

Observe that skirental() is declared as an array of type orderitem with global scope. The constant represents the multiplier for the standard 15 percent discount.

9. In the frmOrder.cmdOrder_Click() event, enter the following code:

```
Private Sub cmdOrder_Click()
    Dim i As Integer
    'Variable for checking array redeclaration
    Dim arraynum As Integer
    'Variable for tracking assignment to global array
    Dim assigncheck As Integer
    arraynum = 0
    For i = chkItem.LBound To chkItem.UBound
        If chkItem(i).Value = 1 Then arraynum = arraynum + 1
    Next i
    If arraynum = 0 Then
        Exit Sub
    Else
        'This sets the size of the array and the type
        ReDim skirental(1 To arraynum) As orderitem
    End If
```

continues

```
            assigncheck = 1
            For i = chkItem.LBound To chkItem.UBound
                If chkItem(i).Value = 1 Then
                    skirental(assigncheck).description =
chkItem(i).Caption
                    skirental(assigncheck).fee = Val(lblPrice(i).Caption)
                    skirental(assigncheck).quantity =
CInt(txtQuantity(i).Text)
                    skirental(assigncheck).Linetotal =
skirental(assigncheck).fee _
                    * skirental(assigncheck).quantity
                    assigncheck = assigncheck + 1
                End If

            Next i
            If chkDiscount.Value = 1 Then
                Call CalculateRental(frmInvoice.InvGrid, True)
            Else
                Call CalculateRental(frmInvoice.InvGrid, False)
            End If
        End Sub
```

This code examines how many items the user has checked, and it redimensions skirental, the array declared as a user-defined type. Each element of skirental is populated with four items of information: the rental item, the rental price, the number of items ordered, and the line total.

The CalculateRental procedure then is called, passing two arguments: The grid on which the results of processing are to be displayed and a Boolean argument indicating whether a standard discount should apply to the order total.

10. Add the CalculateRental() procedure to the standard code module:

```
        Public Sub CalculateRental(grid As MSFlexGrid, Discount As
➥Boolean)
            Dim i As Integer
            Dim RunTotal As Currency
            Dim addstring As String
            Dim TabChar As String * 1
            Dim rowcounter As Integer

            TabChar = Chr(9)

            'Unload all previously loaded items from grid
            Call ClearGrid(grid)
            rowcounter = 1
            For i = LBound(skirental) To UBound(skirental)
                addstring = ""
                addstring = skirental(i).description & TabChar
                addstring = addstring & Str$(skirental(i).quantity) &
➥TabChar
                addstring = addstring & Format(skirental(i).fee,
➥"Currency") & TabChar
                addstring = addstring & Format(skirental(i).Linetotal,
➥"Currency")
```

```
        grid.AddItem addstring, rowcounter
        rowcounter = rowcounter + 1
    Next

    'calculate total
    RunTotal = 0
    For i = LBound(skirental) To UBound(skirental)
        RunTotal = RunTotal + skirental(i).Linetotal
    Next i

    'add underline
    grid.Row = rowcounter - 1
    grid.Col = 3
    grid.CellFontUnderline = True

    'display total on grid

    If Discount Then
      grid.Row = rowcounter + 1
      grid.Col = 0
      grid.CellFontBold = True
      grid.Text = "Total: "
      grid.Row = rowcounter + 1
      grid.Col = 3
      grid.CellFontBold = True
      grid.Text = Format(RunTotal, "Currency")

      grid.Row = rowcounter + 3
      grid.Col = 0
      grid.CellFontBold = True
      grid.Text = "Total w/Discount: "
      grid.Row = rowcounter + 3
      grid.Col = 3
      grid.CellFontBold = True
      grid.Text = Format(RunTotal * StdDiscount, "Currency")

    Else
      grid.Row = rowcounter + 1
      grid.Col = 0
      grid.CellFontBold = True
      grid.Text = "Total: "
      grid.Row = rowcounter + 1
      grid.Col = 3
      grid.CellFontBold = True
      grid.Text = Format(RunTotal, "Currency")
    End If
    'erase the global array

    ReDim skirental(0)    ' clear the array !!
End Sub
```

Using the properties of the grid control, this code loops through the global array, building individual strings to add to the grid control. The total is calculated, and, depending on the value of the discount argument, the order total is displayed or the order total and discount total are displayed. The array is then cleared.

The procedure also contains code to format individual grid cells, such as underlining the last order item and placing the total and discount amounts in bold.

continues

11. Every time the CalculateRental() procedure is called, the grid is cleared with the ClearGrid() procedure. Add it to the standard code module:

```
Public Sub ClearGrid(grid As MSFlexGrid)
    grid.Clear
    Call Addheaders(grid)
End Sub
```

12. The MSFlexGrid control's Clear method clears all text, including text on fixed rows. The fixed row is used for displaying column headers in this application. The Addheaders() procedure resets the values for the fixed row. Add it to the standard code module:

```
Public Sub Addheaders(grid As MSFlexGrid)
    ' insert column headers
    grid.Row = 0
    grid.Col = 0
    grid.CellFontBold = True
    grid.Text = "Item"
    grid.Row = 0
    grid.Col = 1
    grid.CellFontBold = True
    grid.Text = "Quantity"
    grid.Row = 0
    grid.Col = 2
    grid.CellFontBold = True
    grid.Text = "Each"
    grid.Row = 0
    grid.Col = 3
    grid.CellFontBold = True
    grid.Text = "Total"
End Sub
```

13. When the application is first launched, code is needed to set the grid control's properties. Add the following code to the standard code module:

```
Public Sub PrepGrid(grid As MSFlexGrid)
    ' set columns
    grid.FixedCols = 0
    grid.FixedRows = 1
    grid.Cols = 4
    grid.Rows = 100
    ' set width

    grid.Width = 4600
    ' set column widths

    grid.ColWidth(0) = 1800
    grid.ColWidth(1) = 800
    grid.ColWidth(2) = 800
    grid.ColWidth(3) = 800

    ' insert column headers
    Call Addheaders(grid)
End Sub
```

14. Return to `frmOrder`, and add the `form_Load()` event to set up the application:

```
Private Sub Form_Load()
    frmInvoice.Show
    Call PrepGrid(frmInvoice.InvGrid)
End Sub
```

15. Add code to the `chkItem_Click()` event to add a default quantity of 1 when an item is selected and clear the quantity text box when the item is deselected:

```
Private Sub chkItem_Click(Index As Integer)
    If chkItem(Index).Value = 1 Then
        txtQuantity(Index).Text = "1"
    Else
        txtQuantity(Index).Text = ""
    End If
End Sub
```

16. Add code to allow the user to clear choices in the `cmdClear_Click()` event:

```
Private Sub cmdClear_Click()
    Dim i As Integer
    For i = chkItem.LBound To chkItem.UBound
        chkItem(i).Value = 0
        txtQuantity(i).Text = ""
    Next i
    Call ClearGrid(frmInvoice.InvGrid)
End Sub
```

17. Add code to the `txtQuantity_LostFocus()` event to test whether the user has entered a numeric value in the `txtQuantity` text boxes:

```
Private Sub txtQuantity_LostFocus(Index As Integer)
    Dim test As String
    test = txtQuantity(Index).Text
    If Not IsNumeric(test) And Len(test) <> 0 Then
        MsgBox "Please enter an integer value.", 0, "Ski rental
➥order"
        txtQuantity(Index).Text = ""
        txtQuantity(Index).SetFocus
    End If
End Sub
```

As you work with this code, observe that the `CalculateRental()` procedure performs the main business-rule functions. It receives data, calculates the totals checking for discount pricing, and returns the results of processing to the user.

The code is modularized by having frequently called functions placed in a standard code module, such as the procedures formatting the grid control. As more forms are added to this application, these forms would have these procedures available to them.

continues

Exercise 21.6   continued

As lengthy as this exercise is, it does not contain code for dealing with a persistent data layer. Suppose that data on the products offered for rent were maintained in a database, for example. Code to populate the order form would need to be written as would code for modifying the product list.

A real world application also would need to have customer information, including form of payment information. Code to write and read this kind of information normally would be placed in the business-rule layer of an application. Segmenting these procedures in standard code modules makes the code more modular.

Objective 21.4   Using Class Modules in the Processing/Business-Rule and Data Layers

Using modules in applications takes a more complex turn when employing class modules. This requires an analysis of the object classes that should make up the application. Volumes are written on object-oriented design. A wide variety of notation systems exist for modeling object classes and the relationships among classes. These topics go well beyond the scope of this book. You should be aware, however, that the kind of object-oriented analysis that formerly went into large projects coded in C++ is now being used for large scale Visual Basic projects.

You can use class modules to segment an application. Recall from Chapter 20, "Class Modules," that you created an OrderItem class and then placed newly instantiated objects within that class. That objects collection provided the beginnings of an Order class. In Exercise 21.7, you will modify the OrderItem class created in Chapter 20 and build an Order class for the ski rental shop using Visual Basic's intrinsic Collection object.

Think of the different attributes and functions of the Order class as compared to the OrderItem class. The Order class should contain all line item information and display the order when requested. It should be able to total the order and apply a discount if requested. It needs to know on which grid to display the information and be able to manipulate the grid as needed. In contrast, the OrderItem class needs to hold information about the ski items: the unit price, the quantity ordered, and the line item total. It is the responsibility of the OrderItem class to calculate line items by multiplying the quantity by their unit prices.

With these concepts in mind, you will revamp the ski rental shop application using class modules.

Exercise 21.7 Building Classes to Enhance the Ski Rental Shop Application

In this lengthy exercise, you will build two classes: an OrderItem class and an Order class. It uses the same forms as those in Exercise 21.6.

1. Save the two forms, frmOrder and frmInvoice, as **f21-7A.frm** and **f21-7B.frm**, respectively.

2. Add a new standard code module to the project, change its Name property to **m21_7**, and save it to disk as **m21-7.BAS**. (You might want to add the code module from Exercise 21.6 to the project during design time in order to copy and modify its code. Much of the code from **m21-6.BAS** will be placed inside the Order class.) The new standard module, **m21-7.BAS**, contains only a single global declaration:

```
Public RentalOrder As Order
```

3. In the Load() and Unload() events for frmOrder, add code that creates a single instance of the Order class and removes it from memory when the form is unloaded:

```
Private Sub Form_Load()
  frmInvoice.Show
  Set RentalOrder = New Order
End Sub

Private Sub Form_Unload(Cancel As Integer)
  Set RentalOrder = Nothing
End Sub
```

4. Add a class module to the project, name it OrderItem, and save it to disk as **cls21-7A.cls**. (You might want to add the OrderItem class module built in Chapter 20 for Exercise 20.4, "Creating and Using an OrderItem Class," and modify its code.) Following is the entire code for the class module. It comprises only accessor and mutator methods (Property Get and Property Let, respectively) and class initialization code:

```
Private m_ProductName As String
Private m_Quantity As Double
Private m_UnitPrice As Currency
Private m_ItemTotal As Currency

Public Property Get ProductName() As String
    ProductName = m_ProductName
End Property

Public Property Let ProductName(ByVal vNewValue As String)
    m_ProductName = vNewValue
End Property

Public Property Get Quantity() As Double
    Quantity = m_Quantity
End Property
```

continues

521

```
Public Property Let Quantity(ByVal vNewValue As Double)
   m_Quantity = vNewValue
End Property

Public Property Get UnitPrice() As Currency
   UnitPrice = m_UnitPrice
End Property

Public Property Let UnitPrice(ByVal vNewValue As Currency)
   m_UnitPrice = vNewValue
End Property

Public Property Get ItemTotal() As Currency
   m_ItemTotal = m_UnitPrice * m_Quantity
   ItemTotal = m_ItemTotal
End Property

Private Sub Class_Initialize()
   m_ProductName = "Product"
   m_UnitPrice = 0
   m_Quantity = 0
   m_ItemTotal = 0
End Sub
```

Observe that the ItemTotal property is a read-only property because it is derived from the Quantity and UnitPrice properties.

5. In the frmOrder.cmdOrder_Click() event, add code that instantiates new instances of the OrderItem class and adds values to its key properties:

```
Private Sub cmdOrder_Click()
   Dim i As Integer
   Dim numitems As Integer
   Dim Lineitem As orderitem
   numitems = 0

   For i = chkItem.LBound To chkItem.UBound
      If chkItem(i).Value = 1 Then numitems = numitems + 1
   Next i

   If numitems = 0 Then ' check to see that data has been
➥entered
      Exit Sub
   Else
      For i = chkItem.LBound To chkItem.UBound
         If chkItem(i).Value = 1 Then
            Set Lineitem = New orderitem
            Lineitem.ProductName = chkItem(i).Caption
            Lineitem.UnitPrice = Val(lblPrice(i).Caption)
            Lineitem.Quantity = CInt(txtQuantity(i).Text)
            RentalOrder.AddOrderItem Lineitem
         End If
      Next i
   End If

   Call RentalOrder.DisplayOrder
End Sub
```

Observe that the last line invokes the AddOrderItem and DisplayOrder methods of the single instance of the Order class, RentalOrder. Now you begin building the order class.

6. Add a new class module to the project, name it **Order**, and save it to disk as **cls21-7B.cls**.

7. The Order class will have as a private data member an intrinsic Visual Basic Collection object. It also needs to manipulate a grid control in order to display the results of processing. In addition, the class must retain information about the amount of the standard discount, and whether a discount should be applied to an order. Make the following declarations in the General declaration section of the class:

```
Private colOrder As New Collection
Private m_Count As Long
Private m_Discount As Boolean
Private m_grid As MSFlexGrid
Private Const StdDiscount = 0.85
```

8. Initialize these data members and prepare the grid when the Order class is initialized by adding the following code to the Initialize() event:

```
Private Sub Class_Initialize()
   Set m_grid = frmInvoice.InvGrid
   m_Count = 0
   m_Discount = False
   Call PrepGrid
End Sub
```

Observe how the Set statement is used with the MSFlexGrid object. This allows you to reference the grid within the class without passing it to the grid manipulation procedures.

9. The Order class essentially "wraps" a class around the intrinsic Visual Basic Collection object. Because the collection is private to the Order class, you need to replicate some of the collection's methods and properties. Add a read-only Count property and an AddOrderItem() method to replicate the collection's Add method:

```
Public Property Get Count() As Long
   m_Count = colOrder.Count
   Count = m_Count
End Property

Public Sub AddOrderItem(newone As orderitem)
   colOrder.Add newone
End Sub
```

10. Add accessor and mutator methods for the Discount property:

```
Public Property Get Discount() As Boolean
   Discount = m_Discount
End Property

Public Property Let Discount(ByVal vNewValue As Boolean)
   m_Discount = vNewValue
End Property
```

continues

11. Add a `ClearOrder()` method that allows the collection to be cleared of objects and also clears the grid:

```
Public Sub ClearOrder()
  Dim i As Integer
  For i = colOrder.Count To 1 Step -1
    colOrder.Remove i
  Next
  Call ClearGrid
End Sub
```

12. Add the following grid manipulation procedures. (You might want to copy and modify this code from Exercise 21.6.) Observe that all of the grid manipulation procedures are `Private`.

```
Private Sub ClearGrid()
  m_grid.Clear
  Call Addheaders
End Sub

Private Sub Addheaders()
  ' insert column headers
  m_grid.Row = 0
  m_grid.Col = 0
  m_grid.CellFontBold = True
  m_grid.Text = "Item"
  m_grid.Row = 0
  m_grid.Col = 1
  m_grid.CellFontBold = True
  m_grid.Text = "Quantity"
  m_grid.Row = 0
  m_grid.Col = 2
  m_grid.CellFontBold = True
  m_grid.Text = "Each"
  m_grid.Row = 0
  m_grid.Col = 3
  m_grid.CellFontBold = True
  m_grid.Text = "Total"
End Sub

Private Sub PrepGrid()
  ' set columns
  m_grid.FixedCols = 0
  m_grid.FixedRows = 1
  m_grid.Cols = 4
  m_grid.Rows = 100
  ' set width

  m_grid.Width = 4600
  ' set column widths

  m_grid.ColWidth(0) = 1800
  m_grid.ColWidth(1) = 800
  m_grid.ColWidth(2) = 800
  m_grid.ColWidth(3) = 800

  ' insert column headers
  Call Addheaders

End Sub
```

13. As the final piece of the Order class, add the DisplayOrder() method. Again, you might want to copy and then modify code from Exercise 21.6, but note the differences, especially the use of the For Each...Next syntax to iterate through the collection and read Object property values:

```
Public Sub DisplayOrder()
    Dim i As orderitem
    Dim n As Integer
    Dim RunTotal As Currency
    Dim addstring As String
    Dim TabChar As String * 1
    Dim rowcounter As Integer

    TabChar = Chr(9)

    'Unload all previously loaded items from grid
    Call ClearGrid
    rowcounter = 1
    For Each i In colOrder
      addstring = ""
      addstring = i.ProductName & TabChar
      addstring = addstring & i.Quantity & TabChar
      addstring = addstring & Format(i.UnitPrice, "Currency") &
➡TabChar
      addstring = addstring & Format(i.ItemTotal, "Currency")
      m_grid.AddItem addstring, rowcounter
      rowcounter = rowcounter + 1
    Next

    'calculate total
    RunTotal = 0
    For Each i In colOrder
       RunTotal = RunTotal + i.ItemTotal
    Next i

    'add underline
    m_grid.Row = rowcounter - 1
    m_grid.Col = 3
    m_grid.CellFontUnderline = True

    'display total on grid

    If m_Discount Then
      m_grid.Row = rowcounter + 1
      m_grid.Col = 0
      m_grid.CellFontBold = True
      m_grid.Text = "Total: "
      m_grid.Row = rowcounter + 1
      m_grid.Col = 3
      m_grid.CellFontBold = True
      m_grid.Text = Format(RunTotal, "Currency")

      m_grid.Row = rowcounter + 3
      m_grid.Col = 0
      m_grid.CellFontBold = True
      m_grid.Text = "Total w/Discount: "
      m_grid.Row = rowcounter + 3
```

continues

```
            m_grid.Col = 3
            m_grid.CellFontBold = True
            m_grid.Text = Format(RunTotal * StdDiscount, "Currency")

        Else
            m_grid.Row = rowcounter + 1
            m_grid.Col = 0
            m_grid.CellFontBold = True
            m_grid.Text = "Total: "
            m_grid.Row = rowcounter + 1
            m_grid.Col = 3
            m_grid.CellFontBold = True
            m_grid.Text = Format(RunTotal, "Currency")
        End If

        ' remove items from collection

        For n = colOrder.Count To 1 Step -1
            colOrder.Remove n
        Next

    End Sub
```

14. Return to frmOrder and add the following code to the cmdClear_Click() and chkDiscount_Click() events:

```
    Private Sub cmdClear_Click()
        Dim i As Integer
        For i = chkItem.LBound To chkItem.UBound
            chkItem(i).Value = 0
            txtQuantity(i).Text = ""
        Next i
        Call RentalOrder.ClearOrder
    End Sub

    Private Sub chkDiscount_Click()
        If chkDiscount.Value = 1 Then
            RentalOrder.Discount = True
        Else
            RentalOrder.Discount = False
        End If
    End Sub
```

15. Run and test the program. Be sure to remove any extra modules added from Exercise 20.4 and Exercise 21.6.

Although lengthy, this exercise shows how segmenting your application into classes makes the application easier to extend and maintain. As your application expands, adding functionality to the right class makes the application conceptually manageable.

As you work more with classes and include them in larger applications, you will come to appreciate that correct design of classes, correct designation of class functionality, and clear designation of class relationships takes on added importance. In fact, it often is the key to software success.

Chapter Summary

Modular design is the breaking down of a computer program into several discrete units, rather than writing one long application. It also involves using several forms rather than one. Program modules consist of procedures and functions that are either bound to forms, stored in standard code modules, or encapsulated in objects defined by class modules.

Perhaps the most important reason for modular design is to specify the functionality of a coded procedure. Use a form to convey a specific function, and write procedures or functions to perform one and only one task. Often, you might want to think of an application as having a user-interface layer, a processing/business-rule layer, and a data layer. This logical construction can assist you in building modular, readily understood applications.

In multiple-module applications, an initial form often is the login window. This window is used to provide security to a design. Use the PasswordChar property to make a password invisible to the person typing (or to the person trying to steal the password).

Modular design requires an understanding of how to load, show, hide, and unload forms. If a form is hidden, it remains in memory; if unloaded, it is removed from memory.

Call by reference and call by value are essential to modular design. Both allow the Visual Basic programmer to pass values from one procedure to another. Call by reference, the default, passes a copy of the address of the variable to a function or procedure. This allows the value of the argument to be directly altered by the function or procedure. Call by value passes a copy of the variable to the receiving function or procedure. The original value cannot be altered if passed by value, only the copy. To call by value, place the variable to be passed in parentheses, as in the following example:

```
Call Reverse ((my_age), my_name)
```

In this statement, my_age is passed by value; my_name is passed by reference.

Call by value features the ByVal keyword in the called function or procedure:

```
Private Sub Reverse(ByVal my_age, my_name)
```

Both standard modules and class modules can be used to help segment an application, especially in constructing the processing/business-rule and data layers of an application.

Skill-Building Exercises

These exercises ask you to practice your design and programming skills. You begin by designing a login window. Following this, use programming skills to practice passing values and modifying code. The last three exercises ask you to modify the university and the ski rental designs presented in the chapter. When asked to extend a design, remember the importance of good visual presentation and modular design.

1. Design a login window that allows a user to access frmSystem if the password ButterBun is typed, but only frmMain if the password RobRun is typed. The system form gives the user access to the entire design; the main form provides only limited access.

2. Modify Exercise 21.5 to allow you to change your name and address from old to new, showing both on the same display. Name should not be changed, only the address.

3. Modify Exercise 21.4. Use .BAS files to store the functions fun1() and fun2(). As before, display all letters.

4. Pass an array of numbers to a procedure. Within the procedure, sort the numbers from lowest to highest. Return to the calling procedure and display the sorted list of numbers.

5. Using Exercise 21.2 add a new form which allows the user to enter new course location information. Name the form **frmNewCL**. On the form, permit the user to input information on the building, room number, and capacity of the course location. Also enable the user to indicate whether the room has handicapped access and has an LCD projector.

6. Extend the previous exercise by letting the user navigate to frmNewCL from frmNewCourse. Change the text box txtLocation on frmNewCourse to a combo box and name the combo box **cboLocation**.

7. Modify Exercise 21.7 so that the user can select from a range of discounts between 10 and 40 percent. Present the choices in increments of five percent. Also allow the user to have no discount.

CHAPTER 22

CREATING AN ACTIVEX DLL

In Chapter 21, "Modular Design," you used class modules to revamp the ski rental program (see Exercise 21.7, "Building Classes to Enhance the Ski Rental Shop Application"). The class modules defined the properties and methods of the objects created from those classes. In this manner, you made your programs more modular.

Among the many benefits of modular design is the promotion of *code reuse*. In Visual Basic, it is possible to employ a module in more than one application. An existing form module, standard code module, or class module can be added to a project in design-time. Even so, the added module must usually be modified to become fully integrated into the new project. Form module names, for example, often must be changed to make them distinct. Class modules usually require some modification to fit into the new application's design.

Visual Basic also makes the code and capabilities of an entire project available to other applications. You can use the multiple modules of a project to create a custom software component. You already have used components created for you by others. Every time you use a Visual Basic control, you use a component. When you used the MSFlexGrid control, for example, you added this custom control to the Visual Basic toolbox from the Custom Control tab of the Components dialog box. In advanced Visual Basic, you can build your own ActiveX controls. An ActiveX control is a control you design and add to your toolbox. This type of control can be used by you as well as by other Visual Basic developers.

Software components provide the principal means by which Visual Basic promotes code reuse. Creating your own ActiveX control in Visual Basic is a major undertaking, but you can build ActiveX DLLs and ActiveX EXE components fairly easily. Because of a recent development, Visual Basic can now also create ActiveX documents for World Wide Web applications for distribution of computing applications on corporate intranets (see Chapter 27, "Visual Basic Internet Applications").

ActiveX DLLs often are referred to as *code components*. They frequently contain no visual interface at all. Instead, they perform vital processing for any application that chooses to use the services the DLL provides. These functions might involve numerically intense calculation routines, sorting routines, string parsing, or standard database query management.

The exercises in this chapter teach you several tasks. After you work through the exercises, you will be able to perform the following tasks:

- Use the References dialog box to examine type libraries registered on your computer

- Add a reference of a type library to a Visual Basic project

- Examine objects exposed by the type library with the Object Browser

- Learn the difference between in-process and out-of-process servers

- Create an ActiveX DLL server application that performs various string and numeric functions

- Write a client application that uses an ActiveX DLL

- Write a function that parses a delimited string and places it inside an array

- Create a Visual Basic group so that you can work on multiple projects simultaneously

- Write a sort algorithm to return a sorted array from an ActiveX DLL

- Use Visual Basic's application Setup wizard to create a project dependency file, listing the files that need to be distributed with your application

Chapter Objectives

This chapter focuses on the creation of ActiveX DLLs. This type of component is easier to develop than other types of software components. ActiveX DLLs also provide some decided speed advantages over most ActiveX EXE projects. (You will look at using ActiveX EXE components in Chapter 26, "Working with Objects from Microsoft Office," especially the ActiveX EXE components exposed by the Microsoft Office suite.) This chapter is organized around four objectives:

1. Understanding ActiveX components and their type libraries

2. Creating and using an ActiveX DLL

3. Creating and using a Visual Basic group

4. Determining an application's file dependencies

These objectives make a preliminary introduction to the topics that are central to the architecture of ActiveX components and the understanding of how ActiveX components can be used by many applications.

Objective 22.1 Understanding ActiveX Components and Their Type Libraries

How is it that multiple applications can use the same software component? How does an application know the properties, methods, and events of an object if the object isn't first loaded into memory with the application? Isn't it wasteful to have multiple instances of the same component occupying memory?

Answering these questions has occupied developers of systems and application software for more than 10 years. Think of the differences between an old DOS program and an operating system such as Windows. In the DOS world, developers frequently use libraries of reusable code in their applications. There are a handful of sort algorithms that nearly every program uses at one time or another. Why code them again? The same goes for many standard string parsing functions.

In a single-tasking environment, such as older versions of DOS, the linking functions of compilers bring libraries of code into an executable file. They might make the executable file a little larger, but that, after all, is just space on the hard disk.

22.1.1 A Brief Sketch of DLLs

In a shared memory environment, such as Windows 3.0 and 3.1 (or DOS with shared memory manager programs), or a multitasking environment, such as 32-bit Windows operating systems, the situation becomes more complicated. With more than one program running, you do not want them occupying precious memory with the same code. Operating system functions, functions to use the built-in Windows dialog boxes, or common mathematical functions need to be shared by all running applications. This is where *dynamic link libraries* (DLLs) come in.

When programs use a DLL, the functions in the library are not linked to the application when it is compiled. Instead, functions in the dynamic-link library are identified and called when needed by the running application. Multiple running applications can call the same library, but only one instance of the library is loaded into memory. In the Windows operating system, the User32.DLL in the Windows\System subdirectory services every running application with core operating system functionality.

It is important to remember that DLLs are a type of executable. Visual Basic controls have an .OCX extension. This stands for OLE control extension, the predecessor of ActiveX. However, .OCX files are a type of DLL, and sometimes .EXE applications resemble DLLs as well. They are executables that service other applications. In the Windows operating system, the GDI32.EXE application, for example, performs drawing functions on the screen and printer.

When you add a custom control to your Visual Basic toolbox, you essentially identify the library that will act as the engine for that control when it is used by your application. Another running application might be using the same control and the same engine. In this example, the .OCX control (a type of DLL) acts as a server to a client application.

This is the heart of component-based development. Software components act as servers to client applications. Visual Basic enables you to develop these types of servers.

22.1.2   ActiveX DLLs and Type Libraries

ActiveX DLLs are DLLs of a special type. They conform to what is known as the Component Object Model (COM), the technology upon which ActiveX is based. The COM defines a set of protocols (usually referred to as interfaces) by which objects communicate with one another. This communication includes the manner in which objects inquire about each other's properties, methods, and events. The COM also defines how communication will occur within a process and outside a process.

Every time an application is launched in 32-bit Window operating systems, it is launched within a process. The full details of a process are quite complex, but a process includes the executing program, a set of memory addresses, and at least one thread: a part of a process that runs program instructions. A process can have more than one thread, which allows a single process to have different parts of a program running concurrently. All the programs in this text are single-threaded.

ActiveX DLLs are in-process servers. That means they operate within the same process as your application. This usually means dramatically faster program performance than out-of-process communication, the type of communication that occurs when using an ActiveX EXE, a topic covered in Chapter 26.

Because ActiveX DLLs are software components, they can be used by several applications. However, for this to occur, they must make themselves known. Like other software components, ActiveX DLLs make themselves known to other Windows applications by being registered in the Windows Registry.

You probably already have encountered the Windows Registry in working with other Windows programs or when installing new programs on your computer. The Registry essentially is a large database that contains information about the hardware on the computer, the configuration of different peripherals, the different users on the machine, and environmental settings for software on the computer. It also holds information about the various software components on the computer.

Each of the software components registered in the Windows Registry contains a unique identification. The components usually receive their identification when they are compiled, using what is known as the GUID standard, or globally unique identifier. The GUID standard is a long alphanumeric string that identifies a software component, and is created by an algorithm made universally available to software component developers. When you compile an ActiveX DLL, a GUID for that component is automatically created for you. This then allows the software component to be installed on other computers and registered.

By being registered in the Registry, ActiveX software components define object data types that can be declared and bound to object variables. In Chapter 21, "Modular Design," you defined two object data types in class modules: an OrderItem class and an Order class. You made object variable declarations of these objects and bound them with such an instruction as

```
Dim Lineitem as OrderItem
Set Lineitem = New OrderItem
```

or

```
Dim skirental as New Order
```

Your program knew what these datatypes were because you defined them within class modules inside your project.

When you create an ActiveX DLL, other applications know the datatypes and the interface the ActiveX DLL exposes because the DLL also defines a *type library*. There are different type libraries for ActiveX components. These include type libraries for ActiveX controls, ActiveX DLLs, ActiveX EXEs, and explicit libraries that have .OLB or .TLB extensions.

The type libraries available to you on your computer are listed in the References dialog box, which you access by choosing Project, References. After you choose a reference, you can examine the objects described by the type library by using the Object Browser. These two important features are discussed next.

22.1.3 Working with the Reference Dialog Box and Object Browser

You have already used the Object Browser to examine classes that you built in Chapter 20, "Class Modules," and perhaps to examine the classes you built in Chapter 21, "Modular Design." Because those class modules were defined in the projects, references to the classes were already available to the Object Browser. Generally, however, using the Object Browser to examine objects defined in type libraries is a two-step process:

1. Make a reference to the object type library by using the References dialog box.

2. Examine the properties, methods, and events of the object in the Object Browser.

If the type library you are examining is an ActiveX control, you need only select the control from the Components dialog box. A reference to the control's type library is then automatically added to the References dialog box.

Exercise 22.1   Using the References Dialog Box and Object Browser

In this exercise, you will use the References dialog box to select a type library. You then will examine some of the objects described in the type library with the Object Browser.

1. Start a new project. Do not save it to disk because you will only use the utilities associated with type libraries.

2. Choose Project, References. You will see the References dialog box, as shown in Figure 22.1.

Figure 22.1   *Use the References dialog box to select another application's objects that you want available in your code by setting a reference to that application's object library.*

3. Assuming you have either the Professional or Enterprise editions of Visual Basic, select one of the Microsoft DAO libraries (for example, DAO 3.0 or DAO 3.51). Either of these is the type library for Data Access Objects, a topic addressed in Chapter 24, "Using Data Access Objects." It exposes most of the functionality of the Access database, but without the visual interface of Access. This often is referred to as the Access database engine. Select the DAO library and click OK. You now have a reference to this type library in the project.

4. Press F2 and open the Object Browser. Alternatively choose View, Object Browser from the Visual Basic menu.

5. Select the DAO library and examine the Database class; then, examine the OpenRecordset member of this class (see Figure 22.2).

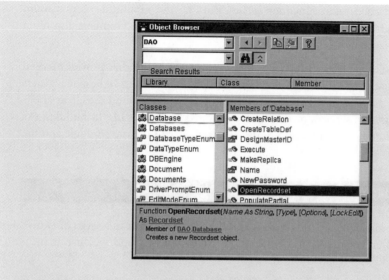

Figure 22.2 *After you set a reference, you can examine objects defined for that library with the Object Browser.*

Objective 22.2   Creating and Using an ActiveX DLL

When you create an ActiveX DLL project, you also create a type library that other applications can use when that project is compiled. These DLLs are referred to as code components. They are often used to encapsulate numerically intensive operations or to provide precoded functions to applications.

22.2.1   The Uses of ActiveX DLLs

The database capabilities of Access are encapsulated in the DAO library. Database functions so often are needed by programs that these libraries are among the most frequently used by Visual Basic programmers. Nearly every program needs to store data to disk. If the program serves a typical enterprise, the database will need to be queried often for data on a regular basis. The power of a relational database to retrieve data with ease makes the DLLs that encapsulate the Access database engine into Data Access Objects (DAO) a premier feature of the Visual Basic language.

Nearly every program needs to use math and string functions. As an example, string functions are used to count the number of specified characters in a string or to find the position of the *n*th occurrence of a character. String functions also frequently work with delimited files. Delimited files are sequential records in which each line in the file has its fields delimited by some character. The delimiter in the line is often a comma, a semicolon, or a tab. Path strings also often need to be parsed.

Frequently needed math functions include finding the minimum or maximum value in an array or finding the average of a set of numbers. Numbers also often need to be placed in ascending order.

In this chapter, you will construct a DLL server application that provides several string and math functions. You then will compile it and observe how it registers itself within the Windows Registry. Following this, you will build the client application and use the services of the newly registered ActiveX DLL. In building the ActiveX DLL, pay close attention to the Name property of the class module and the Name property of the ActiveX DLL project.

Exercise 22.2   Building an ActiveX DLL

This project asks you to build an ActiveX DLL, and is the first in a series of two exercises. After you build and register the ActiveX DLL, you will use it in Exercise 22.3.

1. Create a separate directory for this exercise. Each of the next four exercises in this chapter will have a separate directory. Name the directory **EX22_2**.

2. Start a new project inside Visual Basic. When the New Project dialog box appears, select the ActiveX DLL icon (see Figure 22.3).

Figure 22.3   *The ActiveX DLL icon indicates that you plan to design and register a DLL on your computer.*

3. The new project will include a general section and a single class. Press the F4 key to examine the properties of the Class module. Make no changes at this time. Leave the Name property (Class1) and the Instancing property (5—MultiUse).

4. Perform the following two-step procedure:

   1. Change the name of the Class module to **MiscFunctions1**.

   2. Save it to disk as **clsMisc1.cls** in the directory you have created.

   Important: The Name property of the Class module will become the name of the set of objects that you instantiate from this class.

5. Again, follow a two-step procedure:

   1. Go to the Project Properties dialog box. (Right-click the project in the Project Explorer and select Properties, or choose Project, Properties from the Visual Basic menu.)

   2. Change the Name property of the project to **Misc1**.

   Important: The Name property of the project will become the name of the type library when the DLL is compiled. You need not specify a Startup object for the DLL. The client applications start the DLL when it is needed.

6. Save the project to disk as **Misc1.vbp**. Save the project in the directory you have created.

7. Add two string functions to the MiscFunctions1 class module. One function, GetCharCount, returns the number of occurrences of a single character within a string. The other function, GetCharPos, returns the *n*th position of a single character within a string.

```
Public Function GetCharPos(s1 As String, testchar As String,
➥pos As Integer) As Long
  ' this function tests for the nth occurrence of a character
  Dim i As Long
  Dim slength As Long
  Dim testpos As Long
  If Len(testchar) > 1 Then
    MsgBox "Search item must be a single character.", 0,
    ➥"String Functions"
    Exit Function
  End If
  testpos = 0
  slength = Len(s1)
  For i = 1 To slength
    If Mid$(s1, i, 1) = testchar Then
      testpos = testpos + 1
      If testpos = pos Then
        GetCharPos = i
        Exit Function
      End If
    End If
  Next
  GetCharPos = 0 ' character not found
End Function

Public Function GetCharCount(s1 As String, examinechar As
➥String) As Long
```

continues

537

Exercise 22.2   continued

```
            Dim i As Long
            Dim slength As Long
            Dim charcount As Long
            If Len(examinechar) > 1 Then
              MsgBox "Search item must be a single character.", 0,
              ➥"String Functions"
              Exit Function
            End If
            charcount = 0
            slength = Len(s1)
            For i = 1 To slength
              If Mid$(s1, i, 1) = examinechar Then
                charcount = charcount + 1
              End If
            Next
            GetCharCount = charcount
        End Function
```

8. Compile the DLL by selecting File, Make Misc1.dll from the Visual Basic menu. Click OK to accept the name Misc1.dll.

9. As Visual Basic compiles the application, it provides the DLL a new GUID. This unique naming of the class ID occurs every time the project is recompiled. Don't worry about whether your class module might somehow create a duplicate ID: The algorithm that generates this ID could be run every few seconds for thousands of years before generating a duplicate ID.

10. Do not run the DLL at this time. The next exercise will ask you to do that.

11. To observe that you have created a registered class, you can use the Regedit.exe Windows Registry utility provided with Windows (under the Windows directory). Examine the HKey_Classes_Root tree with this utility. You should see the Misc1 type library registered.

   Important: Do not change settings in the Registry. An errant assignment in the Registry can make your computer, or programs within it, inoperable.

Exercise 22.3   Building the Client Application

To test the newly created DLL, you need to build a client application that uses it. In this exercise, you build a Standard EXE project, set a reference to the type library created by the Misc1 DLL, and then use the string functions the DLL provides.

1. Create a separate directory for this application. Name the directory **EX22_3**.

2. Create the interface you see in Figure 22.4. It consists of a text box (**txtDisplay**) with its MultiLine property set to True, a combo box (**cboSelect**), a command button (**cmdOK**), and two labels (**lblCommaCount** in the upper-right position of the form and **lblCommaPosition** immediately below **lblCommaCount**) with their BorderStyle properties set to Fixed Single. The other labels offering prompts or descriptions retain their default names. Save the form to disk as **f22-3.frm** and the project as **p22-3.vbp**.

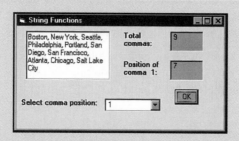

Figure 22.4   *The interface for testing the Misc1 ActiveX DLL is designed to count the total commas and the position of the selected comma.*

3. Choose Project, References to make a reference to the new Misc1 type library by selecting the type library in the References dialog box (see Figure 22.5). The Misc1 type was created in the last exercise.

Figure 22.5   *Find the Misc1 reference and click it to add it to the library for the project.*

continues

Exercise 22.3   continued

4. After a reference has been made, use the Object Browser to examine the `MiscFunctions1` member of the Misc1 type library. You should see listed the two methods you wrote for the DLL: `GetCharPos` and `GetCharCount`. When you select these functions inside the Object Browser, the parameters of these functions should be displayed.

5. At the module level of `Form1`, make the following declarations:

```
Dim strExamine As String
Dim MiscDLL As Misc1.MiscFunctions1
```

6. In the Load event of `Form1`, add the following code to populate the text box with cities, to populate the combo box with numbers, and to create an instance of the `MiscFunctions1` class:

```
Private Sub Form_Load()
  Dim i As Integer
  strExamine = "Boston, New York, Seattle, "
  strExamine = strExamine & "Philadelphia, Portland, San Diego,
  ➡San Francisco, "
  strExamine = strExamine & "Atlanta, Chicago, Salt Lake City"
  txtDisplay.Text = strExamine
  For i = 1 To 8
    cboSelect.AddItem Str$(i)
  Next
  cboSelect.ListIndex = 0
  Set MiscDLL = New Misc1.MiscFunctions1
End Sub
```

7. In the `Form_UnLoad()` event add code to remove the instance of the DLL:

```
Private Sub Form_Unload(Cancel As Integer)
  Set MiscDLL = Nothing
End Sub
```

8. In `cmdOK_Click()`, add code to call the functions in the DLL:

```
Private Sub cmdOK_Click()
  Dim pos1 As Integer, pos2 As Integer
  Dim passpos As Integer
  Dim msg As String
  strExamine = txtDisplay.Text

  passpos = CInt(cboSelect.Text)
  pos1 = MiscDLL.GetCharCount(strExamine, ",")
  pos2 = MiscDLL.GetCharPos(strExamine, ",", passpos)
  lblCommaCount.Caption = Str$(pos1)
  lblPrompt.Caption = "Position of comma " & Str$(passpos) &
  ➡":"
  lblCommaPosition.Caption = Str$(pos2)
End Sub
```

9. Test the program by adding cities with comma delimiters to the text box.

If you run into errors, you might need to go back to the Misc1.vbp project and correct them in the DLL. Remember to recompile the DLL before testing it again in the client application. You will learn how to work with two projects simultaneously in Objective 22.3, "Creating and Using a Visual Basic Group."

22.2.2   Fully Qualified Declarations

Observe the manner in which the module level declaration of MiscFunctions1 was made. It was declared as follows:

```
Dim MiscDLL As Misc1.MiscFunctions1
```

This is referred to as a fully qualified declaration. It specifies both the type library for the object as well as the object name. Suppose that two type libraries had the same name for an object and were referenced within a project. It is possible that an object variable could be bound to the wrong object. By specifying the type library in which the class is defined, you avoid these errors.

22.2.3   The *Instancing* Property of Class Modules in ActiveX DLLs

When you add class modules to Standard EXE projects, no Instancing property appears. A Standard EXE project has only a private instancing capability: Other applications are not given access to type information about the Standard EXE and cannot create new instances of the program. With ActiveX DLLs and ActiveX EXE projects, the way the components are created must be specified.

For most ActiveX DLLs, the instancing should be set to MultiUse. This enables other applications to access the same DLL: One instance of your component can provide services to another application. Table 22.1 explains the different instancing choices.

TABLE 22.1   Instancing Options for ActiveX DLLs

Property	Setting	Description
Private	1	The default. Other applications aren't allowed access to type library information about the class, and cannot create instances of it. Private objects are for use only within your component.
PublicNotCreatable	2	Other applications can use objects of this class only if your component creates the objects first. Other applications cannot use the CreateObject function or the New operator to create objects from the class.

continues

TABLE 22.1   continued

Property	Setting	Description
SingleUse	3	Enables other applications to create objects from the class, but every object of this class that a client creates starts a new instance of your component. Not allowed in ActiveX DLL projects.
GlobalSingleUse	4	Similar to SingleUse, except that properties and methods of the class can be invoked as if they were simply global functions. Not allowed in ActiveX DLL projects.
MultiUse	5	Allows other applications to create objects from the class. A component can provide any number of objects created in this fashion.
GlobalMultiUse	6	Similar to MultiUse, with one addition: Properties and methods of the class can be invoked as if they were simply global functions. It isn't necessary to explicitly create an instance of the class first because one will automatically be created.

It is important to remember that ActiveX DLL projects must include at least one class that is publicly creatable.

Objective 22.3   Creating and Using a Visual Basic Group

Creating a separate ActiveX server application and a separate client application might have seemed a little unwieldy to you. This especially is true if the ActiveX DLL project contains errors. Visual Basic eases this situation by enabling you to gather different projects together into a Visual Basic group. A group allows you to easily switch between projects and to test a DLL as it is developed without compiling.

22.3.1   The Startup Project

Visual Basic groups have a crucial property: You must specify which project is the startup project. This usually is the client application. Pay attention to this important property as you work through the next exercise.

Exercise 22.4   Using a Visual Basic Group to Expand the ActiveX DLL

In this project, you will create a Visual Basic group to expand and test the capabilities of the ActiveX DLL you created in Exercise 22.2. When working with Visual Basic groups and ActiveX DLLs, the names you use for class modules and projects becomes critical. Proper file management and object name management can save you enormous frustration. *Be sure to follow the directory creation and naming suggestions in this exercise carefully.*

1. Create a separate directory for this exercise. Name the directory **EX22_4**.

2. Open Misc1.vbp from Exercise 22.2. Save the clsMisc1.cls file to disk in the new EX22_4 directory as clsMisc2.cls. Rename the class module **MiscFunctions2**.

3. Save the Misc1.vbp project to disk in the Ex22_4 directory as Misc2.vbp. Change the project name to **Misc2**.

4. Close Misc2.vbp and open the project from Exercise 22.3 (that is, p22_3.vbp).

5. Save f22-3.frm as **f22-4.frm** in the EX22_4 directory. Save p22_3.vbp as **p22-4.vbp** in the EX22_4 directory. Change the project name (select Project Properties) from p22_3 to **p22_4**.

6. Choose File, Add Project from the Visual Basic menu. When the Add Project dialog box appears, choose the Existing tab and add the Misc2.vbp project.

   You have now created a Visual Basic group!

7. Choose File, Save Project Group As. Save the project group as **EX22_4.vbg**. (.vbg stands for Visual Basic group.) The Project Explorer should now appear as it does in Figure 22.6.

   Observe the Visual Basic title menu as you set focus on the two projects in the Project Explorer. The title will toggle between the two projects in the group.

Figure 22.6   *With Visual Basic groups, you can work on several projects simultaneously.*

continues

8. Select project p22_3(P22-4.vbp) in the Project Explorer and click the right mouse button. Click the top menu item: Set as Start Up. This specifies the P22_4.vbp project as the startup project in the group. The project should now be in bold inside the Project Explorer.

9. Select Form1 inside the p22_4 project and add a line control to separate the top and bottom portions of the form. Build the interface you see in Figure 22.7.

   Add a list box on the left side of the form lstArrayofNums, a command button (cmdTestMathFunctions), and six labels on the right side of the form. The three labels on the left describe the display of values shown in the three labels on the right. Change the BorderStyle of the three right-hand labels to 1-Fixed Single and name them **lblMin**, **lblMax**, and **lblAvg**, respectively. Change the caption of cmdTestMathFunctions to that shown in Figure 22.7.

10. Add the following code to the cmdTestMathFunctions_Click() event:

```
Private Sub cmdTestMathFunctions_Click()
    Dim pass(1 To 100) As Long
    Dim i As Long
    Dim ret1 As Long
    Dim ret2 As Double
    ' generate 100 numbers between 1 and 100000
    lstArrayofNums.Clear
    For i = 1 To 100
      Randomize
      ret1 = Int(100000 * Rnd + 1)
      pass(i) = ret1
      lstArrayofNums.AddItem ret1
    Next
    ret2 = MiscDLL.GetMin(pass())
    lblMin.Caption = ret2
    ret2 = MiscDLL.GetMax(pass())
    lblMax.Caption = ret2
    ret2 = MiscDLL.GetAvg(pass())
    lblAvg.Caption = ret2
End Sub
```

Figure 22.7   *This interface allows you to test various comma positions and simple math functions.*

This code randomly generates 100 numbers between 1 and 100,000 and places the numbers into an array. The arrays then are passed to three math routines in the `MiscDll` dynamic link library, which creates within it an instance of the `MiscFunctions2` class. The class routines get the minimum value of an array of numbers, the maximum value of an array of numbers, and the average of an array of numbers.

11. Switch the focus in the Project Explorer to the Misc2 project. Notice that the title bar of Visual Basic changes with the changeover. Add the three routines described in Step 10 to the `MiscFunctions2` class module:

```
Public Function GetMin(pass As Variant) As Double
    Dim i As Long
    Dim RidiculousNum As Double

    If VarType(pass) < vbArray Then
      GetMin = -1.1
      Exit Function
    End If

    RidiculousNum = (1000 ^ 32)
    For i = LBound(pass) To UBound(pass)
      If pass(i) < RidiculousNum Then
          RidiculousNum = pass(i)
      End If
    Next
    GetMin = RidiculousNum
End Function

Public Function GetMax(pass As Variant) As Double
    Dim i As Long
    Dim RidiculousNum As Double

    If VarType(pass) < vbArray Then
      GetMax = -1.1
```

continues

```
        Exit Function
    End If

    RidiculousNum = -(1000 ^ 32)
    For i = LBound(pass) To UBound(pass)
        If pass(i) > RidiculousNum Then
            RidiculousNum = pass(i)
        End If
    Next
    GetMax = RidiculousNum
End Function


Public Function GetAvg(pass As Variant) As Double
    Dim SumOfNum As Double
    Dim i As Long
    Dim arraynum As Long

    If VarType(pass) < vbArray Then
        GetAvg = -1.1
        Exit Function
    End If

    SumOfNum = 0
    arraynum = (UBound(pass) - LBound(pass)) + 1
    For i = LBound(pass) To UBound(pass)
        SumOfNum = SumOfNum + pass(i)
    Next

    GetAvg = SumOfNum / arraynum
End Function
```

The GetAvg function is the easiest to understand. It calculates the number of array elements and then divides this number into the sum of the numbers in the array.

The GetMin and GetMax functions are mirror images of one another. The GetMin function posits a ridiculous number as a minimum–1,000 raised to the 32nd power. As the routine loops through the array it compares the number in the array with the RidiculousNumber variable. If it encounters a number that is less than the variable it assigns that value to the RidiculousNumber variable. This occurs with the first comparison. The process continues until the entire array has been walked. At the end of the loop the lowest number has been found and is returned to the calling procedure. The RidiculousNumber variable in the GetMax is the complement of the GetMin procedure.

When passing arrays to DLLs, they must be passed as variants. Each of these functions uses the varType function to test whether the passes value is an array. If not, it exits the function so as not to generate an error when references are made to array with the LBound and UBound functions.

Important: Make sure that the p22_4 project has a reference to the Misc2 DLL. If the DLL project is part of the Visual Basic group, it need not be compiled to test; however, a reference to it still must be made. This greatly speeds application development. Make sure you have a check in the check box at Project|References|Misc2.

12. Test the new program. When you are satisfied with the performance of the DLL, you can compile it. After compilation, check to determine if the correct name has been created. Make sure that all references to Misc1.MiscFunction1 have been updated.

13. Remove the reference to Misc2 and observe the result. Make a new reference to the Misc2 library and then compile the Misc2 project. Save both projects in the EX22_4 Visual Basic Group.

14. Examine the p22-4.vbp file in a text editor, such as Notepad. You should see a reference to the GUID for the Misc2 type library near the top of the file. In the application compiled on the author's machine, the first lines of the P22-4.vbp file include the following reference:

```
Reference=*\G{55D0EE96-FC3C-11D0-A4E0-
00A0C90D3A89}#8.0#0#Misc2.dll#
```

15. Examine the GUID for the Misc2 type library compiled on your computer.

22.3.2   Adding a Sort Algorithm to the ActiveX DLL

DLLs frequently are used for numerically intensive tasks, which makes them ideal for sort routines. With these routines, you often need to return numbers from functions. If you are placing strings inside a list box, the task is easy: The list box can sort the strings for you. If sorted numbers or string need to be placed inside another control, such as a grid, or to be printed, however, you need to sort them yourself.

Exercise 22.5   Adding a Bubble Sort Routine to the ActiveX DLL

This exercise employs a bubble sort algorithm of the type that you used in Chapter 17, "String Functions." In this exercise, you alter the sort routine to handle numeric values. When the user chooses, randomly generated numbers are returned in sorted order.

1. Create a separate directory for this exercise. Name the directory **EX22_5**.

2. Open Misc2.vbp from Exercise 22.4. Save the clsMisc2.cls file to disk in the new EX22_5 directory as **clsMisc3.cls**. Rename the class module MiscFunctions3.

continues

Exercise 22.5   continued

3. Save the Misc2.vbp project to disk in the Ex22_5 directory as **Misc3.vbp**. Change the project name to **Misc3**.

4. Close Misc3.vbp and open the project from Exercise 22.4 (for example, p22_4.vbp).

5. Save f22-4.frm as **f22-5.frm** in the EX22_5 directory. Save p22-4.vbp as **p22-5.vbp** in the EX22_5 directory. Change the project name (select Project Properties) from p22_4 to **p22_5**.

6. Choose File, Add Project from the Visual Basic menu. When the Add Project dialog box appears, choose the Existing tab and add the Misc3.vbp project. Save the Visual Basic Group as **EX22_5.vbg**.

7. Make sure that P22_5 is the startup project. Shift the focus to Form1 in P22_5. Add a check box (**chkSort**) to the bottom area of the form to the right of lstArrayofNums (see Figure 22.8).

Figure 22.8   *This display shows the sorted list following the use of the bubble sort algorithm placed within the DLL.*

8. Change the cmdTestMathFunctions_Click() procedure to read as follows:

```
Dim pass(1 To 100) As Long
Dim i As Long
Dim ret1 As Long
Dim ret2 As Double
Dim ret3 As Variant
' generate 100 numbers between 1 and 10000
lstArrayofNums.Clear
For i = 1 To 100
  Randomize
  ret1 = Int(100000 * Rnd + 1)
  pass(i) = ret1
  lstArrayofNums.AddItem ret1
Next
ret2 = MiscDLL.GetMin(pass())
```

```
        lblMin.Caption = ret2
        ret2 = MiscDLL.GetMax(pass())
        lblMax.Caption = ret2
        ret2 = MiscDLL.GetAvg(pass())
        lblAvg.Caption = ret2
        If chkSort.Value = 1 Then
           lstArrayofNums.Clear
           ret3 = MiscDLL.ReturnBubbleSort(pass())
           For i = LBound(ret3) To UBound(ret3)
              lstArrayofNums.AddItem ret3(i)
           Next
        End If
```

This routine tests whether the user wants to have the randomly generated numbers string returned sorted or unsorted. If the array is to be sorted, the routine passes the array to the Misc3 Dll ReturnBubbleSort function and displays the sorted numbers in the list box.

9. Add the new features to the MiscFunctions3 class. Shift the focus in the Project Explorer to the Misc3 project. In the MiscFunctions3 class module, add the ReturnBubbleSort function:

```
Public Function ReturnBubbleSort(varArray As Variant) As
➡Variant
    Dim topnum As Double
    Dim NextItem As Long
    Dim topindex As Long
    Dim i As Long, j As Long
    Dim temp As Variant
    Dim tindex As Long
    Dim test As Long

    If VarType(varArray) < vbArray Then
       ReturnBubbleSort = 0
       Exit Function
    End If

    tindex = UBound(varArray)
    NextItem = LBound(varArray)

    Do While NextItem < tindex
       topindex = tindex
       Do While topindex > NextItem
         If varArray(topindex) < varArray(topindex - 1) Then
           temp = varArray(topindex)
           varArray(topindex) = varArray(topindex - 1)
           varArray(topindex - 1) = temp
         End If
         topindex = topindex - 1
       Loop
       NextItem = NextItem + 1
    Loop

    ReturnBubbleSort = varArray
End Function
```

10. Run and test the program.

Observe that when an array is returned from an ActiveX DLL, it also is returned as a Variant.

22.3.3   Design and Documentation Considerations in an ActiveX DLL

You have expanded a DLL over the course of this chapter. To make this expansion even more attractive, you can readily add other string and math functions to this ActiveX DLL. It then can be shared with other Visual Basic programmers.

Classes are somewhat self-documenting by being exposed by the Object Browser. ActiveX DLLs, however, require documentation as they become larger and more complex. This especially is true for DLLs made up of multiple class modules. Other programmers will want to know the meaning and use of different function parameters. There often is an interdependency between functions and object properties. This means that certain properties must be set before a function can be effectively invoked. These interdependencies need to be documented.

As you build larger DLLs, you will confront a fundamental design question: Should many arguments be passed to a DLL function or should values for class properties first be set and then functions operate on these class data members? As with most things, there is a tradeoff.

Keeping your DLL easy to use is one consideration. Being able to set properties first and then invoke functions usually makes the DLL easier to understand and work with. If you think your ActiveX DLL might, at a later time, be recompiled into an ActiveX EXE, however, other considerations come into play.

As you will learn in Chapter 26, "Working with Objects from Microsoft Office," ActiveX EXE components provide enormous flexibility. They suffer in performance compared to DLLs, however, because they work as out-of-process servers while DLLs are in-process servers. If there is a chance your DLL will need to be recompiled to become an ActiveX EXE, passing many arguments to a function can dramatically improve performance.

Objective 22.4   Determining an Application's File Dependencies

This final objective deals with files you need to distribute with your application. When you create an ActiveX DLL and use it in a program, you need to be sure that it is distributed and registered on the end user's computer. This is just one of the files to be distributed. Depending on the type libraries that are referenced in your application, the number of files to be distributed can vary dramatically.

Let's be frank: Visual Basic installations can be difficult. Visual Basic provides a Package and Deployment wizard for creating distribution disks or for getting a Visual basic application for deployment from an Internet Server. It usually works well; however, you can encounter problems if there are name conflicts in the libraries, software components fail to register, or the installation program generated by the Application Wizard encounters an unhandled error.

Several third-party tools exist on the market that allow robust installation scripts to be written, and these can more than pay for themselves in a short period. You might have written the best program in the world, but if the user can't install it, all you have done is made the end user angry.

This objective is not intended to provide a thorough review of Visual Basic's application Package and Deployment Wizard. It is intended to show how you can use this wizard to generate a dependency file, so you can examine your program and its dependent files before moving to the creation of installation disks. Visual Basic dependency files have a .DEP file extension.

Exercise 22.6   Generating a Dependency File with the Package and Deployment Wizard

This exercise asks you to use the application Package and Deployment Wizard to create a dependency file. This file lists the supporting files needed by your application when it is distributed to end-user machines and which should be included on your program's installation disks.

1. Make sure that you have compiled the Misc3 project into the Misc3.DLL and Project p22_5 into p22-5.exe.

2. Go back to Start, Programs, Microsoft Visual Basic 6 program group on your computer, and Start the Package and Deployment wizard from the Visual Basic 6 startup directory. If you have Visual Studio installed on your computer, it will be under the Visual Studio directory. You should see the dialog box displayed in Figure 22.9.

Figure 22.9   *This dialog box asks that you choose the project for which to build a dependency file.*

continues

Exercise 22.6   continued

3. Select the Browse button and choose the p22-5.vbp project and click Open.

4. Click the Package button you see on the dialog box shown in Figure 22.9. The wizard will present a dialog box asking which packing script to use. Select None and click the Next button.

5. A dialog box will appear similar to the one displayed in Figure 22.10. In the drop-down combo box, select Dependency File.

Figure 22.10   *This selection will generate a dependency file for the P22-5.EXE application.*

6. Continue clicking through the application Setup Wizard until you are asked to save the dependency file. The file usually is saved in the project directory.

7. Examine the P22-5.DEP file with a text editor. It should contain a list of the file dependencies for your application, including a reference to the Misc3.DLL file. These files must be present on the end users machine for your application to work and should be included in your application's installation program.

Chapter Summary

In this chapter, you developed your first true software component. You defined a component that could be created by other applications and then provided services to those other applications. This component acted as a server to client applications.

Software components are defined in type libraries. ActiveX type libraries can have .OCX, .DLL, and .EXE extensions. Some ActiveX type libraries have .OLB and .TLB extensions. These type libraries define classes of objects and are registered within the Windows Registry. Once registered, type libraries are available for inspection and use by other applications.

You make type libraries available to your project by creating a reference to that type library in the References dialog box. Objects defined in that type library then can be bound to object variables in your application.

ActiveX DLLs created in Visual Basic mainly use class modules to create code components. These components usually provide processor or computationally intensive services to client applications. In an ActiveX DLL project, the `Name` property of publicly instanced modules becomes the class names of objects that can be created from that DLL. The `Name` property of the ActiveX DLL project specifies the name of the type library for those objects when the ActiveX DLL is compiled. The `Instancing` property specifies how the ActiveX DLL can be created. For ActiveX DLLs, the most frequently used setting for the `Instancing` property is `MultiUse`.

Multiple projects in Visual Basic can be placed in Visual Basic groups. These groups, when saved to disk, have a .VBG extension. Visual Basic groups aid the development of ActiveX DLL projects by permitting both the server application (the ActiveX DLL project) and the client application (usually a Standard EXE project) to be worked on simultaneously in the Visual Basic design environment.

ActiveX DLL applications are in-process servers. This enhances their performance because they work within the same operating system process as the client application.

You can use Visual Basic's application Package and Deployment Wizard to create a dependency file. This file lists the supporting files needed by your application when it is distributed to end-user machines and which should be included on your program's installation disks. Dependency files have a .DEP extension.

Skill-Building Exercises

In these exercises, you will create and use new DLLs using the Misc3 DLL as a starting point. Place each exercise in a separate directory and copy and rename files to save time. For each exercise, write a client program that demonstrates the described DLL feature. You may want to start with the form from P22-5.vbp as a starting point.

1. Create a project based upon the Misc3 DLL to count the number of a user specified character in any text file on the computer.

2. Add a function to the DLL that returns the median (midpoint between highest and lowest value) of an array. Write a client program that demonstrates the feature.

3. Add a function to the DLL that returns the initials of any person. (*Hint:* Review the Split string function.)

4. Add a function to the DLL that counts the number of words in any text file on the user's computer. The indefinite and definite articles "a", "A", "the", and "The" do not count for determining total number of words. Pass only the filename to the DLL function.

5. Passing only the filename to the DLL function (this may be any text file on the users computer), write a function that returns a 26 member array of strings listing the number of times each letter of the alphabet occurs in a text file. Treat upper- and lowercase characters the same. Display the returned array in a list box.

6. *Challenge:* Extend the previous exercise so that the user can see the list in either ascending alpha order or in descending order from most frequently used letter to least frequently used letter. (*Hint:* Use a user-defined type in the DLL to hold the character and its frequency together.) Sort an array of the UDT in a private function within the DLL.

7. Generate a dependency file for the project in Skill-Building Exercise 5.

ACCESSING AND MANIPULATING DATABASES WITH VISUAL BASIC

Visual Basic includes a special control for accessing external databases, named, appropriately, the *Data control*. It allows a user to access an existing database and to navigate through the stored data with little or no programming. Visual Basic also contains Visual Data Manager: an application that allows a user to create and repair a database from within the Visual Basic design environment.

When you complete this chapter, you will have a good understanding of what a database is, how it works, and you will be able to perform the following tasks:

- Use the Data control

- Open a database

- Add to a database

- Edit a record stored in a database

- Use Recordset methods

- Write a query to retrieve a set of prescribed facts stored in a database

- Use Visual Data Manager to build a database

- Query a database built using Visual Data Manager

Chapter Objectives

In this chapter, you initially explore the use of the Data control to open existing databases. Following this, you examine building a small database from within Visual Basic using the Visual Data Manager. The objectives of this chapter focus on database concepts and the following use of Visual Basic's database features:

1. Understanding relational database terminology

2. Using the Data control

3. Querying data stored in a database

4. Building a database using Visual Data Manager

Objective 23.1   Understanding Relational Database Terminology

Before learning how to use the Data control and the Visual Data Manager, you need to understand some fundamental terminology and concepts regarding the structure of a database. To Visual Basic, database structure means a relational view or structure. A relational view of a database depicts a database as nothing more or less than a collection of tables, in which the rows of each table represent database records, and the columns of each table refer to the fields or attributes of a record.

Consider the relational database tables shown in Figure 23.1. These tables contain customer information and sales representative information. Information for one customer is placed in a single row. The information shown for a customer includes the customer number, the customer name, the customer telephone number, and the number of the sales representative assigned to the customer. Information for one sales representative is also placed in one row. The information shown for a sales representative includes the sales representative's number, name, and sales volume.

23.1.1   Important Terms

To begin, review the terms that are important to database tables. A database table contains data about a specific type of entity or object, such as a customer or salesperson. Figure 23.1 shows two database tables designed for use with Microsoft Access, a database software package.

Figure 23.1   *The structure of a relational database shows fields as columns and records as rows.*

The following are essential database terms:

- **Table**—A table is a logical structure used to group sets of related information. In the example shown in Figure 23.1, customer information is kept separately from salesperson data. The two types of information are not mixed and placed in a single table.

- **Record**—A record is a grouping of a set of attributes describing each person, place, or item in a database. In Figure 23.1, a record is a collection of data describing each customer. For each customer, there is one and only one record. Likewise, there is one and only one record for each sales representative.

- **Field**—A field is an attribute of a record. For example, an attribute of a customer is the customer name; another attribute is the number of the sales representative. For each field, there is one, and only one, entry.

- **Primary key**—Each record in a relational database must be unique. This is accomplished by assigning a unique ID or number to each record, which is called the *primary key*. Records are stored based on the primary key. For example, in storing a customer's record, a unique customer number is assigned (`Cust_no`). A unique key separates two customers with the same name. Likewise, each sales representative is assigned a unique primary key (`Sales_rep`). No two members of the sales force can have the same `Sales_rep` number.

- **Foreign key**—Foreign keys are fields in common between tables. In your example, the `Sales_rep` number in the sales representative table is a primary key, while the `Sales_rep` number in the CUSTOMER table is a foreign key. By knowing the `Sales_rep` number in the CUSTOMER table, it becomes possible to link to the SALESPERSON table and to retrieve stored information for that number.

- **Indexes**—Access to a database record often is made faster through the use of an index assigned to fields other than the primary key field.

  Suppose that you want to retrieve a customer record by entering the name of the customer, rather than the unique `Cust_no`. To accomplish this, you can create an index based on customer names, keeping this index separate from the database table. Before retrieving a record from the table, the index is searched for the record containing the specified customer name. If the search is successful, the record location of the customer is identified. This allows for direct access of the customer's record.

- **Queries**—Queries are questions asked of a database. In Visual Basic, an English-like language named Structured Query Language (SQL) is used to retrieve data from a database. The following is an example of SQL:

  ```
  SELECT Cust_Name, Cust_phone
  FROM Customer
  WHERE Customer.Cust_Name = 'D.D. Smiley'
  ```

  This SQL query can be read as follows: Display the customer name and the customer telephone number from the table for the customer named D.D. Smiley.

23.1.2   Setting Relationships

Besides defining tables, records, fields, primary and foreign keys, and indexes, constructing a relational database requires the setting of relationships between tables, using primary and foreign keys. The relationships permitted include one-to-one (1:1), one-to-many (1:N), and many-to-many (M:N). The way of depicting a one-to-many relationship is shown in Figure 23.2. This diagram depicts what is termed the database schema.

Figure 23.2   *In this one-to-many relationship, one sales representative is responsible for many customers.*

In this example, each sales representative number can be found in many customer records. Stated as a rule, each sales representative can be responsible for several customers.

For each customer, however, there is one and only one sales representative, as indicated by the number 1. Stated as a rule for each customer, there is one, and only one, sales representative.

Objective 23.2   Using the Data Control

The relational database native to Visual Basic is the *Jet database engine.* This underlying database is the same database engine used by Microsoft Access. With Visual Basic, it is possible to build your own database. Such a database will have an .MDB extension just as an Access database does. It is possible for Visual Basic to open and manipulate a database developed in Access, and the reverse also is true.

The underlying Jet engine also can be used in combination with specially designed software drivers to open and manipulate other databases, including Btrieve, Paradox, dBASE, and FoxPro. Learning to exploit the Jet database engine will take up most of Chapter 24, "Using Data Access Objects," and Chapter 26, "Working with Objects from Microsoft Office."

23.2.1   Data Control Properties

The easiest way to connect to Visual Basic's built-in database capabilities is to use the Data control. By simply setting Data control properties, it is possible to connect to a database without writing a single line of code. Several Data control properties are key to the control's functionality. As you work through these properties, you might want to place a Data control on a form and manipulate it as you read.

The first property to observe is `DatabaseName`. Its complete syntax is the following:

```
[form.]datacontrol.DatabaseName [= pathname]
```

The component `pathname` is a string expression describing the location of the database file. For a database named Design1.MDB, you could assign it to a Data control, named `Data1`, with such an expression as the following:

```
Data1.DatabaseName = "C:\data\design1.mdb"
```

An alternative form is to write the following:

```
Data1.DatabaseName = App.Path & "\design1.mdb"
```

With this form, it is assumed that the database is stored with the Visual Basic application.

In design-time, the default database extension in the `DatabaseName` property dialog box is determined by the `Connect` property. Examine this property and you will see it's possible to connect to Paradox and dBASE databases, Excel and Lotus spreadsheets, and ASCII text databases. It also is possible to connect to ODBC (Open Database Connectivity) databases, such as SQL Server and Oracle. The default is Microsoft Access. With this database, no `Connect` property needs to be set.

After setting the path and the `Connect` properties, a third Data control property, the `RecordSource` property, must be set. The `RecordSource` must correspond to a type of record supported by the database. For example, in a database consisting of several tables, select the table you want to draw records from. The following is the complete syntax for this property:

```
[form.]datactl.RecordSource [= {tablename | sqlstatement | queryname} ]
```

The `RecordSource` can be a specific database table (`tablename`), a structured query language query (`sqlstatement`), or the name of a stored query (`queryname`). In the Jet engine, this last option is known as a `QueryDef` object, which is explored in Chapter 24.

Closely associated with the `RecordSource` property is the `RecordSetType` property. The complete syntax for this property is as follows:

```
datactrl.RecordsetType [= value ]
```

Table 23.1 shows the settings for value.

TABLE 23.1   Settings for value in the *RecordSetType* Property

Constant	Value	Description
vbRSTypeTable	0	A table-type `Recordset`.
vbRSTypeDynaset	1	The default. A dynaset-type `Recordset`.
vbRSTypeSnapshot	2	A snapshot-type `Recordset`.

As specified by the Jet database engine, a `Recordset` can be one of the following types:

- **Table-type `Recordset`**—A data set that is part of the underlying database and can be updated.

- **Dynaset-type `Recordset`**—A data set that is returned from a query and can be updated.

- **Snapshot-type `Recordset`**—A data set that can be from either a table or a query, but is read-only and, therefore, cannot be updated.

The `Recordset` object is explored in detail in section 23.2.4, "Working with *Recordset* Objects," later in this chapter.

23.2.2   Adding Bound Controls

After the properties have been established for the Data control, bound controls can be added to display the contents of database records. A *bound control* is a data-aware control. When a control is bound, Visual Basic provides field values from the database to that control. With a bound control, moving to a different record in the database leads to its display on a form.

Bound controls are not limited to text boxes. Visual Basic allows check boxes, image boxes, labels, picture boxes, text boxes, and other controls to be bound to the Data control.

Two important properties when adding bound controls to the database are the `DataSource` and the `DataField`. The `DataSource` property refers to the source of the database records to be returned and displayed. If the data control is to return customer records and place one field in a text box, for example, the `DataSource` for that text box first must be bound to the data control. The `DataField` property then refers to the specific field within the record to be bound to a control. It specifies a field, such as the customer name, that is to be bound to the text box. The syntax for a `DataField` is as follows:

```
[form.] control.DataField [=fieldname]
```

Thus, if the `txtCustomer` text box is to display the field `customer name`, the property should be set as the following:

```
txtCustomer.DataField = "customer name"
```

Exercise 23.1   A Beginning Database

Design a form to open a database and display the returned records using bound controls. The name of the database is Design1.MDB and is supplied on the disk with this book. Figure 23.3 shows the form that you are to create.

The schema for this database is shown in Figure 23.4. As indicated, a customer places an order for a single product. When placing an order, the order number, customer number, product number, date required, and quantity ordered must be recorded.

Figure 23.3 *The Visual Basic form contains a single Data control named* Customer.

Figure 23.4 *The Design1.MDB schema contains three tables: a customer table, customer orders table, and a product table.*

1. Place a Data control on the form (the default name is Data1), the six text boxes, and the six labels. Add the captions to the labels. The text box names are **txtID**, **txtName**, **txtStreet**, **txtCity**, **txtState**, and **txtZip**.

2. Make sure a copy of the Design1.MDB file is in the same directory as your Visual Basic project (for example, Ch23\Exercises\). In the DatabaseName property of the Data control, click the ellipses button, and select the Design1.MDB database in the dialog box that appears.

   ```
   <drive>:\[<pathname>\]DESIGN1.MDB
   ```

   Alternatively, you can type in the full path for the database. If the database is stored on the C drive, for example, you might type C:\VBTXT6\DATA\ DESIGN1.MDB.

   continues

3. Change the RecordSource property for the Data control to Customer by selecting the table from the drop-down list.

4. Change the RecordSetType to 0 ' table. This indicates that you want to examine the Customer table in the database saved as DESIGN1.MDB.

5. Bind all text boxes to the Data control. This can be done in two ways. Click the form and drag the cursor to enclose all text boxes. Then, set the DataSource property to Data1. The alternative is to set the DataSource to Data1 for each control, one at a time.

6. After the controls are bound, set each data field. For the txtID, set the DataField property to customer number; for the txtName, set the DataField to customer name, and so on. Click the DataField box with the mouse to move to the next setting or make the selection from the drop-down list box.

7. Run and test your design. You should be able to display the six customer records stored in this database by navigating through the database with the Data control.

23.2.3   The *Refresh* Method

When working with the Data control, the Refresh method is needed when opening a database or reopening a database with a different set of Data control properties. Also use Refresh when you want to repopulate a Recordset. With this method, the underlying query is re-executed, and the Data control automatically points to the first record and makes it current. The syntax for this method is as follows:

```
[form.] datacontrol.Refresh
```

The component datacontrol specifies the database name and record source.

If the Refresh method fails to open the database, a trappable error will result. You can use the following code to determine the cause of failure should Refresh fail to open a database:

```
Data1.Refresh
If Data1.Database Is Nothing Then
    MsgBox "Database opening failed"
End If
If Data1.Recordset Is Nothing Then
    MsgBox "Database recordset failed"
End If
```

23.2.4 Working with *Recordset* Objects

When working with a database, Visual Basic treats the rows of data returned to the Data control as a `Recordset` object. This object, like most others, features a number of methods which are explained in Table 23.2.

TABLE 23.2 Methods of the *Recordset* Object

Method	Description
AddNew	Clears the buffer in preparation for creating a new record in a table or dynaset
Delete	Deletes the current record in a specified table or dynaset
Edit	Opens the current record in a specified `Recordset` for editing
Update	Saves the contents of the copy buffer to a specified table or dynaset
FindFirst	Locates the first record that satisfies specified criteria and makes it the current record
FindLast	Locates the last record that satisfies specified criteria and makes it the current record
FindNext	Locates the next record that satisfies specified criteria and makes it the current record
FindPrevious	Locates the previous record that satisfies specified criteria and makes it the current record
MoveFirst	Moves to the first record in a specified `Recordset` and makes it the current record
MoveLast	Moves to the last record in a specified `Recordset` and makes it the current record
MoveNext	Moves to the next record in a specified `Recordset` and makes it the current record
MovePrevious	Moves to the previous record in a specified `Recordset` and makes it the current record
Seek	In a table-type `Recordset`, moves to the indexed record specified by method arguments

Besides methods that are applied to the `Recordset` object, `Recordset` object properties also can be referenced or changed. Consider the following instruction:

```
data1.Recordset("order number") = CInt(txtOrdNum.Text)
```

This instruction assigns the integer value of the string placed in the text box to the order number field of a specific record in a designated Recordset. Recordset objects also have BOF (beginning of file) and EOF (end of file) properties. The following instruction would help prevent navigating past the end of a database:

```
Data1.Recordset.MoveNext
If Data1.Recordset.EOF then
    MsgBox "End of File"
    Data1.Recordset.MovePrevious
Else
'    code to update status bar and/or add a new record
End if
```

As long as you are using the Data control to move through records, you needn't worry about this. The Data control prevents these kinds of errors automatically.

There are three other principal sources of errors that you must remain mindful of when modifying data in database tables, as follows:

- **Data validation errors**—These errors occur when you seek to assign data to a field that the field is not designed to handle. Incorrect data types can generate these types of errors. Assigning a string to a field that expects a numeric value, for example, will usually generate an error of this type.

    Other data validation errors occur when data violates rules put in place when the database table was designed. Suppose that you have a Ship_Date field for the Order table. You might enter a data validation rule that says the Ship_Date value cannot precede the date placed in the Date_Ordered field. Microsoft Access allows you to place these type of range limitations on numeric data fields.

- **Entity integrity errors**—These errors occur when you attempt to add a second record with the same primary key as a record currently stored in the database.

- **Referential integrity errors**—These complex errors occur when you seek to modify data in one table, but it violates the data set in another table. Take another look at the schema in Figure 23.2. If you seek to remove a sales representative who is assigned to a customer, such a deletion will not be allowed. Before the sales representative can be deleted, all references to that person in the Customer table must be changed.

    In the schema shown in Figure 23.4, referential integrity errors also occur if you attempt to add a customer number to the orders table when that number does not represent a stored customer's primary key.

Exercise 23.2 Adding and Deleting a Record in a Database

Besides displaying records stored in a database, you can directly use Visual Basic in modifying the contents of stored records. This exercise asks you to open the customer orders table in the database, add a record, and delete a record. A copy of the database, named Design2.MDB, has been placed on file on the student disk. This database has the same schema as Design1.mdb. Figure 23.5 shows the modified form for this exercise.

Figure 23.5 *The data form layout contains three new buttons: New, Update, and Delete.*

1. Design the form as shown in Figure 23.5. For the Data control, make the following settings:

   ```
   DatabaseName = "C:\Design2.mdb      'or set your own path"
   RecordSource = "Customer orders"
   RecordSetType =  0 ' Table
   ```

   Name the new commands **cmdNew**, **cmdUpdate**, and **cmdDelete**. Name the text boxes **txtOrdNum**, **txtCustNum**, **txtProdNum**, **txtDate**, and **txtQuantity**. Set the DataFields and DataSource for each text box. Add all labels as shown.

2. Write the cmdNew_Click() procedure as follows:

   ```
   Private Sub cmdNew_Click()
      cmdUpdate.Enabled = False
      data1.RecordSource = "Customer orders"
      txtOrdNum.SetFocus
      data1.Recordset.AddNew
      cmdNew.Enabled = False
      cmdUpdate.Enabled = True
   End Sub
   ```

   The keywords important to this code include the following:

   ■ **RecordSource**—Sets the table from which to draw records.

   ■ **Refresh**—Updates the data structure of a Data control and goes to the beginning of the Recordset.

   ■ **RecordSet.AddNew**—Adds a buffer in memory for a new record in the specified RecordSource that clears all bound controls.

   continues

3. Write the `cmdUpdate_Click()` procedure as follows:

```
Private Sub cmdUpdate_Click()
  On Error GoTo cmdUpdateErr:

  Data1.Recordset("order number") = CInt(txtOrdNum.Text)
  Data1.Recordset("customer number") = CInt(txtCustNum.Text)
  Data1.Recordset("product number") = CInt(txtProdNum.Text)
  Data1.Recordset("date required") = CDate(txtDate.Text)
  Data1.Recordset("quantity ordered") = CInt(txtQuantity.Text)
  Data1.Recordset.Update
  cmdNew.Enabled = True
  Exit Sub
cmdUpdateErr:
  MsgBox Str$(Err) & "   " & Err.Description, 0, "Error in
➡Update"
End Sub
```

In this case, the `data1.Recordset.Update` instruction complements the `data1.Recordset.AddNew` instruction. It assigns values to the record in memory and writes the data to the database.

4. Write the `cmdDelete_Click()` procedure as follows:

```
Private Sub cmdDelete_Click()
  data1.RecordSource = "Customer orders"
  data1.Recordset.Delete
End Sub
```

The key instruction is `data1.Recordset.Delete`. The `Delete` method removes the current record from the database.

5. Add a record to the database. To avoid violating integrity rules, the following are the values that can be added for product and customer numbers:

Product Number	Customer Number
5000	1000
5001	1001
5002	1002
5003	1003
5004	1004
5005	

Add the following data to the data entry screen. If order number 10059 already has been entered, delete this order and fill in the new information for 10059.

Order number = 10059

Date required = 7/15/99

Quantity ordered = 500

6. After adding the data, click Update.

7. Find record 10059, and click Delete to remove the record from the database.

8. Place a product number or customer number that does not exist in the Product or Customer tables, respectively, and observe the error that occurs.

Exercise 23.3 Adding Editing to a Design

Add one control to the preceding design: a command that allows you to edit a record, as shown in Figure 23.6. With editing, the Edit method is used, which locks the record to prevent changes by others. After changes are made, the Update method is required. With either Edit or AddNew, the "page" around a record is locked until the Update method has completed writing to the database.

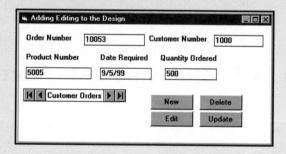

Figure 23.6 *You use the Edit button to lock a record in place while it is being revised.*

1. Add the command button as shown to the design and change the name to **cmdEdit**. This exercise uses Design3.mdb, which is found on the companion disk. Make sure all of the appropriate text boxes are bound to the correct fields of the Customer Order table.

2. Write the following cmdEdit_Click() procedure:

```
Private Sub cmdEdit_Click()
    cmdNew.Enabled = False
    cmdUpdate.Enabled = False
    data1.RecordSource = "Customer orders"
    data1.Recordset.Edit
    cmdUpdate.Enabled = True
    cmdEdit.Enabled = False
End Sub
```

continues

3. Write the following cmdUpdate_Click() procedure:

```
Private Sub cmdUpdate_Click()
  On Error GoTo cmdUpdateErr:
  Data1.Recordset("order number") = CInt(txtOrdNum.Text)
  Data1.Recordset("customer number") = CInt(txtCustNum.Text)
  Data1.Recordset("product number") = CInt(txtProdNum.Text)
  Data1.Recordset("date required") = CDate(Trim(txtDate.Text))
  Data1.Recordset("quantity ordered") = CInt(txtQuantity.Text)
  Data1.Recordset.Update
  cmdNew.Enabled = True
  cmdEdit.Enabled = True
Exit Sub
cmdUpdateErr:
  MsgBox Str$(Err) & "   " & Err.Description, 0, "Error
↳encountered in Update"
End Sub
```

In this example, the instruction Recordset.Edit allows a record stored in the database to be revised. The Edit method alone, however, is not sufficient for updating. After changes are made to the record, the Update method must be employed to record the changes.

Objective 23.3   Querying Data Stored in a Database

Visual Basic supports a query language known as *Structured Query Language* (SQL). Although a complete discussion of this language falls outside the scope of this text, following is an overview of some important query concepts.

SQL is a scripting language you can use to create tables, define the relationship among tables, and, most importantly for Visual Basic developers, manipulate the data held in tables. The most frequent use of SQL is to extract data from a database and place the data in a result set. The snapshot (read-only) and dynaset (updatable) types of Recordsets often are result sets from this type of query. Read-only queries begin with a SELECT statement, which is written to allow you to select a set of records that matches a prescribed set of criteria.

When using SQL, use SQL statements that conform to the following form (using the SELECT statement as an example):

```
SELECT the following items
FROM this table
  [WHERE(match this or these criteria)]
```

Observe that the WHERE clause is optional. For example, the following code features the wild card (*):

```
SELECT *
FROM product;
```

The query can be read as follows: Display all values for all products stored in the product table.

Likewise, consider the following statements:

```
SELECT order_number
FROM customer_orders
WHERE quantity_ordered >= 1000;
```

They can be read as follows: Display all order numbers contained in the customer orders table where the quantity ordered is greater than, or equal to, 1,000.

Exercise 23.4   Using a Query to Retrieve a Set of Records

Use a SQL statement to retrieve a set of records from the product table. Specifically, you are asked in this exercise to examine a subset of customer orders. Figure 23.7 and Figure 23.8 show the designs of the two forms for this exercise. Use Design4.MDB for this exercise, which is found on the companion CD.

Figure 23.7   *The Writing Queries form contains a button showing the name of the query to execute.*

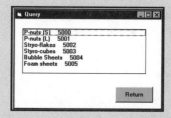

Figure 23.8   *The Query form shows the results of the executed query.*

1. Design **frmOpen** and **frmQuery** as shown, adding the End procedure to frmOpen and the Return procedure to frmQuery. Name the List All Products button **cmdQuery**. The list box on frmQuery is named **lstResults**. The command button on frmQuery is named **cmdReturn**. Save frmOpen to disk as **f23-4a.frm** and frmQuery to disk as **f23-4b.frm**.

2. Set the Data control properties on frmQuery as follows:

```
RecordsetType = 2 ' Snapshot
```

continues

Exercise 23.4   continued

3. Write the `cmdQuery_Click()` procedure as follows:

```
Private Sub cmdQuery_Click()
    frmOpen.Hide
    frmQuery.Show
    frmQuery!Data1.DatabaseName = App.Path & "\Design4.mdb"
    'Execute query
    frmQuery!Data1.RecordSource = "SELECT [Product name],
➥[Product number] FROM Product"
    frmQuery!Data1.Refresh
 ' Clear the List box
  frmQuery.lstResults.Clear
    'Retrieve data from database
    Do While Not frmQuery!Data1.Recordset.EOF
       If Not IsNull(frmQuery!Data1.Recordset(0)) Then
          frmQuery!lstResults.AddItem
➥frmQuery!Data1.Recordset("Product Name") & "     " &
frmQuery!Data1.Recordset("Product Number")
       End If
       frmQuery!Data1.Recordset.MoveNext
    Loop
    frmQuery!Data1.Refresh
End Sub
```

Following are several new concepts introduced by this procedure:

- The record source is represented by the following query:

  ```
  "SELECT [Product name], [Product number] FROM Product"
  ```

  With this syntax, field names with spaces in them must have brackets around them.

- The `data1.Recordset.MoveNext` method moves from one record to the next in the `Recordset`.

- The following statement retrieves the first field from the record:

  ```
  data1.Recordset(0)
  ```

  If the second field is to be displayed, use the following:

  ```
  data1.Recordset(1)
  ```

- The loop continues until the `Recordset` reaches the end-of-file marker (`EOF`). At that point, processing stops.

- The `AddItem` method displays records that match the specifications of the query.

4. On the second form, write the `cmdReturn` procedure as follows:

```
Private Sub cmdReturn_Click()
    frmQuery.Hide
    frmOpen.Show
End Sub
```

5. For the Data control, set the `Visible` property to `False`.

6. Test your query design.

Care must be taken not to enter product numbers or customer numbers that do not already exist in the Product or Customer tables when modifying records in the Customer Order table. Otherwise, errors will result. It is not possible, for example, to process an order for a customer who is not found in the database, or for a product that does not exist. One way to prevent these types of errors is to present data in related tables as combo boxes for the user.

Exercise 23.5   Using Queries to Populate Combo Boxes

Modify Exercise 23.3 to permit a user to navigate through records with the Data control, but not to enter new values for product number or customer number while navigating. Valid choices are presented from which to make selections when a user enters AddNew or Edit mode.

To accomplish these twin functions, replace the text boxes for inputting customer number and product number with labels. On top of these labels, place combo boxes with their Visible properties set to False. When the user enters AddNew or Edit mode, these combo boxes will be made visible. Populate the combo boxes by adding another Data control to the form and setting its Visible property to False. Use DESIGN5.MDB for this exercise. Figure 23.9 shows the interface during runtime in AddNew mode.

Figure 23.9   *The revised form now contains two combo boxes: one for displaying the list of product numbers and one for displaying the list of customer numbers.*

1. Save the form and project from Exercise 23.3 under a new name (for example, save **f23-3.frm** as **f23-5.frm** and **p23-3.vbp** as **p23-5.vbp**). Change the Name property of the project to **P23_5**.

continues

2. Remove the two text boxes txtCusNum and txtProdNum from the form, and add two labels in their places: **lblCustomer** and **lblProduct**. Remove the caption from these labels and set the BorderStyle property to 1 (Fixed Single). Set the DataSource property for these labels to Data1 and the DataField property to customer number and product number, respectively.

3. Add two combo boxes to the form, and size them so they are directly over the labels. Name these combo boxes **cboCustomer** and **cboProduct**. Set the Style property for the two boxes to 0 (Dropdown List) and remove any value from the Text property.

4. Add a second Data control to the form, and set its Visible property to False.

5. In the Form_Load(), event add the following code:

```
Private Sub Form_Load()
  Data2.DatabaseName = App.Path & "\design5.mdb"
  ' populate the product combo box
  Data2.RecordSource = "Product"
  Data2.RecordsetType = 2 ' snapshot
  Data2.Refresh
  Do While Not Data2.Recordset.EOF
    cboProduct.AddItem Data2.Recordset("Product number")
    Data2.Recordset.MoveNext
  Loop
  cboProduct.ListIndex = 0
  'populate the customer combo box
  Data2.RecordSource = "Customer"
  Data2.RecordsetType = 2 ' snapshot
  Data2.Refresh
  Do While Not Data2.Recordset.EOF
    cboCustomer.AddItem Data2.Recordset("Customer number")
    Data2.Recordset.MoveNext
  Loop
  cboCustomer.ListIndex = 0

  Data1.DatabaseName = App.Path & "\design5.mdb"
  Data1.RecordSource = "Customer orders"
  Data1.RecordsetType = 0 ' table
  Data1.Refresh
End Sub
```

6. The cmdEdit_Click() event should now read as follows:

```
Private Sub cmdEdit_Click()
  cmdNew.Enabled = False
  cmdUpdate.Enabled = False
  Data1.RecordSource = "Customer orders"
  Data1.Recordset.Edit
  cmdUpdate.Enabled = True
  cmdEdit.Enabled = False
  cboCustomer.Visible = True
  cboProduct.Visible = True
  lblCustomer.Visible = False
  lblProduct.Visible = False
End Sub
```

7. The `cmdNew_Click()` event should now read as follows:

```
Private Sub cmdNew_Click()
  cmdEdit.Enabled = False
  Data1.RecordSource = "Customer orders"
  txtOrdNum.SetFocus

  Data1.Recordset.AddNew
  cmdNew.Enabled = False
  cmdUpdate.Enabled = True
  cboCustomer.Visible = True
  cboProduct.Visible = True
  lblCustomer.Visible = False
  lblProduct.Visible = False
End Sub
```

8. The `cmdUpdate_Click()` event should now read as follows:

```
Private Sub cmdUpdate_Click()
  On Error GoTo cmdUpdateErr:
  Data1.Recordset("order number") = CInt(txtOrdNum.Text)
  Data1.Recordset("customer number") = CInt(cboCustomer.Text)
  Data1.Recordset("product number") = CInt(cboProduct.Text)
  Data1.Recordset("date required") = CDate(Trim(txtDate.Text))
  Data1.Recordset("quantity ordered") = CInt(txtQuantity.Text)
  Data1.Recordset.Update
  cmdNew.Enabled = True
  cmdEdit.Enabled = True
  cboCustomer.Visible = False
  cboProduct.Visible = False
  lblCustomer.Visible = True
  lblProduct.Visible = True
Exit Sub

cmdUpdateErr:
  MsgBox Str$(Err) & "   " & Err.Description, 0, "Error
➥encountered in Update"
End Sub
```

9. Run and test the program. When you click New, the combo box drop-down arrows appear. Click New and add a new order. Click Edit, followed by Update. Delete the order you added.

Visual Basic also provides special data-bound custom controls to make the type of interface in Exercise 23.5 easier to create. Examine the online Help system of Visual Basic and explore the possibilities with the data-bound Combo Box, List Box, and Grid controls.

Objective 23.4   Building a Database Using Visual Data Manager

Besides opening and changing a database created by an external database application, you can create a database from within Visual Basic. This is accomplished by choosing Add-Ins, Visual Data. VisData, an abbreviation for Visual DataTools, is supplied as an executable with Visual Basic 6 and provides a graphical user interface that allows you to view and edit objects inside ODBC databases. If, for some reason, VisData does not appear, use Windows Explorer to find the file and double-click to start the program.

23.4.1   Creating a Database

When the VisData window appears, choose File, New to open a new database. A dialog box will appear, asking you to choose one of several databases. Select Access and the version supported by your computer. A second dialog box will then ask you to supply the name of the database. We called our database Classes.mdb. A copy of this database is placed on the companion CD. You can examine this copy using Access before you get started. If your version of Access is newer than the copy, you must convert it. Perform the following steps:

1. Close the copy of CLASSES.

2. Choose Tools, Database Utilities, and select Convert Database.

3. Name the database CLASSES1.

The procedure that we used to create this database follows. To replicate this procedure, give your database a new name.

After naming the database, you can add tables. To add a table, click the database window and click the right mouse button to open the dialog box shown in Figure 23.10. We typed ClassList for our table name.

You can define fields for a table after the table is created. To create a field, click Add Field. As shown in Figure 23.11, the field name, field type, and field size are used in defining a field. The field name is a field of your choice. We selected ClassNo for a field in the ClassList table.

Figure 23.10   *The Table Structure dialog box appears by clicking the right mouse button and selecting New_table.*

Figure 23.11   *The Add Field dialog box appears when you click the Add Field button shown in the Table Structure dialog box.*

The field types include Boolean, Byte, Integer, Long, Currency, Single, Double, Date/Time, Text (not string), Binary, and Memo. To add a fixed-length string to a table, select Text. To add an image, select Binary. To add a variable-length string, select Memo. The field size is used with variable length strings. With ClassNo, for example, you can select a field of type Integer.

Notice that you can set field validation rules, designate whether data is required for the field, and specify whether the field can contain zero-length values.

After the fields for the relational table have been established, you can further edit individual fields by making changes directly on the Table Structure dialog box. To do this, highlight the field to change, make the change, and press the Tab key.

After fields and data types have been established, a primary index and secondary indices can be set. Figure 23.12 shows this dialog box, as well as the additional fields we have added to the table. To reach it, click Add Index from the Table Structure dialog box. In Figure 23.12, you see the primary index being set. To set a secondary index, make similar settings, except do not click Primary index because there can only be one primary index for a table.

Figure 23.12   *The Add Index to ClassList dialog box appears when you click the Add Index button in the Table Structure dialog box.*

23.4.2   Entering Data into the Database

You must add data to each table in the database following table, field, and index definitions. To add data to a table, click the Build the Table button in the Table Structure dialog box, and double-click the ClassList icon that appears in the Database window. This opens the ClassList data entry window (see Figure 23.13). Initially, this table will be empty. We show it with data added.

Figure 23.13   *In the Database Window, double-click the ClassList table icon to open the Table:ClassList.*

With the data entry window facing you, click Add to open the Update dialog box (see Figure 23.14), fill in the data shown on Figure 23.13, and click the Update button. At this point, the dialog box shown in Figure 23.13 reappears with the data added. To add a second record, click Add, fill in the data, and click Update.

Figure 23.14   *Click Add on Table:ClassList to move to the Update dialog box, add the data, and click on Update.*

The Table Access window shown in Figure 23.13 contains six buttons, which are explained in Table 23.3. (By now you realize that these are methods that can be applied to a Recordset.)

TABLE 23.3   Table Access Window Buttons

Button	Description
Add	Adds new records to a table
Edit	Revises a record in the table
Delete	Deletes a record from the table
Seek	Invokes a Seek method using the primary index
Filter	Places a filter on the current table-type Recordset and loads the newly filtered Recordset into a dynaset/snapshot form
Close	Closes the table

Exercise 23.6   Using VisData to Create a New Database

This exercise asks you to explore the use of VisData. The database for this exercise is named Classes1.MDB.

1. Choose Add-Ins, Visual Data Manager.

2. Open the database Classes1.MDB stored on disk (an Access database).

3. Double-click on ClassList in the Database Window and scroll through the records stored in this database.

4. Click on Add to add a record to the database, using the data shown in Figure 23.13.

continues

Exercise 23.6   continued

5. Scroll through the database again.

6. Delete the record you added.

7. Do not save this exercise. By now you should have a better understanding of how VisData works.

23.4.3   Building Queries with VisData

In addition to building tables, setting field properties, and defining table relationships, VisData also permits you to test and save queries. A separate SQL Statement window allows you to write, test, and save queries. These saved queries are QueryDef objects, which are explored in greater depth in Chapter 24, "Using Data Access Objects." You can use saved queries to create Recordsets. Once saved, they will appear in the drop-down list box in the RecordSource property of a Data control.

Exercise 23.7   Using the VisData SQL Statement Window

1. Open the Classes.MDB database from VisData.

2. Without opening the ClassList table, enter the SQL statement you see in Figure 23.15.

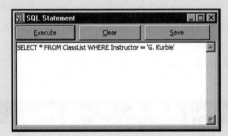

Figure 23.15   *This is one possible SQL query you can write to determine the type of information stored in the ClassList table.*

3. Click Execute to test the query. When the dialog box asks if this is a SQL Pass Through query, click No.

4. Save this query. When asked for a name, call it **Query1**.

5. Return to the Database window to test the saved query. Double-click **Query1** and click Yes when asked, "Use DynaSet?" Experiment with other types of queries.

Exercise 23.8   Combining Visual Basic with the Created Database

You can use a database created by Visual Basic like a database created externally. This exercise asks you to list the records stored in the database Classes.MDB. Figure 23.16 shows the interface you are asked to use.

Figure 23.16   *You can display the Class List by using a query to process the data in the ClassList table.*

1. Create the interface as shown, adding a Data control.

2. Set the following Data control properties:

```
DatabaseName = "C:\Classes.MDB  ' place correct path to your
➥database
RecordSource = "ClassList"
RecordSourceType = 2 ' snapshot
Visible = False
```

3. Write the following cmdSchedule_Click() procedure:

```
Private Sub cmdSchedule_Click()
    data1.RecordSource = "Select * from classlist"
    data1.Refresh
    Do While Not data1.Recordset.EOF
        If Not IsNull(data1.Recordset(0)) Then
            lstResult.AddItem data1.Recordset("ClassNo")
            lstResult.AddItem data1.Recordset("ClassName")
            lstResult.AddItem data1.Recordset("StartDate")
            lstResult.AddItem data1.Recordset("EndDate")
            lstResult.AddItem data1.Recordset("Credits")
            lstResult.AddItem data1.Recordset("Cost")
            lstResult.AddItem data1.Recordset("Instructor")
            lstResult.AddItem ""
        End If
        data1.Recordset.MoveNext
    Loop
End Sub
```

4. Run and test your program.

continues

> ### Exercise 23.8   continued
>
> In this example, a loop reads all records on file. When a null value is found, processing stops. After the contents of a record have been displayed, the `MoveNext` method is required to advance to the next record in the `Recordset`. This method explains how Visual Basic moves from record to record in a relational file.

Chapter Summary

Although this chapter presents many topics, they all center on how Visual Basic implements the relational database model through the use of the Jet engine and makes the database easy to use through the Data control. The chapter also introduces the Visual Data Manager tool for building database tables and testing and saving queries.

In the relational model, databases are constructed from a series of tables. Tables, themselves, are composed of rows and columns in which rows represent individual records and columns represent the fields of those records. Tables have a primary key index, which represents a field that has a unique value for every record in the table. Tables also can have foreign keys, which represent data shared in common between tables. In Visual Basic, queries are written in SQL to retrieve data from the database or manipulate the database itself.

The `Data` control allows easy access to Visual Basic and other databases. Important properties for the `Data` control include the `DataBaseName` property, identifying the path to the database; the `RecordSource` property, identifying whether the `Data` control contains data from a table or a query; and the `RecordSetType` property, identifying whether the data contained by the `Data` control is an updatable data set from a table (table-type `Recordset`), query (dynaset-type `Recordset`), or a read-only data set (snapshot-type `Recordset`).

Data-aware controls can be bound to a `Data` control by setting their `DataSource` property to a `Data` control in design time and their `DataField` property to an appropriate field in the `Data` control's `Recordset`.

Key methods for working with `Recordsets` include `AddNew`, `Edit`, `Update`, and `Delete`—the only one that can write data to the database is the `Update` method. Loops can be used in conjunction with the `Recordset` `Move` methods to iterate through a `Recordset` so that data can be displayed or amended.

The Visual Data Manager tool helps you build Jet engine databases. Table elements can be designed and relationships between tables set. You also can test and save queries. Saved queries become `QueryDef` objects, and can be referenced for use later as `RecordSources` for the `Data` control.

Skill-Building Exercises

These exercises ask you to work with a number of databases stored on the companion CD. The first two exercises ask you to work with the Biblio database to allow the user to examine the author's table. The next three exercises ask you to work with the Cinama2 database. The final two exercises ask you to work with a new database named EinUniv (or Einstein University). Use the forms created for the exercises in Chapter 21 for these exercises.

1. A database called Biblio.MDB comes with Visual Basic 6 software. Add a Data control to a form, and bind three labels to the three fields in the Authors table so that the user can scroll through the table.

2. Using Biblio.MDB, write a program that lists all authors whose last names begin with the letters A–L in one list box, and those whose last names begin with the letters M–Z in another list box.

3. On your disc is a program called Cinema2.MDB. Use VisData to examine this database. Write a program that lists film titles and the years released from the Film Titles table in a list box.

4. Write a program that allows new records to be added to the Directors table in Cinema2.MDB.

5. Write a program that lists film titles from Cinema2.MDB in a list box. When the user clicks a film title, display the director's name by using the Seek method. (Hint: Place the Director ID from the Film Titles table in a separate array. When the user clicks the list box, use the ListIndex property to retrieve the director ID from the array, and the Seek method in the Director's Table to retrieve the Director's name.) This exercise requires two Data controls.

6. In the next two exercises, you use the database EinUniv.mdb, which you can find on the companion disc. Some of the code has been left in for you while other code you are asked to add. The schema for this database is shown in Figure 23.17.

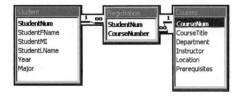

Figure 23.17   *The EinUniv.mdn database schema should assist you in the next two exercises.*

Alter the program on the companion CD (sb23-6.vbp) to allow the user to Enter New Student Data and Add New Courses to the Einstein University database.

7. Extend the Einstein University program by allowing users to make course registrations. Use a single data control on frmRegistration. Call a procedure in the Form_Load event that populates the cboStudent combo box with student name and social security number separated by a colon. Also display the student's social security number in the label lblStudentID whenever the combo box is clicked. Code the cboCourse combo box in a similar manner. Use the Student Social Security number and the Course numbers to update the EinUniv.mdb Registration table.

Examine the code on frmReports in the previous two exercises. Observe how the MSFlexGrid control may be used in bound mode.

USING DATA ACCESS OBJECTS

In Chapter 23, "Accessing and Manipulating Databases with Visual Basic," you used the Data control to open and access the Jet engine. This is the simplest method for opening databases, and the Data control must be used if you want to bind controls to data. However, large data sets bound to Data controls can appreciably degrade performance. For full flexibility and programmatic control, the Jet engine enables the developer to exploit Data Access Objects (DAOs): In large database applications, this is how the Jet engine is used.

Because the Jet engine is a full-featured database, you will perform a large number of tasks relating to DAOs in this chapter. Even with the following extensive list, this book does not cover all of the DAOs. Instead, it covers the essential core of the Jet engine. With this foundation, you should be able to work with the DAOs not specifically addressed. After you complete the eight exercises of this chapter, you will be able to perform the following tasks:

- Review the Jet engine object model

- Iterate through the Jet engine object collection hierarchy using For Each...Next structures

- Use the OpenDatabase method on the Workspace object

- Use the OpenRecordset method with database and other DAO objects

- Use Recordset Move methods

- Understand the varieties of syntax in reading and writing field values

- Use the Seek method on indexed table fields

- Use Find methods on Recordsets

- Use AddNew, Edit, and Update methods with Recordsets

- Open and use a QueryDef object

- Create a QueryDef object

- Open and use a Parameter query

Chapter Objectives

The preceding extensive list of tasks is incorporated into the following four objectives:

1. Understanding the Jet engine and working with DAO collections
2. Opening databases and Recordsets
3. Working with the Recordset object
4. Learning to create, retrieve, and use QueryDef objects

Objective 24.1   Understanding the Jet Engine and Working with DAO Collections

The Jet engine features an object model based on collections. A *collection* is an ordered set of items that can be referred to as a *unit*. It provides a convenient way to refer to a related group of items as a single object.

Implicit in the design of an object model is the notion of a collection hierarchy. An object model contains a set (or collection) of objects. Each of the objects in the set (or collection) also can contain a collection. At the top of the collection hierarchy is a single object. Below that object, a series of other nested object collections can proliferate.

In Chapter 19, "Object Types, Variables, and Collections," you iterated through an application's Forms collection and then through each form's Controls collection. In that hierarchy, the application contained a collection of forms. Each form, in turn, contained a collection of controls. The map of collections in an application is thus called the *application object model*.

24.1.1   The Jet Engine Object Model

The object model for the Jet database engine, like other object models, displays a hierarchy of objects (see Figure 24.1). At the top of the object model is the DBEngine. All parts of the Jet engine are nested collections contained within the DBEngine. In Visual Basic, collections are always referenced with the plural (for example, TableDefs) and individual members with the singular (for example, TableDef).

Examine the Jet database model carefully. The Database object is nested within the Workspace object. The Workspace object acts as a container for open databases and provides security for the database. Users and groups also are collections nested within the Workspace object. These objects (which you will not be working with in this chapter) contain properties and methods for providing user passwords and permissions.

Figure 24.1   *The Jet engine object collection contains a collection of* Workspaces *and within each* Workspace *a collection of* Databases.

Other DAO objects should be familiar to you from Chapter 23, including the following:

- **TableDef**—A stored table definition.

- **QueryDef**—A stored query definition.

- **Recordset**—An object that presents a cursored view into a database table or a query result. Rows of data are stored in a buffer, and one record—the current record—is pointed to at a time.

- **Index**—A stored index associated with a TableDef or table-type Recordset.

- **Field**—A column of data that is contained in a TableDef, QueryDef, RecordSet, or Index.

Appendix B, "Data Access Object Collections, Properties, and Methods," contains a list of the core DAOs. In addition to the tables you define yourself, the Jet engine maintains system tables for each .MDB database that you create. These tables are not generally accessible, and serve such Jet engine tasks as tracking object database structures for database repair and maintaining information on database security. These tables have an MSys prefix.

Although not illustrated, the DAO contains a Connections collection under the Workspace object. A Connection object permits the use of ODBC Direct, a library of database drivers written to bypass the Jet engine and connect directly with large, server-hosted, ODBC-compliant databases, such as SQL Server and Oracle. These new drivers provide much faster performance when accessing these types of databases than earlier versions of the Jet engine. This book focuses on Jet databases exclusively. After you learn to work with the object hierarchy of Database objects and Recordset objects, using ODBC Direct is not difficult.

24.1.2   Collection Syntax and Collection Defaults

A collection behaves somewhat like an array. Unlike the Collection object you have used with objects instantiated from class modules, DAO collections have a zero-based index. You can access individual members by referencing this index and by navigating through nested collections using the dot (.) navigation operator. Consider, for example, the following code fragment:

```
DBEngine.Workspaces(0).Databases(0).TableDefs(0).Fields("ProductName")
```

It refers to the ProductName field in the first TableDef of the TableDefs collection, the first Database of the Databases collection, and the first Workspace of the Workspaces collection of the DBEngine.

Fortunately, fields usually are not referenced this way. Instead, you typically work with Recordset objects that provide an easier syntax.

Referencing individual object values through long nested collections can make code complicated to read and maintain. Most DAOs have default collections that ease this task. The default collection for a Database object, for example, is TableDefs. For TableDef, Index, and Recordset objects, the default collection is Fields. When you create a database, these collections are stored much the way Forms and Controls collections are stored. For QueryDef objects, the default is Parameters. These defaults help shorten the navigational path down the collection hierarchy. To get the value from a field from a table, for example, you can use

```
tblProduct![Product Name]
```

rather than

```
tblProduct.Fields![Product Name]
```

because Fields is the default collection for a TableDef object. Similarly, because TableDefs is the default collection for Database objects, you could use the following expression to read or assign a value to the Product Name field of the current record:

```
db!tblProduct![Product Name]   ' where db is a variable of type Database
```

24.1.3   Iterating Through Database Collections with *For Each...Next* Statements

To work with collections, you can use the For Each...Next statement, as follows:

```
For Each element In group
    [statements]
    [Exit For]
    [statements]
Next [element]
```

In this syntax, element is a counter variable of an object type contained within the collection. To iterate through a database TableDefs collection, you would use code similar to the following:

```
Dim tdef as TableDef
For Each tdef in db.TableDefs
   Print tdef.Name
   ' or other code you want to execute on collection members
Next
```

This syntax and its usage will become clearer when you work through Exercise 24.1. For the exercises that follow, you use the Cinema.mdb database, a sample database that has been placed on the companion disk. This database is a simple three-table database. In one table are listed movie titles and their years of release. In another table are five movie directors and data about them. A third table consists solely of the movie title ID numbers and the directors' ID numbers. The tables, their primary and foreign keys, and their relationships are diagrammed in Figure 24.2.

Figure 24.2   *The Cinema database schema indicates that a film director is associated with one or more films, and that each film has only one director.*

Exercise 24.1   Iterating Database Collections

In this lengthy exercise, you work with the main DAO collections of the Cinema database. You use several DAO methods that have not yet been introduced, but the code should be understandable. Objective 24.2, "Opening Databases and Recordsets," covers these new Visual Basic statements and methods in detail and examines their syntax.

1. Design the interface illustrated in Figure 24.3. Use three list boxes (**lstTable**, **lstFields**, and **lstFieldData**). Use a text box to display query data (**txtSQL**). Name the combo box **cboQueryDef**. Change the Multiline property of txtSQL to True and set its Scrollbars property to 2-Vertical.

continues

Exercise 24.1 continued

Figure 24.3 *This interface is designed to show the internal makeup of the Cinema database.*

2. Important: Examine <u>P</u>roject, Refe<u>r</u>ences and click Microsoft DAO 3.51 Object Library if this reference is not checked.

3. At the form module level, make the following declarations:

```
Dim ws As DAO.Workspace

Dim db As DAO.Database
```

4. In the `Form_Load()` event, enter the following code:

```
Private Sub Form_Load()
    Dim tdef As TableDef
    Dim qdef As QueryDef
    Set ws = DBEngine.Workspaces(0)
    'Set correct path if necessary
    Set db = ws.OpenDatabase(App.Path & "\cinema.mdb")

    For Each tdef In db.TableDefs
        'display non-system tables in list box
        If Left(tdef.Name, 4) <> "MSys" Then lstTables.AddItem
tdef.Name & "," & tdef.RecordCount
    Next
    'display querydefs in combo box
    For Each qdef In db.QueryDefs
        cboQueryDef.AddItem qdef.Name
    Next
    cboQueryDef.ListIndex = 0
End Sub
```

5. In the `lstTables_Click()` event, enter the following code:

```
Private Sub lstTables_Click()
    Dim tablename As String
    Dim testtable As TableDef
    Dim tfield As Field
    Dim position As Integer

    lstFields.Clear            ' clear other list boxes
    lstFieldData.Clear

    ' get tablename from lstbox
    tablename = lstTables.List(lstTables.ListIndex)
    position = InStr(tablename, ",")
    tablename = Left(tablename, position - 1)

    Set testtable = db.TableDefs(tablename)

    For Each tfield In testtable.Fields
        lstFields.AddItem tfield.Name
    Next
End Sub
```

6. In the `lstFields_Click()` event, enter the following code:

```
Private Sub lstFields_Click()
    Dim tablename, fieldname As String
    Dim testtable As TableDef
    Dim tfield As Field
    Dim position As Integer
    Dim dtype As String
    lstFieldData.Clear
    ' get tablename form lstbox
    tablename = lstTables.List(lstTables.ListIndex)
    position = InStr(tablename, ",")
    tablename = Left(tablename, position - 1)
    fieldname = lstFields.List(lstFields.ListIndex)

    Set testtable = db.TableDefs(tablename)
    Set tfield = testtable.Fields(fieldname)
    dtype = GetDataName(tfield.Type)
    lstFieldData.AddItem dtype & "," & tfield.Size
End Sub
```

7. In the `cboQueryDef_Click()` event, enter the following code:

```
Private Sub cboQueryDef_Click()
    Dim qdef As QueryDef
    For Each qdef In db.QueryDefs
        If Trim(cboQueryDef.Text) = qdef.Name Then lblSQL.Caption
        ➥= qdef.SQL
    Next
End Sub
```

continues

589

8. The `GetDataName()` function code is as follows:

```
Public Function GetDataName(dtype As Integer) As String
    Select Case dtype
        Case 1
            GetDataName = "Boolean"
        Case 2
            GetDataName = "Byte"
        Case 3
            GetDataName = "Integer"
        Case 4
            GetDataName = "Long"
        Case 5
            GetDataName = "Currency"
        Case 6
            GetDataName = "Single"
        Case 7
            GetDataName = "Double"
        Case 8
            GetDataName = "Date/Time"
        Case 10
            GetDataName = "Text"
        Case 11
            GetDataName = "OLE Object"
        Case 12
            GetDataName = "Memo"
    End Select
End Function
```

9. Run and test your application.

In this exercise, a `For Each...Next` loop is used to successively iterate through several DAO collections. Examine the various events and functions.

■ **The `Form_Load()` Event**

In the `Form_Load()` event, the database was opened using the `Workspace` `OpenDatabase` method. An object variable of type `TableDef` was declared. It was then set to refer to all members of the database's `TableDefs` collection in a `For Each...Next` loop. Each member's name and `RecordCount` were added to the `lstTables` list box.

Notice that the `For Each...Next` syntax permits you to reference object variables without using the `Set` statement. Remember: Object variables are references to objects, not objects themselves.

■ **Binding DAO Variables**

DAO variables, like any other object variable, must be bound to a particular object before object properties can be read or assigned or object methods invoked. Consider the following code:

```
Dim tdef as TableDef

For Each tdef In db.TableDefs
```

```
        lstTables.AddItem tdef.Name & "," & tdef.RecordCount
    Next
```

This code is the equivalent of the following:

```
    Dim  as integer
    Dim tdef as TableDef
    For  = 0 to db.TableDefs.Count - 1
        Set tdef = TableDefs()
        lstTables.AddItem tdef.Name & "," & tdef.RecordCount
    Next
```

The For Each...Next syntax allows you to iterate through the collection without a counter variable or the Set statement. Of course, you also could use a For...Next loop and simply reference the collection index, as follows:

```
    Dim  as integer
    Dim tdef as TableDef

    For  = 0 to db.TableDefs.Count - 1
        lstTables.AddItem tdefs().Name & "," & tdefs().RecordCount
    Next
```

■ The List Box Click() Events

The list box Click() events perform similar operations down the DAO hierarchy. In the lstTables_Click() event, you set a parent collection reference from the lstTables list box. A For Each...Next loop then lists fields from the selected table's Fields collection. The lstFields_Click() event sets two object variables from list box values. After Table and Field object references are set, you can retrieve individual field properties, such as data type and size.

Alternatively, you could have used nested For Each...Next loops. To list all fields in the table selected by the user in the lstTables list box, you could have written the code as follows:

```
    Dim tablename As String
    Dim testtable As TableDef
    Dim tfield As Field
    Dim position As Integer

    ' get tablename form lstbox
    tablename = lstTables.List(lstTables.ListIndex)
    position = InStr(tablename, ",")
    tablename = Left(tablename, position - 1)
    For each testtable in db.TableDefs
        If tablename = testtable.name then
            For Each tfield In testtable.Fields
                lstFields.AddItem tfield.Name
            Next
        End if
    Next
```

This exercise serves as the beginnings of a generic application that can map any database. You can use Visual Basic code to iterate through any database and examine core DAOs. For example, change the single line of code in the Form_Load() event that references the cinema.mdb to another .MDB database file, such as Design1.MDB. This exercise should be able to list the databases' tables, fields, field data types, field sizes, and stored queries for any .MDB database stored on your computer.

Objective 24.2   Opening Databases and *Recordsets*

In Exercise 24.1, you used several new statements to open databases and Recordsets. These statements are used every time you employ DAO methods, so they deserve careful review.

24.2.1   Opening Databases with the *Workspace OpenDataBase* Method

To open a database, declare a Database object and set that object by employing the OpenDataBase method of the Workspace object. If only one Workspace is used, which is typical for a single user on a workstation, make the following kind of object variable declaration and assignment:

```
Dim db as DAO.database
Set db = DBEngine.Workspaces(0).OpenDatabase("MyDB.MDB")
```

Because the DBEngine is a single object, the following instruction also will work:

```
Set db = Workspaces(0).OpenDatabase("MyDB.MDB")
```

The full syntax of the method is as follows:

```
Set database = [workspace].OpenDatabase(dbname[, exclusive[, read-only
➡[,connect]]])
```

Table 24.1 explains the components of the OpenDataBase method.

TABLE 24.1   Syntax of the *OpenDataBase* Method

Component	Description
database	A variable of a Database object data type that represents the Database object that you're opening.
workspace	A variable of a Workspace object data type that represents the existing Workspace object that will contain the database.
dbname	A string expression that is the name of an existing database file or registered ODBC data source name. If the file name has an extension, it's required. If your network supports it, you also can specify a network path, such as \\MYSERVER\MYSHARE\MYDIR\MYDB.MDB.
exclusive	A Boolean value that is True if the database is to be opened for exclusive (non-shared) access, and False if opened for shared access. If you omit this argument, the database is opened for shared access.
read-only	A Boolean value that is True if the database is to be opened for read-only access, and False if opened for read/write access. If you omit this argument, the database is opened for read/write access.

Component	Description
connect	A string expression used for opening the database. This string constitutes the ODBC connect arguments. You must supply the exclusive and read-only arguments to supply a source string. (See the connect property (DAO) documentation using Help for the appropriate syntax.)

24.2.2 Opening *Recordsets* from a *Database* Object

After a Database object has been set, the Database object's OpenRecordset method is used to open a database. Recordsets can be of three types, with which you should be familiar from working with the Data control: table-type, dynaset-type, or snapshot-type.

The syntax for opening a Recordset for a Jet engine database is as follows:

```
Set variable = database.OpenRecordset (source, [type], [options],
[lockedits])
```

Table 24.2 shows the components of this syntax.

TABLE 24.2 Syntax of the *OpenRecordset* Method When Used with a *Database* Object

Component	Description
variable	A variable that has been declared as an object of data type Recordset.
database	The name of an existing DAO object you want to use to create the new Recordset.
source	A string specifying the source of the records for the new Recordset. The source can be a table name, a query name, or a SQL statement that returns records. For table-type Recordset objects, the source can only be a table name.
type	If you don't specify a type, OpenRecordset creates a table-type Recordset, if possible. If you specify an attached table or query, OpenRecordset creates a dynaset-type Recordset. One of the following Integer constants defines the data type of the new Recordset object: dbOpenTable—Opens a table-type Recordset object. dbOpenDynaset—Opens a dynaset-type Recordset object. dbOpenSnapshot—Opens a snapshot-type Recordset object.

continues

TABLE 24.2   continued

Component	Description
options	Any combination (or none) of the following Integer constants specifying characteristics of the new Recordset, such as restrictions on other users' capabilities to edit and view it:
	dbDenyWrite—Other users can't modify or add records.
	dbDenyRead—Users can't view records (table-type Recordset only).
	dbReadOnly—Limited to viewing records; other users can modify them.
	dbAppendOnly—Limited to appending new records (dynaset-type Recordset only).
	dbInconsistent— Inconsistent updates are allowed (dynaset-type Recordset only).
	dbConsistent—Consistent updates are allowed (dynaset-type Recordset only).
	dbForwardOnly—The Recordset is a forward-only scrolling snapshot. Recordset objects created with this option only support the MoveNext method to move through the records.
	dbSQLPassThrough—The Microsoft Jet database engine query processor is bypassed. The query specified in the OpenRecordset source argument is passed to an ODBC back-end server for processing.
	dbSeeChanges—Generates a runtime error if another user is changing data you are editing.
lockedits	You can use one of the following constants for the lockedits argument:
	dbReadOnly—Prevents users from making changes to the Recordset (default for ODBCDirect Workspaces). You can use dbReadOnly in either the options argument or the lockedits argument, but not both. If you use it for both arguments, a runtime error occurs.
	dbPessimistic—Uses pessimistic locking to determine how changes are made to the Recordset in a multiuser environment. The page containing the record you're editing is locked as soon as you use the Edit method (default for Microsoft Jet Workspaces).
	dbOptimistic—Uses optimistic locking to determine how changes are made to the Recordset in a multiuser environment. The page containing the record is not locked until the Update method is executed.

Exercise 24.2   Using the Three *OpenRecordset* Types

Create the interface shown in Figure 24.4 to open and view a table, a dynaset, and a snapshot.

Figure 24.4   *This interface enables you to compare and contrast the three* Recordset *types.*

1. At the form module level, make the following declarations:

```
Dim db As DAO.Database
Dim ws As DAO.Workspace
```

2. In the Form_Load() event, enter the following code:

```
Set ws = DBEngine.Workspaces(0)
Set db = ws.OpenDatabase(App.Path & "\cinema.mdb")
```

3. In the cmdOpen_Click() event, enter the following code:

```
Private Sub cmdOpen_Click()
    Dim rsTbl As Recordset, rsDyna As Recordset, rsSnap As
    ➥Recordset
    Dim SQL1 As String
    Dim SQL2 As String
    Dim msg As String

    On Error GoTo cmdOpenErr

    SQL1 = "SELECT  [Film Title] FROM [Film Titles] Order by
    ➥[Film Title]"
    SQL2 = "SELECT  [Film Title], [Year Released] FROM [Film
    ➥Titles] Where [Year Released] = 1990"

    Set rsTbl = db.OpenRecordset("Directors", dbOpenTable)
    Set rsDyna = db.OpenRecordset(SQL1, dbOpenDynaset)
    Set rsSnap = db.OpenRecordset(SQL2, dbOpenSnapshot)

    ' clear list boxes
    lstTable.Clear
    lstDynaSet.Clear
    lstSnapShot.Clear

    If rsTbl.RecordCount <> 0 Then
```

continues

595

```
        Do While Not rsTbl.EOF
          lstTable.AddItem rsTbl![Director Name]
          rsTbl.MoveNext
        Loop
      End If

      If rsDyna.RecordCount <> 0 Then
        Do While Not rsDyna.EOF
          lstDynaSet.AddItem rsDyna.Fields(0).Value
          rsDyna.MoveNext

        Loop
      End If

      If rsSnap.RecordCount <> 0 Then
        Do While Not rsSnap.EOF
          lstSnapShot.AddItem rsSnap![Year Released] & _
  ": " & rsSnap![Film Title].Value
          rsSnap.MoveNext
        Loop
      End If

      ' close recordsets
      rsTbl.Close
      rsDyna.Close
      rsSnap.Close
      Exit Sub
  cmdOpenErr:
      msg = "Error: " & Err.Number & " " & Err.Description
      MsgBox msg, 0, "Error in opening Recordset"
  End Sub
```

4. Run and test the program.

When a Recordset is opened and it contains some data, it's RecordCount property shows a value of 1. The total number of records returned is not determined until the entire recordset has been looped through using the MoveNext method or a MoveLast method has been invoked. A RecordCount of 0 indicates no data was returned. This property was tested in this exercise before executing code to loop through the Recordset.

An alternative to testing RecordCount is to test to see whether the BOF (beginning of file) and EOF (end of file) properties are both True. If so, the test indicates no data was returned, as in the following:

```
      If (rs.BOF And rs.EOF) Then
          MsgBox "No Data Returned"
      Else
      Do While Not rs.EOF
          ' code to get data from Recordset
          rs.MoveNext
        Loop
      End If
```

When you no longer need access to a Recordset, it should be closed with the Close method. If you close the database, however, all Recordsets associated with that database also are closed. In this exercise, you could add the instruction db.Close to the Form_Unload() event to ensure that the database closes when you exit the application. Alternatively, you could set the Database object variable to Nothing, as in the following:

```
Set db = Nothing
```

24.2.3   *OpenRecordset* Method for Other DAO Objects

You also can use the OpenRecordset method on existing TableDef, QueryDef, and Recordset objects. The syntax is a little different from that used with a Database object:

```
Set variable = object.OpenRecordset([type],[options],[lockedits])
```

Table 24.3 explains the components of this syntax.

TABLE 24.3   Syntax of the *OpenRecordset* Method When Used with DAO Objects

Component	Description
variable	A variable that has been declared as an object of data type Recordset.
object	The name of an existing QueryDef, Recordset, or TableDef object that you want to use to create the new Recordset.
	If object refers to a dynaset or snapshot-type Recordset object, the type of the new object is the same as that of the Recordset specified by object.
	If object refers to a table-type Recordset object, the type of the new object is a dynaset-type Recordset.

The type, option, and lockedits arguments are the same as in the syntax for opening a Recordset for a Jet engine database (refer to Table 24.2), but often the type argument is omitted. Visual Basic determines the Recordset type automatically. The most frequent use of this OpenRecordset syntax is with a stored query or QueryDef object, as in the following expression:

```
Set rs = QueryDef.OpenRecordset
```

Exercise 24.3 Using the *OpenRecordset* Method with a *TableDef* Object

This exercise employs a small change to Exercise 24.2. It uses the OpenRecordset method of the TableDef object.

1. Change the name of the list box lstSnapShot to **lstTableDef**, and change the code in the cmdOpen_Click() event accordingly:

```
Private Sub cmdOpen_Click()
    Dim rsTbl As Recordset, rsDyna As Recordset, rs As Recordset
    Dim tdef As TableDef
    Dim SQL1 As String

    SQL1 = "SELECT  [Film Title] FROM [Film Titles] Where [Year
    ➥Released] Between 1959 and 1970"

    Set rsTbl = db.OpenRecordset("Film Titles", dbOpenTable)
    Set rsDyna = db.OpenRecordset(SQL1, dbOpenDynaset)
    Set tdef = db.TableDefs("Directors")
    Set rs = tdef.OpenRecordset()

    If Not (rsTbl.BOF And rsTbl.EOF) Then
      Do While Not rsTbl.EOF
        lstTable.AddItem rsTbl![Film Title]
        rsTbl.MoveNext
      Loop
    End If

    If Not (rsDyna.BOF And rsDyna.EOF) Then
      Do While Not rsDyna.EOF
        lstDynaSet.AddItem rsDyna.Fields(0).Value
        rsDyna.MoveNext
      Loop
    End If

    If Not (rs.BOF And rs.EOF) Then
      Do Until rs.EOF
        lstTabledef.AddItem rs![Director Name] & ";  " &
        ➥rs![Years]
        rs.MoveNext
      Loop
    End If

    rsTbl.Close
    rsDyna.Close
    rs.Close
End Sub
```

2. Test this code to determine whether the OpenRecordset method works as you expected.

Objective 24.3   Working with the *Recordset* Object

The Recordset object should be familiar to you from working with the Data control. It is the object you deal with most frequently when working with the Jet engine. It is important, therefore, to review its methods thoroughly.

24.3.1 *Recordset Move* Methods

The Move methods (MoveFirst, MoveLast, MovePrevious, and MoveNext) are similar to those used with the Data control. If you use the visible Data control to navigate through a cursored Recordset, you can easily move to the first record, last record, previous record, and next record.

As you navigate through a Recordset, the BOF (beginning of file) and EOF (end of file) Recordset properties need to be tested. If the values turn to True, you must reset the cursor to the preceding record (in the case of EOF) or the next record (in the case of BOF).

The BOF property does not become True when the cursor arrives at the first record in the Recordset; it becomes True only when on the first record and a MovePrevious method is invoked. The same is true for the EOF property: It becomes True when you are on the last record and a MoveNext method is invoked. Exercise 24.4 shows how you can use the BOF and EOF properties in conjunction with the Move methods.

Exercise 24.4   Using *Recordset* Move Methods

This exercise demonstrates one way of avoiding errors by navigating past the beginning or end of a Recordset. It uses BOF and EOF properties to test the position of the Recordset cursor.

1. Construct the interface shown in Figure 24.5. It consists of four buttons (**cmdFirst, cmdPrevious, cmdNext,** and **cmdLast**) and two labels (**lblTitle** and **lblStatus**).

Figure 24.5   *The* Move *methods enable you to move to the first or last record in a database as well as to the next and previous record.*

continues

---

2. Make the following declarations at the form module level:

```
Option Explicit
Dim db As DAO.Database
Dim ws As DAO.Workspace
Dim rsSnap As DAO.Recordset
```

3. In the Form_Load() event, enter the following code:

```
Private Sub Form_Load()
    Dim SQL As String
    ' open database which is declared at form module level
    Set ws = DBEngine.Workspaces(0)
    Set db = ws.OpenDatabase(App.Path & "\cinema.mdb")

    SQL = "SELECT [Film Title] FROM [Film Titles]
    Where [Year Released] > 1980 Order By [Film Title]"

    Set rsSnap = db.OpenRecordset(SQL, dbOpenSnapshot)

    If Not IsNull(rsSnap.Fields(0).Value) Then
        lblTitle.Caption = rsSnap.Fields(0).Value
    End If
End Sub
```

4. In the first, last, next, and previous command button Click() events, enter the following code:

```
Private Sub cmdFirst_Click()
    rsSnap.MoveFirst
    lblTitle.Caption = rsSnap("Film Title")
    lblStatus.Caption = "Beginning of file"
End Sub

Private Sub cmdLast_Click()
    rsSnap.MoveLast
    lblTitle.Caption = rsSnap("Film Title")
    lblStatus.Caption = "End of file"
End Sub

Private Sub cmdNext_Click()
    lblStatus.Caption = ""
    rsSnap.MoveNext
    If rsSnap.EOF Then
        rsSnap.MovePrevious
        lblStatus.Caption = "End of file"
    End If
    lblTitle.Caption = rsSnap("Film Title")
End Sub

Private Sub cmdPrevious_Click()
    lblStatus.Caption = ""
    rsSnap.MovePrevious
    If rsSnap.BOF Then
        rsSnap.MoveNext
        lblStatus.Caption = "Beginning of file"
    End If
    lblTitle.Caption = rsSnap![Film Title]
End Sub
```

5. Test your code. What are the purposes of the BOF and EOF tests?

24.3.2   Varieties of Syntax in Accessing Field Values

In Exercise 24.4, you used two different means of accessing field values. In the Form_Load() event, you referenced the Fields collection index, while in the command button Click() events, you used the default collection for the Recordset object in the following expression:

```
lblTitle.Caption = rsSnap("Film Title")
```

The syntax varieties for accessing field values are even more numerous. For a field name with a single word, such as Title, the varieties include the following:

```
lblTitle.Caption = rsSnap!Title
lblTitle.Caption = rsSnap!Title.Value
lblTitle.Caption = rsSnap![Title]           ' brackets or quotes
                                            'necessary for field names
lblTitle.Caption = rsSnap![Title].Value     ' with spaces
lblTitle.Caption = rsSnap(0)
lblTitle.Caption = rsSnap(0).Value
lblTitle.Caption = rsSnap("Title")
lblTitle.Caption = rsSnap("Title").Value
```

These examples do not include statements in which the default Fields collection is referenced, as in the following:

```
lblTitle.Caption = rsSnap.Fields("Title")
lblTitle.Caption = rsSnap.Fields("Title").Value
```

Due to greater simplicity in the code, it is generally faster to use the exclamation point operator, as in

```
rsSnap!Title
```

rather than the field name in parentheses, as in the following:

```
rsSnap("Title")
```

24.3.3   Using *MoveLast* Before Checking *RecordCount*

As indicated at the end of Exercise 24.3, when a Recordset is opened, the Recordset's RecordCount property cannot be ascertained unless a MoveLast method is invoked first. This populates the Recordset with data and allows the RecordCount to be determined. Before trying to read the RecordCount property, always use a MoveLast method, but be aware that in large data sets, a MoveLast method can have an impact on performance because the entire Recordset is populated. To determine the RecordCount, use code such as the following:

```
myrecordset.MoveLast
Print myrecordset.RecordCount
```

24.3.4   Using the *Seek* Method with *Recordsets*

You can use the `Seek` method to locate records in a table-type `Recordset` when the search criteria are performed upon an identified table index. It is the fastest means of locating a record. `Recordsets` also have `Find` methods (`FindFirst`, `FindLast`, `FindPrevious`, and `FindNext`), which use criteria equivalent to SQL `WHERE` clauses. Using a SQL `SELECT` query or a `Parameter` query often is faster in these situations. When you need to locate a record and it is possible to open a table-type `Recordset` to retrieve the record, the `Seek` method should be your first choice. The `Seek` method's syntax is as follows:

```
table.Seek comparison, key1, key2...
```

Table 24.4 explains this syntax.

TABLE 24.4   Syntax of the *Seek* Method

Component	Description
table	The name of an existing table-type `Recordset` object or `Table` object that has a defined index as specified by the `Recordset` or `Table` object's `Index` property
comparison	One of the following string expressions: "<", "<=", "=", ">=", or ">"
key1, key2...	One or more values corresponding to the underlying table's `Primary` property setting

This syntax is a little different, especially regarding the placing of the comparison operators within quotation marks. For a `Recordset` object variable named tbl, a `Seek` method would look like the following:

```
Dim tbl as Recordset
Set tbL = db.OpenRecordset("Film Titles", dbOpenTable) tbl.Index =
"Primary Key"
tbl.Seek "=", "Raging Bull"
If tbl.NoMatch = True then
    lblStatus.Caption = "Film not located."
Else
    ' write code to retrieve record field values
End if
```

Using the `Seek` method is a three step process:

1. Identify the `Index` upon which you are using the `Seek` method.

2. Check the `Recordset`'s `NoMatch` property, a Boolean value property, to see whether your search was successful.

3. Retrieve values from the fields of the record if you are successful in locating it.

At first glance, the `Seek` method's syntax is a bit odd, but its speed quickly induces you to use it whenever possible.

Exercise 24.5   Using the *Seek* Method

In this exercise, film titles are selected in a list box. The user then can choose a title to receive more information about the film. The left list box displays film titles; the right list box displays information about the selected film (see Figure 24.6).

Figure 24.6 *The* Seek *method is used to provide details about a selected film.*

1. Create the interface illustrated in Figure 24.6. The list box on the left is named **lstFilmTitles** and has its MultiSelect property set to 0 (None). The list box on the right is named **lstFilmDetails**.

2. At the form module level, make the following object variable declarations:

```
Dim db As DAO.Database
Dim ws As DAO.Workspace
Dim rs As DAO.Recordset
```

3. In the Form_Unload() event, enter the following:

```
db.Close
```

4. In the Form_Load() event, enter code that selects all film titles and orders them alphabetically:

```
Private Sub Form_Load()
    Dim rsSQL As Recordset
    Dim SQL As String
    Dim strSearch As String
    Dim position As Integer

    Set ws = DBEngine.Workspaces(0)
    'change path as necessary
    Set db = ws.OpenDatabase(App.Path & "\cinema.mdb")

    Set rs = db.OpenRecordset("Film Titles", dbOpenTable)
    Set rsSQL = db.OpenRecordset("Select [Film Title] FROM [Film
Titles]ORDER BY [Film Title]", dbOpenSnapshot)

    Do Until rsSQL.EOF
        lstFilmTitles.AddItem rsSQL![Film Title]
        rsSQL.MoveNext
    Loop
    rsSQL.Close
End Sub
```

continues

Exercise 24.5   continued

5. In the lstFilmTitles_Click() event, enter the following code:

```
Private Sub lstFilmTitles_Click()
    Dim tfield As Field
    Dim criteria As String    lstFilmDetails.Clear
    ' set index for Seek method
    rs.Index = "Title"
    criteria = Trim(lstFilmTitles.Text)

    rs.Seek "=", criteria

    If rs.NoMatch = True Then
     lblStatus.Caption = "Film not located"
    Else
      For Each tfield In rs.Fields
         If Not IsNull(tfield.Value) Then
            lstFilmDetails.AddItem tfield.Name & ":   " &
tfield.Value
         End If
      Next
    End If
End Sub
```

6. Run and test your program.

In the lstFilmTitles_Click() event, you identify the index to use for the seek. In this instance, it is an index named "Title." You then use list box values to perform the seek. After the seek is successful, a For Each...Next structure iterates through every field in the Recordset to display values for the current record.

24.3.5   Using the *Find* Methods with *Recordsets*

The Find methods locate records as well. Recordset Find methods work only on dynaset- and snapshot-type Recordsets (not table-type). The search direction for the FindFirst and FindNext methods moves toward the end of the Recordset. Each method stops at the first record that meets the criteria. FindFirst starts the search at the beginning of the Recordset, and FindNext starts the search from the current record.

FindLast and FindPrevious mirror this behavior. The search direction moves toward the beginning of the database with the method starting the search from either the end of the Recordset or from the current record.

If you want to find more than one record using the criteria, it often is faster to use a SQL statement and create a new Recordset. You then can scroll through the Recordset with Move methods. The Find method syntax is as follows:

```
recordset.{FindFirst | FindLast | FindNext | FindPrevious} criteria
```

Table 24.5 explains this syntax.

TABLE 24.5   Syntax of the *Find* Method

Component	Description
Recordset	The name of an existing dynaset- or snapshot-type Recordset, Dynaset, or Snapshot object.
criteria	A string expression (such as the WHERE clause in a SQL statement without the word WHERE) used to locate the record.

Using the Find method rather than the Seek method in Exercise 24.6, you could change the code in the Form_Load() event to open a snapshot-type, instead of a table-type, Recordset. You then could use the following code in the lstFilmTitles_Click() event:

```
Private Sub lstFilmTitles_Click()
    Dim tfield As Field
    Dim criteria As String
    Dim film As String

    lstFilmDetails.Clear

    film = Trim(lstFilmTitles.List(lstFilmTitles.ListIndex))
    criteria = "[Film Title] = " & Chr(39) & film & Chr(39)
    rsFilm.FindFirst criteria
    If rsFilm.NoMatch = True Then
       lblStatus.Caption = "Film not located"
    Else
       For Each tfield In rsFilm.Fields
          If Not IsNull(tfield.Value) Then
             lstFilmDetails.AddItem tfield.Name & ":  " & tfield.Value
          End If
       Next
    End If
End Sub
```

In SQL syntax, you need to enclose string literals in quotation marks. In this case, you concatenated the search criteria using the Chr() function. For search expressions that contain apostrophes, this can be troublesome. You might, for example, encounter an error for film titles that have a possessive adjective, as in the George Cukor film *Adam's Rib*. If possible, try to search on numeric expressions. This avoids inordinate amounts of string parsing and generally is faster and less prone to error. Better yet, use the Seek method.

24.3.6   Using the *AddNew, Edit, Update,* and *Delete* Methods

The DAO methods for adding, editing, updating, and deleting records essentially are the same as those with the Data control. If you use unbound controls, however, more code is required to check data entry errors, ensure data types are not mismatched, and keep controls that provide views of the Recordset "refreshed." If you are familiar with SQL, its syntax often is faster for modifying data than DAO methods. Use the SQL Reference section of Help to investigate the INSERT INTO and UPDATE syntax of SQL to get fast performance.

Exercise 24.6   Editing and Updating a Database Record

In Figure 24.7, you see an interface with added buttons for performing operations to edit and add data for the Film Titles table. Because the code for this application is extensive, most of it has been retained in Exercise 24.6 on the companion disk (P24_6.VBP). The key DAO methods, however, are the same as those used with the Data control.

You cannot update a Recordset unless the Recordset's AddNew or Edit methods have been invoked. In the application, the Update button is enabled only after one of these buttons has been depressed, and at the end of the Update procedure, the Update button is disabled.

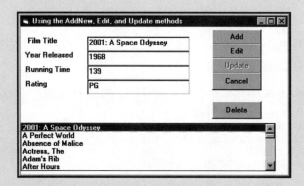

Figure 24.7   *This interface allows you to add or edit a record and to update the database.*

1. Load the project from the companion disk.

2. Write the cmdUpdate_Click() procedure, as follows:

```
Private Sub cmdUpdate_Click()
    Dim DirId As Integer
    Dim dashpos As Integer

    On Error GoTo cmdUpdateErr:

    If Len(Trim(txtTitle.Text)) <> 0 Then
      rsTbl![Film title] = Trim(txtTitle.Text)
    Else
      MsgBox "Please Enter valid data."
      txtTitle.SetFocus
      Exit Sub
    End If

    If Len(Trim(txtYear.Text)) <> 0 And IsNumeric(txtYear.Text)
Then
      rsTbl![Year Released] = CInt(txtYear.Text)
    Else
      rsTbl![Year Released] = 0
    End If

    If Len(Trim(txtRunTime.Text)) <> 0 And
IsNumeric(txtRunTime.Text) Then
```

```
          rsTbl![Running Time] = CInt(txtRunTime.Text)
    Else
          rsTbl![Running Time] = 0
    End If

    If Len(Trim(txtRating.Text)) <> 0 Then
          rsTbl![Rating] = Trim(txtRating.Text)
    Else
          rsTbl![Rating] = "NR"
    End If

    If AddNewRecord = True Then
          dashpos = InStr(cboDirID.Text, "-")
          rsTbl![Director ID] = CInt(Trim(Left(cboDirID.Text,
          ➥dashpos - 1)))
    End If

    rsTbl.Update
    cmdUpdate.Enabled = False
    cmdAdd.Enabled = True
    cmdEdit.Enabled = True
    cmdDelete.Enabled = True
    RebuildList
    ClearText

    If AddNewRecord = True Then
          lblDirIDPrompt.Visible = False
          cboDirID.Visible = False
          AddNewRecord = False
    End If

    Exit Sub
cmdUpdateErr:
    MsgBox Err & "    " & Error.Description, 0, "Error in Data
    ➥Update"
    Resume Next
End Sub
```

3. Run and test your program.

Missing from this exercise are the numerous data access errors that you can trap. Go to the Visual Basic online Help to review the list of these errors.

Objective 24.4   Learning to Create, Retrieve, and Use *QueryDef* Objects

In the Cinema database, there are a number of stored queries or QueryDef objects. Using Access or Visual Data Manager, it is possible to create your own stored queries. One of the easiest ways to build a stored query in a Jet engine database is to use the query building tool included with the Access database. This feature of Access is a query by example (QBE) tool. With this tool, complex queries, especially joins of multiple tables, are easy to build.

The Jet engine SQL syntax is different from other versions of SQL, especially in how joins are handled and variables are passed to queries (parameters). A nested join query in Jet engine SQL can be very difficult to decipher. The Access database makes this type of query easier to write.

24.4.1   Opening and Using a *QueryDef* Object

Retrieving a Recordset based on a SELECT query is a matter of iterating through the QueryDefs collection and using the OpenRecordset method with the identified QueryDef object.

Exercise 24.7   Using a *QueryDef* Object

This exercise opens all stored queries that do not have parameters. The user then can execute these queries and observe the SQL code upon which they are based.

1. Build the interface you see in Figure 24.8. It contains a list box for listing QueryDef objects (**lstQueryDef**) and a list box for displaying query results (**lstResult**). Add labels **lblSQL**, **lblStatus**, and **lblRecordCount**. The label lblStatus appears below the Previous and Next buttons to display the beginning or end of the file.

2. At the form module level, make the following declarations:

   ```
   Dim db As DAO.Database
   Dim rs As DAO.Recordset
   ```

3. In the Form_Load() event, enter code to list QueryDef objects that do not have parameters:

   ```
   Private Sub Form_Load()
       Dim qdef As QueryDef
       ' alter path as appropriate
       Set db = Workspaces(0).OpenDatabase(App.Path &
   \"cinema.mdb")
       For Each qdef In db.QueryDefs
           If qdef.Parameters.Count = 0 Then
               lstQueryDef.AddItem qdef.Name
           End If
       Next
   End Sub
   ```

4. In the lstQueryDef_Click() event, enter the code to identify the query, open a Recordset based on that query, display the query's SQL syntax, and display the first record in the Recordset returned by the query:

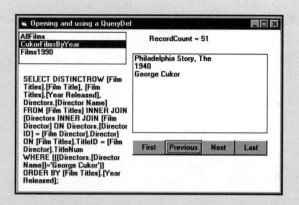

Figure 24.8 *This interface displays the query used in processing and the records found through the use of the query.*

```
Private Sub lstQueryDef_Click()
    Dim qdef As QueryDef
    Dim f As Field
    Dim s As String

    s = Trim(lstQueryDef.List(lstQueryDef.ListIndex))

    For Each qdef In db.QueryDefs
        If qdef.Name = s Then
            Set rs = qdef.OpenRecordset
            lblSQL.Caption = qdef.SQL
        End If
    Next
    lstResult.Clear
    For Each f In rs.Fields
        lstResult.AddItem f.Value
    Next

    rs.MoveLast
    lblRecordCount.Caption = "RecordCount = " & rs.RecordCount
    rs.MoveFirst
End Sub
```

5. Add the appropriate code for the navigation buttons:

```
Private Sub cmdFirst_Click()
    Dim f As Field
    lstResult.Clear
    rs.MoveFirst
    For Each f In rs.Fields
        lstResult.AddItem f.Value
    Next
```

continues

Exercise 24.7   continued

```
                lblStatus.Caption = "Beginning of file"
        End Sub

        Private Sub cmdLast_Click()
            Dim f As Field
            lstResult.Clear
            rs.MoveLast
            For Each f In rs.Fields
                lstResult.AddItem f.Value
            Next
            lblStatus.Caption = "End of file"
        End Sub

        Private Sub cmdNext_Click()
            Dim f As Field
            lblStatus.Caption = ""
            lstResult.Clear
            rs.MoveNext
            If rs.EOF Then
                rs.MovePrevious
                lblStatus.Caption = "End of file"
            End If
            For Each f In rs.Fields
                lstResult.AddItem f.Value
            Next
        End Sub

        Private Sub cmdPrevious_Click()
            Dim f As Field
            lblStatus.Caption = ""
            lstResult.Clear
            rs.MovePrevious
            If rs.BOF Then
                rs.MoveNext
                lblStatus.Caption = "Beginning of file"
            End If
            For Each f In rs.Fields
                lstResult.AddItem f.Value
            Next
        End Sub
```

6. Test your design. Can you understand the logic of the SQL?

24.4.2   Opening and Using a *Parameter* Query

The power of stored queries becomes more impressive the more you work with them. Individual permissions can be granted to individual queries. In this manner, it takes a relatively short amount of time to build a view of a database customized for an individual or group of individuals.

One of the most flexible means of providing users with individual views of a database is to use a Parameter query. In a Parameter query, an individual value is not known until the user provides it. The following exercise shows how the Parameters collection of a QueryDef object can be used to execute a Parameter query.

Exercise 24.8   Using a *Parameter* Query

In this exercise, you simply modify the previous code so that all queries, including `Parameter` queries, are included. The `InputBox()` function serves to retrieve user input for the parameters (see Figure 24.9).

Figure 24.9   *A* Parameter *query requires an input box for the user to supply a needed value.*

1. Change the `Form_Load()` event so that it reads as follows:

```
Private Sub Form_Load()
    Dim qdef As DAO.QueryDef
    Set db = Workspaces(0).OpenDatabase(App.Path & "\cinema.mdb")
    For Each qdef In db.QueryDefs
        lstQueryDef.AddItem qdef.Name
    Next
End Sub
```

2. In the `lstQueryDef_Click()` event, change the code to read as follows:

```
Private Sub lstQueryDef_Click()
    Dim qdef As QueryDef
    Dim param As Parameter
    Dim queryname As String
    Dim f as field
    Dim ret As Variant

    queryname = Trim(lstQueryDef.List(lstQueryDef.ListIndex))
    Set qdef = db.QueryDefs(queryname)
    If qdef.Parameters.Count = 0 Then
        Set rs = qdef.OpenRecordset(dbOpenSnapshot)
    Else
        For Each param In qdef.Parameters
            ret = InputBox("Please enter parameter value " &
param.Name, "Entering parameter values")
            param.Value = ret
        Next
        Set rs = qdef.OpenRecordset(dbOpenSnapshot)
    End If
    lstResult.Clear
    For Each f In rs.Fields
        lstResult.AddItem f.Value
```

continues

Exercise 24.8   continued

```
        Next
        lblSQL.Caption = qdef.SQL
        rs.MoveLast
        lblRecordCount = "Record Count: " & rs.RecordCount
        rs.MoveFirst
    End Sub
```

3. Run the program and click the `FilmsByYearRange` query in the `lstQuery` list box. Enter two dates, such as 1975 and 1992, when the `InputBox()` function requests them.

If you are familiar with SQL, you might have built dynamic SQL statements in which SQL strings are concatenated with user input values. As a general rule, when working with Jet engine queries, it is better to use a `Parameter` query, as these types of queries tend to execute faster.

Chapter Summary

In this chapter, you examined the properties, methods, and functionality of the core objects that make up the Jet database engine.

The Jet engine object model is based on a hierarchy of objects and object collections. At the top of the hierarchy is the single object `DBEngine`. Below it is the collection of `Workspace` objects that provide security, user management, and data transaction functions. Among the object collections contained within the `Workspace` object is the `Database` collection. The `Database` object contains collections of objects that received your major focus: `TableDef`, `Recordset`, `QueryDef`, and `Field`. These objects and others within the Jet engine are known as Data Access Objects (DAOs).

To iterate through Jet engine objects, you can use the `For Each...Next` structure. With this structure, it is possible to map an entire database, examining individual objects and their properties as well as the objects and collections contained within them.

Databases are opened with the `OpenDatabase` method of the `Workspace` object. You can create `Recordsets` (table-, dynaset-, or snapshot-type) with the `OpenRecordset` method of the `Database` object. `TableDef` and `QueryDef` objects have a `OpenRecordset` method. All the results of `OpenRecordset` methods provide a record-by-record or cursored view of data. Whichever record has been moved to or found becomes the current record. The `OpenDatabase` and `OpenRecordset` methods have a list of arguments you can use to determine such behaviors, including whether the opened database or data set should be read-only or read/write.

To navigate through a `Recordset`, you can use the `Move` methods (`MoveFirst`, `MoveLast`, `MoveNext`, `MovePrevious`) or the `Find` methods (`FindFirst`, `FindLast`,

FindNext, FindPrevious). The fastest way to move to a specific record is to use a table-type Recordset and the Seek method on an indexed field.

The process of adding, editing, or deleting records is very similar to the methods used with the Data control. Before a record can be written with the Update method, the AddNew or Edit methods must first be invoked. The Edit and Delete methods work on the current record.

Stored queries in a Jet database are known as QueryDef objects. To create a data set based upon the query, use the OpenRecordset method for the identified query within the QueryDefs collection. For queries that require parameters, use the queries' Parameters collection to identify parameters and assign values to them before the queries are opened with an OpenRecordset method.

Skill-Building Exercises

This set of exercises asks you to work with a number of databases, all of which are stored on the companion disk. Besides the Biblio.mdb database that is shipped with Visual Basic, you will work with the Cinema.mdb database used in this chapter, and a new database entitled pop.mdb. In all cases, use DAO methods in solving these exercises.

1. Use a Common Dialog control accessed through menu items to change Exercise 24.1 so that it displays the principal Data Access Objects for any .MDB database on the user's machine. Test your program by using the sample Biblio.mdb database that comes with Visual Basic.

2. Write a program using a table-type Recordset that displays in a list box all film titles from the Cinema.mdb database.

3. Write a program using a snapshot-type Recordset that displays all film titles, running times, and ratings in a list box.

4. On your disk is a database named Pop.mdb that contains population information on 209 U.S. cities, as well as individual state populations. Write a program that maps the tables and fields of this simple database. Include the indexes of the tables in your program.

5. Based on the information learned in the preceding exercise, write a program that lists each city in a list box. When a city is clicked in the list box, have your program use the Seek method to retrieve the population of the state in which the city is located, and display the retrieved information.

6. Write a program that lists all state abbreviations from the Pop.mdb database in a list box. When the user clicks on the state abbreviation, have all cities and their populations display in an MSFlexGrid control.

7. *Challenge:* Extend the previous exercise so that the percentage of the state population represented by the city population is shown in a third column in the grid control.

ACTIVEX DATA OBJECTS

In the preceding two chapters, you used the Data Access Object (DAO) library to manipulate Access databases. In Chapter 23, "Accessing and Manipulating Databases with Visual Basic," you worked with Data Access Objects as encapsulated in the Data control. In Chapter 24, "Using Data Access Objects," you stepped down one level and worked directly with DAO objects.

This chapter introduces a new data access capability, ActiveX Data Objects (ADO), a library of functions based on a technology called OLE DB. Microsoft intends its OLE DB initiative to serve as the basis for its future data access tools, regardless of whether the data access requirement is for a single workstation, a client/server network, or an enterprisewide information system. The OLE DB technology is designed to access and manipulate heterogeneous data sources within an organization. The data might be stored in a relational database such as Access, SQL Server, Oracle, a spreadsheet, an email repository, an HTML document, or simple text files.

By encapsulating OLE DB technology into easily manipulated objects, ADO is the principal means by which this new technology will be used. This chapter introduces the core ADO objects. ADO's ambitious goals and broad capability preclude a full presentation of ADO within a single chapter. By completing this chapter, you will, however, gain a significant understanding of this new data access method.

On completion of this chapter, you will be able to do the following:

- Use the ODBC utility to make a DSN connection

- Use the DSN connection and ADO objects to access a Jet database

- Use the ADO Recordset and Command objects to retrieve data from a database

- Use the different behavior and characteristics of ADO Recordset cursors

- Combine the ADO Data control with a DataGrid control

- Design a subquery to retrieve a single value for a record lookup

- Use an ADO Command object and INSERT SQL syntax to write data to a database

■ Create and use the Data Environment Designer to connect to a database

■ Add and manage ADO Command objects with the Data Environment Designer

■ Code ADO events

Chapter Objectives

This chapter's objectives introduce core ADO concepts and techniques for working with ADO object properties, methods, and events. The chapter's six objectives as follows:

1. Explaining how ActiveX Data Objects differ from other data access objects

2. Introducing the ADO object model

3. Connecting to data sources through ADO

4. Working with the ADO Command and Recordset objects

5. Using the Data Environment Designer to manage ADO connections

6. Working with ADO events

Objective 25.1   Understanding How ActiveX Data Objects Differ from Other Data Access Objects

The purpose of this objective is to clarify ADO's place among the alphabet soup of data access choices. You have worked with DAO objects, and we made brief mention of ODBC in the previous chapter. You may also have heard of ODBC Direct, RDO, OLE DB, and even VBSQL, an older library for accessing SQL Server directly. If you are confused, you have every reason to be. It's a jumble of choices, and Microsoft may not realize its vision of replacing them all with ADO for some time.

25.1.1   The Role of ODBC

As you examine all the data choices currently available in Figure 25.1, it should become apparent that most recent data access has been designed around the Open Database Connectivity (ODBC) Application Programming Interface (API). This standard is by far the most popular common database access standard today. The ODBC standard defines a set of functions that any database vendor may use to expose its database for programmability. Many databases may be programmed through multiple "drivers" or libraries of functions that permit the database to be manipulated. Often database vendors offer a native driver for directly accessing database functions as well as an ODBC driver, permitting the database to be manipulated through ODBC routines. By learning ODBC functions, a programmer will be able to write code against a wide array of databases. That said, directly coding to the ODBC API is no easy task.

Figure 25.1   *ADO represents an encapsulation of OLE DB, a technology designed to make multiple data sources available via a common interface.*

Consider Access databases. The DAO libraries you used in the previous chapters are native drivers for Access databases. But the DAO libraries also contain ODBC functionality, permitting DAO objects to manipulate other databases through ODBC functions. Through the ODBC functionality in DAO objects, it is possible to attach an SQL Server or Oracle table to an Access database. Rows of data held by the table can then be read, edited, or added to. The reverse is also true. Through an ODBC driver, a developer may also manipulate Access databases.

As you work through different library layers, you pay a price in raw database performance. The trade-off, however, is faster, easier database application development. A common data access library that exposes objects that can be readily programmed means developers need not learn a multitude of native functions for different databases within an enterprise.

The Remote Data Objects (RDO) library available in the Enterprise edition of Visual Basic provides a very "shallow wrapper" over ODBC functions. There is a very minor performance penalty for using easy-to-code RDO against SQL Server and Oracle databases instead of calling a multitude of ODBC API functions. Because ODBC acts as the native driver for Microsoft SQL Server databases, the RDO library represents a very fast means for working with that database. The RDO library has also been optimized for Oracle databases.

25.1.2   The Rationale for OLE DB

As prevalent as ODBC drivers may be, they have one significant limitation: They are optimized for relational databases. Relational databases represent by far the majority of stored data in most enterprises. But the advent of the World Wide Web and the explosion in corporate networks are making data in the enterprise more heterogeneous. Data is stored in Web pages, in email, in word processing documents, spreadsheets, and ASCII log files. In the near future, complex data in the form of objects will be increasingly stored on disk. With object storage not only is data stored, but so is the code that makes that data useful when retrieved.

The OLE DB initiative represents an effort to define a common data access method for this multitude of data sources. It also seeks to take advantage of the improved network communication among software components made possible by newer versions of Windows. The library that provides OLE DB capability to a data source is not referred to as a driver. Instead, it is called an OLE DB *Provider*, reflecting the shift from relational database *drivers* to data source interfaces that *provide* data and other services such as event messaging.

The principal means by which programmers can access OLE DB capability is through ActiveX Data Objects (ADO). We turn to the ADO object model next.

Objective 25.2   Introducing the ADO Object Model

You have worked with object models that feature nested collections. To create and work with an object down the object hierarchy, you must first create objects higher in the hierarchy. The DAO object model in Chapter 23 and the ones in Chapter 26, "Working with Objects from Microsoft Office," feature this type of object model.

The ADO object is different. It is a smaller, flatter model. In some ways, it is a simpler model. The simplicity means, however, that each ADO object exposes a larger set of properties and methods that must be learned. ADO objects differ from nested collection objects most significantly by being created independently and later associated with another ADO object. Consider the object model in Figure 25.2.

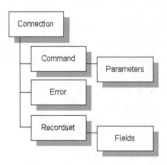

Figure 25.2   *The ADO object model is flat, with the* Connection, Command, Recordset, *and* Parameter *objects capable of being created independently and later associated with other ADO objects.*

Table 25.1 describes these core objects and provides a thumbnail description of each.

TABLE 25.1   ADO Core Objects

Object	Description
Connection	Creates a connection to a data provider. Similar to the DAO database object in this functionality.
Command	The ADO Command object can reference SQL strings, stored procedures, or action queries for execution. Similar to the DAO QueryDef object.
Recordset	Creates a set of records from a query. Like the DAO Recordset object, you can move forward and backward through ADO recordsets unless otherwise specified. Sometimes, ADO recordsets are referred to as *cursors*.
Errors collection	A collection of errors that occurs from a failed data-access attempt. Because multiple errors can occur from a single instruction, the ADO interface defines an Errors collection rather than a single Error object. Similar to the DAO Errors collection.

To get a flavor of the use of ADO data access, consider the following code where ADO objects are independently created and then associated with one another. The database accessed is the same one you used in the previous chapter, Cinema.MDB.

```
Private Sub cmdGetData_Click()
    Dim msg As String
    Dim cn As New ADODB.Connection
    Dim cmd As New ADODB.Command
    Dim rs As New ADODB.Recordset
    Dim sql As String

    On Error GoTo cmdGetDataErr

    cn.Open "DB_Cinema"
    sql = "Select [Film Title] FROM [Film Titles] ORDER BY [Film Title]"
    cmd.CommandType = adCmdText
    cmd.CommandText = sql
    rs.CursorType = adOpenStatic
    cmd.ActiveConnection = cn
    Set rs = cmd.Execute

    ' alternative code w/o use of Command object
    'rs.CursorType = adOpenStatic
    'rs.Source = sql
    'rs.ActiveConnection = cn
    'rs.Open

    Call FillList(rs, 0, lstDisplay)
    rs.Close
```

```
CloseDown:

   If Not cn.State = adStateClosed Then cn.Close
   If Not rs.State = adStateClosed Then rs.Close
   Exit Sub
cmdGetDataErr:
  MsgBox "Error: " & Err.Number & " " & Err.Description
  Resume CloseDown

End Sub
```

Observe that the Command object may be created and property values assigned before a connection is assigned. Similarly, the CursorType property (similar to specifying the Recordset type in DAO) is set before the Recordset object is opened. The independent, nonhierarchical nature of ADO is perhaps easiest to see in the alternative code that is commented out. Here the ADO Recordset object is created, the cursor type designated, the SQL code assigned, and a Connection object is associated with the Recordset. Only then is the Recordset opened. The returned data recordset is then passed to a procedure (FillList), which walks through the Recordset to display the values in the first field.

A major conceptual difference between the ADO library and the DAO library is the idea of a *connection*. The Connection object makes an OLE DB Provider available by specifying key information required by the Provider, including the name of the data source, the user ID, and the user password. In the preceding code, the Connection object used a single argument in its Open method, DB_Cinema. This references a stored file called a *data source name* (DSN) that contains information used to open the database. This represents one of several ways to get connected to an OLE DB Provider. That topic is covered next.

Objective 25.3   Connecting to Data Sources Through ADO

Turn again to Figure 25.1 and examine the different paths from an application to a data source through ADO. If the data source has an ODBC driver, it is possible to use ADO via the OLE DB Provider for ODBC-compliant databases. If the database has a separate OLE DB Provider, the more direct route is to use that Provider. A software layer is thereby removed between the application and the data source.

If your application uses the OLE DB Provider for ODBC, it must pass the ODBC database a string that allows a connection to the database to be established. The specific string required depends on the ODBC data source. All ODBC databases, however, must be supplied with the ODBC driver being used, the database being opened, the user ID, and the password.

25.3.1   Creating a DSN File

To make connections easier, this ODBC connection information is often stored in a DSN file on a client machine. This file may then be referenced when making a database connection. The preceding code illustrates this kind of connection. For databases that have an OLE DB Provider, Visual Basic offers the Data Environment Designer, which helps create a file that holds connection information, and much else. You learn about the Data Environment Designer in Objective 25.5, "Using the Data Environment Designer to Manage ADO Connections."

To manipulate Access databases, therefore, you have at least three choices:

Access Choice	*Comments*
1. Use DAO	The highest performance option for manipulating Access database from within Visual Basic applications.
2. Use the Data Environment Designer to create a connection though the Access OLE DB Currently,	As the OLE DB Provider for Access and ADO is improved, this option is likely to become a higher performing option. Currently, the OLE DB Provider has significant limitations, including the inability to recognize QueryDef objects as stored procedures. ADO's rich interface of properties, methods, and events makes this approach an increasingly attractive option in the future.
3. Use the OLE DB Provider ODBC	With the most software layers to go for through, the least high performance option. But it is very flexible.

Although this book introduces ADO using Jet-compatible databases, ADO's best use today is for larger client/server databases, such as SQL Server and Oracle. Until the Data Environment Designer is introduced later in this chapter, all connections to a data source are through a DSN file.

Exercise 25.1   Creating a DSN File for ODBC Databases

This exercise creates a DSN file. Because you create the file outside of Visual Basic, there is no project file to create or to save.

1. Make sure that the student exercises in the companion CD for this chapter have been installed on the hard disk of your computer. The Cinema.MDB database should be installed in the Chapt25 folder.

2. Go to the Windows Control Panel. Find an icon for the ODBC (32) utility included with Windows.

continues

3. Click on this icon to open the tabbed dialog box shown in Figure 25.3. Select the System DSN tab.

Figure 25.3   *The ODBC utility allows you to create various DSN files for your computer.*

4. Click the Add button on the System DSN tab. The Create New Data Source dialog box shown in Figure 25.4 should appear. Select the Microsoft Access Driver and click Finish.

Figure 25.4   *This dialog box specifies the ODBC driver for the DSN file.*

5. After you select the driver, the dialog box you see in Figure 25.5 should appear. Type in the Data Source Name **DB_Cinema** and then click the Select button. Select the Cinema.MDB database under Chapt25 for the student exercises you have installed from the CD that accompanies this book.

Figure 25.5   *In this dialog box, you assign the DSN name and identify the database with which the DSN links.*

6. After you select the database, click OK. Click OK again on the main ODBC utility dialog box shown in Figure 25.3. You have now created a DSN file. If you want to add a login name and password to the DSN file, you can restart the ODBC utility and click the Advanced button shown in Figure 25.5.

25.3.2   Using a DSN File with ADO to Connect to a Database

After a DSN file has been created on the user's system, the ADO `Connection` object can look for it. Look again at the code sample in Objective 25.2, "Introducing the ADO Object Model." Observe that the `Open` method of the ADO `Connection` object need only specify the DSN name to make a connection to the Cinema.MDB database.

Exercise 25.2   Using a DSN Connection

This exercise gets you started with ADO. First, you employ the code you examined earlier.

1. Open Project P25-2 from the installed exercises that accompany this book or build the form you see in Figure 25.6. Save it to disk as **f25-2.frm**.

Figure 25.6   *Clicking on the Get Data button should establish a DSN connection with ADO.*

2. The name of the command button is **cmdGetData** and the name of the list box is **lstDisplay**.

3. Add a standard code module to the project and save the module to disk as **Mod25-2.bas**. Save the project as **P25-2.vbp**.

4. To the code module, add the FillList procedure. This routine displays in a list box or combo box the values of a specified field of any ADO Recordset passed to it.

```
Public Sub FillList(rs As ADODB.Recordset, f As Variant, c As
Control)
   c.Clear

   If (rs.BOF <> True And rs.EOF <> True) Then
     Do While Not rs.EOF
        c.AddItem rs.Fields(f)
        rs.MoveNext
     Loop

   Else
     c.Clear
     Exit Sub
   End If

End Sub
```

By using a Variant data type for the second argument of this routine and the generic object Control for the third argument, the procedure may be used to fill either list or combo boxes with field values specified by the field name or its ordinal position within the Recordset. For example, either

```
   Call FillList(rs, "Film Title", lstDisplay)
```

or

```
   Call FillList(rs, 1, cboDisplay)
```

5. Add the following code to the `cmdGetData_Click()` event:

```
Private Sub cmdGetData_Click()
    Dim msg As String
    Dim cn As New ADODB.Connection
    Dim cmd As New ADODB.Command
    Dim rs As New ADODB.Recordset
    Dim sql As String

    On Error GoTo cmdGetDataErr

    cn.Open "DB_Cinema"
    sql = "Select [Film Title] FROM [Film Titles] ORDER BY [Film
    ➥Title]"
    cmd.CommandType = adCmdText
    cmd.CommandText = sql
    rs.CursorType = adOpenStatic
    cmd.ActiveConnection = cn
    Set rs = cmd.Execute

    Call FillList(rs, 0, lstDisplay)
    rs.Close

CloseDown:

    If Not cn.State = adStateClosed Then cn.Close
    If Not rs.State = adStateClosed Then rs.Close
    Exit Sub
cmdGetDataErr:
    MsgBox "Error: " & Err.Number & " " & Err.Description
    Resume CloseDown

End Sub
```

6. Run and test the program. With luck, you should get connected!

The error trapping in this exercise is a little different from what you have seen previously. Because of the flat ADO model, you do not work down through an object hierarchy. Instead, the usual practice is to declare and modify ADO objects and later assign them to a Connection object. An error may occur while assigning a property to a Recordset or Command object before it is associated with a Connection.

To make sure things are properly cleaned up if an error is encountered, the Connection and Recordset should be closed. An error is raised, however, if you attempt to close an object that is not open. To avoid an endless bouncing between the code beneath the cmdGetDataErr label and the CloseDown labels, you need to check the State property of the Connection and Recordset objects.

Objective 25.4   Working with the ADO *Command* and *Recordset* Objects

With a connection made, the program developer may use the Command and Recordset object to edit, retrieve data from, and write data to the database. As you saw with the DAO library, the Recordset object represents data retrieved from the database. Depending on the kind of Recordset it is, the Recordset may be read-only or available for editing and updating. A QueryDef in the DAO library represents a stored query that may retrieve data (a SELECT query) or update (an action query).

The ADO Command object is roughly equivalent to a DAO QueryDef object. As with a DAO QueryDef object, an ADO Command object may be created dynamically in memory and executed without being permanently stored in the database. The big difference between DAO and ADO objects is that ADO objects may be declared to receive messages to trigger object events. You examine this ADO capability in Objective 25.6, "Working with ADO Events."

25.4.1   Various Ways to Open a *Recordset*

ADO provides a multitude of ways to open a Recordset. Among the different methods:

1. A Command object's Execute method can return a Recordset for SELECT queries.

2. A Recordset may be declared independently and opened when associated with an open Connection object.

3. The arguments required by the Open method of the Recordset object may be assigned before the Open method is executed.

4. The arguments may be included in the Recordset Open method when executed.

5. You can use the Data Designer.

In Exercise 25.2, you demonstrated the first method of opening a Recordset. In the next exercise, you demonstrate methods 2, 3, and 4. You examine the Data Designer in Objective 25.5, "Using the Data Environment Designer to Manage ADO Connections." First, you examine the ADO Recordset's Open method. The syntax of the Open method is

```
Object.Open([Source], [ActiveConnection], [CursorType], [LockType],
    [Options])
```

The elements of the Open method are described in Table 25.2.

TABLE 25.2   Elements of the *Open* Method and Their Description

Element	Description
Source	A Command object variable name, an SQL statement, a table name, or a stored procedure call. In Access databases, QueryDefs that return data are seen as views, *not* as stored procedures.
ActiveConnection	Either a connection string or a Connection object
Cursor Type	One of the following values: adOpenForwardOnly (default) adOpenStatic adOpenDynamic adOpenKeyset
LockType	One of the following values: adLockReadOnly(Default) adLockPessimistic adLockOptimistic adLockBatchOptimistic
Options	One of the following values: adCommandText adCmdTable adCmdTableDirect adCmdStoredProcedure adCmdUnknown adCmdFile adRunAsync

We examine some of the constant values for these Open method arguments in greater detail later in this section.

Exercise 25.3   Opening *Recordsets*

This exercise examines various ways of opening a Recordset. Figure 25.7 shows the completed application.

Figure 25.7   *The* Recordset Open *method arguments may be designated before the* Open *method is executed.*

1. Open **Project P25-3.vbp** from the installed exercises that accompany this book. You should see the interface displayed in runtime on Figure 25.7. The form has two list boxes on it, **1stDisplay** and **1stDisplay2**, and a single Command button, **cmdGetData**.

2. The project also contains a module, **mod25-3.BAS,** that contains the FillList procedure from the previous exercise.

3. In the cmdGetData_Click event, enter the following code:

```
Private Sub cmdGetData_Click()
    Dim cn As ADODB.Connection
    Dim rs As New ADODB.Recordset
    Dim rs2 As New ADODB.Recordset
    Dim msg As String
    Dim sql as String

    On Error GoTo cmdGetDataErr

    Set cn = New ADODB.Connection
    cn.Open "DB_Cinema"

    rs.Source = "Select [Director Name] From Directors"
    rs.ActiveConnection = cn
    rs.CursorLocation = adUseClient
    rs.CursorType = adOpenStatic
    rs.LockType = adLockReadOnly

    rs.Open

    sql = "Select [Film Title] From [Film Titles] Order By [Film
    ➡Title]"
    rs2.Open sql, cn, adOpenStatic, adLockReadOnly
```

```
            Call FillList(rs, "Director Name", lstDisplay)
            Call FillList(rs2, 0, lstDisplay2)

    CloseDown:

        If Not cn.State = adStateClosed Then cn.Close
        If Not rs.State = adStateClosed Then rs.Close
        If Not rs2.State = adStateClosed Then rs2.Close
        Exit Sub
    cmdGetDataErr:
        MsgBox "Error: " & Err.Number & " " & Err.Description
        Resume CloseDown

    End Sub
```

4. Run and test the program.

Observe the two methods of specifying Open method arguments. For Recordset rs, all properties are assigned before the Open method is called. For Recordset rs2, the arguments are included in the Open method itself. Unlike Exercise 25.2, neither of these methods uses a Command object. Instead, the Recordset objects are associated directly with the Connection object.

25.4.2   A Closer Look at Cursor Locations and Cursors

The cursor argument is important to understand, and it can affect performance dramatically. As you have seen, a cursor is very much like a recordset. In fact, recordsets *are* cursors. Some cursors, such as dynamic cursors, are extremely expensive in terms of system resources such as RAM, network bandwidth, and CPU cycles. Other cursors, such as forward-scrolling, read-only, and static cursors containing a reasonable number of rows are much less expensive on system resources. It is even possible (and advisable) to return data without using a cursor at all. In fact, no cursor is the ADO default "cursor."

In a client/server environment, the cursor may be built on the server or on the client. In ADO this location is specified by the CursorLocation property of the recordset. Choosing where to build cursors depends on a variety of factors, the most important of which is the type of cursor is being built. Some cursors, such as ForwardOnly, KeySet, and Dynamic, must be built on the server. Static cursors may be built on either the server or the client. Choosing cursor location is also influenced by other factors such as the number of simultaneous users, the average power of the client machine, the capability of the server machine, and overall network load. Server-side cursors, for instance, are great for low-power client machines with a fairly capable server. Such cursors are also speedy when writing data to the server machine. As the number of users increases, however, the server can become strained under the increased load.

Cursors determine how a returned data set is handled in three key areas:

Membership   The WHERE clause of an SQL query determines which rows should initially be included in the recordset. As the query processor in the database operates, the cursor type determines when to close membership. When the last row is found and the current row pointer is pointing to the last row, cursor membership is typically closed. Some cursors such as the ForwardOnly cursor try to close membership as soon as possible. Others, such as dynamic cursors, never close membership.

Scrolling   By allowing the current-row pointer to move forward and backward, you place extra requirements on the cursor and system resources. A cursor that scrolls forward only is less burdensome than one that scrolls both ways, but cannot return a RecordCount property.

Updatability   An updatable cursor refers to one that allows rows to be edited or new rows to be added. Making a cursor updatable is also relatively expensive.

With these concepts in mind, the following table re-examines the cursor choices available in the Recordset Open method:

Cursor Type	Behavior
adForwardOnly	The fastest cursor to use. It is identical to a static cursor except that you can scroll only in a forward direction. If made read-only, it is the fastest cursor you can use. A server-side cursor only, a static cursor is the default if the CursorType property is not specified.
adOpenStatic	Membership is frozen after the cursor is populated. Changes (additions, edits, deletions) by other users are not visible. Can be updated and may be placed on either the client or the server. May be scrolled in either direction.
adOpenKeyset	Fully scrollable, updatable server-side cursor. Data changes by others are visible when the current-row pointer is placed on the changed row. New rows added by other users are *not* visible, and rows deleted by others are not accessible.
adOpenDynamic	The most expensive cursor. Membership is never closed, so all additions, edits, and deletions by other users are visible. Fully scrollable.

If providing concurrent data to all users simultaneously is not an absolute application requirement, the best approach is often to present data to the user in a read-only fashion using the adForwardOnly or adOpenStatic cursors. Should the user want to add, edit, or delete rows, a separate action query using INSERT, UPDATE, or

DELETE SQL syntax can write data to or delete data from the database. Although writing this type of code takes longer than using an updatable scrollable cursor, the former is much less stressful on system resources. It also dramatically improves database performance.

25.4.3   Using a *Recordset* with an Unbound *MSFlexGrid* Control

Grid controls are frequently used in database applications. In fact, very few real-world database applications do not use a grid control of some type. Users expect to see data presented in tabular fashion, and grids are among the most efficient ways to present returned result sets for reading or editing.

You have already been introduced to the MSFlexGrid control. A relatively "lightweight" control in its impact on system resources, the MSFlexGrid control is very well suited for use in database applications that present mainly read-only data to the user. Visual Basic also provides a DataGrid control that may be used in bound mode with an ADO Data control. Using the MSFlexGrid control in unbound mode takes a little more code but makes for snappier performance because less expensive cursors may be used.

Exercise 25.4   Presenting an ADO *Recordset* in an Unbound *MSFlexGrid* Control

This exercise asks you to display an ADO Recordset in an unbound MSFlexGrid control (see Figure 25.8).

Figure 25.8   *The MSFlexGrid control in unbound mode offers snappy performance.*

1. Open Project **P25-4.vbp** from the installed exercises. The project consists of one form and one code module. The form should appear similar to the runtime form illustrated in Figure 25.8. The form consists of an MSFlexGrid (Grid1) and a command button (**cmdGetData**).

continues

Exercise 25.4   continued

2. Add a general procedure to the form module to prepare the grid control:

```
Private Sub PrepGrid(g As MSFlexGrid)
    With g
        .FixedCols = 0
        .FixedRows = 1
        .Rows = 2
        .AllowUserResizing = flexResizeColumns
    End With
End Sub
```

3. In the Form_Load event, call the PrepGrid procedure:

```
Private Sub Form_Load()
    Call PrepGrid(Grid1)
End Sub
```

4. In the cmdGetData_Click event, add code to retrieve all data from film titles and pass it to a procedure for filling the grid:

```
Private Sub cmdGetData_Click()
    Dim cn As ADODB.Connection
    Dim rs As New ADODB.Recordset
    Dim msg As String

    On Error GoTo cmdGetDataErr

    Set cn = New ADODB.Connection

    cn.Open "DB_Cinema"

    rs.Source = "[Film Titles]"
    rs.CursorType = adOpenStatic
    rs.ActiveConnection = cn
    rs.Open

    Call FillGrid(rs, Grid1, Me)
CloseDown:

    If Not cn.State = adStateClosed Then cn.Close
    If Not rs.State = adStateClosed Then rs.Close

    Exit Sub
cmdGetDataErr:
    MsgBox "Error: " & Err.Number & " " & Err.Description
    Resume CloseDown

End Sub
```

5. Add the FillGrid procedure to the code module. This procedure is intended to handle the display of any ADODB.Recordset that does not use an adForwardOnly cursor.

```
Public Sub FillGrid(rs As ADODB.Recordset, g As MSFlexGrid,
➥f As Form)
    Dim intFieldNameLen As Integer
    Dim intFieldValueLen As Integer
    Dim wid As Integer, i As Integer
    Dim runwidth As Integer
```

```
                Dim fcount As Integer, rowcount As Long
                Dim holdstring as String

                On Error GoTo FillGridEH

                ' check that recordset contains data
                If rs.BOF = True And rs.EOF = True Then
                   MsgBox "No Data returned"
                   Exit Sub
                End If

                If rs.RecordCount = -1 Then
                   rowcount = 1000
                Else
                   rowcount = rs.RecordCount
                End If

                wid = Screen.TwipsPerPixelX
                fcount = rs.Fields.Count

            With g
                .Redraw = False
                .Clear
                .Cols = fcount
                .Rows = rowcount
                .Row = 1
                .Col = 0
                .RowSel = rowcount - 1
                .ColSel = fcount - 1
                holdstring = rs.GetString(adClipString, , , , "-")
                .Clip = holdstring

                ' add column headers and adjust column widths
                .Row = 0
                For i = 0 To fcount - 1
                  .Col = i
                  .CellFontBold = True
                  .Text = rs.Fields(i).Name

                  If rs.Fields(i).Type <> adBinary And _
                     rs.Fields(i).DefinedSize < 256 Then
                     intFieldNameLen = f.TextWidth(rs.Fields(i).Name)
                     intFieldValueLen = wid * rs.Fields(i).DefinedSize
                     If intFieldNameLen > intFieldValueLen Then
                        .ColWidth(i) = intFieldNameLen + 400
                     Else
                        .ColWidth(i) = intFieldValueLen * 3
                        If .ColWidth(i) > 4000 Then .ColWidth(i) = 4000
                     End If
                  Else
                        .ColWidth(i) = intFieldNameLen + 400
                  End If
                runwidth = runwidth + .ColWidth(i)
              Next

            If runwidth < (f.ScaleWidth - 400) Then
                .Width = runwidth + 400
            Else
```

continues

633

Exercise 25.4   continued

```
            .Width = f.ScaleWidth - .Left
        End If

        .Visible = True
        .Redraw = True
    End With
Exit Sub
FillGridEH:
    MsgBox "Error: " & Err.Number & " " & Err.Description
    g.Clear

    Exit Sub
End Sub
```

This lengthy procedure uses most of its code to format the MSFlexGrid control after the Recordset values have been placed in the grid. First the code checks to see whether the Recordset has returned any data. If the Recordset contains no data, both the BOF and the EOF properties of the Recordset are true. If no data has been returned, the procedure is exited.

This procedure uses the Clip property of the MDFlexGrid control to populate its cells. Controls that can use a Clip string can handle delimited strings for speedy addition of data to the control. The ADODB.Recordset object has a GetString method that creates a delimited string.

Because clip strings must be "pasted" into a preallocated space, the RecordCount property of the Recordset determines the number of rows. Similarly, the Count property of the Fields collection determines the number of columns. Because it references the RecordCount property, this routine cannot use a ForwardOnly cursor.

After you enter the data, the only step left is to set grid column widths. Setting column widths in a grid is a matter of trade-offs. To the degree possible, columns should be wide enough to accommodate all field names, but not so wide that the grid's width extends beyond the bounds of the form.

The code first checks for Binary or Memo data types in a Recordset that extend beyond 256 characters. These fields get an arbitrary width of 400 twips. (These data types should usually *not* be included in Recordsets intended for grid display.) If the FieldName is longer than the value of the data displayed in the column, the column is set to accommodate the FieldName; otherwise the column is set to accommodate data values up to an arbitrary limit of 4,000 twips. The runlength variable helps ensure that the grid does not extend beyond the bounds of the form. The MSFlexGrid control automatically adds a horizontal scroll bar at the bottom of the grid if column widths extend beyond grid width dimensions.

6. Run and test the program.

The *GetString* Method

The `FillGrid` procedure used the `GetString` method of the `Recordset` object. The syntax of this method is

```
Function GetString([StringFormat], [NumRows], [ColumnDelimiter],
[RowDelimiter], [NullExpr]) As String
```

When working with ADODB.Recordsets, you usually need to only specify the string that you want to use to indicate null values included in the `Recordset`. The `StringFormat` argument always takes the `adClipString` constant for the its argument. The default column delimiter is a tab character, and the `GetString` method adds carriage return and linefeed characters as default row delimiters. In Exercise 25.4, you used a dash character to represent null values.

25.4.4   Using a *Recordset* with a Bound *DataGrid* Control

For small recordsets, the convenience of using a bound `DataGrid` control can easily outweigh the resource costs. For a database being used on a single-user machine with adequate memory, you should not hesitate to use a bound `DataGrid` control.

Similar to using the standard Data control, you can bind a `DataGrid` to an ADO `Recordset` by using an ADO Data control. You can use standard ADO methods to open a Recordset and then assign it to the `Recordset` property of the ADO Data control. Assuming the `DataGrid` control is bound to the ADO Data control, the grid automatically fills with the returned data and even automatically assigns field names to the grid column headers.

Exercise 25.5   Using the *DataGrid* Control

In this exercise, you add an ADO Data control and a `DataGrid` to a form. You also open an ADO Recordset and assign it to the data control, filling the `DataGrid` control with returned data.

1. Open **Project P25-5.vbp** from the installed exercises. You should see a form that resembles the one in Figure 25.9. The form includes a command button (`cmdGetData`), an ADO data control (`adoTest`), and a `DataGrid` (`Grid1`). The `Visible` property for the data control has been set to `False`.

continues

Exercise 25.5   continued

Figure 25.9   *Using the ADO Data control and a* DataGrid *facilitates data display.*

2. Examine the selections in the Project|Components|Controls dialog box. You should see the check boxes marked for the Microsoft ADO Data Control 6.0 (OLEDB) check box as well as the Microsoft DataGrid Control 6.0 (OLEDB).

3. Make sure that the DataSource property of Grid1 is set to adoTest.

4. In the cmdGetData_Click event, add the following code:

```
Private Sub cmdGetData_Click()
  Dim cn As ADODB.Connection
  Dim rs As New ADODB.Recordset
  Dim msg As String

  On Error GoTo cmdGetDataErr

  Set cn = New ADODB.Connection
  cn.Open "DB_Cinema"

  rs.Source = "Select * From [Film Titles]"
  rs.CursorType = adOpenStatic
  rs.ActiveConnection = cn
  rs.Open


  Set adoTest.Recordset = rs

  adoTest.Refresh

CloseDown:

  If Not cn.State = adStateClosed Then cn.Close
  If Not rs.State = adStateClosed Then rs.Close

  Exit Sub
cmdGetDataErr:
  MsgBox "Error: " & Err.Number & " " & Err.Description
  Resume CloseDown

End Sub
```

5. Run and test the program.

As you can see, by using the ADO Data control and a DataGrid control, you get an extraordinary amount of functionality with just a little bit of code. The editability of individual cells in the DataGrid depends on the kind of cursor assigned to the Recordset property. Change the LockType and CursorType property settings for the Recordset and observe the different DataGrid behaviors.

25.4.5   Using a *Command* Object to Write Data to a Database

So far, you have only read data from the database. To write data to the database, you must use the ADO Command object. Writing data to the database is often best handled by stored procedures such as QueryDef objects. Here, action queries with specified parameters can be compiled and kept. This approach obviates the need to concatenate long SQL strings on a client application.

Unfortunately, the OLE DB Provider for Jet databases does not recognize QueryDef objects as stored procedures. Instead, they are seen as views. The parameters of a stored procedure that would expose themselves through the OLE DB Provider for other databases such as SQL Server are unavailable.

Exercise 25.6   Writing Data with the ADO *Command* Object

This exercise permits you to add a new director to the Directors table of Cinema.MDB. It also allows the user to show all film titles by director. It uses an SQL subquery in the WHERE clause of a query to retrieve the Director ID value from the Directors table. It then uses that value to select film title data. When adding a new director to the Directors table, the exercise automatically creates a new Director ID by incrementing the highest value currently in the Director ID field.

1. Open **Project P25-6** from the installed exercises. The Project contains two forms, frmMain (f25A.frm) and frmInput (f25B.frm), and a standard code module (mod25-6.BAS). The code has been left in the code module. The two forms are shown in Figures 25.10 and 25.11. On frmMain is a single combo box (cboDirectors), a MSFlexGrid control (Grid1), and a command button (cmdNewDirector). When the user selects a director from the combo box, the films of that director are shown in the grid control. The second form, frmInput, allows the user to enter a new director's name. The Director ID is calculated in code.

continues

Exercise 25.6   continued

Figure 25.10 *This form allows the user to select film titles by director and to add new entries to the Directors table.*

Figure 25.11 *The data entry form for adding new directors.*

2. Make the following declarations at the module level of `frmMain`:

```
Dim cn As ADODB.Connection
Public WriteToDB As Boolean
```

The `WriteToDB` variable acts as a flag so code is not executed if the user decides to cancel data entry on `frmInput`.

3. Add the following code to the `frmMain` `Load()` and `Unload()` events:

```
Private Sub Form_Load()
  Set cn = New ADODB.Connection
  cn.Open "DB_Cinema"
  Call GetDirectors
End Sub

Private Sub Form_Unload(Cancel As Integer)
    If Not cn.State = adStateClosed Then cn.Close
End Sub
```

Notice that you close the connection that was opened when the form is loaded in the form `Unload` event, testing to make sure that the `connection` is not already closed.

4. Add code to populate the cboDirectors combo box with director names.

```
Private Sub GetDirectors()
    Dim rs As New ADODB.Recordset
    rs.Source = "Select [Director Name] From Directors"
    rs.ActiveConnection = cn
    rs.Open
    Call FillList(rs, 0, cboDirectors)
    cboDirectors.ListIndex = 0
    rs.Close
End Sub
```

5. Add code that uses a subquery to populate the grid control with film titles when the user chooses a new director:

```
Private Sub cboDirectors_Click()
    Dim cmd As New ADODB.Command
    Dim rs As New ADODB.Recordset
    Dim dir_id As Integer
    Dim sql As String
    Dim msg As String

    On Error GoTo cboDirectorsClickErr
    sql = "SELECT * FROM [Film Titles] WHERE "
    sql = sql & "([Director ID] = ANY (Select [Director ID] FROM
    ➥Directors "
    sql = sql & "WHERE [Director Name] = '" & cboDirectors.Text &
    ➥"'))"

    rs.Source = sql
    rs.ActiveConnection = cn
    rs.CursorType = adOpenStatic
    rs.Open
    Call FillGrid(rs, Grid1, Me)

CloseDown:

    If Not rs.State = adStateClosed Then rs.Close

    Exit Sub
cboDirectorsClickErr:
    MsgBox "Error: " & Err.Number & " " & Err.Description
    GoTo CloseDown

    End Sub
```

6. Add code to the cmdNewDirector_Click() event that inserts new values into the Directors table using SQL syntax.

```
Private Sub cmdNewDirector_Click()
    Dim answer As Integer
    Dim msg As String
    Dim cmd As New Command
    Dim NewID As Integer
    Dim NewDirector As String
    Dim rs As New ADODB.Recordset
    Dim sql As String

    WriteToDB = False
    frmInput.Show vbModal
    If WriteToDB = True Then
```

continues

639

```
            rs.Source = "Select Max([Director Id]) AS MaxID FROM
            ➥Directors"
            rs.ActiveConnection = cn
            rs.Open
            NewID = rs![MaxID] + 1
            If rs.State = adStateOpen Then rs.Close
            NewDirector = cboDirectors.List(0)
            sql = "INSERT INTO Directors ( [Director ID], [Director
            ➥Name] )"
            sql = sql & " VALUES (" & NewID & ", '" & NewDirector &
            ➥"');"

            With cmd
                .CommandText = sql
                .CommandType = adCmdText
                .ActiveConnection = cn
                .Execute
            End With
        End If

        WriteToDB = False
        Call GetDirectors
    End Sub
```

This code inserts new values into the Directors table *without using a record-set*. A recordset is employed to retrieve a value so a new Director ID may be calculated but is then immediately closed. A Command object is executed to write the data. This approach is much less expensive on system resources than opening an updatable cursor, especially in a multiuser environment.

7. Examine the code in frmInput. It has been left in for you on the student disk. Assuming the user enters data and does not click the Cancel button on frmInput, the code assigns the new director name to the top of the combo box. This value is then used by the INSERT SQL statement. The call to the GetDirectors code at the end of the procedure rearranges directors in the combo box by their Director ID values.

8. Run and test the program.

The ADO Recordset object also has available the AddNew, Delete, Edit, and Update methods, which act nearly identically to their DAO counterparts. These methods may be used only on Recordsets with updatable cursors, however.

Objective 25.5   Using the Data Environment Designer to Manage ADO Connections

Visual Basic 6.0 includes a multitude of wizards and utilities to speed application development. Among the most powerful are the DataView window and the Data Environment Designer. These two utilities are often used in tandem to permit the programmer to see a database structure while in design time and to manage connections and commands in a separate file for use by one or more applications.

This objective introduces the Data Environment Designer. The Data Environment Designer includes a powerful utility for building SQL queries with a query-by-example interface very similar to the one used by the Query utility inside Access. Space limitations preclude a full presentation of this and other Data Environment Designer utilities. Instead, we emphasize using the Data Environment Designer to make database connections and then demonstrate how to address the Data Designer Environment object and its contained Command object in code.

25.5.1 Creating a Direct ADO Connection

Unlike a DSN file, the Data Environment Designer enables you to make a direct connection to the OLE DB Provider with ADO. This feature removes one software layer between your application and the database. Depending on how much of the database functionality is exposed by the OLE DB Provider, you should be able to accomplish nearly everything you wish with ADO.

To create an ADO connection, you add a Data Environment Designer object to a Project. Exercise 25.7 steps you through this process.

Exercise 25.7 Using the *Data Environment* Object to Create an ADO Connection

1. Start a new Project. Remove the default form from the project and save the project to disk as **P25_7**.

2. To add a Data Environment object to your program, select Project|Add DataEnvironment.

3. In your Project Explorer, you should see a Data Environment object with the default name of DataEnvironment1. You should also see the Data Environment Designer displayed in Figure 25.12.

Figure 25.12 *The Data Environment Designer enables you to make connections and to manage* Command *objects.*

continues

Exercise 25.7 continued

4. Select the `DataEnvironment1` object in the Data Environment Designer and press F4. Change the name of the `DataEnvironment1` object to **DEDemo** and save it to disk as **DEDemo.Dsr**. Save the project again.

5. Right-click on the `Connection1` object in the Data Environment Designer and select Properties from the pop-up menu; the tabbed dialog box you see in Figure 25.13 should appear.

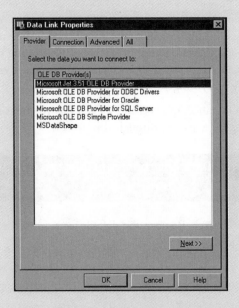

Figure 25.13 *The* Connection *object allows you to select the appropriate OLE DB Provider.*

6. Select the Microsoft Jet 3.51 OLE DB Provider and click on <u>N</u>ext. When the display appears, select the Connection tab as shown in Figure 25.14. Click the button with the ellipse and select the Cinema.MDB database under Chapt25 in the installed exercises directory (the path statement will differ from that shown in Figure 25.14).

Figure 25.14   *After you select a database, you can test the connection.*

7. After you select the database, click the Test Connection button on the Connection tab to be sure you are connected. A message box should tell you that the test succeeded.

8. Click the OK button.

9. Right-click again on the Connection1 object in the Data Environment Designer and change the name of Connection1 to **cnDemo**.

10. Make sure cnDemo has the focus in the Data Environment Designer window. The second toolbar icon should display a ToolTip saying Add Command. Click this toolbar icon or right-click on cnDemo and select Add Command. A Command folder should appear with the default name Command1.

11. Right-click on Command1, and the tabbed dialog box displayed in Figure 25.15 should appear.

    Change the name of Command1 to cmdGetDirectors, select the SQL Statement option and enter the simple SQL statement you see in Figure 25.15. Click OK. Once completed, the Data Environment window should be similar to the one in Figure 25.16. Notice how the returned fields from the query are listed below the Command object.

12. Save the project at this point.

continues

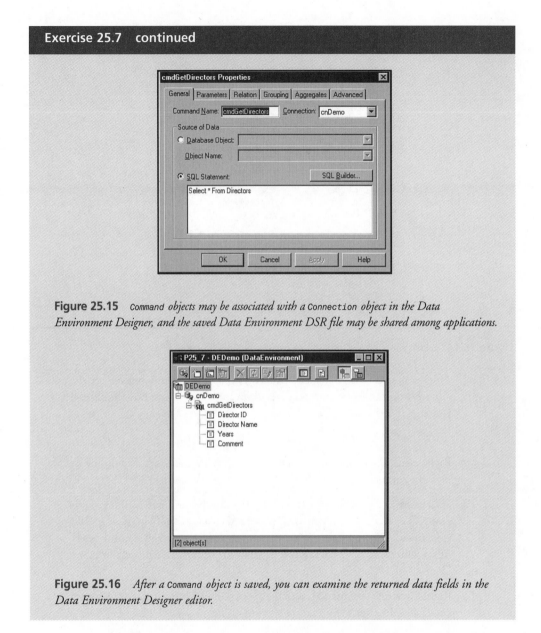

Figure 25.15 *Command objects may be associated with a Connection object in the Data Environment Designer, and the saved Data Environment DSR file may be shared among applications.*

Figure 25.16 *After a Command object is saved, you can examine the returned data fields in the Data Environment Designer editor.*

25.5.2   Adding and Using a Data Environment File

With a saved Data Environment (.DSR) file, it is now possible to add the file to different projects. All Command objects added to the Data Environment Designer become methods of the Data Environment object. For methods that return Recordsets, invoking the method populates a property of the Date Environment object that takes as its name the name of the Command object with an rs prefix.

Exercise 25.8   Adding and Using a DSR File in a Project

This exercise demonstrates how to add and use a Data Environment (.DSR) file in a project.

1. Open **P25-8.vbp** from the installed exercises directory.

2. The project should contain a single form (f25-8.frm) and a code module (mod25-8.bas). The form contains a single MSFlexGrid control (Grid1) and a command button (cmdGetData).

3. To add the DEDemo.DSR file to the projects, select Project, Add File. Select DEDemo.DSR from Add File dialog box and add it to the project. Save the project. Your Project Explorer window should look similar to Figure 25.17.

Figure 25.17   *The Project Explorer window after the DEDemo.DSR file has been added.*

4. At the module level of the form, make the following declaration:

```
Dim ucn As DEDemo
```

5. In the Form_Load event, add code to instantiate the DEDemo object:

```
Private Sub Form_Load()
  Set ucn = New DEDemo
End Sub
```

6. In the cmdGetData_Click event, add code that executes the cmdGetDirectors command as a DEDemo event and then reads the result from the rscmdGetGetDirectors property. Note how the cmdGetDirectors method is presented in the Visual Basic editor when a period is added to the ucn variable.

```
Private Sub cmdGetData_Click()
  Dim rs As ADODB.Recordset

  ucn.cmdGetDirectors
  Set rs = ucn.rscmdGetDirectors
  Call FillGrid(rs, Grid1, Me)

  If rs.State = adStateOpen Then rs.Close
End Sub
```

7. Run and test the program. After the Data Environment object is built, the code is simple!

Objective 25.6   Working with ADO Events

Perhaps the most significant improvements represented by the ADO library are the rich set of events exposed for ADO objects. This section gives you the flavor of working with ADO events, and as you work more with Visual Basic, you will come to appreciate the significant advance these events represent for database application development, compared against other database object libraries.

Most events for ADO Connection and Recordset objects exist in pairs with a Will event and an EventComplete event. For instance, the Connection object has WillConnect/ConnectComplete and WillExecute/ExecuteComplete event pairs. The Recordset object has a WillChangeRecord/RecordChangeComplete pair. The Recordset also has an EndOfRecordset event.

There are two ways of working with ADO events in Visual Basic. If you work with a Data Environment Designer, Connection and Recordset events are exposed within the Designer. Merely right-click on the Designer and select View Code. If you are not working with the Data Environment Designer, you may declare the ADO objects with a WithEvents keyword. For instance, the declaration

```
Dim WithEvents cn as ADODB.Connection
```

would cause the cn object to appear in the Object drop-down combo box in the Visual Basic code window and the Connection events would appear in the Procedure combo box.

Exercise 25.9   Coding ADO Events

In this exercise, you work with events exposed by the Data Environment Designer.

1. Open **P25-9.vbp** in the directory of installed exercises.

2. You should see the interface illustrated in Figure 25.18. The form consists of a single button (cmdConnect), an MSFlexGrid control (Grid1), and three labels from left to right at the bottom of the form (lblStartConnnect, lblConnectionMade, and lblRecordsetComplete).

Figure 25.18   *The* Data Environment *object exposes a rich series of events.*

3. At the module level of the form, make the following declaration:

```
Public ucn As DEDemo
```

4. Add a general procedure called FillOnNotice. This code executes when called by the Data Designer after the connection is complete.

```
Public Sub FillOnNotice()
    Dim rs As New ADODB.Recordset
    lblConnectionMade.Caption = "Connected"
    DoEvents
    ucn.cmdGetDirectors
    Set rs = ucn.rscmdGetDirectors
    Call FillGrid(rs, Grid1, Me)
    If rs.State = adStateOpen Then rs.Close
End Sub
```

5. Add the following code to the cmdConnect_Click event to open the connection:

```
Private Sub cmdConnect_Click()
    Set ucn = New DEDemo
    ucn.cnDemo.Open
End Sub
```

6. Add the following event procedures to the DEDemo Data Connection object. To see the DEDemo code window and the event procedures, select the DEDemo object in the Project Explorer and right-click on it. Choose View Code from the pop-up menu.

```
Private Sub cnDemo_ConnectComplete(ByVal pError As ADODB.Error, _
        adStatus As ADODB.EventStatusEnum,_
        ByVal pConnection As ADODB.Connection)

    Call Form1.FillOnNotice
End Sub

Private Sub cnDemo_WillConnect(ConnectionString As String, _
➥UserID As _
String, Password As String, Options _
As Long, adStatus As _
ADODB.EventStatusEnum, _
ByVal pConnection As ADODB.Connection)
    Form1.lblStartConnection.Caption = "Connecting...."
    DoEvents
End Sub

Private Sub rscmdGetDirectors_EndOfRecordset(fMoreData As _
➥Boolean, _
    adStatus As ADODB.EventStatusEnum, ByVal pRecordset _
    As ADODB.Recordset)

    Form1.lblRecordsetComplete.Caption = "Data Retrieved"
End Sub
```

7. Run and test the program. As the events fire, you should see them reported in the labels on the form.

Chapter Summary

This chapter introduced the use of OLE DB connections to databases managed through ActiveX Data Objects. OLE DB is a new technology and the ADO library is the principal means of exploiting it. OLE DB databases are designed to meet the growing need of enterprises to have a common data access interface to heterogeneous data sources.

OLE DB Providers are available for a multitude of data sources, including ODBC databases. For databases with their own OLE DB Provider, the ODBC OLE DB Provider may be bypassed. For now, Access databases are best developed with the DAO library. The early versions of ADO are optimized for larger databases such as SQL Server and Oracle.

Unlike other object models, the ADO object model is flat with the core ADO objects of Connections, Commands, and Recordsets capable of being created independently and then later associated with one another.

ADO Recordsets have four cursor types: ForwardOnly, Static, Keyset, and Dynamic. These cursors vary in the ways they handle membership, scrolling, and updatabililty. All the cursors are built on the server except for static cursors, which may be built on either the server or the client. The fastest cursor is no cursor at all: a read-only, forward-scrolling record retrieval. This cursor type is the ADO default.

When used in combination with a DataGrid and other ADO-compliant bound controls, the ADO Data control provides an easy way to rapidly present returned records to the user. The behavior of the DataGrid control depends on the kind of cursor used by the Recordset assigned to the control.

Connections to databases may be created and maintained using the Data Environment Designer. The Designer allows Command objects to be added to it for easy programmability. A Data Environment object is saved to disk with a .DSR extension. This file may be shared between projects.

ADO objects expose events. If you are using the Data Environment Designer, these events are presented automatically in the Designer code window. If you are not using the Designer, events may be exposed by declaring ADO Connection and Recordset objects with the WithEvents keyword as in the following example:

```
Dim WithEvents cn as ADODB.Connection
```

Skill-Building Exercises

This set of exercises asks you to practice using ADO in several ways. The first, third, and fifth exercises ask you to use ADO via a DSN connection. The second and fourth exercises ask you to write SQL queries. The final exercise gives more practice in working with the bound DataGrid control.

1. Write a program using ADO via a DSN connection that displays all film titles and the year of release for all films released in 1970 or later in the Cinema.MDB database. Name the DSN file **SB_Cinema**.

2. Write a program that displays the film title and rating for all films rated PG-13 or R in the Cinema.MDB database. (Hint: Consult Visual Basic's online help to see how an OR expression can be used in an SQL WHERE clause.)

3. Create a DSN file for the Biblio.MDB database that comes with Visual Basic. Name the DSN file **SB_Biblio**. Write a program that displays all the data from the Publishers table using this DSN file.

4. Using the DSN connection created in the previous exercise, use an ADO Recordset object to let the user select all author information in the Authors table by the first letter of their last name. (Hint: The WHERE clause of the SQL statement will be similar to "WHERE Author Like '" & variable & "%'". The ADO library uses the standard ANSI wild card operator [%]).

5. Convert the previous exercise using a Command object rather than a Recordset object.

6. Create a DSR file for the Biblio database. Name the file **SB_DE_BIBLIO** and save it to disk as **SB_DE_BIBLIO.DSR**. Add a Command to the Data Environment Designer that selects all Publishers. Write a program that uses the DSR file and displays the Resultset of the Command when it is executed.

7. Using the previous skill-building exercise, display the result set in a bound DataGrid control.

26

WORKING WITH OBJECTS FROM MICROSOFT OFFICE

This chapter introduces utilizing objects contained within the desktop applications of the Microsoft Office suite from within a Visual Basic application. Visual Basic is much more than just a language for developing standalone Windows applications; it also is the scripting or macro language for nearly the entire suite of Microsoft desktop applications, including Word, Excel, Access, and PowerPoint. A version of Visual Basic, VBScript, is designed for use with interactive Internet applications.

Within Microsoft Office applications, you can use Visual Basic for Applications to automate many program actions or to execute independent code. The newest versions of the Microsoft Office applications provide a rich design environment for writing application macros, or for developing custom applications within the framework of the applications. When programming with Microsoft Office applications, you must decide whether you want to work primarily within the programming environment provided by the application and Microsoft Office, or within the Visual Basic design environment.

This chapter focuses on interacting with Microsoft applications from within standalone Visual Basic programs. The concepts and code presented within this chapter will be usable if you choose to work with the Visual Basic editors provided within Microsoft Office. This chapter emphasizes using Visual Basic with two of the Microsoft Office products: Excel and Access. Excel is one of the most frequently used Office products that serves to enhance Visual Basic projects. Excel's built-in functions and charting capabilities make it an extremely useful add-on to all kinds of programming tasks.

You already have used Data Access Objects (DAOs), a library of functions encapsulating the Jet engine of Access. You were able to use DAOs provided by an in-process server because the Jet engine is encapsulated inside a set of DLLs. The desktop program Access, including its user interface, can also be manipulated using Visual Basic. In this case, however, Access acts as an out-of-process server. You will use Access to print a report from a database, illustrating by example the distinction between in-process and out-of-process servers.

The newest version of Word has now migrated to Visual Basic for Applications. Visual Basic for Applications is gradually replacing Word Basic, a subset of earlier versions of Basic. Given the enormous complexity of Word and its object model, the migration of Word to Visual Basic for Applications is proving a gradual one. Word is the flagship application of the Microsoft Office suite, and there is an enormous installed base of Word Basic macros and programs. This chapter, therefore, concentrates on Excel and Access. Needless to say, this chapter assumes that you have the Microsoft Office suite, including Access, installed on your computer.

When you complete this chapter, you will be able to perform the following tasks:

- Use the `CreateObject()` function to create running instances of Excel and Access

- Use the following Excel objects and collections: `Application`, `Workbook(s)`, `Worksheet(s)`, and `Range`

- Use the Excel `Cells` and `Range` methods

- Use the Excel `Average()` function in a formula

- Use the `Shell()` function to launch non-ActiveX executables

- Use the `SendKeys` statement to send keystrokes to other applications

- Use the `AppActivate` statement to shift focus to another running application

- Use the `OpenCurrentDatabase` method of the `Access.Application` objects

- Use the methods of the Access `DoCmd` object

- Use the DAO `Container` and `Document` objects

- Print a stored report from an Access database

Chapter Objectives

The objectives of this chapter center on interacting with Microsoft Office applications from Visual Basic programs, as follows:

1. Understanding Microsoft Office applications as ActiveX servers

2. Using the `Shell()` function and `SendKeys` statement

3. Working with objects from the Excel type library

4. Working with objects from the Access type library

These objectives introduce enhancing Visual Basic applications with objects exposed by Microsoft Office applications. Given the size and complexity of these applications, this chapter cannot provide comprehensive coverage of the object hierarchy of Microsoft Office applications; rather, it gives you a flavor of how Microsoft Office objects can be combined with a Visual Basic application.

Objective 26.1   Understanding Microsoft Office Applications as ActiveX Servers

In Chapter 22, "Creating an ActiveX DLL," you constructed ActiveX DLLs containing string and math functions. These DLL code components operated within the same process as the client application using it, acting as in-process servers. The libraries containing DAOs also act as in-process servers. ActiveX DLL servers contain a type library that allows client applications to know the properties and methods exposed by the DLL.

Using ActiveX technology, free standing executables operating within their own process can also contain type libraries describing objects for use by other applications. These executables, using the underlying Component Object Model (COM) technology, can act as servers to client applications. The major difference between an ActiveX DLL server and an ActiveX EXE server is that the latter operates within its own process. Client applications that use the services of ActiveX EXE applications employ cross-process communication.

In-process communication is faster than cross-process communication; however, cross-process communication adds important flexibility to an application, especially when numerous client machines must access a single-server machine. An ActiveX EXE program on the server running within its own process can provide services to multiple client applications. Unlike an ActiveX DLL, the ActiveX EXE need not be stored on the client machine. Most important, it need not be tied to a single client application: It can service multiple applications. Two or three different database reporting applications, for example, can all avail themselves of the services of an ActiveX EXE running on the server.

Because the Microsoft Office applications are ActiveX EXE servers, they can be used by other applications. This makes possible the rapid development of document processing applications using the constituent applications of Microsoft Office. Suppose that you work in an enterprise in which elements of a spreadsheet, data in a database, and text from a word processing document must all be integrated regularly into a single report. The content varies from day to day, but the same elements are always used. Using the ActiveX capability of the Microsoft Office suite, you could construct a program to generate this report automatically.

26.1.1   Creating Instances of ActiveX EXE Objects

When working with ActiveX DLL objects, first make a reference to the type library of the DLL in the References dialog box (after choosing Project, References). With a reference established in the project, you then can declare objects defined within the type library in one of two ways:

- You can declare the object variable and then bind it with the Set statement, as in the following example:

```
Dim objectvar as myClass.myobject
Set objectvar = New myClass.myobject
```

The new class instance in this code occurs when the Set statement is executed.

- You can make the declaration with the following statement:

```
Dim objectvar as New myClass.myobject
```

In this code, the object is instantiated the first time a reference is made to an object property or method, as in the following example:

```
objectvar.Sort = True
```

Visual Basic provides a special function for creating objects when working with ActiveX EXE projects: the CreateObject() function. This function returns an instance of an object of a specific class. The syntax for the function is as follows:

```
CreateObject(class)
```

The class argument is a string argument that contains a fully qualified reference to the object, including the name of the ActiveX application and the object name. This string reference uses an appname.objecttype syntax. Suppose that you wanted to reference an Excel application. After making a reference to the Excel type library in the References dialog box (after choosing Project, References), you could make the following declaration:

```
Dim xlApp As Excel.Application
```

You then could create an instance of an Excel application with a Set statement and the CreateObject() function:

```
Set xlApp = CreateObject("Excel.Application")
```

The execution of this Set statement starts Excel on your machine. By setting the Visible property of the application to True, a running instance of Excel will appear on the user's desktop. Exercise 26.1 demonstrates working with the CreateObject() function.

Exercise 26.1   Using the *CreateObject*() Function to Create a Running Instance of Excel

In this short exercise, you create a running instance of Excel, using the CreateObject() function, and then terminate it.

1. Create a form with two buttons (**cmdStart** and **cmdStop**), as shown in Figure 26.1. Save the form to disk as **f26-1.frm** and the project as **p26-1.vbp**. Change the Name property of the project to **p26_1**.

2. Choose Project, References, and make a reference to the Excel library on your computer (see Figure 26.2).

Figure 26.1   *This application uses the* CreateObject() *function to start and stop Microsoft Excel.*

Figure 26.2   *The References dialog box allows you to select another application's objects that you want available in your code.*

3. At the module level of the form, make the following declaration:

   ```
   Dim xlapp As Excel.Application
   ```

4. In the cmdStart_Click() event, add the following code:

   ```
   Private Sub cmdStart_Click()
       Set xlapp = CreateObject("Excel.Application")
       xlapp.Visible = True
   End Sub
   ```

5. In the cmdStop_Click() event, add the following code:

   ```
   Private Sub cmdStop_Click()
       xlapp.Quit
       Set xlapp = Nothing
   End Sub
   ```

   In this code, you invoke the Excel.Application object's Quit method, and set the object variable to Nothing.

6. Run and test the program. The Start button should start the Excel application (with no workbook open), and the Stop button should terminate the application.

continues

Exercise 26.1   continued

Using the Object Browser, examine the `WindowState` property of the `Excel.Application` object. Experiment with launching the `Excel.Application` objects with the `WindowState` property set to its three possible settings (`xlNormal`, `xlMaximized`, `xlMinimized`).

Experiment further by commenting out the instruction `xlapp.Visible = True` in the `cmdStart_Click()` event. After clicking the Start button, use the Windows Task Manager utility to determine whether Excel is running.

26.1.2   Object Models of Office Applications

After you create an ActiveX EXE, you must know the object model of the application to navigate the hierarchy to access and manipulate the objects the application exposes. Although there is some similarity among object models, you must know the model and then learn the properties and methods of the objects contained within the application.

The Object Browser lists the properties, methods, and events of objects defined in ActiveX EXE type libraries, but the Object Browser by itself is not enough to work with these objects. You almost always need the programming references that accompany the developer versions of Office products to fully exploit their resources. Each application contains object methods with some of their own idiosyncrasies.

This chapter limits attention to examining some of the major objects contained within Excel and Access. Next, however, you will examine intrinsic Visual Basic commands that permit the developer to launch applications that are not ActiveX-compliant from within a Visual Basic application.

Objective 26.2   Using the *Shell()* Function and *SendKeys* Statement

Not all interapplication communication in Visual Basic involves the use of ActiveX or object linking and embedding (OLE) technology. Before the advent of OLE, Windows included simplified interapplication communication using the Windows Clipboard and a technology known as dynamic data exchange (DDE). You use the Windows Clipboard (a `System` object in Visual Basic) every time you copy and paste. You can easily add Clipboard functions to your Visual Basic applications, including the copying and pasting of graphics files. Visual Basic's documentation and online Help demonstrate how to add this operating system feature to your applications.

DDE, an early attempt to add programmable interapplication communication within Windows, is still available in Visual Basic. It features very fast passing of string data between applications. Because DDE is a receding technology, it is not included in this text. You should know, however, that DDE exists, and you should investigate it seriously if the interapplication communication you require is relatively simple. This technology frequently is used today for handling data transmitted from a serial port, often in applications that monitor and control automated manufacturing processes.

Two other Visual Basic instructions are important when working with interapplication communication: the Shell() function and the SendKeys statement.

26.2.1 The *Shell()* Function

A special Visual Basic function designed specifically to launch another application is the Shell() function. The syntax for this function is as follows:

```
Shell(pathname [,windowstyle])
```

The component pathname refers to the path and the name of the program to execute and any required arguments or command-line switches. It can include the directory and drive names and also the name of a document that has been associated with an executable program.

The component windowstyle refers to the style of the window in which the program is to be executed upon its opening. If windowstyle is omitted, the program is started minimized with focus. Table 26.1 explains the various styles.

TABLE 26.1 *windowstyle* Constants

Constant	Value	Description
vbHide	0	The window is hidden and focus is passed to the hidden window.
vbNormalFocus	1	The window has focus and is restored to its original size and position.
vbMinimizedFocus	2	The window is displayed as an icon with focus.
vbMaximizedFocus	3	The window is maximized with focus.
vbNormalNoFocus	4	The window is restored to its most recent size and position. The currently active window remains active.
vbMinimizedNoFocus	6	The window is displayed as an icon. The currently active window remains active.

As an example of the Shell() function, consider the following statement:

```
X = Shell("C:\windows\Calc.exe", 1)
```

This statement uses Shell() to leave the Visual Basic application and run the Calculator program, an .EXE program included with Microsoft Windows. The value returned (to X) is the task identification number of the started program.

Exercise 26.2   Using *Shell()* to Start Two Windows Applications

In this short exercise, you use the Shell() function to start the Windows Calculator and the Windows Notepad programs. Figure 26.3 shows the simple interface.

Figure 26.3   *This application launches the Calculator and the Notepad .EXE files using the* Shell() *function.*

1. Create the interface shown adding the **cmdCalculator** and **cmdNotepad** commands. Add the form caption. Save the form to disk as **f26-2.frm** and the project as **p26-2.vbp**. Change the Name property of the project to **p26_2**.

2. Write the following cmdCalculator_Click() procedure:

```
Private Sub cmdCalculator_Click()
    Dim X As Long
    X = Shell("c:\windows\calc.exe", 1) ' adjust the path
                                        'statement as necessary

End Sub
```

3. Write the cmdNotepad_Click() procedure:

```
Private Sub cmdNotepad_Click()
    Dim Y As Long
    Y = Shell("c:\windows\notepad.exe", 1) 'adjust path statement
                                           'as necessary

End Sub
```

4. Test your design.

26.2.2   The *SendKeys* Statement

A most useful Visual Basic statement is the SendKeys statement, which, as the name suggests, is a statement used to send one or more keystrokes from a Visual Basic application to another application. The syntax for this statement is as follows:

```
SendKeys string [,wait]
```

The `string` component is the string expression to be sent to the active window. The `wait` component is `True` or `False`. If `True`, keystrokes must be processed before control is returned to the procedure from which the keystrokes were sent. If `False`, control is returned to the calling procedure immediately after keys are sent. `False` is the default.

26.2.3   Dealing with Special Characters

Sending special characters with `SendKeys` requires knowledge of the `SendKeys` codes. The entire list of codes is found in the Help section of Visual Basic under the `SendKeys` statement. For your purposes, codes of special importance are those for the Shift, Ctrl, and Alt keys (see Table 26.2).

TABLE 26.2   *SendKeys* Codes for Special Characters

Key	Code
Alt	%
Backspace	{BACKSPACE}, {BS}, or {BKSP}
Break	{BREAK}
Caps Lock	{CAPSLOCK}
Ctrl	^
Del	{DELETE} or {DEL}
Down Arrow	{DOWN}
End	{END}
Enter	{ENTER} or ~
Esc	{ESC}
F1	{F1}
Help	{HELP}
Home	{HOME}
Ins	{INSERT}
Left Arrow	{LEFT}
Num Lock	{NUMLOCK}
Page Down	{PGDN}
Page Up	{PGUP}
Print Screen	{PRTSC}
Right Arrow	{RIGHT}
Scroll Lock	{SCROLLLOCK}
Shift	+
Tab	{TAB}
Up Arrow	{UP}

As an example, suppose that the Close window command on the Close box is Alt+F4. The following statement closes the active window (meaning the window must have the focus to be closed):

```
SendKeys "%{F4}", True
```

26.2.4   The *AppActivate* Statement

The AppActivate statement is used to activate an application window and is closely wedded to the SendKeys statement. The syntax for this statement is as follows:

```
AppActivate title [, wait]
```

The title component is the string expression that appears in the title bar of the application window to activate. Observe that this is not the name of the application, but the title caption shown in the title bar. The wait component is True or False, as with SendKeys.

Consider the following example:

```
AppActivate "Calculator"
```

This statement gives the focus to the Calculator application, provided it has been opened.

Exercise 26.3   Using *SendKeys* to Close Windows Applications

Create the interface shown in Figure 26.4 to use the SendKeys and AppActivate statements to close Windows applications from within Visual Basic. From this design, you can start and close the Windows Calculator and the Windows Notepad.

1. Design the interface as shown, and add the command buttons (**cmdClose**, **cmdNotepad**, and **cmdCalculator**). Add the form caption (exactly as shown). Save the form to disk as **f26-3.frm** and the project as **p26-3.vbp**. Change the Name property of the project to **p26_3**.

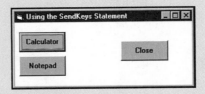

Figure 26.4   *The Calculator and the Notepad applications can be stopped with the* SendKeys *statement.*

2. Declare a flag variable at the module level.

```
Dim Message As String
```

---

3. Write the following `cmdCalculator_Click()` procedure:

```
Private Sub cmdCalculator_Click()
    Dim X As Long
    If Message = "Notepad" Or Message = "Calculator" Then
        MsgBox "Close the Open Windows Application", , "Please"
    Else
        X = Shell("c:\Windows\calc.exe", 1) ' adjust path as
        ➥necessary
        Message = "Calculator"
    End If
End Sub
```

In this procedure, error checking determines whether either the Notepad or the Calculator is already open. If the Notepad is open, the Calculator cannot be used until the Notepad is closed. If the Calculator is open, there is no need to open it again.

4. Write the following `cmdNotepad_Click()` procedure:

```
Private Sub cmdNotepad_Click()
    Dim Y As Long
    If Message = "Notepad" Or Message = "Calculator" Then
        MsgBox "Close the Open Windows Application", , "Please"
    Else
        Y = Shell("c:\Windows\notepad.exe", 1) ' adjust path as
        ➥necessary
        Message = "Notepad"
    End If
End Sub
```

This procedure is identical in form to the Calculator procedure.

5. Write the following `cmdClose_Click()` procedure:

```
Private Sub cmdClose_Click()
    If Message = "Calculator" Then
        AppActivate "Calculator"
        SendKeys "%{F4}", True
        AppActivate "Using the SendKeys Statement"
        Message = ""
    ElseIf Message = "Notepad" Then
        AppActivate "Untitled - Notepad"
        SendKeys "%{F4}", True
        AppActivate "Using the SendKeys Statement"
        Message = ""
    Else
        MsgBox "There is no Windows Application to Close", ,
"Sorry"
    End If
End Sub
```

The procedure first checks to determine what the Message is. If there is no Message, a message box is displayed. If the Calculator Message is assigned, the Calculator application is activated. Once activated, the keys (Alt+F4) are passed to close the application.

A second AppActivate instruction returns the focus to the Visual Basic program. Notice that the string expression in the AppActivate statement must match the title bar of the application to which you want to shift focus, or an error occurs.

6. Run and test your design.

Objective 26.3   Working with Objects from the Excel Type Library

In Exercise 26.1, you launched Excel using the CreateObject() function. To work with Excel, you need to review the Excel object model. Although this section cannot provide complete coverage of the Excel object model, nor cover the different ways you can manipulate these objects using Visual Basic for Applications, it does give you a flavor of manipulating Excel with ActiveX technology.

26.3.1   The Excel Object Model

The Excel object model, like the application, is large and complex. Excel has 150 objects! Like the hierarchy of objects with which you become familiar when working with Data Access Objects, the Excel object model is organized in a hierarchical manner. However, the Excel object model has some features that make working with it a little different from working with the DAO object model.

Consider the objects in Figure 26.5, which represent some of the most frequently used objects in Excel. At the top of the model is a single object: Application. This represents a running instance of Excel with no .XLS files open. Below this single object is a collection of workbooks, with each workbook representing an open .XLS file. Each workbook, in turn, contains a collection of worksheets. Finally, each worksheet contains a grouping of cells (the intersection of a column and a row), which is represented by the Range object.

A range can represent a single Excel cell, such as B3, or a grouping of cells, such as B3:K3. As you probably are aware from working with Excel, the letter represents the column and the number represents the row. The range B3:K3 would represent a row of 10 cells on the third line of the worksheet.

Figure 26.5   *The Excel Object model consists of an application that contains a collection of workbooks, each containing a collection of worksheets, and each worksheet containing a collection of ranges.*

Examine Figure 26.6. You can observe that in this single instance of Excel, the Funds.xls worksheet is open. The range of cells B3:K3 in Funds.xls displays values for the Income Fund; the range of cells E2:E13 displays values for 1995.

	A	B	C	D	E	F	G	H	I	J	K	L
1		1998	1997	1996	1995	1994	1993	1992	1991	1990	1989	Ave
2	Variable Fund	1.22	22.3	6.74	6.7	26.41	3.31	29.06	14.63	5.4	18.97	13.474
3	Income Fund	5.66	8.45	9.68	7.45	19.43	9.11	14.57	7.63	4.52	14.07	8.646
4	Encore Fund	7.23	8.2	3.19	3.67	6.53	8.44	9.39	7.5	6.81	6.88	10.482
5	Advisers Fund	2.33	12.6	9.9	6.39	18.38	5.72	5.33				9.144
6												
7	Alger Fund	-0.5	18.6	13.3	3.55	57.54	8.71	64.48	-3.35			24.035
8	Calvert Fund	2.35	12.66	8.01	7.61	16.4	4.18	20.69	11.75	6.78	3.31	9.84125
9	Franklin Fund	4.55	15.25	7.58	7.66	15.87	10.2	8.9				10.048
10	Lexington Fund	10.5	12.3	10.9	3.22	-4.95	-15					-1.42
11	N & B Fund	8.45	7.45	6.79	9.54	29.73	-8.2	29.47	25.97	-4.9	14.94	10.336
12	Scudder Fund	3.45	18.6	37.8	-3.1	11.45	-7.7	37.79	16.73			15.51
13	TCI Fund	-3.5	14.8	10.3	-1.3	41.86	-1.2	28.7	-2.26	7.2		11.89
14		41.8	151.2	124	51.4	238.7	17.8	248.4	78.6	25.8	58.17	121.9863
15												
16												
17												

Figure 26.6 *The Funds.xls worksheet shows the asset value for a number of mutual funds across several years.*

26.3.2 The *Cells()* Function

A Range object refers to an individual cell or a group of cells. The Application, Worksheet, and Range objects also have a Cells() function that can be used to refer to an individual cell. In this case, the row index value comes first and the column index value comes last. Consider the following code:

```
Dim xlapp As Excel.Application
Dim xlbook As Excel.Workbook
Dim xlsheet As Excel.Worksheet

Set xlapp = CreateObject("Excel.Application")
xlapp.Workbooks.Add
Set xlbook = xlapp.Workbooks(1)
Set xlsheet = xlbook.Worksheets(1)
xlsheet.Cells(2, 1).Value = 45
```

This code places the value 45 in the second row and the first column, namely, the cell that would be referred to as xlsheet.Range("A2"). The Cells() function uses only numeric arguments to specify a cell, unlike the Range function of a Worksheet or Application object, which uses letters of the alphabet to specify columns.

26.3.3   The *ActiveWorkBook* and *ActiveSheet* Methods

As you observed when working with DAOs, it is possible to navigate down the entire object model path to specify a value. Usually, however, object variables are set that allow you to easily reference the subordinate object with which you would like to work. Just as you worked primarily with the DAO.Recordset object in Chapter 24, "Using Data Access Objects," you work mainly with the Worksheet and Range objects in Excel. It is possible to write code like the following:

```
Application.Workbooks(1).Worksheets(1).Range("B2").Value = 56.75
```

However, you more typically bind object variables as you work down the object hierarchy, and work with code like the following:

```
Dim xlsheet as Excel.Worksheet
Set xlsheet = xlapp.Worksheets(1)
xlsheet.Range("B2").Value = 56.75
```

Any subsequent reference to the Worksheet object can use the object variable xlsheet.

Alternatively, you can use the ActiveWorkbook and ActiveSheet methods to refer to the current Workbook and Worksheet objects, depending on the context in which you are working, You can write code such as the following:

```
Dim xlapp As Excel.Application
Dim xlbook As Excel.Workbook
Dim xlsheet As Excel.Worksheet
Set xlapp = CreateObject("Excel.Application")
xlapp.Workbooks.Add
Set xlbook = xlapp.Workbooks(1)
Set xlsheet = xlbook.Worksheets(1)
xlsheet.Cells(2, 1).Value = 45
ActiveSheet.Cells(2, 2).Value = 46
```

26.3.4   Working with the *Range* Object

If you examine the Excel library with the Object Browser, you will discover that most functions that perform calculations on cell or range values are methods of the Application object. These functions are the heart of Excel. By specifying formulas that act on Range objects of values, you make a spreadsheet truly useful. The primary method of employing these functions is by assigning a new value to the Formula property of a Range object.

You will find that when working with a Worksheet object, you typically work with multiple Range objects. These Range objects often are used as arguments in the functions identified for Excel formulas. To make working with these multiple Range objects easier, each Range object has a Name property that is used when specifying a Range object as an argument in an Excel formula function. The next exercise illustrates how Range objects, their Name properties, and Excel functions expressed in the Range object's Formula property can be utilized.

Exercise 26.4   Calculating an Average in Excel

In this exercise, you will launch a running instance of Excel, create a new workbook, display 10 randomly generated integers on a worksheet, take the average of these numbers, and save the workbook to disk as an .XLS file. Figure 26.7 shows the interface you are asked to build.

Figure 26.7   *This application uses ActiveX automation to generate numbers and then add them to an Excel worksheet.*

1. Add the two command buttons (**cmdGenerate** and **cmdAdd**) and a list box (**lstNumbers**). Change the captions of the form and the command buttons as shown. Set the Enabled property for cmdAdd to False. Save the form to disk as **f26-4.frm** and the projects as **p26-4.vbp**. Change the Name property of the project to **p26_4**.

2. Set a reference to the Excel library using the References dialog box (by choosing <u>P</u>roject, Refere<u>n</u>ces).

3. At the form module level, make the following declaration:

   ```
   Dim DataRange(1 To 10) As Integer
   ```

4. Write a procedure for the cmdGenerate_Click() event that will randomly generate 10 integer values between 1 and 100, assign the values to the DataRange array, and display them in the lstNumber list box.

   ```
   Private Sub cmdGenerate_Click()
       Dim i As Integer
       lstNumbers.Clear
       For i = 1 To 10
           Randomize
           DataRange(i) = Int((100 * Rnd) + 1)
           lstNumbers.AddItem Str$(DataRange(i))
       Next
       cmdAdd.Enabled = True
   End Sub
   ```

continues

665

5. Write a procedure for the `cmdAdd_Click()` event that will add these randomly generated numbers to an Excel worksheet and take their average:

```
Private Sub cmdAdd_Click()
    Dim xlapp As Excel.Application
    Dim xlbook As Excel.Workbook
    Dim xlsheet As Excel.Worksheet
    Dim xlrange As Excel.Range
    Dim i As Integer
    On Error GoTo cmdAdderr:
    Set xlapp = CreateObject("Excel.Application")
    xlapp.Visible = True
    xlapp.WindowState = xlMaximized
    xlapp.Workbooks.Add
    Set xlbook = xlapp.Workbooks(1)
    Set xlsheet = xlbook.Worksheets(1)

    For i = 1 To 10
        xlsheet.Cells(i, 2).Value = DataRange(i)
    Next
    Set xlrange = xlsheet.Range("B1:B10")
    xlrange.Name = "myRange"

    xlsheet.Range("A13:B13").Font.Bold = True
    xlsheet.Range("A13").Value = "Avg."
    xlsheet.Range("B13").Formula = "=Average(myRange)"

    xlbook.SaveAs App.Path & "\p26-4.xls"
    Set xlrange = Nothing
    Set xlsheet = Nothing
    Set xlbook = Nothing
    xlapp.Quit
    Set xlapp = Nothing
    cmdAdd.Enabled = False
    Exit Sub
cmdAdderr:
    cmdAdd.Enabled = False
    If Not xlapp Is Nothing Then
        xlapp.Quit
        MsgBox Str$(Err) & "   " & Err.Description
    Else
        MsgBox Str$(Err) & "   " & Err.Description
        Exit Sub
    End If
End Sub
```

6. Run and test the application. The first time you run the program, you will see a worksheet that contains cells similar to those in Figure 26.8.

	A	B
1		83
2		56
3		9
4		52
5		76
6		3
7		68
8		1
9		74
10		59
11		
12		
13	Avg.	48.1
14		
15		

Figure 26.8   *This worksheet shows the result of executing the ActiveX application.*

In subsequent testing of the application, a dialog box will appear, asking whether you want to replace the p26-4.xls file. Select Yes to return to the Visual Basic application without error.

As you study the cmdAdd_Click() event, the code should become more understandable to you. In this code, you launch Excel, create an entire new workbook, and save it to disk. Like the intrinsic Collection object in Visual Basic, collections in Excel are 1-based. After you have bound object variables to the first workbook in the Workbooks collection and the first worksheet in the Worksheets collection, you use the Cells method inside a For...Next loop to populate the cells with the values of the randomly generated number.

The Range object, xlrange, is bound by using the Range method of the Worksheet object xlsheet. The procedure then assigns the value myRange to the Name property of this Range object. This Name property is employed when you specify a formula for the individual cell "B13." This formula uses the Excel Average() function, which expects a range for its single argument.

The workbook then is saved to disk using the SaveAs method.

26.3.5   Opening an Excel File

As you work more with Excel objects and consult the documentation for programming Excel, you will discover the use of a colon with named argument identifiers in Excel object methods. For example, to open an existing Excel file, you use the Open method of the Workbooks collection. The Open method has a long and complex syntax depending on whether the Excel file is linked to other files and is password protected. The syntax of the Excel Workbooks.Open method is as follows:

```
Workbooks.Open(fileName, [updateLinks], [readOnly], [format],
 [password], [writeResPassword], [ignoreReadOnlyRecommended], [origin],
 [delimiter], [editable], [notify], [converter])
```

You can consult the Excel Visual Basic for Applications Help to get a complete description of these method arguments. All arguments are optional except the first one. To assign a value to this argument, use the parameter name followed by a colon.

Consider the following code:

```
Dim xlapp As Excel.Application
Dim xlbook As Excel.Workbook
Set xlapp = CreateObject("Excel.Application")
xlapp.WindowState = xlMaximized
Set xlbook = xlapp.Workbooks.Open(filename:=App.Path & "\p26-4.xls")
```

This code would open the .XLS file you saved to disk in Exercise 26.4. You are asked to use this method of opening a workbook in the third exercise in the "Skill-Building Exercises" section at the end of this chapter.

Objective 26.4   Working with Objects from the Access Type Library

At the start of this chapter, you noted the distinction between DAO objects, which serve an application from a DLL, and Access, which serves your application as an ActiveX executable. If you are familiar with DAO objects, there are very few times you actually need to use Access as an ActiveX EXE server. You get much speedier performance by using DAO objects because you avoid all the cross-process communication.

26.4.1   The Access Object Model

One very useful feature of Access, which is not contained within the DAO DLLs, is the Access reporting capability. Visual Basic comes with third-party report-generating utilities such as Crystal Reports. The Access Report editor, however, is superb and quite easy to use. If you are certain that the end user will have Access installed on the target machine of your application, you can design your program to print stored Access reports (see Exercise 26.5). Figure 26.9 displays a simplified version of the Access object model.

Figure 26.9   *The Access object model contains all objects and collections, including the* Forms *collection, the* Reports *collection, the* DBEngine, *the* Screen *object, and the* DoCmd *object.*

26.4.2   The *DoCmd* Object

The Access object model contains DAO objects. It also contains the DoCmd object as a first-tier object below the Application object. The DoCmd object permits you to execute nearly every Access menu item as well as many other built-in Access commands. The methods of the DoCmd object follow. Of these commands, OpenReport prints a report by default.

ApplyFilter	Maximize	Restore
Beep	Minimize	RunCommand
CancelEvent	MoveSize	RunMacro
Close	OpenForm	RunSQL
CopyObject	OpenModule	Save
DeleteObject	OpenQuery	SelectObject
DoMenuItem	OpenReport	SendObject
Echo	OpenTable	SetMenuItem
FindNext	OutputTo	SetWarnings
FindRecord	PrintOut	ShowAllRecords
GoToControl	Quit	ShowToolbar
GoToPage	Rename	TransferDatabase
GoToRecord	RepaintObject	TransferSpreadsheet
Hourglass	Requery	TransferText

26.4.3   The DAO *Containers* and *Documents* Collections

With DAO objects, you may have noticed the Container and Document object collections in the DAO object model. Each container in the Containers collection holds Document objects describing a particular part of the database, including stored databases, tables, table relationships, and reports. By iterating through the Documents collection of the Reports container, you can list all stored reports in an Access database. Following this, you can use the OpenReport method of the DoCmd object to select and print an individual report.

Exercise 26.5   Using DAO and Access Together

Use the DAO library to help identify stored reports for the Cinema2.MDB database; then, select a report and print it. To work through this exercise, you must have Access 95 or a later verision on your computer and a printer attached to one of your computer ports.

1. From the companion disk, find the Cinema2.MDB database in the Chapt26 folder.

2. Choose Project, References, and select both the DAO type library (DAO 3.51) and the Access type library in the References dialog box. For Access 97, the library should be listed as MSACC8.OLB.

3. Build the interface you see in Figure 26.10. The interface contains two list boxes (**lstContainers** on the left, and **lstReports** on the right) and two command buttons (**cmdShow** and **cmdPrint**). Save the form to disk as **f26-5.frm** and the project as **p26-5.vbp**. Change the Name property of the project to **P26_5**.

Figure 26.10   *This application lists the reports prepared for the Cinema database and enables you to print them using Visual Basic.*

4. In the cmdShow_Click() event, write instructions to list every Container object within the Cinema.MDB database and place them in the lstContainers list box. If the container holds reports, list all the reports within that container and place the report names in the lstReports list box.

```
Private Sub cmdShow_Click()
   Dim db As DAO.Database
   Dim doc As DAO.Document
   Dim con As DAO.Container
   Set db = DAO.Workspaces(0).OpenDatabase(App.Path &
   ➥"\cinema2.mdb")
     For Each con In db.Containers
        lstContainers.AddItem con.Name
        If con.Name = "Reports" Then
           For Each doc In con.Documents
              lstReports.AddItem doc.Name
           Next
        End If
     Next
     lstReports.ListIndex = 0
     db.Close
     Set db = Nothing
End Sub
```

5. Write the `cmdPrint_Click()` event to open Access and print a specified report.

```
Private Sub cmdPrint_Click()
    Dim acApp As Access.Application
    Dim rptname As String
    Set acApp = CreateObject("Access.application")
    acApp.OpenCurrentDatabase (App.Path & "\cinema2.mdb")
    rptname = lstReports.Text
    acApp.DoCmd.OpenReport rptname, acNormal
    acApp.Quit
End Sub
```

This code uses the `OpenCurrentDatabase` method of the `Access.Application` object and the `DoCmd` object to open the report. The `acNormal` constant indicates that you want to have the report printed. Other options include `acPreview` to see the report in Preview mode within Access, or `acDesign` to enter the report design editor within Access.

6. Run and test your design.

Chapter Summary

This chapter introduced you to working with applications of the Microsoft Office suite as ActiveX servers. It also discussed the `Shell()` function and the `SendKeys` and `AppActivate` statements. The `Shell()` function can be used to execute programs from within a Visual Basic program. The `AppActivate` statement shifts focus from one executing program to another. The `SendKeys` statement enables keystrokes to be sent from a running Visual Basic application to another running Windows application.

Applications of the Microsoft Office suite are out-of-process ActiveX EXE servers. Through hierarchical object models, they expose their functionality for use by Visual Basic applications.

To create a running instance of an ActiveX EXE, you use the `CreateObject()` function. The object created is the singular object called `Application`. For Excel, the fully qualified name is `Excel.Application`. For Access, the fully qualified name to use with the `CreateObject()` function is `Access.Application`.

Key objects and collections when working with Excel are the `Workbook(s)`, `Worksheet(s)`, and `Range` objects. The latter can contain one or more cells. To reference a `Range` object, you can use the `Range` method of the Excel `Application` or `Worksheet` objects. `Range` objects have a `Name` property that is commonly used when the `Range` is referred to inside an Excel formula function.

The Access object model allows features of Access that are not included in the DAO library to be used by a Visual Basic application. One of these features is the Access reporting capability.

The DAO Database object includes a Containers collection. Each Container object in Containers holds a collection of Document objects. A Document object describes a single instance of part of the database, including tables and reports. Using the Container and Document objects, it is possible to list all stored reports in an Access database.

Skill-Building Exercises

This set of exercises is designed to give you extra practice in working with Visual Basic and Microsoft Excel and Microsoft Access. In addition, you are asked to use the Shell function and to create a Visual Basic Project Group.

1. Use the CreateObject() function to create a running instance of Excel. Change the caption of the running application to Using ActiveX Automation with the Caption property of the Excel.Application object.

2. Revise Exercise 26.4 so that the Visual Basic application places three rows of randomly generated numbers on a worksheet. Each row should contain 10 randomly generated numbers between 1 and 5,000. At the end of the row, display the sum of the randomly generated numbers in one cell and the average of the randomly generated numbers in another cell.

3. Alter the preceding exercise so that the Visual Basic application opens an existing .XLS file rather than creates a new one. Refer to section 26.3.5, "Opening an Excel File," earlier in the chapter.

4. Create an application that launches the Windows Paintbrush utility using the Shell() function.

5. Create a Visual Basic Project Group containing two standard EXE applications. Name one application **launch.exe** and the other application **receive.exe**. Have launch.exe start receive.exe with the Shell function.

6. Extend the previous exercise by adding a menu to the receive.exe application. Under a File menu, add two subordinate menu items, one with a caption of Fill List Box and the other Exit. Have the mnuFillListBox_Click procedure add 10 items to a list box on the receive.exe form. Have the mnuExit procedure end the receive.exe application. From the launch.exe application, launch receive.exe and execute the mnuFillListBox and mnuExit procedures using the SendKeys statement.

7. Using the Northwind.mdb file that is shipped as a sample .MDB file with Access, write an application that lists the stored reports in the database and prints a report the user selects.

CHAPTER 27

VISUAL BASIC INTERNET APPLICATIONS

This final chapter introduces the newest Internet features provided by Visual Basic. The Professional and Enterprise Editions of Visual Basic now feature three types of Internet applications: ActiveX applications, Dynamic HTML (DHTML) applications, and Internet Information Server (IIS) applications. In addition, all Visual Basic editions feature various Web Publishing Wizards. These wizards enable you to convert Visual Basic applications to Internet applications and to post your Visual Basic designs to a Web site.

This chapter begins with a discussion of the oldest of the Internet applications, ActiveX applications. These produce ActiveX documents that have attributes similar to a Visual Basic form but are more akin to an application. ActiveX documents consist of a UserDocuments interface that holds controls and code. This interface can be executed much like any other Visual Basic program.

This chapter illustrates how an ActiveX document is constructed and how existing Visual Basic applications can be converted to ActiveX applications. It then introduces DHTML and IIS applications. Because each of these Internet applications would require one or more dedicated chapters, we cannot cover all the topics necessary for creating robust Internet applications. However, you will gain an understanding of how Internet applications are built and learn about some of the differences between ActiveX and DHTML applications.

When you complete this chapter, you will be able to do the following:

- Describe key factors affecting client/server design
- Create an ActiveX application
- Use the Hyperlink object to navigate among ActiveX documents and to link to a Web page
- Add a form to an ActiveX document
- Retrieve data from a database using an ActiveX application

- Convert Visual Basic applications to ActiveX document applications
- Construct a small DHTML application
- Link HTML pages using DHTML

Chapter Objectives

The objectives of this chapter include an introduction to acquaint you with some of the design issues surrounding the use of ActiveX technology, DHTML, IIS, and the Internet. Next you complete a single-document design, a multiple-document design, and a combined user document-form design using ActiveX technology. You then convert two Visual Basic applications developed for earlier chapters, including a database application, to ActiveX applications. The last set of exercises features two DHTML applications.

The four objectives of this chapter are as follows:

1. Understanding basic Internet application concepts
2. Creating an ActiveX application
3. Using the ActiveX Document Migration Wizard
4. Creating a DHTML application

To perform the exercises in this chapter, you will need a copy of Microsoft Internet Explorer. This software can be downloaded from the Microsoft Web site at

```
http://www.microsoft.com
```

Another item to download is the Personal Web Server. This server comes with Microsoft Front Page. It can also be downloaded using the URL address shown above.

We have decided not to feature IIS applications in this text. However, if you want to experiment on your own, you will need a copy of the Microsoft Personal Server, which allows you to run Internet Explorer on your personal computer without linking to a network provider. IIS can also be downloaded from Microsoft at

```
http://www.microsoft.com/windows/downloads
```

Warning: This download requires 27MB of disk space and requires 3.8 hours at a 28.8K transmission speed. IIS was also designed to be run on a Windows NT server.

Objective 27.1   Understanding Basic Internet Application Concepts

Visual Basic is a superb language for rapid development of Windows programs. Its market success, however, is attributed to its use as a development language for standalone applications and more recently for Internet-based client/server database applications.

We use the term *client/server* in the sense of hardware and architecture—that is, a client machine on a desktop running a client application and receiving services from a network server. The services in a network environment include file and print sharing as well as program execution services. In the past, the primary network service accessed by a Visual Basic client application received the processing results from large-scale database management systems, such as Microsoft SQL Server, Oracle, Sybase SQL Server, Interbase, and Informix. However, you use Microsoft Access as the DBMS for this chapter.

We also use the term client/server with respect to software components—that is, ActiveX and DHTML applications, in general, are written as client components; IIS applications are written as server components. All the software component servers used for this book are located on the local (client) machine.

The explosion of the Internet and the use of Internet standards within enterprises in the design of company intranets is rapidly changing how Visual Basic is used for client/server application development. What follows is a brief description of how client/server application design has evolved in recent years. This material provides some context for the subsequent discussion of ActiveX applications.

27.1.1   Visual Basic and Two-Tier Client/Server Applications

A typical Visual Basic application in an enterprise is a database application. Update queries (INSERT, DELETE, UPDATE, and so on) and read-only (SELECT) queries are typically submitted by a Visual Basic application on the client computer to a DBMS hosted on a network server. If the query returns data, it is often presented to the user onscreen or processed and formatted for printed output.

This two-tier model describes most client/server applications in use today. In this environment, the application designer has important choices to make about how computing is to be distributed. For instance, will calculations on retrieved data be performed by the client application or by a stored procedure (stored code) on the server? How will new rows of data be added to the database? Will they be added one by one as the client application finishes entering the information required to complete a row of data, or will the data be stored temporarily on the client machine and be updated as multiple rows in a batch operation? Where will validation of field values take place? Should validation occur on the client side or should a stored network procedure check input and return an error for invalid field values? Should validation be performed at both the client and the server side?

27.1.2   Software Components and the Internet

Simultaneous with the evolution of client/server designs, the Internet and the World Wide Web (WWW) have exploded. The Internet and its standard protocols hold an enormous appeal to information managers struggling with multiple platforms in their enterprises (for example, Windows, UNIX, and Macintosh). Just a short while ago, debates raged about the best combination of operating system platforms, back-end DBMSs, and front-end development tools to rapidly deploy client/server applications. These debates have essentially been silenced. There appears to be very little doubt that delivery of distributed information in the enterprise and among enterprises will be dominated by Internet-compliant applications. New debates, however, have taken their place. These debates center on which software component model best suits an Internet-compliant client/server design.

Using Internet protocols and World Wide Web technology for client/server applications holds additional appeal because it suggests a way of lowering the maintenance costs of complex client machines. The typical desktop machine hosting a suite of office productivity applications can prove very costly to maintain. By moving the presentation layer of an application to the Internet, a change to this layer is immediately evident to all users, without the need to ship new disks or even documentation. For performance reasons, software components can be stored on the hard disk of the client machine or loaded into the client machine's memory from the server when needed.

Transforming the Web into the main platform for client/server applications poses some significant challenges. Originally, Web pages were composed of static text and images that a Web browser could read. Hypertext Markup Language (HTML), the standard defining Web documents, evolved to permit limited interactivity between the reader of the Web document and the document. Form fields describing such objects as buttons, text boxes, and list boxes were added to the HTML standard. These built-in HTML objects allow the end user to submit information to the Web server and have data displayed in a fairly primitive interface.

Standard HTML, however, cannot provide the rich user interface of a program written specifically for a native platform, such as Windows. To overcome these limits, DHTML was introduced. DHTML applications allow you to write Visual Basic code to respond to actions on an HTML page without transferring processing to the server. For software development and deployment, this capability is revolutionary. In one sense, Internet Explorer gives you a universal client application or at least a universal client application container.

Objective 27.2   Creating an ActiveX Application

ActiveX applications are entirely different from HTML or software components embedded within HTML pages. ActiveX applications contain no HTML whatsoever. Web browsers that have ActiveX capability can then read ActiveX documents. (The only Web browser at the time of this writing that also serves as an ActiveX container is Microsoft Internet Explorer.) You can use Internet Explorer to navigate from an HTML document to an ActiveX document and back again, but when you load the ActiveX application, you are no longer Web browsing: You are executing a software executable within an ActiveX container.

The *UserDocument* Object

The base object of an ActiveX application is the UserDocument. As an object, it is supported by properties, methods, and events. The UserDocument object resembles a standard Visual Basic Form object with several exceptions. For example, the UserDocument object has only some of the events that are found on a Form object. The events that are not found on the UserDocument include Activate(), Deactivate(), LinkClose(), LinkError(), LinkExecute(), LinkOpen(), Load(), QueryUnload(), and Unload(). Thus you cannot Load() and Unload() a UserDocument.

Events present on the UserDocument include AsycReadComplete(), EnterFocus(), ExitFocus(), Hide(), InitProperties(), ReadProperties(), Scroll(), Show(), and WriteProperties(). You can show and hide a UserDocument.

To load a UserDocument, you must use the Initialize() event (which is also used for a Form object). The syntax for this event is

```
object_Initialize()
```

The following is an example:

```
UserDocument_Initialize()
```

UserDocument Objects and the Internet

When Internet Explorer finds a UserDocument, it checks to see whether the document is currently registered on the client machine. If the document is not registered or if the UserDocument document on the server is a newer version, the UserDocument document and any components the UserDocument document requires must be downloaded to the client machine and registered in the client machine's Registry. The UserDocument document then executes within Internet Explorer.

UserDocuments Are Components

UserDocuments are components within an ActiveX application. You create the component by completing an ActiveX Document EXE project within Visual Basic. The project executable, an .EXE file, defines the type library for the documents that can be read by the executable. When the ActiveX project is compiled, so are the associated ActiveX documents included in the project.

Each ActiveX application is given its own class ID and registered in the Registry of your computer. When the ActiveX application is placed on a server, through a program created by the Setup Wizard, a .CAB (cabinet) file is created. The .CAB file instructs Internet Explorer to download the document and its components and register them on the user's machine.

With this brief background for ActiveX document technology, you are ready to build and view such a document.

Exercise 27.1   Building an ActiveX Application

In this exercise, you build an ActiveX document, compile it to create an ActiveX application, and then read and process the application from within Internet Explorer. As you proceed with the exercise, pay close attention to the file extensions that make up an ActiveX project. You need Internet Explorer installed on your machine to complete this exercise. Figure 27.1 shows the design interface you are asked to create.

Figure 27.1   *This ActiveX EXE interface contains the MSFlexGrid control and two command buttons.*

1. Choose File, New Project. When the New Project dialog box appears, select ActiveX Document EXE.

2. Project Explorer contains a User Documents folder with one UserDocument included in the folder with a default name of UserDocument1 (UserDocument1), as shown in Figure 27.2. Double-click the folder, User Documents, if you cannot see UserDocument1(UserDocument1).

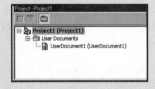

Figure 27.2   *Double-click the User Documents folder if UserDocument1(UserDocument1) is not visible.*

3. Choose View Object (click the icon) in Project Explorer to examine the Project1-UserDocument1 interface. Size the document to make it larger. Press F4 and change its Name property to Axdoc1 (see Figure 27.3).

Name	Size	Type	Modified
Axdoc1.dob	2KB	Visual Basic User Document	11/13/98 3:50 PM
Axdoc1.vbd	2KB	VBD File	11/13/98 4:02 PM
P27_1.exe	20...	Application	11/13/98 4:02 PM
P27_1.vbp	1KB	Visual Basic Project	11/13/98 3:50 PM
P27_1.vbw	1KB	Visual Basic Project Workspace	11/17/98 10:49 ...

Figure 27.3   *Compiling an ActiveX document project creates five files.*

4. Save this UserDocument file to disk as **Axdoc1.dob**. A .DOB file can be read in a text editor similar to the way a form's .FRM file is read.

5. Change the Name property of the project to **p27_1** and save the project to disk as **p27_1.vbp**. The project Name property will now become the name of the type library in which the ActiveX documents will be placed and defined.

6. Choose Project, Components and click the MSFlexGrid control. This step adds the control to the toolbox.

7. Add MSFlexGrid6.0 to the UserDocument and size it so it has a width of about 4,000 twips and a height of 2,500 twips. Change the Name property of the Grid control to **grid1**.

8. Add two command buttons (**cmdFill** and **cmdClear**) to the UserDocument and add the captions as shown (refer to Figure 27.1).

9. Add code that fills the grid with four columns and 10 rows of numbers and also clears the grid.

```
Private Sub cmdClear_Click()
  grid1.Clear
End Sub

Private Sub cmdFill_Click()
  Dim i As Integer, j As Integer

  grid1.Cols = 4
  grid1.Rows = 10
  grid1.FixedCols = 0
  grid1.FixedRows = 0
  For i = 0 To 3
    For j = 0 To 9
      grid1.Col = i
      grid1.Row = j
      grid1.Text = (i + 1) * (j + 1)
    Next
  Next
End Sub
```

10. Run the project. It should load Internet Explorer and allow you to test the application.

continues

11. Choose File, Make p27_1.exe to compile the project. Depending on your version of Windows (95 or NT), an .EXE file and an Internet Explorer file may be created. Windows NT, for example, creates the latter file; Windows 95 does not.

12. Examine the files that have been created in the root directory of the application (see Figure 27.3). For all versions of Windows, you should see the following files:

   ■ **Axdoc1.dob**—The design-time file for editing the UserDocument

   ■ **Axdoc1.vbd**—The compiled ActiveX document, which can be read by an ActiveX container application such as Internet Explorer

   ■ **P27_1.exe**—The executable file that is registered on your computer

   ■ **P27_1.vbp**—The project file to open when you want to change the project

   ■ **P27_1.vbw**—The Visual Basic Project Workspace file

13. Run the Regedit.exe program. (Use Microsoft Explorer and choose Tools, Find to locate this program.) Under the HKEY_CLASSES_ROOT folder, you should see an entry p27_1.axdoc1 specifying that the ActiveX document is now registered for your computer (see Figure 27.4).

Figure 27.4   *ActiveX document applications must be registered for your computer.*

14. Run Internet Explorer. You do not need to connect to an Internet service provider if you have installed Personal Web Server. Rather, click to display your home page. If you are connected to an Internet service provider, click the Stop button on Internet Explorer because you do not need the service provider to build this application.

15. Choose File, Open in Internet Explorer. When the Open dialog box appears, select Browse. Important: When the Browse dialog box appears, be sure to select All Files under the combo box named Files of Type. Move to the folder that contains the saved project.

16. Open the file axdoc1.vbd. If you have trouble in Run mode, exit Visual Basic and open the project with Internet Explorer.

17. The ActiveX document should be displayed within the browser, as shown in Figure 27.5. Test the program by clicking both buttons. If you encounter an error, you must return to Visual Basic, make the correction, and recompile the executable before testing it again from within Internet Explorer.

Figure 27.5   *Internet Explorer allows you to load an ActiveX.VBD file when it knows the address.*

18. With Internet Explorer running, choose File, Close if you plan to quit at this time. In addition, before you shut down your computer, press Shift+Alt+Del to examine the Close dialog box. If an ActiveX document program is still running, click it and click End Task.

Navigating Among ActiveX Documents

Every ActiveX application is a separate software component. As such, it must be registered on the user's computer when it is downloaded. A project can contain multiple UserDocuments defining ActiveX documents. These documents can be navigated in a way similar to navigating among Web documents using hyperlinks.

Each UserDocument has a Hyperlink property that returns a Hyperlink object. The Hyperlink object has three navigational methods: GoBack, GoForward, and NavigateTo. By specifying the path (URL) of the ActiveX document, you can navigate among ActiveX documents with the NavigateTo method.

The *GoBack* Method

The GoBack method executes a hyperlink jump back in the history list, for which the syntax is simply

```
object.Hyperlink.GoBack
```

The object in this syntax is a container that supports OLE hyperlinking. GoBack signifies that the container will jump to the location that is back in the history list. However, if the object is in a container that does not support hyperlinking, then this method raises an error.

The *GoForward* Method

The GoForward method executes a hyperlink jump forward in the history list, provided there is one. Like the GoBack method, the syntax is limited to

```
object.Hyperlink.GoForward
```

The object must support OLE hyperlinking.

As a general rule, use error checking when using GoBack, GoForward, or NavigateTo. As an example, the following code moves to the next UserDocument in the history list if such a document exists:

```
Private Sub cmdGoForward_Click()
    On Error GoTo noDocInHistory
    UserDocument.Hyperlink.GoForward
    Exit Sub
noDocInHistory:
    Resume Next
End Sub
```

The *NavigateTo* Method

The NavigateTo method jumps to a URL. For example, the following code presumes an ActiveX document named axdMyDoc exists:

```
UserDocument.Hyperlink.NavigateTo "c:\mydocs\axdmydoc.vbd"
```

The syntax for this method is as follows:

```
object.Hyperlink.NavigateTo Target [, Location [, FrameName]]
```

Table 27.1 explains this syntax.

TABLE 27.1 The *NavigateTo* Method Syntax

Component	Description
object	An application that is registered as supporting hyperlinking is started to handle the request.
Target	A string expression specifying the location to jump to. This location can be a document, such as axdmydoc.vdb, or a URL.

Component	Description
Location	A string expression specifying the location within the URL specified in Target to jump to. If Location is not specified, the default document will be jumped to.
FrameName	A string expression specifying the frame within the URL specified in Target to jump to. If FrameName is not specified, the default frame will be used.

To link to a URL, either type or code the URL. For example, the following code will jump to the URL placed in the txtURL text box:

```
Private Sub cmdNavigateTo_Click()
    Hyperlink.NavigateTo txtURL.Text
End Sub
```

To jump to the computer science Web site at Willamette University, type:

http://www.willamette.edu/agsm/

The hyperlink will navigate to this Web location.

Exercise 27.2   Using the *NavigateTo* Method of the *Hyperlink* Object

This exercise asks you to use the NavigateTo method to move from one UserDocument (one .vbd file) to a second UserDocument (a second .vbd file). The names of the two UserDocument files are axdoc1A.vbd and axdoc2.vbd, respectively.

1. With Exercise 27.1 open, save axdoc1.dob to disk as **axdoc1A.dob**. Save p27_1.vbp to disk as **p27_2.vbp**.

2. Open project p27_2 and change the Name property of the project to **p27_2**. Change the Name property of the user document to **axdoc1A**.

3. Add a label to axdoc1A and name the label **lblJump**. Change the caption of the label to **Go there**. Make the label look like a hypertext link on a Web page by changing the label ForeColor to royal blue and adding an underline attribute to the font (see Figure 27.6).

continues

Exercise 27.2   continued

Figure 27.6   *Adding a hypertext link to an ActiveX document requires a label and an associated label* Click() *event.*

4. In the lblJump_Click() event, add the following code:

```
Private Sub lblJump_Click()
    On Error GoTo noDocFound
    UserDocument.Hyperlink.NavigateTo App.Path & "\axdoc2.vbd"
    Exit Sub
noDocFound:
    Resume Next
End Sub
```

5. Insert a new UserDocument into the project by choosing Project, Add User Document. Save the new UserDocument to disk as **axdoc2.dob**. Change the Name property of the document to **axdoc2**. Save the entire project.

6. Add two labels to axdoc2 so that it appears similar to Figure 27.7. The upper label (**lblName**) has its alignment centered and its BorderStyle property set to FixedSingle. The caption to this label is set in code. The lower label (**lblJumpBack**) has the caption **return**, ForeColor set to royal blue, and Font set to underlined.

7. In the UserDocument_Initialize() event, add the following code:

```
Private Sub UserDocument_Initialize()
    lblName.Caption = UserDocument.Name
End Sub
```

Figure 27.7 *This second ActiveX document contains a return link to the first ActiveX document.*

Remember that although the UserDocument appears similar to a form, the former is a component and has an Initialize() event rather than a Load() event.

8. In the lblJumpBack_Click() event, add the following code:

```
Private Sub lblJumpBack_Click()
    On Error GoTo noDocFound
    UserDocument.Hyperlink.NavigateTo App.Path & "\axdoc1A.vbd"
    Exit Sub
noDocFound:
    Resume Next
End Sub
```

9. Compile and run the executable. Observe the files created in the application directory and the new entries made to the Registry.

10. Test the application by launching Internet Explorer and opening the file axdoc1A.vbd. Test the design by navigating between the two ActiveX documents. When you are finished, click the back and forward arrows located on the Microsoft Explorer menu bar.

11. With Internet Explorer running, choose File, Close if you plan to quit at this time. Otherwise, continue with the next exercise.

Exercise 27.3   Linking to a URL

This brief exercise is similar to Exercise 27.2 except that here you link to a URL rather than to another ActiveX user document. Figure 27.8 shows the Internet Explorer interface you are creating.

1. Open a new ActiveX document .EXE project and open the UserDocument1 interface.

Figure 27.8   *This interface allows you to type a URL and to navigate to this location.*

2. Change the name of the project to **p27_3**. Change the name of the UserDocument to **URL1**.

3. Add a command button (**cmdNagivateTo**) and a text box (**txtURL**) to the document. Change the caption on the command button to **Link to URL** and remove the text from the text box.

4. Add the cmdNagivateTo_Click() event:

```
Private Sub cmdNavigateTo_Click()
  txtURL.Text = "C:\WEBSHARE\WWWROOT\DEFAULT.HTM"
  Hyperlink.NavigateTo txtURL.Text
End Sub
```

In this code, substitute the txtURL.Text statement to link to a URL address of your choosing. We decided to link to the default home page on our computer.

5. Save the UserDocument to disk as **axURL1.dob** and save the project as **P27_3**.

6. Make the P27_3 executable and run the program.

7. As another test, run Internet Explorer and open the file URL1.vbd. Click the command button to navigate to the URL address indicated by your code.

8. With Internet Explorer running, choose File, Close if you plan to quit at this time. Otherwise, continue with the next section.

Adding a Form to an ActiveX *UserDocument*

In this section, you are asked to add a modal form to an ActiveX UserDocument. Remember, a UserDocument requires a container. Some containers permit modal forms to be displayed. The addition of a form to an ActiveX document is a simple procedure. What is more difficult is deciding on good reasons for adding forms. As the next exercise demonstrates, a form can be added to show special effects or to provide information that might help the user work with a UserDocument.

Exercise 27.4 Calling a Form from a *UserDocument*

Create a UserDocument and add a single form to it, adding command buttons to both the UserDocument (to call the form) and the form (to execute a form-designed event procedure). Figure 27.9 shows the Internet Explorer interface you are creating.

Figure 27.9 *This screen is the final display; however, the application opens with only the* UserDocument *visible.*

1. Open a new ActiveX document .EXE project and open the UserDocument1 interface.

2. Change the name of the project to **p27_4**. Change the name of the UserDocument to **AddForm**.

3. Choose Project, Add Form and select Form. This step adds a new form to the project.

4. Change the name of the form to **frmAdd**.

continues

687

5. On the form, place a label (**lblText**), set WordWrap to True, and remove the label caption.

6. Add a command button to the form (**cmdShow**) and change the caption to **Show Text**.

7. Write the following cmdShow_Click() procedure:

```
Private Sub cmdShow_Click()
    lblText.Caption = "When you click some HELP information could
    ➡be written to appear"
End Sub
```

8. Return to the UserDocument (AddForm), add a command button to this form (cmdShowForm), and change the button caption to **Show Form**.

Write the following cmdShowForm_Click() procedure:

```
Private Sub cmdShowForm_Click()
    frmAdd.Show vbModal
End Sub
```

9. Save the Form as **frmAdd.frm** (a regular form) and save the UserDocument as **AddForm.dob**.

10. Make the P27_4 executable and run the program.

11. As a second test, run Internet Explorer and open the file AddForm.vdb. Click Show Form to open the form. With the form open, click Show Text. Close the form and click Show Form again.

12. With Internet Explorer running, close the form. Then choose File, Close.

Objective 27.3   Using the ActiveX Document Migration Wizard

In some cases, you may want to convert a Visual Basic application you have written to an ActiveX UserDocument. Rather than starting from scratch, you can use an add-in tool, known as the ActiveX Document Migration Wizard, to handle the conversion. The ActiveX Document Migration Wizard performs the following tasks:

■ Copies form properties to a new UserDocument.

■ Copies all controls from the form to the UserDocument and retains their names.

■ Copies all code written for the form to the UserDocument.

■ Copies all event handlers into ActiveX document objects as the code is being copied. For example, the Wizard replaces the word Form with UserDocument. In this case, Form_Click() becomes UserDocument_Click().

■ Comments out illegal code, such as `Me.Left` and `End`.

■ Changes the project type to an ActiveX EXE or DLL.

Exercise 27.5   Using the ActiveX Document Migration Wizard

Refer to Chapter 14, "Lists and Arrays," and convert Exercise 14.8, "Creating an Application with Control and Variable Arrays," to an ActiveX `UserDocument` application. Figure 27.10 shows the converted application running within Microsoft Explorer.

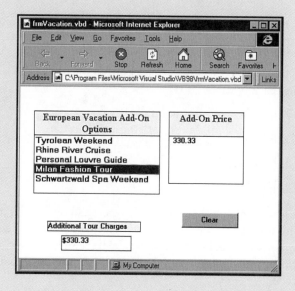

Figure 27.10   *The form used in designing this application has been converted into a* `UserDocument`.

1. Copy Exercise 14.8 and copy and paste files F14_8.FRM, P14_8.VBP, P14_8.VBW into a folder named Exer27_5. If these files do not exist, you must complete Exercise 14.8 first.

2. Open the project file and change the name of the form to **Vacation**. Change the project name to **p27_5**.

3. Save the project as P27_5.vbp.

4. With the project still open, select Add-Ins, Add-In Manager.

5. Double-click the VB ActiveX Document Migration Wizard check box. The text, Loaded, appears. Click OK. This step places the ActiveX Document Migration Wizard on the Add-Ins menu (see Figure 27.11).

continues

Exercise 27.5   continued

Figure 27.11   *Select the ActiveX Document Migration Wizard to start the conversion of a Visual Basic application to an ActiveX document application.*

6. Select the Document Migration Wizard, and perform the following steps:

1. Click Next.

2. Click Vacation to insert a check mark when asked to select a form, and click Next.

3. Click Comment out Invalid Code?

4. Click Remove Original Forms After Conversion?

5. Click Convert to ActiveX EXE?

6. Click Next.

7. Click Yes to review the summary report and then click Finish. During the conversion process, you will receive a message stating that the wizard has found some invalid code. Because not all Visual Basic code works with Internet Explorer, the wizard will comment out invalid code.

7. Examine the converted application. A UserDocument with the name Vacation should have replaced the original form.

8. Save the project.

9. Make a P27_5 executable file and run the program. If you are asked to select a start-up file, select (none).

10. As another test, run Internet Explorer and open the file frmVacation.vbd. Close this application when you have finished.

Exercise 27.6   Using an ActiveX Document to Retrieve Data from a Database

This exercise uses Exercise 23.4, "Using a Query to Retrieve a Set of Records." The application is converted into an Internet ActiveX application, using the ActiveX Migration Wizard. Figure 27.12 shows the converted application running within Microsoft Explorer.

Figure 27.12 *This interface contains a* UserDocument, *which in turn contains the command button List All Products that opens a form named Query with the query results.*

1. Copy the files to a folder named Exer27_6. These include the two form files (F23-4a.frm and F23-4b.frm), the project file (p23-4.vbp), and the database file (Design4.mdb). If you have not completed Exercise 23.4, you must do so to create these files.

2. Rename the form files **F27-4a.frm** and **F27_4b.frm**, respectively.

3. Run the project to determine whether it works as before. Review Figures 23.7 and 23.8 if you need to review the original interface and the results.

4. Rename the project and save it as **p27_6.vbp**.

5. With the project still open, select the ActiveX Document Migration Wizard from the <u>A</u>dd-Ins menu.

continues

Exercise 27.6   continued

6. With the Wizard open, perform the following steps:

   1. Click <u>N</u>ext.

   2. Click frmOpen to insert a check mark when asked to select a form, but do not insert a check mark for frmQuery. Click <u>N</u>ext.

   3. Click <u>C</u>omment out Invalid Code?

   4. Click <u>R</u>emove Original Forms After Conversion?

   5. Click Convert to ActiveX <u>E</u>XE?

   6. Click <u>N</u>ext.

   7. Click Yes to review the summary report and then click <u>F</u>inish.

7. Examine the converted application. A UserDocument with the name frmOpen(frmOpen.dob) and a form with the name frmQuery(F27.4b.frm) should exist.

8. Remove the End command button from the UserDocument.

9. For frmQuery, comment out the line

   ```
   'frmOpen.Show
   ```

10. Click the Data control and check the path for Design4.mdb. If needed, change this path.

11. Place the form inside the UserDocument.

12. Save the project and make p27_6 an executable file. Run the program.

13. As a final test, run Internet Explorer and open the file frmOpen.vdb. Does it work? If it does, you have just simulated a client/server environment in which the database resides on the server and the query instructions reside on the client.

14. Close Internet Explorer.

15. As a final test, run Windows RegEdit.EXE again and check the Registry on your computer. The programs for all six exercises should now be registered on your machine.

Objective 27.4   Creating a DHTML Application

DHTML applications differ from ActiveX applications in that the former can contain both HTML and Visual Basic code. In creating the user interface for your application, you can create pages from scratch by typing in HTML text and formatting it as desired, create pages using an external HTML editor, or create pages using a combination of both methods. Because we cannot assume you know how to write HTML, we ask you to create pages from scratch.

Instead of procedures, DHMTL uses functions placed in .BAS modules for an ActiveX control. The following code placed in a .BAS module, for example, links two HTML pages:

```
Private Function Link1_onClick() as Boolean
   BaseWindow.Navigate "Page2.html"
EndFunction
```

27.4.1   The DHTML Designer Window

To create a DHTML page, click on the DHTML Application icon to start a DHTML project. The project window shown in Figure 27.13 appears. Click on Designers to open the DHTMLPage1(DHTMLPage1) document, which is similar to the UserDocument1(UserDocument) used for ActiveX applications. Double-click on the DTHMLPage1(DHTMLPage1) icon to open the Designer window (see Figure 27.14). This window is complex and contains several parts.

Figure 27.13   *The Project Explorer window for a DHTML page includes a Modules folder and a Designers folder.*

Figure 27.14 *The DHTML Designer window contains a Treeview pane, a Detail pane, and several types of toolbar bands.*

Treeview and Detail Panes of the Designer Window

The Treeview pane on the left displays a hierarchical representation of all the elements within an HTML page, including all HTML formatted code and all ActiveX controls. For each control, the page designer lists the ID (if one exists) and the type of control. For example,

```
txtField1 INPUT()
```

If an element does not contain an ID, you can assign one to it in the Properties window. Elements with IDs are indicated in bold.

The Detail pane on the right presents a drawing surface on which you can create a new page or edit the contents of an existing page. You can add HTML text to the page, add ActiveX controls, and set properties to control physical appearance.

Format Toolbar Band

The Designer window contains a separate toolbar band at the top of the form from which you can make various selections (some of which are outside the scope of this chapter). In the following exercise, you select headings for HTML, make font selections, and make text alignment decisions.

File Toolbar Band

This band opens the DHTML Page Designers Properties dialog box and launches the default HTML editor if one has been designated. The Page Designers Properties box asks you how your page will be saved: as a separate HTML file or as part of a Visual Basic project. The Launch Editor opens Notepad or your computer's default HTML editor and displays the contents of the HTML page you are currently editing in the Designer.

Element Toolbar Band

This portion of the tool band contains buttons that are frequently used when grouping elements on the page or working with tables. With the exception of the Table Operations icon, the options on this band are available only when you have highlighted a selection of text or elements in the Detail pane or when you select the Document or Body object or a DIV HTML element in the Treeview pane. The Table Operations icon is always available.

Design Toolbar Band

The buttons on this section of the toolbar enable you to show table borders; show details such as comments not supported by HTML script; determine whether a selected item is positioned absolutely or relatively; lock an element from being moved; set the page designer in either absolute or relative positioning mode (by default), and control the order in the arrangement of elements on the page.

Exercise 27.7   Creating a DHTML Application

With this brief introduction, you are ready to use the Designer window. This exercise walks you through the construction of a DHTML application. First you type HTML code into the Detail pane, and then you attach ActiveX controls and code to your design. Controls are also added to the Detail pane.

1. Start a new project and select a DHTML application.

2. Click on the Designers folder to display the DHTMLPage1 (DHTMLPage1) document.

3. Click on the DHTMLPage1(DHTMLPage1) icon to open the Designer window (see Figure 27.14).

4. Figure 27.15 shows the design you are creating. Type the text as shown into the Detail pane. Center the title, underline it, and set it to bold.

continues

695

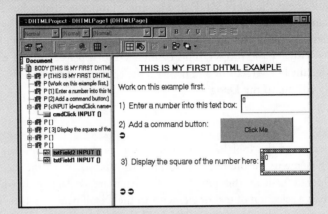

Figure 27.15   *As you type and add controls to the Detail pane, the DHTML document is displayed on the Treeview pane.*

5. Add the ActiveX controls to your design. Name the first text box (**txtField1**), the second text box (**txtField2**), and the command button (**cmdClick**).

6. Add the following cmdClick() event:

```
Private Function cmdClick_onclick() As Boolean
   txtField2.Value = txtField1.Value ^ 2
End Function
```

7. If everything is positioned correctly, run your program. The display shown in Figure 27.16 should appear.

8. Save your DHTML application by placing it in a separate folder.

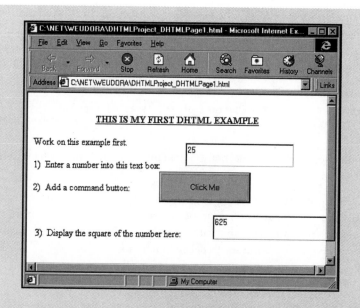

Figure 27.16   *The completed DHTML application contains a mixture of HTML and ActiveX components.*

9. Experiment with your design. It will take you some time to learn to work between the Treeview and Detail panes. To move a control, for example, click on the document text to highlight the control. The control can then be moved with ease.

27.4.2   Linking HTML Pages

This section considers how DHTML pages are linked. However, before you try to link any pages, you must understand more about Internet applications. Typically, Internet applications are *stateless*. That is, the protocol that passes requests and responses between the browser and Web server is not capable of maintaining information between each request. Therefore, the protocol does not "remember" any information from previous requests when it receives a new request.

Because the protocol cannot maintain state, the GetProperty and PutProperty functions are used to store and pass information you want your application to remember. These functions store data as long as the end user's Web browser window is open.

You store information using the PutProperty function. In this function, you identify the name of the property in which you want to store information, and the value to store. The browser stores the indicated data in a client-side *cookie*, a small packet of information used to store persistent state information on a user's computer.

The syntax for the PutProperty function is

```
Private Function StoreButton1_onclick() As Boolean
    PutProperty BaseWindow.Document, "Property1", TextField1.Value
End Function
```

This function stores the information contained in a text field when StoreButton1 is clicked.

You retrieve information using the *GetProperty* function. In this function, you identify the name of an existing property that you want to retrieve from the client-side cookie. You can assign this value to fields on the page or use it in your calculations. The syntax for the *GetProperty* function is

```
Private Function GetButton1_onclick() As Boolean
    MyValue.innerText = "The value of the property is " & _
    GetProperty(BaseWindow.Document, "Property1")
End Function
```

This function uses the stored innerText property of DHTML to replace the contents of a DIV tag, called "MyValue," with a sentence that contains the retrieved property.

For now, all this may be confusing; however, the next exercise illustrates how the PutProperty and GetProperty functions work.

Exercise 27.8   Using DHTML to Link Two HTML Pages

This exercise asks you to design a DHTML application that links two HTML pages and passes information from one page to another. We should note that this project is complex and may require considerable experimentation on your part. The code used to pass a string from one HTML page to another is especially difficult to understand. To protect yourself, save the project after completing page 1, the .BAS module, and page 2.

1. Start a new project and select a DHTML application.

2. Click on the Designers folder to display the DHTMLPage1 (DHTMLPage1) document.

3. Click on the DHTMLPage1(DHTMLPage1) icon to open the Designer window.

4. Design the Data Entry page shown on Figure 27.17. This page contains a text box (**txtName**), a command button (**cmdName**), and a Hyperlink object (**Hyperlink1**). To place the hyperlink on the form, click on the Hyperlink icon and type over the title Hyperlink1. Type **Clickhere**; then backspace to leave a space between Click and here.

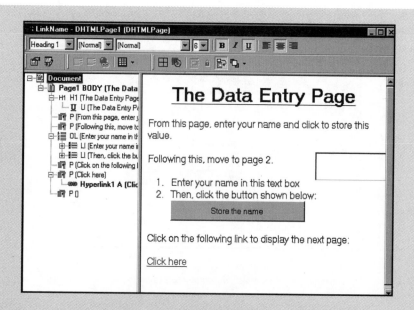

Figure 27.17   *The first page of your design asks you to type your name, to store it, and to navigate to a second HTML page.*

5. Remove the text from the textbox and change the command button caption.

6. Write the following cmdName() function:

```
Private Function cmdName_onclick() As Boolean
    PutProperty BaseWindow.Document, "MyDocument", txtName.Value
End Function
```

BaseWindow.Document specifies the name of the first HTML starting page. The string "MyDocument" is linked to the second HTML page. You add the onClick() function for the hyperlink in step 9.

7. Select Project, Add DHTML Page to add DHTMLPage2 to your project.

8. Design the receiving page shown in Figure 27.18. Type the HTML text and add the command button **cmdDisplay**.

continues

Figure 27.18   *The second page of your design asks you to display the name you typed on the first page.*

9. Write the following onClick() function:

```
Private Function cmdDisplay_onclick() As Boolean
    MyValue.innerText = "Your name is " &
GetProperty(BaseWindow.Document, "MyDocument")
End Function
```

This function uses the "MyDocument" string placed in the PutProperty code.

10. Return to the first page and write the following Hyperlink1_onclick() function:

```
Private Function Hyperlink1_onclick() As Boolean
    BaseWindow.navigate "C:\TEMP\LinkName_DHTMLPage2.html"
End Function
```

11. In a .BAS file, place the following code:

```
Public Sub PutProperty(objDocument As HTMLDocument, strName As
➥String, vntValue As Variant, Optional Expires As Date)

    objDocument.cookie = strName & "=" & CStr(vntValue) & _
    IIf(CLng(Expires) = 0, "", "; expires=" &
➥Format(CStr(Expires), "ddd, dd-mmm-yy hh:mm:ss") & " GMT")
➥' & _
End Sub

Public Function GetProperty(objDocument As HTMLDocument,
➥strName As String) As Variant
    Dim aryCookies() As String
    Dim strCookie As Variant
    On Local Error GoTo NextCookie

    'Split the document cookie object into an array of cookies.
    aryCookies = Split(objDocument.cookie, ";")
    For Each strCookie In aryCookies
      If Trim(VBA.Left(strCookie, InStr(strCookie, "=") - 1)) =
➥Trim(strName) Then
```

```
                GetProperty = Trim(Mid(strCookie, InStr(strCookie, "=")
            ⮎+ 1))
                Exit Function
        End If
    NextCookie:
        Err = 0
        Next strCookie
    End Function
```

This code also uses the PutProperty and GetProperty functions. The PutProperty function stores the string; the GetProperty parses the string array using the Split function.

12. Return to the second page, create a blank paragraph (P()), and click on the Document Body to highlight the Wrap Section in the <DIV>...</DIV> icon.

13. Click on the <DIV>...</DIV> icon and press the F4 key.

14. Type **MyValue** for the element ID.

15. Make sure you save your project. Then run and test your program.

Chapter Summary

ActiveX applications consist of a user document interface that holds controls, including forms and code. An ActiveX container, such as Internet Explorer, can read this interface. ActiveX documents have a .VBD extension. This file, with its extension, is created for you when you create an ActiveX executable.

In this chapter, we strove to simulate a client/server Internet architecture in the sense that a client application running on the desktop can receive services over the Internet from a server application, involving access to a stored Access database.

ActiveX applications contain no HTML and are unlike HTML-based Internet applications. An ActiveX application contains a UserDocument object—an object supported by properties, methods, and events.

Before Internet Explorer can gain access to an ActiveX UserDocument, the UserDocument must be registered on the client machine. Run Regedit.exe to determine whether a UserDocument has been registered.

Building an ActiveX document requires several new steps, including selecting the ActiveX Document Exe when asked to begin a new project. Following this step, a UserDocument object, rather than a form, is displayed. Controls and forms can be added to this new type of object. When the UserDocument is saved, it requires a .DOB extension. A UserDocument is not run. Rather it is compiled into an executable, which leads to .EXE and .VBD files. Because of these requirements, many Visual Basic developers build an application outside ActiveX and then use the ActiveX Document Migration Wizard to transform their forms into ActiveX UserDocuments.

It is possible to navigate between ActiveX documents using hyperlinks. Each `UserDocument` has a `Hyperlink` property that returns `Hyperlink` objects. Three navigational methods are `GoBack`, `GoFoward`, and `NavigateTo`.

Adding a form to a `UserDocument` is straightforward: Choose Project, Add Form. To show the form, use the `Show` method and make the form modal, as in the following example:

```
FrmAdd.Show vbModal
```

The ActiveX Document Migration Wizard is a powerful tool. It allows you to convert a Visual Basic application into an ActiveX application. In conversion, it copies all form properties, controls and their names, code, and event handlers. It even comments out code that is illegal and replaces `Form` with `UserDocument` when appropriate.

DHTML applications contain HTML as well as Visual Basic code. When working with DHTML, you are provided with a Designers page. This page contains a Treeview pane and a Detail pane. When you type in the Detail pane, HTML formatted text appears in the Treeview pane.

The Format, File, Element, and Design Toolbar bands aid in the design of the DHTML document.

The linking of DHTML pages requires the `PutProperty` and `GetProperty` functions. The `PutProperty` function stores the information; the `GetProperty` function gets the stored information. A .BAS module consists of one or more cookies to store persistent state information on your computer.

Skill-Building Exercises

These exercises give you practice with ActiveX applications and DHTML applications. The first five exercises deal with ActiveX applications because this technology is the easiest to work with. The final two deal with DHTML. IIS exercises are not included here because of their complexity.

1. Modify Exercise 27.3 to navigate to a different Web page, such as the Web page for your college or university or a friend's personal Web page. To run this exercise, you will need the services of a Web server. In your design, add error-trapping code. Do not add quotation marks if you type in the Web address.

2. Modify Exercise 27.3 by adding a combo box that allows you to select one URL from several. Use the back arrow to demonstrate that your design is capable of linking to more than one Web site.

3. Convert the third exercise in the "Skill-Building Exercises" section at the end of Chapter 24, "Using Data Access Objects," to run on the Internet. Use the Cinema2.mdb database. Write a program that lists the year of the film's release and its title from the Film Titles table and then place the results in a list box.

4. Modify Exercise 27.6 to allow it to contain two possible query selections: one to list all products and one to list all customers. Use Design4.mdb. Place the results of the all-products query on a form named **All Products**; place the results of the all-customers query on a form named **All Customers**.

5. Refer to Chapter 21, "Modular Design," and convert Exercise 21.7, "Building Classes to Enhance the Ski Rental Shop Application," to run on the Internet. Place the order form on a UserDocument (see Figure 21.9); leave the invoice form as a form (see Figure 21.10).

6. Extend Exercise 27.8 by adding a link to the second HTML page. This new link will return you to the first page.

7. Design a DHTML page by placing a list box on the Detail pane and adding the following text below it: **This HTML page is designed to display a list of your favorite activities and fun things to do.** Add several of your favorite things to do to the list box. To do so, give the list box the focus, right-click, and select Properties. The Property Pages dialog box appears. Use this dialog box to add items to the list box.

APPENDICES

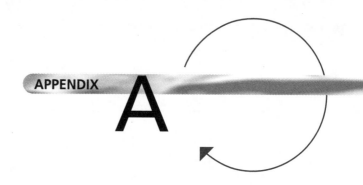

THE ANSI CHARACTER SET

ANSI values 8, 9, 10, and 13 have no graphical representation, but—depending on the application—can affect the visual display of text.

The abbreviation *n/a* indicates characters that Microsoft Windows does not support.

ANSI Code	Character	ANSI Code	Character
0	*n/a*	19	*n/a*
1	n/a	20	n/a
2	n/a	21	n/a
3	n/a	22	n/a
4	n/a	23	n/a
5	n/a	24	n/a
6	n/a	25	n/a
7	n/a	26	n/a
8	[backspace]	27	n/a
9	[tab]	28	n/a
10	[linefeed]	29	n/a
11	n/a	30	n/a
12	n/a	31	n/a
13	[carriage return]	32	[space]
14	n/a	33	!
15	n/a	34	"
16	n/a	35	#
17	n/a	36	$
18	n/a	37	%

ANSI Code	Character	ANSI Code	Character
38	&	71	G
39	'	72	H
40	(	73	I
41	)	74	J
42	*	75	K
43	+	76	L
44	,	77	M
45	-	78	N
46	.	79	O
47	/	80	P
48	0	81	Q
49	1	82	R
50	2	83	S
51	3	84	T
52	4	85	U
53	5	86	V
54	6	87	W
55	7	88	X
56	8	89	Y
57	9	90	Z
58	:	91	[
59	;	92	\
60	<	93	]
61	=	94	^
62	>	95	_
63	?	96	`
64	@	97	a
65	A	98	b
66	B	99	c
67	C	100	d
68	D	101	e
69	E	102	f
70	F	103	g

ANSI Code	Character	ANSI Code	Character
104	h	137	*n/a*
105	i	138	n/a
106	j	139	n/a
107	k	140	n/a
108	l	141	n/a
109	m	142	n/a
110	n	143	n/a
111	o	144	n/a
112	p	145	'
113	q	146	'
114	r	147	n/a
115	s	148	n/a
116	t	149	n/a
117	u	150	n/a
118	v	151	n/a
119	w	152	n/a
120	x	153	n/a
121	y	154	n/a
122	z	155	n/a
123	{	156	n/a
124	|	157	n/a
125	}	158	n/a
126	~	159	n/a
127	*n/a*	160	[space]
128	*n/a*	161	¡
129	*n/a*	162	¢
130	*n/a*	163	£
131	*n/a*	164	¤
132	*n/a*	165	¥
133	*n/a*	166	¦
134	*n/a*	167	§
135	*n/a*	168	¨
136	*n/a*	169	©

ANSI Code	Character	ANSI Code	Character
170	ª	203	Ë
171	«	204	Ì
172	¬	205	Í
173	—	206	Î
174	®	207	Ï
175	-	208	–
176	°	209	Ñ
177	±	210	Ò
178	2	211	Ó
179	3	212	Ô
180	´	213	Õ
181	µ	214	Ö
182	¶	215	x
183	n/a	216	Ø
184	,	217	Ù
185	1	218	Ú
186	º	219	Û
187	»	220	Ü
188	–	221	Y
189	–	222	–
190	–	223	ß
191	¿	224	à
192	À	225	á
193	Á	226	â
194	Â	227	ã
195	Ã	228	ä
196	Ä	229	å
197	Å	230	æ
198	Æ	231	ç
199	Ç	232	è
200	È	233	é
201	É	234	ê
202		235	ë

ANSI Code	Character
236	ì
237	í
238	î
239	ï
240	?
241	ñ
242	ò
243	ó
244	ô
245	õ
246	ö
247	÷
248	ø
249	ù
250	ú
251	û
252	ü
253	y
254	_
255	ÿ

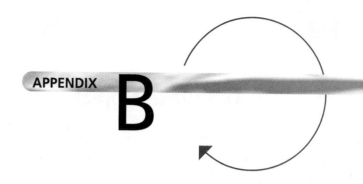

DATA ACCESS OBJECT COLLECTIONS, PROPERTIES, AND METHODS

DBEngine Object

Collections	Properties	Methods
Errors	DefaultPassword	BeginTrans
Workspaces	DefaultType	CommitTrans
Properties	DefaultUser	CompactDatabase
	IniPath	CreateDatabase
	LoginTimeout	CreateWorkspace
	SystemDB	Idle
	Version	OpenConnection
		RegisterDatabase
		RepairDatabase
		Rollback
		SetOption

Workspace Object

Collections	Properties	Methods
Connections	DefaultCursorDriver	BeginTrans
Databases	IsolateODBCTrans	Close
Groups	LoginTimeout	CommitTrans
Properties	Name	CreateDatabase
Users	Type	CreateGroup
	UserName	CreateUser
		OpenConnection
		OpenDatabase
		Rollback

Database Object

Collections	*Properties*	*Methods*
Containers	CollatingOrder	Close
Properties	Connect	CreateProperty
QueryDefs	Connection	CreateQueryDef
Recordsets	DesignMasterID	CreateRelation
Relations	Name	CreateTableDef
TableDefs	QueryTimeout	Execute
	RecordsAffected	MakeReplica
	Replicable	NewPassword
	ReplicaID	OpenRecordset
	Updatable	PopulatePartial
	Version	Synchronize
	V1xNullBehavior	

TableDef Object

Collections	*Properties*	*Methods*
Fields (default)	Attributes	OpenRecordset
Indexes	ConflictTable	RefreshLink
Properties	Connect	CreateField
	DateCreated	CreateIndex
	KeepLocal	CreateProperty
	LastUpdated	
	Name	
	RecordCount	
	Replicable	
	ReplicaFilter	
	SourceTableName	
	Updatable	
	ValidationRule	
	ValidationText	

Recordset Object

Collections	Properties	Methods
Fields	AbsolutePosition	AddNew
Properties	BatchCollisionCount	Clone
	BatchCollisions	Close
	BatchSize	CopyQueryDef
	BOF	
	Bookmark	Delete
	Bookmarkable	Edit
	CacheSize	FillCache
	CacheStart	FindFirst
	Connection	FindLast
	DateCreated	FindNext
	EditMode	FindPrevious
	EOF	GetRows
	Filter	Move
	LastModified	MoveFirst
	Index	MoveLast
	LockEdits	MoveNext
	Name	MovePrevious
	NoMatch	OpenRecordset
	PercentPosition	Requery
	RecordCount	Seek
	RecordStatus	Update
	Restartable	
	Sort	
	StillExecuting	
	Transactions	
	Type	
	Updatable	
	UpdateOptions	
	ValidationRule	
	ValidationText	

Field Object

Collections	*Properties*	*Methods*
Properties	AllowZeroLength	AppendChunk
	Attributes	CreateProperty
	CollatingOrder	GetChunk
	DataUpdatable	
	DefaultValue	
	FieldSize	
	ForeignName	
	Name	
	OrdinalPosition	
	OrdinalValue	
	Required	
	Size	
	SourceField	
	SourceTable	
	Type	
	ValidateOnSet	
	ValidationRule	
	ValidationText	
	Value	
	Visible	

Index Object

Collections	*Properties*	*Methods*
Fields (default)	Clustered	CreateField
Properties	DistinctCount	CreateProperty
	Foreign	
	IgnoreNulls	
	Name	
	Primary	
	Required	
	Unique	

QueryDef Object

Collections	Properties	Methods
Fields	CacheSize	Cancel
Parameters	Connect	CreateProperty
Properties	DateCreated	Execute
	KeepLocal	OpenRecordset
	LastUpdated	
	LogMessages	
	MaxRecords	
	Name	
	ODBCTimeout	
	Prepare	
	RecordsAffected	
	Replicable	
	ReturnsRecords	
	SQL	
	StillExecuting	
	Type	
	Updatable	

INDEX

U-V

W–Z

By opening this package, you are agreeing to be bound by the following agreement:

Some of the software included with this product may be copyrighted, in which case, all rights are reserved by the respective copyright holder. You are licensed to use software copyrighted by the publisher and its licensors on a single computer. You may copy and/or modify the software as needed to facilitate your use of it on a single computer. Making copies of the software for any other purpose is a violation of the United States copyright laws.

This software is sold as is without warranty of any kind, either expressed or implied, including, but not limited to, the implied warranties of merchantability and fitness for a particular purpose. Neither the publisher nor its dealers or distributors assume any liability for any alleged or actual damages arising from the use of this program. (Some states do not allow for the exclusion of implied warranties, so the exclusion may not apply to you.)